EMPIRICAL POLITICAL ANALYSIS

Niko Fischer

Eighth Edition

EMPIRICAL POLITICAL ANALYSIS

QUANTITATIVE AND QUALITATIVE RESEARCH METHODS

Craig Leonard Brians

Virginia Polytechnic and State University

Lars Willnat

Indiana University

Jarol B. Manheim

The George Washington University

Richard C. Rich

Virginia Polytechnic and State University

Longman

Boston   Columbus   Indianapolis   New York   San Francisco   Upper Saddle River
Amsterdam   Cape Town   Dubai   London   Madrid   Milan   Munich   Paris   Montreal   Toronto
Delhi   Mexico City   São Paulo   Sydney   Hong Kong   Seoul   Singapore   Taipei   Tokyo

Acquisitions Editor: Vikram Mukhija
Editorial Assistant: Toni Magyar
Associate Editor: Donna Garnier
Marketing Manager: Lindsey Prudhomme
Production Coordinator: Scarlett Lindsay
Project Coordination, Text Design, and Electronic Page Makeup: Pre-PressPMG
Cover Design Manager: Wendy Ann Fredericks
Cover/Photo: Gideon Mendel/Corbis News/Corbis
Manufacturing Manager: Mary Fischer
Printer and Binder: RR Donnelley & Sons Company/Crawfordsville
Cover Printer: RR Donnelley & Sons Company/Crawfordsville

Library of Congress Cataloging-in-Publication Data

Empirical political analysis : quantitative and qualitative research methods / Craig Leonard Brians . . . [et al.].—
8th ed.
   p. cm.
Includes bibliographical references and index.
ISBN 0-205-79121-2 (alk. paper)
1. Political science—Research. I. Manheim, Jarol B., 1946– II. Brians, Craig Leonard.
JA86.E57 2011
320.072—dc22

2009052074

Longman
is an imprint of

www.pearsonhighered.com

3 4 5 6 7 8 9 10—DOH—13 12 11

ISBN 13: 978-0-205-79121-7
ISBN 10:   0-205-79121-2

BRIEF CONTENTS

Part I   Introduction

Chapter 1   Research as a Process   1

Part II   Preparing to Do Research

Chapter 2   Explaining the Political World: Building Theories and Hypotheses   16

Chapter 3   Developing Your Literature Review: What Others Say about Your Topic   36

Chapter 4   Designing Your Research and Choosing Your Qualitative and Quantitative Methods   75

Chapter 5   From Abstract to Concrete: Operationalization and Measurement   88

Chapter 6   Experimental Research: Attributing Causation through Control   117

Chapter 7   Who, What, Where, When: The Problem of Sampling   131

Part III Quantitative Methods

Chapter 8   Survey Research: Characterizing a Broader Population   151

Chapter 9   Combining Multiple Measures: Using Scaling Techniques   180

Chapter 10   Content Analysis: Researching Textual Material   194

Chapter 11   Aggregate Data: Studying Groups   209

Chapter 12   Comparative Research: Identifying Characteristics across Populations   226

Part IV Analyzing Quantitative Data

Chapter 13 Social Network Analysis: Finding Structure in a Complex World   240

Chapter 14 Coding Data: Preparing Observations for Analysis   252

Chapter 15 Tables and Charts: Visually Describing the Data   265

Chapter 16 Statistics I: Summarizing Distributions on One Variable   278

Chapter 17 Statistics II: Examining Relationships between Two Variables   290

Chapter 18 Statistics III: Examining Relationships among Several Variables   311

Part V   Qualitative Methods

Chapter 19 Direct Observation: Systematically Watching Behavior   324

Chapter 20 Focus Group Research: Guided Conversations   347

Chapter 21 Elite and Specialized Interviewing: Discussing to Garner Knowledge   365

Part VI Conclusion

Chapter 22 The Research Report: Diagramming a Sample Article   377

Chapter 23 Summary: Overview of a Research Project   392

Appendix A Statistical Tables   399

Appendix B Ethical Standards in Empirical Research   408

CONTENTS

Preface   xiii

Part I   Introduction

Chapter 1   Research as a Process   1
Making Scientific Political Theories   1
The Formulation of Theory   5
The Operationalization of Theory   7
The Selection of Appropriate Research Techniques   8
The Observation of Behavior   9
The Analysis of Data   11
Interpretation of the Results   12
Will I Ever Be a Political Scientist?   13
Conclusion   14   •   Key Terms   15   •   Research Examples   15

Part II   Preparing to Do Research

Chapter 2   Explaining the Political World: Building Theories and Hypotheses   16
The Nature of Social Science Theory   18
The Logic of Theory Building   19
Components of Social Science Theory   23
Relationships in Social Science Theory   25
Theory Testing and Elaboration   27
The Role of Hypotheses   29
Formulating Hypotheses   32
Conclusion   34   •   Key Terms   35   •   Research Examples   35

Chapter 3   Developing Your Literature Review: What Others Say about Your Topic   36
Searching and Researching   36
Deciphering Library Records   39
Inside the Physical Library   43
Library Catalog Searching   44
Word Mining: Four Steps to Searching Success   46
Word Mining Step 1: Scanning the Information Environment   47

Word Mining Step 2: Harnessing the Power of Bibliographic
Records   54

Word Mining Step 3: Digging into the Library's Full-Text
Resources   61

Word Mining Step 4: Making the Free Web Work for You   64

Evaluating Information   66

Reviewing and Summarizing the Literature   68

Combining Searches in the Library Catalog (Advanced Tools)   70

Taking Control of Your Search (Advanced Tools)   71
          Conclusion   72   •   Key Terms   72   •   Research Examples   73

**Chapter 4   Designing Your Research and Choosing Your Qualitative
and Quantitative Methods   75**

Research Purpose and Research Design   75

Coping with Alternative Rival Hypotheses through
Research Design   77

Comparing Qualitative and Quantitative Methods   81
          Conclusion   86   •   Key Terms   86   •   Research Examples   87

**Chapter 5   From Abstract to Concrete: Operationalization and
Measurement   88**

Operationalization: The Link between Theory and Observation   89

Operational Definitions   92

Measurement   94

Levels of Measurement   94

Working Hypotheses   99

Measurement Error: The Enemy   102

Validity   105

Factors That Threaten Validity   106

Reliability   107

Types of Validation (Advanced Tools)   110
          Conclusion   114   •   Key Terms   115   •   Research Examples   116

**Chapter 6   Experimental Research: Attributing Causation through
Control   117**

The Classic Experiment   118

Field Experiments   123

Quasi-Experiments   123
          Conclusion   129   •   Key Terms   129   •   Research Examples   129

Chapter 7   Who, What, Where, When: The Problem of Sampling   131

Defining a Representative Sample   132

Procedures for Selecting a Representative Sample   135

Probability Sampling   135

Variations on Random Sampling   137

Nonprobability Samples   143

Determining Appropriate Sample Size   145

Conclusion   149   •   Key Terms   150   •   Research Examples   150

Part III   Quantitative Methods

Chapter 8   Survey Research: Characterizing a Broader Population   151

Stages of the Survey Process   152

Conceptualizing   153

Survey Design   153

Instrumentation   155

Types of Surveys   162

Training and Briefing Personnel   168

Pretesting   169

Surveying   170

Monitoring   172

Verifying   173

Secondary Analysis of Survey Data   174

Conclusion   177   •   Key Terms   177   •   Research Examples   177

Chapter 9   Combining Multiple Measures: Using Scaling Techniques   180

The Art of Scaling   181

Scale Construction: Two Basic Concerns   181

Likert Scaling   183

Guttman Scaling   184

Thurstone Scaling   188

The Semantic Differential   190

Conclusion   192   •   Key Terms   192   •   Research Examples   192

Chapter 10   Content Analysis: Researching Textual Material   194

Preparing to Use Content Analysis   195

Undertaking a Substantive Content Analysis   200

Undertaking a Structural Content Analysis   202

Special Problems in the Use of Content Analysis   204
Conclusion   207   •   Key Terms   207   •   Research Examples   208

Chapter 11   Aggregate Data: Studying Groups   209
Types of Aggregate Data   211
Limitations in the Use of Aggregate Data   214
Sources of Aggregate Data   220
Collecting Aggregate Data   222
Conclusion   223   •   Key Terms   224   •   Research Examples   224

Chapter 12   Comparative Research: Identifying Characteristics across Populations   226
Research across Borders   227
Finding Questions That "Travel"   228
Using Equivalent Measures   229
Choosing Cases to Study   231
Finding Independent Observations   233
Finding Data   234
Conclusion   237   •   Key Terms   238   •   Research Examples   238

Part IV   Analyzing Quantitative Data

Chapter 13   Social Network Analysis: Finding Structure in a Complex World   240
Social Network Data   241
Types of Networks   245
Roles of Participants   247
Conclusion   250   •   Key Terms   250   •   Research Examples   250

Chapter 14   Coding Data: Preparing Observations for Analysis   252
Coding: What Do All Those Numbers Mean?   252
The Codebook and the Coding Sheet   257
Data Entry and Data Processing   261
Conclusion   263   •   Key Terms   263   •   Research Examples   264

Chapter 15   Tables and Charts: Visually Describing the Data   265
The Simple Table   265
The Line Graph   268
The Pie Chart and the Bar Chart   269
The Bilateral Bar Chart   272
The Crosstabulation   273

Creating Tables and Charts   275
Conclusion   276   •   Key Terms   277   •   Research Examples   277

**Chapter 16   Statistics I: Summarizing Distributions on
One Variable   278**

Measures of Central Tendency and Dispersion   279

Measures for Nominal Variables   281

Measures for Ordinal Variables   282

Measures for Interval/Ratio Variables   284
Conclusion   288   •   Key Terms   288   •   Research Examples   289

**Chapter 17   Statistics II: Examining Relationships between
Two Variables   290**

Measures of Association and Statistical Significance   290

Measures of Association and Significance for Nominal Variables:
Lambda   297

Measures of Association and Significance for Ordinal Variables:
Gamma   301

Measures of Association and Significance for Interval/Ratio Variables:
Correlation   303
Conclusion   309   •   Key Terms   310   •   Research Examples   310

**Chapter 18   Statistics III: Examining Relationships among Several
Variables   311**

Tabular Analysis   311

Multiple Regression   314

Interpreting Multiple Regressions Results   316

Solving Common Problems in Multiple Regression   317
Conclusion   321   •   Key Terms   322   •   Research Examples   322

Part V   Qualitative Methods

Chapter 19   Direct Observation: Systematically Watching Behavior   324

Direct Observation and the Scientific Method   325

Degree of Obtrusiveness   327

Degree of Structure   328

Techniques of Unstructured Observation   329

Techniques of Structured Observation   334

Sampling Procedures in Direct Observation   339

Coping with Method Effects in Direct Observation   340
Conclusion   345   •   Key Terms   345   •   Research Examples   345

Chapter 20   Focus Group Research: Guided Conversations   347

Why Use Focus Groups?   348

When Are Focus Groups Useful?   351

Planning and Conducting Focus Groups   353
Conclusion   363   •   Key Terms   363   •   Research Examples   363

**Chapter 21   Elite and Specialized Interviewing: Discussing
to Garner Knowledge   365**

Elite Interviewing   366

Seeking Validity   367

Techniques of Elite Interviewing   368

Conducting Elite Interviews   369

Specialized Interviewing   373
Conclusion   375   •   Key Terms   375   •   Research Examples   375

Part VI Conclusion

Chapter 22   The Research Report: Diagramming a Sample Article   377

The Plan   378

The Structure   378

The Style   381

The Title and Abstract   382
Conclusion   383   •   Key Term   390   •   Research Examples   391

Chapter 23   Summary: Overview of a Research Project   392

Developing Theories, Hypotheses, and a Research Design   392

Data Collection and Analysis   394

A Checklist for Judging Research   395
Conclusion   398

Appendix A Statistical Tables   399

Appendix B Ethical Standards in Empirical Research   408

Glossary   411
Index   419

PREFACE

With this edition, *Empirical Political Analysis* comes full circle. More accurately, the principal author, Craig Brians, has come full circle—from reading a copy of the second edition of this text in his first college methods course, to joining the author team on the sixth edition, to becoming first author of the eighth edition. In fundamental ways, his professional formation has been shaped by—and now helps to shape—this premiere political science methods text, which was originally conceived by Jarol Manheim and Richard Rich a decade before most of today's college freshmen were born.

This edition incorporates a more personal touch, reflecting Brians' experience with (and scholarship on) teaching research methods. Like many of you who teach methods, Brians noticed that his students connect better with methods techniques when he relates how we study political science to his own life experience. Like many of you students reading this book for your first methods course, Brians grappled with the content of this class when he himself was a student. Unlike, say, taking a course that covers U.S. government or comparative politics, he had no idea why he was required to take a course that involved math. Rest assured, you will get through this! When you finish this book, you will have a much better idea why the discipline typically requires a methods course for graduate students and, increasingly, for undergraduates. The skills you gain in this course should help you be more successful in every future course you take (in political science or other fields), in your everyday life, and in your future career. The section below, describing the new features of this edition, outlines some of the techniques we use to deliver on this claim.

NEW TO THIS EDITION

Each chapter has been fully updated and revised to incorporate the most current political science research advancements. New features include:

- ***We Are All Researchers.*** This message resonates in each chapter. The introductory chapter starts with a story that demonstrates to students: "As a small child you were doing research, and you still perform research every day!" In each chapter we teach students to research more systematically and efficiently, yielding more predictable and easier-to-communicate results.
- ***Word Mining.*** A new chapter teaches this newly developed technique for literature reviewing, which capitalizes on tools students already use and *think* they know (e.g., Google) and scholarly tools they usually have not already used (e.g., indexed databases). Here, literature searching leads to writing the literature review.
- ***Choosing Your Methods.*** A new chapter puts the facets of both *qualitative* and *quantitative* approaches at the initial stages of the project, as students are developing their research designs. When students start by thinking more broadly, they research more broadly.
- ***Research Exercise.*** Each chapter features a new "Research Exercise" that directly involves students in demonstrating each step in the research process. Depending on the

chapter's topic, students find themselves standing up individually or in groups to be part of a sampling frame, or role-play a focus group in a circle in front of their class.

- *Lab Manual.* The newly updated companion *Quantitative Analysis Lab Manual* (Brians 2011) teaches hands-on data analysis in SPSS and Excel, as well as enhanced literature searching skills. Carefully selected data sets and tailored exercises illustrate each analytic procedure, from difference of means to crosstabs, and from regression to recoding. This manual provides essential hands-on explanations and practice with the research techniques that depend most heavily on math and computer software.

FEATURES

This edition reflects feedback from dozens of faculty and students from the United States and other countries. In the year before this text was revised, principal author Craig Brians traveled from coast to coast interviewing dozens of professors who teach in a wide variety of settings—from large research universities to small liberal arts colleges. The text you hold also reflects suggestions offered by many undergraduate and graduate students, who graciously responded to Brians' challenge for improvement.

The entire book is structured to follow the research process—not an ideal typical process, but one that more closely reflects what we actually see as students and faculty conduct their research. Although we frame the text in "stages" of research, we also make frequent references to the recursive process. For example, developing theories (Chapter 2) comes before researching the literature (Chapter 3), but they are closely related to one another; we cannot begin looking at research until we have an idea what we are researching, but we rarely know enough to develop a theory from whole cloth without consulting others' research on the topic(s).

Each chapter follows a straightforward path. Beginning with a set of learning goals, we then try to relate research to students' everyday lives through personal anecdotes, where possible. The chapters offer numerous examples, designed to demonstrate each concept and emphasize its importance. Research exercises are interspersed through the chapters to closely follow the topics they elucidate. All of the exercises use readily available resources to illustrate a research technique—some are designed to be 15-minute in-class exercises, while others can be assigned as homework. Ethics are crucial to every stage of the research enterprise; thus, a "Practical Research Ethics" box figures prominently in each chapter. Rather than isolate ethics in a separate location, our pedagogical approach infuses every chapter and every day in class with relevant ethical concerns and examples.

We try to anticipate the questions a student might raise and to respond to them. We introduce necessary technical terms—which is, after all, a central function of a methods text—but we strive to avoid unnecessary jargon. Specialized terms are defined in the glossary at the end of the book and are shown in **bold print** on their first use in context.

Finally, each chapter concludes with an annotated bibliography. The Research Examples are recent articles that feature high-quality articles that illustrate the research method used in the chapter. Faculty have told us they use these examples in two ways.

First, they may bring the article into class and show a portion of the text or a table or figure to demonstrate a facet of the research process. Alternatively, they may assign the articles to their students to read before class; by reading the article, the students get a more concrete feel for the research technique, or at least more concrete questions about the technique, which is an important starting point.

SUPPLEMENTS

Longman is pleased to offer several resources to qualified adopters of *Empirical Political Analysis* and their students that will make teaching and learning from this book even more effective and enjoyable. Several of the supplements for this book are available at the Instructor Resource Center (IRC), an online hub that allows instructors to quickly download book-specific supplements. Please visit the IRC welcome page at **www.pearsonhighered.com/irc** to register for access.

For Instructors

INSTRUCTORS GUIDE FOR THE LAB MANUAL. This guide includes suggestions for classroom exercises and homework assignments using the Lab Manual. Available exclusively on the IRC.

TEST BANK. This assessment resource includes multiple-choice, true-false, and essay questions for each chapter in this text. Available exclusively on the IRC.

For Students

LAB MANUAL. The newly updated companion *Quantitative Analysis Lab Manual* (0-205-79125-5) teaches hands-on data analysis in *SPSS* and *Excel*, as well as enhanced literature searching skills. Carefully selected datasets and tailored exercises illustrate each analytic procedure, from difference of means to crosstabs, and from regression to recoding. This manual provides essential hands-on explanations and practice with the research techniques that depend most heavily on math and computer software. To order the Lab Manual with this book, use ISBN 0-205-78833-5.

MYSEARCHLAB. Need help with a paper? MySearchLab saves time and improves results by offering start-to-finish guidance on the research/writing process and full-text access to academic journals and periodicals. To learn more, please visit www.mysearchlab.com or contact your Pearson representative. To order MySearchLab with this book, use ISBN 0-205-79859-4.

ACKNOWLEDGMENTS

This text represents a collaborative effort of four authors, who hail from a range of political science fields. We publish research on topics ranging from political communications to environmental politics, from international studies to organizational networks, and more. Additionally, we work across the spectrum of methodologies—when we discuss a given research method in this text, we speak from personal experience. For many political scientists, much of that experience has been gained using data obtained from the Inter-University Consortium for Political and Social Research at the University of Michigan (www.icpsr.umich.edu), and through hands-on exposure to qualitative and quantitative research techniques at the ICPSR Summer Program (www.icpsr.umich.edu/sumprog).

Although we collectively possess broad expertise, this text is written for students and has benefited from the useful feedback our own students have offered. Of particular assistance have been Craig Brians' students in the undergraduate (PSCI 2024) and graduate (PSCI 5116) Research Methods courses at Virginia Polytechnic and State University. We also have benefited from the comments we receive from students who use this text at colleges and universities across the United States and throughout the world—this book has been translated into numerous languages, including Arabic, Chinese, and Russian. Student responses have particularly contributed to the many Web-based resources incorporated into this book.

In preparing this eighth edition, we owe a particular debt to Bruce Pencek, Ph.D., College Librarian for the Social Sciences at Virginia Polytechnic and State University's Newman Library, whose expertise in teaching students (and faculty) to locate research and learn to tell stories through their research is reflected in an entirely new Chapter 3. Jessica Folkart, Ph.D., a language professor at Virginia Polytechnic and State University, substantially enhanced the clarity and readability of every part of this text. Additionally, we received detailed suggestions for every chapter from Caitlin Dwyer of the University of Minnesota as well as from Martin G. Evans of the University of Toronto. Also offering important suggestions were Danie Stockmann of Leiden University in the Netherlands, Joseph Fletcher of the University of Toronto, and Lindsey Lupo of Point Loma Nazarene University in California. Daniel Doherty of the College of William and Mary and Yale University provided suggestions that helped refine and clarify the text in the new stand-alone chapter on Experimental Research (Chapter 6). Virginia Polytechnic and State University graduate students who went out of their way to contribute include Burke Thomas, Miranda Canody, and Ted Farmer. Last, but certainly not least, three of Brians' undergraduate researchers contributed to this project: Nelson Gunther, Ryan Mowery, and Tyler Garrafa.

Also, we wish to thank the following reviewers for their helpful comments: Stephen A. Borrelli, University of Alabama; Cynthia J. Bowling, Auburn University; John Calhoun, Palm Beach Atlantic University; Leonard Champney, University of Scranton; Derrick L. Cogburn, University of Michigan; Bruce Evans, Susquehanna University; Kenneth Fernandez, University of Nevada, Las Vegas; Lauretta Conklin Frederking, University of Portland; U. K. Heo, University of Wisconsin–Milwaukee; Pia Kohler, University of Alaska Fairbanks; Edward Kwon, Northern Kentucky University; Donald R. Raber, Presbyterian College; and Matthew M. Shousen, Franklin and Marshall College. Thanks, too, to Vikram Mukhija, Toni Magyar, and Andrew Jones for helping to make this new edition a reality.

We are grateful to Donna Bahry, whose knowledge of comparative politics and contributions to this text over the years are still reflected in Chapter 12, and to the literary executor of the late Sir Ronald A. Fisher, F.R.S., to Dr. Frank Yates, F.R.S., and to Longman

Group, Ltd., London, for permission to reprint Tables IV and VII from its book *Statistical Tables for Biological, Agricultural and Medical Research* (6th ed., 1974).

Finally, we want to thank our families, who, once again, have put up with our undoubtedly intolerable behavior as we came to terms with the fact that signing a publishing contract is not the same as turning in a completed manuscript.

With all of this assistance, the final product is ours. We are responsible for its weaknesses and for continually improving this text's value as a teaching tool. Thus, we welcome your comments and suggestions. Enjoy your research experience!

Craig Leonard Brians
Lars Willnat
Jarol Manheim
Richard Rich

CHAPTER 1

Research as a Process

In this chapter you will learn:

- How we formulate and test theories in everyday life.
- How empirical qualitative and quantitative scientific research differ from normative approaches to knowledge.
- The six steps of the political science research process.

You have always been a scientist, even before you attended school. Watch a small child explore her world. What does she do? She tests, observes, and queries her surroundings. She generalizes the accumulated knowledge into principles that closely resemble what we would call theories.

My younger daughter is now a college student, but when she was 2½ years old we visited my family's farm in Central California. Where I grew up, we did our cooking on a wood stove. My daughter knew not to touch ranges, because they were hot. She had never seen a wood stove before, though, so she walked up to the large white box on one side of the kitchen in the farm house and put her hand directly on the chrome rim to lean against it. I rushed across the room, grabbed her hand, and removed it from the hot stove. As I was putting ice on her palm and drying her tears, she was confused and asked me how she got hurt. I suddenly realized that she had not recognized the wood cook stove as something that could be hot. That day her "theory," which told her what should not be touched because it could be hot and burn her, was expanded to include any large metal box in a kitchen.

This story anecdotally illustrates the idea that children learn to navigate their world more safely through making observations and developing guiding theories from the information they gather. What does children's tendency to generalize from their experiences in the physical world tell us about the study of social relations and politics? This chapter addresses this question, and the entire book will teach ways to formalize the research skills you already possess and relate them to political science.

MAKING SCIENTIFIC POLITICAL THEORIES

Tacit Political Theorizing

In addition to developing theories to explain the physical world around you, as you were growing up you also merged your observations of the social and political world into theories. Here is one student's story describing how he came to distinguish why some people are Republicans and some are Democrats:

> As a child, I grew up in a large extended family—30+, including grandparents, aunts, uncles, and cousins. A quarter of my family lived on the West Coast, a quarter lived in the Northeast, and the rest of us lived in the Mid-Atlantic and the South. Once a year we would all get together for a reunion and rent a few houses on the Outer Banks of North Carolina. During that week, politics was one subject that always seemed to be discussed during dinner. However, not all of us saw eye to eye, and we usually ended up in a lively debate. At some point, I noticed that those who lived on the West Coast and Northeast seemed to be on the same side of issues, and those who lived in the Mid-Atlantic and the South on the other. It wasn't until I was older that I found out that those who lived on the West Coast and Northeast were more aligned with the Democratic Party, and those further south on the East Coast were aligned with Republicans. Since most of the family originally came from the same area, I concluded that people who moved to California became Democrats, or they moved there because they wanted to be Democrats.

Upon reading this student's youthful theory, you may ask yourself: Is this geographic theory of political ideology "true?" This question gains particular salience when you think of contrary examples. For example, both President Nixon and President Reagan were Californians, but also Republicans. When we learn information that seems contrary to our theories, though, we should not discard them. We should refine the theories to account for the new information and make the theories more useful—just as we did when we were young and we learned about the various types of hot kitchen objects (e.g., stoves, rice cookers, hot plates, slow cookers, etc.).

In this text, we claim that we all develop associations to help us interpret the world; thus, we are all scientists. We begin with physical associations (that stoves are hot), and as we gain sophistication we move to interpreting social and political relationships (that people from the West Coast are Democrats). This leads to our ability to categorize political groupings and create useful taxonomies—and test those relationships—as we grow older.

Empirical versus Normative Analysis

Political scientists distinguish between obtaining knowledge and using knowledge. Dealing with how (and what) we know is termed **empirical** analysis. Dealing with how we should use our knowledge is termed **normative** analysis. Empirical analysis is concerned with developing and using a common, objective language to *describe* and *explain* political reality. It can be **quantitative**, based on statistical comparisons of the characteristics of the various objects or cases that are being studied, or it can be **qualitative**, based on the researcher's informed understanding of those same objects or cases. Normative analysis is concerned with developing and examining subjective goals, values, and moral rules to *guide* us in applying what we have learned of that reality.

Thus, although our emphasis in this book is on empirical political analysis, our goal is to develop an appreciation of the larger, normative perspective within which knowledge is interpreted, in addition to a facility with various aspects of empirical technique.

PRACTICAL RESEARCH ETHICS
Ethics in Research and in Life

At each stage of the research process, and in each chapter of this book, you will confront choices that present ethical challenges. As you conduct your research (and live your life), you should keep the potential consequences of your actions in mind. Throughout this book, you will detect the tension that exists in our discipline between our interest in learning about human behavior, and our concern that we may be negatively affecting people through our research. Sometimes your research may directly impact a person when you ask a survey subject about her attitude toward abortion policy, and she recalls a personal experience. Other times, your research may influence human lives more indirectly, such as when your findings are utilized by judges as they wrestle to interpret the law.

The foregoing examples noting the real human impact of political science research make it clear why we discuss ethical research in each chapter. As you are evaluating your behavior, consider the weight that others in society and government give to the importance of ethical conduct. In class, unethical use of others' research in your writings is called plagiarism, and may cause you to receive a failing grade in the course, or even be expelled by your college. In academic research, failing to obtain prior permission to carry out research or not fully protecting human or animal research subjects will lead to sanctions against you, and may well cost you both your reputation and your career. In business, using others' copyrighted material without permission may be punishable with a fine amounting to hundreds of thousands of dollars, and a decade in prison—per offense!

Clearly, our society values your ethical behavior; in this text we will do our part to promote ethical studies at each stage of the research process by suggesting specific strategies you can use to foster and develop your ethical compass.

Carried to the extreme, normative analysis without empirical foundation can lead to value judgments that are out of touch with reality. Empirical analysis in the absence of a sensitivity to normative concerns, on the other hand, can lead to the creation of a fact structure in a vacuum, a collection of observations whose significance we are not prepared to understand fully. The object, then, in undertaking political inquiry is to draw upon both types of analysis—empirical and normative—so as to maximize not only our knowledge but also our understanding of political reality.

the process

Scientific Knowledge

In this context, we can see scientific research as a way of knowing and as a common language of inquiry. Scientific research is certainly not the only way of knowing, but it is in many instances and for many purposes the *most effective*. People can know things through experience, but not everyone shares the same experiences. People can know things by keeping their eyes open, but they cannot be sure that through such unstructured observation they will note all or even a representative group of relevant events. Some people can "know" things by seeing visions or hearing disembodied voices, and others may accept their descriptions and accounts as valid, but not everyone can be trained in visionary methods. Each of these ways of knowing serves a purpose and each has its uses, but none allows for the total sharing of facts or conclusions, as well as the knowledge of how those facts or conclusions were obtained. Each allows communication, but none helps us reach a comprehensive, shared understanding.

Defining the Scientific Method

Scientific research is *explicit, systematic,* and *controlled*. It is explicit in that all the rules for defining and examining reality are clearly stated. Nothing is hidden from view and nothing is taken on faith. Scientific research is systematic in that each item of evidence is linked by reason or observation to other items of evidence. No ad hoc explanations are tolerated and no carelessness of method is permitted. It is controlled in that the phenomena under analysis are, to the extent possible, observed in as rigorous a manner as the state of the art allows. Generalized conclusions are reached only after the most thorough and painstaking assessment, and caution (in the larger sense of exercising great care and attention to detail) is a watchword. Yet for all its constraints, or, indeed, precisely because of them, scientific research opens for those versed in its ways a whole new level of understanding reality. It is for this reason that the scientific method is applied to the study of politics.

Scientific research, meaning inquiry guided by the scientific method, permits us to know reality and to evaluate the ways in which we know, but—because those ways are commonly understood by those trained in the method—it also permits us to improve upon our means of inquiry. Scientific research is a self-correcting, continuously developing way of knowing. Remember that the data you obtain from your scientific research may resemble the quantitative methods on display at the school science fairs, or the data may emphasize qualitative in-depth observation and description.

There are, of course, other ways to analyze political relationships. In this text, though, we confine our attention to qualitative and quantitative methods that subscribe to the assumptions inherent in the scientific method (i.e., there is an observable reality, and we can observe it). Thus, we leave it to others to discuss Critical Studies, Feminist, Interpretive, or Postmodern approaches to research.

Scientific research, or for our purposes, *social* scientific research, is a *method of testing theories and hypotheses by applying certain rules of analysis to the observation and interpretation of reality under strictly delineated circumstances*. These are the rules and constraints that we must learn in order to gain and communicate knowledge in the science of politics.

Six Steps in the Research Process

Political science research is best thought of as a *process* of gathering and interpreting information. This research process generally follows a standard progression, although one often will return to an earlier stage when new information alters our understandings. The six distinct but highly interrelated stages of the research process are:

1. The formulation of theory.
2. The operationalization of that theory.
3. The selection of appropriate research techniques.
4. The observation of behavior.
5. The analysis of data.
6. The interpretation of the results.

These six stages provide the organizing rationale for the rest of this chapter, for much of this book, and for much of your research.

THE FORMULATION OF THEORY

The first step in undertaking political science research is the selection of an appropriate research question, and here we can readily see the importance of mixing normative with empirical considerations. What criteria make one research question more appropriate than another? Although a number of such criteria come to mind, ranging from the personal interests of the researcher to the collective interests of society, most fall into one of two major categories. A question is worthy of research either because it fulfills a scientific need—that is, because its answer will further our theoretical understanding of some phenomenon—or because it fulfills a societal need—that is, because its answer may help us to deal with one or another of the problems faced by our society.

Although these two types of research questions, frequently termed **basic research** and **applied research**, are not mutually exclusive (asking one does not *necessarily* mean you cannot ask the other), they do frequently compete with one another. For example, should we study the hypothetical determinants of aggression under conditions of stress in order to develop a sophisticated predictive model of human behavior, or should we instead focus on the reasons riots occur and on ways to prevent them? Should we examine at length the decision-making processes of national leaders to help us understand leadership, or should we instead concentrate on identifying and avoiding the types of decisions that lead to war? Because too few scientific resources (money, time, and trained personnel) are available to study all potentially interesting or important research questions, there is often a conflict between the need to perform basic research—whose practical payoffs, however great, are almost always felt only indirectly and far in the future—and the need to use our scientific knowledge in the present for the immediate benefit of humanity, even though we may, in the process, delay or prevent the further development of our science. The choice must be made by individual researchers in accordance with their own values.

Once you have identified the problem you wish to tackle and the type of contribution you wish to make, then you need to frame a more specific research question. First, you should identify which aspect of the problem interests you most. Since research projects may be lengthy and no research question can be answered adequately without hard work, you should not take on a task in which you have little interest.

Second, you must sift through the various elements or components of the research topic to identify those that may be important to your research. Draw on your powers of observation, reasoning, and past research to identify the major factors that bear on the behavior you are seeking to understand.

A Research Example

Let us imagine that in the middle of the desert there is a town called Little America that consists of several miles of service stations and restaurants stretching from the exit ramp of an interstate highway to the edge of the horizon.[1] One can do nothing in Little America except eat and buy gas. An image of a location greatly resembling Little America appears in Figure 1.1.

---

[1] This fictional example does not refer to Little America, Wyoming, which consists entirely of a truck stop motel.

FIGURE 1.1   "Little America," as seen near I-81 in Southwestern Virginia.

Now, suppose we have decided to study the voting behavior of Little Americans in presidential elections so that we may explain why one person votes Democratic while another votes Republican. In this simplified example, the subjects of our analysis (Little Americans) differ from one another in only two ways besides their voting preferences: each is either an owner or a worker, and each is associated with either a service station or a restaurant. Each of these factors, which political scientists term *variables*, represents a characteristic of a particular individual. One citizen of Little America might be (1) an employee of (2) a restaurant (3) who votes Democratic, whereas another is (1) an owner of (2) a service station (3) who votes Republican. We wish to explain differences in voting behavior in terms of other kinds of differences among the voters, so we must focus on all the factors that might bear on a person's electoral preference. In this instance, we have only two to choose from: employee or owner status and service station or restaurant affiliation. Let us refer to these respectively as *socioeconomic status* (*SES*)—with ownership representing higher status than employment—and business affiliation. Is there any reason to expect that knowing either characteristic of a particular person will help us predict his or her voting preference?

To answer that question, we must do two things. First, we must *think*. We must ask ourselves: Is there any *logical reason* to expect either of these factors to influence voting behavior? Second, we must consult the political science literature: Is there, in previous studies of this or related topics, any *empirical evidence* that one or the other of these factors influences voting behavior? In reality, there is little reason to expect the business-affiliation variable to make much difference in voting behavior in this instance. Differences may well exist between those associated with service stations and those with restaurants, but these differences are not likely to have much impact on presidential voting preferences. Few presidential candidates run on a pro–service station, antirestaurant platform (or vice versa), and, other things being equal, this variable is not likely to help us explain voting behavior. The second variable, SES, however, is a different story. The Democratic Party is popularly identified as the party of labor and the Republican Party as the party of business, and since persons of higher SES are more likely than those of lower SES to vote Republican, we might well expect that employees will be more likely to vote for the Democratic candidate and owners for the Republican. Indeed, the research literature is replete with examples of precisely this kind of relationship. Thus, logical reasoning and empirical evidence both point in the same direction. Our research question might then become, "does the SES of a voter in Little America influence voting preference in a presidential election?"

In the real world, of course, people differ from one another on more than two or three characteristics, but the problem we face in framing a research question is essentially the same. Because no one has the resources to measure every possible variable, we must choose, from among the thousands of human (or institutional) characteristics, those few that we expect will help us to explain whatever pattern of behavior interests us. With the aid of both logic and literature we try to anticipate and identify the factors that might be related to the behavior of interest. In so doing, we are not prejudging our results, but rather refining our thinking about the research problem to identify those avenues of inquiry most likely to lead to successful explanation. This process of refining our research question through informed selection is what we mean by the term *formulation of theory*.

THE OPERATIONALIZATION OF THEORY

Once we have arrived at one or more research questions and the theory needed to direct our search for answers, we must progress to the next step, that of operationalization— the conversion or redefinition of our relatively abstract theoretical notions into concrete terms that will allow us actually to measure what we are after. Operationalization involves moving from the conceptual level (thinking about a problem) to the operational level (deciding how to solve it); it involves learning to think in *practical* terms.

Defining Terms

Suppose, to continue our example, that we have a hypothesis—a statement of the answer we expect to find for our research question—that Little Americans of higher SES (owners) are more likely than those of lower SES (employees) to vote Republican in the next presidential election. This is in line with the findings of countless other voting studies and is a reasonable expectation in the present instance as well. But how do we find out for sure? We cannot simply walk up to a Little American and say, "Good evening. Are you of higher or lower socioeconomic status?" To begin with, the person we are interviewing probably will not understand what we are talking about, since *socioeconomic status* is a technical term with many variations of meaning. And second, even if we get an answer, we will probably not be able to interpret it. Suppose the respondent replied, "Yes, I am of higher socioeconomic status." Higher than whom? How high? How does that person define socioeconomic status? Does it mean the same thing to the respondent as it does to the researcher? Once we have an abstract concept in mind, we must find a way to define more explicitly what we mean by that concept and then we must form our definition into as clear a question or measure as possible.

The problem here is to make intelligent yet arbitrary choices among numerous shades of meaning. When we use the variable SES, are we thinking about respondents' level of income, occupation, or perhaps even subjective notions of which social class they belong to? Each might be a component of SES, but each has a somewhat different meaning, and each must be measured differently: What was the total income of your family last year? What is your occupation? Would you say that you consider yourself to be a member of the working class, the middle class, or the upper class?

In other words, once we arrive at some hypothesis or research question, we have to examine very closely just what it is that we mean by each phrase we use, and we have to translate that more precise definition into measurable indicators. We seek, in effect, the lowest common denominator of meaning. (Although not everyone would, for example, assign the same meaning to the term *socioeconomic status,* almost everyone would understand *total annual income in dollars.*) In the process our concepts are narrowed and shades of meaning are lost, but because of this our thinking becomes much more precise, and our ability to communicate in clear, unambiguous terms what we have done is greatly enhanced. This process of translation and simplification, which we term *operationalization,* is *the single most important key to conducting meaningful research.*

THE SELECTION OF APPROPRIATE RESEARCH TECHNIQUES

Once we have decided what we want to measure, we must decide how we will measure it. We must devise a research strategy, a plan of attack. Three considerations are of primary importance here.

First, we must select *appropriate measures*—a technique or a combination of techniques that will enable us to ask the particular questions that measure the particular variables of interest to us. Additionally, we must conduct these measurements in ways that are consistent with our operationalizations. We cannot, for example, measure the attitudes of individual voters by analyzing the content of newspaper coverage of a given election, because newspaper content may reflect the views of an editor or of those few people whose letters to that editor are published, without necessarily reflecting the views of most voters. Moreover, analyzing news or editorial content does not permit us to differentiate among different types of voters, such as those of higher or lower SES. Thus, content analysis would not allow us to answer our research question—that is, to test our hypothesis; survey research would be more useful. On the other hand, suppose that we wish to assess the coverage given by a newspaper to a political campaign. We might simply analyze the content of the newspaper itself, counting references to the candidates and interpreting the nature of those stories, or we might survey readers of the newspaper to measure what information they remember reading about the campaign. In the first instance, we would have a direct measure of content from which we are forced to infer impact; in the second instance, we would have a direct measure of impact from which we are forced to infer content. Depending on the precise formulation of our research question, one or the other or the combination of both strategies might be useful. The point is that the appropriateness of a given research technique is, in large part, determined by the particular problem we have selected for study.

Secondly, we must choose the most appropriate *type of data* to study our theory. Sometimes we obtain numerical data and other times we gather non-numerical data. Quantitative and qualitative data, respectively, each have different uses in our scientific research. We will delve much more deeply into each type of data in Chapter 4, but as a general rule when we want greater breadth we count, and when we want greater depth we do not. For example, to return to our Little America example, depending upon our research purposes we might count the number of bumper stickers for candidates of various parties on the cars driven by the gas station attendants, or we might conduct lengthy interviews with service station owners about a lifetime of political experiences.

The third consideration is *feasibility.* This is the stage of the research process at which we prepare to leave our ivory tower and actually go out into the real world. For that reason, we must assure ourselves that whatever method or technique we select can be employed properly under the particular set of conditions we are likely to face. For example, since there is no newspaper in our Little America (only service stations and restaurants), we cannot use content analysis, even if we want to. Similarly, the most direct way to measure the level of tension between the leaders of Iraq and those of Turkey might be through a series of personal interviews with the leaders themselves, but such interviews are difficult to arrange, to say the least. In each instance, we have to find less-than-ideal ways of measuring the key variables. A feasible technique, then, is one that will be maximally effective given the constraints of the research situation.

For student and professional researchers alike, feasibility is most often determined by time and resource constraints. The length of a given term or the years of funding for graduate research or the number years on the tenure clock are time limits. Resources include money to fund original research or lengthy, direct observation fieldwork or personnel to hand-code thousands of pages of text. Ultimately, then, researchers choose techniques that fit within their available time and resources.

To summarize, we must find a way to measure those variables we wish to measure that will be (1) consistent with our working definitions of the variables and (2) practicable. We must be as scientific as possible, but we can only be as scientific as the circumstances allow.

THE OBSERVATION OF BEHAVIOR

The fourth stage of the research process involves actually carrying out the research strategy developed in stage 3. Many factors must be taken into account here, but two in particular are worthy of note. The first is the notion of generalizability; the second that of reactivity.

Generalizability refers to the ability to generalize or extend our conclusions with some confidence from the observed behavior of a few cases to the presumed behavior of an entire population. It is a concern we must take into account in selecting the particular cases (people, decisions, organizations, or nations) that we wish to study. The problem here is basically one of scale. If there are only, say, four or five occurrences of an event or subjects in a group we wish to study, we can examine each of those occurrences or subjects individually and make various general statements about them, with reasonable confidence that our conclusions apply to all the cases. However, if—as is much more frequently the situation—we have so many hundreds or thousands or millions of cases that it is impossible to examine each firsthand, we will have much less confidence that a study of a relative few of these cases—perhaps fewer than 1 in 1,000—will allow us to make accurate statements about the entire group. In such circumstances we must develop a strategy, often termed a *sampling procedure,* by which we can select from the many cases a few to study and come to conclusions that might apply to the entire population of cases. In doing so, we must decide how many cases to study and how these cases should be selected, and we must try to estimate the representativeness of these few cases. The key to generalizability lies in selecting for observation those cases that are likely to represent, or be most typical of, the larger population.

Once we have selected our cases for analysis, we must exercise great care in observing them. We must avoid measuring political phenomena or behavior in ways that display **reactivity**—a situation in which either the person who is doing a study or the actual methods of the study somehow interfere with and alter the way those under observation would behave or think in the absence of the researcher. In other words, a danger exists that the act of observation may itself cause those being observed to change their behavior so that the results of the observation are misleading.

Hawthorne Effect - false reality

The classic case of reactive observation was a 1939 study of the effects that changes in working conditions at a particular factory had on worker productivity. During the 1920s and early 1930s, such factors as hours of work, rest periods, lighting, and methods of pay were varied for a small group of workers. Regardless of what conditions they worked under, whether long or short hours, few or frequent rest periods, or some other variant, this group of workers continually out-produced all other workers in the same factory. The most influential factor in their productivity, it turned out, was an unusually high level of morale associated with the fact that members of this group knew they were being observed and experimented upon (Roethlisberger and Dickson 1939). This so-called Hawthorne effect, named for the factory where it was first observed, meant that no conclusion could be drawn regarding the relationship between working conditions and productivity because the act of observation created a false reality, a work environment unlike the normal one.

Sometimes in undertaking political science research, we encounter similar, obvious examples of reactivity. An overbearing or unfriendly interviewer, a leading question, or a meddlesome observer can so damage the research situation that no confidence can be vested in its outcomes. As often as not, however, the process is more subtle. We might, for example, properly train the perfect interviewer to ask a perfectly good question, yet still incur reactivity: *Q:* "Do you favor or oppose the president's economic policy?" *A:* "I'm in favor of it. I think it is a good idea." But how do we know for sure that our respondent has really given any thought to the president's economic policy before being interviewed? Is it not possible that the interview itself acted as a catalyst, in effect crystallizing the respondent's thoughts and creating an opinion where none had previously existed? This, too, is reactivity, but of a type that is much more difficult to detect and to avoid.

It is not enough simply to march into the field armed with a few questions and start looking around for answers. We must exercise great care in deciding how and where we shall enter the field and how and whom we shall observe. The best theory and the best plan of attack can be squandered if we are careless in our observation.

THE ANALYSIS OF DATA

The bits of information about each case that we gather during our observations are called data and once we have them in hand, the end is in sight. The object at this point is to ascertain what answers we have found to our research question. This may be done in many instances by answering three questions. First, is there some association between, on the one hand, the behavior we are hoping to explain or to understand better and, on the other hand, the factors we think will help us to do so?

Is There a Relationship?

Suppose, for example, that we expect to find that people who differ in their level of formal education will differ systematically in the likelihood that they will vote. Our first question must be, does this happen? Do people who differ from one another on one of these variables tend to differ consistently on the other as well? Are the more educated people consistently either more or less likely to vote than the less educated people? We might find in examining our data, for instance, that less educated people tend to vote about as often as more educated people and that knowing a person's level of education does not help us to predict or explain the difference between that person's likelihood of voting and someone else's. If this is the case, we say that one's level of education does not influence the likelihood of voting or, alternatively, that there is no association between the two variables. Our expectation is not supported by our analysis. If, on the other hand, we discover that six or seven times out of ten, knowing the level of education does allow us to predict accurately the likelihood of a person's voting, this constitutes evidence supporting our expectation that the two variables are related. It tells us that more educated people are systematically different from less educated people when it comes to voting and helps us understand our subjects' voting behavior. The first thing to look for in assessing a hypothesis, then, is whether the two variables are statistically related.

What Type of Relationship?

How are the two variables related? Are more educated people more likely than less educated people to vote? Alternatively, are they less likely to vote? Or is the relationship between the variables even more complex? If we have thought through our hypothesis so that we have some reasons to expect the level of education to be related to voting, we probably have one or another of these possibilities in mind.

We might argue, for example, that having more formal education increases the likelihood of someone having the skills and information needed to support an interest in politics. Accordingly, a more educated person is more likely to vote than is a less skilled or less informed person. Thus, we might expect voting to be more frequent or more common among the more educated of the people we study. This type of relationship is illustrated in Figure 1.2(a), where points on the line represent corresponding values on the two variables.

We might also argue, however, that the more educated one becomes, the more one comes to believe that political activity is futile. Education, in this view, gives rise to disillusionment, which in turn reduces the inclination to vote. Here we expect voting to be more frequent among the less educated of our subjects. This type of relationship is illustrated in Figure 1.2(b).

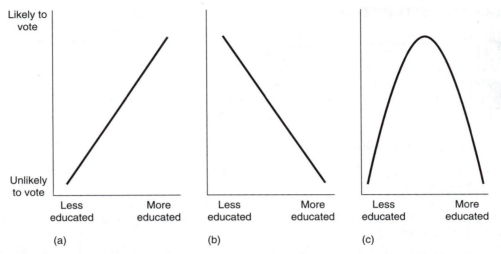

FIGURE 1.2   Possible relationships between individuals' level of education and their likelihood of voting.

Or, we might even argue that education contributes to skills and interests to a point, but that those who are educated beyond that point (for example, those who attend college) become increasingly disillusioned and less interested in politics. Here we expect voting to be most frequent among those of moderate educational attainment, with lower levels of voting at either extreme. This more complex relationship is illustrated in Figure 1.2(c).

In each instance a relationship exists between a person's level of education and likelihood of voting, but clearly the implications of these varying relationships are vastly different. It is possible, then, to find a strong relationship between the two variables and yet fail to substantiate our hypothesis. It should be noted that in each of the graphs in Figure 1.2, it was assumed that we possess numerical data on respondents' educational level and voter turnout.

Confidence in Findings?

How likely is it that the relationships we find in a sample also occur in the population from which those cases were drawn? This is simply a statistical way of asking how good a job we have done in ensuring that our small sample is representative, or typical, of the larger population. If we have properly selected the cases to be studied, then we can say with confidence that our conclusions, though based on but a few cases, may be applied to all. If we have made errors, we may be less confident. Of course, as will be emphasized in Chapter 7, when conclusions are based on a sample of the population, we can never be *totally* certain of them.

INTERPRETATION OF THE RESULTS

Finally, we reach a point where we must put all the pieces together. Have we succeeded in actually asking the research question that we set out to ask? What have we discovered? What is the substantive importance of our findings? How do these results square with our expectations? In essence, we have by this time reduced some aspect of political behavior to a set of observations—detailed and descriptive qualitative data, or numerical quantitative data. Now, though, we must decide what our data tell us about our research question.

But there is more: We must also look back with a critical eye on our research itself. Have we made some fundamental error along the way that may invalidate our findings? Have we managed to keep a close relationship between our theory and our research on the one hand and the reality of political activity on the other? Can we credit any of our apparent findings about the real world to the things we have done (or have failed to do) in our research, rather than to actual events? These are difficult questions to answer, but you must address these issues before you will know how much confidence to place in the product of the research.

WILL I EVER BE A POLITICAL SCIENTIST?

Over the decades that we have been teaching research methods, we have been asked this question countless times by students (and, sometimes, by their parents). This question implicitly poses another question: Will taking this class and studying political science research methods help me in my future life and career? For the following reasons, we enthusiastically answer both of these questions in the affirmative!

1. Yes, because within your political science major, you will be doing research and reading research. Learning how research is conducted through hands-on experience prepares you to read research effectively, efficiently, and analytically in other political science courses.

2. Yes, because all of you will attend graduate school at some point in time. I apologize if you have not heard, but the days when a bachelor's degree was sufficient for an entire career are long past. Graduate programs in management, public administration, medicine, and many others require students to use the skills taught in this book and your course—each of these fields requires students to interpret scientific research.

3. Yes, if you will be a lawyer. Federal judges frequently apply social science data to rulings. As Watson (2009) notes, lawyers who have a strong command of research skills have an advantage in arguing their cases. In *Daubert v. Merrell Dow Pharmaceuticals* (1993), the Court found that judges must determine whether scientific evidence is gathered following appropriate methodologies. Thus, both judges and the lawyers arguing before the judges must be well versed in the relevant research methods.

4. Yes, because we use research skills in daily life—even if you are thinking of living in your parent's basement for the rest of your life (by the way, have you checked with your parents about this plan?). We will teach you research techniques in daily life through a scientific approach. These skills can be used in a variety of ways, from analyzing local crime rates or school quality in certain neighborhoods, to gathering information to help you choose which candidate to support in an election.

RESEARCH EXERCISE

Evaluating Research Evidence: *The Oprah Winfrey Show*

Every day we're confronted with information—some we trust, and some we ignore. We constantly make choices about this information, based upon our evaluation of its plausibility, how well it conforms to our current understandings, or its source. Similarly, in science we filter information—often for those same reasons—but we evaluate the evidence more systematically.

To learn scientific information processing and to get used to evaluating information's trustworthiness:

1. Tomorrow (or the next week day), watch an entire episode of *The Oprah Winfrey Show* on TV, or read three articles from her magazine (*O, The Oprah Magazine*) or from her website (www.oprah.com).
2. Write a brief description of three products or techniques about which medical or health claims are made. This should take no more than three sentences.
3. Answer these questions about each health suggestion or claim that you noted:
   a. Who made each claim?
   b. Was evidence offered to support the claim?
      i. Were these anecdotes?
      ii. Were the claims systematically evaluated?
      iii. Was "science" mentioned? If so, favorably or derisively?
   c. Did the host seem to favor systematic or anecdotal studies or evaluations? To which type of evidence did the studio audience seem to give more credence?
4. Do you find the presented evidence persuasive? Why or why not?

Conclusion

This book will introduce you to a more systematic way to pursue your informal theorizing and continually refine your theories, increasing their usefulness, as you learn new information. We teach you how to frame questions more formally, and present the findings in a more formal or professional and standardized way.

This chapter's brief overview of the six stages of the research process will give you a good idea of what scientific research into politics is like and what this book is about. We shall devote a good many of our pages to learning to perform and evaluate each of these tasks. We know that the same skills that go into creating quality research may also be applied to developing more thorough and critical skills in reading and evaluating the research done by others. This is an ability that anyone with an interest in the study of politics will do well to possess. Social scientific research is increasingly used as a basis for both public policy and legal decisions. It is, therefore, increasingly important that citizens be able to judge the merits of research in order to discharge their responsibilities in a democratic society.

Key Terms

empirical *2*

normative *2*

quantitative *2*

qualitative *2*

scientific research *4*

basic research *5*

applied research *5*

operationalization *7*

generalizability *9*

reactivity *10*

data *11*

Research Examples

Rarely is every part of the research process described in great detail in published work, because many authors reserve scarce printed space for their findings. However, explicitly identifying each of the components of a published research report may serve to guide the reader through the work and make it accessible to a wider audience. For example, in their article on the relationship between who sits (e.g., elected officials or managers) on Metropolitan Planning Organizations and whether they pursue local or regional goals in their distribution of federal transportation funding, Elisabeth Gerber and Clark Gibson (2009) begin by noting each component of the research at the end of the article's introduction. Throughout the article, the authors clearly explain each step in the development of the project, from building the theory from the existing literature, to data coding and merging, to sample selection, to interpreting the results.

References

Gerber, Elisabeth R., and Clark C. Gibson. 2009. "Balancing Regionalism and Localism: Institutions and Incentives Shape American Transportation Policy." *American Journal of Political Science* 53(July): 633–648.

Watson, Wendy. 2009. "Teaching Research Methods to Pre-Law Students." Paper presented at the annual meeting of the Teaching and Learning Conference of the American Political Science Association, Renaissance Baltimore Harborplace Hotel, Baltimore, MD, February 6.

Explaining the Political World: Building Theories and Hypotheses

In this chapter you will learn:

- Why we use theories to guide our research.
- The roles played by induction and deduction in developing theory.
- The characteristics of useful theories.
- The distinction between covariation and causation.
- How we elaborate theories using hypotheses.

Theory building may sound like an alien concept, but you already regularly develop and use your own theories to interpret your world and operate better within it. For example, when you started college, it is unlikely that anyone issued you a dress code, but you still figured out what to wear. Consciously, or unconsciously, you probably started with a **research question**: What do people like me wear in this setting? From this question, you might have developed a theory, such as: Those who wear (flip-flops/hiking boots/dress shoes/sneakers) are seen as (casual/outdoorsy/fashionable/athletic), because their footwear (1) signals their interests and (2) facilitates their preferred recreational activities.

Moving to the political realm, as a youth you likely gravitated toward a certain party, based on your understanding of which party was most similar to your interests. While probably not explicit, this information was interpreted through a theory, such as: Those who favor (personal freedoms/social welfare/international cooperation/national defense) are more likely affiliated with ([party name]), because this party (1) runs candidates who speak about these topics, (2) has a track record of performance on this issue, and (3) those who support this party share my views.

Whether we actively think about it or not, most of us develop and refine our understanding of the political world and our role in it using theories. Based on the first chapter's discussion, we know that scientific research requires systematic observation and analysis. This chapter takes your informal theory-making skills and directs them toward building explanatory research theories, makes this process explicit, and teaches you to derive testable hypotheses from your political theories.

The Purpose of Theory

Transforming our general research question into one or several specific ones requires developing some plausible explanations for what we observe. We might, for instance, reason that people's position on environmental protection is influenced by the nature of their job. Some occupations, for example, benefit from environmental protection measures whereas others are hurt by them (at least in the short run). We might also think that age influences people's attitude toward environmental issues, because younger people have grown up with an awareness of the problems of pollution while older people grew up before these problems were understood.

This reasoning helps us to reduce the complexity of social life and puts us in a position to begin scientific inquiry. We can apply logic and information that we already have about empirical relationships to reason out a set of things we expect to be true if our tentative explanation is valid. Now we can ask questions like these: Do younger people support environmental legislation more often than older people? Do white-collar and professional people support environmental measures more often than blue-collar people? We can devise ways to make observations that will allow us to answer these questions and, when we have explored enough small questions, to answer our initial research question.

When we attempt to create possible explanations for events, we are **theorizing**, or developing a theory. Theories are created in our effort to gain understanding. They help direct the research to determine if our understanding of events is correct. This is why theory building is the first stage in the research process and why it is essential that we understand the relationship between theory and research.

Theories Aid Interpretation

Without a sound theory, we will not be able to tell why our research "findings" provide an answer to the research question. Suppose we begin research with only the general question posed earlier. If we ask, a properly selected sample of 2,000 Americans about their position on environmental protection and a series of questions about their personal characteristics, we can use our results to *describe* the kinds of people who support and oppose environmental legislation, but we cannot tell *why* they support or oppose it.

If, on the other hand, we start with a theory that offers an explanation of why people support or oppose environmental protection policies and ask questions to check on the accuracy of the expectations that logically follow from this theory, our results will contribute to our understanding of why people take the positions they do.

To illustrate, say that we theorize that people's first concern is their economic well-being and that their position on environmental protection is determined totally by their perception of how proposed legislation will affect their income. One expectation or prediction that logically follows from this line of reasoning is that people who expect to be financially hurt by environmental protection laws will oppose them, whereas those who expect to be helped by these laws will support them. If our theory is an adequate explanation of how people develop attitudes about environmental protection, then this prediction should be an accurate statement about real-world relationships. We can then get some idea of the usefulness of our theory by checking on the empirical accuracy of the prediction that logically follows from it. For example, we might ask people about their position on environmental protection and their perception of its effect on their income to find out whether the prediction is borne out by what we learn about actual relationships.

Regardless of the outcome, our research can then tell us something about why people feel as they do about this issue. If the research is correctly done and the prediction is supported, we are encouraged both to believe that we have developed a sound explanation for the behavior in question and to search for further evidence of its utility. If the prediction is shown to be wrong, we at least have reason to believe that this is not likely to be a useful theory for understanding people's position on this matter, and we can begin to explore other possible explanations.

Whether we start our research with a theory or without a theory, it may produce the same facts. But the facts will contribute to our understanding *only* if we can tie them together through a theory. For example, knowing that white-collar people tend to support environmental protection more often than blue-collar people do will provide an explanation of why people take the positions they do only if we can give some reason why occupation and position on ecology should be related. Otherwise, the fact could be a coincidence, and knowing it will add nothing to our ability to explain people's attitudes. Theories provide sets of reasons why facts should be connected in given ways. Therefore, *theories make facts useful by providing us with a framework for interpreting them and seeing their relationships to one another.*

This chapter is designed to help you understand how theories are developed and how they are used to guide research. We will discuss the nature of social science theorizing, the elements of theories, and the relationship of theory to the rest of the research process. When you have finished the chapter, you should be able to begin thinking about political questions that interest you in ways that will prepare you to undertake systematic empirical research in order to find valid answers to those questions.

THE NATURE OF SOCIAL SCIENCE THEORY

Usefulness of Theories

First, theories help simplify reality so that we might understand it in order to control it or adapt to it better. Second, once we have developed such an understanding, theories can guide us in testing its accuracy. Theories do this by providing a logical basis for expectations or predictions about the world that can be compared with reality through research. When our predictions are supported by evidence, the understanding that provides a basis for those predictions is also supported, and our confidence that we have a grasp of the way things work is increased. When our predictions are inaccurate, we begin to question our understanding of events and to look for ways to improve it.

Theories are *sets of logically related symbols that represent what we think happens in the world.* They are simply intellectual tools. Understanding this is important, because it helps us realize that theories are neither true nor false in any absolute sense, but only more or less *useful.* You cannot expect to discover a theory the way an explorer discovers a new island. Why? Because theories do not exist "out there" for discovery. They are the products of human imagination, hard work, and sometimes good fortune.

If theories are essential to sound research but cannot be discovered by simply looking at accumulated data, how can we go about building a theory to guide our quest for an understanding of those aspects of political life that interest us? What processes are involved? The answer is not neat or simple, because theories are developed in a variety of ways. We cannot outline a set of procedures to produce a useful theory in the same way as we might describe how to build a table. We can, however, provide an explanation of the major ideas and stages commonly involved in theory construction. The first of these stages is the *conceptualization of the problem*.

THE LOGIC OF THEORY BUILDING

Beginning with the event or behavior we want to understand, we must first ask ourselves what we know about the phenomenon that might help us explain it. Insights might be gained from personal experience, casual observation, or creative thinking. More often we will find it useful to investigate systematically what others have found about the subject. Useful theories begin from a thorough knowledge of the events we want to explain. Without such knowledge, we might fail to understand what is to be explained or might not have a clue where to begin looking for relationships that can be used to explain the events. An example might highlight the importance of having a thorough knowledge of the facts to aid our research conceptualization.

An Example

The massive riots that took place in many U.S. cities in the late 1960s deeply worried many Americans. Political scientists and other social scientists were asked to investigate the causes of the riots. When the riots first occurred, many public officials said they were the acts of a group of poor citizens without stable ties to society. If we had accepted this interpretation and sought to understand the riots, we would have defined our task as one of explaining why so many of these "riffraff" were concentrated in our cities at that time and how they were moved to riot. Many public officials turned to the alleged presence of "outside agitators" as an explanation. As social scientists conducted interviews in the riot-torn cities, however, we learned that rioting was not restricted to riffraff. In fact, as a group, rioters differed very little from the general black population of those cities (Fogelson and Hill 1986). This fact presents us with a very different research task from that suggested by the riffraff interpretation. We must now seek to understand how average citizens with jobs, families, and other ties to society were motivated to riot. Subsequent explanations have focused on variables such as African Americans' reaction to white racism rather than "outside agitators." The alternative theoretical explanations of urban rioting are diagrammed in Figure 2.1.

   In this case, an inadequate knowledge of the facts could have fundamentally misdirected our theory-building efforts. This exemplifies why **exploratory research**, which is designed to establish the facts in a given case, is important. It is also the reason why we must search the literature for information on the phenomena we seek to explain if we hope to develop sound theories.

   Once we have as many facts as we can find, how do we construct a theory to explain these observations? We generally begin by searching the facts for patterns that can account for the observed events. For example, we might want to know what causes political protests on college campuses. Answering this question involves explaining what leads students to take part in protests. Having been or having known protesters might

A	→	B	*because*	C
1. Poor citizens	are more likely to	riot	because	(1) they lack stable ties to society
2. Marginalized citizens	are motivated to	riot,	because	(1) of outside agitators' encouragement
				(2) those outside the mainstream have little to lose (e.g., jobs, home)
3. Middle class urban blacks	were motivated to	riot,	because	(1) they came to believe that whites placed little value on African Americans' lives
				(2) people who think they have nothing to lose are willing to engage in alternative protest behavior (e.g. Chinese protestors in Tiananmen Square in 1989)

FIGURE 2.1   Alternative theories explaining 1960s urban rioting.

provide us with some insights into their motivation, but to develop an explanation of why large numbers of students participate would require information on a much larger number of people. We would be wise to seek data on the characteristics and motives of student protesters *in general* in order to frame our explanation. If we found among protesters commonalities that set them apart from nonprotesters, we might reason that these characteristics led to their participation in demonstrations. The prominence of these characteristics among college students then becomes part of our explanation of why protests occur.

Induction

The process of generalizing from what we have observed to what we have not or cannot observe is called **induction**. It forms the basis of scientific theory. Theories built through inductions from observations are said to be *empirically grounded*.

In the process of induction, we reason from what we know to be the case in some situations to what might be the case in other, similar situations; we make a logical leap from what we have seen to a prediction about what we have not seen, based on the assumption that there is some constant underlying pattern to events in the world. We all use induction in our daily life. If we observe five consecutive times that the elevator door opens after we push a button on the wall, we will quickly draw the conclusion that pushing the button causes elevator doors to open. This is an inductive generalization from the few cases we have observed (pushing the button five times) to cases we have not (pushing the button on

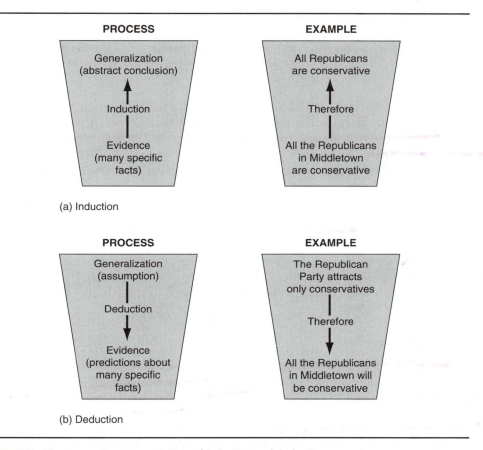

FIGURE 2.2   Diagrammatic representation of inductive and deductive reasoning.

the wall outside of all elevators). The process of induction is diagrammed in Figure 2.2(a). This diagram suggests how inductively constructed theories are grounded in facts.

There is more to theory building than induction, however, because pointing out facts does not provide an explanation unless we can show *why* those facts have led to the observed results. Let us return to the example of student protest. Suppose we find that protesters tend to be more dissatisfied with public policies than nonprotesters and that protesters also tend to have far less faith in the effectiveness of conventional politics in getting policies changed. Stating this fact constitutes an explanation of protest only if we are able to show why such attitudes should lead to protest behavior. Showing this might involve making some *assumptions* about political behavior. Specifically, it might involve assuming that people will act to change policies they strongly oppose and that they will resort to protest behavior if they feel that conventional political participation (voting, letter writing, etc.) will not alter the policies.

These **assumptions** (sometimes called *axioms* or *postulates*) then become part of our theory. Assumptions describe the conditions under which we expect the tentative explanation we have reached to be supported by evidence. They tell why we expect student protest from what we know about students on college campuses by making general statements about political behavior under certain conditions. We can now explain specific behavior (protest) by showing that it follows logically from a set of theoretical assumptions.

Deduction

This process is the reverse of inductive reasoning. Deductive reasoning moves from abstract statements about general relationships to concrete statements about specific behaviors. This process of reasoning *from the abstract and general to the concrete and specific* is known as **deduction**. We all use deductive logic in everyday life. If we have developed a general idea that pushing the button next to elevators causes the door to open, then when confronted with an elevator and a button on a wall, we will deduce that the way to enter the elevator is to push the button. We have moved from a generalization to the prediction of a specific event by deduction. This process is diagrammed in Figure 2.2(b).

Deduction is the process that enables us to use theories to explain real-world events. If we can show by a process of deduction that some observed event can be logically predicted from the set of assumptions that constitute our theory, then the theory provides an explanation for the observed event. The theory helps us to understand the event by giving us a reason why it is as it is. The role of deduction is to provide this link between the theory and our observations.

Theory Construction

The process of theory construction involves the interaction of both inductive and deductive logic in the following stages: (1) we use induction to translate what we have observed into assumptions; (2) we employ deduction to derive predictions; (3) we test these predictions against new observations; and (4) we revise our assumptions to make them consistent with the results of our observations. Then we repeat the process in an effort to make the theory increasingly useful as a tool for understanding events.

Merely devising a theory, however, does not make it valid. We can generally come up with many theories to explain a given event. The question we must ask is, which of these theories is most useful in helping us understand the world? Answering this question will require that we test alternative theories against reality.

Before we can discuss theory testing, it is important to understand two things. First, we have to know what features make a theory useful so that we can know how to go about building theories. Second, we must know how the components of a theory are related to each other and to empirical research.

Characteristics of Useful Theories

For a theory to be useful in explaining observations, it must meet several standards:

1. It must be *testable*. Can we reason from the theory to expectations about reality that are concrete and specific enough for us to make observations that either support the expectations or fail to support them? Can the theory be related to the world in systematic ways, or is it only a set of abstractions?
2. It must be *logically sound*. Is the theory internally consistent? Are its assumptions compatible, and the terms it contains unambiguous?

3. It must be *communicable*. Can other, properly trained people understand the theory in ways that allow them to use it to explain events and to test hypotheses derived from it?

4. It must be *general.* Is it possible to use it to explain a variety of events in different times and places? Can we deduce predictions from it that can be tested in different circumstances, or is it tied too closely to one set of observations?

5. It must be *parsimonious*. Is it simple enough to be readily applied and understood, or is it so complex, so filled with conditions and exceptions, that it is difficult to derive explicit expectations about real-world events from it?

Theories can have each of these desirable characteristics in different degrees, and sometimes we have to choose among them in developing a particular theory. We may have to sacrifice some parsimony in order to obtain more generality or testability, for instance. We have to keep all these desirable features in mind when formulating theories if the products of our labors are to be truly useful.

COMPONENTS OF SOCIAL SCIENCE THEORY

Theories are composed of sets of *concepts* that are related by propositions logically derived from a set of *assumptions.* This is the *logical structure* of a theory. It is this structure that allows us to use the theory to explain events, because it allows us to give reasons why we can logically expect things to be as they are.

Defining Concepts

The quest for useful theory begins with the decisions we make about the building blocks of theories: concepts. A **concept** is merely a *word or symbol that represents some idea.* There is nothing mystical about concepts. We use them every day to help us cope with the complexity of reality by categorizing the things we encounter according to some of their properties that are relevant to us. We classify the four-legged creatures we see into cows, cats, dogs, and other species, and that classification alone provides a basis for some important expectations (for example, dogs are not a good source of milk). Assigning a name to something allows us to predict certain things about it, because the name is a symbol for particular combinations of properties.

Social science concepts serve the same purpose. They point to the properties of objects (people, political systems, elections) that are relevant to a particular inquiry. One observer might be interested in a person's personality structure, another is interested in partisan identification, and a third focuses on the person's level of political alienation. The person has all of these properties (a personality, a party identification, and a degree of alienation) and many more, but only certain of the properties are relevant to any given piece of research. All three observers are dealing with the same reality; they simply choose to organize their perceptions of it differently. Concepts help us to decide which of many traits or attributes are important to our research.

Making Concepts Useful

Concepts, like theories, are tools that we create for specific purposes and that cannot be labeled true or false, but only more or less useful. What makes a concept useful? There are three major considerations.

First, since we are involved in *empirical* inquiry, the concept must refer to phenomena that are at least potentially *observable*. In medieval times, the concept of divine will played an important role in explanations of events. We cannot verify such explanations, however, because we cannot observe divine will to tell whether it is present or absent in any given case. If it is to have any scientific value, a concept must refer to something that can be measured with our ordinary senses.

This does not mean that all concepts must refer to *directly* observable things. Some of the most useful concepts in the social sciences refer to properties we cannot observe directly. For example, people do not have a class status in the way that they have red hair, but if we know certain things about them (their income or their occupation, for example), we can infer what their class status is. Similarly, nations do not have authoritarian or democratic political systems in the way that they have mountains or deserts, but we can *infer* the degree of democracy that exists in a nation by observing certain things about its political life (the nature of elections and provisions for civil liberties, for instance).

The question is: Can we devise a set of procedures for using our senses to gather information that will allow us to judge the presence or absence or magnitude in the real world of the thing to which the concept refers? If we can do this for a concept, it is said to have **empirical referents**; it refers to something that is directly or indirectly observable.

Second, in addition to having empirical referents, concepts must be *precise*. They must refer to one and only one set of properties of some phenomenon. We must be able to know exactly what we are talking about when using a concept to describe an object. For instance, is the degree of inequality of distribution of wealth part of what we are referring to when describing a nation's political system as democratic or authoritarian, or is the nature of the

PRACTICAL RESEARCH ETHICS

How will your work be used?

Beyond learning the characteristics of useful theories, you should also consider how your research will be used. While scientific theory is inherently value-free, you might feel some compunction about the use of your idea.

When critiqued during the arms race, the scientists who developed the nuclear bomb during World War II defended themselves by pointing out that they simply identified atomic properties and capabilities that have always existed. They further suggested that it is up to others—specifically, policy makers—to decide how scientific discoveries are used.

Implicitly or explicitly, political science always involves humans. Thus, it is unrealistic to pretend that people's lives could never be affected by your research, whether it explores media messages, or interest groups, or executive power. How would you feel if someone used your research to manipulate voters through the media during a political campaign? What if a government in a developing nation realized, through your research findings, that its environmental groups' voices may be silenced without popular backlash, as long as the government maintains economic development? Would it make you feel good if, based upon your research findings that people are greatly comforted by a strong executive during times of popular fear, a democratic regime sharply limited judicial oversight in favor of concentrating power in the executive?

Although these examples are intended to represent hypothetical research applications, you should never assume that your own research cannot have consequences for real people's lives—for good or ill.

political system determined exclusively by other factors? Precision is important because it tells us what to observe in order to see how a concept is manifested in any given case. Only if we can determine this can we use the concept in empirically grounded explanations.

Precision also helps us identify our empirical referents and make distinctions among observed phenomena. If democracy means *only* the presence or absence of popular elections for public officials, then the former Soviet Union and the United States both were democracies. Do we want to treat these two nations as examples of the same kind of political system for purposes of our research? If not, then we need to refine the concept, making it more precise, so that we can draw a distinction in our study between the two nations.

Finally, useful concepts have **theoretical import**. A concept has *theoretical import* when it is related to enough other concepts in the theory that it plays an essential role in the explanation of observed events. In our hypothetical explanation of student protest, we employed two concepts. One was *intensity of policy preferences,* and the other was *perception of the effectiveness of conventional political action in changing policies.* These two concepts were tied together by the assumptions that people will act to change policies with which they strongly disagree and that they will turn to protest when they feel that other means of influence will not bring results. Given these assumptions, finding the particular combination of attitudes we have referred to will lead us to expect protest behavior. Each concept is essential to the explanation and is linked both to the theoretical assumptions and to the other concept. Each concept has theoretical import because it plays a necessary role in our explanation.

RELATIONSHIPS IN SOCIAL SCIENCE THEORY

Now we can begin to see that theory makes concepts useful by tying them together so that they can be used in formulating explanations. Theory ties concepts to one another by stating relationships between them. These statements take the form of **propositions** derived from our assumptions. Propositions generally posit one of two major types of relationship among concepts. These are *covariation* and *causation.*

Covariational relationships indicate that two or more concepts tend to change together: As one increases (or decreases) the other increases (or decreases). Covariational relationships tell us nothing about what causes the two concepts to change together. For instance, we might predict that level of political information and likelihood of voting covary, so that as one increases so does the other. But are people more likely to vote because they have more information, or do they gain information because they intend to vote and want to make a sound decision, or are both information level and likelihood of voting the products of some third factor, such as interest in politics or perceived civic duty? The covariational proposition does not tell us.

Causal relationships exist when changes in one or more concepts lead to or cause changes in one or more other concepts. For example, the stronger one's party identification, we might argue, the more likely one is to vote. Feeling oneself to be a member of a party can lead one to vote, but the likelihood of voting does not create one's party identification.

We are accustomed to thinking in terms of cause and effect in our everyday life, and generally use these concepts loosely. In scientific research it is often very difficult to identify the causes or consequences of human behavior; the more important the event, the more difficult isolation of its causes can be. What brings on a war, a social movement, or the creation of a new political party?

Testing Causation

Because of such complexities, we must be careful to postulate causal relationships only when four conditions are simultaneously met. First, the postulated cause and effect must change together, or covary. Second, the cause must precede the effect. Third, we must be able to identify a *causal linkage* between the supposed cause and effect (meaning, we must be able to identify the *process* by which changes in one factor cause changes in another). Fourth, the covariance of the cause-and-effect phenomena must not be due to their simultaneous relationship to some third factor—a condition we discuss next.

Spurious relationships occur when A and B vary together only because they are both caused by C. If they would not covary in the absence of C, the apparent relationship between A and B is termed *spurious*. We must carefully examine the assumptions we are making in an effort to uncover possible spuriousness in relationships before we build them into our theories as though they were the product of causal interaction. A classic instance of spuriousness is the case in which an investigator first finds that the price of imported rum and the salaries of ministers fluctuate together and then reasons that changes in the price of rum cause changes in ministers' salaries. It is more likely that both rum prices and ministers' salaries change in response to changes in general economic conditions and overall price level. The relationship between the first two variables is covariational, but it is not causal.

It is important to recognize two other features of social causation. First, one phenomenon may cause another either directly or indirectly. For example, A may cause B only in that it is the cause of C, which directly causes B. We must be alert to the role of **indirect causation** in attempting to make our theories as complete as possible. Second, we must be sensitive to the fact that human behavior generally has more than one cause. In theorizing, we should avoid oversimplifying and thus recognize the role of **multiple causation** in social life. This simply means that any one event may have several different causes, and that many events sometimes must come together to cause a given occurrence.

To cope with all of these complexities, it is generally a good idea to draw a **causal model** of the theory. This is simply a diagram that clearly specifies all the relationships posited in the theory so that it is easier to see the implications of our arguments. Figure 2.3 presents an example of such a model. Each arrow in the model represents a causal influence, and the direction in which it is pointing indicates which variable is theorized as dependent and which as independent. The theory diagrammed in Figure 2.3 asserts that a variety of factors influence a representative's decision to vote for or against welfare legislation in both direct and indirect ways. For instance, the size of the poor population in the representative's congressional district is depicted as influencing welfare voting both directly (independently) and indirectly through the electoral competitiveness of the district and the seniority level of the representative.

Although our theories typically specify a causal relationship between our concepts, we rarely encounter social science data that can establish definite causation. Later in this text, we will highlight the exceptional degree of control the experimental setting offers, which can help to identify causal relationships.

Positive and Negative Relationships

Both covariational and causal relationships can be either *positive* or *negative*. This means that the two concepts can change either in the same direction or in opposite directions, respectively. An example of a **positive relationship** is: The *higher* the relative deprivation of

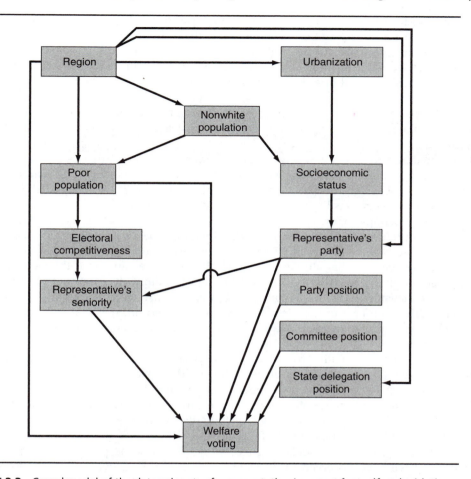

FIGURE 2.3   Causal model of the determinants of representatives' support for welfare legislation in the U.S. Congress.
Source: Rich (1984, 135). Reprinted with permission.

minority groups within a society, the higher the likelihood of political violence. A **negative relationship** may be posited as follows: The *higher* the degree of political alienation one feels, the *lower* the likelihood that one will take part in conventional political activities. Our theories must specify whether we expect positive or negative relationships among concepts. This information can be added to causal diagrams by placing a plus (1) or minus (2) sign on each path in order to indicate whether the relationship is thought to be positive or negative.

THEORY TESTING AND ELABORATION

Theories must never be regarded as finished products, but always as tools that should occasionally be inspected and can often be improved. We start with a research question that asks for an explanation of observed events, select concepts that promise to be useful in explaining those events, and relate the concepts through propositions logically derived from a set of assumptions we choose to make in order to secure an explanation. Now our backs are against the wall. Is this lovely structure any good? It seems to explain what we want to understand, but can we check it in some way? Can we test its utility so that we can know how much confidence to place in it and persuade others of its value?

Theory testing is at the center of the research process. Because our theories are generally developed from bits of knowledge about actual relationships, the tasks of theory testing are essentially those of using the theory to formulate some expectations about other relationships we have not observed and then checking to see whether actual observations are consistent with what we expect to find. We cannot rely on relationships we have already observed, because showing that the theory leads us to expect the very relationships the theory was built to explain would be no test at all.

In our example of the elevator, after observing the elevators in one building, we will be quite confident that the elevators in that building operate in response to a system of wall-mounted buttons. We might even be willing to generalize from our observations to reach the conclusion that all elevators work this way. We can check the validity of that conclusion only by actually trying it out in other buildings. It does not help to double-check the elevators in the building we started in, because we already know that they respond to the buttons and showing that they do does not make us feel any more secure that other elevators do as well. We have to go to other buildings to see how their elevators operate.

We can never actually prove that our theory of elevator operation is correct because we can never observe all the elevators in the world. As we see more and more elevators that do work this way and we never encounter any that do not, our confidence in the validity of our generalization will increase. If we cannot find any other elevators that work by buttons, however, we will quickly conclude that we have been mistaken in generalizing from the initial observations to all other elevators.

Theory testing in the social sciences works by the same principle. We must move from what we have observed in devising the theory to what we have not observed, in order to discover whether or not the theory provides us with an accurate set of expectations about the world.

Suppose, for example, that we want to construct a theory to explain voting behavior. We review previous research on the subject and discover that, for citizens of the United States, higher education is positively related to the propensity to vote. On the basis of these observations, we include in our theory an assumption that higher educational levels lead to a greater likelihood of voting. We know that these factors are related in the United States, but what about in other nations? Could there be something unique to the educational system or the informational complexity of voting in the United States that causes this relationship? The only way we can find out is to observe people and the political systems in other nations, because, as political scientists, we are interested in finding *general* relationships in human behavior.

From the assumption that education increases the likelihood of voting, we might deduce the prediction that people with some college education are more likely to vote than people with no more than a high school diploma. We can test this prediction by seeing whether it accurately reflects relationships found in data from a variety of countries. The more often we find evidence consistent with the prediction, the more confident we will feel that our theory is useful in predicting human behavior. We can never be absolutely certain that the theory is "true," because we can neither observe all cases nor be sure how the empirical relationships might change with time. But we can acquire more or less confidence in the utility of the theory by comparing the predictions derived from it with observations. If it allows us to accurately predict things we have not previously observed, then it is useful.

Theories, as sets of concepts, assumptions, and propositions, are never finally proved or disproved. Rather, our confidence in the *usefulness* of a theory builds as we accumulate observations that are consistent with the expectations or hypotheses derived from it. Alternatively, our confidence diminishes as we accumulate observations that are inconsistent with theoretically derived hypotheses.

RESEARCH EXERCISE

Developing an Explanatory Theory

As noted in this chapter, an explanatory theory includes a relationship between two concepts, and offers at least one plausible explanation of that relationship. For this exercise, you will write an explanatory theory:

1. Your theory will be based upon two concepts mentioned in one of the articles cited at the end of one of the chapters in this book (your instructor may assign you a specific chapter or specific article).
2. Following the guidelines in this chapter, your theory must:
   a. State a relationship between the two concepts from the article's title.
   b. Offer a third concept that plausibly explains the relationship between the first two concepts.
3. Your theory should be one sentence long, but you may offer more than one explanatory concept, if you wish.

THE ROLE OF HYPOTHESES

The above section's **theory elaboration** is based largely on a process of comparing hypothesized conditions with reality and, once we have the results, modifying our theory so that the hypotheses that can be derived from it are more and more consistent with what we observe. Now we consider how our research questions are translated into hypotheses that can guide empirical investigations and provide us with clues to the adequacy of our theoretical explanations.

Hypotheses Defined

A **hypothesis** is essentially a statement of what we believe to be factual. It tells what we expect to find when we make properly organized observations of reality.

- Hypotheses are declarative statements.
- Hypotheses identify a directional relationship.
- Hypotheses are specific.

Hypotheses are usually stated in the following general form:

The higher (lower, greater, larger, slower, etc.) the _____, *the higher (lower, greater, larger, slower, etc.) the* _____.

The blanks are filled in with the names of the phenomena that we expect will change together. For example, let's say we have a theory that those who have a more conservative ideology are more likely to be Republicans, because the GOP is known to promote conservative ideas. From this theory we might construct the hypothesis below. This is a covariational hypothesis. It does not tell us how partisan identification (for the GOP) is determined, but it does point us to something that we can observe in an effort to acquire some evidence on the fit between our theory and reality.

The more likely one is to identify as Somewhat Conservative or Very Conservative, the more likely one is to also identify as a Weak Republican or Strong Republican.

Acquiring that evidence through empirical observation requires that we move from the very general level of theory to a more specific level from which to organize observations. In doing this, we have to begin to think in terms of **variables.** A variable may be defined as an empirically observable characteristic of some phenomenon that can take on more than one value. Sex and nationality are two variables that can take on only a limited number of values and can be "measured" only qualitatively by designations such as "male" or "British." Age and gross national product are two variables that can take on a much wider range of values; they can be measured quantitatively by counting.

Concepts into Variables

To facilitate empirical testing, abstract concepts must be translated into statements with more precisely defined variables. For instance, the concept of *pluralism* is important in political science, but its empirical referents are not particularly clear. In order to test the empirical accuracy of any statement relating pluralism to anything else, we have to translate the concept into some variable or set of variables with clear empirical referents. We might want to use the number of organized interest groups in a nation as a variable to represent the concept of pluralism in our research. We can then reason backward from our observation of relationships among variables to evaluate the empirical validity of statements about relationships between concepts. If we are willing to assume that the variable *number of organized groups* captures the essential meaning of the concept *pluralism,* we will be willing to take evidence that this variable is related to some other variable (such as the level of government expenditures) as evidence that pluralism is also related to that other variable or the concept it represents.

Independent and Dependent Variables

Variables have a central place in the research process for two reasons. First, they help us identify what we will have to observe to test our theory by providing more precise empirical

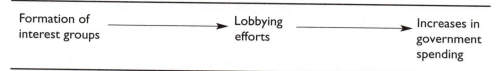

FIGURE 2.4 Interest group activity (independent variable) leads to higher government spending levels (dependent variable).

referents. Second, we can organize our observations by knowing the role variables play in hypotheses. Variables that are thought to change value in response to changes in the value of other variables are referred to as **dependent variables**. Their value depends on the value of other variables. Variables that influence the value of other variables through changes in their own values are referred to as **independent variables**.

An Example

Whether a variable is dependent or independent is determined by the relationship asserted by the hypotheses containing it. The same variable might be dependent in one study and independent in another. For example, a theorist observing the lobbying efforts of interest groups might reason that the larger the number of organized interest groups in a nation is, the higher the level of government expenditures will be. In this case, the number of groups is the independent variable and the level of expenditure is the dependent variable. This relationship is described in Figure 2.4. An independent variable's change in value must precede changes in the dependent variable. For example, if we observe an increase in government spending between 1990 and 2000 and also see a positive change in the number of organized groups between 2000 and 2010. Logically, this subsequent surge in interest group formation cannot have been responsible for a change in the level of expenditures that preceded it. In fact, these observed data should prompt a reconsideration of our hypothesis in Figure 2.4, and (perhaps) a theoretical reformulation that accounts for this phenomenon.

Intervening Variables

A close look at Figure 2.4 alerts us to another type of variable important in social analysis. In the theory summarized by the diagram in Figure 2.4, lobbying activity is an intervening variable; it comes into play *between* the number of organized interest groups and the level of government spending. **Intervening variables** provide the link between independent and dependent variables. In this case, interest groups would not affect the level of government spending if they did not engage in lobbying to get funds appropriated to their cause.

Intervening variables *condition* the relationships between other variables. This means that the value attained by intervening variables can affect the strength and direction of relationships between other variables. If lobbying activity is slight in Figure 2.4, then the relationship of interest group organization to public spending is weak. If lobbying is extensive, the relationship between the other variables will be strong.

Because intervening variables condition relationships between other variables, our knowledge of the role they play will affect our expectations about relationships between variables. If we are theorizing that lobbying intervenes between group organization and increases in spending, then we can make the following predictions:

> *Interest group organization will be positively related to increases in government spending when lobbying activity is vigorous.*
> *Interest group organization will be related only weakly to increases in government spending when lobbying activity is highly limited.*

We will not be satisfied to predict simply that interest group organization will be related to increases in government spending, because we believe that whether the two variables are related depends on the value of the intervening variable—lobbying. For this reason, we must specify the order of relationships and the role played by each variable in our theories.

Antecedent Variables

Whereas intervening variables come between independent and dependent variables, antecedent variables come into play before the independent variable does. For instance, we know that studies of voting behavior in the United States show that people who identify strongly with a political party are more likely to vote than those who do not. We might then want to theorize that party identification leads to or causes voting frequency. But what causes some people to identify strongly with a party while others do not? We might reason that the strength of their parents' party identification plays an important role in people's development of such party identification. Parents' party identification then is an **antecedent variable** in the causal chain that produces voting frequency.

Using both intervening and antecedent variables in our theories helps to clarify the *causal chains* at work in creating the phenomena we want to explain. It gives us more of a basis for deriving hypotheses through which we can test the utility of our theories, because hypotheses are essentially *statements of relationships between variables*. Hypotheses provide a basis for collecting evidence about the empirical utility of our theoretical structure. The more numerous and the more detailed the relationships we postulate, the more predictions we can make about the world and therefore the more potential tests we have of our theory.

This leads to the question of how we decide what relationships to assert in the form of hypotheses around which to build research projects.

FORMULATING HYPOTHESES

We arrive at hypotheses by either inductive or deductive reasoning. Which one we use depends on the stage we have reached in the research process. If we are still using trial and error to construct a theory, we might develop hypotheses by a process of *inductive generalization*. For example, we might observe that among the states in the United States the level of popular political participation varies directly with the extent of industrialization, and we might generalize that this relationship between variables is also found when comparing nations. If we find evidence to support the hypothesis, we will be more confident in including industrialization as a variable in a theory designed to explain political participation. Until we have a theory that shows *why* industrialization and participation are related, however, we cannot use the fact of their relationship as an explanation of political participation.

Hypotheses arrived at inductively can be important in *exploratory research,* which helps us construct theories, but they do not help us explain phenomena. Once we have stated a theory relating our variables in a logically coherent system, we can derive hypotheses from that theory by *deductive reasoning.* Because these hypotheses are predictions about the world that are logically implied by the theory with which we are working, finding support for them does help us explain events, because such findings reflect the validity of the theoretical system from which the hypotheses have been derived.

We cannot learn anything new about relationships from deduction alone. Deductive logic is a process by which the information contained in a set of statements can be made explicit. We use deduction to *clarify the implications of our assumptions,* and it is that clarification that produces hypotheses.

The deduction contained in Figure 2.2(b) shows this. If the assumption stated there is correct, that is, if the Republican Party attracts *only* conservatives, then any subset of the members of that party will be conservative also, and since the Republicans in Middletown are members of that party, they too will be conservative. This is the kind of reasoning referred to when we say that one conclusion "logically follows" from another. The conclusion that all Republicans in Middletown will be conservative is logically implied in the assumption that the Republican Party attracts only conservatives.

Since hypotheses are derived from theories, testing hypotheses indirectly tests our theories. Returning to our example, if we interview a properly drawn sample of Middletown Republicans and find that not all are conservative, we will have good reason to question the validity of our assumption. Finding liberals among Middletown Republicans shows that the party does not attract *only* conservatives. We will then want to modify our assumption so that the theory can more closely reflect reality. We may want to change it to read, "The Republican Party tends to attract more conservatives than liberals." From this assumption we can derive the hypothesis "There will be more conservatives than liberals among the members of the Middletown Republican Party."

If we find a few liberals and many conservatives among Middletown Republicans, we can say that the evidence is consistent with the hypothesis and the modified assumption from which it has been drawn. We still cannot put much faith in the general accuracy of the assumption until it is supported by evidence about the conservative or liberal character of a larger sample of the national Republican Party. After all, Middletown may be unique in some way. Perhaps, for example, there are only ten liberals in the entire city, and the fact that only a few of the Republican Party's members are liberal is a result of this more than of the relative attractiveness of the party to liberals and conservatives.

Indirect Theory Testing

The important point here is that evidence about the accuracy of hypotheses represents evidence about the accuracy of a theory *only when the hypotheses are linked to the theory by deductive logic.* Only when this is the case can we safely reason backward from evidence of the validity of a hypothesis to any judgment about the parent theory. Theories are developed, expanded, and improved by this process of logically deriving hypotheses, checking them against reality, and evaluating the theory in light of the results.

One type of hypothesis that plays an especially crucial role in this process is the **alternative rival hypothesis**. There are many possible explanations for any event. Some of these explanations are fully consistent with one another; more than one may be correct. In some cases, however, the explanations are opposed to one another: if one is correct, the other cannot be. If we state our explanations as hypotheses, then those which are inconsistent with one another are termed *alternative rival hypotheses*. They are alternatives because they provide different ways of looking at or understanding the event to be explained. They are rivals because they cannot both be valid. If one is accurate, the other has to be inaccurate. We cannot test and compare all possible alternative hypotheses relating to any event, but if we are to have faith in the accuracy of any one hypothesis, we must attempt to test the major rival hypotheses to be sure that we are not being misled by our observations.

One common form of alternative rival hypothesis is that which states that the relationship between any two variables is spurious and that changes in both are in fact due to some third factor. This type of alternative rival hypothesis is especially useful in theory testing because it suggests a research finding that gives us a solid basis for judging which of the two hypotheses in question is more accurate.

An Example

In our previous illustration inferring a causal relationship between rum prices and ministers' salaries, one major alternative rival hypothesis is that fluctuations in both measures are caused by changes in general economic conditions, as represented by general price levels. If this hypothesis is correct, then the relationship between rum prices and ministers' salaries will disappear when we "control for" (that is, hold constant) the effect of the overall prices on each of these variables. If the statistical association between rum prices and ministers' salaries vanishes when we control for general price level, we will have a basis for rejecting the original hypothesis in favor of its rival. If the relationship between rum prices and salaries remains even after our imposition of controls for general price level, we have more confidence in the hypothesis that these variables are genuinely related.

Conclusion

Theories demonstrate their usefulness as we find evidence supporting the hypotheses we derive from them, and eliminate alternative rival hypotheses. We must keep in mind, though, that some future research will produce evidence undermining our theory. We must always be open to contrary findings and willing to return to induction to build new evidence into more useful theories. Theory building is a process of constant interaction between conjecture and evidence, and between reasoning and research. It calls for both creative ingenuity and hardheaded empiricism. Although you must provide the former, we hope to provide a good dose of the latter in the chapters that follow.

Key Terms

research question *16*
theorizing *17*
theories *18*
exploratory research *19*
induction *20*
assumptions *21*
deduction *22*
concept *23*
empirical referents *24*
theoretical import *25*

propositions *25*
covariational relationships *25*
causal relationships *25*
spurious relationships *26*
indirect causation *26*
multiple causation *26*
causal model *26*
positive relationship *26*
negative relationship *27*
theory testing *28*

theory elaboration *29*
hypothesis *29*
variables *30*
dependent variables *31*
independent variables *31*
intervening variables *31*
antecedent variable *32*
alternative rival hypothesis *34*

Research Examples

Research in all fields of political science is built on a solid foundation of theory, grounded in the relevant literature. A study of the relationship between presidential discussion of international crises and domestic economic performance develops a theory that predicts declines in consumer confidence in the presence of fears of international conflict (Wood 2009). Brown and Mobarak (2009) compare electrical consumption by industry, agriculture and residential users in democracies and nondemocratic countries in order to test electoral theories postulating that elected politicians maximize their utility by offering legislation that benefits large proportions of society. Discussing the role of theorizing in the social sciences, Ish-Shalom (2009) argues that theorists have a moral responsibility to inject themselves into public social and political debates, particularly when their research is being utilized incorrectly.

References

Berry, Jeffrey M., Kent E. Portney, and Ken Thompson. 1993. *The Rebirth of Urban Democracy*. Washington, DC: The Brookings Institution.

Brown, David S., and Ahmed Mushfiq Mobarak. 2009. "The Transforming Power of Democracy: Regime Type and the Distribution of Electricity." *American Political Science Review* 103(May): 193–213.

Fogelson, R. M., and R. B. Hill. 1986. "Who Riots? A Study of Participation in the 1967 Riots," in *Supplemental Studies for the National Advisory Commission on Civil Disorders*. Washington, DC: U.S. Government Printing Office.

Ish-Shalom, Piki. 2009. "Theorizing Politics, Politicizing Theory, and the Responsibility That Runs Between." *Perspectives on Politics* 7(June): 303–316.

Rich, Richard. 1984. "The Representation of the Poor in the Policy Process: Changes in Congressional Support for Welfare," in Robert Eyestone, ed., *Public Policy Formation*. Greenwich, CT: JAI Press.

Wood, B. Dan. 2009. "Presidential Saber Rattling and the Economy." *American Journal of Political Science* 53(July): 695–709.

CHAPTER 3

Developing Your Literature Review: What Others Say about Your Topic

In this chapter you will learn:

- How you can build on your current searching skills to gather scholarly research systematically.
- The value of having a search plan that builds on your theory or research story.
- A four-step scholarly research discovery process we call *word mining*.
- How to utilize searching skills in scholarly databases and on the free Web.
- The searching and research report-writing benefits of taking accurate notes.

Like most things you study in college, reviewing research literature isn't an entirely new process to you. You already use your research tools to gather information about myriad topics. Whether you *Google* the name of your city and the words "voter registration" or skim this week's issue at *Newsweek.com* to find in-depth analysis and opinions about North Korea's military capabilities, you're gathering information to inform your (perhaps tacit) theories about how the world operates.

In this chapter, we build on your current skills to show you a more systematic way to gather and sort your information, and we streamline the process by teaching you some time-saving tools and techniques. You likely have learned your information-searching skills through a combination of trial and error and being exposed to some assignments in high school. What you currently do is not wrong, but our system will likely make your literature search more comprehensive and faster. Missing fewer key references and getting to the relevant sources more efficiently should reduce the number of searching dead ends you run into, improve your paper grades, and make the research process more fun!

SEARCHING AND RESEARCHING

Literature searching—which for convenience we'll simply call **searching** in this chapter—in many ways parallels the empirical research techniques presented throughout this book. Sound researching and effective searching both require that you clarify and focus the question you intend to address, rather than simply acquiring a little information here and there that broadly relates to a topic. Thus, just as meaningful research requires a research design, efficiently finding relevant information to substantiate and situate your research requires a search design. Just as some data and some methods of analysis are more appropriate for some questions than for others, some information resources will provide better access to relevant literature than others, with different power tools and tricks to get you quickly to the information you need.

Searching does not stop at the beginning of your research, although it is crucial to start searching early in your theory building. You are likely to search for relevant literature during each phase of your project. For example, at the beginning of your project you will refine and focus your research topic and theory, while toward the end of your project you will situate your findings in the context of what previous researchers have published as part of the process of preparing your literature review (see Chapter 22).

Building on Your Skills

In your classes, you will be called upon to read, locate, and retrieve scholarly journal articles. You already do research and gather information daily, and you may naturally tend to apply techniques learned on the free Web to scholarly research. Commercial search engines are often a useful place to start the research process, but they have limitations when you are doing scholarly work.

An Example

Diagramming alternative paths to retrieve a scholarly article, Research Exercise 3.1 illustrates the steps involved in locating and obtaining research in flowchart form. Framed in fairly general steps, the upper path probably uses tools you already know and use daily to find information. As you work through the exercise, you probably will have great success rapidly *finding* the example article, but you may have more trouble *reading* it. This challenge illustrates a basic facet of the free Web: You can locate and obtain many things, but many others are invisible and/or inaccessible to you. The lower path represents several typical approaches to locate materials using academic resources, that is materials or tools your college has paid to access. The crucial difference between the two paths occurs in the section termed "Authentication." Here, you obtain authorization to access proprietary and copyrighted material, which is not freely available. If you normally use a campus network, the entire authentication process may be transparent to you, or you may have logged in using your student ID and password, or some similar identifier. Take a few moments to try each path and each option in Research Exercise 3.1. We recommend that you write on the flowchart the names of indexes and databases you locate in your library resources. Hint: If you cannot find any of the listed article-locating resources, other than the library catalog, you should contact a reference librarian to learn the names of your college's political science article indexes and databases.

RESEARCH EXERCISE 3.1

Alternative Techniques for Retrieving a Scholarly Article

Try each of the sets of steps on the following page to retrieve this scholarly article:

Blattman, Christopher, 2009. "From Violence to Voting: War and Political Participation in Uganda." *American Political Science Review* 103(May): 231–247.

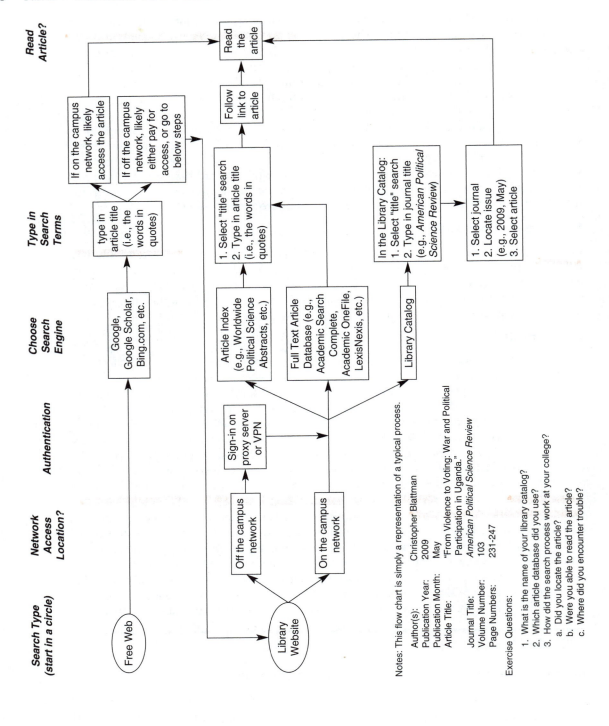

Notes: This flow chart is simply a representation of a typical process.

Author(s):   Christopher Blattman
Publication Year: 2009
Publication Month: May
Article Title: "From Violence to Voting: War and Political
                    Participation in Uganda."
Journal Title: *American Political Science Review*
Volume Numbers: 103
Page Numbers: 231-247

Exercise Questions:

1. What is the name of your library catalog?
2. Which article database did you use?
3. How did the search process work at your college?
   a. Did you locate the article?
   b. Were you able to read the article?
   c. Where did you encounter trouble?

DECIPHERING LIBRARY RECORDS

The previous section established the value of using library searching tools to locate and retrieve scholarly research, but before we can demonstrate a system to maximize your search success we need to explain how research is organized and described. Watching *Question Time* on C-SPAN or the BBC could resemble an unfocused series of softball questions or critical and grunting sounds from Members of Parliament if you do not understand the role of this formal questioning and discussion in the Westminster party structure. Similarly, knowing the organizational rules used by librarians and academic authors will facilitate effective use of articles. First, you need to know that articles are referenced in scholarly research using a **citation** that describes key elements of the article's authorship, title, and publication. Second, when you search for an article, you will see a **bibliographic record** that includes most of the information contained in the citation, as well as information on locating the full text of the article. If you are looking at a bibliographic record in an indexed library database, you also may find special descriptive information categorizing the article's research—these classifications will supercharge your subsequent searches.

Citations. When you searched for the article in Research Exercise 3.1, you knew who wrote the article, its title, what year it was published, where it was published (and more) from looking at the citation, which is located at the top of the page. Citations, broadly speaking, take two forms: those inside an article or book, and those composing the bibliography at the end. In the physical and social sciences, citations appearing inside articles usually identify a source only by author name and publication date, pointing to a "references" or "works cited" list at the end, where the full information is listed. In humanities and history, it is still common to use foot- or endnotes that provide full publication information in the first reference to a work, and to repeat that publication information in a list marked "Bibliography," or "Works Cited." For convenience, we will say bibliography to label the source lists that provide full publication information at the end of an article or book.

Publishers and academic disciplines have developed style manuals that prescribe what information goes into a citation, where it goes, and how it is punctuated. Your professors will probably specify which style manual they want you to follow. In one semester, it is quite possible that you may have to submit one paper that follows the American Psychological Association (APA) style, another that conforms to the Modern Language Association (MLA) style, and yet another that uses the American Political Science Association (APSA) style (2006).

An Example Citation. Here is the citation to the article from Research Exercise 3.1, in APSA style:

Blattman, Christopher. 2009. "From Violence to Voting: War and Political Participation in Uganda." *American Political Science Review* 103(May): 231–247.

This citation gives the basic information you need in order to find, retrieve, read, and record the article: author, publication date, article title, journal title, journal volume, inclusive page numbers. As we will see later in this chapter, author names and words used in article titles will also be important tools for discovering articles and books you don't already know about.

Bibliographic Records. The description of this book in a library catalog is its bibliographic record (or simply, "record"): it provides information about its title and creators, a physical description, a representation of its subject, and its address—its call number—in the library. While the format of library catalog records is consistent, following international rules, there is some variation in the format of the records for individual articles in a library's article **databases**, generally depending on the database provider. There is even less consistency in how Web search engines represent the results they return; it is not strictly correct to treat results lists as bibliographic records, but their functions are similar enough for now.

An Example from the Free Web. If you Google the title of the article in the above citation, you will get a screen full of results, some of them telling you where to get the article, others pointing you to other kinds of documents on the Web. These entries in the results list point to the article in slightly different ways.

From Violence to Voting: War and Political Participation in Uganda
From Violence to Voting: War and Political Participation in Uganda. CHRISTOPHER
BLATTMAN. Yale University. What is the political legacy of violent conflict . . .
journals.cambridge.org/production/action/cjoGetFulltext?fulltextid. . . –Similar
by C BLATTMAN–2009–Cited by 12–Related articles
    CJO–Abstract–From Violence to Voting: War and Political . . .
    Jun 16, 2009 . . . From Violence to Voting: War and Political Participation in
    Uganda. American Political Science Review, 103, pp 231–247 . . .
    journals.cambridge.org/abstract_S0003055409090212–Similar
    by C BLATTMAN–2009–Cited by 12–Related articles
    Show more results from journals.cambridge.org

In these two results, *journals.cambridge.org/* and "CJO" show that *APSR* is a journal published by Cambridge University Press on the Cambridge Journals Online platform. When you see the name of a publishing company, even one associated with a university, in an article URL, assume that someone will have to pay for you to access it. Assuming your library subscribes to *APSR* (most colleges having a political science major do), if you search Google from a computer in a classroom or dormitory, clicking the link should take you to the article; your library pays for your access. If you search without **authenticating** yourself as a person whose access has been paid for, you will be stopped and asked to pay for access yourself. Thus, although the broad Internet is called "the **free Web**," if you want to read copyrighted material, someone probably will have to pay.

In addition to not providing free access to an article's text, the main Google result entry also does not include crucial citation information about the journal in which it was published, nor the second author's name. Instead, the Google record provides a not-very-useful extract from the first line of the article's abstract. You need the indented version, which points to the abstract (i.e., summary) of the article to see that this result matches the citation you were given.

An Example from an Indexed Database. Now, we repeat the same article search using Worldwide Political Science Abstracts, an index database available at most college libraries.

<u>From Violence to Voting: War and Political Participation in Uganda</u>
<u>Blattman, Christopher</u>
American Political Science Review, vol. 103, no. 2, pp. 231–247, May 2009
What is the political legacy of violent conflict? I present evidence for a link from past violence to increased political engagement among ex-combatants. The evidence comes from northern Uganda . . .
<u>View Record</u> I <u>References</u> I <u>Cited by 1</u>

Note that this record provides the full publication information—all you would need to know to cite it correctly in a bibliography for a term paper—but not in the same order or punctuation as the APSA-style citation. The "view record" link tells us that a full record of this article is just a click away, as does the obviously incomplete abstract. In a library subscription database, the full record will add value to the basic publication information by providing several ways to discover quickly other articles that share something in common with this one.

One important bit of added value to look for is an option to save a link to that record with a "persistent URL" (sometimes called a static URL or a permalink). A PURL is a unique address for that source that does not depend on the computer you used or the time you searched—it is the address other people can use to get to that source. PURL options are widely available in library databases and catalogs and in many government-published information sources on the free Web. If your instructor says your citations must include the Web address of the online sources you use, it is always better to copy the persistent URL rather than the session-specific information displayed in your browser's address box.

Worldwide Political Science Abstracts is an **index** database. That is, it identifies where articles are; it does not incorporate the full articles. When you search an index, you search only the information contained in bibliographic records, not in the full text of the articles, dissertations, books, etc. that it identifies. Indexing databases generally try to identify and describe information sources on particular subjects, not on the basis of what any one library may own or connect to. When an entry appears in an index, you should be aware that your library may not own or subscribe to that source, but that it can probably get you a copy from another library if you allow time for **interlibrary loan**.

To connect to the articles from an indexing database, look for links with labels such as "view [or get] full text," "SFX (a brand of software that connects records to online articles), "Article Linker" (a different brand of link resolver software), or an icon or label specific to your library. Clicking that link will either take you to the article or give you a list of options: perhaps a choice among several online providers of that article, a link to the library catalog to search for a print version of the journal it appeared in, or a link to your library's interlibrary loan request system. When you connect to the article, you may have a choice to view it in plain HTML or PDF format. HTML may load faster over a slow

Internet connection and be easier for you to copy and paste from; PDF will be the more faithful version of the article as it was actually published, including illustrations and pagination as they appeared in the original. Think HTML for convenience, PDF for authoritativeness and accuracy.

We've seen some general similarities and differences about how citations, bibliographic records, and search-engine results represent articles. Since details can make a world of difference, let's break the information into the smaller parts, called fields, on which indexes and library catalogs rely. Understanding how records are organized in fields will help you target your further searching and then to put your citations in proper form. While you might not immediately see all the fields used in a database, as you become familiar with them, you will be able to focus your searches on different aspects of information resources, find similarities and differences among them, and manage your results. (It is the use of fields in bibliographic records that allows citation-management software like *RefWorks, EndNote*, or *Zotero* convert your citations from one style to another more or less automatically.)

Annotated below are some of the most important fields from citation of the article as they are represented in the full bibliographic record of the article, which is indexed in *Worldwide Political Science Abstracts*:

TI: Title

From Violence to Voting: War and Political Participation in Uganda
In article databases, "title" means the title of the article, not *the name of the publication in which the article appears. If you don't have a link to the article from a bibliographic record or search-engine result, you should search your library catalog for the name of the publication: "american political science review," not "from violence to voting." (Capitalization does not matter in online searching, and usually you don't need to type out the words at the end of titles.)*

AU: Author

Blattman, Christopher.
In databases and library catalogs, as in citations, authors are identified with the surname first, though in the article they will be listed in conventional order. They might not always have middle initials listed. In the physical sciences, it is common for authors' given (first) names to be reduced to initials. You may have to adjust your searches because of these common variations.

SO: Source

American Political Science Review, vol. 103, no. 2, pp. 231–247, May 2009
This is the main publication information, starting with the name of the journal. (Thus some databases will use "citation" as the name for this field.) In a library catalog you must remember that the field for specifically searching the name of a publication will be called "title."

DO: DOI

10.1017/S0003055409090212
A Digital Object Identifier is essentially a unique Web address for a piece of intellectual property such as an article. A hotlinked DOI will connect you to the article if you have access rights to it.

We have spent a good deal of time getting familiar with the codes and structures used in scholarly articles. Now it is time to locate the article and read it.

INSIDE THE PHYSICAL LIBRARY

The example article published in the *American Political Science Review* will be available online through most academic libraries, but suppose your library does not subscribe to it online. Aside from your grade possibly depending on reading that article, is it worth bothering to figure out and visit the physical library? We say "Yes," for several reasons. First, not all of the relevant articles you may need are available online. Second, while doing periodical research, it is likely that your articles will refer to books that you will want to review personally. Third, you may want additional books, possibly videos or sound recordings, and the library has them laid out nearby so that it is easy to discover them simply on the basis of the book you might have in hand. Finally, if you limit your bibliography to those articles that are available online, you allow an external source of selection bias to distort your research (Chapter 7 will discuss proper sampling techniques).

Libraries organize their collections using two different sets of organizing principles that try to put related materials together. One principle has already been described: subject headings added to bibliographic records are elaborate, standardized systems of labels that describe aspects of the contents of books and the coverage of periodicals. Subject headings make *intellectual connections* among items in the library, even though the items may be physically separated or some of the items may be online. The other principle tries to put related items *physically* near one another, so that if you find one relevant book on the shelf, you can easily browse along the shelf to find others that address the same material. Both principles are implemented according to nationwide, even international, rules, so you can use a catalog record from your library to identify related books in other libraries.

Understanding Call Numbers

The key tool for this physical arrangement is the call number, which the library affixes to the spines (or sometimes the covers or other containers) of the materials in its collection. Think of the call number as the address of the book on the shelf. Two call number systems are widely used in North America: the Dewey Decimal Classification system, used mainly by schools, small colleges, and public libraries; the other is the Library of Congress Classification system, widely used by universities and large research libraries. If the call numbers on a book's spine in your library begin with numbers of the type 320.072, your library uses the Dewey Decimal system. If the call numbers begin with a combination of letters and numbers, such as JA86.M35, your library uses the Library of Congress system. (Both identifiers, incidentally, designate the book you are holding.)

Both systems divide knowledge into big classes, then subdivide it. In a "Dewey library," the 300s are social sciences, the 320s are political science, and the numbers to the right of the decimal point indicate more specific characteristics of the book. The assignment of call numbers in an "LC library" is less rigidly hierarchical: each discipline or group of disciplines is assigned a letter of the alphabet. Thus, H represents social science in general, J political science, K law, and so forth. These larger classes are subdivided alphabetically and numerically: JA is for works about political science in general; the range JA86-88 is reserved for works about studying, teaching, or doing research in political science in general. Each call number consists of two groups separated by a decimal point (*not* called a period; the numbers in that cluster are decimals, not integers, which makes a difference in locating books on the shelves). The cluster of letters and numbers to the left of the decimal point will be the same in all LC libraries. The cluster to the right reflects where the book would be shelved in the context of *your* library: the more books your library has on that topic, the more complex that cluster will be. The net effect of this system is that books sharing a given topic and all books by a particular author that are on that topic are shelved together.

You should also be aware of a third, specialized call number system that may be used in libraries with extensive holdings of U.S. government publications: the Superintendent of Documents Classification system. Government publications are a tremendous, underused source of primary and secondary materials. They include not only "documents" in the sense of dusty official records, but also studies, hearings, raw and compiled data, periodicals, books, maps, and more on any subject of interest to the U.S. federal government—which is to say, almost any subject.

Utilized by the U.S. Government Printing Office, Superintendent of Documents Classification system is organized around the government entity responsible for the document rather than by subject. Sometimes SuDoc numbers are mnemonic, as in A for publications of the Department of Agriculture or *PrEx* for publications from the Executive Office of the President and its many specialized offices, but some important ones are not—notably *Y*, which applies to the published output of the Congress and also to reports submitted to it by federal agencies. The letters in SuDoc call numbers do not correspond to those in LC call numbers. Fortunately, you can distinguish them at a glance because SuDoc numbers include colons and slashes. Do not be dismayed when you see records in your library catalog with SuDoc numbers: the federal government has been putting most of its publications online for free since the mid-1990s. If the materials are older, your librarian can help you locate print or microform government publications.

LIBRARY CATALOG SEARCHING

Online library catalogs allow you to perform searches in several ways: by keyword, title, author, subject, or call number. Additionally, your library catalog may add special features, say, to search exclusively for periodicals or videos, or to limit your search to one branch of a library system. As demonstrated in Research Exercise 3.1, to locate the printed copies of a journal, we *title search* in the library's catalog for the periodical's name—not the article title. Similarly, to find a book that has been cited in your research, start with a *title search*. Use the first few words of the title, in their exact order. However, do not start with *A, An, The*, or their equivalents in foreign languages, as these words are not considered part of the title. On the other hand, you may use the *author search* feature to locate all of the books written by a given author who does research in your field.

An Example

In journal articles you have located while doing your research project, perhaps you have noticed that several articles were written by Ted Jelen. Searching for "Jelen, Ted" in your library's catalog should yield references to several of the books he has written related to abortion policy, as well as others on religion and politics. If a book has a common title, you might use an author search to locate it in your library. *Call number searching* will find the item marked with that call and give you a virtual browse of titles with nearby call numbers. *Subject searching* is not an appropriate tool for locating and retrieving items you know already exist. However, it is a very powerful tool for discovering new materials, so we discuss it at length later in this chapter.

A Strategy to Discover the Relevant Literature

These questions should help you focus your research as well as your searching:

1. **What story is this research trying to tell?** What would a plausible answer to your research question look like? It is not enough to know *that* you intend to write on a topic. You must quickly go out on a limb and articulate a provisional version of *what* you think you can say about it. The story determines everything else as you design your search strategy, conduct your searches, and interpret and apply the results you retrieve. In group projects, it is especially important and helpful for everyone to share a clear vision of the *what* and *why* of a story before dividing responsibilities. Empirical researchers will lay out their stories in the form of theories and hypotheses (recall Chapter 2), but "story" is a useful concept to keep in mind when you work on more historical or text-based research, such as in public law or political theory.

2. **What *kinds* of information do you need in order to tell that particular story?** Secondary or primary sources? If primary sources, do you need statistics (compiled or raw?) or other data? First-person accounts like letters or oral histories? Contemporaneous journalism? Patents? Corporate records? Congressional reports? If secondary, do you need scholarship within an established discipline or across disciplines; in popular periodicals or other media? How might relevant information have been filtered by its creators' viewpoints or intentions? From what date range? In what languages?

3. **Who cares?** That is, who is likely to have the needed information (and where is it likely to be now)? No library will have all the information sources that could be useful for your topic. Lots of important information is not digitized, and if digitized, not available to your library at prices it can afford. Allow time for items not on campus to arrive from interlibrary loan.

4. **What tools will get me to that information most efficiently?** Some will be less obvious than others. Some may not be available to you at your place and moment of need. So think laterally. Most academic libraries will provide some sort of subject guides to their online and/or print tools for finding and retrieving information. Behind them are the library's subject specialists, who generally have extensive experience (and often graduate degrees) in the discipline.

5. **How do you learn to use the tools effectively and efficiently?** Answer: Practice, practice, practice. Library databases have many powerful features for searching and for managing search results—but they often are hiding in plain sight. Start by searching for a book or other document with which you are already familiar. See the different ways you can find it, the different ways it may be described or represented in various resources, the different information sources they suggest it is related to.

6. **Are the information sources you retrieve truly relevant to *your* needs in *this* project?** If you don't have a rough idea of what you need to find, or why and how

the different bits of information you retrieve are likely to hang together, you'll get a bad case of information constipation. If you do have an idea of the what/why/how, you'll be sensitized to cues in your results that will allow you quickly to choose which sources are likely to be highly relevant to your particular project and which ones are too loosely related to fit.

WORD MINING: FOUR STEPS TO SEARCHING SUCCESS

Computers Are Stupid

This is the fundamental challenge with searching in the age of the Internet. But computers are very good at doing huge numbers of simple things extremely rapidly—like matching the letters you type in a search box against "strings" of characters they have stored in memory, which is what online searching really boils down to. Sophisticated programming provides the computer's best guess of that matches are most relevant to your need. Effective searchers know that computers cannot read their minds. Sophisticated computer users appreciate that, while they have specific needs and intentions, computer programmers must write general rules (based on statistical principles) that will not fit every case equally well.

Computers cannot process all the information human brains draw on when we ask questions or make statements. When you are talking with your professor, you know when the "string" *bush* refers to one of several U.S. politicians, a shrub, an arid wilderness, or very minor league baseball. In daily conversation, your professor understands what you mean when you refer to "depression:" a low spot in the earth, a low-pressure area in the atmosphere, a low feeling in your heart, a low spot on a graph of economic indicators, or a low time in twentieth-century history. These are far from isolated examples. Many words used in politics and political science are ambiguous—*power, justice, state, statistics, survey, party, elect, survey,* to name a few—that is, the computer cannot "know" which of several meanings you intend when you enter that word in a search box.

The ambiguity inherent in computerized searching just grows as the World Wide Web becomes ever-more global. The same set of letters may retrieve sources in languages you can't read or that deal with topics you didn't intend. As historical content—newspapers, government documents, manuscripts, and other archival materials—is added to the Web, you will have to grapple with the difference in meaning as well as spelling between the words *you* use and those in the original sources, especially when you are looking at topics relating to race, ethnicity, religion, or gender. Sad to say, if the computer has not been programmed to translate today's publicly acceptable labels into those commonly used in the time or place you are researching, you will have to discover and search with terms you would never utter in polite company.

Computers "understand" your searches because you do things to help them. Notably, you provide a context for the computer in several ways. One is by choosing to search in places where your meaning of the word is more common than the other meanings. Another is by asking the computer to match combinations of words: typing *george bush* gives the computer more information to filter out files (called "documents" by information scientists) that don't contain the strings *george* and *bush*. (Later in this chapter we will discuss ways some online search tools provide to improve the likelihood that you will find documents you want about the former U.S. president you intended, rather than news reports about George Clooney feeling "*bush*ed" after a strenuous day working in rural Sudan.)

A Four-Step Program

We will break your literature search into this sequence:

1. Scan the information environment.
2. Use the power of abstracted information.
3. Dig into the library's full-text resources.
4. Return to uncharted cyberspace.

The kinds of resources you will work with, the tricks you can bring to bear, and even the way you think will differ from one stage to another. The insights you develop and the terms you identify in one stage will help you search efficiently and effectively in the next one. We call this process ***word mining***. Throughout your search/research you should be actively thinking about your story, and about how information you find helps make better sense of your theory and hypotheses, about how refinements in your story help you identify the most appropriate information. The interplay of your speculation, discovery, and reflection make your project interesting—and even fun.

WORD MINING STEP 1: SCANNING THE INFORMATION ENVIRONMENT

In this step you are not merely getting background information that is "sort of" on the general topic. You are looking for ideas to support your research design as well as information to help you structure your search design. In this step, focusing your story or theory and your search for literature converge. The purpose of the **information environmental scan** is to get a sense of what is "out there" in published knowledge that might speak to your story/theory. Is it interesting or old hat? It may sound paradoxical, but when you are doing original research, not just training exercises, you really *do not* want to find many scholarly articles or books that are squarely about your theory. If so, someone else has probably already done your research! This means that you will have to rethink your project. Perhaps you can apply the same theory or methodology but to a different population. Another important question to consider is whether the resources available to you are adequate to conduct sufficiently rigorous research. If they are not, again, you will need to rethink and reconceptualize your project.

Getting Started

Virtually anything goes as a resource to get your thinking and judging started: a comment on TV, a blog, or a remark in class may be enough to get you thinking about how the story you have in mind could hang together. Then start looking more systematically. Use both traditional print sources and online tools like Web search engines, social networking sites, and image/video sharing.

Take notes of everything—of arguments and facts and, crucially, of terms that in some way represent the concepts that your theory or story is trying to relate to one another. At the beginning of your research, you probably don't have a clear idea of how your concepts will fit together, and as a student you might not yet have a set of established ideas to frame the

PRACTICAL RESEARCH ETHICS
Giving credit where credit is due?

This chapter teaches techniques that are designed to uncover prior research on a given topic. Gathering and summarizing the existing literature builds a foundation upon which new research rests, and positions research findings within the discipline. You should use great care to conduct a thorough search of the literature. Although much is freely available online, free information is often poorly organized and may contain hidden bias.

Whether earlier research is found in printed books, or online journal articles, or in a video documentary, it is crucial to never lose sight of the fact that these specific words and the ideas conveyed by those words belong to their authors.

With information so easily accessible in a digital format, some budding researchers simply "copy and paste" material from the Internet directly into research papers. However, if you use others' work without properly citing the source, you are committing plagiarism—something that academically and legally constitutes theft. You must properly attribute all ideas and material that come from others.

Of course, you demonstrate the amount of effort you have expended researching other's findings and your mastery of the extant literature through a well-documented literature review. This means that (1) you may never paraphrase anyone else's ideas without attribution to the original source, (2) you will never quote any verbal or written text without placing the quote marks around the material that is in the original author's own words, and (3) you should use a standard bibliographic style that conveys your references clearly to your reader.

information you come across. (Conversely, professors, working in a context of their chosen disciplines, may have so many firmly established ideas that they may have trouble appreciating new ideas outside those frameworks.) On virtually any interesting topic, there will be too many information sources and too many somewhat relevant words for you to remember them all. Write them down as you go along. Add annotations to them as they come to mind. The lists of terms (nouns, verbs, author names) you generate as you go along will help you unlock information sources during the substantive search phases.

Using a Search Grid

We suggest that you use a **concept search grid** to organize your thoughts and your searches. During this preliminary phase the table is pretty simple: a space for a sentence that lays out your hunch about what your research will demonstrate—your story—followed by several columns, each column corresponding to a primary concept in that hunch. Figure 3.1 presents a sample concept search grid, which is also available for download from the first author's Web site. As an empirical researcher, while your searching gets more intense and focused, that written-out hunch will become the statement of your theory, and your concepts will distill into your variables.

It is fairly common at this stage for your concepts to consist of a few *things* and a *process* or *effect* that would explain how they are connected to one another. Create a column for each concept. In each concept write down a few other words that describe or represent that concept. These might be synonyms, broader terms, or narrower ones. We encourage you to group each concept's words in the same column; start a new column when you explore a new concept.

Search	Theoretical Concept: REPUBLICAN		Link (and/or)	Theoretical Concept: ABORTION
	Related Terms:			**Related Terms:**
1	REPUBLICAN VOTER			PRO-LIFE
2	REPUBLICAN PARTY			PRO-CHOICE
3	PARTY IDENTIFICATION			ABORTION POLICY
4	CONSERVATIVE			
5	RIGHT-WING			
6				
7				

FIGURE 3.1   Sample concept search grid.

Note: Printable copies of this grid may be downloaded from Craig Leonard Brians' Web site: www.psci .vt.edu/brians.

An Example: The Concept Search Grid

Suppose we theorize that *pro-choice voters* with *Republican* partisan identification who favor a *pro-life Republican candidate* are more likely to think (incorrectly) that their preferred candidate shares their abortion policy view, because to think otherwise could cause these voters to experience *cognitive dissonance*. The broader concepts in this theory, italicized in the preceding sentence, include: pro-choice (i.e., abortion), Republican, candidate, and cognitive dissonance. Brainstorming, we develop a list of political synonyms or words that are related to these concepts. For example, the term *Republican* may suggest: Republican voter, the Republican Party, Republican partisan identification, a U.S. political party, conservative ideology, right wing, etc. Notice that few of the related words in our list are truly identical in meaning to the initial word. Some are broader (U.S. political party), some are more specific (Republican Party), and some are related but fundamentally differ from the original term (conservative ideology). Additionally, when thinking of related terms, remember the multiple meanings that many words have— Republican Party versus a republican form of government. At this point, an important part of our brainstorming is to develop a fairly wide list of relevant keywords, because we do not know how the existing research may characterize our theory's concepts.

The grid in Figure 3.1 is used by simply writing your initial concepts (from your theory) on the upper lines, and then listing the brainstormed terms below each concept. These "related terms" may be synonyms, narrower words, broader words, or subject terms from a library's catalog, indexes, or databases. The "Link" between the terms is printed in lighter type because it is optional. Now that you have begun clarifying the parts of your story, you can start visualizing how they might fit together to tell a single story. Rearrange columns, draw in arrows, play with possible alternative relationships.

As you look at the concept search grid rearrangements, you may decide that one concept does not make as much sense as you first thought. When you try to keep the words for a concept all in one column and they simply will not stay lined up only in that one column, it's a sign that you need to rethink your initial hunch: you have probably

---

RESEARCH EXERCISE 3.2

Brainstorming—The Game Show!

This exercise demonstrates the value of thinking broadly and spontaneously to develop a list of synonyms and related words to use with the concept search grid.

1. The instructor chooses a hypothesis (with two variables), perhaps from the week's news. For example, you could state that democracies rarely have civil wars, U.S. conservatives favor less government spending on the economy, wealthier appellants are more likely to get a hearing above the trial court level, etc.
2. The instructor assigns a student to be the "reporter." She or he should go to the front of the room, to facilitate writing out what is said. The "reporter" should write in a place that everyone can see—on the class chalkboard or whiteboard, on an overhead projector, or on a computer projector.
3. The "reporter" will make two columns, with each variable at the top of a column, leaving room to write 8 or 10 more words under the variable.
4. The instructor breaks the class into four groups, numbering them 1 through 4.
5. The groups meet, and in 5 minutes come up with as many words related to variables as they can.
6. The instructor calls "time," and starts the game:
   a. She or he calls on a group.
   b. The group offers one word related to one of the variables.
   c. The instructor evaluates the word, in consultation with the rest of the groups.
      i. Is the word closely enough related to the variable? The team can make a case for this.
      ii. If a team offers a word that is too different from the variables, it loses its turn.
      iii. If a team offers a word already on the list, it loses its turn.
   d. If the word is acceptable,
      i. The "reporter" writes the word under the appropriate variable.
      ii. The "reporter" also writes the number of the group after the word.
   e. The instructor calls on the next group in numerical order.
   f. This process is repeated until there are 8 words under each variable.
7. Winning: The team with the most words on the lists at the end wins!

---

blended together some ideas or phenomena that are distinct. So rethink the concept that does not fit. Break it into more precise concepts and focus on one of them, then add words that more precisely describe that concept—*as that concept fits into your overall story*. Since your theory has at least three concepts and you will probably use several different library tools in your search, you will need to use multiple grids to include all of your concepts. Remember, the grid is simply a tool; use it as long as it facilitates your literature search, modifying it as your search progresses.

This process may make you more aware of your tacit knowledge, the information and opinions you already had but perhaps had not credited yourself with already knowing. Don't be afraid to start with what you already know.

The key to effective searching, in online and print sources, is to search in small chunks (hence your search grid), look at the results of those searches, decide which ones fit best into your theory or story, and then deliberately and systematically combine the best results. As a searcher, you can make many of those combinations through a computer keyboard. As a researcher, you will make the most important combinations and connections inside your own head. This process of division and recombination ultimately saves you time and trouble, and it makes your searching more thorough and thoughtful.

Taking the Notes You Need

The words you enter into your grid are the search terms you use in the tools (see below) to scan the environment of available information. As your searching evolves from this point, you will add new terms as you discover them, include notes about those terms, and perhaps note how you build your search from individual terms to combinations of the terms that work best. Every time you find an encyclopedia entry, an article, or a book—online or on a printed page—that helps you understand and tell your theory or story better, you should at minimum:

- Record the citation for that source, along with the tool you used to find it.
- Write out a one- or two-sentence explanation of how this source might relate to your preliminary story/theory. You would be required to do this if your instructor requires an **annotated bibliography**.
- Record the words (which may include names of authors and other researchers) used in that source that most relate to your preliminary story/theory.
- Record other words that could also describe that source. These might be provided in the bibliographic record's subject terms, by social tagging services such as LibraryThing, Digg, or Delicious (and some online newspapers), or they might be words you recall from other sources that also apply to the one in hand.

Record the reference's citation and annotation in whatever system you use to keep notes. Enter the words you recorded in the appropriate columns on your grid. Add tags to the terms in your grid as they relate to the concept at the top of your column; for example, *NT* for narrower term, *BT* for broader term, *SU* if the word is a subject term in your catalog or an indexing database. You may develop your own coding system or some graphical way of noting relationships.

Many sources are available to you to conduct your scan of the information environment, some freely available online, others through your library. Never be reluctant to ask your instructor or a librarian for help in clarifying your theory or story, choosing relevant resources from those available in your institution, and making the search tools work for you.

Information Scan: Traditional Sources

- ***Library Catalog.*** Your library's catalog is far more than an inventory of how many books, journal subscriptions, films, and so on are available through your library. It is a gateway to the organization of knowledge as maintained by your library. Unlike the computer-generated relevance rankings of Web search engines, which vary from one engine to another, library catalogs follow international standards for describing and classifying materials. The international cataloging rules make possible the existence of union catalogs, which allow you to see the collections of several libraries. The most important *union catalog* for the environmental scan is *WorldCat*, which as the name implies, is global in its coverage. The main shortcoming of library catalogs is the way they treat journal articles, where most of the important empirical research in political science or any other field is first published. You will not discover individual articles with a library catalog. However, once you have citations to articles, you will likely use the catalog to locate the journals in which they appeared.

- *Books.* If your project is for a class, don't overlook books your instructor assigned you. The index in the back of the book shows where the most important ideas in that book are located, which in turn helps you learn how they are used in the discipline. Often, indexes will be arranged hierarchically, showing how major topics in the work are subdivided and interconnected—a good way to discover how a seemingly simple topic may be richer than you suspected. Words used in chapter headings and section headings may be widely used by researchers on that topic—they are often words you can use to mine online resources. Look through the bibliographies and notes that are typical of textbooks and scholarly works.

  Many times you can get a sense of the contours of the literature on your topic simply from the titles of books. Sometimes books will include annotated bibliographies or bibliographic essays. These can be especially valuable because the author expressly addresses the contents, contexts, and connections among books he or she found useful. If an author's work on a subject impresses you, so might his or her sources, which in turn point you to their sources, and so on.

- *Books: Back of Title Page.* An overlooked tool in many books is the "cataloging in publication" information on the reverse side of the title page of many academic books. The CIP is a miniature version of the catalog record, with that book's call number (in Dewey and Library of Congress systems) and subject headings. Just as with a record in your library's catalog, you can use these to find similar works in your—or virtually any other—library.

- *Encyclopedias.* Often overlooked these days, articles in a respectable encyclopedia will, of course, provide an overview of core topics. But beyond that overview, a good encyclopedia article will be signed (so you can look for other works by that author) and include bibliographic references. General encyclopedias, even famous ones like *Britannica*, will usually not address topics in enough detail to be useful to inform college-level research, so be sure to look in a **subject encyclopedia** like the huge *International Encyclopedia of the Social and Behavioral Sciences*, which give deeper, often more sophisticated coverage. Browse the index volume. Entries will generally be in alphabetical order, but with special features such as cross references to related entries and "see also" references that point you to synonyms and related topics (and terms used in the discipline).

- *Subject bibliographies.* These compilations of the literature on a given topic were more often published in the pre-Internet era, but they can still help you identify and analyze comprehensively the literature on a topic. They can save you a lot of work, especially if your topic requires looking at older primary and secondary sources. These bibliographies are often organized in ways that allow you quickly to see what aspects of the subject have interested authors, so you can orient your project in those contexts.

Information Scan: Online Sources

- *Free Web search engines.* Virtually everyone, including professors and librarians, starts here. *Google* is the best known and most widely used (at the time of this writing), but you should familiarize yourself with several. No one search engine captures more than a fraction of the World Wide Web. (In fact, most of the traffic over the Web is invisible to search engines, either because of technologies or because the owners of the information do not want it freely available.) On the freely available portion of the Web, different search engines cover different parts. Crucially for the environmental scan, search engine's relevance rankings—their computers' best guesses of what people like you really want because of the works you use and your location—will list results in different order. For example, a site that could be very important to your particular project might be at the top of a *Bing* search but off the screen in *Google*.

- *Wikipedia.* Wikipedia is another online tool that nearly everyone uses as a starting point. In the environmental scan Wikipedia is especially useful as a source of arguments or positions, whatever the value of the information in the articles you use. Criticisms of Wikipedia as a source of trustworthy information are well known: anyone can create or change an article; articles can be biased or based on incomplete research; information appears and disappears; article lengths do not necessarily reflect the importance of the topic; writing is uneven, sometimes too elementary and other times too technical and jargon-laden for the non-expert.

  There are two key guidelines when reading Wikipedia during your environmental scan. First, always read the discussion tab behind an article. That is where ideas and sources are discussed, biases identified, alternative interpretations presented; the discussion tab can be very useful as a sketch of the intellectual landscape on that topic. Second, keep track of the links among articles, both those created by authors and those you followed because they seemed intuitively appropriate. You may get ideas from the connections among topics that you would not see when reading one article at a time. (This technique also applies to reading the traditional sources listed above. Learning from patterns of linkages or connections among sources, not only from the individual sources, is also the basis of *Google*'s relevance rankings.)

- *Social media.* Social media are filled with assertions, whether comment threads on news Web sites, talk radio, or sites such as *Twitter, Facebook,* or *MySpace.* Some of these claims are substantiated by thorough research, whereas some merely restate (or modify) existing allegations and convictions. While these sources certainly can be problematic as sources of credible information, they can be rich sources of propositions for you to operationalize for empirical testing and to investigate in more authoritative literature.

- *General purpose article database.* Most academic libraries, and many public library systems, will have at least one big (expensive) general-purpose database, such as *Academic OneFile* or *Academic Search Complete.* These resources typically combine the complete text of many periodicals, ranging from the popular press to trade magazines to peer-reviewed scholarly journals, across many academic disciplines and areas of general interest. Newspapers are typically covered as well, though sometimes only by citation information rather than the full text of the articles.

  The breadth of coverage makes general-purpose databases ideal for the information environmental scan: unlike the free Web resources, the publications selected for inclusion in these library databases will be a bit more authoritative. They add value over the free Web tools in other ways: they provide more powerful options for focusing your search and for consistently connecting to similar articles; most importantly, like library catalogs, they use consistent, standardized subject headings to connect you with articles that address the same topics even when their authors used different or ambiguous words.

- *Searching multiple databases.* Many people are tempted to search multiple databases at once. This can be done in many ways, whether the databases are all on the same interface (or "platform") such as *EbscoHost* or *FirstSearch*, or across many separate databases in a "federated search." Searching with single terms across many databases is a good way to scan their content on that one concept (especially if it is a proper noun like the name of an author or an institution), but combining searches can be cumbersome, and you lose the power of special features in each database, especially their distinct systems of subject headings. We would argue that *the worst possible way to run a search is to write out all the terms of your theory into a single search that looks simultaneously in many places.*

- *Advanced search option.* Many online search tools have one or more "advanced search" options that, among other things, give several rows of search boxes and various ways to filter out kinds of information you know you do not need. It is tempting to throw together terms from more than one concept into a single search—after all, the boxes are there to fill. During the environmental scan, it is okay to give in to the temptation to type in a few terms connected by AND. But avoid that temptation later. While you will probably find some sources that relate, more or less, in some respects, to your theory, you will miss even more: the more ANDs, the narrower your search; the more search terms, the greater the likelihood that just one of them will skew your results without your being aware of it.

Utilizing these sources should push your environmental scan into high gear and yield large numbers of search terms for your concept search grid.

WORD MINING STEP 2: HARNESSING THE POWER OF BIBLIOGRAPHIC RECORDS

The second step in word mining acknowledges that in today's research environment, the problem most searchers face is not a shortage of potentially relevant information but rather too much information. Word mining is a sequence of discovering high-value search terms and working through information resources to maximize the relevance of your search results to your particular theory or story, with the least waste of your time and trouble. This section will help you to hone in on the most relevant sources.

So, you have completed your information scan and worked out a basic theory or story. You have discovered and read some sources, discarding some and annotating others because they address some aspect of your story. Your search concept search grid has a few words listed under each concept. The next—and most productive—stage is to exploit the way bibliographic records distill the essence of articles, books, and other sources into small packets that highlight the most useful information for literature searchers. These are incorporated systematically into library catalogs and indexing databases (sometimes called abstracting and indexing databases or simply

indexes).[1] As we mentioned in the section on the information environmental scan, some databases add the complete text of articles to extensive bibliographic records. For now, when you work in these mixed databases, tell the database to search only in the fields that go into the citation and abstract, not the full text. In some databases, this may be the default option. In others, you may have to change the setting; if you cannot search across multiple fields, the most productive one to search is for words appearing in abstracts.

The records in abstracting and indexing databases describe each item, but unlike many full-text databases and most search tools on the free Web, they also describe *relationships and connections*. Because bibliographic records are constructed of numerous fields, library catalogs, and indexes give you levers that can move the information universe the way you want, to have it support your story. If you start your search in a full-text resource that offers few search fields—for example, *LexisNexis Academic*, or *Google Scholar*—you can lose your way in information swamps. Save those full-text sources for later, after you have mined the high-value terms from the library catalog and indexes and the sources they identify.

Navigating across the Country on Abstracted Information

Suppose you live in Virginia and decide to drive to Las Vegas as a graduation present to yourself.

- First, you'd look at a map or GPS navigation system to plot a general route across the United States. Taking into account how long you like to drive in a day, the sights and people you want to see along the way, how much you can afford for the drive, and so on, you pick a general route. (Say, Interstate 40, because it looks relatively direct, and would allow you to take a side trip to the Grand Canyon.)
- Then you decide how far you think you can get in each day, so you can predict how long the drive will take.
- Then you start looking at more detailed maps of the regions and states you'll pass through. Once you decide that the leg between Elk City, Oklahoma, and Santa Rosa, New Mexico, looks manageable, you look for the attractions en route and your lodging and dining options.
- As you drive, you'll adjust the information you look for as you get a clearer idea of where you've been and how close you are to where you intended to go.
- Maybe you even discover that in parts of New Mexico, if you ask how to get to Las Vegas, locals will direct you to Las Vegas, New Mexico, because your search term, Las Vegas, was in fact ambiguous, and the information system made its best guess.

Your map is a representation of the ways across the country—an abstract. It appears to provide less information overall than would a satellite photo, but the information the map presents is more meaningful and useful to reaching your destination precisely because it **omits** information that is not relevant to your needs. Once you are in a locality, however, the aerial image—the full text of the place, so to speak—may help situate you more fully on the ground, and help to guide your activities.

---

[1] "Indexes" is poor Latin but good, unambiguous library terminology, especially for online searchers. The Library of Congress's official cataloging rules prescribe using "indexes" to describe finding aids and "indices" to describe statistical indicators.

Start your word-mining by answering the "who would care about this?" question. Do a quick scan of the subject-based databases available through your library. Many academic libraries will provide subject guides to help researchers get to the library's resources that are most valuable to the disciplines taught in that institution. These guides will describe and point you to the indexing and full-text databases they pay for, to selected resources on the free Web, and to important parts of their print collection.

A Most Helpful Librarian: The Subject Specialist

Your library may employ a subject specialist who is particularly knowledgeable about your discipline as well as about your library. That librarian is there to be a resource for you and your professors. In larger academic libraries, a subject librarian is often expected to have at least a master's degree in an academic discipline as well as the master's in library and information science that is a prerequisite for the job.

If the library subject guides do not include name and contact information for the library's subject specialist, look for a staff directory on the library Web site and see if there are reference or instructional librarians responsible for the discipline. Sometimes the librarians with subject expertise will be labeled bibliographers or liaisons, because they coordinate between the library and academic departments.

Between the library subject guide and conversations with your instructor and a librarian, you will be able to choose the best available indexing database. Start in the database that will produce the least ambiguity about the search terms you have identified for your theory or story. Ideally it will be specifically for political science or a related discipline such as sociology, but broader-based indexing databases can still be useful.

As you work through the indexing databases and eventually the library catalog to discover information, you should practice these three important skills to maximize the power of bibliographic records:

1. Find and use the subject vocabulary within each tool.
2. Mix and match individual searches.
3. Learn from the terms you uncover at this stage so you can save time and trouble when you look in full-text online sources and the free Web.

The next section offers specific guidance and hints that will maximize the effectiveness of your literature searches. Here we describe basic principles and techniques, most of which work in library catalogs and indexing databases. You should always bear in mind, though, that library resources vary greatly from college to college, so we cannot speak to the specific set of tools you have in your library. This makes learning to use those tools more challenging for you, but this process of learning new tools is a skill you will find quite helpful as technologies evolve and change over time.

Find the Subject Headings

Because all your searches on all the terms in your grid are in support of one theory or story, the best way to discover the subject headings in a catalog or index is while you search on each term as a keyword. Look through the results lists, pick ones that seem most useful, and look for the subject (sometimes called descriptor) field in their bibliographic records. Not all the subject headings from a source will be relevant to your particular story, so write down the ones that seem to fit best. Note when terms in your concept grid are subject terms. Most of the time, the database or catalog will show these descriptors in hypertext, so that in one click you can search for every source affixed with that descriptor in the database.

When you encounter a hyperlinked subject term in your search results, your next step depends on the database. In some databases, if you click on that link, it will run an entirely new search and identify all the records in the database that wear that subject label. In other databases, that same click will narrow your existing search and display only the items from that one search that also have that subject heading. Look for labels to tell you if clicking from a list of the subject headings will narrow your results. That narrowing can mislead you about the scope and usefulness of the records in the database. In such databases, we recommend that you note the subject terms and type them into search boxes, as you would when you discover additional keywords. Save the narrowing function for full-text databases.

Unfortunately, subject terms are seldom consistent from one database to another or from a database to the Library of Congress subject headings in your catalog. As you become more expert in the literature of the discipline and more comfortable using indexes, you will learn some core subject terms. You will probably start developing hunches about others. Usually the most convenient way to confirm those hunches is simply to search with them.

- Most library catalogs allow you to search specifically in the subject field. Depending on your catalog, when you do a subject search, the system may provide a list of works that share that heading (or its best guess of works that share the computer's best guess of the heading you intended). More useful, we think, are catalogs that display lists of subject headings instead of books in response to subject searches or clicks on hotlinked subject terms in records. The headings and their "subdivisions"—more specific aspects, set off by dashes—can give you a better idea of the scope of your library's holdings but also deeper insight into how previous writers have approached that topic. The full list of official subject headings is published by the Library of Congress online and in the several large print volumes called *Library of Congress Subject Headings*.
- Some databases include ways to see how subject terms relate to one another in the tool's overall "controlled vocabulary," its system of unambiguous, precise labels. When you do any sort of search, look around the results screen for a list of subject terms for your whole results list, in addition to those that might appear in individual records. Some database interfaces include links next to search boxes for you to see the terms they use. (In addition to subject terms, these might include author names, journal titles, etc.) For the broader overview, look to see if a database provides a link to its thesaurus, which may give you options to search to see if your keyword is also a subject term, or to browse through the subject terms alphabetically and/or thematically. The thesaurus in a database is thus like the index in the back of a book or encyclopedia.

Combining the Best Searches

We have emphasized that you should resist the urge to use *AND* to combine multiple terms in a single search. (Using *OR* to search simultaneously for different spellings and suffixes of the same word is okay.) Searching for each term on its own allows you to see more clearly what kind of literature is attached to that word. You can determine how effective each term is for getting the information you need, and discover related, potentially more effective, terms in the process. Additionally, you can diagnose why your searches are not coming out the way you expected. Perhaps you misspelled the word. Perhaps there are no bibliographic records in that catalog or indexing database that used that word (hence the importance of subject headings/descriptors). Now we will show an efficient strategy for combining those separate searches and narrowing them to find the best results for each concept and the best results linking concepts together.

When searching, it is important to keep in mind the characteristics of two types of searches:

1. A *keyword* (*KW*) search looks for your search term anywhere in several (or perhaps all) fields in the bibliographic records.
2. A *subject* (*SU*) term or *descriptor* defines a universe of information on one topic inside the database or catalog, no matter what other words authors may have used in the article.

Now we will combine these terms into our three basic types of searches. Suppose you have done some searches on two of your concepts, which we will represent by the numbers 1 and 2. The broadest search is to combine keywords for each concept:

$$KW_1 \ AND \ KW_2$$

Keyword-to-keyword searching can be a rather fuzzy search because of the ambiguity of some of your terms. But they probably will not be entirely irrelevant, because words in bibliographic records are more likely than those spread across whole documents to represent the most important content of the documents they represent. And you have already thought about how the concepts are most likely to fit together in your theory or story, so you can relatively quickly look over abstracts and decide which ones fit.

But that can still leave you with a lot of keyword combinations and a lot of results to sort through. So now you can think about your first concept as a whole concept or topic and search to see if some part of the other concept is an aspect of the first one—where the two intersect. That is, you combine subject terms relating to your first concept with keywords relating to the second. This kind of search can be rendered as:

$$SU_1 \ AND \ KW_2$$

What if the subject terms for your first concept are too generic for your particular theory? You reverse the relationships in that earlier search to see how keywords relating to the first concept may be represented in the universe of information defined by the second concept:

$$KW_1 \ AND \ SU_2$$

You will find that you can quickly work through a remarkable number of combinations of searches by using this basic logic. Why not search "SU_1 AND SU_2"? It puts too much faith in the indexers and catalogers to have applied the best subject terms—and it assumes that the meanings of those subject terms perfectly matched your concepts, right down to the variables you might subject to statistical analysis.

Different tools have different ways to combine searches. Your library catalog and some databases may force you to do it manually by entering one word in a keyword field and another in a subject field. (Another good reason to keep notes!) Fortunately, most indexing databases allow you to combine searches with a few mouse clicks and little or no retyping. Look for an option called "search history" or something similar, like "previous searches" or "recent searches." The option may not appear until you have already done at least one search in that database, and it might show only in the search interface screen rather than the screen displaying search results.

Use the search history function as a shopping basket and a database as a supermarket, except that you are selecting searches instead of groceries. Your concept grid is your shopping list. Your dinner plans are your theory or story. You look through the merchandise on display and select products that will allow you to make the dinner you have envisioned. Even as your basket fills, you discover some other products in the store that seem likely to make a better dinner, so you put them in the basket. When you finish shopping and go home, you put your planned ingredients together and experiment with the others, always with the view of what will make the best dinner.

More concretely, to locate the most relevant literature more comprehensively you should

- Do separate searches for each of your search terms, noting how many results each term generates and how well they fit your story/theory. You can do this very quickly: do a search, eyeball the kinds of results it gives you, note subject terms, and move on to another term (or the same term but in a different field: if you searched by keyword and that term was also a subject term, search for it again specifically as a subject; if you began with a valid subject term, search for its broader usage as a keyword).
- Search on additional search terms as you uncover them.
- Select the *search history* function, which will display a list of your searches.
- Choose which of those searches you want to combine with others. Typically, you can simply mark each term in a check box, then select a button to AND them together—there is no need to retype any words. Sometimes you can type in the numbers of the searches and a Boolean operator, or even combine a search number with a new search term.
- Look at the results list and select the records that look relevant to your theory or story. The database should let you save the file to your computer or e-mail the results to yourself.
- Systematically do other combinations.
- Work your way through other indexing databases and the library catalog.

As you grow more familiar with this clicking and mixing technique and see how the sources you identify and retrieve will fit into your theory or story, you are likely to discover that you can complete much of your project's basic literature searching in a couple of hours.

Cited reference searching allows you to trace the influence of an author or work. It is especially valuable for advanced researchers but worth knowing about as you start your career as a researcher. A work that deals with some aspect of your theory or story and has been cited repeatedly may be a work worth reading especially carefully. Although this information originally was restricted to the *ISI Web of Science* database (and before that, the print volumes of the *Science Citation Index, Social Science Citation*

Index, and *Arts and Humanities Index*), other tools have made it possible to see how influential an article is by how many later works cite it. The *Scopus* database competes directly with *Web of Science* in the library marketplace. More limited citation-trackers have been introduced in subject databases for a few years, as well as in *Google Scholar*.

Pause to Evaluate Your Search Strategy

As we have previously suggested, during the literature search, you should develop a habit of reading on two levels. First, you will read your articles and books for what their content has to say about the story or theory your research will lay out. Secondly, you should also be reading to look for sources of additional relevant citations and search terms, which you will now see in the context of how professional scholars communicate their ideas and information to one another.

This is also the stage for you to reflect on the adequacy of your searching so far, so that you can plan your next step. If your research project will need scholarly articles more than about 20 years old, or if you need primary historical sources, you may need to talk to your librarian about print resources: subject-based article indexes, aids to finding periodicals and documents that your library holds in microfilm, and other pre-Internet tools.

The notion that "everything is on the Internet" is a cruel myth. A lot is on the Web, but a lot of that comes with a price tag. Especially for materials published since the early 1920s—which are intellectual property protected by copyright law—the cost of online access to complete, digitized versions of books and periodicals can be too high for your library to afford. Your library may be able to pay only for parts of digital collections like the *JSTOR* archive of leading scholarly journals; when finances are bad, it may be forced to cancel its subscriptions to databases and electronic journals that are not used heavily enough at your institution. Of course, interlibrary loan or your friendly librarian can help you access print information housed elsewhere.

Taking Notes

You have now reached the stage at which you stop searching for a while, record your searches, and start reading and taking notes. Increasingly, library databases will allow you to display citations in the forms prescribed by the principal style manuals, though these are a computer's best guess and should be double-checked for punctuation, capitalization, italicization, and spacing. When the database provides the full text of the article, these database-generated citations will include the persistent URLs of the article as well as the date you accessed it through the database. Nearly all library databases allow you to manage the results of your searching. Experiment with features that allow you to e-mail results lists or individual articles, select and save them to your computer or portable storage media, print them, or export them to citation management software. Most will allow you to create "alerts" associated with search terms and combinations you choose: as new records or documents are entered into the database, you will be notified of those that match your search. Alerts are especially valuable if you are working on an extended project, such as a thesis.

When saving searches or documents you have located:

- Save or send your results in small batches, not in a big lump. They will be easier to work with later—and less vulnerable to computer failure.
- When saving bibliographic records, save the most complete versions available, including abstracts and authors' reference lists if provided.

- If the database permits it, save the full search history list for that session. It may come in handy later to refresh your memory as well as to plan future search sessions.
- Look at the records as soon as you have saved or exported them, to make sure that the date of your search is included. Your instructor may require you to include the date you looked at a document as part of your list of citations.
- When e-mailing, include notes about the search in the message. When the database allows you to create the subject line for the e-mail, create a subject line that will make sense when you look in your inbox. For example: *ABI su = voters kw = advertis** would tell you that the e-mail contains the results of your search in the *ABI/Inform* database using the subject term *voters* and the keyword (with wild-card for multiple suffixes) *advertis.**

What Is in Your Notes?

In addition to copying and pasting or e-mailing your citations to yourself, you should type notes about your sources as you find them. This requires thinking about the material that you record, which is a more effective way of understanding and applying information than merely highlighting your photocopied or printed articles, or copying and pasting chunks of text. Of course, your notes will include the full citation information we discussed at the onset of this chapter, but your notes should also include all of the main points of the book or article, any especially useful tips or facts, a summary of the method the author used and of the findings if research is reported, and any potentially useful quotations. Make frequent page references to the specific locations of the items you record.

Additionally, a thorough job of note-taking at each stage of your research saves time. First, it lets you use, cite, and discuss any of your sources without necessitating a return to the library or rereading the source. Second, if for some reason you must reread a source, the page notations help to pinpoint the portion of the material that is of interest. An investment of a little time and care to document your literature research pays great dividends.

WORD MINING STEP 3: DIGGING INTO THE LIBRARY'S FULL-TEXT RESOURCES

Appearances can be deceptive. Full-text library resources can easily bring a wealth of information right to your computer. Full-text databases of possible interest to you may offer the complete text of popular journalism—newspapers, magazines, transcripts of selected broadcasts, even selected blogs—as well as scholarly journals. Common full-text resources used in political science include *JSTOR*, portals to electronic journal packages like *Cambridge Journals Online* or *Informa World*,[2] and "aggregator" databases such as *LexisNexis Academic*. Full-text tools are available in legal scholarship, laws and regulations, and judicial opinions; for compiled statistics, and for position papers and analyses by think tanks. Your library may have searchable facsimiles of historical periodicals, right down to ads and editorial cartoons. Knowing the conventions of these source documents will help you focus your searches.

---

[2] Because journal package sites are so tied to particular publishers rather than to disciplines, we do not recommend relying on them when you wish to discover articles you do not already know about. Once you become more familiar with the contours of the literature of political science and related disciplines, you will find features in the publisher sites that will facilitate your research.

The Challenge of Full-Text Searching

While the content is there, efficient full-text searching can be challenging and frustrating, especially if you are not already expert on the topic. Additionally, if you have not clarified what kind of information you need, learned the specialized terminology scholars have used to address topics like yours, and chosen which databases are most likely to provide that information, you can waste a lot of time and energy searching and waste even more time hunting through long lists of results. If you have worked through the previous two steps of word mining, though, you should avoid many of these pitfalls.

We pointed out that the abstract of a scholarly article is likely to feature high-value words that represent the whole article. The equivalent in American journalism is the "lede"—the first one or two sentences that summarize the who-what-when-where-how of a news story. You may be able to focus your searches to the lede before looking through the whole article. Conversely, 90 percent of the articles in the *JSTOR* journal archive were not published with abstracts, so if you need to use *JSTOR* as a discovery tool rather than as a repository from which to retrieve articles you already know about, you will have to work creatively with the words you mined from your previous searches. Another reason not to start your literature searching in *JSTOR*: by design, you will not discover the most recent scholarship there. As an archive, it includes all the articles in the most important journals, especially in liberal arts disciplines, from the first issue up to three to five years before the current issue.

Full-Text Database Searching versus the Free Web

Searching library full-text databases is a lot like searching the free Web. But the library products have a number of characteristics that make searching them faster and more effective than using a typical Web search engine. Many full-text library databases have special subject concentrations (e.g., international relations); many comprehensive ones are internally divided by subject. As with indexing databases, take the opportunity to choose full-text resources that are most likely to include content that relates to aspects of your theory or story, so you can avoid irrelevant content.

Moreover, you can think of the library databases as providing a baseline measure of quality control compared to the hodge-podge of sources that Web search engines give. This quality may reveal itself in the features a database provides for searching and managing search results, even when the content may be available on the free Web. Of course, because both commercial database vendors and libraries have an interest in providing quality content, library full-text databases will provide you with articles and other content that are (depending on your purpose) more authoritative and reliable. For example, even historical full-text databases of newspapers from a century ago are authoritative and reliable, despite the fact that individual articles say things we see now to be untrue, offensive, or wacky: the database presents you with the articles exactly as they were printed, in the context of the page and edition, neither hiding nor adding anything.

As we mentioned earlier, many indexing databases mix in lots of full-text articles. These give you the power of indexes for subject searching and mining high-value terms along with the rich opportunities presented by the full-text content. If your first set of searching in this kind of mixed database was limited to subject terms and keywords appearing only in the citation and abstract fields, just extend the process to find keywords anywhere in the database: $subject_1$ AND $keyword_2$, $keyword_1$ AND $subject_2$, $keyword_1$ AND $keyword_2$.

Subject Searching in Full-text Databases?

Unfortunately, at the time of publication, few full-text-only databases have any useful system of subject headings that bring together documents as easily and effectively as those in indexing or mixed databases. When the database does not provide subject headings (and may have fewer fields in which to focus your search for high-value words), you have to do extra thinking to tell the computer to focus on the kinds of information sources that are most likely to be relevant to your theory or story. You should also look back over your concept grid and other notes from your previous searching and think about which search terms are likely to match words actually used in the source documents. Many times, you will not be able to draw upon a search history tool to combine productive searches, so you will have to pay closer attention to the results of your searches, note down the terms that were most productive, and reenter them as combination searches.

Still, good full-text databases do provide many ways to filter out many kinds of irrelevant sources before you start searching. Get to know them. Pay particular attention to default settings—especially dates—that might not match your own needs. Default settings for publication dates and location are probably the most important ones, especially in heavily news-oriented databases like *Factiva* and *LexisNexis Academic*. If the concepts you are researching are associated with hot political topics, and the number of results is more than you can manage at a sitting, run a search with the dates set to one period, then rerun that search for another range of dates, and then again for another, and so on. If your concepts have many international aspects, you might restrict your searches only one continent or region at a time.

Proximity Searching in Full-text Databases

Good full-text-only databases provide a much more powerful search logic than the crude Boolean AND to search for documents that contain two search terms. A tool called *proximity searching* is based on the logic that when two terms are near each other in a document, then the words may be conceptually related to each other in that document. By extension, where these combinations are relevant and meaningful, then the documents in which they appear are more likely to be relevant to what you need. Whereas subject searching is the power tool in indexes and mixed databases, proximity searching is the power tool in full-text-only databases.

Depending on your database, you may be able to tell the computer to search for words within X number of words of one another, in any order. Proximity operators may be available as menu items or manually entered. For example, *Hillary w/3 Clinton* tells *LexisNexis Academic* to retrieve documents with three words (or fewer) between the first name and the second, thus retrieving documents that name *Hillary Clinton, Hillary Rodham Clinton, Hillary R. Clinton*, and also the reverse-order name, *Clinton, Hillary*. You might also be able to search for words appearing in the same sentence or same paragraph. *W* (for *within*) and *NEAR* are common labels for the same operation.

Generally, proximity searching has a companion feature that makes it an efficient search technique: the ability to view search results with the terms highlighted in context. Commonly called a *keyword in context* (KWIC) display, this feature allows you quickly to see if in fact your search terms are meaningful and relevant to your theory or story, or if for your purposes they are merely accidentally near each other. Look for menu options that allow you to change quickly between full-document, KWIC, and other options for viewing the articles or other documents you retrieve. Chapter 10 on Content Analysis discusses KWIC as a data collection tool.

As you work through the list of results of a search, look for ways you can focus on documents in that list that also include another search term. Library databases typically include special features for searching within a list of results, thereby narrowing the number of results you must handle. This permits you to follow a search strategy similar to the one we suggested for working in indexing databases: use one search to define a universe of information inside that database, then search inside that universe with another term. This technique is really the same as *keyword₁ AND keyword₂*, but you may find it refreshes the way you think about how the documents, the search terms, the larger concept, and your theory or story all fit together.

WORD MINING STEP 4: MAKING THE FREE WEB WORK FOR YOU

Once you have exploited your library's subject-oriented resources, with their relatively bounded content and special features for powerful, efficient searching, you are ready to look for remaining sources that might be "out there" in cyberspace but that your library's tools missed. Once again, your searching will build upon the substantive information you found that helps build your theory or story, and also upon the jargon, names, and other searchable terms you have discovered.

Throughout this discussion, we feel safe in assuming that you already have a good deal of experience Web searching, and that you have used at least one general Web search engine like Google or Bing. Given the rate of innovation among Web search engine companies, much we might say about advance features of specific products could be obsolete by the time you read this book. Instead we provide an overview of several kinds of online resources. The tools we discuss will often present you with primary- and secondary-source information. The skills we emphasize will be portable—regardless of the evolutions in Web search products that will occur in the coming years.

The Free Web Defined

Several times we have mentioned the "free Web" and distinguished it from library subscription resources that are delivered through Web browsers. The free Web is that part that is identified by familiar Web search engines and retrieved without charge. Just as the Web is only part of the larger Internet, the content available via free Web is only a part of the content of the whole Web. Most of the information passing over the Web is "invisible" for either economic or technological reasons. While increasingly the owners of valuable intellectual property—such as the publishers of scholarly articles and books—"expose" their content to *Google* and the other search engines for you to discover, they still charge fees to access them. The technologies conventional Web search engines use to identify Web pages often cannot get inside many searchable databases that are made available without charge. These can range from airline-reservation databases, to the congressional information site *THOMAS* (thomas.loc.gov), to the many useful databases maintained by government agencies, to the campaign-finance databases (www.opensecrets.org/) maintained by the nonprofit Center for Responsive Politics.

You may find it efficient to approach the free Web in the same general way as we did our word mining: reduce ambiguity and irrelevant results by starting with the most narrowly focused resources and work outward to the most general.

Subject Directories

A Web subject directory is a collection of sites selected and organized into categories. Resembling library tools, they enable you to apply library-searching techniques in them. They do not try to identify every Web resource on a topic but rather to provide access to sources that meet basic standards of authoritativeness and reliability; this makes them especially valuable to discover what the invisible Web has to offer you. Because they are selective, they resemble the selection of materials in physical libraries, and their classification systems resemble the function of library cataloging. Some have even gone so far as to assign subject headings and call numbers to Web sites as they would books and journals in a physical library. When, as the most useful ones do, the directory includes annotations describing the sites, it works a lot like a library indexing database.

Good academic directories are compiled by experts—librarians and/or professors—and include annotations about the sites they identify. Look for ones that are sponsored or hosted by academic institutions. We have already mentioned the likelihood that your library has created subject guides or directories to identify its databases, print resources, and probably free Web resources that support your institution's teaching and research programs.

Two of the best subject directories are *Intute* (www.intute.ac.uk), a product of a consortium of British universities, and *Infomine* (infomine.ucr.edu), from librarians at the University of California, Riverside, and several other universities. Analogous to a public library, the *Librarians' Internet Index* (lii.org) points to more consumer-oriented Web resources; it was developed at the University of California and moved to Drexel University.

Good subject directories allow you both to search their "Webliographic" records and to browse. When you become familiar with the sorts of resources a directory includes, you will find that "drilling down" from broader categories to narrower ones can be a valuable technique for the environmental scan. Look for the ability to search within categories, not simply across the whole collection. You can use these categories as you use subject headings in indexes and catalogs to define big chunks of knowledge, in which you search with keywords to find resources dealing with some aspect of your concepts and theory or story.

Think of **portals** as specialized kinds of directories specifically designed to be starting points for getting information produced by an institution—a government, a business, a university. The United States government has created many portals, as have many state governments. *USA.gov* is a searchable and browseable gateway to government Web sites, not all of them of interest to you as a political scientist. The federal government has many specialized portals to facilitate access to particular topics or kinds of information. One of the most important is the Government Printing Office's *FDsys (Federal Digital System)* which is superseding GPO Access as the gateway to government information submitted by Congress and federal agencies (www.gpo.gov/fdsys/search/home.action).

Work in Multiple Search Engines

It is easy to get into the habit of using only one search engine. That is unfortunate for several reasons. First, no single search engine covers the entire Web, and even the most popular ones will include links to pages that no longer exist or, worse, that still exist but have been replaced by newer versions with different URLs. Second, different search engines use different techniques to rank the relevance of search results to the string or query you entered. Finally, habitual use of one search engine may make it harder for you to discover innovations in others that might work better for you.

Meta-search engines are a convenient compromise for retrieving the results of many search engines. *Clusty.com* is an especially useful one because it is programmed to arrange search results into clusters of related sites.

Scirus.com is a specialized search engine specifically geared toward academic research. Though developed primarily for researchers in the natural and physical sciences, it has significant content in social sciences and law. Like *Google Scholar* (scholar.google.com), *Scirus* identifies journal articles as well as conference papers, theses and dissertations, and "preprints" of journal articles that are in the process of being published. *Scirus* is produced by Elsevier, a large, commercial journal publisher, which limits its comprehensiveness. Its advanced-search options for focusing searches are richer than *Google Scholar*'s, though it covers fewer resources.

OAIster.org is a specialized search engine that is especially useful for identifying electronic theses and dissertations, technical reports of government agencies like NASA, and the contents of institutional digital repositories. The "OAI" in its name refers to a technical standard for Web publishing, the Open Archives Initiative.

As with library databases, good Web search engines have "advanced search" options that you should familiarize yourself with. When you have already mined library search tools and read the works they pointed you to, you will have a good idea from them of what words to search for and what settings to specify (for example, to limit to pages with .gov, .mil, or .edu Internet domains or to restrict your searched to words in a site's title).

EVALUATING INFORMATION

The World Wide Web is the primary medium for researchers today, at least in the rich countries of the world. Students and faculty consistently praise the convenience of using a Web browser to access journals, digitized primary sources, and increasingly whole books at any time, from any place that has Internet access. Governments across the world use the Web to provide civic information, to distribute official records of legislative, executive, judicial, and administrative proceedings, and to disseminate government-sponsored research and the holdings of cultural institutions.

We need to note that the Web is merely a medium, just as television is a medium. As a researcher, what matters to you is the *content*, not the *medium*. An article in the *American Political Science Review* is the same article, whether you read it in the printed journal, a photocopy, or online. We point this out because you may encounter instructors who will say you can use only *X* number of Web pages in an assignment. It's unlikely they really mean you cannot use good journal articles or publications of the U.S. government. Rather, they probably mean you should restrict your reliance on sites that may have hidden agendas, present bad or wrong information, or make unsubstantiated claims.

The Web has made it cheap and easy for virtually anyone to say virtually anything that virtually anyone else in the world can access. The standard criteria for judging information pulled from the Web are authority, objectivity, accuracy, currency, and coverage (since Alexander and Tate [1999]). But the same problems exist with information distributed over other media, whether print or broadcast, billboard or graffiti, correspondence or word of mouth. We urge you to critically evaluate any piece of information you come across. Here are a few useful assessment criteria:

- Is it truly relevant to the story or theory you expect this particular research project to illuminate? Relevance in part depends on how you will use the information source.
  - o Is it relevant because it provides evidence that (some) people believe or behave in ways your research is testing? Jon Stewart's *America (The Book): A Citizen's Guide to Democracy Inaction* and Stephen Colbert's *I Am America (And So Can You!)*, though plainly satirical, are relevant literature if you are researching the extent to which cable TV comedians may make some voters distrust how journalists report on political campaigns.
  - o Is it relevant because it situates your own research within the context of existing scholarly research? Jamie Warner's (2007) "Political Culture Jamming: The Dissident Humor of the Daily Show with Jon Stewart" [*Popular Communication* 5(1): 17–36] would be relevant to the story sketched in the previous bullet point. (Incidentally, of the 50 sources that article cites, 8 are to the Web site of Stewart's show or to his book, a dozen are to popular news sources in various media, and the rest are academic sources.)
- "Consider the source" remains a valid rule of thumb.
  - o What sort of authority does the author have to say what he or she does on this particular topic? What are the author's credentials to speak about this subject? If the source is not signed, is it clear that an institution (like the *Economist* magazine or a government agency) takes responsibility for it?
  - o Is the information bound to a different place or time? Parts of an article on political behavior in Moscow, Russia, may be applicable in several ways to your work on political behavior in Moscow, Idaho, but that depends on how you use it. The pathbreaking work on how members of Congress relate to their home constituents may have been written in the 1970s, but how well those theories fit evidence from the 2010s (or the 1970s) is always open to reexamination.
  - o How candidly and completely does the information source take previous scholarship into account? Selectively acknowledging and citing previous work is bad scholarship.
  - o Do the conclusions follow from the evidence and the methodology?
  - o What about the larger context in which you found it? What is the purpose of that publication or Web site? If you are dealing with an article, whether published in an online journal or a print one, was it peer-reviewed? If a book, does it come from a publisher with a good reputation for producing scholarly books? If in a popular medium (e.g., TV, radio, newspapers, blogs, social networking sites), are the conclusions and claims of fact grounded in evidence and respectful of other claims, or are they merely the posturing of advocates? In general, information published by academic and government institutions is more reliable than information from interest groups, businesses, or individuals.
- Is the information corroborated? Never hang any important claim you make in your research on only one source. How have other researchers addressed the theory, methods, evidence, and/or interpretation of the source that impressed you?

REVIEWING AND SUMMARIZING THE LITERATURE

The literature review organizes the works you found in searching and places your research into a broader context, justifies the importance of your work, and serves to establish the plausibility of your theory. How much attention others will pay to your research findings may be determined by the quality of your review of the literature.

A literature review that precisely identifies the body of literature within political science to which you are contributing also allows others to incorporate your findings more easily into later research. The literature review establishes the distinct contribution that your research will make to the existing body of research. Since no research stands completely on its own authority, reviewing the literature related to your research establishes the initial plausibility of your theory.

Positioning and Justifying Your Research

The realization that the existing literature may already speak to most questions you might develop does not mean that your research can make no contribution; rather, it means that your contribution will most likely represent an addition to an *existing* body of knowledge instead of the creation of a new one. This fact may cause you to feel that all the really interesting work has already been done, that the field is closed to innovation, and that no individual accomplishment can amount to much. Each of these perceptions is incorrect. The acquisition of knowledge is a cumulative and incremental process, and your knowledge of the existing research allows you to properly position your theory and findings. Contextualizing your work helps others both to locate and to utilize your findings.

Thus, rather than erecting constraints, the research process offers opportunities. Familiarity with past political science inquiry suggests the direction for future inquiry, and the value of individual effort is enhanced by the collective context. The value of a piece of research increases as that research builds upon the existing body of political science knowledge.

Organizing the Literature

The easiest way to begin organizing and writing a literature review is by outlining a chain of reasoning, based upon your theory or story. The chain of reasoning is simply a series of relationships (or hypotheses) that establish the plausibility of your theory, using the existing research. For example, the left column of Figure 3.2 shows summarization of the chain of reasoning from the literature review in the sample article presented in Chapter 22. The right column in Figure 3.2 notes citations to the research literature that support each assertion in the chain of reasoning. In the research described in Figure 3.2, the authors simply broke the theory down into its most basic components. Then the authors used the literature search tools and strategies described earlier in this chapter to locate evidence supporting the ideas in the chain for reasoning.

Unlike how you may have written papers in high school, scholarly literature reviews are not a series of book reports or article synopses. Rather, just like the theory or story underlying your research, the literature review should tell a story, driven by ideas (as opposed to noting a series of authors and summarizing what they said).

In practice, each paragraph in the literature review should be topic-oriented. That is, each paragraph will focus on a different, but linked, topic. In sequence, these paragraphs

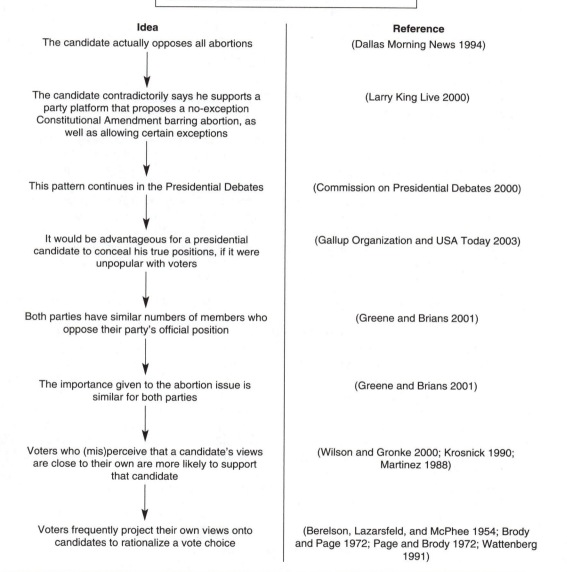

Theory:
A presidential candidate who publicly obfuscates his policy position on a contentious issue can obtain the support of voters who hold opposing policy views, because many voters will project their own views onto the candidate.

Idea	**Reference**
The candidate actually opposes all abortions	(Dallas Morning News 1994)
The candidate contradictorily says he supports a party platform that proposes a no-exception Constitutional Amendment barring abortion, as well as allowing certain exceptions	(Larry King Live 2000)
This pattern continues in the Presidential Debates	(Commission on Presidential Debates 2000)
It would be advantageous for a presidential candidate to conceal his true positions, if it were unpopular with voters	(Gallup Organization and USA Today 2003)
Both parties have similar numbers of members who oppose their party's official position	(Greene and Brians 2001)
The importance given to the abortion issue is similar for both parties	(Greene and Brians 2001)
Voters who (mis)perceive that a candidate's views are close to their own are more likely to support that candidate	(Wilson and Gronke 2000; Krosnick 1990; Martinez 1988)
Voters frequently project their own views onto candidates to rationalize a vote choice	(Berelson, Lazarsfeld, and McPhee 1954; Brody and Page 1972; Page and Brody 1972; Wattenberg 1991)

FIGURE 3.2   A sample theory and chain of reasoning for a literature review, derived from the article in Chapter 22.

build a chain of reasoning (e.g., Figure 3.2). The first sentence of each paragraph should state the main point of the paragraph, but probably will not contain citations. Then, each subsequent sentence in the paragraph elaborates on that first (thesis) sentence and cites references to support it.

Your theory and the chain of reasoning you initially write will undergo many refinements as you read the available literature, just as your outline and first draft only approximately resemble your final paper. In other words, you will start your literature search with a working theory and some idea of how to support it logically, but you also should be prepared to learn and adapt as you read the literature and let the new information you encounter shape the eventual form of your literature review.

COMBINING SEARCHES IN THE LIBRARY CATALOG (ADVANCED TOOLS)

Your library catalog may not permit click-and-combine searching as we have outlined. But you can do a variation that allows you to focus your search for books and other materials that emphasize particular approaches to your topic. When you don't know a main, official subject heading, you can exploit the special, even artificial language of a handful of subject subdivisions in ordinary keyword searches to focus your searches on particular aspects of the topic. Just do a keyword search combining a term from your concept search grid with the exact language of the subdivision. Because of the built-in clumsiness of keyword searching, you will still get some irrelevant results, but you will also get some good ones, including exact matches of subject terms you did not know existed. These suggestions for combining catalog searches were borrowed from Kornegay, Buchanan, and Morgan (2005).

- *Indexes*—Tools for finding what was written on a topic, where: *political science AND indexes*.
- *Bibliography*—Build upon what others have done to identify what sources have been written on a topic: *pro-choice AND bibliography* or *voting AND bibliography*.
- *Encyclopedias*—Important tools for locating basic information on which to build your thesis or theory and identify some search terms: *social science AND encyclopedias* or *elections AND encyclopedias*.
- *Dictionaries*—Reference tools arranged alphabetically; can range from Webster's word lists to small-scale encyclopedias: *gender AND dictionaries* or *religion AND dictionaries*.
- *Handbooks, manuals, etc.*—How-to information. Often you can get by with using only parts of this subdivision, if you remember to type the plurals: *SPSS AND handbooks* or *research AND manuals*.
- *Aspects*—the royal family of subdivisions. Use these to put a spin on any topic. Especially good for unlikely pairings.
  - Economic aspects—Voters AND economic aspects
  - Moral and ethical aspects—Leadership AND moral and ethical aspects
  - Political aspects—Abortion AND political aspects
  - Psychological aspects—Candidates AND psychological aspects
  - Social aspects—*Parties AND social aspects*
- *Sources*—Crucial in the search for the primary documents that historians crave. Most of the time you can replace the subject search, "United States—History—Civil War, 1861–1865—Sources," with *Civil War AND sources*. This abbreviated search for

sources will also yield non-US references, but in a US academic library catalog the US Civil War sources will predominate.

- *Statistics*—Quantitative data. Knowing that the catalog will use *statistics* (not "statistical" or "quantitative") makes all the difference in a search: *abortion AND statistics*.
- *Attitudes*—The opinions belonging to a particular group. *Attitudes AND pro-life* asks how people in the movement feel about, well, anything. For how others feel about pro-life proponents, see *public opinion*.
- *Public opinion*—The attitudes or opinions toward a group or topic. How do people feel about pro-life positions? *Pro-life AND public opinion*.
- *Influence*—Interpretations of the effects of well-known ideas, people, or events, so fuzzier than you'd like when relating variables: *George Bush AND influence*.
- *Sex differences*—For gender issues relating to "individual languages, individual organs and regions of the body," etc.: *communication AND sex differences* or *values AND sex differences*.
- *Cross-cultural studies*—Explores diversity among different cultural and ethnic groups. Best when the topic matters more than the place: *morality AND cross-cultural studies* or *democracy AND cross-cultural studies*.

Bonus: Used in *Google*, this tactic also helps bring relevant scholarly articles and the books digitized by that company toward the top of the results list.

TAKING CONTROL OF YOUR SEARCH (ADVANCED TOOLS)

For the foreseeable future, electronic search and retrieval tools, both those on the free Web and proprietary databases, will use diverse ways to perform similar functions. In their underlying principles they are generally fairly similar, like the Spanish and Italian languages. But to make them work for you, you discover that they are as different as Spanish and Italian. You just have to learn the differences.

Assume that your search tool will be very literal, matching exactly the word you type in. While it is true that some tools are programmed to search for variants of the term you enter (root words, plurals, forms with suffixes, common misspellings), often you will have to instruct the computer. For the broad, fuzzy searching you do in an environmental scan, some tools will let you use **wildcard characters** to stand in for different letters and combinations. The most common one is the asterisk (*) at the end of a set of letters to broaden your search: thus typing "vot*" retrieves documents that include the words *vote, voter, votes, voters, voter's, voters'*, and *voting*.

Some tools will be programmed to interpret a two-word entry in a search box as a phrase and thus put at the top of their results lists documents that include that exact pair. Others will read that same two-word search as in instruction to search for all documents that include the one word as well as the other, whether they are adjacent or not, whether they are in the same order or not. Try a two- or three-word phrase and see how the tool processes it. To make those tools search for phrases, look for a menu option to search for the combination as a phrase (sometimes labeled *exact phrase*) or put the words in double quotation marks ("like this").

Boolean operators (or connectors) give you control over two-word searches. The connector AND tells the computer to retrieve documents that include both the first word and the second word, anywhere, in any order, adjacent or at opposite ends of the document. AND can produce lots of results that are useless to you. For example, the search "Hillary

AND Clinton" could find documents that mention *Hillary* Swank and DeWitt *Clinton* High School. It is good practice to type connectors in all capital letters: it is easier for you to read, and some search tools, especially in some U.S. government agency resources, actually require it. In the environmental scan, it's appropriate to AND together all sorts of terms related to your topic. (As we describe later, when you start your serious searching, it is better to search for each term separately, see what kinds of results it gives, then selectively combine the terms that give results most relevant to your particular theory or story.)

Whereas AND narrows a search, there are two Boolean operators that expand a search: OR and NOT. Use OR to bring together synonyms and variant spellings, as in the difference between U.S. spelling and the spelling used in Britain, in the United Nations, and by most English speakers worldwide: "organize OR organise" (though you might use "program*" instead of "program OR programme"). Use NOT to exclude documents that include words you don't want: "Senators NOT baseball" would find documents that include the word senators except for those that also include the word *baseball*. That would be an effective search if you want to find articles dealing with members of the U.S. Senate rather than members of an old Washington major league baseball team. But it would not be good if you want documents dealing with congressional hearings about the abuse of drugs in sports. Nor would it filter out articles about the Canadian Senate or the Ottawa hockey team. On search engines for the free Web, though typically not library databases, you can use a plus sign to do the opposite of NOT: the plus forces the search engine to identify all documents containing that word.

Conclusion

This chapter offers a brief overview of the basic procedures associated with using online book and article databases to find literature illuminating your theory, and a strategy for organizing the information you find. Because this textbook is used at colleges and universities throughout the United States, and in many other countries as well, it is not possible for us to present a comprehensive primer on the specific resources that your institution's library offers.

Electronic searching looks easier than it is. Still, armed with the basic understanding of literature searching techniques and the literature review organization model this chapter provides, as well as some perseverance, you will be able to get started on building a literature review. To progress beyond our general treatment of literature searching, and to get the most from your library's resources, you should experiment with searches, utilize your search tool's help functions, and contact a librarian with more involved questions that arise in the course of your research. With experience, you will develop your own repertoire of preferred resources and search techniques, but it is unnecessary for you to work completely solo. A reference librarian at your college will be your most authoritative source of information and guidance.

Key Terms

searching *36*
scholarly journal articles *37*
citation *39*
bibliographic record *39*
databases *40*
authenticating *40*
free Web *40*

index *41*
interlibrary loan *41*
word mining *47*
information environmental
  scan *47*
concept search grid *48*
annotated bibliography *51*

subject encyclopedia *52*
indexes *55*
cited reference searching *59*
portals *65*
wildcard characters *71*
Boolean operators *71*

Research Examples

Noting that the research of "academic giants is not generally composed of lengthy literature reviews," McMenamin (2006) nevertheless describes the key value and function of the cited literature as a source for ideas and material to critique in your own work.

To get a sense of the current research in a subfield (and read some high quality literature reviews) try the *Annual Reviews*. Each summer an issue devoted to political science is published containing about two dozen articles summarizing the latest research on a given topic. This publication is available online, or may be found in your library's reference section.

Methodological Readings

For a step-by-step explanation of how to write literature reviews for articles or books, see *Publishing Political Science: The APSA Guide to Writing and Publishing* (Yoder 2008). Additionally, this work offers a comprehensive discussion of various publishing options in political science, as well as specific advice for getting your efforts in print. For a comprehensive, descriptive listing of journals in political science, see *Getting Published in Political Science Journals: A Guide for Authors, Editors, and Librarians* (Martin and Goehlert 2001). Political science journals are ranked using both reputational approaches and "impact measures" in Giles and Garand (2007). Among the most useful general guides to library research are *The Oxford Guide to Library Research* (Mann 2005) and *Doing Honest Work in College* (Lipson 2005).

References

Alexander, Janet E., Marsha Ann Tate, and NetLibrary, Inc. 1999. *Web Wisdom: How to Evaluate and Create Information Quality on the Web*. Mahwah, NJ: Lawrence Erlbaum.

American Political Science Association Committee on Publications. 2006. *APSA Style Manual for Political Science*. Washington, DC: APSA.

Giles, Michael W., and James C. Garand. 2007. "Ranking Political Science Journals: Reputational and Citational Approaches." *PS: Political Science & Politics* 40(October): 741–751.

Kornegay, Becky, Heidi Buchanan, and Hiddy Morgan. 2005. "Amazing, Magic Searches! Subdivisions Combine the Precision of the Cataloger with the Freewheeling Style of a Googler." *Library Journal* 130(Nov 1): 44–46.

Lipson, Charles. 2004. *Doing Honest Work in College: How to Prepare Citations, Avoid Plagiarism, and Achieve Real Academic Success. Chicago Guides to Writing, Editing, and Publishing*. Chicago: University of Chicago Press.

Mann, Thomas. 2005. *The Oxford Guide to Library Research*. New York: Oxford University Press.

Martin, Fenton, and Robert Goehlert. 2001. *Getting Published in Political Science Journals: A Guide for Authors, Editors, and Librarians*, 5th ed. Washington, DC: American Political Science Association.

McMenamin, Iain. 2006. "Process and Text: Teaching Students to Review the Literature." *PS: Political Science & Politics* 39(January): 133–135.

Yoder, Stephen. 2008. *Publishing Political Science: The APSA Guide to Writing and Publishing*. Washington, DC: APSA.

Scholarly Political Science Journals

This list of some of the major scholarly political science journals that regularly publish empirical research is not comprehensive, but many of the more prominent journals appear here.

American Journal of Political Science
American Political Science Review
American Politics Research
British Journal of Political Science
Comparative Political Studies
Perspectives on Politics
Policy Studies Journal/ Policy Review
Political Behavior
Political Communication
Political Research Quarterly

Comparative Politics
Foreign Policy
Harvard International
    Journal of Press/Politics
International
    Organization
International Political
    Science Review

Political Science
    Quarterly
Political Studies
Polity
Presidential Studies
    Quarterly
Public Administration
    Review

International Studies
    Quarterly
Journal of Conflict
    Resolution
Journal of Politics
Legislative Studies
    Quarterly

Public Choice
Public Opinion
    Quarterly
Publius
World Politics

CHAPTER 4

Designing Your Research and Choosing Your Qualitative and Quantitative Methods

In this chapter you will learn:

▪ Why a research plan is fundamental to a successful project.

▪ In explanatory research, the components comprising the research plan.

▪ The key differences in the uses of qualitative and quantitative research methods.

When you gather information in your daily life, you probably do not make a plan. Whether finding movie times for a Saturday evening outing with friends or investigating whether to buy a Zune or an iPod MP3 player, you often conduct research casually. On the other hand, recall the steps you went through to pick your college, choose your apartment, or buy a car—when making these important and expensive decisions, you are more likely to formulate a written plan. Research projects, to the extent that they involve higher stakes (at least in terms of your time) and others have something at stake, require a written plan of attack or *research design*.

"A **research design** is the scheme that guides the process of collecting, analyzing, and interpreting data. It is a logical model of proof that allows the making of valid causal inferences" (Nachmias 1979, 21, emphasis added). Without an adequate and appropriate design for research, the best of measures will be useless, since their meaning cannot be determined. Before undertaking any serious study, you should write out a research design that not only tells exactly what you intend to do in the research process and how you intend to do it, but also tells *why* you are taking each step and why you are taking it in the way that you are, rather than in some other way.

RESEARCH PURPOSE AND RESEARCH DESIGN

The type of research you propose determines the type of methods you will choose. For subjects that are new or yet to be studied, **exploratory research** may be most appropriate. These projects try to provide greater familiarity with the phenomena to be investigated so that we can formulate more precise research questions and perhaps develop hypotheses.

If we have some information on a topic, but need to make our understanding more systematic, we may choose to conduct **descriptive research**. These projects are intended to provide an accurate representation of some phenomenon so that we can better formulate research questions and hypotheses. We may, for example, need to know the frequency, geographic distribution, and sequence of events of a phenomenon or need to know what other phenomena it tends to be associated with before beginning to theorize about what might have caused it.

Finally, research can be intended to test causal hypotheses. If we can use the results of a study to argue that one thing causes another, we can begin to develop explanations of the second event. For that reason, hypothesis-testing research may be described as **explanatory research**. Such research is appropriate when we have enough knowledge about a phenomenon to begin to seek explanations for it.

The significance of this rough typology of research purposes is that research of each type requires different things of a research design, and therefore may tend to utilize data gathered qualitatively (involving detailed, personal observations) or quantitatively (requiring numerical measurement). Exploratory research requires flexibility more than precision, because its purpose is to discover possible explanations rather than to test hypothetical explanations. Exploratory research designs need only provide an opportunity to observe the phenomenon in question, and are normally best conducted using qualitative methods.

Descriptive research, however, requires accurate measurement of phenomena. In descriptive studies, the research design must ensure unbiased and reliable observations if the studies are to produce accurate pictures of the events of interest. These observations may be obtained using either qualitative or quantitative research.

Explanatory research designs must ensure both unbiased and reliable observation and provide a basis for inferring the causal influence of one or more variables on others. A research design provides a basis for causal inferences when it allows us to rule out any plausible explanations for observed results that represent alternatives to the causal hypothesis being tested. Normally, explanatory research is performed using quantitative data.

Regardless of the specific purpose of a study, its research design should include the following *basic elements:*

1. A statement of the purpose of the research.
2. A statement of the theory and hypotheses to be tested (if any).
3. A specification of the variables to be employed.
4. A statement of how each variable is to be operationalized and measured.
5. A detailed statement of how observations are to be obtained and organized.
6. A general discussion of how the data collected will be analyzed.

This text elaborates these research design elements, with each chapter detailing specific facets of the research process and offering options for your project. Background for research elements 1, 2, and 3 is offered in Chapters 1, 2, and 3. Element 4 is discussed in Chapter 5. The procedures used for the remainder of the elements depend upon whether your project utilizes qualitative or quantitative data (or both). The latter half of this chapter details the comparative benefits of qualitative and quantitative data. Chapters 6 through 18 quantitatively elaborate elements 5 and 6, whereas Chapters 19 to 21 detail these elements qualitatively. As you will learn later in this chapter, though, there is no bright line between data types, so you should find something useful in all of the chapters, regardless of which type of data you plan to use.

COPING WITH ALTERNATIVE RIVAL HYPOTHESES THROUGH RESEARCH DESIGN

Science operates negatively. Thus, regardless of the type of data we plan to gather, we do not simply construct a research design that we think "proves" our ideas. Rather, we strive to eliminate plausible alternatives to our (1) suggested understanding of a situation and (2) proposed explanation of its cause. The choices we make in organizing our observations structure our options in testing various hypotheses. A hypothetical research project provides a useful example of this.

An Example

Imagine that the Justice Department in your state has implemented a new program designed to reduce juvenile delinquency. The program involves taking juvenile offenders, as well as potential offenders who volunteer or are volunteered by their parents, into prisons for one-day visits. The program is founded on the theory that glimpsing the horrors of prison life will discourage juveniles from committing crimes that might result in their being sent to prison, because the youths' exposure to incarceration will cause them to fear prison. Let us say that after the program has been in operation for some months, the state government wants to know whether it is having the desired effect, and it hires you, a skilled political scientist, to evaluate its results. How will you go about this?

Because the program, known as Operation Fright, is intended to reduce juvenile delinquency, delinquency will be your dependent variable. You might operationalize it as *being arrested for a criminal offense* and then, one year after their prison visit, simply check on the criminal records of the youths who went through Operation Fright. If they have been arrested during this time, you label them delinquent. If they have not been arrested during this time, you label them nondelinquent.[1]

Let us say that you find that 70 percent of those who have been in the program have *not* been arrested during the following year. Can you then conclude that the program has been 70 percent effective in preventing delinquency? To do so with any confidence, you need to rule out other explanations of why 70 percent of those youths have not been arrested.

Evaluating Alternative Rival Hypotheses

Your *operating hypothesis* is that the Operation Fright experience prevents delinquent behavior. Some possible alternative rival hypotheses that may explain your findings include the following:

1. No more than 30 percent of the youths would have been arrested, even if they had not gone through Operation Fright.
2. The family background of those who were volunteered for Operation Fright is different from the background of those who were not, and it is that background that has prevented their delinquency, not the state program.

---

[1] This simplified operationalization of delinquency treats it as a dichotomous, nominal variable. In practice, you would probably want to use an operationalization that provided more information and was more sensitive to differences between individuals. You might, for example, choose to develop a "delinquency index" that combined the number of arrests in a year with some measure of the severity of the crimes for which the subjects were arrested in order to have an indicator of the *degree* of delinquency.

3. Many of the youths have committed crimes but have not been caught.
4. Though there may be temporary effects from Operation Fright, they will wear off and the youths will revert to criminal behavior. (The program delays delinquency rather than prevents it.)
5. The youths involved in the program have been arrested more often than they would have been had they not taken part in Operation Fright, because participation labels them as potential criminals and subjects them to greater police scrutiny. (The program causes more frequent arrests regardless of its effect on behavior.)

Alternative rival hypothesis 1 essentially asserts that the program has had no impact. With a single observation you cannot demonstrate that this is or is not true. You can never know how those who have gone through the program would have acted if they had not taken part in Operation Fright, but you can include in your research design a check of the criminal records of a group of youths who have *not* gone through Operation Fright but who are otherwise similar in as many respects as possible to those who have. You can then compare the delinquency rate of those who have been in the program with that of those who have not and argue that any difference in the two rates can be attributed to the program, since we can assume that those in the program would have acted essentially the same way as their peers in the absence of Operation Fright. Observing the control group (those not participating in the program) allows us to assert a causal link between the program and delinquent behavior.

Rival hypothesis 2 is a claim that any apparent relationship between program participation and delinquent behavior is spurious. It holds that family background causes both program involvement and subsequent nondelinquency. This reasoning suggests that there is a selection process in which those who have the family support to help them avoid

PRACTICAL RESEARCH ETHICS

Is your research worth pursuing?

Before planning a research project, the single overarching consideration in designing research is whether a given project will require a breach of personal or professional ethics.

Perceived past abuses of human subjects by researchers in the social sciences include Zimbardo's Stanford (University) Prison Experiment and Stanley Milgram's work in *Obedience to Authority* (1974). Concerns about long-term harm to people involved with both of these experiments have made them emblematic of some of the potential dangers inherent in conducting social research. A film and a very informative Web site (www.prisonexp.org) document the former study, and the latter is described in the cited book.

Scholars causing harm to human subjects, through research that seemed to serve little legitimate purpose, led professional organizations to adopt recommended standards of research ethics, and also prompted federal government regulations protecting research subjects. The ethical standards endorsed by the leading professional association in political science are reproduced in Appendix B.

It is very likely that your institution has a research review board, as required by federal regulations of organizations that receive grant funding. Before approaching the review board with your design, ask yourself: Do the benefits of this research to society outweigh the human costs? If your answer is not an unequivocal "yes," then do not pursue your research.

criminal behavior are also the ones most likely to have gone through the program and that this creates an *apparent* relationship between Operation Fright and nondelinquency.

A single observation will not allow you to rule out this possibility, but having a control group including youths with family backgrounds similar to those who have gone through Operation Fright does, as in the case of rival hypothesis 1, allows you to determine whether this is the case. You can check to see whether program participants and nonparticipants do in fact tend to have different family backgrounds, and whether those with similar family backgrounds tend to have the same delinquency rate regardless of participation in Operation Fright.

Ruling out rival hypothesis 2, like dealing with hypothesis 1, requires that you make a second observation (checking the criminal records of some youths not involved in the program). In addition, however, coping with hypothesis 2 requires that you make a third observation, in which you collect data on the subjects' family backgrounds. You may be able to obtain some objective indicators of this variable (for example, presence of both parents, parents' educational level and occupation, and family income) from public records, but you may also have to conduct interviews with family members or the youths themselves. Operationalizing family background to include attitudes and the character of personal interactions will make such interviews necessary. You will therefore not only increase the amount of data you collect but also adopt another method of data collection—the personal interview.

Rival hypothesis 3 reinforces the need for this additional data collection method. It poses the possibility that Operation Fright has made its participants more cautious and perhaps even more clever criminals rather than reducing the number of crimes they commit. It questions the adequacy of the operationalization of the dependent variable. As long as official arrest records are the only measure of delinquency, you cannot have any confidence that this is not the case.

One way to cope with rival hypothesis 3 is to operationalize delinquency so as to include reports of criminal actions from the youths themselves and to conduct interviews both before and after they go through the program. You will have to interview both participants and nonparticipants and include information on family background for each group to be sure that your results cannot be explained by hypotheses such as 1 or 2 phrased in terms of this new indicator of delinquency. With this action you have added not only another **observation point** (the preprogram interview) but also another mode of operationalization for the dependent variable.

Rival hypothesis 4 adds a time dimension to the study. To discount it, you will have to interview and check on the criminal records of both program participants and the control group, not just one year after the prison visit but also two and perhaps three years after as well. The reason for making subsequent observations of program participants should be clear, since hypothesis 4 contends that participants will eventually become delinquent. You will also need to observe the control group in order to ensure that changes in delinquency rates for program participants in later years are not the result of other factors, such as maturation, changes in family situation, or worsening economic conditions. Only if program participants have a subsequent delinquency rate similar to (or worse than) the delinquency rate for nonparticipants *at the same time* can you conclude that the program has been ineffective (or that it has had a negative effect).

Unlike the others, rival hypothesis 5 argues that Operation Fright has been *more* effective than your results suggest. It raises the possibility that by using arrests as the measure of delinquency, you have introduced an additional independent variable (selective treatment from authorities) whose effects cover up the actual influence of Operation Fright on delinquent behavior.

One way to cope with this possibility is to include yet another operationalization of the dependent variable. Looking at *convictions* as well as arrests for both participants and nonparticipants, you will have some evidence of whether the cases brought against program participants are any less valid than those brought against youths who have never gone through Operation Fright, and you may infer from this whether or not the police are any more likely to arrest those who volunteered for Operation Fright. If participants are arrested without ultimately being indicted or convicted significantly more often than are nonparticipants, you will have reason to believe that rival hypothesis 5 is correct.

This brief examination of a few of the possible rival hypotheses that can challenge the value of your results has provided the basis for developing a much more elaborate research design than that first suggested. If you want to be able to rule out these five alternative interpretations (and you must do so if your study is to be of any value), you will have to move from a single operationalization of the dependent variable and a single observation to a research design involving multiple modes of operationalization, multiple methods of data collection, and several observation points. The revised research design might involve the following major steps:

1. Select a sample of youths who have been designated to take part in Operation Fright and a sample of youths who have the same mix of characteristics relevant to delinquency (e.g., sex; age; race; education; parents' occupation, education, and income; living situation; and place of residence), but who are not to participate in the program.
2. Interview those subjects designated to participate in the program before they take part in Operation Fright, and at the same time interview the control group to obtain self-reports of delinquent activity and information on family background.
3. Interview members of all subjects' families to obtain information on family background.
4. One year after the subjects have visited the prison, interview both participants and nonparticipants to obtain self-reports of delinquent activity and to find out whether family circumstances have changed.
5. At the time you perform step 4, check the arrest and conviction records of both program participants and nonparticipants.
6. Two years after the subjects have taken part in Operation Fright, repeat steps 4 and 5.
7. Three years after Operation Fright, repeat steps 4 and 5.

In analyzing the data, you will want to compare the arrest rates, the conviction rates, and the differences between arrest and conviction rates for the program participants and the control group, being careful to eliminate any members of the control group who have taken part in Operation Fright after their initial selection for the study. By employing appropriate statistical procedures in the analysis of the data produced by these observations, you should be able to reach highly defensible conclusions about the value of Operation Fright as a deterrent to juvenile delinquency. Because of your ability to rule out major rival hypotheses, the state's justice department may place a good deal of confidence in your conclusions—a confidence they could not have if those conclusions were based on the first research design.

Adequacy of Design

The purpose of this exercise is not to argue that complex research designs are preferable to simple ones. The important consideration is the *adequacy* of the design, not its complexity. If a research design provides a logical basis for the kinds of inferences the researcher wants to make, it is adequate.

The discussion of this hypothetical study provides an example of how adequate research designs are developed. In planning a research project, you will go through the same kind of reasoning that we have just laid out. *Research design is a process of formulating alternative rival hypotheses and reasoning through the kinds of observations that are needed to test those hypotheses so that they can be ruled out as explanations for potential findings.*

Alternative rival hypotheses are arrived at in the same manner as operating hypotheses. They result from logical analysis of our theories and from thorough knowledge of the facts that surround the events we are trying to explain. A true alternative rival hypothesis predicts the *same relationship* as our main hypothesis but explains it in terms of a different causal process.

Alternative Rival versus "Other Hypotheses"

It is important not to confuse true alternative rival hypotheses with what we can call *other hypotheses*. Due to the existence of multiple causation in social phenomena, it is usually possible to come up with a variety of equally valid explanations of any given event. Identifying another cause of the observed relationship simply produces another hypothesis that may not be a rival to the original. *A hypothesis is an alternative rival hypothesis only if it is logically impossible for both that hypothesis and the original hypothesis to be true at the same time.*

Identifying crucial rival hypotheses is principally a creative activity. There are no hard-and-fast rules to ensure that you will identify all the rival hypotheses that can challenge the value of your research, but the more thought you put into developing and evaluating possible alternatives, the more powerful your hypothesis becomes. Ultimately, this process of thought and analysis will yield more useful theories, as well.

COMPARING QUALITATIVE AND QUANTITATIVE METHODS

The biggest decision you will make in developing your research design is how you will gather data and what types of data you will gather and analyze. Scientific research is generally conducted using either qualitative or quantitative data. As noted earlier in the chapter, both types of data are collected using a plan, but the plan's specificity varies depending upon the type of data.

Quantitative methods emphasize detached observation and documenting phenomena numerically. Did you participate in a science fair when you were in school? If you even toured the projects and looked at them, you are familiar with quantitative research. **Qualitative methods**, on the other hand, study social phenomena *in their entirety, in the context in which they occur*, while *considering the meanings which those being studied give to their actions and to the actions of others*. Qualitative research "entails immersion [of the researcher] in the everyday life of the setting chosen for study, values and seeks to discover participants' perspectives on their worlds, views inquiry as an interactive process between the researcher and the participants, is both descriptive and analytic, and relies on people's words and observable behavior as the primary data" (Marshall and Rossman 1999, 7).

The key point to remember is that *empirical research can be either quantitative or qualitative* so long as its purpose is to characterize real-world phenomena rather than to interpret them in a normative context. In broad strokes, the following section compares qualitative and quantitative methods, effectively laying out the entire research project or design. Before comparing, it is important to recognize that the distinctions discussed are generally more matters of degree than absolutes; the two types of methods often require only different *forms* of work, but are working toward similar objectives. Table 4.1 offers examples of qualitative and quantitative approaches to research in various fields of political science.

Empirical Focus of Research Questions

Both qualitative and quantitative research begin with a research question, because both approaches are designed to produce knowledge of the empirical world. Both rely on concepts that are, at least in principle, observable with ordinary human senses.

TABLE 4.1 **Quantitative and Qualitative Approaches to Research in Various Fields of Political Science**

Field	Quantitative	Qualitative
International Relations	A trust game where each participant chooses whether or not to gamble their experimental money on cooperation or isolation, depending upon which strategy they believe will earn them more money. In this economic experiment, each participant's actions simulate the choices made by world leaders when they negotiate.	Personal observation of meetings of the European Parliament committee on Industry, Research and Energy, specifically noting how issues concerning new technologies that differentially impact countries are handled.
American Politics	During a midterm election campaign, compute the percentage of yard signs supporting incumbent House of Representatives members versus challengers in five cities that had closely contested partisan voting in the previous presidential election.	Bring together several groups of eight to ten citizens in each of several different cities to discuss the U.S. House of Representatives' midterm election campaign. Each group consists of people who all have the same candidate's yard sign.
Comparative Politics	Compute the ratio of street vendors to population in urban areas of fourteen countries, depending upon licensing requirements and enforcement and the history of street businesses.	Read historical documents to build a series of case studies tracking the development and evolution of street vending in four countries in Africa during and after colonization. The documents include letters from ordinary citizens, journalists' accounts, official reports, etc.
Public Law	Compare whether a federal judge was nominated by a Democratic or Republican president and the proportion of cases the judge decided with outcomes in the direction supported by Democratic politicians, with support determined through the content analysis of news stories. Control for the number of years on the bench.	In-depth interviews with half a dozen high-profile federal judges (retired and serving), documenting their political activity prior to presidential appointment.

Theorizing

Qualitative research is less likely than quantitative work to be interested in testing preformed theories constructed in advance. Qualitative research attempts to gain insights into some phenomenon while developing a conceptual understanding. Thus, qualitative theories are often elaborated as observations are made.

In contrast to quantitative theories postulated in advance, the qualitative process may produce theories that are more firmly grounded in reality, or this practice may open the door to unintentionally shaping a theory that fits observations, leading to an untestable theory. Critics of qualitative work also contend that such "theories" apply only to the cases actually observed and, as a result, are of limited usefulness.

Research Design

Whether doing qualitative or quantitative research, you need to be clear about your research question and know what you seek to learn from your study. Quantitative research tries to establish cause-and-effect relationships, whereas qualitative studies are more concerned with viewing people or events as they "naturally" occur. Thus, qualitative research is far less likely to emphasize research designs that allow researchers to "hold constant" some factors in order to make causal inferences. A qualitative research design will generally focus on who or what is to be observed, in what settings they are to be observed, how observations are to be conducted, what methods will be used to secure the information needed, and how data (often referred to in qualitative research simply as "information") will be recorded.

Sampling

Whereas quantitative research is concerned with generalizing conclusions to large populations, qualitative work is more concerned with gaining insights into specific cases from which they can construct a detailed understanding of broad phenomena. In quantitative research, sampling is often based on the logic of probability and designed to produce statistical representativeness. It is usually done in advance of data collection. By contrast, the sample for a qualitative study often emerges as the study progresses. That is, researchers will select an initial case to observe and then let what they learn from those observations determine whom or what they observe next. This strategy reflects their belief that we can determine where to look for the answers we seek only after gaining a partial understanding of the subject by direct experience with it. This is consistent with qualitative researchers' view that each case is unique and should not be treated in a standardized way (as is done in quantitative research).

Qualitative researchers are also often far less concerned with observing "representative" cases than with observing cases that will yield the insights they seek. To illustrate, a quantitatively oriented scholar might try to understand the fundamental assumptions that constitute a "political culture" by surveying a representative sample of thousands of "ordinary" citizens, whereas one pursuing qualitative research might conduct in-depth interviews with several people who do not share these assumptions and reject the dominant political culture. By understanding the political thought of these "outsiders," the qualitative researcher hopes to see how accepting the assumptions of the prevailing political culture influences the majority's thinking about politics.

Data Collection

Among the most dramatic differences between qualitative and quantitative methods appear in the data collection stage. On the surface, there is the fact that data in qualitative research usually consist of words (or sounds and images translated into words) rather than quantitative numbers.

The underlying difference in data relates to the *means* of collection. Whereas a quantitative researcher typically spends little time with each experimental subject or interviewee, qualitative researchers' data collection usually involves extended observation of (or even participation in) the phenomenon under study. Rather than standing apart from the people or events to be studied, the qualitative researcher is often intimately engaged with them. Only in this way can researchers probe for the information they need to understand, for example, why people act as they do, how complex processes unfold, or what impact some specific event had on those who experienced it.

You may recall the concerns over reactivity raised by the discussion in Chapter 1 of the Hawthorne effect, and wonder how researchers deal with this. Quantitative research typically addresses reactivity in one of two ways: (1) experimental work assumes that all will react, but controls will determine what should be attributed to the treatment—we will say more about this in Chapter 6; or (2) in the case of surveys, it is assumed that many will react to being studied (particularly if sensitive questions are involved), so relationships *between* variables are of greatest interest. Qualitative researchers take two other approaches to the problem of reactivity. First, they may conceal the observer or the purpose of the research from the subjects (as we explain in Chapter 19). Secondly, many qualitative researchers take the opposite approach to reactivity. Since researchers have to interact with those they are studying, they depend not on deception or concealment, but on trust (and their own perceptiveness) to avoid artificial reactions.

The goal of qualitative research is for the researcher to build a strong enough relationship with those being observed that they will reveal their true feelings or reasoning and will act "naturally" because they feel that the researcher will not judge or harm them. At a minimum, the researcher will learn enough about the subjects and their context to know when they are not being truthful or are modifying their behavior because of the researcher's presence.

Data Analysis

The distinction between the data collection and data analysis phases of research is far less clear for qualitative studies than for quantitative ones. In quantitative studies, data analysis is planned in advance so that data can be obtained in the necessary form. The analysis is then carried out after all the data are gathered. In studies using qualitative methods, data collection and analysis generally proceed together. Since data collection in qualitative research consists primarily of observing and recording those observations, the very act of deciding what to pay attention to and how to record it involves some analysis.

To illustrate the interaction between observation and analysis, consider a qualitative researcher who seeks to understand the political power structure in a voluntary organization by observing its meetings. This observer will see, hear, and feel a great deal at each meeting—for example, the temperature in the room, noises from outside, whether or not people bring small children to the meeting—but may regard most of it as irrelevant to the research. However, some seemingly irrelevant things may be important in understanding the power structure. Deciding whether to record and how to describe such things as what clothes different people wear to the meeting, the order in which they arrive, or the tone of voice they use in asking questions involves deciding what each of these things means in the context of the study. That requires analysis on the spot as well as when writing up the notes later.

Failing to recognize the importance of an event when it is observed or transcribed can lead to a failure to understand accurately the subject under study. Thus, some level of analysis must begin immediately. As a result, qualitative researchers often modify their data collection techniques in the course of the project as a result of new insights gained from this early analysis.

Another distinction between qualitative and quantitative research is the use of computerized data analysis. With large numeric datasets, statistical software is central to most quantitative analysis. Qualitative researchers are far less likely to make much or any use of them because the form of data they have (narratives) does not lend itself to computerized manipulation. A number of computer programs have been developed to assist in the analysis of qualitative data, so this distinction is not as stark as it was previously. However, it is highly unlikely that computerized analyses will ever be used as extensively in the interpretation of qualitative data as they are in quantitative research.

Standards of Evidence

Quantitative researchers are usually able to employ some well-established rules of analysis in deciding what is valid evidence for or against their theory. These include such tools as measures of statistical significance and statistical tests of validity, as well as formal logic.

On the other hand, qualitative researchers generally lack this type of commonly agreed-to "objective" tool. Rather, they must rely on their ability to present a clear description, offer a convincing analysis, and make a strong argument for their interpretation to establish the value of their conclusions. Advocates of qualitative methods argue that this is an inevitable result of seeking to deal with the richness of complex realities rather than abstracting artificially constructed pieces of those realities for quantitative analysis. Critics of their approach contend that the vagueness and situational nature of their standards of evidence make it difficult (if not impossible) to achieve scientific consensus and, therefore, to make progress through the accumulation of knowledge.

Reporting the Results

Reports of quantitative research usually rely heavily on presentations of numerical data in the form of tables or charts. Direct and detailed presentation of these data are necessary to make the case for the quantitative interpretations being offered. In contrast, reports of qualitative projects often include long quotations from the people being studied, or present the "stories" they told the researcher about their "lived experience." This is necessary not only to capture the full complexity of the subject matter, but also to give readers a way to judge the validity of the researcher's interpretations (as explained in the discussion of rules of evidence above). Qualitative researchers must very carefully document their methods and processes as they decide what evidence (quotations, observations, etc.) to include to allow readers a chance to evaluate the conclusions critically.

RESEARCH EXERCISE

Qualities and Quantities

As you have learned in this chapter, the data used to investigate scientific theories generally fall into two broad categories: qualitative or quantitative. In essence, they are distinguished by whether phenomena are described or counted, respectively. This exercise further illustrates this distinction.

1. Choose a current political issue in the news (e.g., a court decision, an election, a bill, an international conflict, etc.). State the main characteristic of the issue in one sentence.
2. Find one example of each of these two types of data about the issue:
   a. Qualitative (e.g., interview, transcript, editorials, blog posting, etc.)
   b. Quantitative (e.g., proportion of justices supporting decision, numbers who voted on one side of issue or polling percentages, vote in legislature, numbers in international community on one side of the issue, etc.)
3. Compare what the two types of data tell you:
   a. How are they complementary?
   b. How do their findings conflict or speak to cross-purposes?

Conclusion

Even a perfect research design is useless unless we have the resources necessary to execute it. As a student, you may construct practice research designs incorporating each element of the research design, assuming unlimited funding and time. As you begin to conduct your own research, or even build on others' work, you will quickly discover that the design phase is a crucial time to dream big, but plan realistically. Retain your broad ambitions to employ all relevant methodologies in your study, while considering which scientific techniques are most applicable and will most efficiently evaluate your theory and resultant hypotheses.

Our goal in reviewing some of the key differences between qualitative and quantitative methods is to convince you to be open to using the most appropriate method(s) for your research question and theory, as you construct your research design. Rather than posing a stark choice between two divergent methods, qualitative and quantitative methods are often best used as complements to one another in a single study, with the results from each approach providing a form of validation for findings generated from the other.

Key Terms

research design *75*
exploratory research *75*
descriptive research *76*

explanatory research *76*
observation point *79*
quantitative methods *81*

qualitative methods *81*

Research Examples

Examining the relationship between being the victim of violence and abduction in a developing nation and one's subsequent level of political participation, Blattman (2009) presents a report that lays bare its entire research design. Utilizing both the quantitative data and qualitative data he personally gathered in Uganda, Blattman's original research demonstrates the value of both nationally representative data to demonstrate relationships, as well as in-depth qualitative interviews to delve deeper into the reasons underlying behaviors.

A pathbreaking argument against the artificial barriers between qualitative and quantitative empirical political science research is found in *Designing Social Inquiry: Scientific Inference in Qualitative Research* (King, Keohane, and Verba 1994), and is worth a close reading by both experienced and novice researchers. Forming the basis for our modern understanding of study reactivity, the official company report on the experiments done by the Western Electric Company at its Hawthorne assembly plant in Illinois is documented in the book *Management and the Worker* (Roethlisberger and Dickson 1939).

Those interested in pursuing qualitative research will find like-minded individuals in the Organized Section on Qualitative Methods of the American Political Science Association (APSA). The Section publishes a semiannual newsletter (*Qualitative Methods*), which features discussion of current topics in the field as well as research notes utilizing qualitative methods. Information on membership in the Section may be obtained from the APSA (www.apsanet.org).

References

Blattman, Christopher. 2009. "From Violence to Voting: War and Political Participation in Uganda." *American Political Science Review* 103(May): 231–247.

King, Gary, Robert Keohane, and Sidney Verba. 1994. *Designing Social Inquiry: Scientific Inference in Qualitative Research*. Princeton, NJ: Princeton University Press.

Milgram, Stanley. 1974. *Obedience to Authority: An Experimental View*. New York: Harper & Row.

Roethlisberger, Fritz, and William Dickson. 1939. *Management and the Worker*. Cambridge, MA: Harvard University Press.

CHAPTER 5

From Abstract to Concrete: Operationalization and Measurement

In this chapter you will learn:

- How theories are operationalized.
- The qualities of each of the three levels of measurement.
- How error creeps into measurements.
- The importance of internal validity, external validity, and reliability to accurate measurement.

Empirical research is a means of obtaining answers to questions about our observable reality. Our questions may be primarily practical, or they may be principally of academic interest. In either case, they will probably be stated in abstract terms. Yet the answers we want are usually concrete and specific. One of the first challenges in research is to devise ways of getting from the abstract level of our questions to some concrete observation that will allow us to answer them.

To take a nonpolitical example, suppose we want to resolve a debate between roommates about which of the grocery stores in their neighborhood is preferable. Obviously we will need to compare the two in some way to settle the argument, but on what grounds shall we compare them? We want to determine which one exhibits more of the qualities of a great store, but *grocery store excellence* is an abstract concept. In order to evaluate each store in terms of this quality, we may choose to *quantify* the concept of grocery store excellence. We might agree to compare their prices on a fixed set of items, and to let the resulting quantity stand for grocery store excellence. Or, more likely, we might perform several such operations on different aspects of the stores' performance so that we can get a more complete picture of how well they perform, and then combine them in some way. Once we have these numbers, we will be ready to make concrete comparisons and attempt to resolve the dispute.

What we have just described is essentially the process by which we proceed from abstract concept to concrete observation in quantitative social science research. It is a crucial phase in the research process, for only if it is done correctly will the information we gather represent evidence about the utility of our theories or provide answers to our questions. The process of selecting observable phenomena to represent abstract concepts is known as **operationalization,** and the specification of steps to take in making observations is called **instrumentation.** The application of an instrument to assign numerical values to cases results in a **measurement,** and it is this measurement that we finally use as evidence in making decisions and answering questions.

In this chapter we describe these processes in detail and discuss the problems you may encounter in attempting to operationalize and measure concepts. Upon completion of this chapter, you will be ready to state the explanations devised from your search of the literature in a form that will allow you to test them through actual observations.

It should be noted that this chapter primarily focuses on answering research questions using *quantitative* data rather than employing *qualitative* methods; the focus on numerical measurement in the chapter is intentional, but is not intended to exclude qualitative research. We start with numerically based research because it is likely that you have been using quantitative data to address a science fair project or other physical science research questions since you were in grade school. This chapter seeks to build on your familiarity with these methods. Techniques for qualitative operationalization are integrated directly into the chapters on interviewing, direct observations, and focus groups, applying the distinct approaches to each method.

OPERATIONALIZATION: THE LINK BETWEEN THEORY AND OBSERVATION

In Chapter 2 we stressed the importance of having a theory to guide observation. The research process was described principally as a matter of comparing actual observations with the expectations about reality that we derive from our theories in order to judge how much theories are relied on as explanations of political phenomena. These expectations are stated in the form of hypotheses, which predict relationships between variables that represent the concepts in the theory. The object of this chapter is to describe how we can devise observations that will make these comparisons possible. The question is how to quantify our concepts in order to make precise statements about whether or not our theoretically derived expectations are supported by what we observe. The problems encountered in doing this in the social sciences are basically the same as those encountered in the physical sciences. A simple example will help make some of the issues clear.

An Example

Let us say that we want to test experimentally the hypothesis that a chemical fertilizer spread in one cornfield will stimulate more growth than the natural nutrients found in another field. Growth is an abstract concept; it is not seen directly. We need to translate *growth* into an empirically observable variable so that we can determine when one plant has shown more of it than another.

Variable *height attained* represents the concept *growth* because relative heights are empirically observable. But corn plants do not wear signs telling their height; we have to ascertain it for ourselves. How? We could use human judgment and have observers rate plants in the two fields as tall or short. Such a procedure would allow only crude comparisons between plants and would be subject to all kinds of errors, because people differ in their perceptions. We need a more precise and dependable means of determining heights to make meaningful comparisons.

Implementing Instruments

To quantify our measurements, we must translate the variable height into terms of *an instrument* that can be used to yield precise, standardized indications of the extent to which the characteristic is embodied in individual corn plants. We can let height be represented by an **indicator,** such as *length in inches,* and measure the plants with a tape measure. The readings from the tape measure then become the **values** we assign to plants on the variable *height*, and these values are what we actually compare in attempting to assess the accuracy of our theoretical prediction of greater growth in one field than in another.

We have moved, then, from the abstract concept *growth* to the variable *height*, and then to the indicator *length in inches.* This transformation is known as *operationalization*, because an abstract concept has been reduced to a set of values that can be obtained through specifiable operations.

Observing Indicators

We finally make the comparisons on which we will judge the accuracy of our hypothesis about relative growth by comparing the values that result from the measurement process (in this example, the readings from the tape measure). When we speak of **observation** in research, we are referring to *the process of applying a measuring instrument in order to assign values for some characteristic or property of the phenomenon in question to the cases being studied.* In other words, observation means using an instrument to measure a trait or behavior.

This is an important point to understand. It makes clear the significance of operationalization and measurement in the research process. We can never actually compare concepts, even though our theories and our research questions will be stated in concepts; instead, we compare *indicators of concepts*. In our example, we cannot compare the growth of plants in the two cornfields. We can compare only the readings we get from the tape measures—the measures produced by the indicator that represent the concept.

This means that our *comparisons can be accurate only to the extent that the indicators selected mirror the concept we intend them to measure*. If we have improperly operationalized our concepts, the relationship between our indicators may not be an accurate reflection of the relationship between the concepts they are supposed to represent. As a result, any conclusions drawn from our observations about the concepts or the theory of which they are a part will be faulty.

Figure 5.1 illustrates this situation. Our theory posits a relationship between two abstract concepts. Our hypothesis predicts a relationship between two empirically observable variables, which we reduce to measurable indicators, and our observations reveal a relationship (or lack of relationship) between two sets of values on these indicators. Obviously we can infer something about the reality of the theoretical relationship only if the variables accurately represent the concepts *and* the indicators accurately represent the variables. (Note: For simplicity, Figure 5.1 omits the theory's explanatory component.)

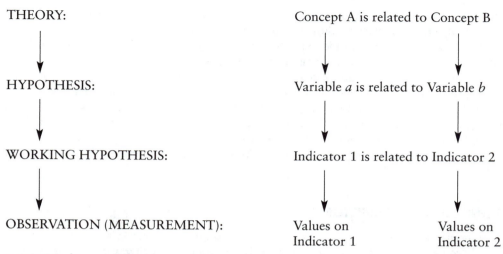

THEORY: Concept A is related to Concept B

HYPOTHESIS: Variable *a* is related to Variable *b*

WORKING HYPOTHESIS: Indicator 1 is related to Indicator 2

OBSERVATION (MEASUREMENT):   Values on   Values on
                                 Indicator 1   Indicator 2

FIGURE 5.1 Operationalization: The relationships of concept, variable, and measure.
Note: This simplified example omits the theory's explanatory component.

Operationalization almost inevitably involves some simplification or loss of meaning, since indicators seldom reflect all that we mean by a concept. Since we almost always have to accept some loss of meaning, we need to operationalize so as to minimize that loss. We have to seek indicators that encapsulate as much of the meaning of the concept as possible and that represent at least some aspects of our concepts as accurately as possible.

Using Multiple Indicators

Our agricultural example illustrates the implications of a single indicator that fails to fully capture our concept. Once we have begun the research, we may realize that there is more to the concept *growth* than height and that the indicator *length in inches* does not fully capture what we want to measure. For instance, it may be that the amount of growth in the two fields is substantially different, but all the difference is in stalk diameter, width of leaves, and weight of corn ears; the height of the plants in the two fields may not be noticeably different. In that case, if only the height is considered in evaluating the effects of the fertilizer, we will be seriously misled, because the link between the concept (growth) and the variable that represents it (height) is imperfect. The variable used here does not *fully operationalize* the concept it represents. It does not capture all the meaning in the concept, and using it misleads us about the relationship that exists in the real world.

This is an especially common situation in the social sciences since most important social science concepts are **multidimensional** in that they have more than one aspect or component. Our measures of these concepts must reflect their diversity if they are to be useful indicators of the concepts. For example, if we operationalized the concept of democracy only in terms of the holding of regular elections, we might classify dictatorial regimes that hold elections with only one candidate per office and do not allow freedom of expression as being just as democratic as the nations of Western Europe. To obtain an accurate measure of the degree to which nations are democratic, we obviously need indicators that reflect the various dimensions of the concept.

The fact that even Iraq under Saddam Hussein held regular elections should help to clarify why operationalization is crucial to theory testing and the research process in general. It is not as easy to explain how to ensure proper operationalization. This is because selecting variables to represent concepts and devising indicators for the variables involve a good deal of creativity and cannot be reduced to a set of standardized steps that will unerringly produce good measures. What we do here is point out some of the pitfalls to be avoided in the process and to describe ways of evaluating the adequacy of operationalizations once they have been selected. We do this in the sections on measurement in this chapter.

OPERATIONAL DEFINITIONS

Before moving to a discussion of social science measurement, however, we should consider what is involved in operationalizing a concept. This is done by specifying a set of procedures to be followed or operations to be performed in order to obtain an empirical indicator of the manifestation of a concept in any given case. These procedures then provide an **operational definition** of the concept and its variable counterpart. The process of operationalization essentially reduces to a matter of selecting operational definitions for concepts.

To be useful—that is, to provide valid and reliable measures of our concepts—operational definitions must tell us precisely and explicitly what to do in order to determine what quantitative value should be associated with a variable in any given case. They should specify a complete set of steps to take in the process of measurement.

Importance of Precise Definitions

We need precise definitions for at least three reasons. First, we want to be able to tell others exactly what we have done to obtain our measures, so that they can evaluate our work and possibly repeat our study to verify its results in another setting. Second, if assistants are actually gathering the information, we will want our instructions for them to be detailed and precise enough to ensure that each one takes the measurements in exactly the same way as the others do. If our instructions are vague and our assistants go through slightly different sets of steps in obtaining measures, their results will not be comparable and we will be unable to draw valid conclusions from them. Finally, precise and detailed statements of how to operationalize a variable will help us in evaluating the results obtained and in eliminating rival explanations of those results that essentially claim that the "findings" have been produced by flaws in the measurement process. (We will have more to say about this in subsequent sections of this chapter.)

When devising operational definitions for variables, you should routinely write out a description of the procedures you will use to obtain measurements. Every step should be detailed. This not only provides a record of your research and ensures standardization of measuring procedures, but also gives you an opportunity to think through the act of obtaining a measurement in order to discover possible errors that can damage the reliability of the results.

An Example

Suppose we want to measure the degree to which members of the two main parties support their own party in a state legislature. We can operationalize the concept *party unity* as *voting together on roll call votes* and then use the percentage of the average member's votes that agree with those of the majority of his or her party as our indicator of *voting together*. Having decided to do this, however, we face a number of critical choices in actually operationalizing our variable.

Before doing anything else, we must initially define both voting and unity. We might get information on how each legislator votes from the records of the legislature, but we will then have to decide which of the many recorded votes to include in our count. Some votes are unanimous (such as a vote to issue a proclamation of praise for some national hero) and do not reflect party unity because they do not involve partisan issues. Thus, including all votes reduces the extent to which our measure reflects our concept. We have to state criteria for selecting votes to include. In order to focus only on controversial issues, therefore, we might, for instance, choose to include only those roll calls in which at least two-thirds of the legislators vote and in which the losing position gets no less than 30 percent of the vote.

We also have to decide how to devise a procedure for determining how a majority of the party has voted in order to classify each member's votes as consistent or inconsistent with that majority position. We need to decide how to treat abstentions. Do they count as a failure to support the party, or do we exclude them from our count? In addition, we have to specify a procedure for first computing and then averaging the percentages of agreeing votes for each legislator.

With every operationalization, we face similar decisions about exact procedures to follow in obtaining measures. A well-constructed, complete operational definition reveals how we have decided to handle such problems and leaves no ambiguity about what we actually did in taking our measures.

Developing Instruments

Building an operational definition results in the development of an **instrument** for taking measurements. In the physical sciences, such instruments as scales, light meters, and micrometers are used to obtain indicators of the degree to which things exhibit some property. In the social sciences, measuring instruments take different forms. Typical social science instruments include a series of questions on a survey form, instructions on how to make and record observations of certain events (such as a debate on the floor of the United Nations), and sets of numbers to be taken from a sourcebook and the rules for combining them into a measure.

Proper instrumentation is as important in the social sciences as it is in the physical sciences. Just as we would not attempt to measure weight with a ruler, we would hesitate to measure *political alienation* solely using demographic questions, such as age or family size. In discussing the validity and reliability of measures in the next section, we also suggest some ways to test the instruments developed in the process of operationalization in order to increase our confidence that they measure what we want.

Choosing Appropriate Measures

The choice of which measures to use for concepts in your theory depends upon several factors, including what other concepts are in the theory, the desired degree of broader generalizability or detailed description, and the resources you have available (e.g., time, personnel, funding, etc.). Thus, there are no "ideal" measures, simply different ones with varying qualities for different situations.

In light of the need to evaluate measures to determine which trade-offs are most suitable for a given project, describe each of the below measures, with one sentence for each measure's costs and a sentence for each measure's benefits or advantages:

- In-depth interviews with 12 members of a national assembly
- Representative polling data comparing environmental attitudes in 20 democracies
- National vote count for an election to join a transnational organization
- Daily observations of the members of a fringe political group that protests international organizations

---

MEASUREMENT

We operationalize variables in order to have a way to concretize abstract concepts so that we can make meaningful comparisons between real-world phenomena in terms of the properties suggested by those concepts. This assigning of numerals to represent properties is known as measurement. The result of measuring is that we have a *value* to associate with some variable for a given case.[1]

This means simply that we can speak with more precision about the extent to which a given unit of observation (for example, a person, a city, a nation, or an organization) exhibits the property represented by the variable being measured. Rather than say that a city has a "bad crime problem," we can speak of specific crime rates. Rather than say that a person is a "devoted Republican," we can say that one has scored a 7 out of 7 on our *strength of party identification* measure.

LEVELS OF MEASUREMENT

Measuring procedures provide a means of categorizing and ordering phenomena. Some procedures, however, produce more precise and detailed distinctions between events than do others. When we say a procedure produces a given **level of measurement**, we are classifying it according to how much information it gives us about the phenomena

---

[1] It is crucial that we appreciate the difference between a variable and its *values*. We recognize a variable because of its capacity to take on different values. The variable is a concept translated into empirical terms. A value is some magnitude or quality of the variable that individual cases can reflect. For example, Lutheran is a value for the variable *religious denomination*; upper class is a value for the variable *socioeconomic status*; and 23 years is a value for the variable *age*.

being measured and their relationship to one another. The levels of measurement are referred to as *nominal, ordinal,* and *interval/ratio.*

Nominal measurement provides the least information about phenomena; it gives only a set of discrete categories to use in distinguishing between cases. Nominal measurement is obtained by simply naming cases by some predetermined scheme of classification. Nationality is generally "measured" at the nominal level by classifying people as Swiss, Brazilian, and so on. However, that "measurement" neither tells us how *much* of the characteristic "nationality" different individuals have nor allows us to rank-order them. Using nominal measurement is simply a way of sorting cases into groups designated by the names used in a classificatory scheme.

To be useful, nominal measurement schemes must be based on sets of categories that are **mutually exclusive** and **collectively exhaustive**. This means (1) it must not be possible to assign any single case to more than one category and (2) the categories should be set up so that *all* cases can be assigned to some category. If we want to classify voters in the United States by use of a nominal measuring scheme, the categories *Democrat, Republican, liberal,* and *conservative* cannot be used successfully, because these categories are not mutually exclusive. Since each U.S. political party appeals to a broad spectrum of voters, it is possible for a person to be both a Democrat and a conservative or liberal, or both a Republican and a conservative or liberal. The categories do not allow us to differentiate among voters in all cases. Similarly, if we try to categorize voters by party affiliation using only two categories—*Republican* and *Democrat*—we will find that our categories are not collectively exhaustive, because some voters consider themselves independents or members of other parties.

In order to facilitate analysis, we will probably want to substitute a number for each category in a scheme of nominal measurement. It is important to recognize, however, that such numbers have no real meaning in this context; they are simply symbols. Just because we choose to substitute a 5 for the *Republican* category and a 1 for the *Democrat* category, it *cannot* be assumed that Republicans have five times as much party affiliation as Democrats. Any number can be substituted for any category of a nominal measurement so long as each category has a unique number associated with it.

Ordinal measurement provides more information because it allows us both to categorize and to order, or rank, phenomena. Ordinal measurement allows us to associate a number with each case. That number tells us not only that the case is different from some other cases, and similar to still others, with respect to the variable being measured, but also how it relates to those other cases in terms of how much of a particular property it exhibits. With ordinal measurement we can say which cases have more (or less) of the measured quality than other cases, and we can rank cases in the order of *how much* of the quality they exhibit. That ranking gives us more detailed and precise information about the cases than we would get from a nominal measurement. The concept *social class* is often measured at the ordinal level, with individuals being ranked as lower, middle, or upper class.

Interval/ratio measurement provides even more information. Not only can we classify and rank-order cases when they have been measured at the interval level, but we can also tell *how much* more (or less) of the measured property they contain than other cases. Ordinal measurement is not based on any standardized unit of the variable in question and does not allow us to tell how far cases are from one another in terms of that variable. It allows us only to say that some have more or less of it than others. Interval/ratio measurement is based on the idea that *there is some standard unit of the property being measured.*

Whereas ordinal measures give us only a rough idea of the relationship between cases with respect to a variable, interval measures provide information on the "distance" between cases. The variable *income* is a clear example. Income is usually measured in units of currency (for instance, dollars in the United States). Because we use *standard units* in our measurement, the difference in income between $10,000 and $11,000 a year is exactly the same as the difference in income between $50,000 and $51,000 a year (i.e., $1,000). We cannot do that with ordinal measurement. If income is measured ordinally by dividing people into such income categories as *under $10,000* and *$10,000 to $19,999,* we can say that one person has more or less income than another, but we cannot say exactly how far apart they are in income because we cannot tell where an individual falls within the category. The income difference between a person in category 1 (under $10,000) and a person in category 2 ($10,000 to $19,999) can be as little as one dollar ($10,000 minus $9,999) or as much as $10,000 ($19,999 minus $9,999), depending on their exact incomes, but we cannot make this distinction from an ordinal measure.

In addition to giving us precise information on the absolute differences between cases, interval measurement lets us make accurate statements about the *relative* differences between concepts. We can, for instance, agree that 50,000 people is twice as large a population as 25,000 people because we can speak meaningfully of a place that has no population. There is a *zero point* in true interval/ratio measures and it is at least conceivably possible for a case to score zero on such measures. Because there is no meaningful zero point on an ordinal scale, we cannot say, for example, that upper-class people have twice as much "class" as lower-class people, because we do not know what it means to completely lack any standing in social class.

It should be noted that we have merged interval and ratio as a single level of measurement. They actually differ based upon the meaning of a variable's zero point, but this distinction is rarely a factor in political science.

Distinguishing between Levels

A handy acronym to remember the levels of measurement in order uses the acronym NOIR (pronounced: no-ear). Simply recalling the names of each level, though, is insufficient to operationalize measurement in research. Still, knowing the names and a working definition of each level are the first steps toward employing appropriate analyses of your measures. Examples and definitions for each level of measurement are provided in Table 5.1.

Increased Precision Is Advantageous

The benefit of increasing precision suggests an important point about levels of measurement. Nominal-level measurement is the least useful form of measurement when comparing phenomena. If we use it when we can use a "higher" (more precise) level of measurement, we may be wasting potentially valuable information. If, in a study of voting behavior, people are categorized only as Republicans, Independents, and Democrats when we can ask a different set of questions and produce a rank-ordering of them as strong to weak party identifiers, we may be giving up information that will help us understand the relationships observed. Ordinal-level measurement is more useful than nominal, but it too has limitations. Interval/ratio-level measurement is the most desirable form of measurement both because it provides the most detail and because of the mathematical procedures it allows us to perform on our data.

TABLE 5.1   NOIR: Summarizing Levels of Measurement

Level of Measurement	Definition	Examples of Variables
Nominal	Unable to rank-order	Race, Gender, City, Employed/Unemployed
Ordinal	May be rank-ordered	Support for increased taxation (1–6 scale), Approval of the president (1–4 scale)
Interval/Ratio	Known distance between ranks	Feeling thermometer rating of Republican Party, Age in years

The point is that we should strive for operationalizations that allow interval-level measurement whenever possible and appropriate. But how do we decide which level of measurement is appropriate for the particular concepts we want to operationalize? This is a matter of both conceptualization and measurement technology.

In the theory-building stage of research, we must first ask ourselves if there is a continuum underlying the differences seen in cases. If there is, we can devise ordinal and even interval measurements for a concept that might otherwise be measured only by nominal classification. An historical example will help clarify the significance of this.

An Example

Suppose we are studying the effects of immigrants' nationality on the degree of their support for big-city political machines in the early twentieth century in the United States. If we operationalize nationality at the nominal level and categorize city voting precincts' support for the machine, we might get a picture like that presented in Figure 5.2(a). There is no apparent relationship between nationality and voting behavior, because knowing a precinct's dominant nationality does not help us rank it relative to the others.

When examining our reasoning, however, we might conclude that the reason we expect nationality to be related to support for the machine is that countries of origin differ in the opportunities they allow their citizens for political participation. When people have had little experience with democratic politics in their native land, we might reason they will be more willing to give up to a political boss their right to self-government. If we can follow this reasoning and rank-order the nations of origin by the extent of political participation they allow their citizens, we can construct a graph like that shown in Figure 5.2(b). In that graph, a relationship between nationality and support for the machine is apparent. The ordering of categories on our independent variable helps us discover a pattern in its relationship to the dependent variable.

If we are bold enough, we may even upgrade our measurement of the independent variable to an interval/ratio level. For example, we might count the number of legal provisions for political participation in the statutes of each country in question for the

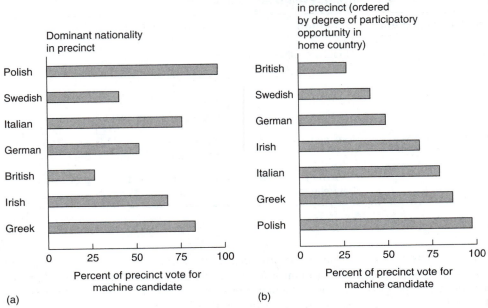

FIGURE 5.2 An example of how level of measurement can affect the interpretation of data.

years just prior to the beginning of significant immigration to the United States. We can use the resulting numbers to rank nationalities along an interval scale and make even more precise comparisons of independent and dependent variables.

Whether or not upgrading of variables can be achieved from the nominal to the ordinal or interval/ratio level depends both on developing a theoretical rationale for doing so and on the technical possibility of applying the operational procedures that produce the higher-level measurements. Even if we can conceptualize *nationality* in interval terms

PRACTICAL RESEARCH ETHICS

How will you explain your choices?

In the process of defining terms and choosing measurement types, researchers make decisions that fundamentally determine the (eventual) research interpretation. During operationalization, an awareness of the limits and strengths of each level of measurement, as well as an appreciation of the measures' reliability and validity, will maximize the interpretability of the research and its acceptance by others.

Later, when writing your research report, you will need to articulate each choice made during operationalization. Documenting each of the reasons for these choices as you are making them will streamline writing, and limit the likelihood that you will accidentally make excessive claims about the power of the measures. Instead of developing your own instrument, you may choose to employ measures tested and used by other researchers. Using measures with known reliability and validity may greatly simplify operationalization, as long as you are fully aware of measurement levels and fully attribute your use of other researchers' measures.

in our example, we may not have access to the legal records necessary to place countries along the interval scale. In that case, *measurement technology* limits what we can do to strengthen our measures.

These situational factors make it difficult to set down rules about operationalizing concepts to achieve certain levels of measurement. We do, though, suggest that you use the most precise measures possible, given the subject you are studying.

Excessive Precision Is Disadvantageous

At this point, we need to add a qualification to our general interest in greater precision. There are cases in which too much precision in measurement is actually undesirable. In Figure 5.3 we see data on the relationship between age and presidential election voting is presented in two different ways. In Figure 5.3(a), age is measured in single years. Because there is greater volatility due to the few people in each age group (for example, 21–22, 35–36, 50–51), the chart reveals no clear pattern in the relationship between the two variables. In Figure 5.3(b), age is measured less precisely, in five-year groupings. With more cases in each group, we can see that there is a broad pattern to the relationship, with voting likelihood increasing to age 75 and then generally declining.

Giving up some precision in our measurements may provide clearer results, but if taken too far we may lose sight of relationships. Using twenty-year groupings to measure age will mask each age group's turnout differences, and we might falsely conclude that age is unrelated to the likelihood of voting. Because we generally do not know in advance of actual data analysis how much precision will be needed to discover relationships, we should follow the rule of operationalizing our concepts as precisely as possible. We can always discard unnecessary precision by "collapsing categories" (moving to larger units of differentiation), if necessary. If detailed information is not collected in the first place, though, we limit our future options.

WORKING HYPOTHESES

Measurement assigns values to cases with respect to given variables. These values are what we use to represent concepts when comparing observations. Before we can understand the implications our observations have for our theories, we have to translate our hypotheses concerning relations between variables into working hypotheses, which state the expected relationships between measures or indicators. The next-to-last line in Figure 5.1 suggests the form that **working hypotheses** take. These hypotheses force us to state explicitly the linkages between indicators and variables that are implied by the operationalization of our theory.

Consider an example from the study of international relations. Suppose we are interested in a theory of dominance in the international sphere. We start with the theoretical proposition that *the more dominated a nation is, the more conformist its foreign policy will be because the nation economically depends upon its patron state*. From this theory we can hypothesize: *As a nation's economic dependency increases, its support for the international policies of its patron state will increase*. We can operationalize *economic dependency* as the percentage of the nation's exports that go to the patron country. The percentage of exports becomes our indicator of the independent variable *dependency*. *Support* can be measured by the percentage of votes in the United Nations General Assembly in which the

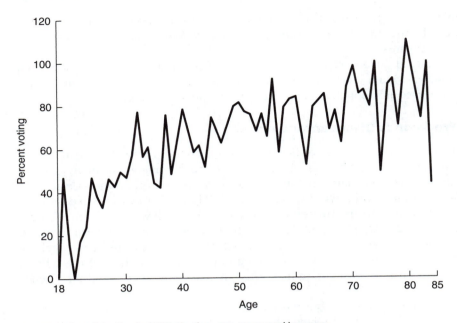

(a) Age and participation in 2002 election: age measured by years

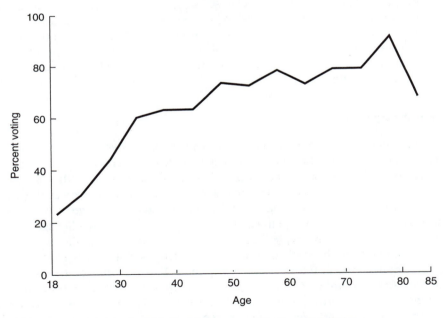

(b) Age and participation in 2002 election: age measured by half-decades

FIGURE 5.3   An example of how level of measurement can affect interpretation of data.

Source: W. Philips Shively, *The Craft of Political Research,* 7th ed. Upper Saddle River, NJ: Pearson Prentice Hall, 2009, pp. 59–60. Reprinted with permission.

client nation's vote differs from that of the patron state. A percentage of votes in the United Nations becomes our indicator of the dependent variable *support for the patron state's policies*. We can now set out a working hypothesis that states the positive relationship expected between indicators: *The higher the percentage of exports going to the patron state, the higher the percentage of votes in the United Nations that agree with the votes of the patron state.*

This working hypothesis tells us what observations are consistent with our hypothesis and theory. It also suggests the relationship we envision between our variables and indicators. That relationship is diagrammed in Figure 5.4.

When doing research, in addition to your theory about political phenomena, you should be able to state a **measurement theory** that sets out *why you expect your indicators to be related to your concepts*. In this example, why should we expect economic dependency to be related to concentration of exports? What is there about the distribution of exports that makes it a reflection of what is meant when we refer to dependency? These are the types of questions a well-developed measurement theory helps us answer. A measurement theory consists of the assumptions that explain why our indicators should change values as the degree to which cases manifest our concepts changes.

Indicators cannot be casually selected but must be chosen as a result of careful reasoning about the way things are related in the world. That reasoning is much like what we go through in constructing theories about political phenomena. This issue of whether or not there is any correspondence between our concept and variables on the one hand

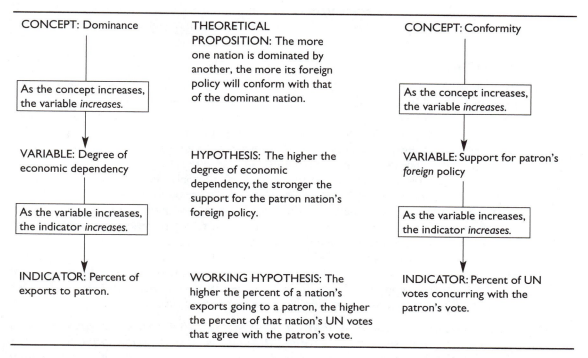

FIGURE 5.4 Specification of the relationships of concepts, variables, and indicators.
Note: This simplified example omits the theory's explanatory components.

and our indicators or measures on the other is the central problem of measurement in science. The question of whether changes in our indicators are actually the result of changes in the concepts they represent gives rise to the problems of reliability and validity that are discussed in subsequent sections of this chapter.

MEASUREMENT ERROR: THE ENEMY

The process of measurement determines the values of cases depending upon how they score on our indicators. The differences in the scores can be entirely attributed to two basic sources. First, the cases really exhibit different degrees of the property in which we are interested. Different scores occur when our measures actually pick up those differences. In this case, *actual* differences in the concept are reflected in our measures. Second, something about the measure itself or the setting in which it is applied causes different cases to get different scores. In that instance, our measures are showing differences between cases that are *not* real—that is, the measurement difference is an artifact, rather than reflecting authentic differences in the concept we want to measure.

If our measures were perfect, they would reveal only the first kind of differences between cases, but our measures are rarely flawless. Differences in the values assigned to cases inevitably reflect not only real differences in the degree to which those cases manifest the concept, but also "artificial" differences created by the measurement process. Any differences in the values assigned to cases that are attributable to anything other than real differences are known as **measurement error**. They are not real differences between cases, but differences that are erroneously recorded because of flaws in the measuring process.

An Example

This distinction between true variations in scores and variations due to measurement error is similar to the distinction between differences in objects viewed directly and differences seen when we look only at their reflection in a mirror. The mirror used may be a precision-ground, optically correct mirror or a funhouse mirror, but we do not know through which we are observing our phenomena. To the extent that the mirror distorts the images, it either masks differences seen when viewing the images directly or creates an impression of differences we would not otherwise perceive. In the social sciences, we rarely can observe our key concepts directly and must rely on measurement procedures analogous to the mirror to reflect these concepts in any given case. Consequently, the accuracy of our impressions of the two depends on the precision with which our measures reflect reality.

What are some of the sources of distortion in the images our measures provide? The answer to this question is needed if we are to control measurement error or recognize it when it is present in our data. We can list several of the primary sources of measurement error by identifying common sources of differences in the scores assigned to cases *other than true differences in the characteristics we want to measure*.

1. ***Differences in the distribution of other, relatively stable characteristics among the cases that are unintentionally revealed by our measures:*** For example, the questions representing our measure of political ideology may require a given level of intelligence to interpret and answer. If this is the case, responses will reflect not only differences in people's political ideology, but also differences in

their intelligence. When looking at the resulting data, the effects of intelligence and political ideology will be confused, and we will be unable to distinguish differences in scores that reflect ideological difference from those that reflect differences in intelligence. Similarly, other characteristics of our units of analysis (such as the regional location of cities, the cultural traits of nations, or the sources of documents) can be inadvertently reflected in our measures and distort our perceptions of the manifestation of the target concepts. When these "contaminating" influences can be identified and measured, we should check to see whether holding their values constant wipes out, reduces, or increases differences in the scores that cases receive on our measures.

2. ***Differences in the distribution of temporary characteristics among the cases that are reflected in our measures:***   A person's mood or state of health can affect the way one responds to items on a questionnaire. The recent political history of cities (the revelation of corruption among public officials, for instance) can create systematic but temporary differences in the way those cities' citizens answer survey questions. A massive natural disaster can produce a drastic but temporary change in the statistics we are relying on to indicate the level of economic development. The effects of such temporary "abnormalities" are more difficult to identify and control than the effects of the stable characteristics in our cases. The only approaches for guarding against them are being alert to signs that individual cases are subject to such transient influences (for example, studying the recent political history of the cities included in our sample or advising our interviewers not to attempt to interview a person who is temporarily bedridden) and following the procedures for checking the reliability of measures described in the section of this chapter discussing reliability.

3. ***Differences in subjects' interpretation of the measuring instrument:***   This is a problem only when people must respond directly to questions, as opposed to when the researcher constructs measures by observing behavior. If questions are ambiguously worded, the different interpretations our respondents place on them can produce differences in their scores on the measures composed of those questions. Suppose, for instance, we are careless enough to ask the question *Did you vote in the last election?* in a study of voting behavior. If some of the interviewees do not know that a city election has been held the prior week, they may answer that they *have* voted because they think the question refers to the last national election, even though they have not voted in the election to which our questions referred. We can guard against this source of unintended differences in scores by pretesting questions and testing our measures for reliability.

4. ***Differences in the setting in which the measure is applied:***   This is a source of measurement error principally in research that relies on individuals' responses to questions as its measures. One well-established fact in survey research, for example, is that the race, sex, and age of interviewers can affect responses. Answers (and therefore scores on measures) can differ among interviews on the basis of the characteristics of the interviewer alone. Similar problems can arise outside survey research. For instance, we may make the mistake of doing a content analysis of one country's domestic newscasts and another's newscasts intended only for foreign nations. We will then be applying the same instrument in very different settings and can expect some differences in scores from this fact alone. This source of

measurement error can be avoided only by making every effort to see that the situations in which we measure are standardized.

5. ***Differences in the administration of the measuring instrument:***   The scores assigned to cases can differ as a result of a variety of errors that occur in collecting and recording information. Interviewers may misunderstand instructions and ask questions in ways the researcher might not intend. Poor lighting may cause a respondent to mismark a questionnaire. Pencils can break and pens run out of ink at crucial moments so that observers fail to record key events in a group interaction. These kinds of variations in the administration of measuring instruments cause differences in scores independent of any differences in real values for the variable under investigation. Beyond employing only dependable assistants, the primary way to guard against such sources of measurement error is through *pretesting* our instruments. A trial run will help us discover potential "mechanical" problems with the instrument (such as insufficient space for recording typical answers on a coding form) and human factors that may affect results (such as length of time observers can work without fatigue).

6. ***Differences in the processing and analysis of data:***   Information has to undergo a great deal of handling before it can be analyzed; it often changes form several times. For example, interviewers may record responses by writing down every word an interviewee says in answer to a question. Those written passages may subsequently be reduced to a single number as responses get coded. The written number may be transferred to a computer file as an entry in the appropriate column of a spreadsheet. In each of these steps, data analysis has been made simpler, but with each step there is a chance of errors that can cause cases to appear to differ on a variable when they do not. The possibility of such errors makes it a good idea to always double- and triple-check each transformation of data and to keep the original form for future reference.

7. ***Differences in the way individuals respond to the form of the measuring instrument:***   This is especially a problem when our units of analysis are people, rather than countries or news articles or the like. Measuring instruments can take such different forms as oral interviews, questionnaires to be filled out by the respondent, and observation by a trained researcher. The different forms place different demands on the people under study. An interview requires ease of speaking, and a questionnaire requires an ability to read and write, for example. If people differ in these abilities, their scores may differ even when the people are actually alike on the variable being operationalized. The best guard against this source of measurement error is the use of more than one form of measure meant to operationalize each concept. We say more about this in the next section of this chapter, which discusses validity.

All of these factors can introduce measurement error into our research. The various errors that arise from these seven sources are generally categorized as either *systematic* or *random* errors.

Systematic errors are those that arise from a confusion of variables in the world (as discussed in item 1 in the preceding list) or from the nature of the instrument itself. They appear in each use of the instrument and are constant among cases and studies in which the same measure is used. Constant errors cause *invalid* results, in that the differences (or similarities) our measures seem to reveal are not accurate reflections of the differences we think we are measuring.

Random errors affect each application of the instrument differently. These errors occur as a matter of chance and are due to transient characteristics in our cases, situational variations in application of the instrument, mistakes in administration and processing, and other factors that vary from one use of the instrument to the next. They make our measures invalid in much the same way that systematic errors do. Random errors also make our measures *unreliable,* in that we cannot consistently get the same results when we use the measure if random errors are occurring.

How do we avoid having measurement error distort the results and render our research useless or misleading? To answer that question we must give careful attention to the issues of validity and reliability.

VALIDITY

We can seldom obtain direct measures of the concepts used in social science theories. Such concepts as power, democracy, and representation cannot be quantified as simply as the concepts of length and weight. We have to use indicators that correspond only indirectly to the concepts they represent. There is always a chance then that the indicators chosen will not adequately reflect the concepts we want to measure. **Validity** is the term used to refer to *the extent to which our measures correspond to the concepts they are intended to reflect.*

To be valid, a measure must be both *appropriate* and *complete*. If, for example, we are interested in comparing the quality of public education in different cities, we may be tempted to use the number of teachers in those cities' schools as an indicator of the quality of educational services. This measure is *inappropriate* because the number of personnel in a school system is determined largely by the number of students and the size of the city and may have little to do with the quality of education. If the ratio of students to teachers is used as our indicator of educational services, we will have a more appropriate measure, in that differences caused by city size will be reduced or eliminated. The measure, however, will still be *incomplete*. Education involves more than teachers; it also involves school buildings, films, books, labs, and a variety of other factors. Looking at any one of these factors by itself might leave us with a false impression of the total quality of educational services. A school system may have a highly desirable student–teacher ratio but inadequate facilities and learning materials. It is a mistake to say that such a school system is equal to one with an identical student–teacher ratio *and* excellent facilities and learning materials. To achieve validity, we must strive to construct measures that are both appropriate and complete.

Internal versus External Validity

There are two primary types of validity associated with empirical research: internal and external. **Internal validity** involves accurate measurement of our theoretical concepts. In other words, *are we measuring what we think we are measuring?* A later section in this chapter examines types of validation, which seek to answer this question. **External validity** pertains to the *generalizability of our results*. Can we reasonably expect to find the same causal influences at work in other settings? Does this study tell us anything about people, governments, and situations *not* included in it? A field experiment on the effects on the public's driving habits of adding a dollar-a-gallon surcharge to the price of gasoline, for example, has little external validity if it is conducted in a community where the average family's annual income is above $100,000, because we cannot expect middle- and low-income people to react to increased prices in the same way as upper-class people.

FACTORS THAT THREATEN VALIDITY

The major categories of threats to both internal and external validity include the following (Campbell 1969, 407–429):

Factors That Threaten Internal Validity

1. *History:* Events other than the Independent Variable (IV) that can alter posttest scores and that occur between the pretest and posttest. For example, a well-publicized statement by a political leader can alter subjects' attitudes independently of some long-term experimental treatment they are undergoing.

2. *Maturation:* Natural changes in the subjects that alter scores on the Dependent Variable (DV) over time independently of the IV (for example, human fatigue, population growth in geographically defined units of analysis, aging of physical facilities).

3. *Instability:* Random changes in recorded values due to unreliable measures, inconsistent sampling of subjects, or other causes.

4. *Testing:* The test effect described in this chapter.

5. *Instrumentation:* Differences in the measuring devices used that produce differences in scores independently of the effects of the IV (for example, different biases among interviewers, an improperly calibrated machine, or inconsistent precision among coders).

6. *Regression artifacts:* Changes due to regression toward the mean, discussed in Chapter 6.

7. *Selection:* Differences in scores resulting from differential recruitment of test and control groups (for example, when members of a test group are forced by law to be exposed to the IV, whereas members of one of the control groups volunteer to be exposed).

8. *Experimental mortality:* Different rates of loss of subjects from test and control groups (for example, those cases that can make the control group as a whole respond to the IV in the same way as the test group may drop out of the experiment before posttest).

9. *Selection-maturation interaction:* Biases in selection processes that lead to different rates of maturation in test and control groups (for example, in a study involving juvenile delinquents in a deterrent study, test subjects may be older because they have volunteered for the program only after a series of juvenile arrests, and they may thus outgrow juvenile delinquency faster than the younger control group).

Factors That Threaten External Validity

1. ***Interaction effects of testing:***   Posttest scores of the pretested subjects may be rendered unrepresentative of the unpretested population because of the way in which the pretest has sensitized the subjects to the IV.
2. ***Interaction of selection and experimental treatment:***   Biased selection processes may produce a test group that responds to the IV in ways atypical of the larger population.
3. ***Reactive effects of experimental arrangements:***   Conditions of the experimental setting may be unrepresentative of real-world conditions.
4. ***Multiple-treatment interference:***   The simultaneous application of more than one treatment may create changes that are different from what would occur if any one treatment or IV were used alone.
5. ***Irrelevant responsiveness of measures:***   All measures pick up multiple aspects of the environment, and some may include irrelevant components that give the appearance of change when none has occurred or that obscure actual changes.
6. ***Irrelevant replicability of treatments:***   When IVs are complex events (as is a college education), researchers may not be aware of what aspect causes the change in subjects, and they may fail to include the relevant aspect of the IV in all experimental exposures to it.

RELIABILITY

Whereas validity considers how closely the measured values correspond to the true values of the variable, when we ask about the **reliability** of a measure, we are assessing how *stable* the values it yields are. Can we get the same value for any given case when we apply the measure several different times, or does each application result in the assignment of a different value to each case? If we do not get substantially the same value for any given case from successive applications of a measure, that measure is *unreliable* as an indicator of the concept. Rulers are made of inelastic materials in order to ensure reliability. If rulers were made of elastic materials, they might very well show different lengths for the same object—even when the object's true length has not changed—simply because the ruler stretches and contracts.

Reliability versus Validity

If a measure is unreliable, it cannot be valid because at least some of the differences in the scores assigned to cases result from measurement errors rather than from true differences between cases. Recall our example of the study of street lighting. What if the light meter we use is so sensitive that in addition to recording the light from the streetlights, it picks up light from the moon? Then the values assigned to each street on the variable *quality of street lighting* will depend both on the brightness of the street lights and on such random factors as the fullness of the moon and the density of the cloud cover. To the extent that these random factors influence our results, the measure will not be a valid reflection of actual differences in the quality of street lighting. In this case, unreliability produces invalidity.

A measure may be quite reliable and yet invalid. Recall our example of the study of the extent to which people in different nations agree with the policies of their government. We said that survey questions may give invalid measures because people in authoritarian countries are afraid to tell the truth about their opinions. Because this factor produces a systematic rather than a random error, the questions might produce very stable results. No matter how many times they are asked, people might give the same "safe" responses. This does not, however, make the measure valid.

Thus, a measure may *be reliable without being valid, but it cannot be valid without being reliable.* Whereas validity is challenged by both systematic and random error, reliability is jeopardized only by random error. This means that if a measure has been convincingly validated in prior studies we can use it without being worried about its reliability; it has to be reliable if it is valid. But demonstrating reliability does not guarantee validity.

Testing Reliability

How do we guard against unreliability? How do we determine whether or not a given measure is reliable? Preventing unreliability depends on our being aware of the various sources of random measurement error described earlier in this chapter and doing what we can to control them. This involves thinking through the actual measurement process and pretesting our measuring instruments to discover previously unrecognized causes of random error.

It is often quite difficult to determine whether or not we have devised a reliable measure in the social sciences. This is because the true value of the variables with which we are concerned can change dramatically with time and circumstance—people change their opinions in response to experience, nations alter the way they allocate resources between social services and defense efforts in response to perceived military threats, and so on. When real values are changing, it is hard to distinguish the effects of random measurement error from genuine fluctuations in the concepts being measured. This means that tests of reliability should be conducted over as short a time span as possible.

There are essentially three broad methods of assessing the reliability of measures in the social sciences. The first is the *test-retest method.* Here the same measure is applied to the same set of cases again and again, over time. To the extent that cases get the same score each time, the measure is considered reliable. A difficulty with this technique arises when our measure involves interviewing people (as opposed to measuring inanimate objects or making concealed observations of people). If we repeat questions in a short time, interviewees may remember their first answer and, in an effort to be consistent, repeat that answer rather than respond truthfully in answering the question. If this happens, we cannot get an accurate picture of the questions' reliability as an indicator of the concept. In an effort to avoid this test effect, we might let a good deal of time pass before asking the questions a second time. In doing that, however, we will run into another problem: true values on the variable may have changed with the passage of time, and we may be unable to distinguish differences in scores caused by unreliability in the measure from actual changes in the variable.

Because of that difficulty, a second type of reliability test has been developed: the *alternative form method.* Different forms of the measure are applied to the same group of cases, or the same measure is applied to different groups *at the same time.* In this way there can be no reaction to being measured because no case will be measured more than once and, because no time lapses between applications of the measure, actual changes in the variables under study cannot affect the results. The success of this strategy, however, depends on the alternative forms of the measure being perfectly comparable to each other as a measure of the concept, or on the two groups being virtually equivalent with respect to the distribution of the measured variable. If we can assume that these conditions are met, the more the scores on the two measures, or the scores of the two groups, are alike, the more confidence we have in the reliability of our measure. If we cannot come up with comparable measures or groups, however, the method cannot be used properly.

The final basic approach to testing the reliability of a measure is known as the *subsample method.* In it we draw one sample of cases and divide it into several subsamples in such a way that each is highly similar to the others in composition. Then, the same measure is applied to all subsamples and we use the similarity or difference of responses from subsample to subsample as an indicator of the reliability of the measure. Because the same measure is used, we do not have to be concerned about comparability, as in the alternative form method, and because we can rely on sampling theory to ensure the equivalence of our subsamples, we do not have to worry that the groups selected for measurement will not be sufficiently alike. Because no case is measured twice, we can discount reaction to testing as a threat to the accuracy of our reliability test, and because the measures are administered simultaneously, actual changes in the variable cannot create problems for this method as they can for the test-retest method. However, use of the subsample method depends on our being able to draw a large enough sample that we can divide it and still have subsamples large enough for our statistical tests to be meaningful. This is not always possible and can represent a barrier to the use of the subsample method in testing reliability.

There are many variations on these methods. Which one is most appropriate for any given research project will depend both on the time and resources available to complete the research and on the nature of the study. For instance, if we want to measure street lighting by having trained observers rate the lighting on various blocks, the test-retest method can easily be used without concern about a test effect. Street lighting will not change simply because it is measured by someone, and so we can have different observers independently rate the same street on the same night. We cannot have the same confidence in this method if our measure of street lighting quality is based on citizens' responses to interview questions.

Regardless of the reliability test we choose to use, it is important to establish the reliability of our measures *before* actually beginning research. This involves pretesting the measure by collecting the data necessary for the purpose of assessing the instruments we will use in the final study. Failing to do this, we may find only *after* the study is complete that our measures of key variables are unreliable (and therefore invalid). This means that we will not be able to place any faith in the results of the research and that our energies will have been partially or totally wasted. *Pretests of the validity and reliability of measures should be part of any research project that either uses measures that have not been convincingly validated elsewhere or relies on measures that have been validated only in settings very different from those in which they will be used.*

TABLE 5.2 Types of Validation

Pragmatic Validation	Construct Validation	Discriminant Validation	Face Validation
Check results obtained from use of the indicator against results obtained from use of another indicator that is known to be a valid measure of the concept, or test the *predictive validity* of the indicator by using it to predict events that reflect the concept being measured.	*Internal (convergent) validation:* Infer validity of the indicator from its relationship to other indicators of the same concept using *multiple indicators.* *External validation:* Infer validity of the indicator from its relationship to indicators of *other* concepts to which the concept being measured should *theoretically* be related.	Infer validity of the indicator from the degree to which it is *unrelated* to indicators of other concepts that are theoretically distinct from the concept being measured.	Assume validity from the self-evident character of the indicator. (Can knowledgeable persons be persuaded that this is a valid indicator of the concept?)

TYPES OF VALIDATION (ADVANCED TOOLS)

Achieving appropriate and relatively complete operationalizations depends both on knowing a good deal about the subject of our study and on conducting a careful, logical analysis of alternative operationalizations. Unfortunately, we can check the validity of our measures in order to determine whether or not we have developed sound measures only *after* we have collected data. The process of evaluating the validity of our measures is referred to as **validation**. There are four basic approaches to validation summarized in Table 5.2.

Pragmatic Validation

The degree to which a measure allows us to predict behavior and events establishes **pragmatic validation**. For example, say that we devise a measure of how appealing candidates for public office are to voters. We can get some indication of the validity of this measure by applying it to all the candidates for seats in the U.S. Senate in a given election year and predicting their chances of being elected on the basis of their relative scores on our "voter appeal" measure. The more successful we are at predicting the candidates' electoral fate, the more confident we become that we have a valid measure, one that accurately reflects the intended concept. Measures that allow us to predict future events accurately are said to have **predictive validity**.

Pragmatic validation requires that there be some alternative indicator of variables that we feel fairly certain is a valid reflection of them. We check our measures against this alternative as we might check the accuracy of verbal reports of age against birth certificates. Unfortunately, there are seldom any clearly valid alternative indicators for the concepts used in social science research. As a result, we generally have to rely on the second type of validation—*construct validation.*

Construct Validation

We *infer* the validity of a measure to develop **construct validation**. Essentially, we determine the extent to which a variety of measures are consistent with what our theory predicts. This involves two lines of reasoning.

First, we might say to ourselves, "If concept X has a positive relationship to concept Y and a negative relationship to concept Z (as our theory says it does), then it will also be true that scores on a valid measure of X will have a positive relationship to scores on a valid measure of Y and a negative relationship to scores on a valid measure of Z." The measure cannot be validated by comparing scores on it to scores on some other measure of the same variable that we know to be valid (as in the case of the birth certificate). We can, however, judge its validity by the extent to which using it as an indicator of our variable produces the kinds of relationships that our theory leads us to expect between that variable and other variables.

An Example

To study international alliances, we might create a measure of the strength of an alliance based on a content analysis of newspaper articles from the countries involved. Is what the newspapers of one nation say about another nation a valid indicator of the strength of the alliance between the two countries? We might get an idea of whether it is by reasoning as follows: "Our theory tells us that the stronger an alliance between two nations is, the more often they will vote together in the United Nations and the fewer restrictions they will place on trade with each other. Therefore, scores on a valid measure of *strength of alliance* will be positively related to scores on measures of *voting together in the United Nations* and negatively related to scores on measures of *number of trade barriers.*" We then proceed to do the data analysis necessary to see whether this expectation is supported by our observations. If the relationships are as expected, we will have greater confidence in the validity of our measure of *strength of alliance*. If they are not as we have expected, we will question whether we have a sound measure of this concept.

What we have just described is often referred to as **external validation**. It involves comparing scores on the measure being validated with scores on measures of *other* variables. To use this method of validation, of course, we have to include measures of the other variables in our research. This means that *we have to begin thinking about ways to validate our measures early in the research process*. Certainly by the time we are ready to develop a research design, we have to know how to check the validity of our measures so that we can be certain to gather any needed information.

Our efforts at external validation will produce convincing evidence about the validity of our measure of one variable only if we can have a high degree of confidence in the validity of the measures used for the other variables. In the previous example, for instance, we could not conclude anything about the validity of our measure of *strength of alliance* from the relationships between scores on it and scores on the other two variables if we did not believe that our indicators of *voting together* and *trade barriers* were valid.

Because it is often difficult to find clearly valid indicators of variables to which our key variable should be related, external validation procedures must be used with caution. This is very much like testing a hypothesis. No single result guarantees the validity (or invalidity) of the measure. Rather, as instances of successful validation attempts accumulate, our confidence in the validity of our measure grows. For that reason, it is wise to seek out as many theoretically predictable relationships as possible to use in external validation. The more different tests of validity we have, the stronger our case will be.

This same logic applies to the second type of construct validation—**internal or convergent validation**. This type of validation involves devising several measures of the *same* variable and comparing scores on these various measures. We reason that if each of the indicators provides a valid measure of the concept in question, the scores individual cases receive on the measures should be closely related. If A, B, and C are all valid measures of X, then any individual's scores on A, B, and C should be highly similar.

An Example

Suppose that we want an indicator of the quality of street lighting in residential neighborhoods as part of a study of the distribution of public services. We might want to use citizens' perceptions of the adequacy of street lighting (as revealed in survey interviews) as that indicator. A sample of citizens in a neighborhood can be asked how adequate they think the area's streetlights are and we can take the average evaluation as our measure of *quality of street lighting.* In order to perform an internal validation, we may also measure street lighting quality (1) by using a light meter to get a physical measure of the brightness and distribution of lighting, (2) by having trained observers rate the lighting, and (3) by having citizens compare their street lighting with that pictured in a series of photos showing streets with different qualities of lighting and then averaging their rankings to get a measure for the neighborhood. This gives us four measures of the variable. If each is valid, all should be strongly related.

We can check this with appropriate statistics. If we find that scores on the measure based on responses to interview questions are weakly related to scores on the other three measures *and* that scores on those other measures are strongly related to one another, we will have reason to suspect that our first measure is not valid.

This is much like weighing the same object on three different scales. If each of the scales gives an accurate weight and we have no reason to assume that the object has changed weight in the course of the test, we expect the weights obtained from the three scales to be identical. If one gives a different weight, we suspect it of being out of adjustment.

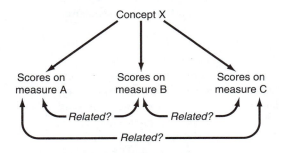

(a) Internal (convergent) validation

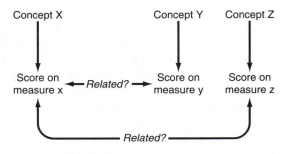

(b) External validation

FIGURE 5.5 Forms of construct validation.

Figure 5.5 suggests the differences between internal and external forms of construct validation. In Figure 5.5a, we see that internal validation is achieved by checking the correspondence of scores on several different measures of the *same* concept. The more closely they correspond, the more justified we feel in claiming that any of the measures is valid. In Figure 5.5b, we see that external validation involves determining whether our measure of one variable shows it to be related to *other* variables as we expect it to be from our theory. If the expected relationships do not appear, we have reason to suspect that the indicator we have selected does not provide valid measures of the concept.

The same caution that applies to the use of external validation procedures applies to the use of internal validation. We cannot always be certain that our measures of the key concept are valid, and should therefore always be careful about concluding that a measure is valid or invalid from any one test of validity. We can significantly increase our confidence in the results of an internal validation if a simple rule is followed: *The alternative measures of the concept should be based on as many different types of operationalization as possible.*

In the street lighting example, our measures come from four distinct types of operationalization: citizens' verbal ratings, physical measurements, observers' judgments, and citizens' selection of photographs. Each of these represents a different *mode of operationalization*. The more different modes we can use and the more independent they are of each other, the more confidence we can place in our validation. Why? The logic is as follows:

The principal source of invalidity is systematic and random measurement error. Different measures are subject to different kinds of measurement errors. The more indicators we have for any variable and the more they differ from one another, the less likely it is that all the indicators will be affected by the same measurement error. If this is true, we will have a better chance of both recognizing measurement error as a source of differences in the scores on any one of our measures and getting an accurate measure of our variable if we use **multiple indicators**. These indicators may be combined into a scale, a topic discussed in great detail in Chapter 9.

An Example

The factors that may invalidate our physical measure of street lighting quality (such as a faulty light meter) are likely to be quite unrelated to any factors that might introduce systematic errors into the measure based on citizens' evaluations (such as a tendency for people to claim, out of a sense of community pride, that public services in their neighborhood are as good as those in other areas). If we use only one mode of measurement, any source of measurement error may affect the scores on each measure, giving us a consistently invalid indicator and not allowing meaningful comparisons among measures. If, for example, we rely only on the physical measure of lighting but take readings in several different ways (say, on the sidewalk, on the curb, and in the street), then any flaw in the measuring instrument (the light meter, in this case) will affect all measures and none can be used to check another.

This logic suggests the great value of having multiple indicators for our variables. The availability of multiple measures not only gives us an opportunity to *test* the validity of our indicators, but also *improves our chances of obtaining a valid measure* of our variables in the first place. Multiple measures can actually increase the validity of

ement by allowing us to combine the results of several different measurement pro-
so as to produce a *composite score* that is more likely to be a valid reflection of
ual value of our variable than any of the measures taken alone. This is because
s a chance that the errors that cause each measure to be invalid will cancel out
the results of several measurement procedures are combined. (In Chapter 9, the
s on scaling describe some possible methods of combining scores to produce a
osite measure.)

Discriminant Validation

A third approach to validation is referred to as **discriminant validation**. When we ask
whether a measure exhibits *discriminant validity,* we are essentially asking whether
using it as an indicator of a given concept allows us to distinguish that concept from
other concepts. For example, we might want to measure the concept *trust in political officials* through a series of questions in a survey. If we also have on the questionnaire a
series of questions designed to measure *trust in people* (in general), scores can be compared on the two measures to ask whether our first set of questions actually reflects simply another way of measuring trust in people. If scores are highly similar, we say that the
political trust measure does not have discriminant validity because it does not permit us
to distinguish the concept of *trust in political officials* from the concept of *trust in
people.*

Face Validation

A final approach to validation relies on the concept of **face validity**. Some measures are
based on such direct observation of the behavior in question that there seems to be no
reason to question their validity; such a measure seems valid "on the face of it." For example, suppose we want to measure compliance with a state law, requiring each business
establishment to display its operating license on its front door. Having trained observers
simply note the presence or absence of such licenses seems to provide an obviously valid
measure of compliance. Though we should always ask ourselves if the measures selected
appear valid on their face, it is generally a mistake to rely on face validity alone to ensure
accurate results from research. We should attempt to ascertain the validity of our measures through established procedures, such as those already described.

Conclusion

At this point we have introduced all the basic elements of the research process. Figure 5.6 depicts
their relationships to one another. The operationalization of our concepts through the development of measurable indicators prepares us to enter
the field to make the observations on which we
will base our conclusions. Before we can make

those observations, however, we need a "plan of
attack"—a scheme for making the observations in
a way that will maximize the number of conclusions we can confidently draw from them. This
plan, or *research design,* is the subject of the next
chapter.

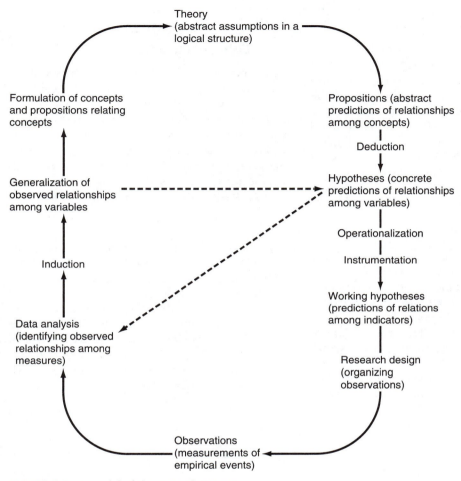

FIGURE 5.6 A model of the research process.

Key Terms

operationalization *89*
instrumentation *89*
measurement *89*
indicator *90*
values *90*
observation *90*
multidimensional *91*
operational definition *92*
instrument *93*
level of measurement *94*
nominal measurement *95*
mutually exclusive *95*

collectively exhaustive *95*
ordinal measurement *95*
interval/ratio measurement *95*
working hypotheses *99*
measurement theory *101*
measurement error *102*
systematic errors *104*
random errors *105*
validity *105*
internal validity *105*
external validity *105*
reliability *107*

validation *110*
pragmatic validation *110*
predictive validity *110*
construct validation *111*
external validation *111*
internal (convergent)
    validation *112*
multiple indicators *113*
discriminant validation *114*
face validity *114*

Research Examples

Brownlee (2009) offers a clear example of transparent research, with several pages devoted to a careful description of the operationalization and measurement of variables associated with the transition from authoritarian to democratic regimes. Confronting and reformulating Edmund Burke's classic distinction between delegates and trustees, Rehfeld (2009) proposes a new set of typologies. Toward this end, he creates a detailed textual table that clearly operationalizes his conception.

Methodological Readings

Many explanations of measurement in the social sciences are found in literature that reports research results or develops sophisticated measurement techniques. An excellent general introduction to measurement strategies is in W. Phillips Shively's *The Craft of Political Research* (2009). A more detailed discussion of measurement error, from the psychology research tradition, is found in *Research Methods in Social Relations* (Hoyle, Harris, and Judd 2002).

References

Brownlee, Jason. 2009. "Portents of Pluralism: How Hybrid Regimes Affect Democratic Transitions." *American Journal of Political Science* 53(July): 515–532.

Campbell, Donald T. 1969. "Reforms as Experiments." *American Psychologist* 24(April): 407–429.

Hoyle, Rick H., Monica J. Harris, and Charles M. Judd. 2002. *Research Methods in Social Relations*, 7th ed. Pacific Grove, CA: Thompson Wadsworth.

Rehfeld, Andrew. 2009. "Representation Rethought: On Trustees, Delegates, and Gyroscopes in the Study of Political Representation and Democracy." *American Political Science Review* 103(May): 214–230.

Shively, W. Phillips. 2009. *The Craft of Political Research,* 7th ed. Upper Saddle River, NJ: Pearson Prentice Hall.

CHAPTER 6

Experimental Research: Attributing Causation through Control

In this chapter you will learn:

- The principal characteristics and benefits of experimental research.
- The limitations that make experimental research particularly challenging.
- The most commonly used experimental methods in political science.

You probably try to avoid wrongly accusing someone of causing a problem. When you return to your room, and you see muddy footprints on your carpet, you can be pretty confident about asking your roommate to clean up the floor, if you only have one roommate and your apartment or dorm was locked since you last saw your clean floor. You feel okay about concluding that she or he must be responsible, because you cannot imagine how anyone else could have caused the mess. On the other hand, when you put the campaign sticker for your candidate on your bedroom window, what effect does it have on the election outcome? Or, when you write an article in the campus newspaper decrying the use of sweatshop workers to make the t-shirts that display your campus team's name, and the administration subsequently cancels its contract with that supplier—did your story lead to your preferred outcome?

Undoubtedly, you hope that your political actions produce your desired results, but how do you know what causes a given outcome? We are much more confident of causation with research designs that give us higher degrees of **control** over the conditions under which variables interact.

Control: An Example

Imagine that voter turnout in the precinct that includes a college's dorms is much higher in the current election after a series of campaign ads promising students student aid benefits, in contrast to that precinct's turnout in the previous presidential election. We do not know that the ads caused the turnout bump, or even if students are the source of the precinct's higher turnout. Turnout could increase due to a variety of factors: (1) this national election may have received greater media attention than did the previous one; (2) there could be an issue in this particular election of great interest to college-age citizens (e.g., the draft, the economy, etc.); (3) one of the candidates might have specifically targeted college students in voter registration efforts; or (4) professors, most of whom hold a liberal ideology and also happen to live in the precinct, might have responded to the ad campaign and voted in higher numbers.

On the other hand, if the students who are shown the advertising campaign in a media research lab show much higher levels of political engagement than those shown other video material, the researcher is more confident that the campaign is stimulating student participation. That is, when we can control the environment and ensure that subjects are *not* exposed to any other new influences during the observations, we are more confident that the treatment (i.e., ads) *caused* the effect (i.e., political engagement and voting).

THE CLASSIC EXPERIMENT

The *experiment* is the classic model of developing scientific causation. It is based on an hypothesis that changes in the value of one variable cause changes in the value of another variable (for example, *changes in temperature result in changes in the viscosity of oil*). The experiment allows us to test this hypothesis by exposing those cases or **subjects** manifesting the dependent variable to the independent variable under conditions that allow us to be relatively sure that any observed change in the dependent variable is a result of changes in the independent variable.

The basic **experimental design** involves three things: (1) an **experimental group** composed of subjects who will be exposed to the independent variable, or **stimulus**, (2) a **control group** of subjects, who will not be exposed to the stimulus, and (3) the random assignment of subjects to each group. The value of the dependent variable in each group is measured prior to introduction of the stimulus in what is called a **pretest,** and is again measured after the experimental group has been exposed to the stimulus using a **posttest.** The impact of the stimulus (independent variable) is inferred from a comparison of the pretest and posttest scores for each group. The greater the difference in values between pretest and posttest in each group, the greater the effect attributed to the independent variable. Table 6.1 shows the logic of the experimental research design. The advantage of this research design is that it allows us to achieve two conditions that facilitate valid causal inferences: *comparison* and *manipulation*.

The assertion that one thing has caused another is based on the concept of change. We must be able to show that some change has occurred before claiming that causal

TABLE 6.1 The Classic Experimental Design

Group	Time 1	Time 2	Time 3	Effect Formula
Experimental	Pretest	Stimulus	Posttest	Effect (of experimental variable) =
Control	Pretest	—	Posttest	$(posttest_E - pretest_E) -$ $(posttest_C - pretest_C)$ where E refers to the experimental group and C to the control group

forces have been at work, and the idea of change implies comparisons. Also, we must be able to compare values of the dependent variable before the subjects have been exposed to the independent or causal variable with values of the dependent variable after such exposure, and if possible, compare values of the dependent variable after exposure with some indicator of what those values might be if exposure had never occurred. The experimental design, with its pretest-posttest procedure and its test and control groups, provides an opportunity for both types of comparison.

In order to feel confident that one variable has a causal influence on another, we must be able to know which subjects have been exposed to the independent variable and which have not, in order to make the appropriate comparisons. The classic experiment provides this knowledge because it is the researcher who introduces the independent variable. The scientist manipulates the subjects' environment so that their exposure to the causal influence is not left to chance. In addition, the researcher manipulates the subjects' environment to ensure that all other possible causes of a change in the dependent variable are removed from the experiment at the time of the subjects' exposure to the independent variable.

A variety of other research designs build on the logic of the classic experiment but add modifications that are especially relevant to social scientists. Social scientists' need for more elaborate research designs is largely due to the facts that (1) the objects of their research are often affected by the very act of studying them (for example, people's behavior may change if they know they are being watched) and (2) the objects of their research are not static but ever changing (for example, people's values may change as new situations arise). Two experimental designs developed by R. L. Solomon (1949) illustrate ways of dealing with these facts.

Illustrated in Table 6.2, Solomon's first design addresses a type of reactivity known as the **test effect.** When experimental subjects are pretested, it is always possible that their score on the posttest will be a result of both their reaction to the stimulus *and* a reaction to the pretest itself. Any difference between pretest and posttest scores that is due solely to reactions to the pretest is known as a test effect. If we are to get an accurate picture of the impact of the stimulus on behavior, we must be able to remove this test effect from the scores. The **Solomon two-control-group research design** in Table 6.2 allows us to do this.

This design is just like the classic experiment except that a third group is added. The third group (Control 2) receives the stimulus and posttest, but no pretest. Though changes from pretest scores to posttest scores in the experimental group can be due to both the pretest and the stimulus, changes from pretest scores to posttest scores in Control 1 can be due only to the pretest and in Control 2 only to the stimulus. If we can assume that all groups have had essentially the same value on the dependent variable

TABLE 6.2   The Solomon Two-Control-Group Research Design

Group	Time 1	Time 2	Time 3	Effect Formula
Experimental	Pretest	Stimulus	Posttest	Effect = $[(\text{posttest}_E - \text{pretest}_E) -$
Control 1	Pretest	—	Posttest	$(\text{posttest}_{C1} - \text{pretest}_{C1})] -$
Control 2	—	Stimulus	Posttest	$(\text{posttest}_E - \text{posttest}_{C2})$

TABLE 6.3   The Solomon Three-Control-Group Research Design

Group	Time 1	Time 2	Time 3	Effect Formula
Experimental	Pretest	Stimulus	Posttest	Effect = $[($posttest$_E$ − pretest$_E) −$
Control 1	Pretest	—	Posttest	$($posttest$_{C1}$ − pretest$_{C1})] −$
Control 2	—	Stimulus	Posttest	$[($posttest$_E$ − posttest$_{C2}) +$
Control 3	—	—	Posttest	$($posttest$_{C3}$ − pretest$_E)]$

initially and have reacted to the stimulus in the same way, then the difference in the posttest scores of the experimental group and Control 2 represents the test effect. The effect of the independent variable (stimulus) alone can then be gauged by subtracting this test effect from the total effect of the experiment, which is computed by the same formula used to evaluate the results of the classic experimental design. The effect formula in Table 6.2 summarizes this logic algebraically.

In addition to the test effect as an alternative explanation of observed changes in subjects' scores, there are other possible causes of change in the groups' scores on the dependent variable (DV) from pretest to posttest. One is the influence of *external factors* not under the control of the experimenter. Another is natural changes in the subjects that proceed independently of the experiment (such as aging—in long-term experiments—or mental fatigue). The impact of such erroneous factors can be judged (and therefore ruled out as a rival explanation of the experiment's results) by use of the **Solomon three-control-group research design,** depicted in Table 6.3.

This design adds a third control group, which receives neither pretest nor stimulus. Any difference in pretest and posttest scores in this group can be due only to the influence of extraneous factors. If we can subtract this change from the effect of the experiment, we can remove from our results the effects of extraneous factors and changes in the respondents, and can hope to rule out the alternative hypothesis that it is these influences rather than the independent variable that have caused the change in the experimental group's score from Time 1 to Time 3.

The difficulty is that Control 3 is not pretested. How can we determine how much these subjects' scores have changed from Time 1 to Time 3? If all of our groups are essentially alike, we can assume that their pretest scores will have been highly similar and simply assign Control 3 a pretest score equal to the average of the scores for the experimental and first two control groups. We can then subtract this score from Control 3's posttest to obtain a measure of the change due to extraneous factors and natural changes in the subjects. With this change removed, we can see more clearly the effects of the independent variable on the dependent variable.

Assigning Cases to Groups

Each of the experimental designs described above is intended to provide a sound, logical basis for conclusions about the effects of one variable on another. To be successful in this, each design fundamentally depends on the assumption that all groups in the study are essentially the same with respect to those factors that might influence their response to the experiment. If we cannot assume that the groups are essentially the same, there is no logical basis for inferring that observed differences in their scores are the result of differences in the way they have been treated in the experiment (for example, whether or not they have been pretested), and we cannot make sound arguments about the causal influence of our independent variable.

Randomly Assigning Groups

In **randomization,** a subject selected from a list of all eligible subjects is assigned to a group by a random process, such as use of a table of random numbers. True randomization is *not* achieved by chance procedures (such as taking the first thirty people who apply for the experiment as the test group and the next thirty as the control group).

Randomization has the great advantage of allowing us to feel quite confident that all of our groups are highly similar in *all* respects, not just in terms of the variables we identify as relevant to the experiment, because random assignment ensures that differences in subjects will cancel out *when large numbers of subjects are chosen.* Randomization, then, allows us to rule out any alternative rival hypothesis that contends that some systematic difference in the groups has produced the observed results. It is *the key to successful laboratory experiments.* In Chapter 7 we discuss detailed procedures for the random selection of cases.

Assigning Groups by Characteristics

If it is not possible to utilize random assignment, it may be possible to minimize the likelihood of bias through two other systematic case assignment approaches. The first technique utilizes **precision matching.** After deciding what characteristics might influence subjects' response to the independent variable, we select a set of subjects for the experiment. For each subject selected, we locate for the control group another subject who has exactly the same combination of relevant characteristics. The result is two groups that are identical in the characteristics that might influence their response to the experiment. Ideally, their pretest scores will be highly similar, and we can use the degree of similarity actually found when pretesting them to judge how well our matching efforts have worked.

There are several problems with this procedure. First, if we need to control for a large number of characteristics, it may be extremely difficult to find subjects who are matched in all the characteristics, as they must be in precision matching. We might, for instance, be able to find people of the same sex, age, and race but have difficulty finding people who share those characteristics *and* have the same occupation, educational background, and length of residence in the community. In addition, if we want to use a research design calling for more than two groups, it may be difficult to locate three or four subjects with identical characteristics. Unless we have an extremely large pool of potential subjects or a very simple experiment, matching may be impracticable as a means of assigning subjects to experimental groups.

A second method of obtaining similar groups is **frequency distribution control.** Here we do not match each subject with another on all characteristics. Rather, subjects are assigned to groups in such a way as to ensure that the groups have the same average characteristics and the same distribution of each characteristic. There may be no two subjects with the same combination of sex, age, race, and occupation, but each group will

PRACTICAL RESEARCH ETHICS
Too much control?

The virtue of the experiment can also be its downfall. A great deal of control and subjects being removed from their natural social setting can lead to dangerous outcomes in the experimental setting.

In the history of psychological experiments, none is more infamous than Stanley Milgram's 1961 laboratory experiments in which many participants were convinced that they had physically harmed other people or even killed them, after being told to do so by an authority figure. Milgram's work is documented in his book *Obedience to Authority* (1974). Decades after his death, Milgram's work continues to generate controversy, much of which is compiled in a book by Blass (2000). Blass (2004) has also written an engaging biography of Stanley Milgram.

In 1971, another controversial research project, the Stanford Prison Experiment, explored people's situational and group behavior in detention settings (www.prisonexp.org).

While your institution's research review board is a safety valve on potentially dangerous or harmful research, you (the researcher) are the real protection against poorly conceived or unnecessary research.

As you gain more control over research subjects' environment, you need to think of their welfare first. If they fully understood all of the implications of your research, would they participate? If you cannot answer "yes," you need to discontinue this research until you can honestly do so.

have the same proportion of males and females, the same average age, and so on. Moreover, the groups will have highly similar distributions of these characteristics among their members.

Frequency distribution control is more often practicable than precision matching, but it has two significant defects. First, it allows us to control for only one variable at a time. Frequency distribution assignment may produce, for example, two groups with equal numbers of subjects over forty years of age and equal numbers of women, but there is no guarantee that all the over-forty subjects will not be men in one group and women in the other. If it works out this way, the two groups will not be truly similar. Second, the method offers no control over any factors that influence subjects' reactions but have not been identified by the researcher. If our theory of the phenomenon under study is incomplete (and it almost *always* is), we may have failed to control the frequency distribution of an important variable. If the control and experimental groups happen to differ systematically on this uncontrolled variable, our results may be distorted.

Clearly, each of the techniques for assigning cases by characteristics is inferior to random assignment. Still, they may be useful when we are unable to use a random approach.

Political Communication Experiments: An Example

Political communications researchers are particularly likely to utilize laboratory experiments to study perceptions and effects of media messages. In these experiments subject treatments may include viewing or reading political content ranging from press releases to campaign ads to news broadcasts. The laboratory environment permits controlling exposure, as well as manipulating content message and formatting. Researchers may evaluate major content effects by varying specific text in ads, making the same advertisement carry a positive or negative tone, for example. Production effects may include controlling for male or female advertising voice-overs, evaluating the type of photos, or colors of circulars. All of this research assumes that certain types of images or messages may differentially influence citizens.

FIELD EXPERIMENTS

Political scientists rarely are able to work in laboratories, due to the nature of their subject matter. Rather, these researchers often observe events in natural settings, where they can exercise less control over the factors that might influence the results of the study. Many of the causal advantages of experimental research may be exercised in the field, though.

As the name implies, a **field experiment** occurs out of the laboratory, but it retains the experimental characteristics of manipulation of the treatment and random assignment to treatment or control groups. For example, field experiments are a logical means to assess the general turnout or persuasive effects of mail, e-mail, phone, and door-to-door canvassing. Campaigns are increasingly dependent upon electronic communications (i.e., televised ads) and direct-mail circulars, but little research has compared the *relative* effectiveness of various media.

In a number of pathbreaking experiments conducted by Green and Gerber (2004), cities and communities were divided into quadrants, and citizens in each area were contacted using different methods (or no method, in the control condition). Not surprisingly, the researchers found that personal contact carried the strongest mobilization or (candidate-specific) persuasive message. Green and Gerber's work employing field experiments at Yale has spawned a renaissance of this approach, with this method being used in communities throughout the United States and beyond.

Of course, the field setting makes it more difficult to isolate the effects of the treatment (contact) from other possible causes of changes in subjects' behavior, but it offers the distinct advantage of giving a realistic test of how mobilization efforts would work in practice. A laboratory experiment, even if it could have been arranged, would not have been as satisfactory, because we cannot be sure that the results obtained in such an artificial environment accurately represent what happens in the outside world. This is a general advantage of field experiments over laboratory studies.

In field experiments, researchers use careful selection of the subjects and random assignment of subjects to the test and control groups in order to gain control over background characteristics that may influence results. They also keep a close check on subjects' circumstances throughout the experiment to rule out alternative hypotheses that attribute observed results to outside events that may occur during the experiment.

QUASI-EXPERIMENTS

Most of the research schemes employed by political scientists can be classified as **quasi-experimental designs.** In these studies, researchers cannot control exposure to the independent variable or the conditions under which it occurs, but they attempt to simulate an experimental design either by gathering additional data or by data analysis techniques. Properly constructed quasi-experimental designs allow us to proceed *as if* we had exercised all the control characteristic of a true experiment, and they provide a sound, logical basis for causal inferences.

Perhaps the most common type of quasi-experimental design in political science is the **ex post facto experiment.** In it researchers make a single observation and collect data about the independent and dependent variables and any other variables they feel should be controlled for. If we want to investigate the effects of college education on voting behavior, for instance, we may conduct a survey of randomly selected subjects. Then we analyze our data in such a way as to determine whether people who are similar in other regards (for example, race, sex, age, and region of residence) but have different educational backgrounds vote differently. There are sophisticated statistical techniques for doing this, but at the simplest level we may sort out our respondents in contingency tables so that we can examine the relationship between education and voting in different categories of other variables, looking, for example, only at women who have and have not gone to college or only at men who have and have not gone to college.

This procedure allows us to act *as if* we had set up an experiment years ago in which we had assigned people to experimental groups, had exposed some to college education (the independent variable), and were now testing them to see what impact this had had on their voting.

The members of our sample who have had less than a college education but are similar in other respects to those in our sample who have had a college education serve as a "control group." Because there was not a pretest, we cannot be sure that it is college education that has created any observed differences in voting, but we can use the additional data gathered in the survey to rule out some plausible rival hypotheses.

There are some situations in which we cannot use random sampling and cannot select comparable control groups. We will find this to be the case if our units of analysis are few in number or unique in many relevant regards. An example is the situation in which a city government wants to know what effect an administrative reorganization has had on the costs of city services. To fulfill the request, political scientists might use another common research design known as a *time-series design*.

In **time-series designs,** the researcher makes several observations both before and after the introduction of a causal phenomenon and compares values on the dependent variable before and after. In our example, political scientists might use city records to compare the per capita costs of municipal services before and after the administrative reorganization. (They will have to use per capita costs and control for inflation in order to rule out the possibility that either an increasing city population or rising prices have affected the costs of public services independently of the impact of the reorganization.) Figures 6.1 through 6.3 illustrate some possible results of this study.

In a sense, time-series designs use as a control group the *same* subject or set of subjects, but at an earlier time. If there is a clear trend in the values of the dependent variable prior to introduction of the independent variable, it is assumed that the trend would continue were it not for the independent variable, and as an indicator of the effect of the IV, we use the difference between observed values of the DV and the values that it would have if the trend continued.

Figure 6.1 illustrates this logic. If the data come out as presented in that figure, city officials will be delighted to learn that the reorganization not only has reduced the cost of services but also has reversed the trend toward steadily increasing costs. The effect of the reorganization in any given year can be measured *by the difference between the value predicted for that year from the original trend line and the observed value.*

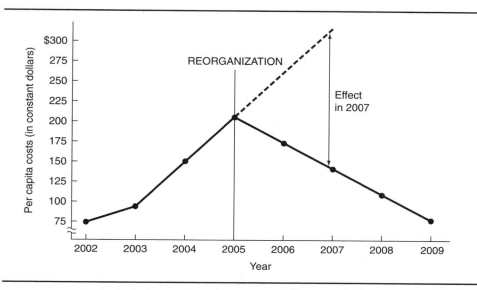

FIGURE 6.1   Hypothetical trend in public service costs showing that reorganization has reversed the original trend.

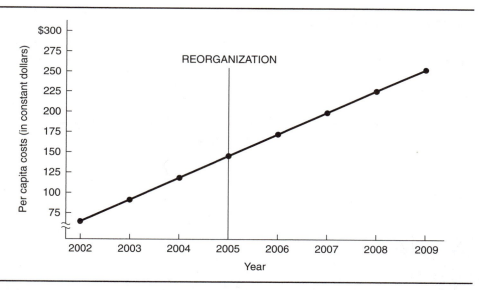

FIGURE 6.2   Hypothetical trend in public service costs showing no effect from reorganization.

If the data come out as in Figure 6.2, the predicted and observed values will be the same, and reorganization will be judged to have had no effect on costs. Figure 6.3 illustrates a case in which the reorganization has initially reduced costs but has had no effect on the trend.

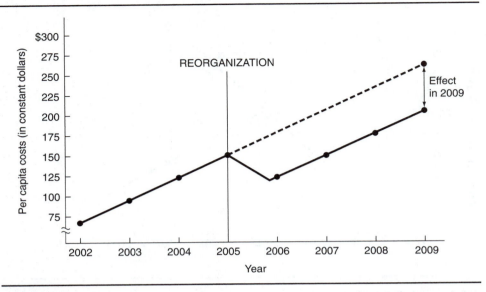

FIGURE 6.3 Hypothetical trend in public service costs showing that reorganization has changed the level of costs but has not interrupted the trend.

Fluctuating Trends: An Example

In most instances, the trend we are dealing with is not as clear and steady as in this example. For instance, let us say that state prosecutors, alarmed by a rise in delinquent court-ordered child support payments to single parents, institute a crackdown to collect the owed money from these deadbeats and subsequently want to know the success rate. Figure 6.4

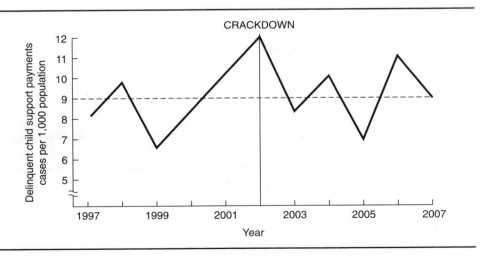

FIGURE 6.4 Hypothetical trend of delinquent child support payments to single parents, showing no effect from the crackdown.

shows the kind of data that might be collected over a ten-year period. The values of the dependent variable (delinquent child support payments) rise and fall from year to year throughout the period. The researcher's task is to determine whether the *general* post-crackdown trend is significantly different from the general precrackdown trend. One way to do this is to compare the average annual delinquent payment rate prior to the crackdown with the average annual rate in postcrackdown years. (Both are nine in this example.) Assuming that the original trend would continue without a crackdown, we can use any difference between the two averages as an indicator of the impact of the crackdown on the *level* of delinquent child support. Another approach is to compare trend lines (represented by a dashed line in Figure 6.4) passed through the precrackdown and postcrackdown scattering of values for the DV to determine whether the general trend differs.

This example illustrates one of the important advantages of time-series designs. If we observe delinquent child support payment rates only in 2001 and 2003, as in a typical before-after study, we may conclude that the prosecutor's crackdown has reduced nonpayment of child support. The time-series data, however, allow us to see the 2001–2003 drop in delinquencies as *a normal fluctuation around a general trend* (represented by a dashed line), which remains unaffected by the government action.

Despite this strength, time-series designs have a weakness. In many instances, there is no control group and therefore we cannot be sure what the effects of the IV are because we cannot be sure what the value of the DV would be without the IV; only a guess can be made that the original trend would continue. There are many reasons why this can be a mistake. One of the most important is *regression toward the mean.*

Regression toward the mean is basically a process by which subjects who have extreme values on a dependent variable at any one time tend naturally to return to a more nearly average value on that variable in subsequent measurements *regardless of any exposure to some hypothesized independent variable.* If this regression toward the mean occurs at the time of a study, the researcher might mistake the natural regression for an effect of the IV. This can be a special problem in cases when subjects are exposed to the independent variable precisely because they have extraordinary values on the dependent variable.

In our last example, prosecutors instituted a crackdown because of an exceptionally high number of cases of nonpayment of child support. This was a deviation from what was normal for the state, and it might have corrected itself even if the government had done nothing.

One way to rule out regression toward the mean as an alternative explanation is to employ a *controlled time-series design.* In **controlled time-series designs,** we gather data on a case or set of cases that are as similar as possible to our test case or group in all relevant respects but are not exposed to the IV, and use that case or group as a control in assessing the effects of the IV. In our example, we can select one or more states very similar to the one conducting the crackdown that have not changed their policies toward collecting child support payments and observe their delinquency rates in the same years. Figure 6.5 shows some possible results.

By comparing the test (crackdown) state with a group of similar states, we can see that, although the pre-2002 trend in child support delinquency continues unchanged in the test state, the average delinquency rate rises dramatically in the control states. This suggests that while the crackdown has failed to change the trend in the test state, it may be preventing it from being changed by the same events that are driving child support nonpayment rates up in other, similar states. In this case, we use the difference between

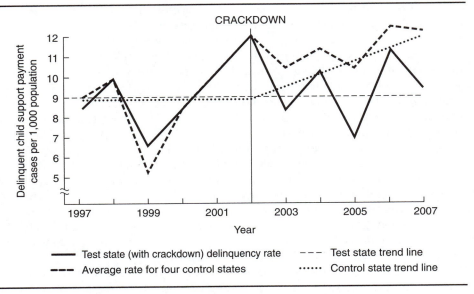

FIGURE 6.5 Hypothetical trend of delinquent child support payments in a test city and a group of control states.

RESEARCH EXERCISE

Controlled or Treated: Being a Subject

If research is conducted at your college, it is likely that you or one of your fellow students has been a research subject. Whether participating in psychological experiments for extra credit or playing a role in an economic experiment where real money is at stake, college students frequently are research subjects. For this exercise, you will describe either your own experiences as a research subject, or the experiences of an acquaintance. If you have been a research subject, you may interview yourself. If you haven't been a subject or if you prefer to relate another's experiences, you may interview another student you identify who has participated in college research as a subject.

1. In what department was the research conducted?
2. How long did the experiment take?
3. What did the subject do or see or experience in the experiment?
4. What was the subject told the experiment was studying?
5. Does the subject think that the experiment was studying something else? If so, what?
6. Would the subject participate in similar research again? If so, why? If not, why not?

---

the test state's postcrackdown rates and those of the control states in the same year as a measure of the effect of the IV, on the assumption that the test state would follow the trend of its companion states were it not for the crackdown. In 2007, for example, the effect of the crackdown is assessed as three child support delinquencies per 1,000 population (i.e., subtract the trendlines: $12 - 9 = 3$). Thus, adopting a stronger research design would prevent us, in this example, from reaching the apparently incorrect conclusion that a program had no impact, when it actually served as an effective deterrent.

Conclusion

Experimental research offers many advantages, but also challenges to political science researchers. The biggest challenge faced by anyone doing a classic experiment is establishing external validity. In light of what you learned about external validity in Chapter 4, you might imagine that the settings offering the highest levels of control are also the farthest removed from the real political world. Thus, as a researcher it is your job to ensure that your variables will travel from the lab to the setting where people actually experience politics. This concern has made field experiments an attractive compromise: some control, lots of reality.

Whether you ever conduct any experiments or not, you should keep in mind the advantages of establishing scientific causation as well as the challenges in getting too far from the real world. The lessons learned in this chapter will serve you well as you design and explain both your quantitative and qualitative research.

Key Terms

control *117*
subjects *118*
experimental design *118*
experimental group *118*
stimulus *118*
control group *118*
pretest *118*
posttest *118*
test effect *119*

Solomon two-control-group research design *119*
Solomon three-control-group research design *120*
randomization *121*
precision matching *121*
frequency distribution control *121*
field experiment *123*

quasi-experimental designs *123*
ex post facto experiment *124*
time-series designs *124*
regression toward the mean *127*
controlled time-series designs *127*

Research Examples

Using laboratory software that recorded reading patterns, Knobloch-Westerwick and Meng (2009) found that subjects spend more time reading political material that reinforced their views than looking at contrary information. A field experiment evaluated whether having personal contact with homeless people altered subjects' stereotypical attitudes (Knecht and Martinez 2009). To evaluate whether black men applying for low-wage jobs would be treated differently than white men, Pager, Western, and Sugie (2009) sent matched research subjects to employers, controlling the applicants' resume characteristics in this field experiment. Results of field experiments comparing the effectiveness of voter mobilization by mail, e-mail, phone, and door-to-door canvassing are contained in *Get Out the Vote! How to Increase Voter Turnout* (Green and Gerber 2004). Applying experimental techniques to the nature of legal reasoning, Eileen Braman (2009) studied the importance of personal views in determining whether a case was a relevant precedent. Interestingly, she used both undergraduates and law students in her randomized subject samples. A brief account of the research project appears in Braman and Nelson (2007).

Methodological Readings

A wide variety of experimental and quasi-experimental designs are described in the *Handbook of Research Design and Social Measurement* (Miller and Salkind 2002). A new volume from Morton and Williams (forthcoming) documents the history of experimental research in political science, and explains how researchers are currently using this method. Many applications of experimental designs in political science can be found in *Experimental Foundations of Political Science* (Kinder and Palfrey 1993). A classic text devoted entirely to real-world research design issues is *Quasi-Experimentation* (Cook and Campbell 1979). Richard L. Solomon (1949) describes two of the most important and frequently used experimental designs, which he created.

References

Blass, Thomas. 2000. *Obedience to Authority: Current Perspectives on the Milgram Paradigm*. Mahwah, NJ.: Lawrence Erlbaum Associates.

Blass, Thomas. 2004. *The Man Who Shocked the World: The Life and Legacy of Stanley Milgram*. New York: Basic Books.

Braman, Eileen. 2009. *Law, Politics, and Perception: How Policy Preferences Influence Legal Reasoning*. Charlottesville, VA: University of Virginia Press.

Braman, Eileen, and Thomas E. Nelson. 2007. "Mechanism of Motivated Reasoning? Perception in Discrimination." *American Journal of Political Science* 51(October): 940–956.

Cook, Thomas D., and Donald T. Campbell. 1979. *Quasi-Experimentation*. Chicago: Rand McNally.

Green, Donald P., and Alan S. Gerber. 2004. *Get Out the Vote! How to Increase Voter Turnout*. Washington, DC: Brookings Institution Press.

Kinder, Donald R., and Thomas R. Palfrey. 1993. *Experimental Foundations of Political Science*. Ann Arbor: University of Michigan Press.

Knecht, Tom, and Lisa M. Martinez. 2009. "Humanizing the Homeless: Does Contact Erode Stereotypes?" *Social Science Research* 38(September): 521–534.

Knobloch-Westerwick, Silvia, and Jingbo Meng. 2009. "Looking the Other Way: Selective Exposure to Attitude-Consistent and Counterattitudinal Political Information." *Communication Research* 36(June): 426–448.

Milgram, Stanley. 1974. *Obedience to Authority: An Experimental View*. New York: Harper & Row.

Miller, Delbert C., and Neil J. Salkind. 2002. *Handbook of Research Design and Social Measurement,* 6th ed. Thousand Oaks, CA: Sage.

Morton, Rebecca, and Kenneth Williams. 2010. *From Nature to the Lab: Experimental Political Science and the Study of Causality*. New York, NY: Cambridge University Press.

Pager, Devah, Bruce Western, and Naomi Sugie. 2009. "Sequencing Disadvantage: Barriers to Employment Facing Young Black and White Men with Criminal Records." *The Annals of the American Academy of Political and Social Science* 623(May): 195–213.

Solomon, Richard L. 1949. "Extension of Control Group Design." *Psychological Bulletin* 46(January): 137–150.

CHAPTER 7

Who, What, Where, When: The Problem of Sampling

In this chapter you will learn:

- What sampling is and why we sample populations.
- The characteristics of a representative sample.
- To differentiate among the different types of probability and nonprobability samples.
- How to determine the appropriate sample size for your study.
- The relationship between confidence interval, confidence level, and sampling error.

You might not have been aware of it, but chances are that you have used some form of sampling before in your life. You might have "sampled" grapes in the grocery store before buying an entire bag, for example, or you might have listened to a selection of songs before downloading an entire music album. Sampling is an extremely useful everyday procedure because it allows us to understand something large by looking at only a small part of it. Thus, sampling is the act of taking a small portion, or sample, to learn about some much larger population. If chosen carefully enough, the sample should reflect the characteristics of the population from which it is drawn.

The advantage of sampling becomes clear when you consider the potential cost and time that are required to look at an entire population. Once every ten years, for example, the Census Bureau, a part of the U.S. Department of Commerce, conducts a census in an attempt to identify, count, and measure certain characteristics of every individual living in the country at a given time. In the 2010 census, it is estimated that the federal government will employ 1.4 million clerks, interviewers, and others over a period of five months to obtain the information. In all, approximately 310 million residents of the United States will be located and studied. Over the ten-year cycle, the total cost of the 2010 count will be between $13.7 and $14.5 billion.

Needless to say, few political scientists are able to marshal such vast resources in pursuing their own research interests. Yet the objects of those interests may be, for all practical purposes, equally numerous: 100 million voters, 500 million residents of Western democracies, 100,000 documents—each might be the focus of political science research, yet each consists of far too many individual cases to permit a comprehensive analysis. Even the Census Bureau, with all its thousands of workers and millions of dollars, found it impossible to ask every one of its questions of each person it located. Instead, it developed a short questionnaire for most people and a longer one for a *select few*. Like political scientists and many other researchers, the bureau found it necessary to employ a *sample*.

In this chapter, we examine the uses and the mechanics of sampling—of choosing a relatively small number of cases that may tell us much about the larger population from which they have been selected. In doing so, we are concerned with **generalizability**—the ability to draw general conclusions based on an analysis of only a few cases.

DEFINING A REPRESENTATIVE SAMPLE

We begin with three questions: What is a sample? When is it representative? What does it represent?

A **population** is any group of people, organizations, objects, or events about which we want to draw conclusions; a *case* is any member of such a population. We should emphasize here that populations may consist not only of people but of anything we wish to study. Thus, we may speak of a population of governments, of decisions, or of court documents as readily as of a population of unemployed males living in Massachusetts. Whenever we refer to a population of any kind, however, all identifying characteristics of that population must be stated, and all members of that population must share them.

A **sample** is any *subgroup* of a population of cases that is identified for analysis. If we want to study and reach conclusions about the decision-making behavior of state legislatures, for instance, we might do so by examining such behavior in the legislatures of Wyoming and Montana rather than in those of all fifty states, and from these we might *generalize* our findings to the larger population from which the two have been selected. To study the issue preferences of voters in, say, Pennsylvania, we might do so by asking questions of fifty millworkers in Pittsburgh and generalizing these results to all voters in the state. Similarly, if we wish to measure the intelligence of college students, we might test all defensive linemen enrolled at Ohio State University during a given football season and then generalize our findings to all U.S. college students. In each instance, our procedure is to identify a subgroup of a larger population; to study that subgroup, or sample, in some detail; and to generalize our results to the population as a whole. These are the basic steps involved in sampling.

It should be quite obvious, however, that each of these samples has a fundamental weakness. Although the legislatures of Wyoming and Montana are, for example, indeed part of the population of state legislatures, they are, for reasons of history, region, and political culture, quite likely to operate in a manner very similar to one another and very different from the legislatures of such diverse states as New York and Texas. Although the fifty millworkers in Pittsburgh may indeed be Pennsylvania voters, they are, for reasons of socioeconomic status, education, and life experience, quite likely to have different views from those of many other such voters. And in like manner, although Ohio State's football players are indeed college students, they are, for a variety of reasons, likely to be different from other college students. In other words, even though each of these subgroups is a sample, the members of each are systematically different from most other members of the population from which they are drawn. As a group, none of these is typical of the distribution of attributes (opinions, behaviors, characteristics) in the larger population with which it is associated. Accordingly, political scientists would say that none of these samples is *representative*.

A **representative sample** is one in which every major attribute of the larger population from which the sample is drawn is present in roughly the proportion or frequency with which those attributes occur in that larger population. Thus, if 50 percent of all state legislatures meet only once every two years, roughly half the bodies in a representative sample of state legislatures should be of this variety. If 30 percent of the voters in Pennsylvania are blue-collar workers, then about 30 percent of a representative sample of those voters should be blue-collar workers. And if 2 percent of all college students are athletes, roughly the same proportion of a representative sample of college students should be athletes.

In other words, a truly representative sample is a microcosm—a smaller, but accurate, model—of the larger population from which it is taken. To the extent that a sample is truly representative, conclusions based on a study of that sample may be safely regarded as applying to the original population. This extension of findings is what we mean by *generalizability*.

An Example

Suppose we want to study patterns of membership in political groups among adults in the United States. Figure 7.1 shows three circles, each of which has been divided into six equal segments. Figure 7.1(a) represents the population in question. Members of the population have been classified according to the number of political groups (such as parties and interest groups) to which they belong. In the example, every adult is assumed to belong to at least one and not more than six groups, and these six levels of membership are equally distributed throughout the population. Suppose that we wish to study people's motivations for membership, choices of groups, and patterns of participation, but because of limited resources, we are able to examine only one of every six members of the population. Which individuals should we select for analysis?

The shaded area in Figure 7.1(b) illustrates one possible sample of the size we have specified, but one that is clearly atypical of the population. Were we to generalize from such a sample, we would conclude that (1) all American adults belong to five political groups and (2) all group-related behavior of Americans is like that of those who belong to precisely five groups. Yet we know that the first conclusion is not accurate, and we may hold suspect the validity of the second as well. The sample illustrated in Figure 7.1(b), then, is not representative, because it does not reflect the distribution of this *population*

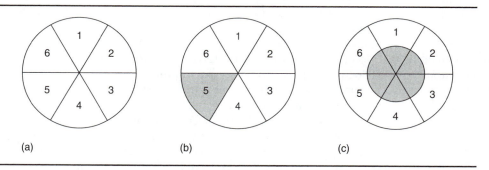

(a)   (b)   (c)

FIGURE 7.1 Sampling from a population with six population types.

attribute (often called a **parameter**) roughly in proportion to its actual incidence. Such a sample is said to be *biased toward* members of five groups or *biased against* all other patterns of group membership. Reliance upon such a biased sample will usually lead us to draw erroneous conclusions about the larger population.

The *Literary Digest* Fiasco

The potential problems of biased samples were clearly illustrated in a public opinion polling disaster that befell a magazine called the *Literary Digest* in the 1930s. The *Literary Digest* was a periodical compilation of newspaper editorials and other opinion pieces that enjoyed a wide readership in the early years of the last century. Beginning in 1920, the magazine conducted a large-scale, nationwide straw poll in which postcard ballots were sent to more than a million people asking them to state their candidate preference in the upcoming presidential election. During a succession of previous election years, the *Digest* poll had proved so accurate that its release in October seemed to make the actual election in November anticlimactic. With such a large sample, how could the poll miss? Yet in 1936, it did just that in predicting a 60 to 40 percent landslide victory for Republican candidate Alf Landon. In the election, however, Landon lost to incumbent Franklin D. Roosevelt by almost precisely the margin by which he was expected to win. So great was the shock to the credibility of the *Literary Digest* that the magazine was forced to cease publication shortly afterward.

What went wrong? Quite simply, the *Digest* poll had used a biased sample. The postcards had been issued to persons whose names were drawn from two sources: telephone directories and automobile registration lists. And whereas this method of selection had not made much difference earlier, it did in the Depression year of 1936, when less affluent voters—those most likely to support Roosevelt—could not afford telephones, let alone automobiles. In effect, then, the sample used by the *Digest* poll was biased toward those most likely to be Republicans.

Avoiding Bias

Returning to our illustration, compare the sample in Figure 7.1(b) with that in Figure 7.1(c). In the latter, one-sixth of the population is again selected for analysis, but each of the major population types is present in the sample in the same proportion in which it is present in the entire population. Such a sample tells us that one in six American adults belongs to one political group, one in six to two groups and so forth. It will also permit us to recognize other differences among members of our sample that might correspond with their varying numbers of affiliations. The sample illustrated in Figure 7.1(c), then, is a representative sample of the population in question.

This example is, of course, simplified in at least two very important ways. First, most of the populations that political scientists wish to study are more diverse than the one in the illustration. People, documents, governments, organizations, decisions, and the like differ from one another on many more than just one attribute. Thus, a representative sample must be one that provides for *each* of the principal areas of difference to be represented in proportion to its share of the population. Second, more often than not the true distribution of the variables or attributes we wish to measure is not known in advance; it may not have been measured previously by a census of the population. Thus, a representative sample must be drawn in such a way that we have confidence in its ability to reflect accurately this distribution even under circumstances when we cannot directly assess its validity. A sampling procedure must have an internal logic that assures us that if we *were* able to check the sample against a census, the sample would prove to be representative.

In order to provide both the capability to reflect accurately the complexities of a given population and some measure of confidence in their procedures for doing so, researchers draw upon certain techniques developed by statisticians. They do so in two ways. First, they follow certain rules in deciding which specific cases to study, meaning, which to include in a particular sample. Second, they follow still other rules in deciding how many such cases to select. Though we do not examine these various rules in detail here, we do consider their practical implications for political science research. Let us begin by looking at strategies for selecting the cases that make up a representative sample.

PROCEDURES FOR SELECTING A REPRESENTATIVE SAMPLE

As we can see from the examples in the preceding section, not all samples are equally representative. Straw polls, in which individuals select themselves as participants and may vote for a favored position or candidate more than once; street-corner interviews, in which selection of location and lack of control over passersby may strongly influence the findings; legislators' questionnaires, the results of which depend heavily on the views of the more articulate and more politically interested few who are most likely to respond; analysis of the foreign press, of propaganda messages, or of some variety of published materials that is restricted to sources available in English, which may be systematically different from other sources of the same type; and blind sampling, in which a researcher simply leaves a stack of questionnaires at a given location with instructions for their completion and surrenders all control over the selection of respondents, all provide common examples of sampling bias. In part, these difficulties may be resolved by a careful definition of the population to which we intend to generalize. In the case of street-corner interviews, for instance, we might want to generalize only to all persons passing a particular location between 10 A.M. and 11 A.M. on March 4. But in far larger measure, these difficulties may be resolved only by developing a systematic and relatively more sophisticated procedure for selecting the cases to be analyzed.

PROBABILITY SAMPLING

Probability sampling involves randomly selecting cases from the population so that all potential cases have an equal chance of being selected for the study. The goal of random sampling is to create samples that are representative of the populations from which they were drawn. The advantage of representative samples, of course, is that they allow researchers to generalize their findings to the overall population. There are four basic types of probability samples, which will be discussed in the next section: (1) random samples, (2) systematic random samples, (3) cluster or multistage random area samples, and (4) stratified samples.

Random Samples

The guiding principle underlying such a procedure is that of *randomization*. A sample is said to be a **random sample** (sometimes referred to as *simple random sample*) if two conditions are met. First, the sample must be chosen in such a manner that each and every individual or case in the entire population has an equal opportunity to be selected for analysis. Second, the sample must be chosen in such a manner that each and every possible combination of *n* cases, where *n* is simply the number of cases in the sample, has an equal opportunity to be selected for analysis.

It sounds a bit complicated and is in fact a more rigorous definition of randomness than we use in everyday conversation, but it is at heart a rather simple and straightforward notion. Random selection amounts to little more than selection by lottery. If we have a population of 1,000 persons whose behavior we wish to examine by studying a representative sample of 100, we might write the names of all 1,000 members of the population on equal-sized pieces of paper, place them in a hopper, mix them well, and draw the names of the 100 persons in our sample. Through such a procedure, each individual has an equal chance of being selected (100 chances in 1,000, or 1 chance in 10), and every possible combination of 100 individuals has an equal chance of selection as well. It is this dual equality that makes the sample a random one.

Often, random samples are employed in studying populations that are too large to permit such a physical lottery procedure. Writing out the names of several hundred thousand cases, entering them in a hopper, and drawing out several thousand, after all, would be a very cumbersome process. In these instances, an alternative, but equally valid, approach is employed. Each case in the population is assigned a number. The numbers of the particular cases to be included in the sample are then identified using a *random number table*, such as Table A.1 in Appendix A, a portion of which is reproduced in Figure 7.2. The arrangement of numbers in such tables is usually created by a computer program called a *random number generator*, which, in effect, places a great many numbers in a hopper, draws them randomly, and prints them in the order in which they were drawn. In other words, the lottery process still takes place, but the computer, using numbers rather than names, conducts an all-purpose drawing. We are able to make use of this drawing simply by numbering each of our cases.

A random number table, such as that illustrated in Figure 7.2, may be used in several different ways, each of which involves the combination of three decisions. First, we must decide how many digits we shall use; second, we must develop a decision rule for using them; and third, we must select a starting point and a system for proceeding through the table.

The first decision is simply a function of the number of cases in our population. If the population consists of fewer than 10 cases, we use single digits; 10 to 99 cases, double digits; 100 to 999 cases, three-digit combinations; and so forth. In each instance, we must take care to allow each of our numbered cases a chance to be selected.

Once this has been accomplished, we must devise a rule to relate the numbers in the table to the numbers of our cases. Two choices are available here. The easiest and most straightforward approach, though not necessarily the most correct, is to use only those numbers that fall within the range of our number of cases. Thus, if we have a population of 250 and choose to begin at the top left of the table and work down each column, we will include in our sample those cases numbered, say, 100, 084, and 128, and we will ignore cases

10097	32533	76520
37542	04805	64894
08422	68953	19645
99019	02529	09376
12807	99970	80157

FIGURE 7.2   Portion of a random number table.

numbered, say, 375 and 990, neither of which corresponds to any of our cases. We will continue this procedure until we have identified the number of cases needed for our sample.

A more cumbersome, but technically more correct, procedure arises from the argument that *every* number of a given magnitude (for example, every three-digit number) in the table must be used to preserve the underlying randomness of the table. Following this logic, and again assuming a population of 250, we must break the range of three-digit numbers from 000 to 999 into 250 equal parts. Because there are 1,000 such numbers, we divide 1,000 by 250 and find that each equal part comprises four numbers. Thus, table entries 000 to 003 correspond to case 1, entries 004 to 007 to case 2, and so forth. In order to identify the case number that corresponds to an entry in the table, then, we divide a three-digit table entry by 4 and round to the lower integer. When this method is used, the same portion of the table that we used earlier leads us to include in our sample cases 025(100 ÷ 4), 093(375 ÷ 4, rounded down), 021(084 ÷ 4), 247(990 ÷ 4, rounded down), and 032(128 ÷ 4), and to ignore none of the entries in the table.

Finally, we must select a point of entry into the table and a system of use. The point of entry might be the upper left-hand corner (as in the previous example), the lower right-hand corner, the left end of the second row, or *any* other location. This decision is strictly arbitrary. Once in the table, however, we must proceed systematically. We might select the first three digits of each five-digit set, as in the previous examples; the middle three digits; the last three digits; or even the first, second, and fourth digits. (In the first five-digit set, these various procedures yield, respectively, the numbers 100, 009, 097, and 109.) We might work these procedures backward getting 790, 900, 001, and 791. We might work across rows, taking each digit in turn and ignoring the groupings of five (getting 100, 973, 253, 376, and 520 for the first row). The possibilities are many and varied, and each is equally appropriate. Once we have decided upon a pattern of use, however, we must follow it systematically so as to maximize the randomness of the entries in the table.

VARIATIONS ON RANDOM SAMPLING

As you can see from even this brief discussion, the drawing of a simple random sample may be no simple matter. In addition to other problems, which we will discuss, the technique involves a great deal of clerical work, especially when it is employed on a large scale. For this reason, random sampling procedures are often modified to enhance their manageability.

Systematic Random Samples

One common variation is called the **systematic random sample** and is used when we wish to study a relatively large population whose members are individually listed in some central location, such as a telephone book, a student directory, a list of registered voters, an index or a table of contents, an agenda, or a membership roster. The procedure is as follows:

Count (or estimate) the number of cases in the population, and divide this by the desired number of cases in the sample. If we label the result k, we are saying, in effect, that we wish to select one case out of every k; or to put it another way, we wish to select every kth case. A concrete example should help to make this clear. Suppose that from a population of 10,000 public statements issued by the Department of Defense we wish to draw a sample of 500, and suppose further that we have a chronological listing that includes all 10,000 documents. To select a systematic random sample:

1. We divide the number of cases in the population by the desired sample size to determine k (in this case, $k = 10,000 \div 500 = 20$).
2. With the assistance of a random number table, we select a case number in the range 1 to k (in the example, 1 to 20) to be included in our sample.
3. We proceed through the listing of documents, selecting every kth (20th) case.

Thus, if k is equal to 20 and we use the portion of the random number table illustrated in Figure 7.2, entering at the top left, seeking two-digit numbers (k here lies between 10 and 99), and using only table entries that correspond to actual case numbers (that is, only those in the range from 01 to 20), the first case selected will be 10. We then include in our sample cases 10, 30 (10 + k), 50 (10 + 2k), 70 (10 + 3k), and so forth, all the way up to case 9,990 (10 + 499k). This upper limit of the sample may be stated generally as $j + (n - 1)k$, where j is the randomly drawn first selection and n is the desired sample size. In this way, we can use the random number table in combination with a centralized list to select a sample of 500 documents for analysis.

The technique of systematic random sampling has one major advantage over simple random sampling—ease of application to large populations that meet the criterion of central listing—and it has many potential uses. Still, we must keep in mind that systematic random sampling is less random than is a straight lottery selection, and it may therefore yield a less representative subgroup. We can see this at both the definitional and operational levels. To begin with, recall that a random sample is one that permits every individual case *and* every possible combination of n cases an equal opportunity of selection. Systematic random sampling meets only one of these criteria. Because we begin to draw such a sample by using a random number table to select the first case, any case in the population has an equal chance of ultimately being included in the sample (though not necessarily on the first draw, because this is limited to the range 1 to k). However, because we then select only additional cases that are k numbers apart from one another, not every possible combination is allowed.

Thus, in the example where $k = 20$, any case from 1 to 20 may be selected to begin with, but once we select case 10, it becomes impossible for us to include, say, cases 11, 237, and 5,724, simply because those cases do not differ from 10 by a multiple of k. A systematic random sample is at best, then, only an approximation of a truly random sample.

Systematic Bias

This observation becomes especially important when the list from which we are sampling contains a **systematic bias**. In alphabetical or chronological lists, this is generally not a problem, but in other kinds of lists it may be a significant one. For example, let us say that, as part of a study of political socialization, we wish to measure the intelligence level of a sample of students at a particular school where every class consists of twenty children. The school contains 100 classes, or 2,000 students in all. In response to our request, the principal of the school provides us with a roster of all students in the school, from which we hope to draw a systematic random sample of 100. However, rather than an alphabetical listing, the roster consists of a compilation of individual class rolls listed one after another. Moreover, each class roll is arranged not alphabetically but in order of the students' class standing, with the best students listed first and the lists continuing in order of decreasing accomplishment. In such a circumstance, if we take every 20th (2,000 ÷ 100) case beginning from a randomly drawn case 1, we will have a sample of only the 100 best (and, possibly, most intelligent) students in the school. If we randomly select case 10, we will sample only the middle range of students. And if we begin from case 20, we will sample only the worst students in the school.

In other words, an underlying bias in the list upon which our sample is based will lead to the selection of an unrepresentative sample. Ultimately, this will either preclude our generalizing to the larger population or, if the problem escapes notice, will result in our drawing potentially incorrect conclusions. Although this particular example is an extreme one developed for the purpose of illustration, similarly biased lists do exist, and the researcher who employs systematic random sampling procedures must be aware of the potential danger.

Random samples, then, are an ideal to which we aspire, and systematic random samples are approximations of that ideal that are often quite useful. Very often, however, a research situation does not readily lend itself to either technique. This is particularly true in the case of survey research. For one thing, centralized lists of the population to be studied are frequently nonexistent (for example, there exists no list of all U.S. voters or of all residents of a particular city), and even the number—not to mention the identity—of all the cases may not be known in advance. Thus, one of the major preconditions for simple or systematic random sampling—the existence of individual cases that can be identified in advance—may not be met. Moreover, even when this problem can be overcome, logistical difficulties and limited resources may render either of these sampling techniques impractical. This is true because random selection of individual cases requires that *specific individuals*, who may live great distances from one another or who may be very difficult to contact, *must be included in the sample*. In a strictly random process, no substitutions are permissible. These considerations can lead to massive diseconomies of time and money that might be so great as to preclude conducting the study at all.

Cluster or Multistage Random Area Samples

Fortunately, an alternative technique has been developed that preserves the quality of randomness desired but overcomes most of the objections we have just noted. This technique, termed either **cluster sampling** or **multistage random area sampling**, has found wide application in survey research and may, by analogy, be applied elsewhere as well. The idea behind multistage random area sampling is that, rather than identifying members of a sample as individuals, we identify them as residents of particular housing units. The reasoning here is that people move from place to place, whereas housing units remain fixed. In addition, the location of virtually every housing unit in the country is known and has been mapped, and each is part of a variety of geographically distinct areas including, among others, blocks, census tracts, precincts, legislative districts, cities, townships, counties, congressional districts, and states.

We shall see that certain types of these areas have characteristics that aid greatly in drawing a representative sample. For the moment, however, the point is that by focusing on the resident of a housing unit, a unit that is always in the same place, rather than on a particular individual, who may be more mobile, we are able to stabilize and localize our sampling procedure. In effect, we are simply redefining our population. Rather than speaking of all persons living in the United States, we speak of all residents of housing units in the United States. Because both groups are, for all practical purposes, the same, however, we may sample the latter and generalize to the former. We avail ourselves of the much simpler and, for reasons to be discussed later, much less expensive technique of sampling locations, yet we are able to generalize not to places, but to the people who inhabit them. This is the principal value of multistage random area sampling.

The procedure itself is illustrated in Figure 7.3. For the purpose of illustration, let us assume that we wish to conduct a nationwide sample survey. The same procedures that we set forth here may, of course, be modified for use on smaller-scale projects.

The Multistage Process

We begin with a map of the United States, which we divide into a large number of equally populated areas (also called primary sampling units, or PSUs). It is less work than it sounds like, because the government has already made this division (or at least approximated it) in the form of 435 congressional districts, each populated with somewhat more than half a million people. We assign a number between 1 and 435 to each such district and, using a random number table, select several congressional districts for analysis. The exact number selected is a function of both the ultimate size of the sample to be drawn and the available resources, but in general, the more districts selected, the better the sample.

At this point, the principal cost saving of the multistage random area technique becomes apparent, for rather than having to track down respondents all over the country, we may focus our attention (and money) on a relatively few areas, most of which are of manageable size.

Once the subject congressional districts have been identified, each is further divided into still smaller but equally populated areas. In many instances, these may correspond to political boundaries, such as precincts or electoral districts, whereas in others we may find it necessary to create our own divisions. In any event, once these areas have been identified, one or more (depending again on sample size) are randomly selected within each congressional district by the random selection procedures we have outlined. These precincts or other areas are then further divided, first into census tracts, then into blocks, and finally into dwelling units (houses and individual apartments), with the random selection process employed at each stage of selection. In the end, we shall have identified a number of individual dwelling units that should correspond roughly to our desired sample size. The residents of these dwelling units will become the subjects of the research.

There is, however, one additional complication. Although, for a number of reasons, we generally wish to interview only one person at a given address, more than one person is likely to reside in any particular dwelling unit. Which one do we interview? Most researchers who use sampling procedures of this type provide their interviewers with a series of decision rules to apply at this point, the net effect of which is to create a set of quotas based on the age, sex, and/or family standing of the respondent. In one home, the interviewer might be instructed to seek out the youngest adult male, in another the oldest adult female, and so forth.

We can see, then, that the term *multistage random area sampling* is truly descriptive. At each of several stages, equally populated areas are selected at random until, ultimately, individual dwelling units have been identified. In each instance, the geographic location is the subject of the sampling procedure, and at each stage, several clusters of locations are identified (hence the alternative term, *cluster sampling*). Only in the final

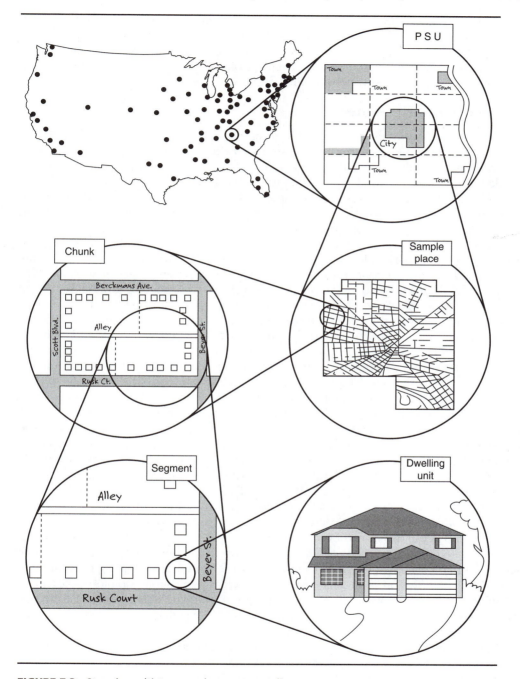

FIGURE 7.3 Steps in multistage random area sampling.

Source: Interviewer's Manual: Survey Research Center. Ann Arbor, MI: Institute for Social Research, University of Michigan, 1969, pp. 8–12. Reprinted by permission.

stage—identifying specific respondents—does the procedure diverge from the principle of randomness, but at so local a level, and with the use of such carefully constructed quotas, that the effects on the representativeness of the sample are probably minimal. In many instances, multistage random area sampling offers a reasonable approximation of a truly random sample at a lower cost in time and resources.

Stratified Random Samples

We should mention one other technique, though it is less a selection procedure than a strategy. This technique is known as **stratified sampling** and is used primarily when we wish to study in detail a population subgroup that is so small that a random sample will include too few members of that subgroup to permit detailed analysis.

Suppose, for example, we wish to study the hypothesis that presidents are more open with the news media during the first two months of their administration (often termed a *honeymoon period*) than at all later times and that we wish to test the hypothesis by analyzing the content of the transcripts of presidential news conferences. Suppose further that we are able to identify 500 such transcripts for a given period, of which only 25 (or 1 in 20) are news conferences from the honeymoon period, and that we wish to sample 100 of these conferences. Using either a simple or a systematic random sample in this instance, we might expect that sample to include approximately 5 honeymoon-period transcripts and approximately 95 posthoneymoon transcripts. The very small number of the former makes a meaningful comparison very difficult, because it may provide too few examples to reflect accurately the range of presidential responses to reporters' questions.

Under such circumstances, to enhance the importance of a particular subgroup, we may choose to *stratify* our sample. In doing so, we choose not one but *two separate samples*. The first is a simple or systematic random sample of the smaller subgroup (transcripts from the honeymoon period) and is *larger* than the expected frequency of occurrence of the subgroup in the original sample (here, perhaps 15 rather than 5 cases). The second is a simple or systematic random sample of the larger subgroup (transcripts from all subsequent periods) and is *smaller* than its expected frequency of occurrence in the original sample (here, perhaps 85 rather than 95 cases). In the example, our sample can be described as stratified according to the date of the news conference. The effect is to provide us with relatively more cases of honeymoon-period transcripts for analysis and comparison with those from later periods than we would otherwise select.

Three observations should be made at this point. First, stratification is not a substitute for simple random sampling or some other form of sampling, but an additional step used under particular circumstances. In effect, it is a second-order sampling procedure. In this context, stratification is frequently used, particularly by public opinion pollsters, at the late stages of a sample in order to ensure an appropriate balance of, for example, men and women. It is thus similar in purpose to the quotas that are applied in the final stage of a multistage random area sample.

Second, because it requires the drawing of separate samples, stratification may be used only when we are able to identify the relevant subpopulations *in advance*. In our example, this is not a source of difficulty, because before sampling, we can easily distinguish the honeymoon-period transcripts from those of later periods. In much survey research, however, when we may wish to stratify along less evident variables, serious problems can be encountered.

Third, because stratified sampling uses separate samples and because one can generalize from a sample only to the particular population (or subpopulation) from which it is drawn, we must exercise great care in stating our conclusions from a study based on such a sample. The reason for this is quite clear. In stratifying to increase the number of cases of a particular type in our study, we are in effect biasing our total sample in the direction of those cases. To overcome that bias, we must state our conclusions in one of only two ways. First, we may compare with one another our findings for the groups by which we have stratified (for example, comparing our findings for honeymoon-period conferences with those for conferences from later periods). Here we are simply comparing the results of separate samples without drawing any conclusions about news conferences as a whole. Second, we may differentially weight the groups by which we have stratified in proportion to their overall share of the population and then draw general conclusions about the population. In this case, we are taking advantage of our detailed knowledge about the smaller subgroup (honeymoon-period conferences) but are reducing its importance vis-à-vis the population of all news conferences. Under the latter procedure, a stratified sample may be used to approximate a simple random sample while providing more complete information.

NONPROBABILITY SAMPLES

Samples that are *not* selected randomly are known as **nonprobability samples**. Because the selection of cases for these samples is not random, there is a greater chance for bias and distortion. As a result, nonprobability samples are generally less likely to be representative of their corresponding populations. Why then would anybody use such samples in their research? The answer is simple: It is often impossible to ensure that all cases of a given population actually have an equal chance to be selected (as would be required in random sampling). To draw a truly random sample of American university students, for example, we would first have to have a complete list of all university students in the United States from which we would then randomly select our sample. Obviously, this would be very difficult to accomplish. Thus, in cases where we cannot ensure an equal chance of selection for all cases, it will be necessary to rely on nonprobability samples that might not be as representative as random samples. Anybody who uses such samples in their research therefore should be aware of their potential limitations. There are five basic types of nonprobability samples: (1) convenience samples, (2) volunteer samples, (3) purposive samples, (4) snowball samples, and (5) quota or judgmental samples.

Convenience Samples

The easiest way to draw a sample is to rely on participants that are readily available. For example, professors often ask their students to participate in experimental studies because students are required to attend classes and therefore are easy targets for sample recruitment. This selection of participants based on their availability results in so-called **convenience samples**. While the creation of these samples might be easy, it is usually more difficult to generalize their results to the overall population from which they were drawn. This is because participants were not selected randomly and therefore might share certain (often unknown) nonrandom characteristics. Students at private universities, for example, might differ significantly from students who study at public universities in terms of their socioeconomic background—but, unless we ask them, we can never be certain that this is actually the case. For most study subjects, selection bias is a serious problem and should be considered carefully when drawing a sample. In some cases, however, it might be justified to rely on convenience samples even though they might contain some type of selection bias. Studies that investigate basic psychological or physiological responses, for example, are often based on student samples because there is (usually) no reason to suspect that their reactions would be any different from those of the "average person." Thus, as long as we can reasonably assume that a selection bias will not influence the results, we might be able to use convenience samples in our research. Unfortunately, we often cannot be sure that our research findings actually are immune to selection bias.

Volunteer Samples

It is quite common that people volunteer to participate in a study or in a survey without being specifically selected to do so. In most cases, people agree to become part of a **volunteer sample** because they are promised some money or a small gift in return for their time. Volunteer samples are commonly used in experimental studies because the researcher can randomly assign subjects to treatment or control groups, and note any self-selection bias by asking participants questions about factors that might affect the results. Any anomolies will be noted in the research report. One of the biggest advantages of such samples is that people who volunteer to be part of a study are usually more willing to participate than, for example, respondents who are called during dinner to answer a telephone survey without compensation. An obvious disadvantage of volunteer samples is the fact that only those people who actually know about the study can also become participants. This self-selection bias is especially a problem in surveys that ask everybody who happens to see the invitation to participate. Since there is usually no control over who actually sees the invitations, findings of such studies cannot be used to make any reliable or representative conclusions.

Purposive Samples

In situations where the researcher needs to select participants who share a certain experience or characteristic, **purposive samples** are employed. Surveys conducted in shopping malls, for example, usually target shoppers who are asked questions about their shopping experience at the malls where the interviews take place. While the selection of respondents in this example is *not* random (only people who happen to be at the mall at the time of the interview can be selected into the sample), the findings can be used to draw conclusions about the mall where the interviews were conducted. Thus, purposive sampling focuses on participants who are representative of a very specific target population only (for example, anybody who bought a BMW last month). This means, of course, that results from purposive samples cannot be generalized beyond its target population.

Snowball Samples

For some study topics, it might be difficult to find appropriate participants. A researcher who wants to study the social interactions of *Star Trek* fans, for example, might be hard pressed to find enough subjects that could answer a survey questionnaire. In cases where it is difficult to identify or to locate a target population, it is often useful to start with a small number of participants who have the desired characteristics (for example, *Star Trek* fan) and then ask them to identify other possible participants they know. Since it is likely that a *Star Trek* fan knows other *Star Trek* fans, who, in turn, know even more *Star Trek* fans, such **snowball samples** are an efficient method to quickly recruit participants with very special characteristics. Since this sampling method relies on participants to identify other participants they personally know, snowball samples are likely to suffer from selection bias and therefore might differ significantly from the overall target population.

Quota Samples

When samples need to be balanced by a certain characteristic, such as race or gender, researchers often choose to rely on **quota samples**. To create a quota sample, members of a population are classified according to several relevant characteristics (such as sex, age, or race) and individuals displaying these traits are selected in proportion to their share of the population. While quota samples might not be representative of the population from which they are drawn, they do ensure that all relevant characteristics are present in the sample according to their proportions in the population. This can be important, for example, in studies that focus on small subpopulations (for example, Asians) that might not be included in the final sample if random sampling procedures were used.

DETERMINING APPROPRIATE SAMPLE SIZE

Having defined our terms and considered our selection procedures, we are now left with the question of how many cases to sample. In many ways, an answer to that question draws upon some sophisticated statistical concepts that lie beyond the scope of this text. However, much of the rationale underlying the determination of an appropriate sample size is more readily understood and is worth some attention before proceeding.

Homogeneity

Several factors help us to determine an appropriate sample size. One of the most important of these is **homogeneity**, the degree to which the members of a given population are like one another with regard to the characteristics we are interested in studying. If every individual in a population is *exactly like* every other individual, then by sampling only one individual we can obtain a truly representative sample. If, on the other hand, every individual in the population is *completely unlike* every other individual, we will be required to conduct a census of the entire population before claiming to have a representative group. In the first instance, the population is described as completely *homogeneous*; in the second, as completely *heterogeneous*. In reality, of course, most populations lie between the two extremes.

The closer a particular population is to homogeneity—that is, the fewer the differences among its members—the smaller the sample required to represent it. Conversely, the closer a particular population is to heterogeneity—that is, the more diverse its members are—the larger the sample required to represent it. This has implications in particular for stratified sampling, because by the very act of stratification, we create subgroups that are more homogeneous than the overall population. We can thus use smaller samples within strata than we could for the overall population without a loss of representativeness.

Number of Categories

Similarly, the more categories (variables and response options) we wish to study, the larger the sample must be. This is true because increasing the variety and sensitivity of our measures will tend to accentuate the heterogeneity of the population we are studying. In other words, the more questions asked or the more types of answers allowed, the more likely we will be to find differences among our subjects. The more differences examined among our subjects, the more subjects we must examine to claim a representative sample.

Sampling Error

Another important consideration is the degree of accuracy required. We use a sample to *estimate* the characteristics of a larger population, but any estimate is likely to include some margin of error. How much of this **sampling error** are we willing to tolerate? The answer is often determined by how we intend to use our results. If we are public opinion pollsters being paid to predict the outcome of a close election, we might be unwilling to accept more than the slightest margin of error. If we are political researchers attempting to spot general trends in attitudes or behaviors, we might tolerate considerably more. In general, the more accuracy we want, the larger our sample must be.

Related to this is a second question, that of just how confident we are that our estimates of the margin of error are correct. Most samples of a given size taken from the same population are very similar to one another and to the population itself, but once in a while a sample is drawn that happens, by chance, to be different. A sample of college graduates, for example, might be far out of proportion to that group's true share of the original population. Thus, while each sample provides us with an estimate of the characteristics of a population, such estimates differ somewhat from one another and from the population as a whole because no two samples are *exactly* alike.

The problem is that in the real world, we do not always know the underlying population parameters our sample is intended to estimate, and we do not draw a great many samples. We draw only one. And though we may be able to check the face validity of our sample by comparing it with those used in other studies of the same or a similar population, *we cannot know for sure* that the sample we have drawn is not the odd one out—an unlikely yet possible unrepresentative sample. We know from a study of statistics, however, that we may reduce the likelihood that ours is the bad apple in the barrel by increasing the size of our sample. The more cases included, the more likely we are to have a truly representative sample—one that does in fact fall within the error range specified.

Confidence Interval

We can make this discussion less abstract by considering the summary of sample sizes presented in Table 7.1 (based on Tables A.2 and A.3 in Appendix A). The table lists appropriate *minimum* sample sizes for several levels of sampling error and confidence for a *random sample* of a relatively heterogeneous population of more than 100,000 cases.

TABLE 7.1 Summary of Sample Sizes

Percentage Sampling	Level of Confidence	
Error Tolerated	.05	.01*
1	10,000	22,500
2	2,500	5,625
3	1,111	2,500
4	625	1,406
5	400	900
10	100	—

*Rounded from the source table for purposes of explanation.

Note: .95 is equivalent to p = .05
.99 is equivalent to p = .01

The table may be used in either of two ways. First, we may wish to specify the particular level of sampling error we are willing to tolerate and the confidence level at which we shall operate. Suppose that these figures are +/−4 percent and p ≤ .01, respectively.

The first tells us that any measurement of our sample we might make is within 4 percentage points above or below the true distribution of the same attribute in the larger population. This range is referred to as a **confidence interval**. If, for example, we find

RESEARCH EXERCISE

Sampling in Today's Social Environment

You are planning a study of student use of social networking media (Facebook, Twitter, etc.). Develop practical alternative strategies for sampling the students at your college or university, using each of the following six sampling methods: (1) simple random sampling, (2) systematic random sampling, (3) stratified sampling, (4) purposive sampling, (5) quota sampling, and (6) snowball sampling.

For each sampling method:

1. Describe how you would select students in your sample.
2. Explain the basic characteristics of each sample (representative or not, user of Twitter only, students who know each other, etc.).
3. Summarize the advantages and disadvantages of each approach.
4. Given the research topic, which sampling method would you recommend using? Why?

that 43 percent of our respondents in a survey report identifying with the Democratic Party, we will assume that a full census of the population would show the true percentage of Democratic identifiers to be 43 percent $+/-4$ percent, or somewhere in the range from 39 percent to 47 percent. The table tells us (reading across at 4 percent and down at .01) that to achieve that degree of accuracy with 99 percent confidence, we must select a sample of at least 1,406 cases. To narrow the margin of error (increase our accuracy) to, say, $+/-2$ percent (that is, to refine our estimate to the range from 41 percent to 45 percent Democrats), we have to increase our sample size to at least 5,625 cases. At both levels of confidence, the table clearly demonstrates that increased accuracy requires an enlarged sample.

Confidence Level

The second number that we began with refers to the likelihood that our sample is in fact representative of the larger population within the degree of accuracy we have specified and is called the **confidence level**. In this context, with $p \leq .05$ (95 percent confidence), out of 100 samples of a given size that are drawn from the same population, 95 will meet this test for accuracy, and with $p \leq .01$ (99 percent confidence), 99 out of 100 samples of a given size drawn from the same population will be as accurate as claimed. The chances that any particular sample will achieve the desired accuracy, then, are 95 to 5 and 99 to 1, respectively.

As one might expect, for each level of sampling error the sample size required to attain 99 percent confidence is substantially larger than that for 95 percent confidence. By convention, in political science research a probability that your confidence is misplaced of less than or equal to either .05 or .01 are considered acceptable. Looking again at our Democrats with a margin of error of $+/-4$ percent, for instance, we find that a sample of 625 cases allows us to say with 95 percent confidence that somewhere between 39 percent and 47 percent of the whole population are Democrats, whereas a sample of at least 1,406 cases is required before we can make the same statement with 99 percent confidence. In general, the lower the percentage of sampling error and the greater the level of confidence, the better a piece of research will be.

This type of table may be used in a reverse manner. If, for example, we encounter a study that employs a sample of 2,500 cases, we may consult the table to ascertain the corresponding sampling error and level of confidence. A glance at Table 7.1 shows that multiple interpretations are possible. We may interpret 2,500 cases to yield a sampling error of $+/-3$ percent with $p \leq .01$, or alternatively, to yield a sampling error of $+/-2$ percent with $p \leq .05$. Either interpretation is equally appropriate, and the two together help to make clear the trade-off between accuracy and confidence. With the same number of cases, we may be extremely confident of a relatively less precise result or somewhat less confident of a higher order of precision.

Ideally, of course, we always prefer to operate with minimum error and maximum confidence. Unfortunately, practical considerations frequently intervene. A single personal interview in a survey project, for example, may cost as much as $100 or more in labor, transportation, and other expenses. This means that with $p \leq .01$, the cost of reducing our margin of error from $+/-3$ percent (2,500 interviews) to $+/-2$ percent (5,625 interviews) may be more than $300,000. In many instances, the difference in the quality of the results is not worth the added expense, and in far more instances, the money is

PRACTICAL RESEARCH ETHICS

How do you describe your sample?

If you are using samples to generalize your findings to the overall population, it is important to remember that you must disclose how you selected your sample and how precise your results might be based on the particular sample used. The goal of such a disclosure is to allow other scholars to evaluate the overall representativeness and relevance of your findings.

The **Code of Professional Ethics and Practices** (see Appendix B) promoted by the American Association for Public Opinion Research (AAPOR) calls on researchers to disclose the following information about their samples and sampling procedures used: (1) a definition of the population under study, and a description of the sampling frame used to identify this population; (2) a description of the sampling procedure; (3) the sample sizes and, where appropriate, eligibility criteria, screening procedures; and response rates; (4) a discussion of the precision of the findings, including estimates of sampling error, and a description of any weighting or estimating procedures used; (5) which results are based on parts of the sample, rather than on the total sample, and the size of such parts; and finally (6) the method, location, and dates of data collection.

simply not available. Limits on resources thus play an important role in limiting the size of samples. Most national public opinion polls, as well as major political science survey research projects, use samples of approximately 1,200 to 1,600 respondents. Such studies yield results to within 3 to 5 percent accuracy with $p \leq .01$ and are regarded as both affordable and sufficiently precise.

One other point should be noted before concluding our discussion of sample size, though it is, no doubt, less obvious and less intuitively appealing than others we have raised. As an examination of Tables A.2 and A.3 in Appendix A makes clear, once it reaches a certain limiting point, the size of a population *does not* affect the size of the sample chosen to represent it. And though the proof of this assertion is beyond the scope of this book, its implications are not. In effect this upper limit on sample sizes means that very nearly the same size sample may be equally representative of the population of Roanoke, Virginia; of New York City; of the United States; or of the entire Western Hemisphere, so long as that sample is properly drawn. Only for relatively smaller populations is population size a significant factor in determining sample size.

Conclusion

An important point that is often overlooked by the novice political researcher is that *any* time you gather data by *any* method from *any* source, if you wish to generalize at all beyond the particular cases examined in the research, then the data set constitutes a *sample* and its constituent cases should be selected with an eye toward the considerations raised in this chapter. Whether the subject of the research is elections, political advertisements, news accounts, political jurisdictions, organizations, or anything else, you must be aware of the importance of the selection process and its implications for the meaning and usefulness of your research.

ey Terms

generalizability *132*
population *132*
sample *132*
representative sample *133*
parameter *134*
probability sampling *135*
random sample *135*
systematic random sample *137*
systematic bias *138*

cluster sampling *139*
multistage random area
   sampling *139*
stratified sampling *142*
convenience sample *143*
nonprobability sample *143*
volunteer sample *144*
purposive sample *144*
snowball sample *145*

quota sample *145*
homogeneity *145*
sampling error *146*
confidence interval *147*
confidence level *148*
Code of Professional Ethics
   and Practices *149*

Research Examples

A variety of recent studies provide comparisons of different sampling techniques. Link et al. (2008), for example, compare address-based sampling (ABS) with random-digit dialing (RDD) sampling for general population surveys. They find that ABS mail surveys generate significantly higher response rates than RDD surveys in five of the six states studied (provided that a second questionnaire is mailed). Forgette et al. (2008) employ a cluster sample and sampling data from a housing census to explore racial differences in satisfactions toward local, state, and federal governments among Hurricane Katrina survivors. To measure the skills of Dutch citizens in using online government information and services, van Deursen and van Dijk (2009) use a randomly selected sample of telephone subscribers and then draw a quota sample with the strata of gender, age, and educational level.

Methodological Readings

Discussions of sampling procedures appear regularly in the pages of the academic journal *Public Opinion Quarterly*. The statistical procedures underlying the determination of an appropriate sample size are discussed in a number of sources, including Levy and Lemeshow's (2003) *Sampling of Populations: Methods and Applications*, Thompson's (2002) *Sampling*, and Lohr's (1998) *Sampling: Design and Analysis*. Several variations on sampling techniques are described, and their respective strengths and weakness summarized, in Miller and

Salkind's (2002) *Handbook of Research Design and Social Measurement*.

References

Forgette, Richard, Marvin King, and Bryan Dettrey. 2008. "Race, Hurricane Katrina, and Government Satisfaction: Examining the Role of Race in Assessing Blame." *Publius: The Journal of Federalism* 38(4): 671–691.

Levy, Paul S., and Stanley Lemeshow. 2003. *Sampling of Populations: Methods and Applications*, 3rd ed. New York: Wiley-Interscience.

Link, Michael W., Michael R. Battaglia, Martin R. Frankel, Larry Osborn, and Au H. Mokdad. 2008. "A Comparison of Address-Based Sampling (ABS) versus Random-Digit Dialing (RDD) for General Population Surveys." *Public Opinion Quarterly* 72(Spring): 6–27.

Lohr, Sharon L. 1998. *Sampling: Design and Analysis*. Pacific Grove, CA: Duxbury Press.

Miller, Delbert C., and Neil J. Salkind. 2002. *Handbook of Research Design and Social Measurement*, 6th ed. Newbury Park, CA: Sage.

Thompson, Steven K. 2002. *Sampling*, 2nd ed. New York: Wiley-Interscience.

van Deursen A.J.A.M., and J.A.G.M. van Dijk. 2009. "Improving Digital Skills for the Use of Online Public Information and Services." *Government Information Quarterly* 26(April): 333–340.

CHAPTER 8

Survey Research: Characterizing a Broader Population

In this chapter you will learn:

▪ How to plan, pretest, and conduct a survey.

▪ The characteristics of good survey questions.

▪ How to design a survey questionnaire.

▪ How to choose an appropriate survey methodology (e.g., personal interviews, mail, telephone, or online).

Public opinion polls have become an important part of our social and political life. To know what most other people are thinking can help us to judge public support for certain ideas and to put our own opinions and attitudes in perspective. Polls provide information that cannot be obtained by simply talking to our friends and relatives, especially if we want to know what an entire population or a large group of people thinks. Only representative polls summarize reliably what the public thinks. Acceptance of this fact has made survey research one of the most fully developed and extensively used of social science methods.

Anybody who has watched an episode of *American Idol* knows how popular polls can be. Each year, millions of people call the show and vote for their idol—"America has voted!" That, of course, is not true. Only the *fans* of this popular television show actually pick up the phone and cast their votes. In fact, nobody really knows who these "voters" are and how many times each of them voted. In other words, these call-in "polls" are *not* representative and thus have entertainment value only. Nevertheless, many of us follow such polls in the media because we like to know who is ahead and who is behind.

The same is true during elections, when people try to gauge which political candidate might win the election and how much support their policies might have in the general public. The difference here, we hope, is that people rely on *representative* polls that provide a fairly reliable and accurate depiction of public opinion. Thus, unless we just want to be entertained by meaningless polls that are based on questionable samples, we need to understand how "good" polls are conducted. This chapter provides an overview of what this method involves, when it is appropriate, and what its principal strengths and weaknesses are.

Survey research is *a method of data collection in which information is obtained directly from individual persons who are selected so as to provide a basis for making inferences about some larger population*. It is important to note that this definition excludes "surveys" not based on scientific sampling procedures. Public opinion polls and "person-in-the-street" interviews, which are based on chance samples, provide no information other than the fact that the particular individuals interviewed gave certain answers; there is no reason to believe that others would respond in similar ways.

The information collected in surveys may be obtained by direct questioning through *face-to-face* or *telephone interviews* or by having the subjects complete *mailed* or *self-administered questionnaires*. In recent years, *online surveys* administered through the Internet have become another common methodology to measure public opinion. Those who answer survey questions are generally referred to as **respondents**.

Surveys provide five types of information about respondents: facts, perceptions, opinions, attitudes, and behavioral reports. *Facts* include background characteristics (age, occupation) and personal history (place of birth, first political involvement) that may be relevant to the interpretation of the other data collected. *Perceptions* are statements of what individuals know (or think they know) about the world, such as the names of public officials or the federal government's current policy toward trade with China. *Opinions* are statements of people's preferences or judgments about events and objects. Such questions as *Do you favor legalization of marijuana?* and *Whom do you want to win the upcoming local election?* tap opinions. *Attitudes* are relatively stable evaluations of and orientations toward events, objects, and ideas. When we want to know about people's support for civil liberties or government regulation of the economy, for example, we are asking about the attitudes on which specific opinions are often based. *Behavioral reports* are simply statements of how people act (for example, how often they vote or read newspaper editorials).

In survey research, concepts are operationalized through questions, and observation consists of recording respondents' answers to these questions. The method, therefore, is especially suited for studies in which individual persons are the units of analysis and the principal concepts employed pertain to individuals. If our research involves concepts, such as the average daily importation of foreign oil by the United States or the number of crimes committed with handguns each year, survey research is inappropriate, because average citizens are not likely to have the information we seek. If research focuses on the opinions, attitudes, or perceptions of individuals, a survey may well be the best method of data collection. It is, however, a very expensive and time-consuming method. Therefore, researchers should be certain that there is not some other, less expensive way of gathering the necessary data before proceeding with a survey.

STAGES OF THE SURVEY PROCESS

Having decided to use a survey as a data collection method, we must now decide what steps to go through. Survey research can be divided into fourteen basic activities. In practice more than one of these may be going on at any one time, and the researcher may, on occasion, move back and forth between activities as the survey develops. Conceptually, however, the stages of survey research can be described as follows:

1. *Conceptualizing:* Specifying the purpose of the research, developing hypotheses, clarifying concepts, and operationalizing the concepts through survey items.

2. *Survey design:*   Establishing the procedures to be used and deciding on the general nature of the sample to be drawn.
3. *Instrumentation:*   Drafting the questions and other items that will appear on the survey instrument (the questionnaire or interview schedule) and planning the format of that instrument, as well as designing any visual aids or other devices that will be used.
4. *Planning:*   Developing methods of managing the survey and anticipating the materials and personnel that will be needed.
5. *Sampling:*   Selecting the persons to be interviewed according to the method that best fits the purposes and resources of a given study.
6. *Training or briefing:*   Preparing interviewers, coders, or other personnel to properly contact respondents and administer the instrument to them.
7. *Pretesting:*   Administering the instrument to a small sample similar to the larger sample to be contacted so as to ensure that instructions can be correctly interpreted and that items produce the desired type of response.
8. *Surveying:*   Administering the instrument (by mail, phone, or personal interview) to members of the sample.
9. *Monitoring:*   Ensuring that the proper persons are being contacted as respondents both by requiring records of contacts and refusals, and by checking on the administration of instruments.
10. *Verifying:*   Using follow-up contacts to make sure that interviews have actually been performed, that mailings have reached potential respondents, and that questionnaires have been returned.
11. *Coding:*   Reducing to numerical terms the data collected.
12. *Processing:*   Organizing the data for analysis.
13. *Analyzing:*   Working the data with statistical and other tools in order to reach conclusions about their content.
14. *Reporting:*   Summarizing findings into research reports.

The remainder of this chapter highlights some of the primary points the survey researcher should take into consideration when engaged in each of these activities.

CONCEPTUALIZING

In this stage, a general research question is reduced to a far more specific set of questions that can be addressed through empirical investigation. Decisions made in the conceptualizing stage have important implications for the choices that are available in sampling and survey design. For instance, in deciding to whom our theory applies, we determine what our sampling frame should be. In selecting an operationalization that requires personal interviewing, we are dictating the level of research support needed. Even when first thinking through the theoretical aspects of the project, then, we have to be sensitive to the issues of resources and accessibility of respondents.

SURVEY DESIGN

Most surveys either are exploratory, descriptive, or explanatory in purpose. *Exploratory* surveys help us acquire information that can be helpful in formulating research questions and hypotheses more precisely when we know little about a phenomenon we want to study. *Descriptive* surveys provide precise measurement of variables that may be important in theorizing but provide no basis for making causal inferences. *Explanatory* surveys test causal hypotheses and help us understand observed patterns in terms of a theory. They must be designed so as to allow us to rule out alternative rival hypotheses. Data for each type of survey can be collected through *personal interviews, mail questionnaires, telephone interviews*, or *self-administered questionnaires*. Deciding on the objective of the survey and choosing the appropriate data collecting method are the first steps in survey design. The purpose will be dictated largely by our level of theoretical and empirical knowledge of the subject. Which data collection technique is appropriate will be determined by the operationalizations we have chosen and by the resources that are available.

Cross-Sectional Surveys

We must next select a way to organize the survey. The basic choice is between *cross-sectional* and *longitudinal* designs. In **cross-sectional surveys**, data are collected from respondents only once. If we have a representative sample, this design allows us to describe populations and relationships between variables in those populations at a given time, but it does not allow us to say how the characteristics or relationships have developed or will develop over time. Cross-sectional surveys offer a snapshot of a moving target. They are best suited to exploratory and descriptive studies, but together with a strong theory and proper data analysis, cross-sectional surveys can provide some basis for explanation. For example, in a study of the relationship between personality and political behavior, we may be willing to assume that a person's level of self-esteem is a relatively stable personality trait that precedes one's level of political involvement. If we find, then, that those with a high level of self-esteem tend to be more politically involved than those with low self-esteem, we might feel safe in arguing that high esteem leads to or causes high political involvement, even though we have data from only one time.

Longitudinal Surveys

Longitudinal surveys are those in which data are collected from respondents on more than one occasion. The main types of **longitudinal surveys** are *trend, cohort*, and *panel* studies.

In **trend studies** samples are drawn from the same population at different times and surveyed. *Different persons* may be included in each survey, but the results will be representative of trends in the *same population*, because, as was explained in Chapter 7, each properly selected sample will be equivalent to every other sample from that population. Thus, if we find different degrees of partisan identification in two samples of the same population surveyed at different times, we may infer that there has been a change in the level of partisan identification *in the population* during the time that separates the surveys. We might also explore changes in the relationship between variables through trend studies. If we find, for instance, that the relationship between gender and political activity is weaker in the second of two surveys of samples from the same population, we might conclude that there is a trend toward the breaking down of sex roles in the political life of that population.

Whereas trend studies are representative of a *general* population at different times, **cohort studies** focus on the same *specific* population over time. Members of the population sampled in trend studies will change with time, but cohort studies draw samples from the *same* population each time even though different members might be included in the samples. For example, we might want to draw a sample among Mexican citizens who legally immigrated to the United States in 2007 and sample that same group again three years later to study these immigrants' adaptation to life in the United States. Though there may be some loss from this population as members die or move out of the United States, no new members will be added.

Both trend and cohort studies allow us to document change in a population over time, but because different samples are drawn for each survey, we cannot identify *which* members of the population are changing. This makes it more difficult to discover causal patterns. **Panel studies**, by contrast, use the *same sample at different times*. This allows us to see which members of a population are changing and to identify the characteristics or experiences that are associated with those changes; for example, we might interview the same sample of registered voters before, during, and after an election campaign in an effort to determine what aspects of a campaign are most likely to lead people to change their choice of candidates.

This important advantage of panel studies must be weighed against some disadvantages. First, panel studies are very costly, because the expense of keeping track of sample members over time must be added to the costs of conducting several interviews. Second, there can be problems of reactivity of the type discussed in Chapter 6. The very fact that people are being interviewed, perhaps repeatedly, about a subject may cause them to alter their behavior or attitudes with regard to that subject in ways they would not were they not being interviewed. This creates a kind of test effect that can distort results. At the very least it means there is a risk that the sample will become *unrepresentative of the larger population* by virtue of being included in the study. Third, *attrition* from the sample can compromise the validity of panel studies. Attrition occurs when respondents in the first wave of surveying do not respond in subsequent waves. If those who drop out of the panel share characteristics that are relevant to the study but not shared by those who do not drop out, their withdrawal may create a highly biased sample that both distorts results and prevents generalizing to the larger population.

Despite these drawbacks, panel studies are still the strongest design for most explanatory purposes, and they often justify their expense by the additional information yielded.

INSTRUMENTATION

Whatever study design is employed, the survey researcher will have to develop a set of questions to use as tools in obtaining measures. This is an extension of the operationalization process begun in the conceptualization stage and produces a *survey instrument*, which may be either a **questionnaire**, to be filled in by the respondent, or an **interview schedule**, which guides an interviewer in a personal or telephone interview. When developing these instruments, the researcher must consider (1) the content, (2) the form, (3) the format, (4) the wording, and (5) the order of questions.

The *content* of questions determines what information can be obtained from responses. It is dictated by the hypothesis being tested or the question being studied. What must we know to resolve the research question, and what must we ask to obtain that information? These are the questions that should guide the choice of what to ask. It is essential to be very clear both about what information is expected from responses to each item on a survey instrument and about how that information will be used in data analysis. What will it contribute to our ability to answer the research question?

There are an infinite number of questions to be asked about almost any important subject, but survey instruments must be kept relatively short if respondents are to complete them. Personal interviews should last no longer than 45 minutes under most circumstances, and telephone interviews no longer than 20 minutes. Mail questionnaires should generally be no more than four pages long. The need for brevity, however, must be weighed against the need to obtain all the information necessary to rule out the various rival hypotheses encountered in data analysis or the need to seek explanations for unanticipated results. One way to approach this problem is to follow two general rules. First, keep the number of hypotheses tested or research questions addressed in a survey very limited. This will restrict the number of variables on which information is needed. Second, when selecting items for inclusion, exclude any for which there is no clear and immediate role in the anticipated data analysis.

Surveys usually contain both questions that are specific to the study and general background questions that measure characteristics that past research has shown to be strongly associated with differences in the political behavior under study. The latter items are included to allow us to rule out rival hypotheses pertaining to background characteristics and to refine our understanding of relationships by seeing how they differ in different **demographic groups**. Questions that seek information on the following characteristics are often at least *considered* for inclusion in any survey instrument:

Sex	Marital status
Age	Home ownership
Race	Household composition
Income	Party identification
Religion	National origin
Education	Length of residence
Occupation	Organizational memberships

Types of Questions

Survey questions can be either *open-ended* or *closed-ended*. **Open-ended questions** allow respondents to answer in their own words; no options are imposed on them. For example, *What do you consider to be the most important single issue in this year's local election?* is an open-ended question. Such questions have the advantage of allowing the researcher to discover unanticipated patterns in people's answers. They also prevent the researcher's selection of response options from biasing answers or concealing information. Open-ended questions have some disadvantages, however: They make comparison of respondents' answers extremely difficult, because each person may not use the same frame of reference in answering. In addition, they could encourage long or irrelevant answers, which are often difficult to analyze.

Closed-ended questions force the respondent to choose an answer from a limited number of options and have the advantages of making comparison of responses simple, allowing quick processing, and ensuring the relevance of responses. For example, *Do you consider yourself to be a conservative, a moderate, or a liberal?* is a closed-ended question. The options offered in closed-ended questions should be *exhaustive* (they should include all possible responses that might be expected) and *mutually exclusive* (they should not allow more than one choice as a response to any single question). The options should also allow respondents to express differences in the *intensity* of their response when this might be relevant. A question like *Some people feel that the federal government should sponsor free abortion clinics for low-income women. Do you agree or disagree with this position?* calls for a more complex set of choices than just agree and disagree. *Strongly agree, agree, neutral, disagree, strongly disagree,* and *no opinion* would better reflect the range of opinions people are likely to hold.

Even when well constructed, closed-ended questions run the risk that the researcher's choice of options may influence responses. A question like *Which of the following would you say is the most important issue facing the United States today?* assumes that the researcher can list all the issues people will consider the most important. Use of this closed-ended form may prevent our discovering something we have not anticipated about public opinion. The choice between open- and closed-ended questions must be made on the basis of both the resources that will be available for data processing (open-ended requiring more) and the theoretical and empirical knowledge we have of our subject (closed-ended requiring more).

It is also important to think about how a question is presented and answered. Though the straightforward oral or written question-and-answer format is most common, a variety of other techniques are available to help respondents conceptualize choices and understand what is being asked. Many of these involve visual aids, such as charts, photographs, or cards that can be sorted into boxes. One example is the "feeling thermometer" developed at the Survey Research Center of the University of Michigan. Respondents are shown a card with a drawing like that in Figure 8.1 and asked to report how warm or cold they feel toward an object or a person by choosing a temperature reading from the thermometer. This instrument facilitates the ranking of more cases (potential presidential candidates, for example) than respondents could reasonably be expected to rank in an abstract mental exercise. The researcher simply asks about each case individually and compares thermometer readings. The more complex the mental task respondents are being asked to perform, the more useful visual aids and other variations on the question-and-answer format can be.

100° Very warm or favorable feeling

85° Quite warm or favorable feeling

70° Fairly warm or favorable feeling

60° Slightly warm or favorable feeling

50° No feeling at all

40° Slightly cold or unfavorable feeling

30° Fairly cold or unfavorable feeling

15° Quite cold or unfavorable feeling

0° Very cold or unfavorable feeling

FIGURE 8.1   The feeling thermometer is a visual aid for surveying attitudes toward groups or individuals.

Question Wording

Careful and proper **question wording** is crucial to the success of a survey. Researchers can make it easier for an interviewer to do a good job by providing clear instructions and by carefully wording questions. Properly phrased questions can often prevent problems in the field. For example, it is easier for the interviewer to establish a good relationship with the respondent and to avoid the appearance of "grilling" if questions are phrased so that respondents do not have to admit that they do not know some fact or have given no thought to the subject. A phrase such as . . . *or haven't you had a chance to read about that?* at the end of a question can considerably ease potentially tense situations.

No one can provide precise guidelines for correct wording, because the questions that have to be asked are determined by the subject under study. We can, however, describe some common errors in question wording. Here are some qualities that questions should *avoid*:

1. ***Excessive length.***   If there is a general rule about question wording, it is to use the shortest form of the question that communicates effectively. Longer questions not only consume more time but are also more likely to lose or confuse respondents. Avoid conditioning phrases and unnecessary adjectives. For example, the question *If the presidential election were to be held at this point in time, rather than in November, which of the following several candidates do you think you would vote for?* can profitably be shortened to *If the presidential election were held today, whom would you vote for?* followed by a list of candidates.

2. ***Ambiguity.***   The quest for brevity should not lead to incomplete or imprecise wording. To be certain that questions contain all the information necessary to elicit an informed response, ask yourself whether the respondent might have to answer the question with a question. For instance, when asked, *Do you ever complain about public services?* a respondent might answer, *Complain to whom? Public officials? Neighbors?* Questions are often ambiguous if they are too general (*Do you feel that people think too much about politics?*) or indefinite about time, location, or point of comparison (*Did you vote in the last election? Do many Asians live here? Do you think Smith is the best candidate?*).

3. ***Double-barreled questions.***   These questions are often impossible to answer with a single response because they contain two distinct questions. For example, *Do you feel that we are spending too much on the military, or do you feel it is important to maintain a strong national defense?* cannot be answered with "yes" or "no" if the respondent feels that it is important to have a strong defense but also thinks that current expenditures are higher than necessary for that purpose. To avoid double-barreled questions, examine any question containing *and* or *or* to be certain it does not combine two questions that should be asked separately.

4. ***Bias.***   Questions can be worded so as to encourage one response rather than another. Such questions are often referred to as *loaded questions*. When asked, *You are opposed to bussing innocent schoolchildren all the way across town just to achieve racial balance in the schools, aren't you?* respondents will be far more inclined to agree than if asked, *Do you favor or oppose the use of bussing to achieve racial balance in the public schools?* Phrases that evoke social norms (such as, *How often do you fulfill your civic duty by voting?*) clearly bias responses. Phrases

that associate a position with authority figures or socially disapproved persons or groups can also distort results. For example, questions that begin with, *Do you agree with the Supreme Court that . . .* or *Do you share the neo-Nazi view that . . .* will probably produce biased results.

If there are opposing positions on an issue, it is important that questions be worded so as to make each seem legitimate. A useful approach here is to word items as follows: *Some people feel that the federal government should take control of the nation's oil companies and operate them as public utilities. Others think that would be a serious mistake. How do you feel about it? Do you think the federal government should take control of U.S. oil companies?*

5. ***Response set bias.***   People have a tendency to agree with statements, regardless of their own positions. Question items that fail to take this into account are said to exhibit a *response set bias*. We can see the effects of this bias if we measure political conservatism first by using six statements with which we expect conservatives to agree, and then again by using six statements with which we expect them to disagree. The first measure will almost always "show" that there are significantly more conservatives than will the second regardless of the actual number of conservatives in the sample. Items should be mixed so that we sometimes expect agreement to reflect a given attitude or position and sometimes expect disagreement to reflect that attitude or position.

6. ***Argumentativeness.***   Though it is sometimes necessary to provide background for questions, it is a mistake to argue a position. For instance, it is not wise to ask, *Since there are so many dangers associated with the operation of nuclear power plants, some people argue that it is foolish to invest so much in developing nuclear power when we could be devoting resources to the development of safe and inexhaustible energy sources such as solar or wind power. Do you agree that our nation should sharply curtail its investment in nuclear energy?* In addition to being far too long, this question will probably bias responses because it omits alternatives to the position stated.

7. ***Encouragement of conditioned responses.***   Special problems of wording are posed when questions are asked that touch on sensitive subjects. Most people are reluctant to talk to strangers about such matters as their income, family life, sexual behavior, or even political preferences in some cases. For example, consider the case of questions for which society largely prescribes certain responses. Unless questions are carefully phrased, respondents will tend to give the socially acceptable answer regardless of their own opinions. Racial prejudice is a case in point. Since bigotry is generally condemned in American society, people may be reluctant to express prejudiced views.

We can suggest a couple of tactics to use in getting genuine responses rather than conditioned or socially approved answers. First, you might suggest that socially unacceptable views are widely held or can be viewed as legitimate. For instance, ask, *Many people feel that having Asian Americans in a neighborhood causes it to go downhill. Others don't think Asian Americans make that much difference in a neighborhood. Do you agree or disagree with the idea that Asian American residents generally cause neighborhoods to decline?* A second approach is to word questions so as to appear to assume that respondents engage in socially proscribed behavior or hold unpopular views so that they are forced to deny it if they do not. This makes it easier for them to "confess" to socially unapproved opinions. For instance, the question *How much harm do you think it would do to this neighborhood if Asian Americans began to move in?* makes it easier to express prejudice than a more neutral wording such as, *Do you think it would be harmful to this neighborhood to have Asian Americans move in?*

8. *Forcing a response.* Many people feel that it is socially undesirable not to have an opinion on political issues and may express opinions on matters to which they have given no thought. This can distort survey results. To avoid such responses, it is generally wise to provide a no-opinion category in response options or to word questions so as to make having no opinion seem acceptable. For instance, try opening a question with wording such as, *Some people consider the national debt to be an important political issue while others are not too concerned with it. Do you think . . . ?*

Questionnaire Structure

In addition to constructing individual items, survey researchers must be concerned with the overall format and organization of the survey instrument. Sound questionnaires or interview schedules generally consist of four main parts: the explanation, some warm-up questions, the substantive questions, and the demographic questions.

The *explanation* informs respondents of the purpose of the study, and it should convince them that the survey is important enough to warrant their time and attention. This can often be done by associating the study with a respected authority or with a worthwhile goal. If the survey has a prestigious sponsor, a line such as, *We are conducting a study for the Center for Survey Research . . .* can have the desired effect. In stating the purpose of a study, the researcher should not use terms beyond the everyday language of respondents. It would be unwise, for example, to say, *We are conducting a study of mass-elite linkages to determine the extent to which formal mechanisms of representation are a facade for social control by political elites,* even if this were the purpose of the study. A more effective statement would be, *We want to know what kind of contact people like you have with their elected representatives, and we hope that the results of this study will help improve the operation of our government.* Though it is never advisable to lie to respondents, the explanation should not reveal study information that would bias responses. If respondents are told that a study focuses on racial prejudice, they may give different answers from those they would give if told only that the study deals with citizens' attitudes or some other neutral term. The explanation can help interviewers establish a good rapport with respondents or encourage respondents to complete a questionnaire by assuring them that the researchers are open about what they are doing and by eliminating any fear that the study might be a front for a sales pitch.

Warm-up questions, too, can help establish a good relationship with respondents. These are impersonal, nonthreatening items used to initiate an interview or questionnaire. Asking respondents about their length of residence in their present location or what they think are the most important problems in their community or in the nation can be useful warm-ups. Any questions that are selected for this purpose, however, should be relevant to the study and have a definite role in the analysis. Otherwise, they are wasted. Warm-up questions should not be created especially for that purpose but should be selected from questions that are to be asked anyway.

Substantive questions constitute the bulk of the items on most instruments. The ordering of items within this group is determined principally by the need to achieve a logical flow in the questioning. Question ordering is not always neutral, however. For instance, researchers often want to ask the same question in different ways. When this is done, the different forms of the question should be separated so that respondents do not find the interview repetitious. Similarly, if both general and specific questions about a phenomenon are asked, it is usually best to ask the general questions first in order to get a response that has not been conditioned by a series of specific inquiries. It usually makes sense to place open-ended questions about a subject before closed-ended questions on that same subject in order to prevent the options offered in the closed-ended items from biasing responses to the open-ended items.

Demographic items seek factual information about respondents that is often regarded as personal or sensitive. They are usually placed at the end of an instrument to prevent having other parts of the interview or questionnaire affected by respondents' being ill at ease or feeling as if the researchers are snooping. Though people are generally willing to provide information on such personal matters as their income or marital status, getting adequate answers to demographic questions requires careful wording.

Placing demographic questions at the end of an instrument has the added advantage of postponing, until more interesting questions have been asked, what some people consider dull questions of the sort they frequently have to answer in filling out official forms. This can be especially important with self-administered questionnaires, because a set of routine questions at the outset can make completing the form seem like work and lead respondents to abandon the questionnaire.

Questionnaire Format

Once the principal sections of the instrument have been designed, decisions about how they will be placed must be made. These decisions determine the *format* of the instrument. Earl Babbie (1990, p. 135) argues:

> The format of a questionnaire can be just as important as the nature and wording of the questions asked. An improperly laid out questionnaire can lead respondents to miss questions, confuse them as to the nature of the data desired, and, in the extreme, result in respondents throwing the questionnaire away.

The format of an interview schedule can be just as important. A poorly laid out schedule can confuse interviewers in ways that lead them to skip items, incorrectly record responses, and alienate respondents by appearing clumsy. We can offer some guidelines for setting up both questionnaires and interview schedules.

The first rule for both types of instruments is *Do not crowd items*. It is difficult to overstress the harm that can be caused to a survey by crowding print on a page. To prevent errors, leave plenty of white space on each page of the instrument. Especially in self-administered questionnaires, this helps respondents avoid misreading or mismarking and can give them the sense that the questionnaire is easy to complete. It is better to have a few questions on each of a large number of sheets in a questionnaire than to have many questions on each of a few sheets. The total number of pages matters less than the clarity of each page, but a rule of thumb is that it will take approximately 30 minutes to administer an instrument of ten well-spaced pages, and 30 minutes is about as long as researchers can count on to hold their respondents' attention under most circumstances.

9. Have you ever complained to local officials about public services?   Yes 1   No 2

9a. To which type of official have you complained most often?

Mayor 1
Council member. 2
City agency head 3
Other official 4

9b. How many times have you complained to local officials about poor public services in the past year?

Once or twice. 1
Three or four times 2
Five to ten times. 3
More than ten times. 4

10. How would you say the public services in your neighborhood compare with the services found in other neighborhoods of this city?

Much better than in other neighborhoods 1
Somewhat better than in other neighborhoods. . . 2
The same as in other neighborhoods 3
Somewhat worse than in other neighborhoods. . . 4
Much worse than in other neighborhoods 5

11. How would you rate the quality of each of the following public services as they are delivered *in your neighborhood* today?

	Excellent	Good	Fair	Poor	Very bad
Fire protection	1	2	3	4	5
Police protection	1	2	3	4	5
Streets and sidewalks	1	2	3	4	5
Trash collection	1	2	3	4	5
Street lighting	1	2	3	4	5
Animal control	1	2	3	4	5
Recreational facilities	1	2	3	4	5

FIGURE 8.2   Excerpt from a hypothetical mail questionnaire.

TYPES OF SURVEYS

The type of survey required is determined by the research question being addressed, and the type *possible* is dictated by the resources available. But the basic choice is always among four options: *personal interviews, mail surveys, telephone surveys*, and

Internet surveys. In making that choice, the researcher should consider the following features of each type of survey.

Personal Interviews

One of the most flexible of survey methods is the **personal interview** because it allows the use of a variety of questioning techniques (visual aids, for example) and gives interviewers a chance to pursue questions in order to ensure appropriate responses and prevent respondents from misunderstanding questions or instructions. Personal interviews also provide the largest amount of data per interview, because an interviewer can normally hold a respondent's attention longer in face-to-face interaction than over the phone or through a questionnaire. The response rate is also generally higher for personal interviews.

These interviews are not without disadvantages, however. In the first place, they are very expensive, and only the most important of projects can generally command the funds necessary to employ the technique. Second, personal interviews can produce biased data because of the features of the interview process itself. Responses recorded by interviewers may reflect real-world facts or attitudes less than they reflect the effects of the setting in which the interview occurs, the reactions of respondents to a given interviewer, the biases of the interviewer, the liberties the interviewer takes in asking questions, or the interview style employed. In addition, personal interviews are difficult to monitor to ensure quality control. The researcher is unable to observe the interviewers in the field and must rely on a variety of postinterview techniques to ensure that interviews were properly conducted. Though such techniques as contacting respondents to see if they were actually interviewed and comparing the responses reported by different interviewers can be effective, they are not foolproof and are costly and time consuming.

Mail Surveys

In cases where personal interviews are impractical, **mail surveys** are a good alternative and offer several advantages:

1. Because mail surveys cost much less to conduct, larger samples can be drawn and a wider distribution of the instrument can be achieved.
2. Many of the biases in distribution of the instrument can be avoided. Among these are biases relating to the reluctance of interviewers to work in certain types of neighborhoods and their inability to obtain interviews with certain types of individuals.
3. Response biases associated with the interviewer are avoided.
4. There is a greater chance of obtaining truthful responses both because a greater anonymity is implied by a mailed instrument and because the biasing effects of respondent-interviewer interaction are removed.
5. Respondents have more time to give thoughtful replies that may reflect their true feelings more accurately than do the hurried responses given in an interview.
6. Fewer personnel need be involved in the survey. This saves money and time.

Unfortunately, mail surveys have their limitations as well. In the first place, they require a mailing list that can be used as a sample frame and provide a representative sample. No such list exists for many of the populations to which researchers may want to generalize.

Second, questionnaires have to be kept short if an adequate response rate is to be obtained. This means that less information can be secured from each contact. Third, the researcher has little control over who responds to the questionnaire. This can pose problems both because someone other than the person to whom it is addressed can complete a questionnaire and because it is difficult to obtain an adequate response rate with a mailed instrument.

The most significant problems associated with mail surveys are low response rates, biased response patterns, and improperly completed questionnaires. In general, a response rate of 40 percent is considered acceptable for mail surveys. A demonstrated lack of bias in responses (which is sometimes imputed through the representativeness of respondents' demographic qualities) is more important than a high response rate, however, because low response rates challenge the value of results chiefly by rendering the sample unrepresentative. The following techniques are available for encouraging better response rates.

The usual procedure for mail surveys is to send a questionnaire, a letter explaining the purpose of the survey, and a return envelope all in one envelope. Research has shown that using *self-mailing questionnaires* increases response rates. Self-mailing questionnaires can be folded, sealed, and mailed without an additional envelope. That seems to make it easier for respondents to return the instrument and averts the problem of respondents losing the return envelope.

Follow-up mailings can substantially increase return rates both by reminding respondents of the survey and by locating people who, for some reason, have not received the initial letter. Generally, three mailings (an original and two follow-ups) are best. If individual respondents can be identified from returned questionnaires, then mailing follow-ups only to nonrespondents can save money. If respondents cannot be identified, it is a good idea to do a blanket mailing to all members of the sample, thanking those who have responded and encouraging those who have not to do so. The follow-up mailing should contain both a letter reminding people to send in their completed questionnaire and a second questionnaire in case the first was lost or never arrived.

It is often wise to include in all mailings a phone number that respondents can call to get answers to questions about the survey. This can both increase the response rate and reduce the number of returned questionnaires that were improperly completed. Response rates can also be enhanced by carefully avoiding any marks on the questionnaires (sequence numbers, for instance) that respondents could interpret as a device for identifying their questionnaire. People are generally more likely to cooperate if they feel their responses will be anonymous.

Telephone Surveys

The commonly used **telephone surveys** fall between personal and mail surveys in many ways. The number of questions that can be asked is generally larger than for mail instruments but shorter than for personal interviews. Response rates are usually lower than for personal interviews but higher than for mail surveys. Though interviewer-related sources of bias are not totally removed, a voice over the telephone is normally less likely to create biasing effects than is a person in the respondent's living room. Finally, the personnel requirements of telephone surveys are between those of mail and personal surveys.

The advantages of telephone surveys include the speed of completion, the control provided over who responds, and the flexibility offered in allowing an interviewer to ensure appropriate responses. Their chief limitation arises from the possibility that an unbiased sample cannot be obtained. Those who do not have a telephone or who have an unlisted number may also be distinctive in ways that are relevant to the study. If so, leaving them out of a sample may provide misleading results. For example, many service professionals (doctors and lawyers, for example) have an unlisted home telephone number in some communities, and very poor people often do not have a telephone. This can be crucial to a study of the relationship between income and political attitudes.

A sampling technique known as **random-digit dialing (RDD)** has enabled survey researchers to overcome the bias associated with unlisted numbers and inaccurate listings, and has significantly increased the speed with which telephone surveys can be conducted. Surveys conducted with the RDD method rely on random samples of computer-generated telephone numbers. This is usually done by combining the three-digit telephone exchanges (or prefixes) of the geographic area where the survey is to be conducted with randomly generated four-digit root numbers. The advantage of such RDD samples is that they not only guarantee a completely random selection of households to be contacted, but also contain numbers of unlisted households which would be otherwise unreachable.

Internet Surveys

The growing popularity of the Internet and the continuing decline of telephone poll response rates have led to the development of surveys that can be distributed through the Internet. In recent years, **Internet surveys**, which usually are administered through e-mail, Web pages, or a combination of both, have become a standard research tool in government, business, academia, and the mass media.

The proliferation of Internet surveys is driven by a number of important advantages this type of survey has over more traditional interviewing methods. First, Internet surveys allow cost-efficient access to potentially millions of national or international respondents. Since Internet surveys are self-administered and distributed online, they eliminate the need for interviewers, long-distance phone charges, or printing and mailing costs. Thus, it is fairly cheap to administer Internet surveys to a large number of respondents regardless of where they live or work. Moreover, because in most online surveys data are entered directly by the respondents (by clicking on answer choices provided on a survey Web page), there is no need for additional data entry, again saving money.

Second, Internet surveys allow a variety of instrument designs that can be tailored to the specific needs of the research project or the targeted respondents. Questionnaires administered through the Internet can, for example, incorporate images or short video clips—something that is impossible in telephone surveys. This enables researchers to expose respondents to visual cues such as videos or images of different product designs. In addition, to accommodate the needs or preferences of specific respondents, the format of Internet questionnaires can be easily adapted to feature, for example, different colors and designs (appealing to men rather than women, for instance), various languages (for non-English speakers), or larger type fonts (for people who cannot read small print).

Third, Internet surveys permit respondents to complete the questionnaire whenever it is convenient for them—and not when an interviewer calls them or knocks on their door. Since many people are annoyed with the often intrusive and repeated calls by marketing and surveying organizations, surveys delivered through e-mail or the Internet might offer a solution to the declining response rates that have been observed in more traditional telephone surveys.

Fourth, most Internet surveys allow researchers to monitor the progress of their online survey in real time. Because all respondent data are instantly recorded and saved on a central computer, it is possible to track who is answering the survey and what answers have been provided at any given time during the survey period. This can be extremely useful when only a certain number of responses is needed (for example, in quota samples), or when researchers need partial results for an interim report.

Fifth, Internet surveys are especially suited for research involving international respondents. The logistics of conducting international surveys is often underestimated, especially when questionnaires need to be administered in various languages and across different time zones. Internet surveys, however, make it fairly easy to write and administer different language-versions of the same questionnaire to respondents living in various nations around the globe. Since all respondents can answer the questions whenever it is convenient to them, there is no need to worry about the actual timing of the interviews. Thus, unlike international telephone surveys, which need to be conducted in each nation at the appropriate time and with language-proficient interviewers, Internet surveys (theoretically) can be carried out by one researcher who controls the distribution of all online questionnaires from a central computer system located in one country only. Moreover, the fact that all survey responses are collected on the same computer system puts the researcher in total control of the data gathering, no matter how many different types of samples are used in each study. This ability to conduct online surveys on a global scale has significantly reduced the cost of international survey research, even though samples are restricted to online users who are often not representative of the overall population.

Finally, it should be mentioned that advances in Internet programming have made it fairly easy for the average scholar (even those with little computer knowledge) to conduct online surveys. Popular survey software packages such as SurveyMonkey (www .surveymonkey.com) or SurveyGizmo (www.surveygizmo.com) allow the design of professional-looking surveys that incorporate various types of survey questions and measurement scales. Most of these survey programs also manage the central storage of the questionnaire and the survey data on the company's server and offer basic statistical analyses of the responses. The cost for running these online surveys depends on the company chosen and the total number of responses required, however, an average cost of 2 cents per response should be a reasonable target price.

Although Internet surveys are attractive because of their low cost and simple administration, this survey method has significant drawbacks which severely limit the type of data that can be gathered. The biggest disadvantage of Internet surveys is related to the fact that not everybody has access to the Internet. Although Internet usage has increased in recent years, and you probably do not know anyone who does not have access, many people from specific groups are still not online. In the United States, for example, only about seven in ten people used the Internet in 2007. Moreover, those who are online tend to be younger, more educated, and wealthier than those who do not have Internet access (Pew Internet & American Life Project; see www.pewinternet.org). Both of these factors make it extremely difficult to obtain a nationally representative sample of survey respondents. After all, even if we were able to obtain a complete list of Internet users in the United States (or anywhere else, for that matter), randomly selecting respondents from such a list would result in strongly biased samples that are not representative of the overall population. Such a sample would not only exclude all those who do not use the Internet, but also would contain more younger, educated, and wealthier people than can be found in the general population.

Because of the difficulties associated with drawing representative samples for Internet surveys, it is advisable to verify whether existing Internet surveys rely on self-selected respondents (as many do), or whether they are based on truly representative samples. Many of the online "polls" that are published by media organizations such as CNN.com, for example, are based on responses from people who happen to visit a particular Web page at a certain time—and who actually decided to answer the poll questions. It is no surprise then, that Internet surveys that are based on such self-selected respondents provide virtually no information about the opinions or attitudes of any group or population. On the other hand, Internet polls conducted among a self-contained group of people (for example, all employees of Microsoft) can be representative if the sample has been drawn from a complete list of possible respondents who have access to the Internet.

It should be noted here that some survey companies have successfully provided access to representative samples of respondents through the Internet. Knowledge Networks (www.knowledgenetworks.com), for example, relies on samples of respondents who are first chosen through traditional random-digit dialing procedures (as in telephone surveys) and are then provided with Internet access in return for their cooperation with surveys sent to them via the Internet. Such a methodology is obviously very expensive and requires the periodic replacement of those people in the sample who have become "professional" survey respondents.

Other survey companies, such as Harris Interactive (www.harrisinteractive.com), rely on respondents who have voluntarily agreed to participate in Internet surveys and have provided extensive information about their personal background. In the case of *Harris Poll Online*, for example, this allows researchers to draw specialty samples of respondents who share certain interests or characteristics (for example, people with pets). The problem with such voluntary samples is the fact that they cannot be representative of the overall population—or even people with common characteristics—because of the **self-selection bias** mentioned above. *Harris Poll Online* tries to get around this problem by using a "propensity weighting" technique that adjusts survey results *ad hoc* by factors such as age and sex in order to match them with their actual proportions in the population of interest. Although such weighting procedures are common in survey research, the question remains whether it is appropriate to rely on samples that exclude large portions of the overall population (in this case, all people who do not use the Internet).

Another big disadvantage of Internet surveys is the lack of control over the administration of the instrument. Since most online polls are self-administered, there is no possibility for interviewers to answer potential questions respondents might have about the survey, or probe any of the respondents' "don't know" or "refusal" answers. In addition, the survey administrator has to make sure that the questionnaire is completed by the targeted respondent and not somebody who happens to stumble across the questionnaire while surfing the Internet (this is usually accomplished by using password-protected survey Web sites).

Finally, researchers interested in using Internet surveys should be aware of the fact that the technology used to access the Internet can differ significantly from one user to the next. For example, although a significant number of people have fast broadband Internet access either at work or at home, some still use the much slower telephone modems to go online. Thus, it might be difficult for respondents with slower Internet connections to receive and answer questionnaires that contain, for example, large video clips or images that cannot be downloaded within a reasonable amount of time. In addition, there are potential technological problems with different browsers or hardware configurations, which can significantly affect the way survey questionnaires are displayed on respondents' computer screens.

Overall then, Internet surveys are most suited to collect data from respondents who belong to finite groups with complete access to the Internet. Research projects that require representative samples of the general population, however, are better served with more traditional forms of surveys, such as personal interviews or telephone surveys based on random-digit dialing procedures.

TRAINING AND BRIEFING PERSONNEL

The personal interview is simultaneously one of the worst and one of the best data collection tools available to political scientists. The most significant disadvantages of the interview stem from the fact that the interview situation is rich with opportunities for *reactivity* to affect measurement. Respondents' reactions to the appearance or behavior of the interviewer, to the wording of questions, or to the interview setting can create artificial data that contain less information about the real world than about the interview process itself.

Because respondents react not only to questions but also to the person asking the questions and the manner in which they are asked, characteristics of interviewers that should be totally unrelated to the interview can, in fact, be crucial to its success. In order to minimize error in survey research, the interviews must be standardized. This means that each question should mean the same thing to each respondent, and that each response must mean the same thing when given by different respondents. The presence of an interviewer, ideally, should not affect the respondent's perception of a question, nor the kind of answer that is given. In order to increase response rates and accuracy, interviewers should do what they can to persuade respondents to complete the interview. It is important to interview busy and less cooperative people as well as people who willingly complete the survey.

Interviewer Guidelines

The following guidelines should help to reduce interviewer error considerably:

1. Use an informal, conversational style when asking the questions in the survey. You should be matter-of-fact and casual in your approach to questioning, as if there were absolutely no reason to expect people to refuse to answer.
2. You should be sufficiently familiar with the questions so that you sound as if you are not reading them. Do not conduct the interview in a monotonous voice, since this might make you sound disinterested in the respondents' answers. Try to make the respondents feel that you are listening to what they say by using affirmations such as *I see* or *okay*.
3. Do not express your own opinions during an interview by expressing agreement or disagreement with the respondent. Remain neutral and never suggest answers to the respondent even if you think you "know" what the respondent thinks. Also, do not allow yourself to be drawn into conversations with the respondent about the subject of the survey, because your remarks may bias responses.

4. Let the respondents determine the speed at which you read the survey. It is, how-ever, important to move the interview along as quickly as possible in order to avoid opportunities for the respondent to terminate the interview.

5. Do not intentionally alter the wording or the order of items. All questions should be read exactly as they are written and in the order in which they are presented. Just as survey results can be distorted when questions are reworded, they can also be distorted when questions are asked out of sequence.

6. Do not attempt to interview from memory. Always have the questionnaire before you, and refer to it for question wording and order even if you are so familiar with the instrument that it takes only a glance to remind you of the items.

7. If you are to record respondents' comments, record them in exactly the words the respondents use rather than summarizing them.

8. If respondents give indefinite answers, probe for more specific responses. Your probes should be neutral and should not suggest answers. The most effective neutral probe is repeating the original question or response categories. In well-constructed surveys, appropriate probes are indicated on the questionnaire for any question that is likely to require them.

9. Do not accept *I don't know* or *no opinion* as a response without at least one probe. Repeat the question and perhaps offer a little encouragement such as *I know some of the questions might be difficult to answer, but what is your best guess?*

10. If respondents object to question wording or the alternative answers offered, do not defend the survey instrument but merely explain that you must ask the questions as written and that you are not responsible for them.

11. Never tell respondents what others have answered in response to a given question even though respondents may ask.

12. Be prepared to answer any questions the respondent asks you about who is doing the survey and why. Each study should have a sheet prepared by the project man-ager that provides brief answers to these questions.

PRETESTING

Pretesting a survey instrument and all the accompanying procedures of data management is as important to successful survey research as a test-drive is to buying a good used car. Also called a **pilot study**, this trial run helps identify problems that will show up only under actual field conditions.

Pretests are conducted by administering the survey to a small sample of respon-dents similar to those who will be in the larger sample. The pretest sample need not be representative of the larger population. It is more important to draw the pretest sample in such a way as to ensure that members of all groups of respondents that may react dif-ferently to the instrument be included in the pretest than it is to draw a representative sample for the pretest. If, for example, less educated people are likely to have difficul-ties with the instrument, the researcher should take special pains to include respondents with little education in the pretest, even if they represent only a small portion of the population of interest.

Pretests can serve both to verify the utility of an instrument in which the researcher has a good deal of confidence and to help in the development of an instrument when the researcher knows less about the phenomena under study. In the former case, the instrument should be administered in the pretest in what is expected to be its final form. In the latter case, however, the researcher might want to experiment with different forms in order to learn what works best. A pretest of that type can involve:

1. Different versions of the instrument that test different question wordings or instrument formats.
2. Administering a final questionnaire through actual interviews in order to identify problems in communication.
3. Open-ended questions that help develop response categories for closed-ended questions to be used in the final version.

When these types of devices are used to refine an instrument, the researcher should pretest the instrument that is finally developed, so as to identify any remaining or newly created flaws.

When pretesting an instrument that calls for interviews, researchers often find it useful to conduct a number of the interviews themselves in order to get a feel for the dynamics set up by their instrument and a sense of whether or not it communicates effectively with typical respondents. At the very least, the researcher should meet with the interviewers as soon as they return from the field and go over the instrument and accompanying procedures in detail in order to identify any points at which instructions are unclear, specified procedures are awkward, or respondents seem confused by questions.

Often a pretest is as much a test of the sampling technique as it is of the survey instrument. If interviewers using the specified sampling procedure turn up an unusually small number of qualified respondents or an obviously unrepresentative sample in the pretest, the applicability of the sampling technique to that research situation should be reexamined. If personnel find it difficult to record data using the procedures selected for the pretest, then other procedures should be developed for the full-scale survey.

Pretesting is costly and time consuming, but it is an absolutely essential investment, because without it the researcher risks producing useless or misleading data. Think of it as buying insurance against finding yourself with a mountain of very expensive data that are useless because of flaws in the survey—flaws that you could have corrected had you been aware of them.

SURVEYING

After all these preparations, we are ready to conduct the actual survey. This is the heart of the study because it is where the data are actually collected. What is done in this stage depends on what type of survey is being conducted.

Most surveys are based either on personal interviews or on telephone interviews. Researchers generally prefer to use face-to-face interviews for longer surveys or questionnaires that contain sensitive topics that respondents might be reluctant to talk about on the telephone. Of course, personal interviews are relatively expensive because interviews have to be conducted at the respondent's home or at a central interviewing facility to which each respondent has to be invited. In addition, surveys that rely on personal interviews can be difficult to conduct in certain areas of the United States (in high-crime neighborhoods or extremely rural areas, for example) and usually take much longer to complete than telephone surveys. Based on the assumption that almost all Americans can be contacted by telephone, a large number of surveys carried out in the United States are conducted by telephone.

Computer-Assisted Telephone Interviewing (CATI)

Most survey organizations use computers in order to manage and conduct telephone interviews. **Computer-assisted telephone interviewing** has mostly replaced the traditional "paper-and-pencil" method, which forced interviewers to read printed questionnaires to respondents and then manually record their answers.

A typical CATI system consists of twenty or more networked computers that are controlled by a server (or main computer) that functions as a central storage location for the sample and the data. The server controls and displays the interview schedule on each interviewer's computer screen, selects telephone numbers, and dials them automatically for the interviewer. As soon as somebody answers the telephone, CATI prompts the interviewer to take the call and then read an introduction to the study (*Hello, my name is . . .*). The introduction typically identifies the survey organization and the study sponsor, in addition to briefly explaining the purpose of the survey. If respondents agree to participate in the survey, interviewers start to read each question directly from the computer screen and enter responses with their keyboards.

Although most questions require the interviewer to enter only numerical codes for each answer (for example, 1 for *agree* and 2 for *disagree*), interviewers can also record longer responses by typing them into blank boxes displayed on their screens. As soon as the interviewer has entered a response, the CATI system automatically displays the next question until the end of the survey has been reached. After completion of the interview, respondents' data are saved on the server and are available for immediate analysis.

The CATI system offers several advantages over the paper-and-pencil method of conducting telephone interviews. First, it increases the efficiency and accuracy of surveys by displaying question-and-answer categories on the interviewer's computer screen. Since the CATI program automatically guides the interviewer through the questions and records responses as they are entered, the possibility of interviewer error is greatly reduced.

Second, CATI systems allow survey organizations to administer very complex and individualized interview schedules. Based on responses to previous questions, for example, CATI can adjust the interview schedule and skip over questions not intended for certain respondents. This so-called **question branching** would be difficult to implement if an interviewer had to flip through pages of a printed interview schedule in order to get to the next appropriate question. CATI also has the ability to take responses and automatically insert them in subsequent questions, thus allowing the interviewer to ask highly individualized questions that are appropriate to each respondent. In addition, most CATI systems allow multilingual interviews (important for surveys targeting non-English speakers), voice capturing of open-ended question responses (eliminating the need to type them), and the playback of short audio clips (to test commercial jingles, for example).

Third, CATI systems are able to monitor and control interviewers unobtrusively during the interviews. Researchers can listen in on any interview at any time to catch and correct interviewers' mistakes. Interviewers who, for example, mispronounce names or forget to probe *don't know* answers can then be retrained or pulled entirely from the study.

Finally, because respondents' answers are directly entered into the computer during the interview, researchers can request distributions or tabulations of responses at any point during a survey project. Most CATI systems feature integrated statistical software packages that allow instant analysis of the survey data, thus eliminating the need to reformat and then export data into other statistical programs.

Whereas the introduction of CATI systems has improved and automated the way telephone interviews are conducted, computers have also simplified the administrative functions associated with interviewing, such as scheduling of callbacks, interviewer productivity reporting, and sample management. Moreover, integrated text editors enable researchers to write, test, and revise questionnaires easily and quickly within CATI, thus reducing the time needed between the development and implementation of new survey schedules.

MONITORING

Surveys are monitored to ensure the validity and generalizability of results. Low or unbalanced response rates can be identified and, perhaps, corrected through careful monitoring. For all types of surveys this involves keeping careful records of completed instruments as they come in.

With mail surveys, returned questionnaires should be opened, checked for proper completion, and filed. Each questionnaire should be assigned a serial identification number so that the time of its return can be determined later. The number of questionnaires that is received each day should be logged so that the researcher can keep track of the response rate. If respondents can be identified from the returned questionnaires, the researcher should record incoming questionnaires in a manner that will reveal imbalances in the return as they develop. If a certain geographic or demographic group is making an extremely low response, some extra follow-up mail effort may be called for to keep the sample from becoming unrepresentative. In addition, examination of the incoming questionnaires may reveal mistakes made by respondents, such as overlooking the last page of the instrument or misreading directions about how to mark items. If respondents are identified, a phone call or second mailing can sometimes save questionnaires that otherwise must be discarded.

With personal surveys, monitoring is done principally through a debriefing session as interviewers return from the field. The researcher or a trusted assistant should check the completed interview schedules to determine whether (1) the correct people in the correct households have been interviewed, (2) all completed interview schedules have been returned, (3) each instrument fully identifies the respondent and provides information on the time and date of the interview, (4) each instrument contains an identification number for the respondent and for the interviewer, and (5) all refusals are explained and any outstanding callbacks have been made. All of this helps ensure proper sampling and assists in verification.

Monitoring telephone surveys usually involves the researcher or field director listening in on interviews randomly without being detected. This provides both an incentive for interviewers to be responsible and a means of detecting and subsequently correcting flaws in interviewers' administration of the instrument.

Internet surveys are routinely monitored by checking the received data for possible problems with the sample or the questions themselves. Since most Internet surveys allow "peeks" at the data even while the survey is in progress, it is relatively simple to get information about who is responding and how questions are answered. Potential problems such as nonresponse, for example, can then be easily addressed by contacting respondents with reminders or sending the survey questionnaires again.

RESEARCH EXERCISE

Conduct a Mini-Survey

You can conduct your own surveys, and learn a lot about gathering and using survey research in the process.

1. First, select a politically relevant topic of interest to you. Identify a dependent variable and three independent variables you might want to use in a study of the subject. Think in terms of an effects model—three independent variables that have an effect on (or are associated with) one dependent variable. Choose variables that can be measured adequately with survey questions (for example, media use and attitudes toward the president). Develop a set of hypotheses that describe the expected relationship(s) between the independent and the dependent variables.

2. Design a questionnaire that provides measures of these four variables, and write it out in a form that can be used in an online survey. Think carefully about the wording of your questions and make sure that the questions actually measure the variables you have included in your effects model. All closed-ended questions should have appropriate answer choices, including a separate "don't know" choice, if necessary. Make sure that the meanings of the answer choices do not overlap and that all necessary answer choices are included in each questions. Pretest your questionnaire with a couple of friends who are not part of your class to ensure that none of the questions has a problem.

3. Use one of the free Internet survey sites (SurveyMonkey and SurveyGizmo, for example, allow you to collect a limited number of responses for free) to create the online questionnaire. After you are satisfied that the online questionnaire actually works (click a few times through the survey to make sure), e-mail a survey invitation with a link to your survey to your friends. Ask them to answer the survey as a favor and then to forward the survey invitation to their friends as well. This "snowball sampling" technique should result in a decent sample size, even if you only start with a few initial friends as respondents.

4. Let the survey run for a couple of days and then download the collected data for analysis on your own computer. Try to test your initial hypotheses and see if the independent variables had any effect on (or are associated with) the dependent variable.

5. Finally, think about how your findings might have been influenced by the type of people who respond to your survey (young, educated, etc.).

VERIFYING

Verification is especially important with personal surveys, when unethical interviewers have both an opportunity and an incentive to falsify interviews and when even well-meaning ones can interview the wrong people. Verification procedures allow researchers to catch this type of error and to be sure that the sampling procedure is followed correctly.

Verification of personal interviews usually involves contacting the intended respondent to determine (1) whether the interview has occurred and (2) whether the interviewer has asked and correctly recorded answers to all questions. To do this, ask when the interview occurred and approximately how long it took. If respondents report that the interview has been conducted, ask them to reanswer two simple questions—one from the middle and one from near the end of the questionnaire—under the pretext that the answers were not clearly recorded in the field. Then check their answers against those that were recorded.

In large surveys, verification is done on a spot-check basis because contacting all respondents would be too costly. If spot-checks reveal falsifications or significant errors in any of an interviewer's forms, all of his or her interviews should be verified.

SECONDARY ANALYSIS OF SURVEY DATA

It is important to recognize that most political scientists, perhaps even most political scientists who publish books and articles based on survey data, *never conduct a survey*. They do not conduct surveys both because it is difficult to obtain the necessary funding and because it is often possible to answer the research question they want to explore by using survey data others have collected. Studying data collected by someone else is called **secondary analysis**. Such analysis is very common with survey data because they are so expensive to collect.

Secondary analysis is highly desirable for several reasons. In the first place, the results of almost any survey contain data that are never used by the original researchers because they turn out to be only marginally relevant to the particular research question under study. Another researcher may find these data perfectly suited to answering some other research question. Secondary analysis allows fuller use of data and conserves resources by saving the cost of new surveys when sufficient data already exist. Second, surveys run the risk of *contaminating the population*. This means that repeated studies of some subject among a population may actually cause changes in the phenomena in question or make people reluctant to cooperate with future research. By allowing research to be conducted without yet another survey, secondary analysis minimizes the risk of contamination. Third, although there are a great many data analysis techniques available to political scientists, any one researcher is likely to use only a few in a single study. Secondary analysis allows other researchers to apply different techniques that may expand our understanding of the subject or may even produce different answers to the original research question.

The most fruitful approach to secondary analysis is to select a research question, devise hypotheses to be tested, and then seek completed studies that contain the data necessary to test those hypotheses. Working in reverse (locating a sound data set and examining it in hopes of coming up with valuable research questions it can help answer) can sometimes pay off, but it significantly constrains the range of questions that can be investigated.

The first requirement of a useful data set is that it be based on a sample of the *appropriate population*. If we want to generalize to women in the United States, a study sampling voters in Kansas will be of no use. The second requirement is that the survey instrument contains *appropriate operationalizations* of the key variables in the hypotheses to be tested. If, for example, differences between African Americans and whites are central to an investigation but the data set has recorded race only as "white" and "nonwhite," it will be of little use, as racial groups other than African Americans (for example, Asians and Native Americans) are included in the nonwhite category.

How do we find out if a study is usable? Good reports of research state what sample has been used and describe the operationalizations of key variables that have been employed. Consequently, books and journal articles sometimes provide enough information about a data set for us to judge its suitability, and a literature search can turn up a source of data for secondary analysis. Individual political scientists are often willing to share data sets with others when asked, so it is sometimes possible to obtain a data set through a letter to an author.

Data Archives

Fortunately, there is a more systematic and reliable way to locate and gain access to data for secondary analysis. There are a number of institutions that collect data sets in the same way that libraries collect books. These institutions are generally referred to as **data archives**. They classify data sets for easy location and put them in a form that facilitates the sets' use by people who were not involved in the original project in which the data were collected. Some of the more important social science data archives are listed here, along with brief descriptions of their holdings.

- *The American National Election Studies (ANES)* produce data on voting, public opinion, and political participation that serve the research needs of social scientists, teachers, students, policy makers, and journalists (www.electionstudies.org).
- *The Association of Religion Data Archives (ARDA)* provides free access to about 400 national and international data sets on religion (www.thearda.com).
- *The Data & Information Services Center (DISC)* is the central repository of data collections used by the social science research community at the University of Wisconsin–Madison (www.disc.wisc.edu).
- *The European Union (EU)* provides access to European public opinion data including *Eurobarometer* and offers links to other social sciences data archives (ec.europa.eu/public_opinion).
- *The International Social Survey Programme (ISSP)* is an annual program of cross-national collaboration on surveys covering topics important to social science research (www.issp.org).
- *The Inter-University Consortium for Political and Social Research (ICPSR)* at the University of Michigan, Ann Arbor, maintains a large collection of surveys conducted in the United States and abroad that stress political variables (www.icpsr.umich.edu).
- *The National Opinion Research Center (NORC)* at the University of Chicago conducts the General Social Survey (GSS), an almost annual survey of U.S. households that has been conducted since 1972 (www.norc.uchicago.edu).
- *The Odum Institute for Research in Social Science* at the University of North Carolina, Chapel Hill, maintains a collection of surveys of the U.S. population, including those conducted by the Louis Harris polling organization (www.irss.unc.edu).
- *The UK Data Archive* at the University of Essex possesses "the largest collection of digital data in the social sciences and humanities in the UK" (www.data-archive.ac.uk).
- *The Pew Research Center for the People & the Press* in Washington, D.C., is an independent opinion research group that studies public attitudes toward the press, politics, and public policy issues. The center offers free access to its own poll data (www.people-press.org).
- *The Roper Center for Public Opinion Research* at the University of Connecticut, Storrs, is one of the nation's largest archives containing data from national and international surveys on a wide variety of subjects (www.ropercenter.uconn.edu).

PRACTICAL RESEARCH ETHICS
How should you protect survey respondents?

The fact that survey researchers ask individuals to talk about their personal attitudes, opinions, and beliefs requires them to be especially sensitive to the possible consequences of their questions. In general, researchers need to protect their respondents from harm and ensure that all survey findings are reported accurately. The following ethical considerations should be observed carefully when conducting survey studies:

- *Respondents' right to know:* Survey respondents should provide their permission to be interviewed, affirming that their participation in the survey is voluntary and that they do not have to answer all questions. In addition, respondents should have enough information about the purpose of the study, the sponsor (if any), and the organization that conducts the survey in order to make an informed decision about their participation.
- *Respondents' right to protection:* Survey researchers have an obligation to ensure that the survey questions do not cause physical or emotional harm to their respondents. This includes practices or methods that may humiliate or mislead survey respondents. Researchers should also consider whether their questions might have any legal consequences for the respondent (for example, workers participating in a survey that was not sanctioned by the employer).
- *Respondents' right to privacy:* Survey respondents have a right to either give or withhold information during an interview. In other words, respondents do not have to answer questions that they consider too personal or private.
- *Respondents' right to confidentiality and anonymity:* Unless waived by the respondent for specified uses, survey researchers are obligated to ensure that the information provided by the respondents will be kept confidential and anonymous. This means that individual survey answers will not be available to people outside the project and that all personal identifiers will be removed from the completed questionnaires in order to ensure that answers cannot be traced to individual participants.
- *Accurate reporting of results:* Survey researchers also should make an effort to fully and accurately represent the results gathered by the survey. Many survey reports do not provide enough information about their data gathering procedures, which might make it difficult to assess the quality of the survey itself. AAPOR's *Code of Professional Ethics and Practices* specifies that survey reports must include the following information: (1) who sponsored and conducted the survey; (2) the exact wording of questions asked; (3) a definition of the population and the sampling frame; (4) a description of the sample design; (5) sample sizes, eligibility criteria, screening procedures, and response rates; (6) estimates of sampling error and a description of any weighting or estimating procedures used; (7) which results are based on only parts of the sample; and (8) method, location, and dates of data collection (see Appendix B for AAPOR's complete "Standard for Minimal Disclosure").

Each of these institutions publishes a list of the data sets it has and provides a general description of the data. Once a promising-sounding study has been located in a listing of archive holdings, we can determine the actual utility of the study by obtaining the **codebook** for the survey. This lists all questions asked and tells how the responses have been coded, and it will allow us to judge the fit between the study's operationalizations and the hypotheses to be tested.

Conclusion

Without question, surveys are the most efficient way to collect information about how people think. Technological developments, such as computer-assisted telephone interviewing and online polling, have increased the number of surveys conducted each year. In fact, there are now so many surveys that many people have become annoyed by the seemingly constant intrusion into their private lives. Successful survey studies therefore have to be planned carefully to ensure that the data collected will provide enough information to answer research questions or to test hypotheses. In the planning phase of a survey, researchers have to consider the conceptualization of hypotheses and concepts, the type of survey required, the design of the survey instruments, the required sample and sampling procedures, the interviewer training, and the pretesting of the instrument. During the designing phase of the survey the researcher needs to pay special attention to the development of the questionnaire and the interview schedule. Survey questions can be either open-ended or closed-ended and should be worded carefully in order to avoid bias and other related problems. The structure of the questionnaire should encourage respondents' participation. Finally, the required survey type is determined by the research question and by the resources available. Each survey type has distinct advantages and disadvantages that have to be considered before the start of any research project. Surveys are conducted either by personal interviews, mail, telephone, or through the Internet. The surveying process requires monitoring and verification of the conducted interviews, data coding, processing, and analysis.

Key Terms

survey research *152*
respondents *152*
cross-sectional surveys *154*
longitudinal surveys *154*
trend studies *154*
cohort studies *154*
panel studies *155*
questionnaire *155*
interview schedule *155*
demographic groups *156*

open-ended questions *156*
closed-ended questions *156*
question wording *158*
personal interview *163*
mail surveys *163*
telephone surveys *164*
random-digit dialing (RDD) *165*
Internet surveys *165*
self-selection bias *167*

pilot study *169*
pretests *169*
computer-assisted telephone interviewing (CATI) *171*
question branching *171*
secondary analysis *174*
data archives *175*
codebook *176*

Research Examples

The literature on survey research is one of the largest in the social sciences. Most of it reflects the fact that the method is widely used in sociology and psychology as well as in political science and other fields. The following studies were chosen as examples because they represent a variety of survey methodologies. Binder et al. (2009), for example, rely on a nationwide mail panel survey to analyze the relationships between discussion networks and extreme attitudes toward stem cell research during the 2004 presidential election. Barth et al. (2009), on the other hand, analyze factors influencing public support for an antigay rights referendum in South Carolina with data from a telephone survey. Johnson and Kaye (2009) use an online survey of Internet users during the period of the 2004 presidential election to explore how users judge the Internet's credibility for political information.

Studies based on representative online polls are still the exception. However, good examples of such polls can be found in reports by the Program on International Policy Attitudes (PIPA), which frequently publishes public opinion reports that are based on representative online surveys conducted by Knowledge Networks. You can find their most recent reports at PIPA's Web site (www.pipa.org).

Methodological Readings

A relatively comprehensive overview of survey methods is provided in *Survey Research Methods* (Fowler 2001). Other excellent introductions are found in *An Introduction to Survey Research, Polling, and Data Analysis* (Weisberg et al. 1996), *Designing and Conducting Survey Research: A Comprehensive Guide* (Rea and Parker 2005), and *How to Conduct Surveys: A Step-by-Step Guide* (Fink 2005).

The subjects of question wording and questionnaire design in general are addressed in *Questionnaire Design and Attitude Measurement* (Oppenheim 1999) and *Improving Survey Questions: Design and Evaluation* (Fowler 1995). Interviewer skills are covered in *Standardized Survey Interviewing: Minimizing Interviewer-Related Error* (Fowler and Mangione 1990).

A very detailed discussion of how to conduct surveys by mail rather than through personal interviews is found in *Mail Surveys: Improving the Quality* (Mangione 1995). Telephone survey methods are covered in *How to Conduct Interviews by Telephone and in Person* (Frey and Oishi 2004). One of the most widely referenced books on these techniques is Dillman's (2006) *Mail and Internet Surveys: The Tailored Design Method*.

A good introduction to the practical applications of Internet surveys is provided in *Internet Data Collection* (Best and Krueger 2004), *Conducting Research Surveys via E-Mail and the Web* (Schonlau et al. 2002), and *Internet Research Methods: A Practical Guide for the Social and Behavioural Sciences* (Hewson et al. 2002). All three books contain a good selection of references for methodological issues in Internet research.

References

Babbie, Earl R. 1990. *Survey Research Methods*. Belmont, CA: Wadsworth Publishing Co.

Barth, Jay, L. Marvin Overby, and Scott H. Huffmon. 2009. "Community Context, Personal Contact, and Support for an Anti-Gay Rights Referendum." *Political Research Quarterly* 62(2): 355–365.

Best, Samuel J., and Brian S. Krueger. 2004. *Internet Data Collection*. Thousand Oaks, CA: Sage.

Binder, Andrew R., Kajsa E. Dalrymple, Dominique Brossard, and Dietram A. Scheufele. 2009. "The Soul of a Polarized Democracy: Testing Theoretical Linkages Between Talk and Attitude Extremity During the 2004 Presidential Election." *Communication Research* 36(June): 315–340.

Dillman, Don A. 2006. *Mail and Internet Surveys: The Tailored Design Method*, 2nd ed. New York: Wiley.

Johnson, Thomas J., and Barbara K. Kaye. 2009. "In Blog We Trust? Deciphering Credibility of Components of the Internet Among Politically Interested Internet Users." *Computers in Human Behavior* 25(January): 175–182.

Fink, Arlene. 2005. *How to Conduct Surveys: A Step-by-Step Guide*, 3rd ed. Thousand Oaks, CA: Sage.

Fowler, Floyd J. Jr. 1995. *Improving Survey Questions: Design and Evaluation*. Thousand Oaks, CA: Sage.

Fowler, Floyd J. Jr. 2001. *Survey Research Methods*, 3rd ed. Newbury Park, CA: Sage.

Fowler, Floyd J. Jr., and Thomas W. Mangione. 1990. *Standardized Survey Interviewing: Minimizing Interviewer-Related Error*. Newbury Park, CA: Sage.

Frey, James H., and Sabine Mertens Oishi. 2004. *How to Conduct Interviews by Telephone and in Person*. Newbury Park, CA: Sage.

Hewson, Claire, Peter Yule, Dianna Laurent, and Carl Vogel. 2002. *Internet Research Methods: A Practical Guide for the Social and Behavioural Sciences*. Thousand Oaks, CA: Sage.

Mangione, Thomas W. 1995. *Mail Surveys: Improving the Quality*. Thousand Oaks, CA: Sage.

Oppenheim, Abraham N. 1999. *Questionnaire Design and Attitude Measurement*. New York: Continuum International Publishing Group.

Rea, Louis M., and Richard A. Parker. 2005. *Designing and Conducting Survey Research: A Comprehensive Guide*, 3rd ed. San Francisco, CA: Jossey-Bass.

Schonlau, Matthias, Ronald D. Fricker Jr., and Marc N. Elliot. 2002. *Conducting Research Surveys via E-Mail and the Web*. Thousand Oaks, CA: Sage.

Weisberg, Herbert F., Jon A. Krosnick, and Bruce D. Bowen. 1996. *An Introduction to Survey Research, Polling, and Data Analysis*, 3rd ed. Thousand Oaks, CA: Sage.

CHAPTER 9

Combining Multiple Measures: Using Scaling Techniques

In this chapter you will learn:

- The benefits of scaling for your research.
- When you should use scales rather than individual measures of concepts.
- The available types of scales (e.g., Likert, semantic differential, Guttman, Thurstone, etc.).

One of the most common problems we encounter in designing surveys or other instruments arises when we must find a way to assign a single representative value or score to a complex attitude or behavior. As an example, consider how one might go about measuring the degree of people's prejudice toward college students. Such prejudice can take a number of forms, depending on which attributes of college students a particular individual might focus upon. That is, some people might judge college students by students' dress, others by their mannerisms, and still others by their behavior, their social or economic status, or even their personal hygiene. Some people might hold stereotypic views based on one or two encounters, either pleasant or unpleasant, with specific students, and others may barely differentiate between college students and other members of the community. These elements of judgment may vary quite widely in substance, direction, and degree, but each is, at least potentially, a component of the larger concept *prejudice*.

Political researchers often face the problem of having to measure complex, vague, or multidimensional concepts such as a person's *political leaning* or the level of *anti-Americanism* found in countries other than the United States. These concepts obviously cannot be measured with one simple question, and, to make matters even more complicated, often have different meanings in different nations or different cultural settings. The concept of *political participation*, for example, traditionally has been measured in the United States by asking people whether they voted in the last election, whether they have previously contacted their political representatives, whether they have donated money to a political organization, and so on. While these questions might successfully measure political participation in the United States, asking such questions in countries with different political systems (such as China or North Korea, for example), would not make much sense. It is therefore important to remember that scale construction is very much dependent on the political and cultural context in which it takes place.

As researchers hoping to measure these concepts, we must design an instrument that is at once sufficiently broad to detect and measure as many of these component elements as possible and sufficiently concise to allow us to summarize in some meaningful way the extent to which the more general concept in question is present. Put another way, we need a device that captures or represents a notion such as prejudice in all its complexity *and* tells us how much of it each respondent (or case) has. One important means by which we can accomplish this is through *scaling.*

THE ART OF SCALING

Scaling is a procedure in which we combine a number of relatively narrow indicators (in the example, survey questions about specific perceived traits of college students) into a single, summary measure that we take to represent the broader, underlying concept of which each is a part (prejudice). Thus, we might measure a respondent's attitudes about various behaviors of college students (that they drink too much or have too many loud parties, for example) or about their mannerisms (that they are snobbish or self-important or inconsiderate), but we would not take any one of these items *alone* to stand for so broad a concept as prejudice. Rather, we must pull together *several* of these narrow measures in some way that allows us to draw conclusions about the more general point of view to which each may contribute or that each may reflect. And more than that, we must accomplish the task so that we can compare the amount of prejudice (or whatever it is we are measuring) that characterizes one respondent with the amount that characterizes another, in effect making a judgment (in the example) about which is *more* prejudiced. The unifying measure that represents a given underlying concept is called a **scale**. The individualized assessment of the degree to which any given case manifests that underlying concept is called a **scale score**. Scaling, or scale construction, is simply the procedure by which scales are built and individual scale scores are assigned.

SCALE CONSTRUCTION: TWO BASIC CONCERNS

Scaling, then, seems to be a fairly straightforward process. The task of the researcher is simply to identify several components of the underlying concept, to develop indicators to measure each, to combine those indicators into a summary score by reciting a few magic words or statistical incantations, and—presto—it is done. Unfortunately, this apparent simplicity is deceptive, for there are some potential dangers to which we must be especially sensitive when selecting and interpreting scale components. Most important among these are two with which we are already familiar: the concerns posed by the notions of validity and reliability.

Validity

In the present context, validity questions whether there is reason to believe that each of the individual components (specific questions) in a given scale is actually related directly to the underlying concept and whether, collectively, those components capture the full essence of it. Put another way, we must ask ourselves whether it really makes sense to combine a particular set of indicators *and*, once we have done so, whether it really makes sense to attach to this set of indicators the particular label we have chosen. Thus, in our example, we must ask ourselves first whether persons' attitudes toward student behavior really have anything in common with their attitudes toward student mannerisms or styles of dress, and second whether all these attitudes together can really be considered to reflect the degree of those persons' prejudice toward students.

Reliability

In scaling, reliability becomes a concern with whether the various component indicators of a scale are in fact related to one another in a consistent and meaningful manner. In effect, we are asking not whether a particular set of questions or indicators differentiates between apples and oranges, but rather whether, once the apples have been identified, it provides us with consistent standards for sorting them by size, color, and variety. If so, then combining the measures will tell us more about apples than will any single measure. But if our standards are inconsistent or ambiguous, then our observations based upon them may prove misleading.

An Example

Consider a scale in which each respondent is instructed to express either agreement or disagreement with each of the following statements:

1. The North Koreans are evil and cannot be trusted.
2. The French are evil and cannot be trusted.
3. The Japanese are evil and cannot be trusted.
4. The Chinese are evil and cannot be trusted.

Let us suppose that this scale is intended to measure *xenophobia*—the fear and distrust of foreigners. Presumably, the more statements with which particular respondents agree, the more xenophobic we may take them to be. But is that really the case? A person who believes only the North Koreans and the Chinese are evil and not to be trusted may, in effect, be expressing anticommunism rather than xenophobia. A person who believes only the Japanese and the Chinese are evil and not to be trusted may, in effect, be expressing racism rather than xenophobia. Even a respondent who regards all four groups as evil and untrustworthy may, upon closer inspection, be expressing not xenophobia but a feeling that *all* people or *all* governments, even the respondent's own, are evil and not to be trusted. Because we cannot say with any assuredness that this scale measures xenophobia per se, the scale lacks validity.

And what of reliability? Even if the scale were measuring xenophobia, could we claim that its components measured consistently? Fear and distrust of the Chinese, for example, may be an indicator of at least two very different characteristics—one ideological and the other racial—and two respondents might give the same answer for very different reasons. Is our anticommunist respondent in some meaningful sense *equally* as xenophobic as our racist respondent? Probably not. To combine these particular items into a single measure by simply adding them together, then, is at best an exercise in futility and at worst a source of erroneous conclusions.

Problems of this type cannot always be overcome easily, and as a result, scaling must be used with great care in some instances and must be forgone in others. Yet the overriding advantages inherent in the ability to develop a single number or score to represent a complex attitude or behavior provide a substantial incentive to employ scaling techniques in a great many instances. In the remainder of this chapter we discuss four different approaches to the development of meaningful scales. Each of these should be viewed not only in terms of its procedures but also in terms of its strengths and weaknesses in overcoming the problems of validity and reliability.

LIKERT SCALING

The first such technique, and probably the least satisfactory in these terms, is **Likert scaling**—a simple technique by which each respondent is presented with a series of statements requiring a value judgment. Figure 9.1 illustrates a typical series of such items, which might constitute a measure of prejudice toward college students. In each instance, respondents are asked whether they agree strongly, agree, neither agree nor disagree, disagree, or disagree strongly with the statement. Each such respondent is assigned a numerical score, with 5 representing the strongest agreement and 1 representing the strongest disagreement.

A middle or neutral response is assigned the value 3. To obtain the summary measure of prejudice for a particular individual, one adds all the individual scores and divides by the number of statements. Thus, a respondent who has answered questions 1 through 6 as follows:

> Item 1: Agree (4)
>
> Item 2: Strongly agree (5)
>
> Item 3: Neither agree nor disagree (3)
>
> Item 4: Agree (4)
>
> Item 5: Disagree (2)
>
> Item 6: Agree (4)

is assigned the summary score 3.67 (i.e., $[4 + 5 + 3 + 4 + 2 + 4]/6$), which might be rounded to 4.

In general, the higher a person's scale score, the more of the measured characteristic (in this case, prejudice toward college students) he or she is presumed to have. The challenges of interpreting these data are the same as those already noted in our xenophobia scale, which

---

Please indicate whether you *agree strongly, agree, neither agree nor disagree*, or *disagree strongly* with each of the following statements:

1. There may be a few exceptions, but in general college students are pretty much alike.
2. The trouble with letting college students into a nice neighborhood is that they gradually give it a typical student atmosphere
3. To end prejudice against college students, the first step is for the students to try sincerely to get rid of their harmful and irritating faults.
4. There is something different and strange about college students; it is hard to tell what they are thinking and planning, and what makes them tick.
5. Most college students would become overbearing and disagreeable if not kept in their place.
6. College students prove that when people of their type have too much money and freedom, they just take advantage and cause trouble.

FIGURE 9.1 Typical Likert scale items.

Source: Adapted from the E (Ethnocentrism) Scale used by Theodore Adorno et al. in *The Authoritarian Personality* (New York: Harper & Row, 1950).

Note: In this figure, statements have been worded in only one direction (that is, all agreements with the items reflect the presence of prejudice) for purposes of illustration. In practice, some items would be reworded so that the negative responses evidence prejudice, and the score values would be reversed accordingly. The goal of such a procedure is to minimize *response set bias*— the tendency of some respondents to give the same answer to every question.

was, in fact, an oversimplified Likert-type scale. For one thing, we know nothing about the relationships among the component items. Each may in fact measure different aspects of the same underlying trait, and on its face each appears to do so, but we cannot be sure.

The items that compose a good (or reliable) scale should have high internal consistency—that is, they should be highly correlated with each other. Different statistical models exist for measuring internal consistency. Probably the most commonly used reliability coefficient for items that have three or more answer categories is **Cronbach's alpha**, which is based on the average inter-item correlation. For items with two answer categories (true/false or agree/disagree, for example), the related **Kuder-Richardson 20 (KR20)** coefficient usually is used.

One point that should be clear even now, however, has to do with the way in which the summary (average) score is determined: one simply adds the individual item scores and divides by the number of items. But if we look more closely at the response categories (that is, *strongly agree, agree*, etc.), we find that they represent measurement at the ordinal level. That is, they distinguish between mutually exclusive categories and rank each relative to the others. They do not, however, establish known and equal intervals (the difference between *strongly agree* and *agree* is not always the same, either from item to item or from one respondent to the next). Accordingly, it is meaningless and misleading to add these numbers together, let alone to average them. A more appropriate procedure, but not a commonly used one, is to calculate a different kind of average, called a *median*, for each respondent's answers and to assign this as the scale score. Determination of the median is discussed in Chapter 16.

GUTTMAN SCALING

Many of the problems associated with Likert scaling can be overcome in certain circumstances by using a more sophisticated technique known as *Guttman scaling*. **Guttman scaling** begins from the assumption that certain attitudes (and behaviors) are related to one another in such a way that holding (or engaging in) one is more difficult or requires more effort than holding (or engaging in) another. Perhaps the best analogy here is to a person standing on a ladder. A person standing on the fifth rung quite likely has climbed there by stepping on the first, second, third, fourth, and fifth rungs. It is possible but less likely that the person skipped one or more of the lower rungs on the way up. It is most unlikely that someone would step directly from the ground to the fifth rung of the ladder, at least without enduring some pain. In effect, then, our climber has reached the fifth rung by engaging in a series of progressively higher-order behaviors and can reasonably be *assumed* to have traversed the lower positions to reach the highest one.

Similarly, even if we know that a particular person has voted in a presidential election—an act known from many studies to be one of the most common and least demanding in politics—we cannot assume with any degree of assurance that the same person has also participated actively in some political organization—a far more demanding and much less common action—or has run for public office—one of the most demanding and least common political acts of all. Yet if, on the other hand, we know that an individual has been active in a political organization, it *may* be assumed, with some degree of confidence, that that person has also engaged in such lesser political acts as voting, though not that the person has taken the further step of running for office. And by extension, if an individual has been a candidate for office, we have reason to assume that the person has also voted and engaged in organizational activity. These assumptions will not always prove correct, but they will be supported far more often than not.

Certain attitudes may be seen to relate to one another in much the same way. We can see this illustrated in Figure 9.2, which represents an alternative approach to measuring a person's degree of prejudice against students. In a procedure similar to Likert scaling, respondents are asked whether they agree or disagree with each item in a series of statements. The response that most reflects the trait being measured (for example, prejudice) is scored with a plus ($+$), and alternative responses are scored with a minus ($-$). Thus, agreement with item 1 would be scored plus ($+$) as reflecting prejudice, and agreement with item 2 would be assigned a minus ($-$), reflecting its absence. The statements themselves may be seen to bear a relationship with one another such that the various responses reflect the degree of one's prejudice or freedom from it. In effect, the closer a perceived threat comes to one's own family or self, the more difficult it presumably is for one to remain free of prejudice. What this means is that there is, at least potentially, a logical, ordinal relationship among the items in the scale—a factor that is missing with the Likert procedure.

Moreover, Guttman scaling provides appropriate procedures not only for summarizing the degree of a characteristic possessed by a given respondent but also for assessing the degree to which a particular set of components meets the assumption of ordinality in the first place. These procedures are illustrated in Table 9.1, which reports the responses of 170 hypothetical persons to the statements presented in Figure 9.2.

TABLE 9.1 Hypothetical Distribution of Guttman Scale Responses*

Item 1	Item 2	Item 3	Item 4	Item 5	Item 6	n	Error (e)	$n(e)$	Scale Score
$+$	$+$	$+$	$+$	$+$	$+$	10			7
$-$	$+$	$+$	$+$	$+$	$+$	20			6
$-$	$-$	$+$	$+$	$+$	$+$	30			5
$-$	$-$	$-$	$+$	$+$	$+$	30			4
$-$	$-$	$-$	$-$	$+$	$+$	10			3
$-$	$-$	$-$	$-$	$-$	$+$	10			2
$-$	$-$	$-$	$-$	$-$	$-$	5			1
$+$	$-$	$+$	$+$	$+$	$+$	30	1	30	(7) or (5)
$+$	$+$	$+$	$+$	$-$	$-$	5	2	10	(7)
$-$	$+$	$-$	$+$	$+$	$+$	20	1	20	(6) or (4)
45	55	95	145	150	160	170		60	

Marginals
(used for ordering items)

Totals

* $+$ Indicates a response reflecting prejudice.

Please indicate whether you *agree* or *disagree* with each of the following statements:

1. Given a choice, I would like to see college students kept out of my community.
2. It is okay for college students to visit my community.
3. If a college student wanted to live in my community, that would be okay with me.
4. I would not want to see a college student living in my neighborhood.
5. I would have no objection to someone in my family bringing home a college student as a guest for dinner.
6. I would be displeased if someone in my family were to marry a college student.

FIGURE 9.2 Typical Guttman scale items.

Source: Adapted from the Social Distance Scale developed by E. Bogardus in *Social Distance* (Yellow Springs, OH: Antioch Press, 1959).

Note: In this figure, the statements have been arranged in order of their degree of difficulty for purposes of illustration. In practice, their order should be mixed to obscure any implicit ranking.

Several points in the table are worthy of note. To begin with, the items are ordered on the left-hand side of the table in ascending order according to their number of supportive responses (+). This number is ascertained by summing the number of cases (*n*) for which a plus (+) has been recorded for a particular item. The assumption here is that the number of agreeing responses will decrease as the difficulty of holding a particular attitude increases. In the example, this ranking happens to correspond with our expectations in that the observed ranking is in the same order as our initial ranking, but this is not always the case.

Each line in the table represents a group of individuals who have given a particular combination of responses to the six items. Thus, the first line represents those ten people (*n* = 10) who have responded to each of the six questions in a manner reflecting prejudice toward students. The second line represents those twenty respondents whose answers indicate prejudice on items 2 through 6, but not on the more extreme item 1, and so forth. The first seven lines in the table represent those combinations of responses that are wholly consistent with the assumption that the six items are ordinally related with one another. Persons displaying any one of these combinations of responses are termed *perfect scale types*.

In Guttman scaling, there will always be one more perfect scale type than there are items in the scale, because the total absence of the characteristic being measured (*no prejudice*, as in line 7) is regarded as a perfect score. Each perfect score is assigned a number from 1 to *i* + 1, where *i* is the number of items, with 1 identifying those respondents possessing the lowest level of the trait in question and *i* + 1 those possessing the highest. The appropriate score is then recorded for each respondent. Thus, in the example, each of the ten persons in line 1, whose responses reflect the highest degree of prejudice, are assigned the score 7 (*i* + 1 = 6 + 1 = 7), each person in line 2 the score 6, each in line 3 the score 5, and so on, until the five respondents in line 7 are each scored 1. These scores rank each respondent vis-à-vis every other respondent according to his or her degree of prejudice.

We have yet to account, however, for the fifty-five respondents represented by lines 8, 9, and 10 in the table. One or more of the responses of these individuals do not fit the pattern predicted by our ordering of the items. These are, in effect, people who skipped one or more steps while climbing the ladder. Accordingly, these sets of responses are said to contain one or more *errors*. The term *error* here refers not to a mistake by the respondent but to a failure of the assumptions of Guttman scaling to apply to these cases. When such errors occur, and they are quite common, we proceed on a line-by-line basis as follows. First, we count the *minimum* number of changes in the line that, if made, would result in a perfect scale score. In line 8, for instance, we can change the plus (+) in column 1 to a minus (−) to obtain a response of 5, or alternatively, we can change the minus (−) in column 2 to a plus (+) to obtain a response of 7. In either event, only one item is changed and so we say line 8 contains one error. This is indicated in the column labeled "error (*e*)." We then multiply the number of errors (1) by the number of cases in which the error occurs (30) and enter our result in the next column. Finally, we assign to each case the scale score it would receive if the error did not occur. Though we have only one error in line 8, we have a choice of two possible corrections, one of which yields a score of 5 and the other a score of 7. Unless there is some compelling reason to choose one of these scores over the other, the standard practice is to assign each of the 30 cases randomly to one or the other scale category.

We move next to line 9 and repeat the procedure. Here we are required to make a minimum of two changes, because we must convert both minus (−) scores to plus (+). Again, we note the number of errors, multiply by the number of cases, and assign a scale score. Here, however, only one score is possible, since we have no options when making our corrections. The procedure is then repeated for line 10, as it is for any additional nonscalar combinations.

In proceeding through lines 8, 9, and 10, we have, of course, assigned scores to each case as if it fitted our scale perfectly, though we know for a fact that it does not. This means that to the extent that we rely upon our scale scores to describe those fifty-five cases, we risk reaching an improper conclusion. How serious is this risk? Fortunately, Guttman scaling procedures suggest an answer.

Recall that we have kept track of the total number of errors in the scale. In effect, an assessment of risk requires us to ask whether this total error is relatively small and therefore unimportant or whether it is so large as to invalidate the scale itself. We may answer this question by calculating a statistic called the *Guttman coefficient of reproducibility* (C_R), using the following formula:

$$C_R = 1 - \frac{\sum n(e)}{i(N)}$$

where n = the number of cases in lines in which errors occur
e = the number of errors in each line
i = the number of response items
N = the total number of cases

For the example, the coefficient of reproducibility is determined by substituting the appropriate values:

$$C_R = 1 - \frac{30 + 10 + 20}{6(170)} = 1 - \frac{60}{1,020}$$
$$= 1 - 0.06 = .94$$

> **PRACTICAL RESEARCH ETHICS**
>
> *Do your scale items work together?*
>
> ---
>
> The creation of scales provides researchers with a convenient method to combine a number of variables into one overall measure that can reflect a rather abstract concept. Because scales often combine very different measures, it is important to remember that each individual measure must logically relate to the overall concept to be represented. Although such a combination of measures might be perfectly logical to you, others might disagree or at least have questions about the measures included in your scale.
>
> In order for others to be able to evaluate your scale and its components, you must therefore not only list all measures that have been incorporated into your scale, but also explain how these measures were conceptualized and operationalized. This also will allow other scholars to replicate your scale for their own research.

In this formula, the quantity $\sum n(e)$ represents the total number of "mistakes" in the scale, and the quantity $i(N)$ represents the total number of possible mistakes if *no* items or respondents fit the scale. The fraction

$$\frac{\sum n(e)}{i(N)}$$

thus tells us what proportion of all possible mistakes have in fact been made. By subtracting this proportion of error from one, we ascertain the proportion of scale entries that are error free. As a matter of convention, any Guttman scale with a C_R of .90 or higher is accepted as sound, and any scale with a lower C_R is considered suspect and is generally not used for purposes of analysis.

We can see, then, that for items that meet the criterion of inherent ordering by degree of difficulty, Guttman scaling is a potent technique by which we may bring together a number of indicators into a single summary value that meaningfully represents a more general characteristic of a respondent.

THURSTONE SCALING

Yet another technique for creating summary measures, though one intended to solve a rather different problem, is the *Thurstone equal-appearing interval scale.* You will recall from our earlier discussion that in phrasing questions to measure such variables as social class, the researcher may choose to measure respondents' characteristics according to some externally imposed criterion, such as income or occupational prestige, or may alternatively permit respondents to apply their own standards of judgment, as by asking them what social class they *identify* with. The first approach enhances the comparability of data from case to case; the second may yield less comparable but more meaningful data. **Thurstone scaling** is a procedure for pursuing the second strategy (but with improved comparability) by letting a few members of the population to be studied actually participate in designing the scales that will be used to measure the characteristics of the population itself. By providing for the internal definition of the meanings of indicators, the Thurstone technique enhances the validity of a scale. By eliminating from consideration all but the most widely agreed-upon scale items, we enhance the reliability of the scale as well. The technique is rather complicated, but once we have these goals clearly in mind, it is not difficult to understand.

In constructing a Thurstone scale, the researcher first gathers a large number of statements, perhaps as many as one hundred, that reflect a variety of attitudes about some object. A number of "judges" is then selected at random from the population to be studied. These are simply individuals on whom the list of statements will be tried out. The judges usually number at least fifty, and they may include as many as several hundred persons when resources permit. Each judge is presented with an 11-point scale—ranging from *favorable* (11) to *neutral* (6) to *unfavorable* (1)—and with a stack of cards on each of which is printed one of the statements. The judge is asked to examine each statement as it relates to the object in question and to place each card in one of eleven piles corresponding to his or her evaluation. Thus, those statements a judge regards as most favorable toward some object, such as college students, may be placed in pile 11, those slightly less favorable in pile 10, and so forth. In this manner, the researcher obtains every judge's understanding of the evaluative meaning of each statement.

At this point, each statement is assigned a scale score indicating its relative position on the favorable–unfavorable continuum, with higher scores going to those statements that are seen as more favorable. Many researchers assign these scores by calculating a mean, that is, by summing all of the individual scores for each item and dividing by the number of judges. A more appropriate procedure is to find the median value assigned to each statement (see Chapter 16) and to treat this as the scale score. Those items that are assigned widely divergent scores by different judges (for example, those that are spread over five or six categories) are eliminated at this point. From the remaining list, some fifteen to twenty final items are selected for inclusion in the questionnaire. The items should be those on which the judges most closely agree, and they should collectively cover the full spectrum of evaluations. Figure 9.3 illustrates a few typical statements that might be included in a Thurstone scale of attitudes toward college students.

When these final items reach the interview stage, respondents in the study sample are asked either which of the statements they agree with or, alternatively, which two or three statements are closest to their own view of the object in question, in this case, college students. The median value of the items so designated by each individual is then determined and is assigned as that respondent's scale score, the summary of his or her views toward the object. When the responses of a given individual are scattered widely over several noncontiguous items, the researcher generally concludes either that the individual has no attitude toward the object in question or that his or her attitude is organized differently from the structure assumed by the scale. In such cases, no scale score is assigned. But when, as is much more often the case, the responses do cluster tightly in one portion of the continuum, the researcher can have reasonable confidence in the validity and reliability of the measure. This is due in no small part to the role of the judges in designing the research instrument.

Please consider each of the following statements and indicate which ones you *agree* with:

1. It may not be widely known, but far more college students have volunteered for the military services than one would expect on the basis of their percentage in the population as a whole.
2. Some college students are definitely much superior in intelligence to other people in this community.
3. Whatever their faults, college students contribute a great deal to the quality of life in this community.
4. There is little truth in the image of college students in this community as being less ambitious or hard-working on the average than many other groups.
5. Some college students are clean and some are dirty, but the average college student does not differ in any way in his personal habits from the average person.
6. When you come right down to it, college students are just like anybody else in this community; they have their good points and they have their bad points.
7. While there are no doubt a few exceptions, in general college students tend to be especially clannish and to stick together.
8. While every group has a right to get ahead, college students are a little apt to disregard the rights and possessions of other people.
9. College students sometimes try to enter stores, hotels, and restaurants where they are just not welcome.
10. Many people in this community would accept college students more easily if there were less drunkenness, self-righteousness, and public demonstrations of sexual looseness and immorality among them.
11. It is a fairly well-established fact that college students have a less pleasant body odor than other people in this community.

FIGURE 9.3 Typical Thurstone scale items.

Source: Adapted from a scale reported by H. Schuman and J. Harding (1964) in "Prejudice and the Norm of Rationality," *Sociometry,* 27(September): 353–371.

Note: These statements have been ordered from most favorable through neutral to most unfavorable for purposes of illustration. In practice, their order should be assigned randomly to obscure any systematic relationships. Scale values should not be shown on the questionnaire.

THE SEMANTIC DIFFERENTIAL

The fourth and final scaling procedure we shall discuss is termed the **semantic differential**. This procedure, which is quite different in structure and purpose from those already discussed, relies on a series of adjective pairs to bring out the meaning a given individual attaches to a particular concept. A typical series of these adjective pairs is illustrated in Figure 9.4. Respondents are presented with such a list, usually on a separate card, and are asked to rate a particular object, again in the illustration using college students, on a 7-point scale from one adjective to the other. Measurement of this type allows for variation in both the intensity and the direction of the attitude being measured, with neutrality being represented by the midpoint on the scale. The ordering of adjectives in each pair is determined randomly to prevent response set bias.

Although some researchers do break such scales into various underlying dimensions and sum the responses within each, most agree that semantic differential scales do not readily yield scale scores in the same way as the other techniques we have discussed. Rather, semantic differential scales are useful primarily either for purposes of comparison

Listed below are several pairs of words that could be used to describe college students. Between the words in each pair are several blanks. Please put an X on the blank for each pair that best describes how you feel about college students.

In general, college students are:

1. Boring	— — — — — — —	Interesting
2. Clean	— — — — — — —	Dirty
3. Emotional	— — — — — — —	Rational
4. Gentle	— — — — — — —	Violent
5. Good	— — — — — — —	Bad
6. Dishonest	— — — — — — —	Honest
7. Serious	— — — — — — —	Humorous
8. Idealistic	— — — — — — —	Realistic
9. Noisy	— — — — — — —	Quiet
10. Pleasant	— — — — — — —	Unpleasant
11. Rich	— — — — — — —	Poor
12. Pleasing	— — — — — — —	Annoying
13. Sincere	— — — — — — —	Insincere
14. Superficial	— — — — — — —	Profound
15. Valuable	— — — — — — —	Worthless

FIGURE 9.4   Typical semantic differential items.

RESEARCH EXERCISE

Playing with Scales

Identify twenty survey items that might be considered indicators of the concept "trust in government." Before you start selecting the indicators, make sure you have clearly defined what you mean by trust (whose trust, what kind of trust, etc.) and government (city, local, national, etc.).

1. Construct both a Thurstone scale and a Likert scale from these twenty items.
2. Administer the survey items to ten friends or classmates and assign each a score on both the Thurstone and the Likert scales.
3. Compare the results with others in your class.
   When carrying out the exercise, also ask respondents for information on their actual behavior that can be used to check the validity of the scale scores you obtain as indicators of the concept. (For example, do people who score high on trust act as we would expect trusting people to behave—whereas those who score low on trust exhibit what we would regard as nontrusting behavior?)
4. Now compare the scale scores with the behavioral reports and write up your findings by comparing the Thurstone and Likert scales for validity.

from object to object (are ostensibly similar objects viewed by respondents in similar terms?) or for the development of scales measuring more general concepts (for example, what types of actions or views are regarded as either liberal or conservative?). In effect, then, the semantic differential serves a somewhat different and more fundamental purpose in the research process—that of helping to construct and evaluate definitions—than do the Likert, Guttman, and Thurstone techniques.

Conclusion

Researchers often use scales to assess "unmeasurable" constructs such as political participation or social power. Since most complex constructs cannot be measured with a single indicator, one simple solution is to combine a number of related indicators into a single measure that is assumed to represent a broader construct. Thus, scales allow the creation of a single indicator for potentially complex concepts that are based on a large number of individual, but related, measures. The scales used most frequently in political science research are Likert scales and semantic differential scales.

Other, but less frequently employed scaling techniques are Guttman and Thurstone scales.

There are, we should note, several other scaling techniques that one might employ in survey research. Those we have discussed are the most common and, within the limits noted, among the most useful. Together they should suggest the types of options available, and the criteria one must consider, when it becomes necessary to develop multiple but narrow measures of broad, underlying concepts.

Key Terms

scaling *181*
scale *181*
scale score *181*
Likert scaling *183*

Cronbach's alpha *184*
Kuder-Richardson 20 (KR20) *184*
Guttman scaling *184*

Thurstone scaling *188*
semantic differential *190*

Research Examples

Good examples of scale construction can be found in explorations of commonly used social or political concepts. Lala et al. (2009), for example, developed a scale for "country image," which contains seven dimensions: economic conditions, conflict, political structure, vocational training, work culture, environment, and labor. Bakke et al. (2009), on the other hand, mapped dimensions of "social distance" among 4,000 survey respondents in Bosnia-Herzegovina and the North Caucasus region of Russia but do not find significant attitudinal cleavages among members of

different ethnic groups. Raab et al. (2008) propose a multidimensional measure of "globalization," including economic, technological, cultural, and political dimensions of global change.

Methodological Readings

For a comprehensive survey and discussion of many specific scales found in the literature of social science, see *Measures of Political Attitudes* (Robinson et al. 1999) and *Measures of Personality and Social Psychological Attitudes* (Robinson et al.

1991). Application-oriented introductions to scaling are provided by *Scale Development: Theory and Applications* (DeVellis 2003) and *Scaling Procedures: Issues and Applications* (Netemeyer et al. 2003). In the chapter titled "Undimensional Scaling" in *Quantitative Applications in the Social Sciences*, McIver and Carmines (1981) provide succinct overviews of Likert, Guttman, and Thurstone scaling at a slightly more sophisticated level than that presented here.

References

Bakke, Kristin M., Xun Cao, John O'Loughlin, and Michael D. Ward. 2009. "Social Distance in Bosnia-Herzegovina and the North Caucasus Region of Russia: Inter and Intra-Ethnic Attitudes and Identities." *Nations & Nationalism* 15(April): 227–253.

DeVellis, Robert F. 2003. *Scale Development: Theory and Applications*, 2nd ed. Thousand Oaks, CA: Sage.

Lala, Vishal, Anthony T. Allred, and Goutam Chakraborty. 2009. "A Multidimensional Scale for Measuring Country Image." *Journal of International Consumer Marketing* 21(January): 51–66.

McIver, John P., and Edward G. Carmines. 1981. *Quantitative Applications in the Social Sciences*. Beverly Hills, CA: Sage.

Netemeyer, Richard G., William O. Bearden, and Subhash Shama. 2003. *Scaling Procedures: Issues and Applications*. Thousand Oaks, CA: Sage.

Raab, Marcel, Michael Ruland, Benno Schönberger, Hans-Peter Blossfeld, Dirk Hofäcker, Sandra Buchholz, and Paul Schmelzer. 2008. "Global Index: A Sociological Approach to Globalization Measurement." *International Sociology* 23(4): 596–631.

Robinson, John P., Phillip R. Shaver, and Lawrence S. Wrightsman, eds. 1991. *Measures of Personality and Social Psychological Attitudes*. San Diego, CA: Academic Press.

Robinson, John P., Phillip R. Shaver, and Lawrence S. Wrightsman, eds. 1999. *Measures of Political Attitudes*. San Diego, CA: Academic Press.

CHAPTER 10

Content Analysis: Researching Textual Material

In this chapter you will learn:

- The uses of content analysis.
- The research process for content analysis.

Every day you evaluate communications. You analyze what others say, you critique what you read online, or you may complain that a new song you downloaded is too long or repetitive. You have analyzed the content of communications since you before you learned to talk. Early in school, you learned that your teachers would test you on the structure of your writing, and perhaps even speaking, teaching you that *how* you say things is as important as what you say. Since you have so much experience in evaluating communication and source material may be found all around you, these same techniques may be used to generate your own data sets—rapidly and at little cost.

Political scientists may learn a great deal about individuals, groups, institutions, or even nations through a careful examination of their communications. How much do campaign advertising and election year news reports tell us about candidates' attitudes and how close observers perceive them? Do the internal memoranda of a large corporation reveal a systematic plan on the part of management to bribe representatives of foreign governments with whom they wish to deal? What does the *Congressional Record* tell us about the relative influence or importance of each U.S. senator? Do diplomatic communiqués between the United States and Russia reflect the public perception of a lack of conflict between these two nations?

Questions concerning the content of communication may best be answered by a direct examination of the items of the source material. In general, these items fall into one of three classes, depending upon the source and intended audience of the material: (1) those that are internally generated and internally directed by the individual, organization, or government we are studying (such communications as corporate memoranda, which represent or reflect the decision-making process itself); (2) those that are internally generated and externally directed (such publications as the *Congressional Record*, which are purposefully molded to create a particular image for the source among outsiders and which may reflect or obscure the process and outcome of decision making); and (3) those that are externally generated and externally directed (such as campaign news stories that are read by potential voters). Each class of communication may be different in purpose or effect, as well as in accessibility and usefulness for research, but each provides potential opportunities to further our understanding of political behavior.

Defining Content Analysis

In each instance, the most appropriate technique for pursuing these opportunities is **content analysis**—the systematic counting, assessing, and interpreting of the form and substance of communication. Content analysis provides us with a method—really a set of methods—by which we may summarize fairly rigorously certain direct physical evidence of the behaviors of, and the relationships between, various types of political actors.

In this chapter we shall discuss when it is appropriate to use content analysis, how the technique is applied, and how the results of content analysis should be interpreted, as well as certain limits of content analytic procedures.

PREPARING TO USE CONTENT ANALYSIS

Content analysis may be used to answer research questions whenever there is a physical record of communications by, to, within, or among the political actors that interest us, as long as the researcher has access to that record. Examples of such a record include books, pamphlets, magazines, newspapers, CDs, audiotape, videotape or DVD recordings, photographs, Web pages, transcripts of meetings or proceedings, government documents, memoranda, films, diplomatic communiqués and instructions, political posters and cartoons, political advertising, speeches, and even letters and diaries. Some of these records may be extremely detailed and precise (as is a verbatim transcript of a congressional hearing), whereas others are much less so (for example, the agenda for the same hearing). Many will have been created independently of the research process (as are newspaper articles by or about the person or group we wish to study), whereas others must be created by the researchers themselves (for example, videotapes of television news programs). But all sources of data for content analysis will have in common one principal characteristic: the existence of a physical record of communication. Whenever such a record exists or can be created, content analysis may serve as an appropriate research method.

Choosing a Population

The first step in preparing to undertake a content analysis is to define the population of communications we want to study. Here we have a number of options. Which is the best will be determined by our particular research question. For example, if we are interested in studying the development of political themes in post–September 11th American novels, we might define our population as all novels (the type of communication) written by Americans (the type of communicator) and published in the United States (the location of communication) between January 1, 2002, and December 31, 2009 (the time period of communication). If we wish to study newspaper coverage of a congressional campaign conducted in the shadow of a presidential campaign, we might define our population as all campaign-related newspaper articles (the type of communication) of 2 column inches or more in length (the size of the communication) published in daily newspapers (the frequency of communication) that are home delivered (the distribution of the communication) in the Sixth, Seventh, and Eighth Congressional Districts of Ohio (the location of the communication) between September 1 and the first Tuesday after the first Monday in November of the election year (the time period of communication). Or, similarly, if we want to study the level of tension between the leaders of the United States and those of Iran, we might define our population as all diplomatic messages (the type of communication) passed between the governments of the United States and Iran (the parties to the communication) during a given time period.

In each instance, we define the population of messages to be studied by establishing sets of criteria to be met by each item. In the examples, these criteria include the type of communication (novels, newspaper articles, or diplomatic notes); the type of communicator; the parties to the communication (the sender or the receiver or both); and the location, frequency, minimum size or length, distribution, and time period of the communication. Although other criteria may be used on occasion, some or all of those listed here will be found in most studies that employ content analysis. The first task in preparing for a content analysis is to choose those criteria that relate most directly to the research question at hand.

Once the population is defined, we are faced with the problem of deciding which particular cases we shall examine in detail. Because the cases to be analyzed are often limited in number and relatively accessible, and because content analysis is generally less expensive per case than other methods (most notably survey research), we are sometimes able to examine every case in a given population—to conduct a census of the material. Indeed, the opportunities it offers for the examination of large numbers of cases is one of the major attractions of content analysis as a research technique. More often than not, however, even content analysis must be based on a more limited sample drawn from the larger population. Since documents, newspaper articles, and the like are frequently indexed or otherwise listed in a central location and since such indexes or lists may easily be created by the researcher, the most common sampling procedures used in content analytic studies are the simple random and systematic random techniques. Even when sampling is required, however, the accessibility and relatively low cost of researching messages of various types come into play, and the sample sizes drawn for content analysis may be substantially larger than those employed in other types of research. The result, of course, is a reduction in sampling error and an increased level of confidence in generalizing from our results.

Choosing a Unit of Analysis

Finally, in preparing to undertake a content analysis, we must decide on our unit of measure, or, as it is more commonly termed, our *unit of analysis*. The **unit of analysis** for content analysis is simply the particular element or characteristic of a given communication that we shall examine, count, or assess. The most basic element of a communication, for example, is the *word*, and it may be employed in a fairly straightforward manner. For example, in speeches delivered to the United Nations between 1975 and 2007, which country was most conciliatory on questions of eliminating conflict in the Middle East: Israel, Egypt, Syria, or Saudi Arabia? We might simply examine the record of all such speeches and count references to such words as *peace, brotherhood,* and *compromise*. In each instance, we identify certain important words and count the frequency with which they appear.

Even in so simple a procedure, however, we must take care to avoid at least two pitfalls. First, we must remember that nonstandardized measures can lead to biased results. If over the years in question, the Israelis have uttered a total of 100,000 words, including 50 salient references (to the words we wish to count), and the Egyptians have uttered some 200,000 words, including 100 salient references, we might reach either of two conclusions from a study of these speeches, depending on whether or not we have chosen to standardize our indicator. If we simply count salient references, we will conclude that the Egyptians have been twice as concerned as the Israelis with procuring a settlement. If, however, our measure is standardized to obtain the *proportion of* all words that are in fact salient (for example, salient references *per 1,000 words*), we will conclude that both sides have shared an equal concern about settling their differences. Which approach is better? This is a fundamental problem in operationalizing variables, and the answer is best determined by looking closely at how we have conceptualized the research question initially. The point here is that the use of even such a seemingly concrete indicator as *number of salient words spoken* can entail some ambiguity. The researcher must recognize and deal with that ambiguity, because the decisions made (or overlooked) can have a substantial impact upon the conclusions one draws.

A second potential pitfall in a reliance upon raw word counts arises because any word may have different meanings, depending upon how it is used: "We seek peace, *but . . .*"; "The Arab brotherhood *can never allow . . .*"; "There will be *no* compromise." In the absence of any sort of control, references such as these to peace, brotherhood, and compromise will be included as positive references and will, at the very least, inflate our assessment of the interest on the part of one or both sides in reaching an accommodation. If such usages are sufficiently common, they may well mislead us altogether. For this reason, if we choose to count words, we should in most instances choose to count them in context.

To assess word meanings, we may either (1) read each passage and interpret it, or (2) broaden the unit of analysis. First, we may use *judges* or **coders**—people who are part of the research team or are employed by it—to read each salient reference *in context* and to judge that context as positive, neutral, or negative. This contextual judgment can then be used to enrich our data by allowing us to count and interrelate not only all references to the words we are focusing on but also the proportions of positive and negative references. Typically, more than one coder reads each reference, and a relatively high level of agreement among coders should be required before a final determination is reached. (We say more on this point later in this chapter.) Along with introducing additional subjectivity, using interpretive coders may increase the cost of our analysis, and require additional training time.

A second unit of analysis, the *theme*, may also partially address the problem of interpreting individual words in context. A theme is a particular combination of words or ideas, such as a phrase, a sentence, or even a paragraph. In effect, when counting themes, we search for recurring subjects in a text, as, for example, the expressions *cold war, refugee problem, national health insurance*, or *faith-based politics*. The procedure is similar to that for counting words and represents an improvement to the extent that themes incorporate the modifiers (adverbs, adjectives) and explanatory text that both accompany usage of a particular word and help to establish its meaning.

Unfortunately, although analysis at the thematic level makes clear the context in which individual words are used, it does so at the cost of much added complexity. This is true in that the same theme may be referenced in very different ways and by very different sets of words. Sometimes these references may be very subtle, displaying few or none of the overt characteristics we are looking for. References to immigration issues, for example, may be veiled in conciliatory words about political asylum, whereas those applied to religion in politics may be cloaked in nationalistic rhetoric. Do such words and rhetoric constitute salient references? Is the theme present, or is it not? These questions do not have simple answers. On the contrary, they generally require us to arrive at some clearly stated but potentially limiting definitions and to develop a series of highly formalized decision-making rules (for example, allowing only overt references that contain one or more words or phrases from a given list to be counted), which may make our findings more reliable but at the same time less meaningful.

A third unit of analysis commonly used in content analysis research is the *item*—the communication itself taken as a whole. What proportion of *books* published in the United States in 1935 advocated socialism? Which presidential candidate in 2008 was the subject of the greatest number of favorable newspaper *editorials*? How did *letters* written by Richard Nixon after his resignation from office differ from those written earlier? In each instance, we treat the item of communication as a unit and examine its *overall* character-istics. Does it or does it not deal with a particular issue? Does it or does it not reflect a cer-tain set of values or preferences? Such questions lose some of the subtlety of judgment required by lesser units of analysis and they necessitate the making of summary evalua-tions. For precisely these reasons, however, their analysis is generally more manageable than is that of words or themes, in a sense making fewer demands of the researcher. This is true because variables may be operationalized at a less specific level, one on which events (that is, occurrences of a salient reference) are often more apparent and on which measurement is often more reliable.

An Example

In recent years, item-based studies of the use of words and themes have become much easier to perform due to the availability of online, searchable databases such as *LexisNexis*, which was introduced in Chapter 3. Suppose, for example, we wanted to know how often Senator Obama's name was associated with its campaign themes (e.g., change or hope) in the news during the 2008 presidential campaign versus how frequently press coverage mentioned Senator McCain's campaign foci (e.g., experience or ear-marks). First focusing on coverage of Obama in *The New York Times* (or any of a large number of other newspapers, magazines, newswires, or broadcast transcripts), we could request a full-text search from *LexisNexis* to count all of the articles in which the words *Obama* and *change* or *hope* appeared for each given month of the period under review. Depending on the interface one uses for access, once you set the appropriate "Source" (e.g., which publications or sites to search), and the date range noted above, the *LexisNexis* Power Search instruction might look something like this:

(((Barack Obama) OR (Senator Obama)) w/10 ((change) OR (hope)))

This string of terms would identify any article published between January and November 2008 in which Mr. Obama's name appeared *and* one of the Obama campaign themes was mentioned *within ten words in either direction* from the word *change* or *hope*. Then we could perform a similar search for Mr. McCain and his campaign taglines, and use the re-sults to compare which presidential candidate more effectively placed his message in the press. Additionally, you might want to conduct additional searches to test (1) whether either candidate was referred to by his first name, last name, or U.S. Senate title when his theme was mentioned; (2) if candidate titles varied during or after the primary campaign; or (3) numerous other hypotheses related to the framing of each candidate's campaign in the press.

The results of item analysis may be at least as meaningful as those of component analysis in many instances. Is it more important that the Egyptians have made, say, seven conciliatory references in a given speech at the United Nations, or simply that they have made a conciliatory speech? Is it more important that the United States has sent a note to Iraq with four overt references to military intervention, three veiled references to the failure to disarm, and two sharply critical references to the possible presence of weapons of mass destruction, or that the United States has issued a note that can be characterized as contentious in tone? In content analysis we always risk losing sight of the forest for the trees or, more precisely, of the overall significance of a communication for its component parts. Thus, we must use great care in selecting the unit of analysis. We should choose the unit that best tests our hypothesized relationship(s), given the content we are using.

Computer-Based Content Analysis

Whereas *LexisNexis* provides basic word counts for text within its own database, those who are interested in analyzing text from other sources (for example, transcripts of speeches, e-mail messages, or Web pages) have to use more specific software packages written for content analysis of digital documents. Among some of the better-known programs for sale are, for example, *Concordance* (www.concordancesoftware.co.uk), *Diction 5.0* (www.dictionsoftware.com), and *WordStat* (www.provalisresearch.com/wordstat/wordstat.html). Other programs are free for academic use; these include the popular *General Inquirer* (www.wjh.harvard.edu/~inquirer).

All of these content analysis programs provide basic text analysis functions such as *word frequency counts* and *category frequency counts*. **Word frequency counts** provide a list of all the words that occur in a text and the number of times they occur. In most of these programs, text can be split into subparts and then compared either visually or statistically to see if there are significantly more mentions of particular words in one part or the other. Another advantage of these software packages is that they often make use of synonym lists in order to merge word counts. Thus, instead of counting all words in a

PRACTICAL RESEARCH ETHICS
No people, no ethical concerns?

Although humans are not being directly studied in content analysis, a human product is being examined. This indirect source of information limits explanations from those producing the communications, at least at the time they were recorded, making accuracy a paramount concern.

You, the researcher, must ensure that the communications are being fairly represented by the research design, coding, data analysis, and interpretation. Since all humans have biases, you should utilize a manifest and transparent coding process. The veracity of the results is elevated (for you and your readers) by using outside coders who do not know the purpose of the research. The documentation you use to instruct these coders, or the software commands you use, should become part of your research record and be included in your written research report.

given document, the program first removes the grammatical structure and then counts as identical those words that share the same stem. In such a frequency count, for example, "politics" and "political" would be counted as the same word. In **category frequency counts**, on the other hand, a set of words or phrases are first grouped into categories, then the program shows how many times each category occurs in the document. For example, the category "election" might consist of the words *voting, vote, voter, election, electorate, choice, participation, ballot, poll,* and *survey,* which would then be counted as part of one category only. Thus, category counts allow a slightly more sophisticated text analysis, because users can define more specific or complex models of content.

Some of the programs also allow the user to generate so-called concordances (or KWIC, as in "key word in context"), which basically analyze the context in which certain keywords appear in the text. For example, a concordance analysis of the key word *liberal* might provide some important insights about how often this term has been used to describe either a politician or a policy. Concordances also are useful for finding lists of words that co-occur reliably in a particular text that then can be combined and used in the category frequency counts described above.

The main advantage of such computer-based content analyses is the fact that as long as the unit of content is short, simple, and well-defined (such as words or small group of words), it is relatively easy to analyze a lot of information. Thus, as long as the text is available in digital form, even documents spanning many thousands of text pages can be analyzed in only seconds. In addition, since the drudgery of content analysis is done by the computer, there is no need to train and employ human coders.

A disadvantage of software-aided content analysis is that computers cannot easily code and analyze latent content, such as meaning or bias. An analysis of whether President Barack Obama has been portrayed by *The Washington Post* in a more positive or negative light, for example, still requires the input of the researchers (defining the codes for "favorable" and "unfavorable") and human coders (evaluating the text as favorable or unfavorable).

UNDERTAKING A SUBSTANTIVE CONTENT ANALYSIS

Once we have settled upon a population, a suitable sample, and an appropriate unit of analysis, we need to choose whether we will study the substance of the communication or its structure—or both. Our theory and hypotheses will guide whether we need to offer primary attention to the meanings of the words or focus on the structure and quantity of a given type of content. The next section delves into structural concerns, while here we discuss the techniques for substantive analysis. **Substantive content analysis** is based on a study of words, themes, and items that focuses on the *substantive content* of a given communication. Thus, in preparing to analyze these elements, we must anticipate their substance and define each possible observation in accordance with our expectations.

Creating a Dictionary

What this means, in effect, is that as the first step in undertaking a content analysis of this type, we must create a sort of dictionary in which we define each and every observation we might make according to the particular category it fits. Suppose, for example, we are interested in studying all of the sixth-grade schoolbooks used in Havana, Cuba, last year and in identifying in them all references to Americans and the United States. Before proceeding with such an analysis, we must define just what constitutes a salient reference. Do we look only for the words *American* and *United States?* In doing so, we may miss a great many salient references using such derogatory terms as *Yankee aggressors, northern imperialists, gringos, invading forces at Guantanamo,* and *the outlaw regime in Washington.*

A parallel but more difficult problem arises when the *absence* of a word or phrase has substantive meaning and must be captured. For example, in a twelfth-grade civics text published in 2006 for use in Palestinian schools, the maps either failed to label Israel, or portrayed Palestinian territory as covering the entire area (Lackner 2007). These omissions are meaningful and significant, and a content analysis scheme for studying such books must capture them.

The point is that we must anticipate not only the references likely to be encountered but also the contextual elements of their use, and we must devise a thorough and systematic set of decision rules for judging each usage as it occurs. This problem is usually resolved by a combination of pretesting the population of communications to be analyzed (that is, reading through a selection of items to identify the types of salient references most likely to be encountered in a subsequent and more thorough analysis) and developing informed judgments about the contexts and uses of terms. Here, as in the later formal analysis, the observations of several researchers are preferred over those of one.

A more difficult problem arises when we must assign *evaluations* to salient references—when we must decide whether a particular reference is good or bad, favorable or unfavorable, pro or anti, and so forth—and when a series of such references must be ranked according to their intensity (which is most favorable, which is next most favorable, etc.). Here we are concerned with developing and applying indicators that are sufficiently refined to tell us not only how the political actor feels but also how strongly the actor feels that way. A situation of this type is illustrated in Figure 10.1. The figure summarizes a number of ways in which a newspaper might endorse a candidate. If our goal is to determine which of several newspapers most strongly supports that candidate, then our immediate task is to decide how to rank these statements according to the intensity of support that each reflects.

Best of a bad lot	Best available
Better than the opponent	Our first choice
Urge you to vote for	Finest candidate in a crowded field
Everything the people of this state could ask for	Woman (Man) of the hour
An outstanding leader	Promising
One of the nation's best	Lesser of two evils
Best the selection process could produce	Our perennial favorite
Acceptable	Most acceptable
Recommend with reservations	Recommend without reservations
Wholeheartedly endorse	Warmly recommend
Offer our support	Enthusiastically commend to your attention

FIGURE 10.1 Sample phrases in newspaper editorials endorsing a candidate (random order).

Pair-Comparison

Several techniques are available to assist us in making these decisions. One of the most prominent of these ranking techniques is **pair-comparison scaling**. Like the Thurstone scaling technique described in Chapter 9, it relies upon the decision of a group of judges about the meaning or intensity of a term, though here the judges may be drawn from the issuers of the communication, the receivers of the communication, a group of scholars familiar with the general subject area under study, the general population, or the researchers themselves.

The goal of pair-comparison scaling is the same as Thurstone scaling, but the procedure itself is rather different. Each item to be evaluated by the judges is paired with *every* other item, in a series of comparisons, and each judge is asked to decide which word or phrase in each pair is the stronger or more intense. Thus, if we have five statements for comparison, each judge compares item 1 against items 2, 3, 4, and 5; item 2 against items 3, 4, and 5; and so forth—in each instance designating one or the other as more intense. By counting the number of times each statement is so designated by each judge, by totaling these numbers for each item for all judges, and by dividing by the number of judges (that is, by calculating the average score the judges as a group have assigned to a particular statement), we are able to arrive at a quantitative ranking of the intensity of each item. The higher its mean score, the stronger the judges consider a statement.

One of the problems associated with the pair-comparison procedure is the fact that it relies entirely on the decisions of judges whose criteria for judgment may or may not be appropriate or consistent. The standards for expertise in such undertakings are not always clear, or at least are not always clearly stated, and as a consequence, the judgments themselves are open to question. Indeed, it is not uncommon for a single judge to assign different scores to the same statement in a series of identical tests. Because we are sampling content and not humans here, there is neither a clear reference population, as there is in Thurstone scaling, nor a set of underlying parameters to be approximated. The selections made by judges are necessarily arbitrary. Consequently, the reliability of results derived by depending upon such judges may be minimal.

UNDERTAKING A STRUCTURAL CONTENT ANALYSIS

In addition to, or in lieu of, words, themes, or other elements that denote the substantive content of a communication, several units of analysis are available that allow **structural content analysis**. Here we are less concerned with *what* is said than with *how* it is said, and while we must retain a concern with the subject matter, we measure something else.

We may be concerned, for example, with the amount of space or time devoted to a given subject in a particular source. How many words or column inches of newspaper coverage have been accorded each candidate in a particular election campaign? How many articles or pages in political science journals published in the United States are devoted each year to an analysis of governments and politics in Africa? Has the number changed, or has it remained constant over the past three decades?

Alternatively, we might be concerned with other, and perhaps more subtle, aspects of the communication format. Is a particular news item accompanied by a photograph or illustration of some sort? Those with an illustration have been found to attract more attention

ID Number		Article type	Publication Date	Candidate	Newspaper	Preference	Prominence	Graphics	Headline	Content	Total	Column	Inches	Candidate	Column	Inches

FIGURE 10.2 Typical coding sheet for structural content analysis.

from readers than those that do not. How large a headline accompanies a news item? Does coverage of a particular subject receive front-page prominence, or is it buried among the truss ads? In answering questions like these, we are less concerned with subtleties of meaning than with styles of presentation. We watch for the presence or absence, the prominence, and the extent of treatment of general themes rather than for substantive nuance. The result in many cases is an analysis whose measurements are much more reliable than those employed in a more substance-oriented study (since there is less ambiguity built into the indicators), but one whose lessons may, as a direct consequence, be less rich.

Figure 10.2 illustrates a typical coding sheet for recording data from a structural analysis of content. Drawn from a study of newspaper coverage of congressional elections (Manheim 1974), the unit of analysis for this particular study was the *candidate insertion*, which was defined as any newspaper item that mentioned by name or implication any candidate for Congress in the district in which the newspaper was distributed. Thus, each row on the coding sheet summarizes the characteristics of a single candidate insertion. After each item was assigned a unique identification number, it was classified according to type (news story, feature article, editorial, letter to the editor), the date of publication, the candidate it referred to, the newspaper in which it appeared, the general preferences expressed in the item (if any), its prominence of placement (front page, inside page), the presence or absence of accompanying photographs or drawings, reference to the candidate in the headline of the item, the primary content of the item (news of a campaign event, content of a speech, endorsement), the overall size of the insertion, and the proportion of the insertion actually relating to the candidate in question.

Structural versus Substantive Content Analysis

Identifying the frequency of occurrence of a name or other item requires only a general concern with the actual substance of each insertion rather than the highly detailed and specific judgment necessary in the substantive approach discussed earlier. As a result, structural content analysis is usually easier to design and carry out, and therefore less expensive and often more reliable, than is substantive content analysis. And though its results may be less satisfying in that they provide us with what amounts to a sketch of a communication rather than a finished portrait, those results often prove entirely adequate in answering a particular research question.

Hands-On Content Analysis

1. The instructor selects a current news topic (e.g., economy, terrorism, election campaign, trade, energy policy, etc.).
2. The class is divided into groups of four or five students. Each group needs to have a computer with an Internet connection.
3. Each group of students locates three different news articles from a single news outlet from the past week.
4. Working together, the group identifies several facets of this topic's news coverage that might likely be incorporated into a coding sheet:
    a. General topic: _____
    b. Specific issue: _____
    c. Dates of articles: _____, _____, _____
    d. Length of articles (word count): _____, _____, _____
    e. Common themes shared by the articles:
        i. _____
        ii. _____
        iii. _____
    f. Information sources (named or implied):
        i. Article 1: _____
        ii. Article 2: _____
        iii. Article 3: _____
    g. Article tone (e.g., critical of government, supporting source, etc.):
        i. Article 1: _____
        ii. Article 2: _____
        iii. Article 3: _____
5. Describe advantages and/or disadvantages of generalizing from this news source: _____
6. Name one other type of data that could be used to supplement this content analysis: _____

SPECIAL PROBLEMS IN THE USE OF CONTENT ANALYSIS

Although content analysis is a relatively inexpensive technique that draws on a relatively accessible database, and although there are few special ethical dilemmas that are likely to be encountered in undertaking it (unless we are analyzing confidential or classified communications), we must still be careful to avoid several potential difficulties when using this method.

Biased Content

We must be aware that communications are issued, and may be specifically designed, for a purpose, whether it be description, persuasion, exhortation, direction, self-protection, or even obfuscation. In analyzing such communications, therefore, we must attempt to interpret their content in the context of their apparent purpose. For example, it is common to find in the Chinese press statements of the type, "*All of the Chinese people believe* that membership in the World Trade Organization is a major step forward in the progress toward social revolution." Taken at face value, such statements are demonstrably false, since not every one of many millions of people would be aware of, let alone agree upon the value of, any single policy. From this perspective, we might be inclined to view these statements as the most blatant form of propaganda. We have learned from studying the Chinese press, however, that statements of this type are not printed for purposes of external propaganda at all, but rather are intended to suggest to the Chinese people themselves the beliefs that their government wishes them to hold. In other words, the purpose of such statements of consensus is not descriptive, but directive. Knowing this, we may interpret them as useful indicators of the policy interests of the Chinese leaders rather than as meaningless items of propaganda, and we may employ them to some advantage. The purpose of a communication, then, can provide an important context for understanding its content, and we must attempt, when possible, to ferret out this information.

Intended Audience

The distribution that is accorded a particular item of communication can have significant implications for its meaning. A pamphlet that circulates only among Chinese dissidents, a solicitory letter from a candidate or special-interest group that reaches only those people on a particular mailing list, a document that circulates only among a small group of persons—each is an example of a communication with a limited or specialized distribution. Even a newspaper that is generally available may have a limited or specialized clientele. *The New York Times*, for example, has a readership that is generally more affluent and better educated than that of the *New York Daily News*, yet both are readily available to all of the city's newspaper readers. *The Wall Street Journal* has nationwide distribution, but its readership does not extend equally to all socioeconomic classes. Very often, in order to assess properly the significance of a communication, we must know whom it reaches. Whether by judgment (rendered, for example, by knowledgeable experts, as might be the case in studying communication among Chinese dissidents), by inquiry (as when we ask a candidate or group which mailing lists were used), by self-evidence (which we have when a document is accompanied by a routing slip listing, and perhaps initialed by, all who have read it, or when a Web page includes a counter showing the number of visitors), or by reliance on an audience survey (such as the kind usually taken by newspapers to document their circulation claims), we must attempt to measure or to estimate how widely a message has been disseminated and to whom. Having this information enables us to judge the value or the importance of the material we analyze.

Representative Sample

We must try to gauge the degree of our own access to the items at issue. Have we been provided with free choice over the materials to be analyzed? Are those materials available in an unbiased manner (that is, do we have access to *all* of them), or has some external control been imposed by someone other than the researcher? Do we, for instance, have access only to documents that have been declassified, only to Chinese newspapers that are published for and distributed primarily to foreigners, only to records of *formal* meetings of a government commission? The issue here is one of generalizability, and the question is whether the research population itself, not to mention the sample, is truly representative. If it is not, the researcher may, if not exercising care, at the very least be misled and at the worst be manipulated.

The difficulty in overcoming these challenges to a successful content analysis is that the information we require in order to make informed judgments may simply be unavailable. We may not know, and may be unable to ascertain, the purpose of a communication, its distribution, or the degree of access to it that we have been accorded. The dangers here are manifold, and the content analyst must be sensitive to them. We must not allow appearances to cloud our judgment but must maintain a healthy skepticism regarding our data as long as these questions remain unanswered. That is not necessarily to say that we should not undertake content analysis under conditions of uncertainty, but merely that we should not lose sight of the uncertainty itself once the analysis is under way.

Intercoder Reliability

We should say a few words about *intercoder reliability*. With the exception of raw word counts and other content analysis procedures that have been thoroughly computerized (several programs embodying concept dictionaries and search or count procedures have been developed), all content analysis depends on human judgments about communication content. Messages, after all, do not analyze themselves. They are poked and prodded, counted and classified by *Homo sapiens* in the form of the researcher. Therefore individual researchers may differ from one another in their understanding of the content of a given communication. Indeed, only when some degree of consensus can be reached about that meaning can we have real confidence in our measurements. **Intercoder reliability** is the term political scientists use to describe the degree of that consensus. The higher it is, the better. In general, intercoder reliability may be promoted by taking three basic steps:

1. Operationalize all variables carefully and thoroughly. Make sure that all meanings have been clearly stated and as many ambiguities as possible have been eliminated. In effect, this will create *common standards of judgment* that can be used consistently in classifying and measuring content.
2. Use as many observers (coders) as possible. The larger the number of subscribers to the consensus, the more confidence we can have in it. This may, of course, mean more work and considerable duplication of effort (and, if proper training is not provided, it carries a risk of increased measurement error), but the payoff can be substantial. The limiting factor here is usually cost.
3. Maximize the interaction among the observers. Hold common practice sessions and argue out all differences of interpretation so that ultimately the consensus extends not only to the data but also to the real meanings of the operational definitions themselves.

Calculating Reliability

The success of this process can be measured in either of two ways, both of which draw upon statistical concepts that we develop more fully in Chapters 16–18. One approach, used primarily in substantive content analysis, is to have all observers who are working on a given project analyze and code independently (assign their own numerical values to) the same communication, then to calculate a statistic called a correlation coefficient (Pearson's r)

among the codes recorded by each pair of observers. This coefficient (discussed in detail in Chapter 17) measures the degree of correspondence in the judgments of the researchers on whether and how often a particular word or theme is present. The coefficient ranges from −1 to +1, and readings of +.90 or better are usually interpreted as indicating a high degree of intercoder reliability. Unfortunately, the correlation coefficient only measures the degree of directional agreement between the coders; in other words, if one coder's values were always the same amount greater than the others, they would rate an *r* of 1.0.

An alternative measure may be more useful for structural content analysis, in which we are less concerned with the treatment of themes than with their presence or absence, and in which duplicated measurement is less necessary. Here the differences between observers are treated as a variable in their own right, and we ask whether that variable is associated with systematic differences in any other variable we have measured. In other words, we are concerned with the possibility that one or more observers have recorded results consistently differently from the others. If it can be assumed that all cases have been distributed to the observers in an unbiased manner (some effort is generally made to distribute them *randomly*), any systematic differences we observe are more likely to be the result of differences between coders than of underlying differences in the cases that happen to have been assigned to the aberrant observer. The coefficient of intercoder reliability here takes the form $(1 - \eta^2)$, where η^2 is a measure of the variance in each subject variable that is accounted for by differences between coders (Freeman 1965, 120–129). By subtracting this "observer error" from 1, we obtain the proportion of error-free observations. The coefficient is calculated separately for each variable and should exceed +.90 if we are to have confidence in the reliability of our measures.

This brief treatment of intercoder reliability is intended to suggest that the subject is quite complex, and a thorough examination requires more space than is available here. An excellent overview of the most popular methods for measuring intercoder reliability, including computational equations and examples, may be found in Neuendorf (2002, ch. 7).

Conclusion

In sum, content analysis is a widely applicable technique with advantages in cost, sample size, and, often, access to data. Perhaps more than any other technique, however, it demands careful operationalization of all variables and constant monitoring of the process of observation. Its results may be highly informative, but they must be understood in a context that it is often beyond the scope of the content analysis technique itself to describe. For this reason, content analysis is often used to best effect in combination with other data gathering methods (surveys, direct observation) in what are termed *multimethod designs*.

Key Terms

content analysis *195*
unit of analysis *196*
coders *197*
word frequency counts *199*

category frequency counts *200*
substantive content analysis *200*
pair-comparison scaling *202*

structural content analysis *202*
intercoder reliability *206*

Research Examples

Content analysis can only identify the frequency of concepts, not the meaning received by the audience. The best analyses find ways to substantively interpret these concepts' meaning to their readers, listeners, or viewers. In their research to evaluate whether the volume, breadth, or prominence of news stories about a given topic is most closely related to citizens' political knowledge on that issue, Barabas and Jerit (2009) link content analyses with survey data measuring familiarity with the policy area. Analyzing hundreds of ads run in campaigns between black and white candidates, McIlwain and Caliendo (2009) find that racially coded messages commonly occur in these spots, but the type of messages varies depending upon the candidate's race. This study reported intercoder reliability using Cohen's Kappa, based upon a 15 percent sample of the articles evaluated by the three coders.

Methodological Readings

The two most thorough and accessible content analysis texts available today are written by communications professors: Kimberly A. Neuendorf (2002) and Klaus Krippendorff (2004). Neuendorf also offers a Web site that features updated information and an extensive flowchart describing an entire content analysis project (http://academic .csuohio.edu/kneuendorf/content/). Krippendorff's Web site (www.asc.upenn.edu/usr/krippendorff/) includes links to his content analysis work and documents explaining the computations for his reliability measure, *Krippendorff's Alpha*.

References

Barabas, Jason, and Jennifer Jerit. 2009. "Estimating the Causal Effects of Media Coverage on Policy-Specific Knowledge." *American Journal of Political Science* 53(January): 73–89.

Freeman, Linton C. 1965. *Elementary Applied Statistics: For Students of Behavioral Science*. New York: Wiley.

Hoddie, Matthew. 2006. "Minorities in the Official Media: Determinants of State Attention to Ethnic Minorities in the People's Republic of China." *The Harvard International Journal of Press/Politics* 11(Fall): 3–21.

Krippendorff, Klaus. 2004. *Content Analysis: An Introduction to Its Methodology*, 2nd ed. Thousand Oaks, CA: Sage.

Lackner, Chris. 2007. "Palestinian Textbooks Biased: Study: Grade 12 Book Depicts Israeli Conflict as 'Religious Battle,' not Land Dispute." *The Ottawa Citizen* (February 9): A11.

Manheim, Jarol B. 1974. "Urbanization and Differential Press Coverage of the Congressional Campaign." *Journalism Quarterly* 51: 649–653, 669.

McIlwain, Charlton D, and Stephen M. Caliendo. 2009. "Black Messages, White Messages: The Differential Use of Racial Appeals by Black and White Candidates." *Journal of Black Studies* 39(May): 732–743.

Neuendorf, Kimberly A. 2002. *The Content Analysis Guidebook*. Thousand Oaks, CA: Sage.

CHAPTER 11

Aggregate Data: Studying Groups

In this chapter you will learn:

- The distinguishing characteristic of aggregate data.
- To avoid the most common pitfall when analyzing aggregate data.

Undoubtedly you value your personal interactions, and draw insights from learning about your friends' lives. Still, you probably have had the experience of knowing a friend who was from a certain town, state, or country, and of becoming familiar with that area—how people speak, how things are done, and what the families there are like. Then, you meet someone new from the same location. You realize—much to your surprise—the limitations of your specific knowledge about whether the residents typically go to college, or work in white-collar jobs, or even how large their families are. If you had only researched the location using the aggregate data compiled by governments on people in each village, state, or country, you could have saved yourself the disillusionment!

Political scientists use aggregate data to avoid becoming too focused on individuals, and to gain more general knowledge of groups or collections of persons or institutions, such as American voters, South African peasants, Russian bureaucrats, or European parliaments.

Defining Aggregate Data

Sometimes, in order to study these groups, we have to gather information on the individual members of the groups (or a representative sample of them) and combine or *aggregate* that information to obtain information about the group *as a group*. Often, however, there already exists aggregated information about the group. Data on the characteristics of an entire group or aggregate of individuals are referred to as **aggregate data**.

Technically, there are two general categories of aggregate data. The first category—**summative indicators**—includes large sets of measures of group characteristics that are created by combining the behavior of all members of the group. For example, the population of a nation is an aggregate datum derived by adding inhabitants as units. Birth, death, literacy, suicide, and crime *rates* are aggregate data created by adding up the number of particular events (births, deaths, crimes, etc.) in a group and expressing it in a standardized unit such as *per thousand persons in the population*. In each case, the aggregate datum quantifies some *group* characteristic that individual members of the group cannot possess. Individuals may be born or learn to read and write but cannot have a birth or literacy *rate* in the same sense that a nation does. These data are measures of aggregate characteristics. A second general category of aggregate data consists of those measures that quantify group characteristics that are derived not from any combination of individual members' characteristics but from qualities of the group *when acting as a group*. They are often referred to as **syntality indicators**. For example, *form of government* is a system-level variable, and a given nation may have a democratic or a nondemocratic form of government regardless of whether its individual citizens hold democratic or nondemocratic values and attitudes.

When most researchers refer to aggregate data they are thinking of *summative indicators*, thus that is the focus of this chapter. Still, it is useful to be aware of both types of aggregate data, since the nature of data specifies how you may analyze it and the conclusions you may draw from it.

Types of Groups

Data from each category are available on many different kinds of groups from a variety of sources. Such groups may be broadly classified into **areal groups** (those defined by residence within a geographic area, such as a nation, city, or census tract) and **demographic groups** (those defined by personal characteristics, such as age, race, or occupation).

In this chapter you will learn that proper use of aggregate data involves solving some challenging methodological problems. The advantages of using such data, however, often far outweigh the costs. Political scientists may find the use of aggregate data necessary or desirable because individual-level data are either unobtainable or too expensive to obtain.

As examples of studies for which individual data might be impossible to obtain, consider the following cases. (1) If we want to do a historical study, at least some of the groups on which we need data (for example, the population of Chicago in 1880) may be dead. (2) Members of some politically important groups, such as international terrorist organizations, may absolutely refuse to be identified or interviewed. (3) Often, political scientists find themselves in situations in which it is theoretically possible to collect individual-level data, but such collection is prohibitively expensive. This is especially likely to be the case when we are interested in comparing nations, because the cost and logistical problems of multinational survey research are enormous.

If you are interested in research questions for which individual-level data are unavailable, you may find it worthwhile to search for aggregate data that contain the basic information needed. In this chapter we introduce you to the types of aggregate data that are available, suggest some sources of these data, discuss some of the methodological problems encountered in using aggregate data, and, finally, offer some guidelines for collecting aggregate data. You will soon recognize that the proper use of aggregate data requires the mastery of data collection, processing, and analysis techniques. As a student and as a professional political scientist, however, you are more likely to work with aggregate data than with data collected through any of the methods described in preceding chapters, because aggregate data are so readily available.

TYPES OF AGGREGATE DATA

Most of the aggregate data available to political scientists are gathered by nonsocial scientists for reasons unrelated to research. In fact, one of the most challenging aspects of aggregate data analysis is finding a way to use existing data as indicators of concepts of theoretical interest to the researcher. For example, at first glance there is little reason to believe that a political scientist will be concerned with the percentage of short-wave radios or televisions or how many people have newspaper subscriptions in some nation. We are not, after all, marketing agents for the press. But these figures may be useful as partial indicators of the amount of political communication that goes on within a nation or of its level of economic development, and these clearly are appropriate concerns for political scientists. Similarly, the number of hospital beds per thousand persons in the population takes on political significance when it is viewed as an indicator of, say, the distribution of health care facilities among groups within a city or state.

The point is that aggregate data are often of no intrinsic interest and have to be transformed in some way to be of use. Do not look only for ready-made indicators of concepts, but be alert to the possibility of combining seemingly unrelated measures into useful indicators.

We can identify six types of aggregate data (Merritt 1970). They are explained here in roughly *descending* order of the extent to which they are likely to be valid and reliable.

1. ***Census data.*** Many of the world's nations attempt to survey their entire population (or at least all households) periodically in order to gather information to be used for such purposes as levying taxes and planning public policy. The data commonly collected includes such information as number of people in the family, sex of the head of the household, length of residence, educational levels, family income, and condition of housing. Though census data are collected from individuals, by the time they become available to researchers as part of the public record, the data usually appear as summary figures (the total number of persons who own a car in a given geographic area, for instance).

   Census data have several desirable characteristics that make them extremely valuable in aggregate data analysis. First, although errors can occur, census data are generally quite reliable. Second, because the variables measured are normally straightforward, census data are usually regarded as highly valid. Third, some nations have been collecting relatively standardized data for many years. Thus, census data provide an opportunity to trace historical trends or to test hypotheses about change over time. Fourth, because census data are generally standardized—that is, they contain responses to the same questions and classify responses in the same categories—within nations and are often comparable between nations, they are useful in comparing different cities, regions, or nations. In addition, census data are easily available. Many nations publish reports of both major census projects (generally undertaken once every ten years) and any of a wide variety of specialized surveys undertaken in between. The United Nations (unstats.un.org/unsd/) publishes the annual *Demographic Yearbook*, describing the census data available from various countries. A plethora of UN Statistics Division data is available online, frequently in downloadable, spreadsheet form. In the United States, the Bureau of the Census (www.census.gov) maintains a large User Services Division that can assist social scientists in gaining access to and working with the wide variety of data available from the bureau.

2. ***Organizational statistics.*** In every nation, the various levels of government, businesses, and organized groups such as labor unions and professional associations gather data related to their own operations. If these statistics happen to fit the requirements of a particular social scientist's research project, they can be of great value.

Some organizations collect their own data, as does a multinational corporation keeping a record of its capital investments, a hospital recording information on patients, or a city government recording property assessments for tax purposes. Others use data generated by other agencies, such as the United States Department of Commerce (www.doc.gov), to create data in the form of various indices of, for example, economic performance or population shifts.

With either type of official statistics, there can be problems. The first, and perhaps greatest, problem is that of gaining access to the data. Data compiled by government agencies are generally part of the public record and readily available, but data collected by nongovernmental organizations are private property. Some organizations, especially businesses, consider their data sensitive and are most reluctant to share them. Often the problem is less one of gaining access to the data than one of simply learning of their existence. There are no central listings of the statistics collected by the thousands of public and private organizations engaged in such record keeping. Researchers may, therefore, miss major opportunities because of a lack of information about the existence or content of particular statistics.

A second problem is that the content and quality of the data may vary greatly, making comparisons and generalizations difficult. If teachers' unions in Indiana and Ohio do not collect comparable information about their members, we cannot use their statistics to make meaningful comparisons between them. In addition, if we do not know how data have been collected, we may not know how much confidence to place in the figures.

Finally, data may not be in a usable form. A local government's vital statistics (records of births, deaths, marriages, deeds) may be available only in unaggregated form and only in a central location, so that a researcher has to sit for countless hours in a government office tediously hand-recording the data so that they can be converted to a machine-readable (i.e., computerized) form and totaled. This can require an unjustifiable investment of time and money.

These problems are not found in all official statistics, and even when they are encountered, the potential payoff in economical research is generally worth the effort required to solve them.

3. ***Sample surveys.*** Survey research is designed to gather individual-level data. When surveys are based on samples that are representative of a population of interest, it is often possible to use their results as aggregate data. Suppose, for example, we want to compare the political information level of two nations' citizenry. If each nation has a public opinion polling organization that regularly surveys a national sample (as Gallup and Roper do in the United States) and that asks questions about such behavioral matters as frequency of watching TV news reports or subscriptions to news magazines, we might use the results to construct aggregate measures of our variable. Similar use can sometimes be made of individual surveys conducted for academic purposes. Survey data, if properly collected, have the advantage of being quite reliable, and they can be as valid as the researcher is wise in constructing indicators. Data are also generally available (at least for a price)

from the agencies or scholars who have collected them, and they are often in a readily usable form.

4. *Publications' content.* In a construction of aggregate data, content analysis can be applied to publications sponsored by or distributed among particular groups. For example, if we are examining political socialization processes in Great Britain, we might content-analyze the textbooks used in civics courses to determine the extent to which they stress democratic values, and we might then use the combined results as one indicator of the nation's democratic orientation. Similarly, we might rely on content analysis of the major newspapers of developing nations to derive an indicator of those nations' relative attention to international and domestic events or of their support for the United Nations. In each case, the product of the content analysis is an indicator of a group characteristic.

   This type of aggregate data is generated by the researcher specifically for the purpose of a given research project instead of being collected from a primary source, such as a census report. As a result, access to such data depends on the availability of the publications or databases (such as *LexisNexis*) needed for a content analysis and on the researcher's having the resources necessary to perform the content analysis. Aggregate data collected through content analysis of publications have the advantage of being adaptable to an individual study but generally provide only highly imperfect indicators of underlying concepts. Ask yourself, for instance, how confident you would feel in making statements about the kind of political values British schoolchildren learn from an analysis of their civics texts. It is worth remembering that the reliability and validity of these content-derived aggregate data depend on the skill with which the researcher applies the rules discussed in Chapter 10.

5. *Event data.* Often, political scientists are interested in the occurrence of discrete events that are not recorded in census reports or organizational data because they are too infrequent or fall outside the responsibility of any one agency. Riots, revolutions, assassinations, the breaking of diplomatic ties, protest demonstrations, indictments of public officials for crimes in office, *coups d'etat*, and the creation of new political parties are all examples. Information on these events can be useful in the construction of indicators of group properties. For instance, we might want to measure a nation's political stability by counting the number of acts of political violence occurring there in a given time period or we might want to compare the level of political corruption in several cities by counting the number of indictments of public officials for bribery.

   There are a number of event data sets that may be used for such studies. One of the best known is the *World Handbook of Political and Social Indicators*, into which researchers have been compiling tens of thousands of world events since its inception in 1963 at Yale. Currently it documents political events, coded by country, from the 1940s to the present. These data are available to researchers at member institutions through the Inter-University Consortium for Political and Social Research (www.icpsr.umich.edu).

   If not available from others' research, event data are gathered by a process very similar to content analysis. Guided by our theory and hypotheses, we decide what events are relevant to our study and, carefully operationalizing them (for example, deciding what actions constitute a riot), we systematically survey sources such as newspapers, yearbooks, and radio broadcast transcripts that are likely to contain reports of them, and we take a tally (being careful to avoid double-counting the same event when it is reported in more than one source). In addition, content-analysis techniques can be used to produce more detailed data about these events. We can, for example, classify terrorist bombings according to their type (e.g., suicide, car, etc.), the number of injuries, the number of deaths, the location (e.g., democratic or not, world region, etc.), and whether responsibility was claimed in order to develop a taxonomy of terrorist attacks.

Event data can be made relatively reliable by careful training and supervision of those who read and code the source materials, but it is extremely difficult to make event data *valid*. The major challenge to validity is comprehensiveness in reporting. Even when all known sources or reports of some type of event have been reviewed, the researcher cannot be sure that some such events have occurred but have not been reported. In some nations the government carefully controls reports of political events in order to present the preferred image to the world, so that many important happenings, such as the use of troops to break a strike, may not be reported and no valid measure of the events can be constructed. A second and related problem grows from the potential inaccuracy of reports. Even when events are recorded, the details of their occurrence can be distorted intentionally or unintentionally. Such problems are not insurmountable, but researchers must be aware of them in designing their studies around event data, and they must realistically assess their chances of acquiring valid measures by this means.

6. *Judgmental data.* Occasionally there simply are no data available to use for construction of measures of particular aggregate properties. In these cases, researchers can sometimes use as data the opinions of experts or persons with special knowledge.

Consider the example of a study of the lobbying efforts by several interest groups for and against environmental protection legislation. There may be no public record on the subject, but researchers can ask key legislators about their judgment of whether and how strongly each group supports or opposes such legislation in its lobbying efforts. Similarly, if researchers are unable to gather data on the force governments employ to stay in power in various nations, they can ask other scholars who have studied those nations' political systems for their judgment about the coerciveness of the governments.

Obviously, judgmental data suffer from serious limitations. In the first place, their accuracy is subject to the biases and limited experiences of the judges. Using many judges and checking their estimates against one another represents one way to avoid relying on false or partial judgments. It is often difficult, however, to find several qualified judges who differ in their background and their experience with the subject matter, so that even using multiple judges is no guarantee against inaccurate data. Second, even when judges provide perfectly accurate information, judgmental data are generally imprecise. We are, after all, asking for opinions and impressions of complex phenomena, not counts of discrete events. It is important that researchers recognize these limitations in designing studies and in analyzing judgmental data.

LIMITATIONS IN THE USE OF AGGREGATE DATA

From the foregoing discussion you can see that the specific types of problems encountered in aggregate data analysis vary with the types and sources of data being used. There are, however, some general problems that may be confronted in any use of aggregate data analysis. We will discuss two. Our purpose is not to provide solutions but to alert you to the need to be on the lookout for these problems in your research and the research of others.

Ecological Fallacy

It is important to consider first the general problem referred to as the **ecological fallacy**, because knowledge of it should guide the design of research and the specification and operationalization of variables, as well as the very decision to use aggregate data to address a specific research question.

Researchers run the risk of committing one of several types of ecological fallacy anytime they attempt to generalize to one level of analysis from data collected at another. For example, if we collect data on the racial characteristics of individual welfare recipients in each *state* in the United States and find a strong positive relationship between being nonwhite and receiving public assistance, we may be tempted to generalize "up" to the national level, claiming that this relationship holds for the nation as a whole, or to generalize "down" by assuming that the relationship found in any given state will also be found in each of its counties. If, however, we actually do aggregate our data at the national or county level, we may find that the relationship is significantly different from that found when data are aggregated at the state level. Empirical studies of the ecological problem have shown that relationships may not only be weaker or stronger at different levels but may even change directions. When researchers generalize from one level of analysis to another, they run the risk of seriously misinterpreting their data and reaching conclusions that are simply wrong.

Does this mean that we must use only data that are aggregated at the level of whatever units of analysis we choose for our studies and can never generalize up or down in research? No. There are techniques of data analysis that, under some conditions, can at least minimize the risks involved in making inferences between levels of analysis. If researchers find that they must use data aggregated at a level other than that with which they are concerned, they should plan to employ one or more of these data analysis techniques outlined by King (1997) or Achen and Shively (1995), and should take care that their data meet the requirements of this type of analysis before investing time and resources in gathering them.

Whenever possible, though, you should avoid selecting indicators that require inferences between levels of analysis. For example, suppose we are studying the relationship between union membership and support for the Democratic Party in the United States, and we discover aggregate data for congressional districts that give the percentage of each district's labor force holding union memberships and the percentage of each district's voters that have voted Democratic in recent elections. We will be able to use these data if congressional districts are our unit of analysis and our goal is to be able to make statements such as, *Those districts with proportionately more union members tend to elect Democratic candidates*. However, if individual voters are our units of analysis, we will want to be able to make statements such as, *Labor union members tend to support Democratic candidates*. In this case we *cannot* use, with any confidence, the aggregate data from congressional districts, and we will be wise to seek data on *individuals'* union membership and voting behavior.

Variable Precision

A second, and related, set of problems often encountered in aggregate data analysis relates to the difficulties of creating valid indicators from aggregate data. It is rare to find aggregate figures that can be used directly as a measure of some concept of interest to political scientists. Most frequently, we find numbers representing variables that can be viewed as part of the larger phenomena to which our concepts refer. In studying the political impact of modernization, for instance, researchers may not be able to find aggregate data that directly report the level of modernization of various nations. They might, however, be able to find information on the proportion of each nation's population that lives in communities of more than 25,000, is engaged in nonagricultural employment, or is literate, all of which can be considered components of modernization. Such figures are often referred to as **raw data**; they are of no intrinsic interest by themselves but can be used to create indicators of concepts that are of interest.

Developing Useful Measures

The challenge that aggregate data analysts face is one of finding theoretically and methodologically justifiable ways of converting raw data into useful measures. Two basic approaches to this are the creation of indices and the transformation of data.

Index construction is a means of reducing complex data to a single indicator that more fully captures the meaning of a concept than does any of its components. Three commonly used types of index are additive, multiplicative, and weighted. An **additive index** is appropriate when available data represent different measures of the *same* underlying variable. For example, we might want simply to add together reported numbers of exported bushels of wheat, corn, and soybeans in order to obtain an indicator of the concept *agricultural exports*.

Often, however, aggregate data represent measures of *different* aspects of a phenomenon and cannot be added. There is, for instance, no mathematical logic by which we can add the number of people involved in a riot to the number of hours it lasts in order to create an index of riot severity. Number of participants and length of duration are nonadditive elements of the phenomenon called *riots*. We can, however, argue that those two elements interact with one another to determine how severe a riot is. By this logic we might *multiply* the number of participants by the number of hours of duration to create an indicator of the severity of the riot by measuring the "demonstrator hours" devoted to it. Such an indicator is called a **multiplicative index**. Indices of this type are called for anytime we have measures of different aspects of a concept.

In some circumstances raw data have to be weighted by some standard to become useful indicators of concepts. For example, the *number* of persons attending antigovernment rallies is a useful indicator of the legitimacy accorded a government only when it is expressed as a percentage of the population. By doing this we are weighting one variable (the number attending antigovernment rallies) by a second (the population) to create a **weighted index**. Similarly, we might want to weight the number of antigovernment demonstrations by the variable *time* to create an index of demonstrations per year on the assumption that ten demonstrations in one year indicate more political unrest than ten demonstrations spread over ten years. This particular type of weighting is known as *standardization*.

Weighting is technically simple to do, but it is often conceptually difficult to determine whether a measure should be weighted and by what it should be weighted. For instance, it is not clear whether arms races are triggered by the absolute level of armaments held by nations or by the ratio of one nation's armaments to another's. Should a nation's armament level be weighted by its opponents' armament level before the figure can be used as an indicator in a study of arms races? Answers to such questions are often found in an empirical examination of how the use of weighted and unweighted indicators affects the results of statistical analysis.

Often, in the use of aggregate data, measures are encountered that cannot be made useful simply by combining them with others, but that must be individually modified. Sometimes even indices can be made more useful if they are modified. Such modifications are referred to as **data transformations**. Data are transformed principally in order to meet the requirements of certain statistical procedures that researchers want to employ in data analysis. In general, the justification for transforming data is to avoid having the results of statistical analyses distorted by features of the distribution of the raw data.

There are many techniques of data transformation, and each is designed to correct different flaws in raw data. However, the *logarithmic transformation* can serve as an example of how transformations work. Some of the most useful statistical procedures can legitimately be applied only to data that are normally distributed. (We discuss normal distributions in Chapter 16.) Application of these procedures to data that are not normally distributed can result in serious underestimates of the strength of relationships between variables, as well as other misleading results. Yet raw aggregate data are often not normally distributed. Logarithmic transformations are designed to make data more nearly approximate a normal distribution. The basic procedure is to add a constant to the score for each case on the raw data and then substitute the appropriate logarithm for the original score by using a log table. The effects of such a transformation on data are suggested in Figure 11.1, which shows the results of transforming hypothetical data on the number of people taking part in abortion rights demonstrations in fifty-seven U.S. cities. The distribution of the transformed data in Figure 11.1(b) does not form a normal, or bell-shaped, curve, but it is much more nearly normal than the distribution of the raw data in Figure 11.1(a).

You should not interpret anything we have just said as meaning that having multiple measures of some concept is a problem that must be solved. On the contrary, it is highly desirable to have *multiple indicators* of concepts, and though it is often useful to combine measures into indices, it is usually wise also to record the individual measures and examine them separately at some stage of the data analysis. The reason is that multiple indicators can be used to check the validity of our operationalization of concepts.

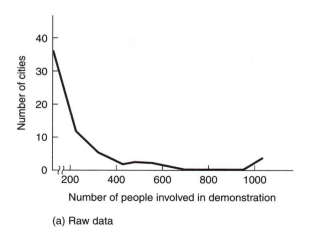

(a) Raw data

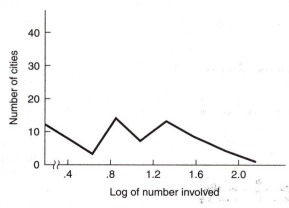

(b) Transformed data

FIGURE 11.1 Effects of logarithmic transformation on hypothetical data from abortion rights demonstrations in fifty-seven U.S. cities.

For example, suppose we want to measure the concept *gender discrimination in employment* among the American states. We might be able to find aggregate data on the following variables:

- The ratio of the average salary paid to women to the average salary paid to men
- The proportion of all professionals in the state who are female
- The ratio of the unemployment rate for women to the unemployment rate for men

We can use all three indicators by scoring each state on each variable and comparing the results. If those states that appear to have the most discrimination by one measure also rank high on discrimination by the other measures, we will feel more confident that each measure is a valid indicator of the underlying concept *gender discrimination in employment.* If, on the other hand, we find that those states that rank high on discrimination as measured by two of the indicators rank low on discrimination as measured by the third, we will be reluctant to use the deviant measure as an indicator of our concept.

The more independent indicators we can locate for each concept, the better, for with more indicators we can provide more convincing tests of the validity of each. For instance, in the preceding example, with only three measures, we might not be altogether sure that the deviant measure is not, in fact, the valid one and the other two invalid. It may be its very validity as an indicator of our concept that makes it stand apart from the others in the way it ranks states. If, however, we have five or ten measures that produce consistent rankings of states and one that stands apart, we can feel quite confident that it is the deviant measure that is invalid. A variety of techniques are available for using multiple measures to test and enhance the validity of our indicators (see Suggested Readings and Examples).

There is one additional important issue to consider when using aggregate data. This potential problem stems from the fact that aggregate data are often available in a form that does not allow valid comparisons across units. For example, if we are interested in the degree to which different states in the United States exhibit a commitment to public education, we might find data on how much each state spends on education each year. It would be inappropriate, however, to compare the total number of dollars Texas spends on education to the total number of dollars Rhode Island spends, because the two states differ so radically in size and wealth. Rhode Island may spend only a fraction of the amount Texas does and yet exhibit a stronger commitment to education because it is spending far more *per school-age child* or a far greater *portion* of its total state budget on schooling. To make a valid comparison among the states, it would be necessary to restate the amount they spend on education in some way that controls for differences in population and wealth. Unless we do this, we will not have a valid indicator of our concept, and our conclusions will be determined by the relative size and wealth of states rather than by their relative commitment to education. Additionally, of course, our research report will have to justify the apparently logical connection between the concept of "commitment to education" and the variable "per child public school spending."

Situations like this require that we *standardize* our measures in some way. A **standardized measure** is one that is stated in a way that, in order to allow valid comparisons, takes into account the differences that might exist among cases on variables other than the one it represents. It is very often necessary to standardize aggregate data prior to making comparisons among units of analysis. This may involve collecting data on variables that are of no direct relevance to the project. For example, in a study of commitment to education, we might need to collect data on the populations and total governmental expenditures of the states in order to standardize their educational expenditures by stating them as dollars per school-age child or a percentage of total state expenditures. Similarly, if we wanted to measure the concept *militarization* by observing the amount of money nations spend on the military, we would need to standardize the measure by stating it as a percentage of a nation's gross national product (the total value of all goods and services produced in the country) before making comparisons. Unless we did this, a wealthy nation might look more militaristic than a poor nation even though it devoted only a tenth as much of its total wealth to the military as a poor nation did.

Whenever you anticipate making comparisons among groups (nations, cities, organizations, etc.), you must be alert to the need to standardize your measures and must plan to collect the additional data necessary for this standardization. Standardization is generally achieved by stating measures either as a percentage or proportion of some other variable or as so many units per unit of some other variable. This often results in the computation of a *rate* such as a crime rate (crimes per 10,000 persons), literacy rate (literate persons per 1,000 population), or infant mortality rate (infant deaths per 1,000 live births). The additional work of collecting data on the variables on which your key variable must be standardized is *absolutely necessary* for valid comparisons among cases that differ significantly in theoretically relevant ways.

The point of this section is that aggregate data analysts should not only be cautious about using raw data as indicators of concepts, but must also be alert to the potential uses of multiple indicators and the possibility of improving indicators by combining, standardizing, or transforming measures.

RESEARCH EXERCISE

Analyzing Relationships at the Data's Aggregation Level

This chapter emphasizes that relationships should not be analyzed at a more refined level than the level at which your data contain information. For example, it would be risky to draw conclusions about state-level relationships from national survey data on age and income. For this in-class exercise, you will locate country data and answer questions about what can be studied with it.

1. Your instructor will break you into equally sized groups. One person in each group will have Internet access. Your instructor will assign two countries to each group.
2. For each of your two countries, locate recent data on:
   a. Crime level
   b. Population density
   (Hint: These country-level data may be obtained from the United Nations Web site.)
3. Compare your two countries:
   a. Which one has a higher population?
   b. Which one has a higher crime rate?
   c. If you observe that the country with the higher density also has more crime, can you reasonably conclude that packing people together causes crime? If the country with a lower density has more crime, does being farther from others in your country make you antisocial?
4. To appropriately analyze the question in 3.c., what level of data aggregation would be required?

SOURCES OF AGGREGATE DATA

The amount of aggregate data available in the world is so great that one is inclined to believe it possible to find indicators for almost any empirically useful concept. In fact the very abundance of the available data sometimes poses problems as researchers find themselves having to search scores of sources to find all available indicators. Yet, even with this reservoir of data, researchers are sometimes unable to locate exact indicators of the concept they want to measure, for exactly the right time period, and aggregated at exactly the right level.

We cannot begin to list *all* the sources of aggregate data here. We can, however, list those sources of general data that are most likely to be of use to political scientists. Whereas some data sources contain data on a variety of subjects and cannot be neatly characterized as a source of one particular type of data, we have classified the sources listed here by the major type of data they are likely to yield. Most college and university libraries have the publications listed here or are able to help you locate them.

The key to successful use of any of the documents or data archives described here is knowing precisely what type of measures you are seeking. The hypotheses you are testing, the theory you are working from, or a precise statement of your research question can tell you what type of data, such as a measure of nations' economic productivity or of the size of their military forces, is needed to operationalize the concepts utilized in your research. Simply going to the library with the idea of poking around in available data sources until you run across some indicators that look useful will almost certainly cause you to meet with failure. If, on the other hand, you approach the task of gathering data with a clearly conceptualized research strategy in mind, you should be able to tell the reference or social science librarian what you need.

1. ***Demographic and related data on the United States.*** All statistics released by agencies of the federal government are indexed in the *American Statistical Index*, which can be used to locate sources for specific measures. In addition, statistics on economic and population trends, foreign trade, energy use, and other issues collected for more than 100 federal agencies can be accessed through the Internet at FedStats (www.fedstats.gov). The publications of the Bureau of the Census are indexed in the *Catalog of United States Census Publications*, which describes the data available from the censuses of housing, population, governments, and agriculture, among others. Many of these data are summarized each year in the publication *Statistical Abstract of the United States*, which presents selected statistical profiles of the United States and its subdivisions and contains an extensive guide to public and private data sources. Many of these tables are also available in downloadable spreadsheets (www.census.gov/compendia/statab/population/). Each of the various censuses of the United States is summarized in *Subject and U.S. Area Reports*.

Some frequently used sources of specialized data about the United States are the *Congressional District Data Book*, which provides demographic and economic information and voting records for United States congressional districts, and the *County and City Data Book*, which contains demographic and economic data for states, counties, cities, unincorporated places of more than 25,000 in population, and urbanized areas in the United States on an annual basis. Similar data are presented in the *State and Metropolitan Area Data Book* from the Bureau of the

Census. Voting data are summarized by Congressional Quarterly in the *Guide to U.S. Elections,* which gives returns for presidential, Senate, House, and gubernatorial races since 1824.

2. ***Demographic and related data on other nations.*** Recognizing the difficulties in locating comparable measures of any given variable for different countries, a variety of sourcebooks contain data collected by different nations and international bodies. Researchers who use these must be especially sensitive to the need to ensure the comparability of reported figures before basing comparisons on them.

The United Nations Statistics Division (unstats.un.org/unsd/) publishes three especially useful documents: The *Statistical Yearbook* summarizes data on population characteristics, economic activity, education, communications, and other matters for the world's nations each year; the *Yearbook of National Accounts Statistics* reports detailed information on economic activity; and the *Demographic Yearbook* gives historical data on population characteristics and annually examines a special subject, such as population distributions, mortality rates, or ethnic compositions. In addition, the United Nations Educational, Scientific, and Cultural Organization (UNESCO) publishes the *Statistical Yearbook* (www.uis.unesco .org/), which summarizes data on education, communication, science, and technology in more than 200 countries.

The *Statesman's Yearbook* provides detailed information about nations that has been compiled from a variety of national and international sources. The European Union publishes the *Eurostat Yearbook*, which provides demographic, social, political, and economic data for EU member states and candidate countries for leading EU economic partners (ec.europa.eu/eurostat/). Further summary figures on national characteristics can be found in the *World Almanac* and *Worldmark Encyclopedia of Nations* in well-indexed form. A good deal of economic data can be found in the *Yearbook of International Trade Statistics.*

3. ***Data on governments in the United States.*** U.S. federal, state, and local governments turn out thousands of publications reporting figures on their own operations and on the social conditions that either call forth or result from public policies. The federal government is by far the most prolific producer of data. Its many publications are listed in the *Monthly Catalog of U.S. Government Publications* (MOCAT). An online version of MOCAT can be accessed through the Government Printing Office (www.gpo.gov). If you know what agency or branch of the government is likely to produce the data you are seeking, you can locate its publications in the *Monthly Catalog.* Correspondingly, if you know what you are looking for, the index of the *Monthly Checklists of State Publications* can be used to direct you to specific state publications. The *County Yearbook* and the *Municipal Yearbook* provide data on political, economic, and demographic variables at local levels.

4. ***Event data.*** By their nature, event data are not reported in regular, summary form. They have to be discovered in running records of daily events that are not necessarily compiled with the social scientist in mind. Two of the most comprehensive reference sources for events reported in newspapers are the indexes for the *Times of London* and *The New York Times. Facts-on-File* is a weekly digest of current events classified by subject and compiled into the annual *News Dictionary*, which stresses events in and related to the United States. Perhaps the most extensive general news digest is *Keesing's Contemporary Archives: Weekly Diary of World Events*, which

PRACTICAL RESEARCH ETHICS

Using group-level data?

There are three principal ethical factors to bear in mind when using aggregate data: 1) You need to document how the data were originally gathered and coded; 2) you should clearly credit the primary sources of the aggregate data; and 3) you will generally want to restrict your analyses to the appropriate group level, using caution if individual-level inferences are desired.

Additionally, you should construct a codebook for all data to provide documentation for those wishing to replicate your study, which may well have combined data from more than one source. This codebook should be available on your Web site, or at the archive where you place your replication data.

contains transcripts of important speeches, some election and statistical data, and news summaries, and is indexed by subject and proper name.

5. ***Survey data.*** Many of the sources named thus far present data in printed form. Using them for large studies requires recording the data and transferring them to machine-readable form. The most useful sources of survey data, by contrast, are electronic data sets. These are available from a variety of data archives, several of which were identified in Chapter 8.

In addition to these sources, it is important to recognize the rich variety of private sources of data. Which of these is appropriate to any given study will be suggested by the subject of the study. For a study of the investment patterns of West European firms, for example, useful data may be held by individual banks or by national and international associations of banks.

COLLECTING AGGREGATE DATA

If data are not available electronically, researchers face the task of transferring the data from a source to their records in a machine-readable form. The basic challenge is one of systematically coding and recording data.

Though transferring data takes only a fraction of the time required to collect the same data through field research, it can be a very time-consuming task. It is important, then, to do it as efficiently as possible. The way to begin is by carefully thinking through in advance the research design and the data analysis you intend to perform so that you can specify exactly which cases you want data on and what measures you want to record for each. Failure to do this advance preparation will often lead to wasting time recording data for which you ultimately have no use. Moreover, by carefully planning the study, you can list all cases and variables in some order of importance so that if you run short of time or funds in the data collection stage, you can make a rational choice to leave out certain cases or variables in order to terminate data collection in the least harmful manner. Keeping this option open means that you must proceed sequentially, either collecting all data on each case one at a time (if you want to be able to drop cases but need all variables) or collecting data for all cases on each variable one at a time (if you need all cases but want to be able to leave out some variables).

In either event, you need two basic tools for data collection: a set of *data specifications* and a *recording form*. **Data specifications** are simply detailed descriptions of the data that are to be recorded for each case and variable, including any coding instructions.

Sometimes a single phrase will serve as a data specification for census data or organizational statistics—for example, *total number of municipal employees in 1905* or *adult population in 2009*. However, apparently simple pieces of data can require extensive qualifications. For instance, if we want a figure on total state expenditures for public welfare programs in a given year, we have to identify those programs that qualify as welfare for purposes of the study. If we want a measure of the number of persons in nations' armed forces, we have to include instructions for excluding domestic police from the count for countries in which the police are formally part of the military. Being able to provide these details in data specifications requires prior study of the subject and the reporting systems of your units of analysis. Even then, unexpected difficulties can arise. You may, for example, discover that budgeted and actual welfare expenditures differ considerably or that corrections for inflation have to be added in time-series studies. The adjustments you make in response to these problems must be both technically correct and consistent with the meaning of the concept operationalized by the measure.

When collecting event data, a coding manual will help to document your data specifications, particularly noting essential distinctions in definitions. You will want, for instance, to be able to distinguish between riots and peaceful demonstrations or between pro-government and anti government demonstrations. The most dependable way of doing this is to develop a **coding manual** (or **codebook**) that records the details of those characteristics that distinguish events in which we are interested from one another. (We say more about the use of coding in Chapter 14.)

The coding manual is then used in completing each **recording form**. It is similar to an interview schedule in survey research in that it is a means of systematizing and coding observations. You will undoubtedly save considerable time by entering your data directly into an electronic spreadsheet or database. Software bundles frequently include both; for example, *Microsoft Office Professional* includes *Excel* and *Access*. Some time spent learning to use these programs before entering data may well pay handsome dividends when you complete your data collection and you have a data set that is ready to be analyzed.

Conclusion

In closing, we want to encourage beginning researchers not to overlook the potential of aggregate data as a *supplement* to other forms of data. There are countless studies that can be based exclusively on aggregate data, but it is also often the case that aggregate data can be used to check the accuracy of results obtained from other forms of data. For example, students of voting behavior are sometimes faced with the problem created when people who are eager to associate themselves with a winner falsely report, in interviews conducted after the election, that they have voted for the successful candidate. In this case, aggregate voting data can be used to estimate the level of misreporting present in a sample. If responses from a sample show that 75 percent of a district has voted for the winner of a recent presidential election but voting statistics show that only 25 percent of that district actually voted for the winner, we have to consider that district's survey responses to be at least potentially an invalid indicator of support for the winner in that district.

In addition to this use, aggregate data can often be relied on to provide additional indicators of concepts so that the multiple indicator approaches to validity discussed earlier can be employed. For instance, in a study of neighborhood stability, we might ask residents about their commitments to stay in the neighborhood and, as an additional indicator, seek aggregate data on the frequency of turnover in home ownership in the neighborhood in recent years. When the findings of a study are confirmed by data collected by such diverse methods, confidence in those findings is greatly enhanced.

Key Terms

aggregate data *209*
summative indicators *209*
syntality indicators *210*
areal groups *210*
demographic groups *210*
ecological fallacy *215*

raw data *216*
index construction *216*
additive index *216*
multiplicative index *216*
weighted index *216*
data transformations *217*

standardized measure *218*
data specifications *222*
coding manual
   (codebook) *223*
recording form *223*

Research Examples

Combining data on the number of Jewish voters in several states with presidential election outcomes, Lieberman (2009) utilizes aggregate data in his argument that Jewish and pro-Israel political power is much weaker in the United States than some would claim. A common use of aggregate data is to set the stage for further analyses. Alvarez, Hall, and Trechsel (2009) present official Estonian government data on the number of Internet voters, their gender, and partisan affiliation before examining survey data on voters' individual characteristics.

Methodological Readings

A bold and controversial claim for the usefulness of aggregate data in individual-level analyses is made in Gary King's 1997 book. His proposed technique to reduce the likelihood of the ecological fallacy in *A Solution to the Ecological Inference Problem* continues to generate controversy and interest, leading to a follow-up work (King, Tanner, and Rosen 2004). Difficulties with analyzing groups using individual-level data, as well as using aggregate data to study individuals, are addressed by Achen and Shively (1995).

It is rare to find textbooks that are solely devoted to aggregate data analysis. Most of the material is scattered among the literature-reporting studies that have employed the various techniques of aggregate data analysis. Drawn primarily from texts produced many years ago, the best general discussions of how to use aggregate data

for beginning political scientists are probably *Politimetrics* (Gurr 1972) and *Systematic Approaches to Comparative Politics*, ch. 2 (Merritt 1970). In *Secondary Research*, Stewart and Kamins offer some practical tips and an excellent review of the issues surrounding the use of aggregate data in research. More advanced discussions of the problems and techniques of using aggregate data and some examples of its uses are found in *Aggregate Data Analysis* (Taylor 1968). Some valuable hints on data transformation (and on the collection and use of aggregate data generally) are offered in *Unobtrusive Measures* (Webb et al. 2000).

References

Achen, Christopher H., and W. Philips Shively. 1995. *Cross-Level Inference*. Chicago: University of Chicago Press.

Alvarez, R. Michael, Thad E. Hall, and Alexander H. Trechsel. 2009. "Internet Voting in Comparative Perspective: The Case of Estonia." *PS: Political Science & Politics* 42(July): 497–505.

Gurr, Ted Robber. 1972. *Politimetrics*. Englewood Cliffs, NJ: Prentice Hall.

King, Gary. 1997. *A Solution to the Ecological Inference Problem*. Princeton, NJ: Princeton University Press.

King, Gary, Martin Tanner, and Ori Rosen, eds. 2004. *Ecological Inference: New Methodological Strategies*. New York, NY: Cambridge University Press.

Lieberman, Robert C. 2009. "The 'Israel Lobby' and American Politics." *Perspectives on Politics* 7(June): 235–257.

Merritt, Richard L. 1970. *Systematic Approaches to Comparative Politics*. Skokie, IL: Rand McNally.

Stewart, David W., and Michael A. Kamins. 1993. *Secondary Research*, 2nd ed. Newbury Park, CA: Sage.

Taylor, Charles L., ed. 1968. *Aggregate Data Analysis*. Paris: Mouton.

Webb, Eugene J., Donald T. Campbell, Richard D. Schwartz, and Lee Sechrest. 2000. *Unobtrusive Measures*, rev. ed. Thousand Oaks, CA: Sage.

CHAPTER 12

Comparative Research: Identifying Characteristics across Populations

In this chapter you will learn:

- How comparative research across borders can provide new insights and generalizations.
- What considerations you should take into account when designing comparative studies.
- How you decide which cases to include in a comparative study.
- How to find appropriate data for comparative research.

All of the research strategies we have dealt with thus far could easily be carried out without ever setting foot outside our country. On most questions we can obtain more than enough data from our own nation's experience to help us explain political life. But an exclusive focus on one nation has some limitations. If we want to improve our ability to explain and predict political events, then one way is to take a comparative approach. This offers a broader range of information about the issues we want to study and in fact allows us to pose some kinds of questions that data from a single country might not answer.

If you have ever traveled outside your own country, you probably noticed that many things are done differently in other nations. People from other cultures might eat food you have never seen or tasted before, their daily routines might be very different from yours, and some of the people you encountered probably acted in ways you never anticipated. The point is, unless you have traveled beyond your own country's border, you probably would have never noticed these differences (or similarities) at all. Thus, only those who are willing to engage with people from other nations will learn to understand the thought processes of another culture and to see it from the native's viewpoint. Moreover, these cross-cultural experiences also will allow people to reconsider their own country from the perspective of an external, and thus possibly less biased, observer.

In politics, social or cultural differences between nations can have an enormous influence on the political process. Presidential elections in the United States, for example, differ greatly from the parliamentary elections that are conducted in most European countries.

Political protests in the streets of Teheran certainly differ from political protests that take place in London or Paris, even though some of the images we see of these protests might look the same on television. Thus, whether the question is about the causes of political violence, the way people vote for their political leaders, the effects of different kinds of political organization on public policy, or something else, comparative research can significantly increase our chances of reaching valid conclusions.

RESEARCH ACROSS BORDERS

Why Comparative Research?

You might ask yourself why there should be any limitations in studying only one country. First, our results are likely to be *culture-bound*. That is, each nation has certain unique traits that can bias the findings. Suppose, for example, we want to explore the connection between socioeconomic class and voting choice. Looking only at data from the United States, we are likely both to conclude that class and voting are only modestly related and to question the notion that political preferences are shaped by the socioeconomic conditions in which voters must live and work. If, on the other hand, we expand our sample to include other Western countries—say, Britain, France, or Germany—we are likely to find a far stronger link, partly because of differences in the historical development of social classes in those countries. Thus, the United States might not be a representative example.

To take another case, suppose that we focus on voter turnout in national elections. For the United States, we will find that close to half of all eligible voters typically stay home on Election Day (however, about 62 percent voted in the 2008 U.S. presidential election). We may explain this by arguing that democratic elections, especially at the national level, tend to discourage voter participation because the large number of voters makes any individual ballot almost meaningless. But that conclusion, too, will be quite different if our sample includes other nations. Electoral turnout at parliamentary elections averaged 86 percent of eligible voters in Sweden since 1945, and almost 90 percent in Italy during the same period (International IDEA 2004). Thus, there must be other reasons for the lower rate of participation within the United States, and these come into sharper focus when we add data from other nations. A comparative analysis shows that electoral competitiveness, and institutional features such as electoral laws and the existence of a two-party or multiparty system go a long way toward explaining different rates of voter turnout (Jackman 1987). These examples suggest that there are specific features in the U.S. system—or in any system—that can distort our conclusions about political relationships.

Focusing on only one country also limits us in another way: It prevents our drawing conclusions about **system-level traits**. In other words, there are some variables, such as type of political system or type of territorial organization, that describe whole countries, and their effects can be studied only by comparing two or more nations. Consider, for example, the impact of federalism. We might argue that federal arrangements—in which power is shared between two or more levels of government—make for an inequitable distribution of public funds among localities. When regions or localities have power independent of the national government, they are likely to have different views about how much public money to spend and how to spend it.

In order to test this, we need to study at least one unitary system (in which regions and localities have no formal power independent of the national government) as a standard of comparison. Only if we found significant differences between nations with federal systems and those with unitary systems could we conclude that federalism was an important variable influencing the distribution of public funds. Similarly, we might make a case that economic growth in newly industrializing countries hinges on a government's ability to coerce and control the labor force. Our test of this proposition requires a sample that includes countries with varying degrees of control over labor. Of necessity, then, any concern with system-level attributes implies a cross-national study.

Requirements in Comparative Research

Comparative analysis is an important part of political research because it allows us to generalize beyond the sometimes narrow confines of a single culture and because it permits us to test for the effects of system-wide characteristics. Needless to say, it should meet all the standards for good research that we have discussed in other chapters. But cross-national studies also require sensitivity to some additional issues. The first lies in conceptualizing what we want to address: *We need to ensure that the questions we pose actually permit cross-national study*. The second lies in operationalization: *Each variable we use must be an equivalent measure of the same concept for every culture in our sample*. The choice of a sample raises a third issue: *Countries should be chosen to minimize cultural biases that can affect our conclusions*. Finally, the sample must also satisfy another rule: *Observations must be independent from one country to another*.

The following sections explain each of these requirements in turn, describing how they can influence the results we obtain and offering examples of questions that invite comparative analysis.

FINDING QUESTIONS THAT "TRAVEL"

The first requirement in cross-cultural research is to pose questions that *apply* from one culture to another. The simplicity of this statement is deceptive, because many of the questions we raise in political science are applicable only to a very select group of countries. Take, for example, the case of explaining electoral behavior—one of the mainstays of political science research. Our long-standing interest in the reasons why people cast a ballot and in the factors that influence their choices has produced a rich body of theory and a set of sophisticated methods that should be applicable in any setting, domestic or otherwise.

Yet questions about why and how people vote do not "travel" well, because they restrict us to studying countries that have regular, competitive, free, and fair elections—a qualification that automatically eliminates many of the world's nations. We would, for example, be likely to exclude consideration of single-candidate or single-party elections, since there would be little variation in electoral behavior and basically no choice other than to abstain. Without variation, there is not much to explain. The factors that lead people to cast a ballot in a certain way in a country with competitive voting appear to make no difference in a noncompetitive election.

Thus, by choosing to analyze elections, we have set up a research question in terms that are specific to certain countries. This in itself might not seem too big a drawback, because we still have a large number of countries in our potential sample. But there is a second problem, one that relates to our ability to draw more general conclusions from voting data. If we assume, as many researchers do, that ballots reflect support for, or alienation from, the political system or reflect a preference for a certain candidate, party, or policy, then we have, in effect, equated elections with political expression. We are treating votes as measures of the more general concept of political participation. Almost by definition, this excludes the possibility that countries without regular and competitive elections provide their populations with a way to express satisfaction with, alienation from, or preferences for the government. Do they? Or are we unnecessarily limiting ourselves by framing our research around competitive electoral behavior? Will we come to different conclusions by redefining what we want to study?

An Example

We might want to explore the patterns of court cases among different countries as a means to test for the connections between democratic political institutions, the frequency of litigation, and the outcomes of court decisions. However, the question of courts and litigation might not travel well, because societies can have very different modes of resolving disputes. In some countries, the emphasis may be on mediating conflicts through local notables rather than bringing them before a formal court, and such countries would be omitted from our analysis of formal court activities. If, like most political scientists, we are interested in drawing valid conclusions that are not culture-bound, then our initial research question must be phrased to allow us to generalize beyond one or a few countries.

Our initial question must also be appropriate to the countries included in the study. Suppose that we are studying the development of women's rights. One approach might be to explore how workplace grievances are resolved, since questions about pay equity and working conditions are a central concern for many women's groups. Yet, if we focus on jobs alone, we overlook a critical issue. In some countries, especially those with strong traditions of social democracy, campaigns for women's rights may focus much more on social policies—parental leave, child care, or other benefits—rather than on individuals at work. Thus, the more appropriate question for us to pose is, *What kinds of women's rights issues are on each nation's political agenda?* Our original question needs to be recast in terms that are appropriate to the countries we study.

In this brief discussion, we have not touched on all the possible biases that might color our initial research questions. We have, for example, dealt only with cases involving advanced industrial societies, in which government is embodied in the work of large, highly specialized bureaucracies. Clearly, the modes of political expression, and the provision of public goods and services, take quite different forms in societies without such institutions, such as many of the developing countries, and these are things we need to consider when forming the questions that will guide our research. Whatever the issue, and whatever countries are studied, we need to be sure that our research is constructed in a way that permits us to generalize about our conclusions and in a way that fits the context of the countries we want to explore. In effect, our design should be able to travel and to focus on questions appropriate to the sample we ultimately choose.

USING EQUIVALENT MEASURES

Once we have settled on a question that allows cross-national study, we will need **equivalent measures** in each country we observe. In other words, comparative research should measure the same concept from one culture to another. There are two ways we can do this: (1) by using the same variable everywhere and (2) by choosing variables that are specific to each country. At first glance, this might appear to be a lopsided choice, for nothing should ensure equivalence between countries better than using the same variable in each one. But this is true only if our "identical" variable means the same thing in every country we study.

Using Identical Variables

Suppose that we want to compare levels of tolerance for minority rights across nations. We might adopt one of two approaches. In one, we might compare the degree to which people in each nation are willing to grant political rights to particular groups, such as a religious sect. Based on this measure, we are likely to conclude that citizens of some nations are more tolerant than others. However, if people in the nations under study are more or less hostile to the specific group in question, this measure might reveal how the group under study is perceived by people in different nations and *not* how tolerant they are of minority rights. This means that our "identical" measure of tolerance does not have the same meaning in each nation.

Alternatively, we might ask people about their willingness to grant political rights to the groups *they most dislike*. This would allow us to control for differences in the acceptance of different groups across nations. This raises another question, however. In some nations, the most disliked groups are larger and more powerful than in other nations, where they may be tiny minorities with little power. If so, the degree to which people are willing to grant political rights to a group may reflect the degree of threat the group poses to the majority. In that case, our measure might reflect fear of a given group rather than citizens' general level of political tolerance. Thus, for comparisons to be valid, *we need measures that tap the same underlying concept*, whatever countries are included in our sample.

Similar problems may arise no matter what question we take up or what countries we study. Suppose, for example, we want to compare the relative commitment to social welfare between nations at different levels of development. We might predict that the more developed a country, the more resources it will commit to social programs. Our measure of commitment to welfare should be relatively easy to define: We can look at expenditures on social welfare programs (such as pensions and aid to the disabled and poor) as a share of a country's total government spending or a share of all the goods and services it produces (as measured by its gross national product). With this measure, we are likely to discover that our prediction holds true: More developed countries devote a greater share of resources to welfare.

Yet here, too, our measure may not be equivalent for all the countries we might want to study. By defining it in terms of formal programs, such as government pensions and aid to the disabled and poor, we may be underestimating the degree of noninstitutional, local effort that aids the most needy in countries where formal government programs either do not exist or are limited in scope. If farmers and local villagers in less developed countries organize to contribute food, shelter, and other kinds of assistance to their indigent relatives and neighbors, then they are, in effect, redistributing community resources in the same basic sense that welfare programs do in more developed systems. Thus, different communities may rely on different methods of providing for the needy, so that a measure based only on formal programs may well exclude informal but significant redistribution. If this is the case, then our measure of welfare provision is more a reflection of a society's degree of institutionalization than of its commitment to aiding the indigent.

Using Country-Specific Variables

Both examples illustrate how the use of identical measures in all countries can lead to serious problems when our variables take on different meanings from one country to another. As an alternative, we may decide on measures that are *country specific*; that is, we may use a different variable for each nation studied, with the choice depending on the local culture. In this case, we need to be sure that every indicator reflects the same underlying concept. As with the selection of identical or common indicators, this can create a problem, since there is no guarantee that our choices will in fact be equivalent.

As evidence of this, consider the issue of political protest. Clearly, if each political system has somewhat different rules governing political life, then protest against the system may take different forms from one country to another. Although one government may permit open dissent or demonstrations, another may impose severe penalties for the same behavior, forcing people to vent their dissatisfaction by other means. Thus, where open dissent is costly, we may anticipate that people protest through indirect methods, such as evasion of government demands and regulations. The discontented may avoid overt ways of expressing antisystem attitudes and may turn instead to beating the system by misappropriating funds, evading taxes, or bending bureaucratic rules. Thus, in order to compare the extent of antisystem activity between countries, we may look at open dissent in one place and noncompliance or evasion (assuming that we can measure it) in another.

We can thus make a plausible case that the two are equivalent measures of protest, but we cannot prove it conclusively. Another researcher may argue that the two activities really reflect different things: Open dissent may actually be a good barometer of our underlying concept, whereas white-collar crime is not. People may misappropriate funds, evade taxes, or bend bureaucratic rules for any number of reasons, none of them directly related to protest against, or dissatisfaction with, the political system. If this is the case, then our two measures are not equivalent, and we are not really tapping the same thing in each country. In other words, white-collar crime may not be a valid indicator here, because it may not reflect what we want to measure. Our use of country-specific variables, then, is not necessarily a guarantee that we have comparable data for all the nations included in our sample.

This suggests that both of our options for choosing variables—the use of identical or country-specific indicators—have their limitations. Neither guarantees equivalence. But we can offer some ways to minimize the problem. First, we clearly need a good, basic knowledge of the culture of each country we study, so that we can determine when a given measure is appropriate. Second, we need multiple measures or indicators. If we can define several different ways of measuring protest, for example, and if those ways tend to produce the same conclusions, then we can have some confidence that we are in fact tapping the right dimension. Using these strategies can help to give us equivalent or comparable data for all the countries studied.

CHOOSING CASES TO STUDY

Given an appropriate question and a sensitivity to the problem of equivalence, we need to be sensitive as well to the problems involved in selecting a sample. Ideally, we should not have to choose among countries: The best way to keep our results from being culture-bound is to include data from every possible nation. But in practice, our range of options is much narrower, because the data available to us are limited. If, for instance, we rely on data provided by each individual country, we are limited by the fact that many nations publish little or no information about the issues we want to study. In some countries, accurate and timely publication of political, economic, and social data remains a luxury. And even where resources are available, some topics may be considered too sensitive (such as data on political unrest) or not salient (such as statistics on domestic violence) to warrant publication. Countries that do provide information often use different ways of defining and reporting data, so that published information might not really be useful for comparison. If, on the other hand, we want to collect our own data—for example, with a survey—the costs of research abroad can be prohibitive and the amount of data collected will be limited.

Most Similar Systems Design

These constraints mean that for most questions studied, we have to work with a sample of a few select countries chosen expressly to minimize bias. Our choice thus has to be made with some care because it can have a significant effect on what we find. We might follow one of two strategies common in comparative research. The first, called a **most similar systems design**, focuses on countries that are very similar, on the grounds that the characteristics they share can thus be held constant. Then, if the countries differ in some other trait, we can eliminate the shared characteristics as explanations for the variation.

To picture how this might work, imagine that we have decided to explore differences between countries in the scope of government activity. Why do governments play a much larger role in the economic and social life of some nations than of others? There are several possible explanations, ranging from differences in levels of economic development to differences in cultural norms about politics. Cultural norms, though, are sometimes difficult to measure precisely. Accordingly, we might control for their effects by looking at variations in the scope of government action among countries with similar cultures, such as the United States and Britain. Whatever differences we find in the reach of political institutions cannot be attributed to cultural factors, because such factors are, in effect, roughly constant across our sample. To put it another way, focusing on countries that have similar traits means that we can safely rule out these specific factors in explaining the differences we find.

Most Different Systems Design

Alternatively, we might adopt the opposite strategy: choosing countries that are different in as many ways as possible. This is referred to as a **most different systems design**. In this case, if we find a common characteristic across our sample, we can rule out the differences between countries as explanations. As an example, consider our earlier question about social welfare. We might choose a set of countries at different levels of economic development and with different types of political systems but, using an equivalent measure for each, discover that they devote roughly the same share of resources to welfare. If so, the differences between them must not affect what each country spends to help needy citizens. Thus, choosing countries that differ on several characteristics allows us to eliminate these characteristics while explaining some shared trait.

Which of the two options should we choose? The answer depends in part on how well we have developed the theory that guides our research. For example, the most

TABLE 12.1 Most Similar System Design versus Most Different System Design

	Most Similar	**Most Different**
Comparing polities with substantial apparent:	Similarities	Differences
Hypotheses focuses on relationship:	Differences	Similarities

similar systems design is appropriate when we can identify all of the important factors that might influence our findings and can locate a set of countries that share them. But because few countries are likely to be so well matched, it is normally much easier to find a sample that differs on the important dimensions. In that case the most different systems design is likely to be more suitable. This design also makes it less likely that we will find a common pattern between widely different countries. It thus gives more credibility to the results when we do find a common pattern. In effect, a most different systems design offers us somewhat better control over the factors that might influence or bias what we find, as well as more assurance that our results are valid. The key characteristics of these two comparative designs are summarized in Table 12.1.

FINDING INDEPENDENT OBSERVATIONS

In choosing a sample, we are usually guided by the notion that the more countries we include, the more confidence we can have in our results. A large sample increases the chance that we have included a representative range of values for key variables and lends more weight to whatever statistical procedures we might employ. This is true, though, only when each observation is *independent*. The advantages of a large sample hold only when data from one country are not influenced by events in another. If the two are not independent, then we really do not have two separate pieces of information backing up our results.

RESEARCH EXERCISE

Most Different Designs versus Most Similar Designs

1. Choose four countries to include in a *most different systems design* to study the relationship between economic development and press freedom in each nation. Explain why you would choose each nation.
2. Now, select three possible indicators you might use to measure the extent of economic development and press freedom in each nation.
   a. Would these necessarily be equivalent measures in a study that includes countries at different levels of development and with different types of political systems?
   b. What effect might differences in definitions have on the comparative analysis?
3. Repeat this exercise using a *most similar systems design* for four countries.

The process whereby events in one country affect the life of another is referred to as **diffusion**, and testing for its effects on cross-national research is referred to as **Galton's problem**, after the author who first described it. It suggests that we may see a strong causal connection between two variables—such as a country's reaching a certain stage of development and its experiencing shifts in policies—where none really exists, all because several countries in our sample are jointly influenced by another country. If so, having a large sample is of no real value because all the extra observations really add no new information.

Actually, we would be hard-pressed to find a sample in which all of the data are completely independent. It is almost inevitable that some degree of diffusion influences virtually everything we study in cross-national research. If this is true, we need strategies that can minimize diffusion's effects. One, of course, is to look for explicit signs that one country in our sample has been influenced by another and to exclude it from our analysis. Another is to adopt a most different systems design, choosing countries that are as divergent as possible and choosing observations from different time periods. Based on the assumption that diffusion effects diminish with distance and time, this strategy can help to increase the chance that each piece of data in our sample is independent of the others.

FINDING DATA

Each issue that we have discussed corresponds to a stage in comparative research, from developing the appropriate question to deciding how best to choose measures and select a sample. In theory, at least, the last stage is to locate the actual data (though sometimes the whole sequence is reversed). If our goal is to find consistent and comparable information, we will need to take several issues into account.

Aggregate Data

There are substantial variations in the scope and quality of aggregate information from one country to another, and even more variation in the availability of data on different topics. Not surprisingly, more developed countries generally have better infrastructure and resources for assembling and publishing national data. They are also likely to face more domestic demand for such information. Thus, comparable aggregate data are far easier to find on the United States, Western Europe, and other developed states than on poorer countries. The CIA's *World Factbook* (www.cia.gov/library/publications/the -world-factbook/), for example, offers comprehensive country-by-country overviews of political structures and economic conditions such as GDP per capita and percentage of the population living in poverty. But the data are much more complete for wealthier states than for poor ones. Even for wealthier countries, we are likely to encounter differences in definitions and coverage of ostensibly identical data. To take our earlier example of public spending on social welfare programs, each country may include different types of expenses or programs in its national statistics, and some may include state and local spending, whereas others may not.

Data availability also differs by topic. Data on election results, for example, have become increasingly easy to locate and are accessible online (one good source is the *International Foundation for Electoral Systems* at www.ifes.org). Other types of information can be more difficult to collect. As one example, consider the question of whether democratization breeds greater income equality. To answer it, we would need data on the timing of democratization and on the distribution of incomes during and after the shift from authoritarian rule. For measures of democratization, we might tap data from *Polity IV* (www.systemicpeace.org/polity/polity4.htm), a widely used data set with country-by-country evidence on regime changes extending back to the 1800s, or *Freedom House*'s annual ratings of civil liberties and political rights (www.freedomhouse.org). However, comparable measures of income inequality are far harder to locate. Even if the data exist, they may be issued sporadically, making it difficult to determine how inequities respond to changes in the political system.

Survey Data

Limitations arise in using survey data. Such data are generally far easier to find for wealthier countries, where resources, logistics, and political stability facilitate individual interviews. Many major cross-national survey projects have thus focused predominantly on more developed states. And, as with aggregate data, coverage varies by topic. It can be much easier to find cross-national surveys on elections and partisan choice, or on core attitudes and values than on individual political behavior, or on interethnic relations. Thus, we are generally limited to the topic and questions defined by other researchers.

The alternative, collecting new survey data, does give us control over the choice of sample and variables employed. But as with aggregate data, the more countries and time periods we include, the more difficult it becomes to guarantee that we are measuring the same thing in each one. In fact, collecting data on individuals in other cultures can be an extremely complicated task. Assuming that we have the resources to carry out a cross-national study—say, a survey of political alienation or of participation—and that we have the cooperation of the government in each of our sample countries (which should not be taken for granted), we need to consider several issues.

First, we need to be confident that our survey ensures **linguistic equivalence**— that is, questions we use in one language are translated accurately into others. Moreover, questions should have a broadly equivalent meaning in all included cultural populations to ensure that differences in the distribution of answers are not due to the respondents' interpretations of the questions (Jowell 1998). This clearly requires fluency (or translators who are fluent) in the language of each individual we interview, as well as back-translations to ensure that the questions are indeed equivalent. Even the most fluent researcher, though, may still have some difficulty in expressing some concepts. Certain ideas or terms derived from one culture may simply have no counterpart in another. Take, for example, the notion of an interest group (that is, a collection of like-minded individuals who attempt to influence government policy) and the notion of pluralism (a political order in which different groups compete and cooperate to influence the government's actions). Because the two notions are products of Western democratic theory, both may have equivalents in Western democratic systems. But in other cultures, neither idea may even exist because each derives from the experience of highly institutionalized political systems that give rise to formally organized groups. When such differences occur, our survey questions will have to be rewritten in terms that allow equivalent translations between cultures.

PRACTICAL RESEARCH ETHICS
How well do know your countries?

Comparative research involves the same ethical considerations that are present in other types of research. However, because cross-national studies often bring together scholars with very different cultural, social, or political backgrounds, ethical standards might differ greatly among those who work together on such projects.

In general, it is best not to assume that scholars from different countries share the same ethical principles, such as the rights of study participants or the ethical conduct of research. Scholars who conduct studies in other countries or cultures should therefore discuss the ethical principles of all participating researchers at an early stage in the project in order to ensure that all research is consistent with the ethical standards of both the home and the host country.

Comparative researchers also need to be aware of, and comply with, the requirements of data protection laws and other relevant legislation that might differ from country to country. Particular attention should be paid to different legal standards that might be applied to issues such as privacy, informed consent, or confidentiality of records. Ignoring these differences can cause unforeseen problems later in the research process, either during the data collection, the analysis, or the interpretation.

Finally, like in any other research project, comparative scholars must carefully consider the risks and benefits of their studies, especially when they involve human subjects. As a general rule, researchers should limit their intrusion into the lives of the individuals or communities they study and protect them from any potentially harmful effects of participating in their studies.

In addition to the possibility of differences in language and concepts from one country to another, there is the possibility that **cultural traits** may influence the way people respond. Thus, for example, respondents in some countries may view the survey as a game in which their role is simply to string along an interviewer, whether their answers are accurate or not. Others may place a high value on cooperation or deference to authority and thus may be inclined to give the responses they think the interviewer wants to hear. Finally, some may not acknowledge having certain reactions or values, because they go against what local society prescribes (for example, racial or ethnic stereotyping). In each case, culture produces a bias that influences the responses obtained.

As with other aspects of the equivalence problem, part of the solution lies in in-depth research on each country to help identify factors that might influence the way people answer. Another lies in the use of multiple measures of what we want to study. If other types of evidence support our survey results, then we have more reason to believe that our findings are valid.

Focus Groups. One of the least used methods for gathering data in cross-national research is **comparative focus groups**. The lack of comparative focus group research can be explained by the fact that it is often difficult for researchers to ensure the equivalence and comparability of data collected from oral statements of culturally and linguistically diverse populations (Colucci 2008). However, comparative focus groups can offer invaluable data about the effectiveness of international marketing campaigns, development, and education efforts in different nations, or of political campaigns that must traverse cultural borders—to mention just a few examples. Thus, comparative focus groups allow researchers to probe for differences and communalities that might exist in the perception of people with different cultural or national backgrounds.

If you are considering using focus groups in a cross-national or cross-cultural context, however, you need to pay attention to a number of potential issues that are typical in international research. First, the use of focus groups as a research method may not be acceptable in some cultures. For example, Yelland and Gifford (1995) found that Cambodian women were reluctant to meet in formal groups because such groups were linked with a repressive government and work camps in their home country. Other respondents simply might find it strange to get together with people they do not know in order to talk about an issue they have discussed previously only with friends and relatives. Liamputtong and Ezzy (2005), for example, found that in Thailand, strangers are usually not trusted. Therefore, it would be inappropriate to invite Thai participants who do not know one another into a focus group to discuss personal matters. In Western nations, on the other hand, anonymity in group discussions is commonly accepted. It is therefore important to consider how focus group meetings might be perceived within each nation or cultural group.

Second, researchers should be sensitive to the ways participants commonly conduct group discussions within their own cultural setting. Vissandjee et al. (2002), for example, showed that people in rural India preferred to sit on the ground with their shoes off and legs crossed when attending focus group discussions. Thus, researchers need to be aware of local customs and must follow them carefully when conducting focus groups in different nations.

Conclusion

As this chapter has shown, comparative analyses are necessary to develop generalizations that apply beyond national borders if we want to study system-level traits. Cross-national research must be designed in accordance with several considerations, including the framing of truly comparative questions, the use of equivalent measures, the choice of an appropriate sample, and the inclusion of observations that are independent from one country to another.

This very short overview of comparative research identifies neither all of the data sources available for cross-national research nor all of the problems we might encounter in using them. But it does suggest that each source has different strengths and weaknesses, and these are factors that we need to recognize in any comparative study. The availability and accessibility of comparative data differ from country to country. Generally, it is easier to find data for industrialized rather than developing nations. Increasingly, however, international organizations provide access to comprehensive country-by-country overviews through the Internet.

Given the state of our theories about politics and our access to information, we obviously do not have perfect solutions for each of the problems that comparative research might raise. Yet we still need to take each one into account when designing a study and interpreting its results. The more clearly we recognize and control for possible biases, the more confidence we can have that our conclusions are accurate.

Key Terms

system-level traits *227*
equivalent measures *229*
most similar systems
   design *232*

most different systems
   design *232*
diffusion *234*
Galton's problem *234*

linguistic equivalence *235*
cultural traits *236*
comparative focus groups *236*

Research Examples

Cross-national analyses allow us to evaluate political issues or systems with a comparative perspective, thus avoiding a narrow understanding of "how things work." Baek (2009), for example, analyzes how political communication institutions affect the differences in voter turnout in seventy-four nations. The author finds that variations in voter turnout can be explained by media systems, access to paid political television advertising, and campaign finance laws. Ormrod and Henneberg (2009) discuss the concept of political market orientation in the context of UK and German political parties and argue that certain aspects of the concept may be mediated by electoral system and other structural variables. Finally, Sawer and Laycock (2009) analyze and compare the political discourse of market populism in Australia and Canada and explore the adaptation of the discourse in local circumstances. If you are interested in reading other examples of research on comparative politics, a good source is the academic journal *Comparative Political Studies*.

Methodological Readings

For a general discussion of comparative methods, consult *Innovative Comparative Methods for Policy Analysis: Beyond the Quantitative-Qualitative Divide* (Grimm and Rihoux 2006), *The Logic of Comparative Social Inquiry* (Przeworski and Teune 2000), *Issues and Methods in Comparative Politics: An Introduction* (Landman 2000), or *Comparative Politics: Theory and Methods* (Peters 1998).

References

Baek, Mijeong. 2009. "A Comparative Analysis of Political Communication Systems and Voter Turnout." *American Journal of Political Science* 53(April): 376–393.

Colucci, Erminia. 2008. "On the Use of Focus Groups in Cross-Cultural Research." In Pranee Liamputtong, ed., *Doing Cross-Cultural Research: Ethical and Methodological Perspectives* (pp. 233–252). New York, NY: Springer.

Grimm, Heike, and Benoit Rihoux, eds. 2006. *Innovative Comparative Methods for Policy Analysis: Beyond the Quantitative-Qualitative Divide*. New York, NY: Springer.

International IDEA. 2004. *Voter Turnout in Western Europe Since 1945: A Regional Report*. Stockholm: International IDEA.

Jackman, Robert W. 1987. "Political Institutions and Voter Turnout in the Industrial Democracies." *American Political Science Review* 81(June): 405–423.

Jowell, Roger. 1998. "How Comparative Is Comparative Research?" *American Behavioral Scientist* 42(2): 168–177.

Landman, Todd. 2000. *Issues and Methods in Comparative Politics: An Introduction*. London: Routledge.

Liamputtong, Pranee, and Douglas Ezzy. 2005. *Qualitative Research Methods*, 2nd edition. South Melbourne: Oxford University Press.

Ormrod, Robert P, and Stephan C. Henneberg. 2009. "Different Facets of Market Orientation: A Comparative Analysis of

Party Manifestos." *Journal of Political Marketing* 8(3): 190–208.

Peters, B. Guy. 1998. *Comparative Politics: Theory and Methods*. New York: New York University Press.

Przeworski, Adam, and Henry Teune. 2000. *The Logic of Comparative Social Inquiry*. Melbourne, FL: Krieger Publishing Co.

Sawer, Marian, and David Laycock. 2009. "Down with Elites and Up with Inequality: Market Populism in Australia and Canada." *Commonwealth & Comparative Politics* 47(April): 133–150.

Vissandjee, Bilkis, Shelly N. Abdool, and Sophie Dupere. 2002. "Focus Groups in Rural Gujarat, India: A Modified Approach." *Qualitative Health Research* 12(6): 826–843.

Yelland, Jane, and Sandra M. Gifford. 1995. "Problems of Focus Group Methods in Cross-Cultural Research: A Case Study of Beliefs about Sudden Infant Death Syndrome." *Australian Journal of Public Health* 19(3): 257–263.

CHAPTER 13

Social Network Analysis: Finding Structure in a Complex World

In this chapter you will learn:

- The characteristics of social networks.
- The principal facets of social networks.
- The basic techniques for analyzing social networks.
- Several types of data that are used in social network analysis.
- Different forms social networks can take.

When you were in grade school and a classmate was teased, do you recall being surprised by *which* fellow student came to his defense? You thought you knew who was linked and the intensity of those connections, but this episode opened your eyes to a newly visible connection. The world is filled with social networks, some highly visible, others closely concealed. A **social network** is a group of actors—people, organizations, governments—who are linked together by some common actions, common membership, shared communication, or some other form of exchange.

An Example

The directors of corporations, for example, often are members of the same trade or business organizations, such as the National Association of Corporate Directors, or read the same magazines, such as *Corporate Board Member*—patterns that might increase their cohesiveness as a group. At the same time, many corporate directors serve on the boards of more than one company, which can produce communication flows and even perhaps common perspectives across those companies.

Similarly, those who may be at odds with business leaders also form organizations with overlapping memberships. Environmental and other activist groups participate in coalitions with overlapping membership and frequently share directors or advisors with other organizations. The result can be information sharing, commonality of perspective, or even coordinated action. Networks of donors to political campaigns often give to the same candidates,

PRACTICAL RESEARCH ETHICS
How to handle personal contacts?

Some networks are openly observable, whereas others may be closely concealed. Following the flow of money or tracing overlapping boards of directors between organizations is substantially simpler and less ethically challenging than recruiting and interviewing confidential informers who reveal the presence of alliances between politicians or internal agency policies that skirt administrative rules or laws.

Civil servants and potential sources in private organizations may welcome your research in much the same way they would react to the scrutiny of an investigative reporter.

If your research involves personal contacts, be honest in your interviews about the amount of confidentiality you will be able to guarantee. Remember that most of your research will be publicly available (whether as a thesis or a book or article), and other insiders may be able to identify your (even unnamed) sources simply by what they know.

political action committees, or advocacy organizations. Activist foundations of the left and right contribute funds to advocacy groups that may, themselves, form activist networks.

Participants in criminal conspiracies are, by definition, members of a network, and demonstrating the nature of that network is often an important part of prosecuting them. Even terrorist organizations such as Al Qaeda are constructed in the form of networks through which resources such as money, plans, and instruction flow.

The Key Facet of Networks

Not all of these networks have the same structure and not all function in the same ways. But at their core is a common fact: They are based on patterns of exchange—money, information, influence, leadership, programmatic objectives, and the like—that can be usefully summarized in the form of maps of these various relationships. Social network analysis is the method by which such maps are produced and analyzed.

This chapter provides some very basic information about the development and analysis of social network maps. The introductory treatment here is restricted to some very basic graphic and generally nonmathematical applications of the technique. In point of fact, social network analysis is a highly developed quantitative methodology that is based, among other things, on the analysis of matrices. If you are interested in more sophisticated applications of social network analysis, the bibliography at the end of the chapter includes references to several key works.

SOCIAL NETWORK DATA

The data employed in social network analysis consist of two types: nodes and links. **Nodes** are the actors or participants in a network. For example, if we are studying networking structures associated with the Republican Party, our nodes might include the Republican National Committee (RNC), the Senate and House Republican Caucuses, the Republican Governors' Conference, the Ripon Society (a group of moderate to liberal Republicans), the Federalist Society (an influential conservative group with ties to the Republican Party), and the Log Cabin Republicans (an organization of gay and lesbian Republicans). Nodes can be of different types. The RNC, for example, is a direct arm of the party itself, whereas the Federalist Society is not.

Links are the connections among the actors. In the present example, this might include such elements as shared members or leaders, the flow of funds to or from each organization, and the sources and movement of policy proposals.

Links may also have different intensities. The ties between the Republican Governors' Conference and the RNC, for example, are likely to be much stronger than those between the RNC and the Log Cabin Republicans. Strength can be measured in a variety of ways, such as the number of personnel interlocks, the value of dollar flows between the nodes, and the number of messages or policy proposals. When constructing a map of such a network, then, we have a number of choices to make: *which nodes we want to include* (all? only those that share a particular characteristic?), *which resource flows we want to include* (money? information? interlocking directorships? direct membership?), *the extent or intensity of the flows* (we can represent this in our map by the size or number or color of the links), and *the direction in which those resources flow* (only toward one or another key participant? only from that participant? both? or do we simply ignore the direction of flow?). As we make each of these choices, we begin to develop the appearance of our network map and, in the process, shape both the information it conveys and the analysis it supports.

Social Network Matrices

All social network analysis begins with a data matrix that represents both the nodes of the network and the relationships, or links, among them. Although these tables contain detailed information, the data will also be placed into more intuitive figures. Examples of matrices are provided in Tables 13.1(a), and 13.1(b). In the tables, the letters represent the nodes in a five-member network. Where the nodes have some form of relationship with one another, the corresponding cell in the table shows a where there is no connection, the cell shows a "0."

The matrix in Table 13.1(a) is known as a **symmetrical matrix**. That means that the relationships represented in the table are reciprocal—if A is linked with B, then B is also linked with A. For example, if the connection between Company A and Company B is provided by Jane Smith, who serves on the board of directors of each company, then Ms. Smith also provides a linkage in the opposite direction (i.e., between Company B and Company A). In the table, this means that if there is a "1" in cell AB (row A, column B), there must also be a "1" in cell BA (row B, column A). In a basic symmetrical matrix, the direction of exchange is not an important consideration.

The matrix in Table 13.1(b) is known as an **asymmetrical matrix**. Here the relationships are not necessarily reciprocal, though some of them may be. For example, if the Progressive Policies Foundation gives money to Environmentalists to Save the World, but the environmental group does not give money to the foundation, then the flow of money is in one direction only, which is to say nonreciprocal. In this instance, if the foundation were represented in the matrix by "A" and the environmental group by "B," then the table would have a "1" in cell AB, but a "0" in cell BA. In a basic asymmetrical matrix, the direction of exchange is an important consideration.

Finally, consider the matrix in Table 13.1(c). This is a symmetrical matrix that is similar to that in Table 13.1(a) in all ways but one—the entries in the cells are not all

TABLE 13.1

(a) Matrix of Symmetrical Relationships

	A	B	C	D	E
A		1	1	1	1
B	1		0	0	1
C	1	0		1	1
D	1	0	1		1
E	1	1	1	1	

(b) Matrix of Asymmetrical Relationships

	A	B	C	D	E
A		1	1	1	1
B	0		0	0	1
C	0	0		1	1
D	0	0	1		1
E	0	1	1	1	

(c) Matrix of Symmetrical Relationships Showing Intensity

	A	B	C	D	E
A		1	3	1	5
B	1		0	0	1
C	3	0		1	1
D	1	0	1		4
E	5	1	1	4	

equal to "1." Rather, they take on different values that represent the amount or intensity of the connection between each pair of nodes. Suppose, for example, that A and C are activist organizations that share five members in common, D and E share four members, A and C share three members, and the other combinations of activist groups share either one or no members in common. If our objective is to analyze patterns of political activism, that information might be well worth capturing. Table 13.1(c) captures it by assigning different values to the cells depending on the number of shared members. These entries could be actual counts of members in common (and, hence, interval data) or simply a ranking from lowest to highest overlap (and, hence, ordinal data). Though not illustrated here, asymmetrical matrices can also capture variable degrees of interconnectedness among the nodes.

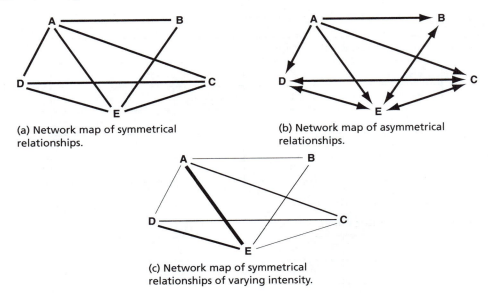

(a) Network map of symmetrical relationships.

(b) Network map of asymmetrical relationships.

(c) Network map of symmetrical relationships of varying intensity.

FIGURE 13.1 Sample network maps of relationships.

Mapping a Network

Working from a matrix like those we have just constructed, it is then a simple matter to draw a map of a given network. As specified in the matrix, the nodes are represented as points in space and the links as lines that connect them. Figure 13.1 illustrates network maps that correspond, respectively, with the matrices in Table 13.1.

Notice that in Figure 13.1(a) there are five nodes, corresponding to the five participants in the network, and that lines have been included to connect each pair for which a "1" appeared in the matrix in Table 13.1(a). So, for instance, A is shown as being connected with each of the other participants, while B is connected—or *linked*—only with A and E.

In Figure 13.1(b), we have the same five nodes, but rather than using simple lines to represent the relationships among the nodes, we have employed arrows.[1]

Recall that in the asymmetrical matrix in Table 13.1(b) the exchanges were in one direction only. The arrows capture that additional directional information.

Finally, in Figure 13.1(c), we return to a symmetrical network, but one in which some relationships are stronger (or larger and more important) than others. In this instance, we capture the additional information by increasing the thickness of the connecting lines, or links. If the links were of different types—say, money, common programs, and interlocking directors—we could also capture their variations by using multiple lines (in different forms, e.g., solid, dashed, or dotted), each of which could vary in thickness.

---

[1] Often symmetrical networks are shown with arrows in both directions rather than with simple lines. We have chosen not to do so here in the interests of clarifying the basic dynamics of network analysis.

RESEARCH EXERCISE

Tracing Information Paths

To illustrate the political information channels traced by network analysis:

1. Ask a friend how she or he gets local political information. Continue your queries until he or she names a specific person as an information source. Record this person's name.
2. Note the type of information this person provides (e.g., official city rules, days/times of the community farmers' market, location of neighborhood polling place, etc.).
3. Contact the politically informed person by phone. Introduce yourself, explain that you are working on an exercise for a college class, and ask where he or she obtains local (to your college area) political information.
4. Repeat this process two more times.
5. Draw a diagram linking the flow of information.
6. Using your interviews and the diagram, answer these questions:
    a. How authoritative do the people you contacted feel their information is?
    b. Which of your contacts get their information from the same source?
    c. Have the people higher up the information chain lived in your college community longer, or do they possess more trusted information?
    d. What makes these individuals more trusted?

TYPES OF NETWORKS

Networks can be simple and straightforward or complex and convoluted. The more members (nodes) included, the more types of linkages we incorporate and the further out we extend our notions of connectivity (e.g., including other networks in which our principal nodes may participate), the more complicated things become. But at the same time, networks tend to display certain structural characteristics that can help us to analyze and understand them. Figure 13.2 illustrates some of these basic configurations.

The first type of network structure shown in Figure 13.2(a) is the **chain** or **linear network**. In this structure, each participant has contact with only two others. Typically, this would be an asymmetrical arrangement in which one participant passes resources or instructions to another (hence the arrows). Although Participant A has a natural power advantage here as the initiator of all exchanges, a network of this type is highly

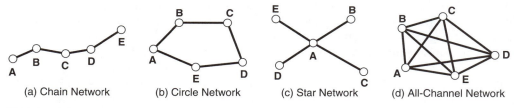

(a) Chain Network   (b) Circle Network   (c) Star Network   (d) All-Channel Network

FIGURE 13.2 Basic network configurations.

decentralized—indeed, there is no central, controlling authority—and the members do not actually know who their co-members are at more than one degree of separation. And because Participant A has no direct links to any participants beyond B, and thus has no way to monitor or adjust subsequent exchanges, even A's power is limited.

As an example, consider a terrorist network in which plans and goals are set by A and sent into the network. By the time D and E have their exchange, both plans and goals may have been modified in ways unknown to, and inconsistent with the wishes of, Participant A. At the same time, should some portion of the network be compromised, the fact that no participant can identify more than two other participants—if certain precautions have been taken in communicating (e.g., through blind drops), each participant may actually only know the identity of the next participant downstream—provides a measure of security against the network being fully dismembered.

A variant on the chain network is the **circle network** shown in Figure 13.2(b). Here the flow remains asymmetrical, but Participant E closes the loop with Participant A. This structure can provide some measure of feedback to A, who can then make adjustments as necessary. But in the previous example, because it requires that E possess some means of exchanging with A, it can also compromise the security of the network at the highest level.

A **star network** shown in Figure 13.2(c) is one in which a central actor—Participant A—is linked with every other actor, but none of the other actors is linked with one another. This is very much the opposite of the chain network, because here there is a single, centrally located participant who controls, and is a party to, every exchange that takes place. In fact, in a star network the identities of the other participants may be entirely unknown to any of them. Each deals only with A. Modifying the previous example, a terrorist network organized in a star pattern would have substantial security at its periphery because no individual cell has any contact of any kind with other cells. Such a network could be easily and effectively controlled because each cell depends on the central participant for its resources and instructions. But, should Participant A ever be compromised, the entire network would be destroyed for the simple reason that no combination of other participants could communicate with one another because each participant other than A operates in virtual isolation.

Finally, there is the **all-channel network** shown in Figure 13.2(d). Here, every participant is linked with every other participant in a thoroughly decentralized structure. In this form of networking, rather than limiting, masking, or controlling exchanges, every member interacts more or less openly and more or less extensively with every other member.

Consider the previous example using the Republican Party. Broadening the range of connections to include not only common membership but also communication between organizations, support for common policies, campaign contributions, and other types of financial support, you can see that the organizations in question have a variety of contacts with one another. Some contacts are stronger or more frequent than others. Some are of one type, some of another. But the participants in the Republican network know and engage in exchanges with one another more or less independently of any central authority. Similarly, we can think of the nations of the world as participants in an all-channel network. They all belong to international organizations like the United Nations, but also retain direct diplomatic relations with one another. Not all of these channels will be equally important, but together they do very closely resemble a large-scale version of an all-channel network.

ROLES OF PARTICIPANTS

In addition to documenting the overall structure and functioning of the network *per se*, researchers are often interested in the functions of individual participants. The most basic question, of course, is which individuals, organizations, or other kinds of entities are members of a given network and, conversely—but also often equally as interesting—which ones are not. This is important, for example, in determining which actors are likely to have an influence on the actions of others within the network and which are not.

Analyzing Influences

Similarly, an examination of the particular role(s) played by a participant within a social network can often help us to understand the behaviors and influence possessed by that particular actor. In the star network depicted in Figure 13.2(c), for instance, there is a clear difference between the roles of Participants A and D. Participant A is more centrally located, more influential, and presumably more important in determining the actions of the network.

In the circle network depicted in Figure 13.2(b) and the all-channel network in Figure 13.2(d), on the other hand, every participant appears to have roughly co-equal influence. Factors determining a particular participant's role and influence would be such things as the participant's number of network links relative to other nodes, the types of exchanges in which the participant engages (e.g., a participant may be involved in exchanges of money but not information), and the direction in which resources flow (e.g., whether a given participant is a major source of funds for the network or, alternatively, a major recipient of funds from others; whether a participant originates most of the plans for the network or receives direction from others). In effect, then, social network analysis provides a tool for gauging and characterizing the relative power of each participant.

Outside Links

It may also be worth noting which nodes in a network provide links to other networks. Some participants may be relatively isolated, interacting only with other members of the original network. Others may provide connections to outside sources of money, information, or other resources. And some may be highly integrated into a large number of networks, which would permit them to serve as conduits through which networks might exchange resources with one another, in effect creating a network of networks. Participants that perform this external integrative function may not be powerful within the structure of any given network, yet may exercise considerable power through their ability to control the flow of exchanges *between* networks.

Example: Networking for the Environment. We can illustrate the use of social network analysis by examining some of the relationships among environmental activists, social responsibility investors (those who invest based on the social policies of companies as well as their financial prospects), and religious organizations. This is accomplished in Figures 13.3–13.5. For purposes of this example, we will not show the underlying matrix of relationships. It is important to note, however, that compiling such a matrix was the first step in the analysis.

We begin by examining three organizations, the Coalition of Environmentally Responsible Economies (CERES), the Social Investment Forum (SIF), and Co-op America.

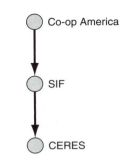

FIGURE 13.3 Origins of CERES.

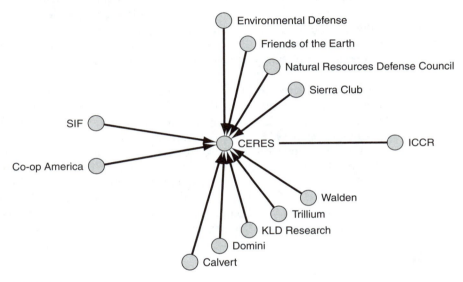

FIGURE 13.4 CERES members.

CERES is a prominent group of environmental organizations and others that has created a set of environmental business practices that its members ask companies to follow. Searching Web sites to research CERES (see Chapter 3 for Internet research techniques), we can easily learn that CERES was established in 1988 and was originally begun at the initiative of another group, SIF. SIF, in turn, is a part or project of yet another organization, Co-op America, a relatively little-known environmental group. Applying this information, Figure 13.3 illustrates the networking origins of CERES. The network is directional because each group acted in turn to create the next. Figure 13.3 is a basic chain network.

Next, let us consider the membership of CERES itself. CERES is a coalition of more than eighty organizations, including well-known environmental advocates, social responsibility investment companies, and others. You will find these members listed on the group's Web site. The star network illustrated in Figure 13.4 shows a few of these members. Since all are members of CERES rather than the reverse, we have, again, included directional links. To help facilitate the analysis, we have organized the network into clusters. On the left are the two companion organizations (Co-op America and SIF) that founded CERES. On the bottom are several of the more prominent social responsibility research and investment companies. At the top are several of the better known environmental activist groups. To the right is yet another organization, the Interfaith Center for Corporate Responsibility (ICCR). Organizing the network in this manner helps us begin to understand the nature and role of CERES, about which we will say more.

Figure 13.5 adds two new sets of information, both, again, based on readily available information from the Internet. ICCR is a coalition of approximately 275 faith-based organizations and others that tries to influence corporate policies. We have included a few of the organization's church-based members to represent its membership, and we have also added links from three of the social investment companies to the Social Investment Forum. Each of these three companies is represented on the organization's board of directors. (Because the network is now becoming more complex, we have eliminated the arrows to reduce visual clutter.)

What can be discerned from Figure 13.5? We can see that CERES has been constructed as a diverse coalition that includes policy-oriented environmental groups, investors who value environment-friendly business practices, and faith-based activists who share an interest in corporate policies. As political scientists, this might suggest to us that the group relies on the environmentalists for its policies, on faith-based activists for its moral authority, and on social responsibility investors for its financial clout. If we were to take such additional steps as including more members of each coalition in the network, examining patterns of cross-membership (one group belonging to two or more coalitions) more extensively, examining different kinds of links (money, leadership, and so forth), and examining other affiliations of the members of this particular network (that is, links to other outside networks), we could learn a great deal more still.

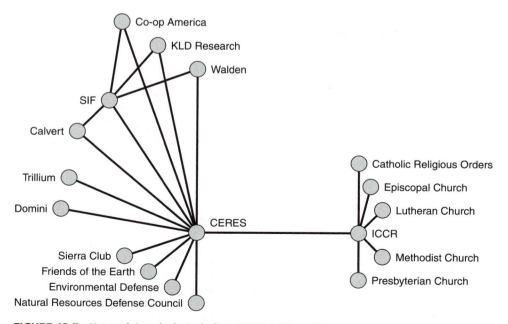

FIGURE 13.5 Network interlocks including CERES, ICCR, and SIF.

Conclusion

To the extent that power relationships drive politics, a set of techniques that systematically characterizes patterns of exchange among groups of political actors clarifies these relationships. Social network analysis advances political science research by focusing on the structure and character of political relationships.

This form of analysis addresses such research questions as:

1. Does a network exist among some group of political actors, be they individuals, organizations, or governments? Who are the members? What do they have in common?
2. What form does the network take? What resources flow through it? How extensive is it?
3. What is the respective role of each participant? Which participants, if any, are positioned to have greater influence within the network? How and why?
4. What does the network's structure indicate about the relative and absolute relationships among the participants?
5. Which key actors have been excluded from the network? What, if any, light does this shed on the nature of the relationships?

6. Does the presence of actors holding membership in multiple networks effectively link the networks to one another? How many (and which) members have such dual linkages? What are the implications of either the isolation of individual networks or their linkage one to another?

The examples in the preceding discussion have only begun to suggest the types of networks that could be explored using this analytic approach. Networks of activists of various stripes, funding networks, terrorist or criminal networks, governmental networks in the international system, networks of political organizations with governments or political parties, networks of parties and interest groups, networks of citizens joined together through memberships in organizations or through their exposure to the same television broadcasts or magazines—these are but a few of the potential sets of relationships that can be studied using social network analysis.

Key Terms

social network *240*
nodes *241*
links *242*

symmetrical matrix *242*
asymmetrical matrix *242*
chain or linear network *245*

circle network *246*
star network *246*
all-channel network *246*

Research Examples

Tracking relationships between regional transportation organizations in two cities, Weir, Rongerude, and Ansell (2009) identify the value of vertical power structures using network analysis. Fowler et al. (2007) use a database of tens of thousands of U.S. Supreme Court cases to construct a network analytic framework that predicts lower court outcomes.

Methodological Readings

A thorough and concise conceptual overview of social network analysis is provided by Monge and Noshir (2003). Castells (2000) offers a sweeping, even visionary, account of the increasing importance of networks in *The Rise of the Network Society*. An early and influential work on political networks is Knoke (1990). Those interested in understanding the mathematics associated with social network analysis will want to consider Pattison (1993).

Software

An example of the specialized software that facilitates large-scale and complex social network analysis is UCINET 6.233, a package developed by Steve Borgatti, Martin Everett, and Linton C. Freeman. UCINET is available online from Analytic Technologies (www.analytictech.com), which offers student pricing. Accompanying the software is an excellent introduction to the technique, *Introduction to Social Network Methods* (Hanneman and Riddle 2005). The text is also available online (www.faculty.ucr.edu/~hanneman/). In this chapter, Figures 13.3–13.5 were prepared using the UCINET software.

References

Castells, Manuel. 2000. *The Rise of the Network Society*, 2nd ed. Oxford: Blackwell Publishers.

Fowler, James H., Timothy R. Johnson, James F. Spriggs II, Sangick Jeon, and Paul J. Wahlbeck. 2007. "Network Analysis and the Law: Measuring the Legal Importance of Precedents at the U.S. Supreme Court." *Political Analysis* 15(Summer): 324–346.

Hanneman, Robert A., and Mark Riddle. 2005. *Introduction to Social Network Methods*. Riverside, CA: University of California, Riverside (published in digital form [www.faculty.ucr.edu/~hanneman/]).

Knoke, David. 1990. *Political Networks: The Structural Perspective*. New York: Cambridge University Press.

Manheim, Jarol B. 2004. *Biz-War and the Out-of-Power Elite: The Progressive Left and the Attack on the Corporation*. Mahwah, NJ: Lawrence Erlbaum Associates.

Monge, Peter R., and Noshir S. Contractor. 2003. *Theories of Communication Networks*. New York: Oxford University Press.

Pattison, Philippa. 1993. *Algebraic Models for Social Networks*. New York: Cambridge University Press.

Weir, Margaret, Jane Rongerude, and Christopher K. Ansell. 2009. "Collaboration Is Not Enough: Virtuous Cycles of Reform in Transportation Policy." *Urban Affairs Review* 44(March): 455–489.

CHAPTER 14

Coding Data: Preparing Observations for Analysis

In this chapter you will learn:

- The value of proper data coding techniques.
- The key characteristics of useful data coding formats.

When you visit a friend's apartment for the first time, can you always immediately locate the trash can, silverware, can opener, or sugar—without asking? It is normal to ask for directions when in a new kitchen, since drawers and cabinets are rarely labeled and many people organize things differently. The data we have collected are like the contents of a kitchen: We have many choices of how to categorize and label them, but we should follow some standard conventions and we must use great care to document our choices carefully. Just as you probably prefer to have your potholders close to the oven to protect your hands from heat, each guideline of data coding has had its genesis in a painful lesson.

Our principal motivations in coding data are: (1) accurately reflecting the underlying nature of the data, (2) facilitating useful analysis, and (3) preserving as many analytic choices as possible. It will be helpful to keep these objectives in mind as you work through this chapter.

CODING: WHAT DO ALL THOSE NUMBERS MEAN?

The process of assigning numerical values to our observations is termed **coding**. Coding is to measurement what the alphabet is to speech: a mechanism for making a precise and lasting record of information. Just as each letter or combination of letters in the alphabet represents a certain sound, each number or combination of numbers in a code represents a particular characteristic or behavior of a research subject. And just as letters allow those who know the alphabet to communicate complex ideas with one another without speech, numbers allow those who know the codes to communicate complex ideas to one another in a much abbreviated form. However, numerical **codes** allow the researcher to go one step further, for coded information, precisely because it is in numerical form, can be transformed and manipulated according to the rules of mathematics so that the findings may yield meaningful conclusions that might remain obscure were there no resort to numerical representations. Proper coding, in other words, allows us to learn more from our research than might otherwise be the case.

The Role of Coding

The codes we assign to each variable's values are determined by level of measurement of each variable, as well as how we plan to analyze the data. Thus, if we measure the educational achievement of members of a given population in which each respondent is scored either as not having completed high school, as having completed high school but not college, or as a college graduate, we might assign the numbers 1, 2, and 3, respectively, to represent the three levels of achievement. Alternatively, if we wish to score each respondent on the number of years of schooling completed, we might assign to each a numerical code equivalent to that number (for example, the code 7 might represent seven years of schooling). Either coding scheme accurately summarizes the findings of our study, though each conveys a meaning different from the other. Once we have assigned one or another set of such numbers, we may process and analyze the data to our heart's content before reconverting our codes into verbal expressions as we prepare our research report. This process of translation from concept to number and back may be summarized, as shown in Figure 14.1.

The most important thing to keep in mind as we develop data codes is that our numerical representations must always be consistent with the measurement characteristics of the variables we are researching. That is, nominal-level variables should have nominal codes, ordinal-level variables should have ordinal codes, and interval/ratio-level variables

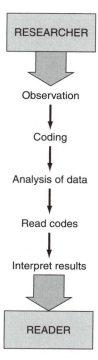

FIGURE 14.1 Coding in research.

should have interval/ratio codes. The numbers may *look* very much the same in each instance, but their meanings will differ substantially. Once words or concepts are converted into numbers, we may be tempted to analyze or manipulate our data in ways that simply cannot be supported by their underlying level of measurement (this problem becomes more apparent in later chapters, when we focus more directly on techniques of analysis). Such temptations must be resisted in order to preserve the usefulness of our research, for, as we learned in Chapter 5, not all numbers are created equal, depending upon level of measurement.

Nominal Data

The mechanics of encoding (or decoding) data are really quite simple. We begin from the values (categories) of each variable in our study. In the case of *nominal* variables, when our numbers need distinguish only between mutually exclusive categories without respect to rank, we merely assign scores in whatever manner is convenient. If, to choose a relatively typical example, our subjects' religious affiliation is to be classified as Protestant, Catholic, Jewish, or Muslim/Islam, we might assign codes according to any of the following schemes:

1 Protestant	1 Jewish	1 Muslim/Islam	43 Catholic
2 Catholic	3 Catholic	2 Protestant	17 Protestant
3 Jewish	5 Muslim/Islam	3 Jewish	27 Muslim/Islam
4 Muslim/Islam	8 Protestant	4 Catholic	07 Jewish

In each instance, a unique numerical value is used to represent one value or category of the variable. Since religious affiliation is a nominal characteristic, the order and magnitude of the codes have no significance whatsoever. We can use one-, three-, or even ten-digit numbers in our codes if desired. It is, of course, best to keep the codes as simple and manageable as possible, and we will generally opt for the lowest numbers and the fewest digits possible, but this is a function of our concern for **parsimony** rather than of any mathematical requirement.

It is possible to use slightly more sophisticated nominal coding schemes in order to convey more complete information. Suppose, for instance, that we wish to further categorize our Jewish and Protestant subjects by their specific denominations. Here we might use a two-digit code that builds on our earlier classification. The first digit would be selected as above (for example, 1 representing Protestants; 2, Catholics; and 3, Jews). The second would add the new information. Consider the following scheme:

10 Protestant	20 Catholic
11 Baptist	30 Jewish
12 Methodist	31 Orthodox
13 Presbyterian	32 Conservative
14 Lutheran	33 Reform

Here our codes preserve (in the first column) the gross differences between the categories but allow as well (in the second column) for some fine-tuning. The result is a more complete record of our subjects' characteristics, which still preserves the essence of the less precise variable with which we began.

Were we to list all of the Protestant denominations, of course, the "10" codes (those from 10 through 19) would soon be exhausted and we would be forced to modify our scheme. Either of the following alternatives can easily meet this challenge, though the desirability of choosing one or the other may vary depending on one's analytical requirements.

10 *Protestant*		100
11 Baptist		101
12 Methodist		102
13 Presbyterian		103
14 Lutheran		104
15 Episcopalian		105
16 Church of Christ		106
17 Latter-day Saints		107
18 Church of God		108
19 Christian Science		109
20 Wesleyan		110
21 Assembly of God		111
30 *Catholic*		200
40 *Jewish*		300
41 Orthodox		301
42 Conservative		302
43 Reform		303
50 *Islam/Muslim*		400

In the first instance we simply expand the number of decades (sets of ten codes) assigned to the Protestants; in the second we add a digit. Again, since the variable in question is nominal, neither the specific numbers nor the number of digits has any significance. As long as our coding system is parsimonious, and as long as the coding categories are mutually exclusive, any numbers will suffice.

Ordinal Data

When coding *ordinal* variables, we are a bit more constrained. Because ordinal measurement does not include equal, or even known, intervals between values, we remain free to employ numbers of any magnitude. But because ordinal measurement requires that we preserve in our codes the relative positions (rankings) of these values, we must, at the very least, take care that our numbers are properly ordered. Thus, for the variable *level of political development* or any variable entailing differences of level, degree, or likelihood, either of the coding schemes in the two left columns might be equally correct (and equally meaningful). Each preserves the order inherent in the variable. Neither is in any way more precise than the others, because precision is a function not of the numbers themselves but of the underlying ordinal measurement. As was true earlier, our concern with parsimony might well lead us to select the first of the two schemes, but beyond that, our choice is strictly arbitrary.

Appropriate Rankings		Inappropriate Rankings	
1 Lowest	1 Lowest	1 Lowest	1 Highest
2 Low	6 Low	9 Low	6 High
3 High	7 High	6 High	7 Low
4 Highest	9 Highest	7 Highest	9 Lowest

In contrast, neither of the schemes in the two right columns is appropriate. Though the relative magnitude, or ordering, of numerical codes (and therefore the direction of their ordering) has no significance for nominal measurement, it is very important when we work with ordinal data. In the second column from the right, the ranking of the numbers has been mixed; in the far right column, it has been reversed. As a result, neither of the right hand coding schemes satisfactorily preserves the relative position and magnitude of the values on the variable. Thus, the codes are an inaccurate translation of our observations. Either they deprive us of the opportunity to rank our cases one against another, or they mislead us about the nature of any ranking we develop. Accordingly, such schemes are to be avoided with ordinal data.

Interval/Ratio Data

Developing codes for interval/ratio measures may prove the easiest. Here numbers take on more precise meanings, and our options in assigning them are substantially reduced. A dollar is a dollar, a year is a year, and the difference between 47 percent and 43 percent is the same as that between 73 percent and 69 percent. In interval/ratio measurement, not only are values mutually exclusive and indicative of rank, but also the distances between any two sets of adjacent categories are constant and equal. The coding of interval/ratio variables must preserve these characteristics.

In order to code scores on an interval/ratio, we must find a set of numbers such that each is mutually exclusive of the others, each corresponds to a value of the variable, each is equally distant from its nearest neighbors, and the distance between any two adjacent values is known. Finding such numbers is generally an easy task, for unlike most nominal or ordinal scales, for which the researcher must, in effect, invent numerical equivalents for observations, many interval/ratio codes are naturally occurring. That is, interval/ratio codes are far more likely than those at lesser levels of measurement to derive *directly* from the operational definitions of variables. If we define a person's income as the number of dollars earned in a given period, then each specific quantity of dollars earned constitutes not only a value of the variable income but also a code for that value as well. As a result, the emphasis in the coding of interval/ratio data is generally less on *creating* meaningful codes than on recognizing and preserving them.

As we pointed out in Chapter 5, situations occur in which the researcher may, in order to enhance the manipulability or the explanatory power of a data set, wish to collapse interval/ratio data into ordinal categories. It may, for example, be both easier and more meaningful for us to compare respondents according to their general level of income than to focus on each dollar of difference. In such instances, it may be that the initial coding of the data will preserve their interval/ratio character and that these categories will subsequently be reaggregated according to the needs of the researcher (for example, we might record the actual number of dollars earned by respondents and then later group these earnings into larger categories), or the design may be to collapse the data at the time of acquisition (as when we simply classify respondents into general income categories [e.g., $20,000–$49,999] and make no record of their specific earnings). Each method entails both advantages and disadvantages, which should be weighed in the context of the research question at hand. Whichever is selected, however, researchers should be sure that their ultimate coding scheme meets the measurement requirements of the indicator in question.

As should be evident by now, the assignment of appropriate codes to data is inseparable from the process of operationalizing variables. Indeed, *codes are nothing more than numerical manifestations of our operational definitions.* Decisions about what codes to associate with values on a variable must be made early in the research process. Such decisions are merely one more important part of proper planning. Yet the real usefulness of codes does not become apparent until later in the research process, for it is when we begin to analyze our data that codes come to bear most directly on our enterprise. It is here that coding provides for the transition first from observation to data processing and then from data processing to interpretation. To understand how this transition takes place, let us now consider the structures and uses of several code-related mechanisms.

THE CODEBOOK AND THE CODING SHEET

The first such device we must examine is the codebook. A **codebook** is simply a listing of each variable to be employed in a study, of each value the variable might take on, and of the numerical scores—the codes—associated with each of these values.

An Example

Suppose that we are investigating a theory that governments can shape foreign press coverage of them through using public relations firms to manipulate the news. Furthermore, let's say that on July 1, 2003, in reaction to President Bush labeling them the "Axis of Evil" in his State of the Union address on January 29, 2002, the governments of Iran and North Korea hired public relations firms to improve their images in the U.S. press. (In our example, the other country identified in the speech, Iraq, is not participating in the PR effort.) We wish to design a study to determine the effect these efforts have had on news and editorial content. In such a study we might compare the periods before and after the starting date of these campaigns to see whether, after the contracts took effect, (1) the amount of coverage of each nation increased or decreased significantly and (2) the various nations were presented more or less favorably than they had been in the earlier period. (In reality, we would also have to control for such additional factors as the occurrence of newsworthy events such as political upheavals or natural disasters, but for purposes of illustration let us assume these are not concerns.)

To assess the effects of these image-enhancing efforts, we can turn to any of a number of indexes of news coverage and either analyze the index entries, which will be in the form of either titles or abstracts of various news articles and may, in fact, convey a good deal of information, or use them to identify the actual articles themselves. For purposes of illustration, let us design a project using index entries in Infotrac *Expanded Academic ASAP* (which indexes the contents of a large number of popular magazines) under the headings "Iran" and "North Korea." Our independent variable is the introduction of professional public relations activities or, more correctly, their absence (before July 1, 2003) or presence (after that date).

Following on the two questions identified, we will have two sets of dependent variables. The first set will measure the *quantity* of news coverage and might include the number of index entries each month in the pretest and posttest periods, and the proportion of such entries (as evidenced by their titles or index classifications) that refer to the political, economic, or social system of each country. We might further classify these as focusing on domestic or international concerns. The second set of variables will measure the *quality* of news coverage through judgments on such matters as whether the article (again, as evidenced by its title) suggests progress or decline in the nation's fortunes. Finally, in any such study we should include codes identifying each individual article, the country to which it refers, the date of publication, its length, and the specific publication or type of publication in which it appears.

Creating a Codebook

An abbreviated codebook for this hypothetical study is illustrated in Table 14.1. As you can see, the codebook summarizes the indicators to be used in the study and their associated values. It is, in fact, little more than a formal statement of the operational definitions with which any piece of research begins. Here, however, these definitions are set

TABLE 14.1   Abbreviated Codebook for a Hypothetical Study of Public Relations of Foreign Nations

Variable Label	Variable Label	Values	Code
var001	Article (CaseID) number		—
var002	Nation referenced	Iran	1
		North Korea	2
var003	Month of publication	February 2002	01
		March 2002	02
		April 2002	03
		.	
		.	
		.	
		June 2003	17
		July 2003	18
		August 2003	19
		.	
		.	
		October 2009	93
		November 2009	94
		December 2009	95

TABLE 14.1 (Continued)

Variable Label	Variable Label	Values	Code
var004	Reference to political system in title (including references to government, political leaders or events, political parties, public policies, etc.)	No reference	0
		Reference present	1
var005	Reference to economic system in title (including references to industry, the currency, the workforce, production, markets, trade, economic opportunity, etc.)	No reference	0
		Reference present	1
var006	Reference to social system in title (including references to cultural, religious or social institutions, social events or actors, social structure, etc.)	No reference	0
		Reference present	1
var007	Reference to domestic or international context	Exclusively domestic	1
		Both domestic and international	2
		Exclusively international	3
		Does not apply, NA	9
var008	Reference to progress or decline	Reference exclusively to progress	1
		Reference to both progress and decline	2
		Reference exclusively to decline	3
		Does not apply	9
var009	Number of pages in article		—
var010	Type of magazine	News weekly (*Newsweek, U.S. News & World Report,* or *Time* only)	1
		Other, primarily political (including opinion magazines and those featuring primarily political news and analysis)	2
		Other, primarily nonpolitical (including general audience magazines and those with specialized but primarily nonpolitical coverage)	3

out in complete detail, including instructions for their interpretation, and are organized not with respect to our hypotheses *per se* but with an eye toward facilitating the actual gathering of information. The codebook provides step-by-step guidance to what we are looking for and how to recognize it when we find it.

The codebook identifies the variable names, variable labels, values, and the numerical codes we will assign to each value. It also tells what codes were used to represent nonnumeric data. For example, the codebook depicted in Table 14.1 indicates that a number 1 for *var010* signifies that the type of magazine in which the article in question was found is a news weekly (such as *Time* or *Newsweek*). Having this information in a central location helps researchers correctly record data, and, later, accurately interpret the results of data analysis. It also makes it possible for others who use the data set to see how data are organized and to interpret the results of data analysis without relying exclusively on the original researcher.

Creating a Coding Sheet

Once the codebook has been prepared, it is a quick and easy step to the next stage of data preparation—the development of a coding sheet. A **coding sheet** is a data recording device whose structure is based on the codebook and whose form will aid in data entry and analysis in our statistics program. It should be noted that we act as if we will be gathering data by hand when creating our coding sheet. This is simply a heuristic to help us develop the most useful electronic form, since manual entry would waste time and increase the opportunity for errors to enter our data. Thus, we will enter our data directly into an electronic coding sheet of our own design. Incidentally, the survey questionnaire described in Chapter 8 is an example of a coding sheet, as is the form presented in Figure 14.2 for our study of coverage of foreign nations in the American press.

In Figure 14.2 the column labels correspond to the indicators developed in the codebook. Each row represents one case, and each numerical entry represents a value on the indicator in question for that particular case. Thus, we see that case number 0742 is an article about Iran that appeared in a news weekly in November 2009, focused exclusively on the political system, and made reference to the nation's declining fortunes and to certain weaknesses in its domestic situation. Such scores might derive, for example, from an article in *Time* entitled "Iran in Chaos: Leaders Unable to Halt Executions, Stability Threatened." In this manner, relevant characteristics of each article title encountered can be recorded on the coding sheet, with each case taking up one row or line. Thus, if we study, or *code*, 821

Identification number	Country	Month of publication	Reference to political system	Reference to economic system	Reference to social system	Domestic/international context	Progress/decline	Number of pages	Type of magazine	
0 7 4 2	1	9 4	1	0	0	1	3	0 0 3	1	

Coding sheet number ____________

Date coded ____________

Coded by ____________

FIGURE 14.2 Coding sheet for studying effects of public relations efforts by foreign nations.

RESEARCH EXERCISE

Usefulness of Codebooks

Without a codebook to help interpret it, a data set may not be very useful.

1. Locate an online data set (e.g., UN health statistics from a year ending in the same number as your student ID number, county-by-county registration, and voting data for a state starting with the same letter as your first name, etc.).
2. Record the data's Web address, and save the data set to your computer.
3. Choose a single variable (with at least thirty cases) and write a description of the variable in your own words, noting:
   a. Is there a detailed description of the variable's source and coding (i.e., a codebook entry)?
   b. Who gathered the data?
   c. Why did they gather data on this variable?
   d. Are the data part of a long-term study, or a one-time data collection?
   e. From the organization's Web site, does it appear that this variable is used by the agency that gathered it? If so, how? If not, why do you suppose they gathered data they don't use?

cases, we can expect to end up with 821 rows of data. In each instance, corresponding data about the various cases will appear in the same column(s) on the coding sheet.

Finally, when printed, all coding sheets should be numbered (to ensure that none has been lost), dated (dates are often useful, for example, if we are forced to alter a definition or add a variable in midstream and must recode or add codes to all previous cases), and signed or initialed by the coder (as a basis for measuring intercoder reliability, as discussed in Chapter 10). If more than one coding sheet is required for each case, as when the number of indicators to be measured is quite large, all sheets for the same group of cases should be both stapled together and numbered identically. This minimizes the chances of their being separated and mixed up during processing.

DATA ENTRY AND DATA PROCESSING

Once the recording of data has been completed, we turn our attention to processing or manipulating our numbers to arrive at our findings. You can well imagine that in a study with large numbers of indicators and cases, the jumble of numbers can be absolutely overwhelming. This demonstrates the value of familiarizing yourself with a statistics package. Rather than an additional complication in the research process, correctly employed statistics software will aid in summarizing the characteristics of your data and greatly simplify their analysis.

Many software packages are available for performing statistical analysis. Arguably the most common in academic, business, and government settings is SPSS. Available for many operating system platforms (for example, Mac OS X, Microsoft Windows, and Unix), this software program combines a spreadsheet view of your data with the most common analytic tools you might find useful in testing your hypotheses. Other common statistical programs are, for example, SAS, Statistica, Genstat, or Minitab. Software packages with full statistical programming languages like S-Plus, STATA, or SHAZAM can provide more flexibility for creating graphics and using new statistical methods. In the end, choosing a program will depend on the analyses you want to do, your statistical background, and which programs are readily available. SPSS and many of these other programs offer student versions at a discount, or your institution may have a site license agreement that reduces the cost of student purchases.

Entering Data

All of the most common statistics programs allow the user to enter data directly into a spreadsheet or data-editing screen. When using such a spreadsheet to enter data, you should first define and label one column for each variable of interest. Then you enter the data, with each row representing a different case or observation. If, for example, you would like to analyze ten characteristics (your variables) of 200 newspaper stories (your cases), you would use one line of data for each of the 200 newspaper stories. In this example, each line of data would use ten columns, one for each of the ten variables. In addition to the columns that represent the variables in your analysis, you should also add one column for a case identification number in order to keep track of your data. This should sound familiar, since it is directly analogous to the coding sheet described previously.

Although manual data entry has become easier due to the availability of spreadsheet-like data entry systems, other methods of data entry are available. Optical scan sheets, with which most students probably are familiar ("fill in the bubbles with a number two pencil . . ."), are also popular due to the increased availability of optical scanners and new software that allow the creation and scanning of questionnaires to produce data files. Optical scan sheets are especially useful for recording large amounts of data that have been initially recorded on predesigned, standardized forms, thus avoiding the arduous task of entering the data manually. There are, however, a few disadvantages of using optical scan sheets for data entry. First, scan sheets only allow data to be entered in a predetermined way. Notes in the margins of the scan sheet, for example, will not be recognized by the scanner and therefore will not appear in the final data file. Second, optical scanners often do not recognize markings on scan sheets that do not conform with the predesignated option. Thus, scan sheet bubbles that are not completely filled, or are smudged or wrongly marked, will probably not be recognized correctly by the scanner. Finally, some people may easily lose their place on scan sheets because of the generic layout or the difficulty in identifying the appropriate space for marking the data on the sheet.

Once your data are in the format of your statistics software, the next step is to check them carefully for errors, a process that is also called "data cleaning." Manual data entry can easily lead to errors because of typos, incorrect reading of the codes, or simply a tired person entering the data. The simplest check for erroneous entries is to print out the distribution for each of the variables in your data set and then look for inappropriate codes. For example, you might have decided to code the variable *party identification* as 1 for Republicans, 2 for Democrats, and 3 for Independents. If you see in the printed distribution that one of the cases has been coded as 5, it is obvious that an error has been made during the data entry. After identifying an error, simply review the original questionnaire

PRACTICAL RESEARCH ETHICS

How thoroughly should you document your coding?

A fundamental quality of scientific research is replicability. That is, can others reproduce a project's research results? An answer of "yes" to this question is obtained, in part, through careful documentation of data coding by researchers. Replication has such value in the discipline that certain journals publish replication articles, often written by graduate students.

To ensure transparent coding, you should fully document the creation of each variable. Recording each variable's construction in a codebook helps people to perform many important tasks, such as:

1. Your instructors to assess your research skills.
2. Reviewers to evaluate your analyses.
3. Subsequent researchers to build upon your work.
4. You to supplement your own memory of how each variable was constructed.

responses and find the correct codes. Unfortunately, erroneous entries within the range of designated values for a given variable can only be found by comparing each entry in the data set to the original data source.

Conclusion

Three final points are in order. First, it is not unusual for those without prior statistical software experience to be both overwhelmed and intimidated by these programs. Such feelings are understandable, but they should not be allowed to stand in the way of learning, since all programs include help menus. Additionally, many useful guidebooks exist, including the Quantitative Lab Manual that supplements this text.

Second, do not be ashamed if you make mistakes. Careful data entry and proofreading eliminate many errors, but as with any new skill you will invent ways to make more. This is a common pattern and should not trouble you. When you think about it, making and correcting mistakes represent two of the most important ways that we learn. Track down your own errors when you can, get help when you must, and keep trying.

Finally, do not get carried away. Computers are inherently stupid; they process information and they follow instructions precisely, but they do not think. By using the software packages we have described here, you can easily get a computer to perform the most elaborate statistical analyses imaginable on data of such low quality that the results, though impressive-looking, are meaningless. Accordingly, it is important that you think through and understand the statistical and analytical procedures that you call upon the computer to perform, and that you select only those that fit your needs and your data. Those procedures are the subjects of the next several chapters.

Key Terms

coding *252*

codes *252*

parsimony *254*

codebook *257*

coding sheet *260*

Research Examples

Examples of coding schemes, and their authors' rationale, may be found in the appendices of the quantitative data analysis articles in the current issues of the political science journals listed in Chapter 3.

In recent years, several massive projects have coded large numbers of factors linked to international conflicts. The Correlates of War project covers the breadth of history, while the International Crisis Behavior Project is a more temporally constrained study that analyzes conflict in the twentieth century. The Web site for the former study (www.correlatesofwar.org) includes exceedingly detailed codebooks, which offer numerous examples of coding techniques. The latter study's Web site (www.cidcm.umd.edu/icb) also offers codebooks and data, with data also available from ICPSR.

Atteveldt, Kleinnijenhuis, and Ruigrok (2008) employ an innovative technique to "teach" a computer program to code using pattern matching and testing against human coders, as they demonstrate the viability of computerized coding of Dutch news articles. Turning their attention to conflicts in the Middle East (and sporting one of the longest article titles ever published in political science) Hudson, Schrodt, and Whitmer (2008) automatically code news items using the Kansas Event Data System (KEDS). In an earlier work, King and Lowe (2003) make a strong case in favor of using coding formulas for very large data collection projects, suggesting that automation permits researchers to utilize data that would be impractical with hand coding.

Methodological Readings

Although from another era, a still-relevant discussion of coding procedures is found in *Data Processing: Applications to Political Research* (Janda 1969).

References

Atteveldt, Wouter van, Jan Kleinnijenhuis, and Nel Ruigrok. 2008. "Parsing, Semantic Networks, and Political Authority Using Syntactic Analysis to Extract Semantic Relations from Dutch Newspaper Articles." *Political Analysis* 16(Autumn): 428–446.

Hudson, Valerie M., Philip A. Schrodt, and Ray D. Whitmer. 2008. "Discrete Sequence Rule Models as a Social Science Methodology: An Exploratory Analysis of Foreign Policy Rule Enactment within Palestinian-Israeli Event Data." *Foreign Policy Analysis* 4(April): 105–126.

Janda, Kenneth. 1969. *Data Processing: Applications to Political Research*, 2nd ed. Evanston, IL: Northwestern University Press.

King, Gary, and Will Lowe. 2003. "An Automated Information Extraction Tool for International Conflict Data with Performance as Good as Human Coders: A Rare Events Evaluation Design." *International Organization* 57(July): 617–642.

CHAPTER 15

Tables and Charts: Visually Describing the Data

In this chapter you will learn:

- Techniques to visually communicate information.
- Some standard guidelines for visual information presentation.

Did you vote in the 2008 presidential election? Did you follow the 2008 campaign in the United States? You probably recall that, even before the party primaries in January, this campaign drew unprecedented attention to the interactions of gender, race, and politics. In the Democratic Party primaries, Senator Hillary Clinton faced off against Senator Barack Obama, pitting the best-financed major party campaign of a female candidate against an African American candidate. In the end, of course, Senator Obama received the party nomination. At the Republican National Convention that summer, presidential nominee John McCain chose Alaska Governor Sarah Palin as his running mate, leading many to believe that he was trying to court disaffected female voters.

Thus, the November election pitted Barack Obama, who had defeated Hillary Clinton, against John McCain, who was running with Sarah Palin. There was widespread speculation in the fall that Obama's victory over Hillary Clinton and Sarah Palin's presence on the GOP ticket would reduce Obama's support among female Democrats in the general election. This chapter attempts to illuminate the electoral role of gender, using tables and charts.

THE SIMPLE TABLE

We begin our analysis of trends in partisan voting by gender using a device with which you are probably already familiar—the simple table. A **simple table** is little more than a tabular presentation of research data in what is essentially the form of a list.

An Example

Table 15.1, for example, summarizes the Democratic presidential vote and its gender components for the period 1980 to 2008.[1] Each column in the table represents a different

---

[1] Just as gender is commonly used in the literature to denote differential partisan voting by females in the term gender gap, sex and gender are used interchangeably here, although sex is a biological characteristic and gender a social construct.

TABLE 15.1　Size and Gender Composition of the U.S. Democratic Vote, 1980–2008*

Year	Democratic Vote (%)	Male Democratic Vote (%)	Female Democratic Vote (%)
1980	44	39	47
1984	42	37	45
1988	47	44	50
1992	58	55	61
1996	58	51	64
2000	53[†]	47	57
2004	49	46	52
2008	55[‡]	52	57

Source: Data reported in this table are computed from the quadrennial surveys of the American National Election Studies (ANES), available at www.electionstudies.org. Any opinions, findings, and conclusions or recommendations expressed in these tables are those of the authors and do not necessarily reflect the views of the ANES funding organizations.

*Data on minor party voting have been excluded from the present analysis.

[†]In the regionally divided electorate of 2000, this national survey somewhat overstates the Democratic vote percentage.

[‡]The 2008 figures are weighted to represent the population more accurately, because the 2008 ANES employs a substantial African American and Latino oversample (Lupia, Krosnick, Luevano, DeBell, and Donakowski 2009).

variable (there are four variables in all). Specifically, the table reports the share of the total (two-party) vote received by the Democratic presidential candidate each year, as well as the percent of the men's and women's vote received by the Democratic candidate. The fact that the table is ordered by the variable year, which appears in the first column, provides a cue for the interpretation of the data. It suggests that the table has been constructed to answer the question, *How has the Democratic presidential vote varied from year to year?*

Table 15.1 can be used to test several hypotheses, which may or may not be supported by the data. For example, (1) Women cast more of their votes for the Democratic Party. (2) The "Gender Gap" between women's and men's support for Republican candidates is growing. (3) It takes more than 50 percent of the both the women's and men's vote for a Democrat to be elected. (4) A Republican is elected if women's support for the Democratic candidate falls below 60 percent. These are just some of the hypotheses that could be tested using these data; several will be examined later in the chapter.

Although the findings reported in Table 15.1 are easy to digest, you should not expect such clearly distilled results directly from a statistics program such as SPSS or even Excel. For example, the data in this table came from eight different surveys. That is to say, after obtaining your data analysis, often you will need to compile new summary tables that condense data from several sources into a simple presentation. When combining, though, great care must be used to accurately represent your data.

A close examination of Table 15.1 reveals a number of points about the proper format for tabular presentation. As in the example, all tables should be numbered consecutively. In a lengthy paper with several numbered sections (or in a thesis or book with several chapters), these numbers may take the form of Table 3.1, Table 3.2, and so forth, or Table III:1, Table III:2, and so forth. In a shorter or more simply structured paper, single-numbered listings (Table 1, Table 2) are quite sufficient. When tables appear in the same work with charts, graphs, or other illustrations, they are usually numbered separately. Graphic presentations are generally referred to as, for example, Figure 1 or Figure 3.1.

Titling Tables

Each table should have a title that accurately summarizes the nature of the data it reports. This title should give the reader enough information to decide whether to examine the table in detail, but it should not go so far as to save the reader the trouble of doing so. Thus, a title for Table 15.1 such as *Data Showing That Democrats Polled More Than Half of the Votes Four Times from 1980–2008 and Did Better Among Women Than Men* would be inappropriate. In general, a title should simply indicate the major variables for which data are reported in a given table. When, as in Table 15.1, these data represent a geographic or political subdivision (e.g., the United States) or cover a particular time period, those characteristics should be incorporated into the title as well. When a table is drawn in whole or in part from another source, the reference should be placed immediately below the table (e.g., the American National Election Study). Explanatory references pertaining to the table as a whole (the first footnote in the example) should be indicated with superscript lowercase letters or other symbols following the title. Those pertaining to parts of the table (the second footnote in the example) should be placed appropriately within the table. The footnotes themselves should be located immediately below the table and should follow a source identification when one is present.

Other points to keep in mind when preparing tables:

1. The table number and title should be separated from both the preceding text and the table itself by open space. Place each table on a separate page at the end of the research report, after the list of references. At the point in the text where the table is discussed, skip a line, type <Table 1 about here> in the center of the page, skip another line, and continue the text.

2. Normally we avoid drawing vertical lines to separate cells within the table. The Table function available in most graphics, word processing, or database programs simplifies the creation and editing of tables. Microsoft Word, for example, allows you to create tables quickly and automatically format them with a variety of borders, fonts, and shading. This feature is especially useful for "hiding" vertical lines in tables and giving all of your tables a consistent look.

3. Labels and data within the table should be double-spaced to facilitate reading, except that titles and category labels that will not fit on one line may be single-spaced. Category labels should describe as briefly as possible the variables or values in question, but they should always be sufficiently complete to clarify the meaning of the data simply by reading the table.

Tables should only be included if they advance the analysis presented in the research report. The key finding(s) of each table should be discussed in the text, but your reader should be able to fully interpret the findings of each table without looking at the description in the report. Avoid overloading the discussion with percentages or other quantitative terms, though these can be used sparingly. Rather, the discussion of a table should make clear any relationships demonstrated in the table and should focus the reader's attention on the highlights and particularly noteworthy findings. The discussion may also be used to report the results of any statistical tests one has performed on the data in the table (see Chapters 16–18).

An Example

A discussion of Table 15.1, for example, would probably touch on the overall level of changes in the Democratic vote during the period in question and on the relative contributions of male and female voters to that vote. Additionally, the discussion of alternative explanations for this gender-based vote disparity might lead to the next table or chart that explores other hypotheses. Specific points to be discussed might include the range of variation and the consistency (if any) in the pattern of variation for the variables, any notable inconsistencies in the data, and even the reliability of the source from which the data have been obtained.

THE LINE GRAPH

Sometimes we may wish to augment or replace tabular presentations with visually simpler graphics. This may be done either to clarify the presentation (consider the difficulty of interpreting Table 15.1 if it covered the period of 1896 to 2008) or to illustrate a particular aspect of the data.

An Example

One of the simplest graphical presentation formats is the line graph, as illustrated in Figure 15.1. A **line graph** connects with a continuous line all the data points for a given indicator and provides for a comparison of data points across indicators by representing each in a separate corresponding line, often in a contrasting style. Line graphs are especially useful for representing trends.

The chart in Figure 15.1 reports the same data as does Table 15.1, but in graphic form. In contrast to the table, which requires a thorough reading, a quick glance at Figure 15.1 is sufficient to tell us that between 1980 and 2008 Democrats polled, in general, between 40 and about 60 percent of the vote in presidential elections; that they did better in 1992, 1996, 2000, and 2008 than in 1980, 1984, 1988, or 2004; that the pattern of male and female voters' support for the party followed very much the same path as its overall fortunes (males and females deserted the party in 1980 and 1984, but returned strongly in 1992 and 2008); and that support for the Democratic Party among female voters was consistently higher than among males. The fine detail available in Table 15.1 is less evident in Figure 15.1, but the overall lessons of the data emerge much more readily.

In general, graphs should be formatted similarly to tables. Each figure should be numbered separately and titled appropriately. Both the vertical and horizontal axes, when present, should be labeled. Vertical-scale labels should be placed to the left of the vertical scale numbers. Horizontal-scale labels should be placed below the figure. If the horizontal-scale numerals are years (as in the example), further labeling is optional. In the

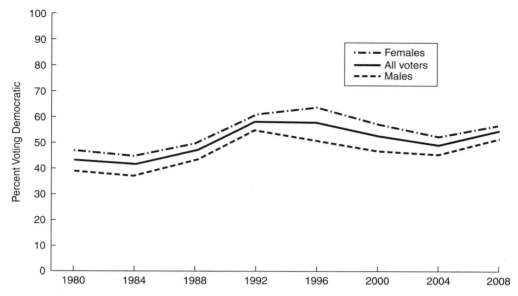

FIGURE 15.1 Line graph: Size and gender composition of the Democratic vote, 1980–2008.

case of a complex line drawing, a **key** (an itemized explanation) to the lines should be placed below the figure. Alternatively, explanatory labels may be placed on the graph.

Just as great care should be exercised to ensure that each figure you create is properly and consistently scaled, attention should also be given to scaling when reading others' charts. Improperly or inconsistently scaled axes can confuse the reader, or even the researcher, by either overstating or understating orders of magnitude or degrees of change. Indeed, truncated graphs (those on which lower values are not included) or stretched graphs (those on which the scale is smaller for one range of values and larger for another) may be deliberately employed to misinform a careless reader. Fortunately, use of these devices is less common in the academic research literature than in advertisements or commentaries.

THE PIE CHART AND THE BAR CHART

Both the simple table and the line graph are useful primarily for describing and summarizing information. With some slight transformation of the data, however, it is possible to use graphic techniques to analyze or interpret these numbers as well. Suppose, for example, we are interested in highlighting the relative importance of women and men voters to the fortunes of Democratic presidential candidates. In particular, we might be interested in such questions as whether females' or males' support is more crucial to Democratic victories and whether (as was widely argued at the time) women voters put Bill Clinton in the White House in 1992, and why Democratic candidates failed to win the White House for the first two elections of the 2000s. Let us suppose further, to keep our argument simple, that in each of the six election years we are considering, 47 percent of all voters were males and 53 percent females. In reality, since the 1980s, women typically

PRACTICAL RESEARCH ETHICS

Fair representation of your data?

Tabular and graphical devices must be used appropriately. As should be evident from this chapter's brief treatment, it is quite easy to present research results deceptively. Misleading presentation of findings is harmful, whether accomplished through the subtle abuse of these techniques or through careless misuse.

You have an ethical obligation to report your findings accurately and fairly. Your colleagues have an intellectual obligation to examine your research rigorously. Together, these obligations are the cornerstones upon which to build your research.

do account for roughly 53 percent of voters, but turnout rates vary from one election to the next (Center for American Women and Politics 2006). Combining this pattern of turnout with the data presented in Table 15.1, we can identify the components of the Democratic vote in each election in terms of their proportional support.

In 1992, for example, we know that 55 percent of male voters supported the Democrats and that 47 percent of all voters were male. Taking 55 percent of 47 percent, we find that 25.85 percent of all voters were males who voted Democratic. Similarly, we know that 61 percent of women voters supported the Democrats and that 53 percent of all voters were female. Taking 61 percent of 53 percent, we find that 32.43 percent of all voters were women who voted Democratic. Together these figures account for the roughly 58 percent of all voters who went Democratic in 1992. (*Note:* The total figure is actually 58.28; these numbers are fractionally different from those in Table 15.1 because of rounding error and because the actual turnout rates that underlie the data in the table only approximate 53 percent for women and 47 percent for men.)

Let us carry this calculation a step further. We know that these male and female voters constituted around 58 percent of the two-party vote in 1992. What proportion of its support did each contribute to the Democratic Party? To ascertain this we simply divide each individual figure by 58 percent (25.85 ÷ 58 and 32.43 ÷ 58) to find that in 1992 around 44 percent of Democratic votes came from males and around 56 percent from females. Similar calculations for each of the five other elections show females have contributed 58 percent, 58 percent, 56 percent, 58 percent, 58 percent, 57 percent, and 55 percent of all Democratic votes in 1980, 1984, 1988, 1996, 2000, 2004, and 2008 respectively; males contributed 42 percent, 42 percent, 44 percent, 42 percent, 42 percent, 43 percent, and 45 percent. These figures may be illustrated graphically by a pie chart, as shown in Figure 15.2.

Using Pie Charts

A **pie chart** is a figure in which a circle (or in this case, a series of circles) representing a given population has been segmented to show the distribution of particular attributes. In Figure 15.2, each circle represents 100 percent of the Democratic presidential vote in a given year. The shaded area represents the proportion of that vote provided by women voters. Note that the title and key to the figure are similar in style and placement to those in Figure 15.1 and that each circle, or pie, is labeled individually at the bottom of the

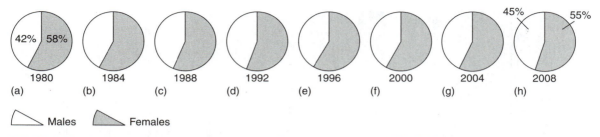

Males   Females

FIGURE 15.2 Pie charts: Gender components of the Democratic coalition, 1980–2008.

figure. Percentages of the pie taken up by each segment may be labeled either within the graph, as in Figure 15.2(a), or outside it, as in Figure 15.2(g), whichever is clearer. Alphabetic labels (a, b, c, and so on) for separate elements within the figure often make it easier for the researcher to discuss the chart in the text and for the reader to follow the discussion.

Limitations of Pie Charts

Looking at Figure 15.2, one may be struck by the seeming lack of change in the proportion of Democratic votes contributed by women between 1980 and 2008, which is consistently about 58 percent. Using Figure 15.2 (and assuming the accuracy of the underlying data), one might thus be tempted to argue in answer to one of the questions posed earlier that in fact Bill Clinton was not put into office by women's votes. Indeed, substantiation for this argument is apparent from even the most cursory inspection of the pie charts.

Unfortunately, in the present instance, the pie charts, although quite accurate, offer evidence that is incomplete and that consequently may prove misleading. This is true because the size of the Democratic vote varied from election to election (47 percent one year, 58 percent the next), whereas the size of the circles in the chart—representing 100 percent of that vote regardless of size—remains fairly constant. Thus, for accuracy and completeness the pies themselves should vary in size to account for variations in the overall Democratic vote. Unfortunately, few people are good at visually judging the relative size of changing pie chart circles.

Using Bar Charts

An alternative graphic device that can illustrate the proportion of women's votes for the Democrats in a given year while at the same time making clear the fluctuations in the overall level of Democratic votes is a segmented bar chart like that illustrated in Figure 15.3. A **bar chart** is a graphic representation in which the height, and occasionally the width, of a series of bars illustrates a set of observations on one or more variables. In a **segmented bar chart**, each individual bar is subdivided to illustrate an additional set of observations relating to the distribution of attributes among the population represented by the bar itself. Note once again that the format is similar to those of Figures 15.1 and 15.2 except that in a bar chart, the key is typically found *above* rather than *below* the chart itself. (Occasionally, bar charts are drawn horizontally beginning at the left margin rather than vertically as in Figure 15.3. In such instances, the key should be placed either below the chart or to the right.)

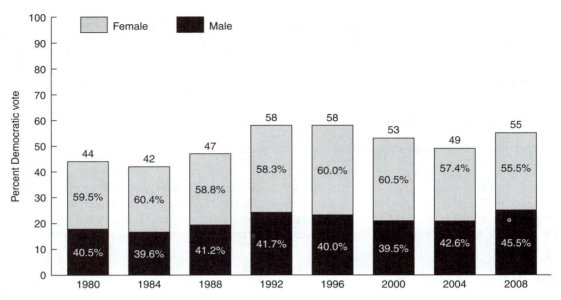

FIGURE 15.3 Bar chart: Gender components of the Democratic vote, 1980–2008.

In Figure 15.3, the female vote is again represented by the shaded area of the chart. The bars, however, vary in size according to the overall percentage of the Democratic vote. This percentage is evident both in the scale along the left-hand margin of the chart and in the labels atop each individual bar. As a result, the impression one gets from the figure is rather different from that suggested by the pie charts, for here we see that though the female Democratic vote did shift up and down a bit, it did so within a relatively narrow range. Instead, it was the overall Democratic vote that proved most volatile, expanding and contracting in concert with the party's fortunes. Returning to our research question of whether female or male support is more crucial to the Democrats, we are now able to answer that the party wins when *both* genders are mobilized. The data used to arrive at this conclusion are essentially the same as those reported in Figure 15.2, but they are more complete. As a result, the conclusions drawn from them are both more sophisticated and more satisfying.

THE BILATERAL BAR CHART

Another type of chart commonly found in the research literature of political science is the **bilateral bar chart**—a two-directional figure that is used to illustrate variation above or below some norm as represented by a center line. Two typical bilateral bar charts are illustrated in Figure 15.4. In Figure 15.4(a), the center line represents the average (mean) percentage of males who voted Democratic in presidential elections from 1980 to 2008 (46 percent). The bars represent variations around that average in each of the eight elections, with bars to the right of the line signifying above-average support among male voters for the Democrats and those to the left signifying below-average support. The length of the bars represents the degree of variation from the average, and the numerals indicate the precise degree of difference. For example, the average of 46 percent minus the variation of

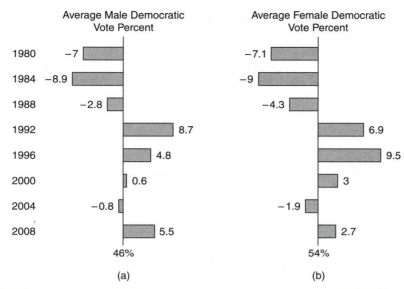

FIGURE 15.4 Bilateral bar chart: Variations in presidential voting by gender, 1980–2008.

7 percent in 1980 yields the 39 percent support by men noted in that year in Table 15.1. Figure 15.4(b) presents a similar analysis of women's votes, based on an average level of Democratic support of 54 percent.

These figures add yet another dimension to our analysis of the data reported in Table 15.1; taken together, they suggest that Democrats can only win the presidency with both men's and women's support. In 1992, a majority of both males and females supported Bill Clinton, the Democratic presidential candidate. In 1996, women maintained strong support, whereas men drifted away from the Democrats. Between 2000 and 2004, on the other hand, women's support for Democrats slipped by 5 percentage points, whereas men's support for Democrats slipped only about 1 percentage points. In 2008 the story was different: Support from women for the Democratic candidate equaled their votes for Al Gore in 2000, and was coupled with well-above-average support for Senator Obama from men. Looking at the overall pattern, the Democratic party captures the White House in the years in which it recruits above-average numbers of male voters (i.e., 1992, 1996, 2008). While Democrats can ill-afford to take women voters for granted, we can see that the type of information available from a bilateral bar chart complements and supplements that which can be developed by using other graphic devices.

THE CROSSTABULATION

One other form of tabular presentation deserves attention before we move on to a discussion of statistics. Indeed, it is perhaps the single most common form of table used in contemporary political science research and provides the basis for a number of the statistical calculations we examine in the next chapter. This form of presentation is known as the **crosstabulation** (or **crosstab**) and is illustrated in Tables 15.2 and 15.3.

TABLE 15.2   Crosstab: Percent of Major Party Vote by Gender, 1980

| | Gender | | |
Presidential Vote	Male	Female	All Voters
Democratic	39	47	44
	(155)	(228)	(383)
Republican	61	53	56
	(239)	(255)	(494)
Total	100	100	100
Number of cases	(394)	(483)	(877)

Source: Warren E. Miller and the National Election Study (1980).

TABLE 15.3   Crosstab: Percent of Major Party Vote by Gender, 2008

| | Gender | | |
Presidential Vote	Male	Female	All Voters
Democratic	52	57	55
	(341)	(506)	(698)
Republican	48	43	45
	(317)	(381)	(847)
Total	101	100	100
Number of cases	(658)	(887)	(1,545)

Source: The American National Election Study (2009).

In format and structure, the crosstabulation resembles the simple table presented earlier, but its substance is different. Crosstabs are based more directly upon hypotheses and are structured to facilitate an examination of the relationships between variables. Table 15.2, for example, summarizes the relationship between gender and the presidential vote for 1980; Table 15.3 summarizes the comparable data for 2008. In each instance, the data are drawn from the National Election Study, and the sample sizes are noted in the table. These tables are organized so as to permit us to examine the hypothesis that women, for one reason or another, are more likely than men to vote Democratic in any given year.

Each entry (exclusive of totals) in each table is termed a *cell*. The tables may be described by the number of rows and columns that they contain, where each row represents a particular value on one variable and each column a particular value on the other. Thus, Tables 15.2 and 15.3 are each referred to as a 2 × 2 (two-by-two) table, since each table has two rows of cells and two columns of cells, excluding totals.

Crosstabs are always arranged so that the data total on the independent or explanatory variable's column or row. In the present instance, that variable is gender (in the columns). This means that if the table contains percentages, they will be based upon and sum to 100 percent along the independent variable. Thus, Table 15.2 tells us that in 1980, 39 percent of males voted Democratic—not that 39 percent of all Democrats were male. The columns for gender total 100 percent, indicating that gender is the independent variable, since one's party preference *invariably* is acquired later than one's gender. The sum of all of the percentages in column 1 of the table accounts for all (100 percent) male voters, in column 2 for all female voters, and in column 3 for all voters. The row labeled "number of cases" reports the number of respondents to our survey who were classified as members of each group. These numbers constitute a *frequency distribution* (discussed in the next chapter) and because of their position in the table, are often referred to as the *marginals*. The numbers in parentheses beneath each percent are the frequencies for that cell.

In examining tables such as these, it is often possible to tell in general terms whether or not your hypothesis is supported by the data. In both Table 15.2 and Table 15.3, for instance, it is evident that women did vote consistently more Democratic than males. Although a majority of women voted Republican in 1980, even in that year female voters were 8 percentage points more likely to vote Democratic (47 minus 39). The data demonstrate that John McCain was able to somewhat narrow the gender gap in 2008, when women were only 5 percentage points more likely to support candidate Barack Obama (57 minus 52). Still, such simple measurements only give us a rough idea of basic relationships, and may be unreliable. In the next three chapters we consider some statistics that enable us to state more precisely the degree of harmony between hypotheses and data.

CREATING TABLES AND CHARTS

Now that you have a sense of how you can present your results, how do you make the charts or tables? Given the capabilities of the analytic software available today, this process is much easier than you may think.

Available Software

A tremendous variety of tabular and graphic presentations may be created using standard software packages. Common programs such as Microsoft Word, Excel, or PowerPoint, for example, have interactive tools and templates to produce a wide range of presentation-quality tables and charts. Similarly, statistical programs such as SPSS make it very easy to display data in the form of bar or pie charts, histograms, or scatterplots, to name but a few options. In most of these programs you must first enter the data for the table or chart into a worksheet or spreadsheet and then build the table or graph through a graphical menu or "wizard" tool. Once your chart or table is created, modifications can be made interactively by changing the data or the graph or table itself. For example, you can insert or delete graphical elements, change colors and textures, rotate three-dimensional graphs, and adjust lines and surfaces.

RESEARCH EXERCISE

Comparing Tables with Text

Locate an article having at least one table, preferably relating to gender and politics, in a recent issue of the journal *PS: Political Science & Politics*.

1. Record:
   a. The full citation for the article
   b. The page number of the table
2. Compare the table data to the information about the table in the text. That is, how is the table described in the text?
   a. Which values or cells from the table are mentioned in the article text?
   b. What is said about these values?
   c. What data from the table are omitted in the text of the article?
   d. Why do you suppose the author(s) did not describe all of the table data in the text?
3. In what way does the table advance the article's examination of its theory or research question?

Conclusion

In conclusion, remember these three important points about the use of tabular and graphic presentations.

First, these devices should be used both imaginatively and constructively. As part of the research process itself, they can be extremely helpful in developing your concepts to the fullest and in bringing you to a firm understanding of what the data really mean. Flexibility and an openness to new forms of analysis can contribute greatly to expanding your knowledge of political phenomena, and techniques as simple as those discussed here can help you shape your discoveries.

Second, in the presentation of research, tables and graphics should be used parsimoniously. Too many such materials in a research report clutter the text and detract from its readability. Your decision to include a table or chart is taken by the reader as an indication of the importance attached to the particular information contained therein. You must make those choices deliberately, rather than simply offering your reader a smorgasbord of information. Such discretion not only enhances your report, but forces you to think more clearly and decide what is important, thus contributing directly to the quality of your research.

Finally, the best way to learn data presentation is through hands-on use and experimentation. Tackling unfamiliar software may be daunting, but it is the best way to add weapons to your research arsenal. If you run into difficulty, programs such as Excel or SPSS have useful help functions, offering step-by-step instructions for constructing charts and tables. While this chapter has presented a first cut at some data on gender and party voting, Chapter 22 features an article that presents a more in-depth examination of this issue.

Key Terms

simple table *265*

line graph *268*

key *269*

pie chart *270*

bar chart *271*

segmented bar chart *271*

bilateral bar chart *272*

crosstabulation (or crosstab) *273*

Research Examples

The uses of graphical data are endless, and often visual data can summarize a great deal of information. To offer an overview of the escalating trend of economic news during the 2008 presidential campaign, Holbrook (2009) offers a graph of the number of articles in *The New York Times* that discuss the U.S. economy from August through the end of October 2008. To predict the range of choices made by voters who are looking ahead and voting for the long run, Penn (2009) graphs density plots depicting hundreds of thousands of iterations of a game theoretic simulation on a range of controversial policies. Quantitative analyses typically include tables, which range from very complex to quite simple. Opening the most recent issue of any political science journal will yield a wide variety of such tables.

Methodological Readings

More theoretical discussions of the use of graphics can be found in William Jacoby's works on univariate and bivariate data presentation (1997) and multivariate presentation techniques (1998). The second edition of Tufte's (2001) classic *The Visual Display of Quantitative Information* is a lovely book, moving beyond simply presenting data to design and aesthetics. Tufte also teaches workshops throughout the country that examine information accessibility in graphical data presentation. For insights into the subtleties and potential abuse of graphic presentation, see *How to Lie with Charts* (Jones 2006).

References

The American National Election Studies (ANES; www.electionstudies.org). 2009. *The ANES 2008 Time Series Study* [data set]. Stanford University and the University of Michigan [producers].

Center for American Women and Politics (CAWP). 2006. *Fact Sheet: Sex Differences in Voter Turnout.* Eagleton Institute of Politics, Rutgers University.

Holbrook, Thomas M. 2009. "Economic Considerations and the 2008 Presidential Election." *PS: Political Science & Politics* 42(July): 473–478.

Jacoby, William G. 1997. *Statistical Graphics for Visualizing Univariate and Bivariate Data.* Newbury Park, CA: Sage Publications.

Jacoby, William G. 1998. *Statistical Graphics for Visualizing Multivariate Data.* Newbury Park, CA: Sage Publications.

Jones, Gerald E. 2006. *How to Lie with Charts*, 2nd ed. Sedona, AZ: La Puerta.

Lupia, Arthur, Jon A. Krosnick, Pat Luevano, Matthew DeBell, and Darrell Donakowski. 2009. *User's Guide to the ANES 2008 Time Series Study.* Ann Arbor, MI and Palo Alto, CA: University of Michigan and Stanford University.

Miller, Warren E., and the National Election Studies. 1980. *The 1980 National Election Study* [data set]. Ann Arbor, MI: University of Michigan, Center for Political Studies [producer and distributor].

Penn, Elizabeth Maggie. 2009. "A Model of Farsighted Voting." *American Journal of Political Science* 53(January): 36–54.

The National Election Studies (www.electionstudies.org). 2005. *The 2004 National Election Study* [data set]. Ann Arbor, MI: University of Michigan, Center for Political Studies [producer and distributor].

Tufte, Edward R. 2001. *The Visual Display of Quantitative Information*, 2nd ed. Cheshire, CT Graphics Press.

CHAPTER 16

Statistics I: Summarizing Distributions on One Variable

In this chapter you will learn:

- The three measures of central tendency.
- The level of measurement most associated with each measure.
- How to measure a variable's dispersion.

Often in political science research, charts and tables alone do not tell us enough about our data to permit a satisfactory answer to our research question. In part this is a problem of complexity (our variables may have either too many values or too many cases—or there may even be too many variables involved—to lend themselves to ready analysis) and in part a question of precision (degrees of difference or subtle variations among variables may be important, and they are often difficult to assess accurately by simply eyeballing a table or chart). In instances such as these, as well as others that call for highly sophisticated analysis, political scientists employ *statistics*.

In this context, **statistics** are numbers that summarize either the distributions of values on, or the relationships between, variables. They are a form of mathematical shorthand capable of telling us at a glance and with great precision what our data show (or, in many cases, what they do not show). What is the political ideology of the typical college student? Do Hispanic voters differ systematically in their party preferences from African Americans? What kinds of actions or situations in the world community are most likely to give rise to armed conflict? If the proper data are applied for analysis, statistics can answer these questions and many more.

Statistics can be extremely complex. It is equally true, however, that many of the primary concepts and techniques of statistical analysis are extremely simple, can be learned in a short time, and can get you a good deal further into the subject than you might imagine. In fact, your knowledge of high school algebra arms you with just about all the mathematics you will need, and you may be surprised at how intuitive many statistical concepts really are.

We should make clear that this chapter and the two that follow will not teach you all there is to know about statistics, nor even all there is to know about the particular statistical measures we discuss. Still, upon completion of these chapters, you should have a good sense of what statistics are and of how to use them, you should have some understanding of the concepts that lie behind the numbers and the calculations, and you should have a reasonable facility in the use of several specific statistics. Together, these skills will enable you to employ statistical analysis in your own research and to comprehend more fully and more critically what you read in scholarly journals and other reports of political science research.

In this chapter we examine statistics that answer the following types of questions about a given set of data: How are the cases distributed among the values of each of our variables? What does the typical case look like? How typical is it?

Statistics and Level of Measurement

In each instance, we examine a different statistic for each level of measurement: nominal, ordinal, and interval/ratio. You will recall from Chapter 5 that these levels differ from one another in that the first merely differentiates categories, the second ranks them, and the third assumes constant degrees of difference between them. In effect, then, *nominal*, *ordinal*, and *interval/ratio* numbers are different kinds of numbers with different qualities. In a sense, nominal numbers are soft numbers; they do not tell us very much. Because they merely separate objects into groups and serve as no more than labels for those groups, nominal numbers cannot even be added or subtracted. Accordingly, we cannot use very sophisticated statistical methods in analyzing nominal data. On the other hand, interval/ratio numbers are much harder, or more concrete, in that these values convey a great deal more information about the data they represent. They can be added, subtracted, squared, and variously transformed. As a result, they offer much more flexibility and an opportunity for far more sophisticated analysis. It is for this reason that different techniques are applied to different levels of measurement. For the same reason, of course, one must take care to use each technique appropriately.

MEASURES OF CENTRAL TENDENCY AND DISPERSION

Two types of statistics are used to describe the distribution of cases over the values of a single variable. The first—the measure of **central tendency**—helps us to identify the most typical value: the one value or score that best represents the entire set of cases on that variable. Suppose we were told that the average American female employee is a white-collar worker, is a high school graduate, and has 1.86 children. Clearly not every American woman fits these categories, but when we look at all American females in a summary manner, this set of characteristics might well come closest to a general description of the findings. It is this same notion of an average, or typical, case that we employ in calculating a measure of central tendency. Indeed, it was precisely such measures that identified these particular traits of American females in the first place.

As we have noted, however, not every member of the female population fits this description. Many are blue-collar or professional workers or perhaps even unemployed, some have finished only grade school whereas others hold advanced degrees, and some may have 10 or 15 children whereas others are unmarried and childless. In other words, the "typical" American female may well represent the *tendencies* within the population, but she does not accurately reflect each individual case. For this reason, once we have

PRACTICAL RESEARCH ETHICS

What are the proper tools for the job?

The primary ethical responsibility that will be emphasized in the three chapters on data analysis is each researcher's duty to utilize the proper techniques.

Of course, which techniques are most appropriate depends upon the nature of the research and the variables' qualities. For example, you are only likely to use the univariate statistics described in this chapter to initially describe and evaluate each of your variables. Assessing relationships between variables requires the type of tools described in the following two chapters.

identified such a typical case, we must ask follow-up questions: How typical is it? How good a job does this average score do of summarizing the distribution of scores for all the cases on a given variable? We answer these questions by using a second type of statistic—the measure of dispersion. The measure of **dispersion** tells us whether the variation around the average value identified is limited, in which case we can have confidence that our average is a meaningful one, or whether that variation is so great that the most typical case is not really representative of the population after all.

This raises an important point, which should be explained before we proceed any further. Statistics are powerful tools of analysis; they can tell us a great deal about our data that we could not otherwise ascertain. But statistics, on their own, are mindless. One can calculate and report *any* statistic on *any* set of numbers and in the process appear to be wringing the last drop of knowledge from one's data. For two reasons, however, many of these "results" may be meaningless. The first reason is one we have discussed already and whose logic should become more evident as we go. Put most simply, the level of sophistication of our statistics may exceed the level of sophistication of our data. If our statistic requires us to add two numbers, but our data are based on nominal-level measures for which the whole concept of addition is inappropriate, we could in fact go through the mechanical process of combining the coded values, but the result would be worthless. Thus, if the score 1 represented blue-collar workers; 2, white-collar workers; and 3, professional workers, we could add 1 and 2 and get 3, but would we really want to argue that one blue-collar worker plus one white-collar worker *equals* one professional? Certainly not.

The second reason that statistical results may be less than meaningful is that one statistic, by itself, often cannot tell the whole story. If the single *most* typical level of education of American females is completion of high school, but only 30.5 percent of women have both reached that level and stopped there, how much does this average really tell us? Not much. And how many people do you know who actually have an average of 1.86 children? Thus, although we can calculate and report these figures accurately, they should not be allowed to stand alone. Each measure of central tendency should be qualified or evaluated with an accompanying measure of dispersion. And similarly, as we shall argue later, whenever we are dealing with a sample, each measure of association between two variables should be accompanied by a measure of statistical significance, which is an indication of how likely that finding is to represent a substantive relationship between the variables in question. Thus, statistics must be not only appropriate to the level of measurement of the data but substantively meaningful as well if they are to prove of much value.

TABLE 16.1   Frequency Distribution: Type of Occupation of Respondents

Code	Value	Number of Cases
1	Blue collar	25
2	White collar	23
3	Professional	22
4	Farm	20
5	Unemployed	10

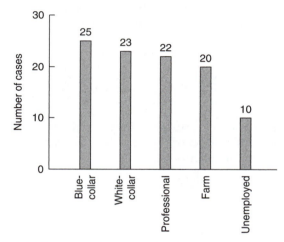

FIGURE 16.1   Histogram: Type of occupation of respondents.

All measures of central tendency and dispersion are based on a summary of values and cases termed a *frequency distribution*. A **frequency distribution** is simply an ordered count of the number of cases that take on each value of a variable. For example, suppose we ask one hundred people to tell us their present occupation and then classify their responses according to type. For the variable *type of occupation*, we might arrive at the frequency distribution shown in Table 16.1. The frequency distribution simply lists each value on the variable and reports the number of cases that take on that value. The same information may be communicated by a bar graph, which, when used for this particular purpose, is often called a **histogram**, as illustrated in Figure 16.1. Using this information, we may identify the most typical case and determine its descriptiveness.

MEASURES FOR NOMINAL VARIABLES

As we suggested earlier, different measures of central tendency and dispersion are appropriate for different levels of measurement. Since *type of occupation* is a nominal variable, let us begin to examine these calculations by focusing on statistics appropriate for nominal-level measures.

The Mode

At this level, where numbers represent merely category labels without regard to order, the only available measure of central tendency is the mode. The **mode** is simply *the most frequently occurring value*—the one which is taken on by the greatest number of cases. In the example, this is category 1, or the value *blue-collar*. We refer to this as either the mode or the modal category. (A distribution in which two categories tie for the greatest number of cases is said to have two modes, or to be *bimodal*, and it is possible to have a tie between even more than two categories.) Blue-collar employment, then, is the single most typical type of occupation among our sample of one hundred persons.

But clearly, most people in this sample (in fact, fully 75 percent) are not blue-collar workers, so even though we can identify the most typical value in this distribution, that information may not be very meaningful. We can be more precise in judging just how meaningful it is by calculating the appropriate nominal-level measure of dispersion—the **variation ratio**—the formula for which is as follows:

$$v = \frac{\Sigma f_{\text{nonmodal}}}{N} \quad \text{or} \quad v = 1 - \frac{f_{\text{modal}}}{N}$$

where $\Sigma f_{\text{nonmodal}}$ = the sum of all cases not falling into the modal category
f_{modal} = the number of cases in the modal category
N = the total number of cases.

In effect, this statistic tells us the *percentage of all cases that do not fit into the modal category*. In the example,

$$v = \frac{23 + 22 + 20 + 10}{100} = .75$$

or, in the simplified form,

$$v = 1 - \frac{25}{100} = .75$$

The variation ratio ranges between 0 (when all cases take on the same value) and $1 - 1/N$ (when each case takes on a different value). In general, the lower the variation ratio, the more typical or more meaningful the mode. In the case of bimodal or multi-modal distributions, one modal value is arbitrarily selected for purposes of calculation, and N is determined precisely as above.

MEASURES FOR ORDINAL VARIABLES

When dealing with ordinal-level data, we have a bit more information, since our codes represent not only categorization but relative position or ranking as well. Our selection of measures of central tendency and dispersion should both reflect and take advantage of this fact.

The Median

The appropriate measure of central tendency for ordinal data—the median—does precisely this. The **median** is simply *the value of the middle case in a distribution*—the

TABLE 16.2 Educational Achievement in Three Samples

Code	Value	Sample 1 (*n*)	Sample 2 (*n*)	Sample 3 (*n*)
1	Grade school	25	25	10
2	Some high school	23	23	40
3	High school graduate	22	22	35
4	College graduate	20	20	10
5	Advanced degree	9	10	5
Total *n*		99	100	100

case above and below which an equal number of other cases lie. Obtaining the median, then, requires only that we count from either end of the distribution toward the center until finding the middle case and then ascertaining the value associated with that case. When we have an odd number of cases, we will be able to locate one middle case (for example, for 99 cases, the 50th case from either end of the frequency distribution will have 49 cases both above and below it). The value of this case is the median. When N (the number of cases) is an even number, two middle cases will emerge (for example, for 100 cases, the 50th and 51st cases from either end together constitute the midpoint of the distribution). If both of these cases take on the same value, that value is the median. If they take on different values, the median is the midpoint between those two values.

An example may help to make this clear. Let us consider the distribution of educational achievement in three samples (Table 16.2). In the first, we identify the middle case (the 50th from either end), note its value, and determine the median level of education to be 3, or *high school graduate*. In the second, we identify two middle cases (the 50th and 51st from either end), note that each takes on the same value, and determine the median once again to be a score of 3. In the third sample, however, the middle cases split between the *some high school* and *high school graduate* categories. Here the median is the midpoint between the two values in question, or $(2 + 3)/2 = 2.5$. Because fractional values have no meaning in ordinal measurement, this figure merely tells us that the midpoint of the distribution lies somewhere between 2 and 3.

Using Quantiles

Any of several measures of dispersion for ordinal variables, termed **quantile ranges**, tells us how tightly the various cases cluster around the median or, again, how typical or representative the median is of the whole distribution. A **quantile** is a measure of position within a distribution. For example, a percentile divides a distribution into 100 equal parts such that the first percentile is the point or value in that distribution (counting from the lowest score up) below which 1 percent of all the cases lie, the second percentile that point or value below which 2 percent of all the cases lie, and so forth. Or, to use what may be a more familiar example, the prospective college student who scores in the 85th percentile on the SAT has achieved a test score that is higher than the scores of 85 percent of all who took the test. Similar to a percentile, a decile divides the distribution into tenths (for example, the third decile would be the point below which 30 percent of all the cases lie), a quintile into fifths, a quartile into fourths. Any of these can be used to indicate dispersion around the median, though the decile and quintile ranges are most commonly found in the literature.

An Example

Let us use the quintile range to illustrate the procedure. The quintile range (q) is defined as follows:

$$q = q_4 - q_1$$

where q_4 = the fourth quintile (the value below which 4/5, or 80 percent, of the cases lie)

q_1 = the first quintile (the value below which 1/5, or 20 percent, of the cases lie).

The narrower the range of values separating these two points in the distribution, the more tightly clustered the cases are about the median and the more truly representative of the distribution the median will be. In sample 2 in Table 16.2, for instance, where $n = 100$, we calculate q by locating the 81st case (below which 80 percent of the cases lie) and the 21st case (below which 20 percent of the cases lie), starting our count within the frequency distribution from the lowest scores. We then subtract the value associated with the 21st case from that associated with the 81st ($q = q_4 - q_1 = 4 - 1 = 3$) to obtain the quintile range. In sample 3, the equivalent computation yields a quintile range of 1 ($q = 3 - 2 = 1$), suggesting by comparison that this distribution is better typified by its median of 2.5 than is sample 2 by its median of 3. An examination of the two frequency distributions will confirm the validity of this conclusion.

One difficulty in interpreting quantile ranges is that they are extremely sensitive to variation in the number of categories on a given variable. The more categories there are, the greater the range is likely to be. For this reason, quantile ranges can prove difficult to interpret for comparison between variables that differ in their number of categories. For similarly coded variables, for longitudinal or cross-sectional comparisons of the values of any single variable, or for some absolute indication of variability around the median, however, they are generally quite adequate.

MEASURES FOR INTERVAL/RATIO VARIABLES

Interval/ratio data, of course, provide us with the most complete information of all, including categorization, rank, and distance. Interval/ratio values can be subjected to any arithmetic manipulation. Consequently, our measures of central tendency and dispersion for interval/ratio data can and should take this added information and capability into account.

The Mean

The measure of central tendency for interval/ratio data is the **mean**—a measure that locates *the central point of a distribution* in terms of both the number of cases on either side of that point and their distance from it. The mean of a distribution is the statistic many people commonly associate with the term *average*.

Let us visualize the nature of the mean by using Figure 16.2. If all the cases in a distribution are represented by equal weights, and if they are arranged on a board at fixed intervals so that those with the most extreme values are farthest from the center in one or

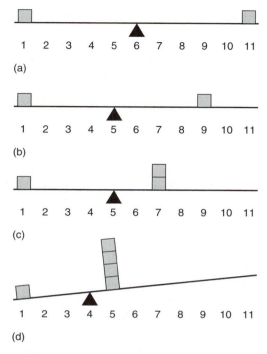

FIGURE 16.2   The mean as a point of balance.

the other direction and those with equal values are placed at the same point on the board, the mean value of the distribution will be the fulcrum point—the value at which the combined weights and distances to one side precisely balance those to the other. As illustrated in the figure, both weight (number of cases) and distance (extremity of the scores) are important in ascertaining the mean.

The mean of a distribution, designated $\overline{X}$ (or X–bar), is calculated by taking the sum of the values of the individual cases and dividing by the number of cases. This procedure is summarized in the following equation:

$$\overline{X} = \frac{\displaystyle\sum_{i=1}^{N} X_i}{N}$$

where X_i = the value of each individual case
   N = the number of cases
   $\displaystyle\sum_{i=1}^{N}$ = an instruction to take the sum of all the individual values of cases 1 to N.

Note, too, however, as illustrated in Figure 16.2(d), that precisely because it is sensitive to distance, the mean is subject to distortion in a distribution that has a few, or even one, very extreme case(s). That is, a small number of cases with very extreme scores can cause the mean to be less than a truly typical value. Let us see how this might occur.

Consider a group of 11 persons, 10 of whom earn $10,000 a year and 1 of whom earns $1 million. The mean income for this group equals $100,000, but 10 of the 11 members of the group actually earn one-tenth of that amount. Thus, the mean, although correctly calculated, is not as representative as, say, the median, which in this case is $10,000.

$$\overline{X} = \frac{(10 \times \$10,000) + \$1,000,000}{11} = \$100,000$$

It would seem at first glance that to determine how typical of a distribution a given mean is, all we need to do is measure the distances of all cases from that point (taking account of direction), add these together, and divide by N (the number of cases). In effect, we would calculate the mean of the distances around the mean as in the formula

$$\text{Dispersion} = \frac{\sum_{i=1}^{N} (X_i - \overline{X})}{N}$$

The greater the dispersion for a given distribution, then, the *less* typical the mean; and the less the dispersion, the *more* typical the mean.

But when we try this with, for example, the three cases illustrated in Figure 16.2(c), a problem emerges. Applying the formula to the example, we find

$$\text{Dispersion} = \frac{(1 - 5) + (7 - 5) + (7 - 5)}{3}$$

$$= \frac{-4 + 2 + 2}{3} = 0$$

Even in a distribution with such clear divergence as our income example, we find

$$\text{Dispersion} = \frac{10(10,000 - 100,000) + (1,000,000 - 100,000)}{11}$$

$$= \frac{-900,000 + 900,000}{11} = 0$$

Indeed, for *any* mean in any distribution the result is the same. The reason is a simple one. We have, in effect, *defined* the mean as precisely that point where these weights and distances cancel out, or the point or value about which all variations are balanced. Therefore, after calculating the mean, we should hardly be surprised to find exactly the effect we have intended. Yet the notion that we ought to be able to measure dispersion by comparing the closeness of cases to, or their remoteness from, the mean retains its appeal. Enter the standard deviation.

Calculating the Standard Deviation

The **standard deviation (s)** employs a mathematical device to accomplish our purpose. In effect, it is a procedure that eliminates the tendency of opposing distances to cancel one another out by the simple expedient of squaring those distances (thereby eliminating all negative signs), averaging the *squares* of the distances around the mean, and then taking the square root of the result so as to return to the original units of distance. The formula by which all of this is accomplished resembles the rejected formula except for the use of the squared distances and the square root of the result. That formula is

$$s = \sqrt{\frac{\sum_{i=1}^{N} (X_i - \overline{X})^2}{N}}$$

where X_i = the value of each individual case
$\overline{X}$ = the mean
N = the number of cases
$\sum_{i=1}^{N}$ = an instruction to take the sum of the individual values for cases 1 to N.

Thus, in the example from Figure 16.2c,

$$s = \sqrt{\frac{(1 - 5)^2 + (7 - 5)^2 + (7 - 5)^2}{3}}$$
$$= \sqrt{\frac{16 + 4 + 4}{3}} = \sqrt{\frac{24}{3}} = \sqrt{8} = 2.8$$

It is expressed in the same units as the original data.

When two variables are measured by the same or comparable scales, the standard deviation provides a basis for comparing the representativeness of the means: The greater the standard deviation, the less representative the mean. But when scales differ substantially or when a single variable is being analyzed, the interpretation of the standard deviation is less clear.

The Normal Distribution

One exception to this applies to variables whose values closely approximate a **normal distribution**, or one in which there is *a single mode in the very center of the distribution and in which the frequencies decline symmetrically as the values become more extreme in each direction*. (The bell-shaped curve with which you may be familiar is simply a graphic representation of a normal distribution, and appears in Chapter 17.) In these cases, we know that 68.3 percent of all cases will lie within +1 and −1 standard deviation from the mean, 95.5 percent will lie within +2 and −2 standard deviations from the mean, and 99.7 percent will lie within +3 and −3 standard deviations from the mean. (The derivation of these mathematical properties lies beyond the scope of the present discussion.) In fact, for such distributions, we can locate the exact number of standard deviation units any particular value lies above or below the mean, then use this information for comparing the relative position of two cases on the same variable or, alternatively, the relative scores on two variables for the same case. The measure that allows us to do this is called the **standard score** (or **z-score**), and it is calculated by simply subtracting the mean ($\overline{X}$) from the score (X) and then dividing by the standard deviation (s):

$$z = \frac{(X_i - \overline{X})}{s}$$

What makes the standard scores so useful is the fact that they allow us to compare scores that are based on very different units of measurements (for example, age measured in number of years and height measured in inches). Since z-scores all have a mean of 0 and a standard deviation of 1, each score simply tells us how many standard deviation units a variable (age, height, etc.) is above or below the mean.[1]

Suppose, for example, that we have data showing the per capita spending by each state for education, the number of teachers per 1,000 students each state employs, and the number of high school degrees per 100,000 population awarded by each state in a given year, and that values on these variables are distributed among the states in a manner approximating the normal curve. Suppose further that we wish to use these data to examine educational policy in, say, Arizona and Virginia. We first calculate the mean $(\overline{X})$ and standard deviation (s) for each variable for all fifty states and then determine the respective standard scores (z) on each variable for the two states of interest. The result will be two sets of scores in standard units (no longer dollars, teachers, and certificates, but the number of standard deviations about the mean) that can be used to construct indices of educational policy, determine an average position for Arizona or Virginia among the states, or provide for standardized comparisons across substantively different measures. As the basis for the standard score, then, the standard deviation may be an especially useful statistic.

Conclusion

In this chapter we have focused on statistics that summarize the distribution of scores on one variable. Because these statistics describe the characteristics of individual variables, they are often called **univariate statistics**. We have seen that different univariate statistics are appropriate for variables with different levels of measurement: nominal, ordinal, and interval/ratio. In the next chapter we examine what are termed **bivariate statistics**—those that summarize the relationship between *two* variables.

Key Terms

statistics *278*
central tendency *279*
dispersion *280*
frequency distribution *281*
histogram *281*
mode *282*

variation ratio *282*
median *282*
quantile ranges *283*
quantile *283*
mean *284*
standard deviation (*s*) *286*

normal distribution *287*
standard score (*z*-score) *287*
univariate statistics *288*
bivariate statistics *288*

---

[1] Table A.6 in Appendix A summarizes the area between the mean and z, as well as the area beyond z in the distribution, for standard scores between 0 and 4, which is to say, for all values between the mean and a distance of four standard deviations in either direction around it. The values in the table can be used to locate (for purposes of comparison) any number of cases relative to the means on different variables.

Research Examples

Finding examples of political science research using the mean is difficult, because most research focuses on hypothesis testing. These studies, by definition, examine relationships rather than calculating univariate statistics on individual variables. Researchers sometimes report mean values as a precursor to more direct comparisons, and sometimes use mean values to make implicit comparisons. For example, in considering whether the arrival of casinos on their reservations have altered Indians' lives, Conner and Taggart (2009) note the mean values of a wide variety of measures for Indians and those of all races in the area of the reservation.

Methodological Readings

At the conclusion of Chapter 18 we suggest several books you might read to begin learning about statistics in more detail. At this point, though, it might be more useful to start with books that can put you at ease about using statistics and at the same time help you grasp some important basic concepts. These books are somewhat dated, but the information is still relevant and the writing is often more engaging than the writing in other works. For this purpose, we suggest *How to Lie with Statistics* (Huff and Geis 1993), a classic and lighthearted examination of the uses and abuses of statistics, or what the authors term "statisticulation." For those who prefer to absorb their statistics through the medium of cartoon drawings, we recommend *The Cartoon Guide to Statistics* (Gonick and Smith 1993).

References

Conner, Thaddieus W., and William A. Taggart. 2009. "The Impact of Gaming on the Indian Nations in New Mexico." *Social Science Quarterly* 90(March): 50–70.

Gonick, Larry, and Woollcott Smith. 1993. *The Cartoon Guide to Statistics*. New York: HarperPerennial.

Huff, Darrell, and Irving Geis. 1993. *How to Lie with Statistics*. New York: Norton.

CHAPTER 17

Statistics II: Examining Relationships between Two Variables

In this chapter you will learn:

- How to define association.
- What chi-square represents.
- Which measure of association is most appropriate when comparing variables with different levels of measurement.

In political science research, we are generally less concerned with describing distributions on single variables than we are with determining whether, how, and to what extent two or more variables may be related to one another. It is these bivariate (two-variable) and multivariate (more-than-two-variable) relationships that usually cast light on the more interesting research questions.

When examining the relationship between two variables, we typically ask three important questions. The first is whether and to what extent changes or differences in the values of one variable—generally the independent variable—are associated with changes or differences in the values of the second, or dependent, variable. The second question examines the direction and form of any association that might exist. The third considers the likelihood that any association observed among cases sampled from a larger population is in fact a characteristic of that population and not merely an artifact of the smaller and potentially unrepresentative sample. In this chapter we introduce some of the statistics that are most commonly used to answer these questions, and we explain when it is appropriate to use them and what they tell us about relationships.

MEASURES OF ASSOCIATION AND STATISTICAL SIGNIFICANCE

An **association** is said to exist between two variables when knowing the value of one for a given case improves the odds of our guessing correctly the corresponding value of the second. If, for example, we examine the relationship between the size of a country's population and the proportion of its adults who are college educated, we may variously find

(1) that larger countries generally have a greater proportion of college-educated adults than smaller ones, (2) that smaller countries generally have a greater proportion of college-educated adults than larger ones, or (3) that there is no systematic difference between the two—that some countries from each group have relatively high proportions of such people but that some from each group have low proportions as well. If our research shows that either case 1 or case 2 holds, we can use our knowledge of values on the independent variable, *size of population*, to guess or predict values on the dependent variable, *proportion of adults who are college educated*, for any given country. In the first instance, for any heavily populated country, we predict a relatively high proportion of college-educated adults, and for a less populous nation, we predict a lower proportion. In the second, our prediction is precisely reversed. In either event, although we may not guess every case correctly, we will be right fairly often because of the underlying *association* between the two variables. Indeed, the stronger the association between the two variables (the more the individual countries' educational level values tend to align on each in precisely the same order), the more likely we are to guess correctly in any particular instance. If there is total correspondence in the alignments on the two variables, high scores with high scores or, alternatively, high scores on one with low on the other, we can predict one from the other with perfect accuracy. This contrasts sharply with the third possibility, which permits no improved prediction of values on the education variable based on our knowledge of populations. In such instances, when cases are, in effect, randomly distributed on the two variables, there is said to be no association.

To get a mental picture of what a strong association might look like, consider the two maps presented in Figure 17.1, which relate to the murder rate in Washington, DC, during the "crack wars" of the 1980s. Figure 17.1(a) shows the location of known drug markets in the nation's capital; Figure 17.1(b) shows the location of homicides. Both are based on information provided by the DC Metropolitan Police Department. The apparent similarity in the locations of clusters of drug dealing and murders suggests an *association* between the two phenomena.

Measuring Association

Clearly there can be more or less association between any two variables. The question in each instance then becomes, *Just how much association is there?* The answer is provided by a set of statistics known as coefficients of association. A **coefficient of association** is a number that summarizes the amount of improvement in guessing values on one variable for any case based on knowledge of the values of a second. In the example, for instance, such a measure would tell us *how much* our knowledge of a country's population size helps us in guessing its proportion of college-educated adults. The higher the coefficient, the stronger the association and, by extension, the better our predictive or explanatory ability. In general, coefficients of association range from 0 to 1 or −1 to 1, with the values closest to unity indicating a relatively strong association and those closest to 0 a relatively weak one.

In addition to the magnitude of association, it is also useful to know the direction or form of the relationship between two variables. Take another look at the earlier example about level of education of a nation's adults, and most particularly at options 1 and 2. We have already suggested that the closer we get to either case, the higher will be our coefficient of association and the better our chances of guessing a particular country's proportion of college-educated adults based on our knowledge of its population size. It should

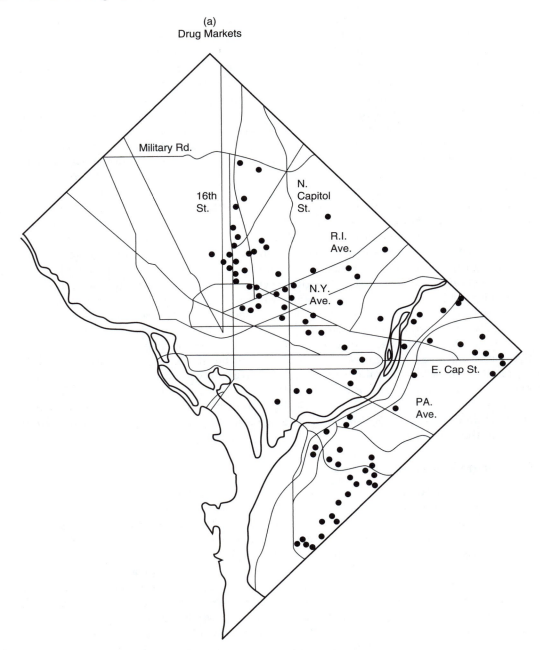

**(a)
Drug Markets**

FIGURE 17.1 Drug markets and homicide locations, Washington, DC, 1988.

Source: Reprinted from the *Washington Post,* January 13, 1989, p. E1, with permission of the publisher.

(b)
Homicide Locations

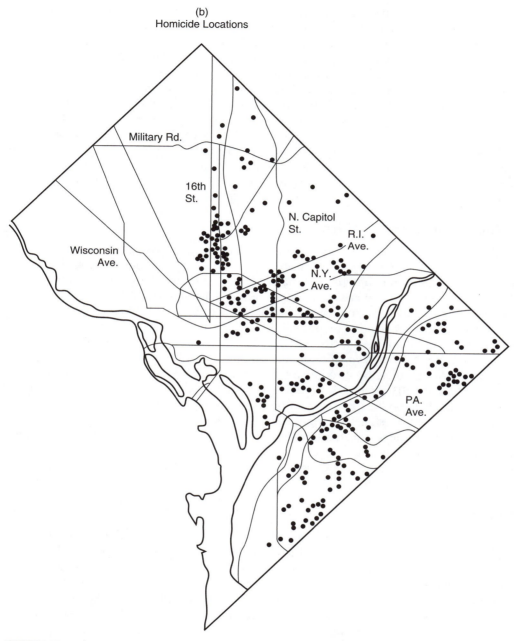

FIGURE 17.1 (Continued)

be obvious, however, that our predictions in the cases are precisely opposite. In the first instance, higher values of one variable tend to be associated with higher values of the other, and in the latter instance, higher values of one tend to be associated with *lower* values of the other. Such relationships are said to display differences in *direction*. Those like the first, in which both variables rise and fall together, are termed *direct*, or *positive*, associations. Those like the second, in which scores move systematically in opposing directions, are termed *inverse*, or *negative*, associations. This additional bit of information, which is represented by a plus or a minus sign accompanying the coefficient of association, makes our guessing even more effective. Thus, a coefficient of −.87 (negative and relatively close to negative 1) might describe a relatively strong relationship in which the values on the two variables in question are inversely related (moving in opposite directions), whereas a coefficient of .20 (positive—the plus sign is usually omitted—and rather close to zero) might describe a weak direct association.

Defining Statistical Significance

Finally, we should say a word about tests of *statistical significance*, though our discussion of the topic will be purposely limited.[1] You will recall from our discussion of levels of confidence and sampling error in Chapter 7 that when we draw a presumably representative sample and use that sample to develop conclusions about the larger population from which it is drawn, we run some risk of coming to incorrect conclusions. This is true because there is a chance that the sample is not in fact representative and that the actual error in our measurement exceeds that specified for a given sample size (Tables A.2 and A.3 in Appendix A). The *chance* of such improper generalizing is known, but we cannot tell whether or not it has occurred in any particular instance. For a level of confidence of .95, that chance is .05, or 1−.95. For a level of confidence of .99, it is .01. These values represent the likelihood that any generalization from our sample to the larger population, even allowing for the estimated range of sampling error, is simply wrong.

Tests of **statistical significance** perform the same function in evaluating measures of association. They tell us just how likely it is that the association we have measured between two variables in a sample might or might not exist in the whole population. Let us see if we can clarify this point.

An Example

Suppose, to continue our example, we have a population of 200 nations for which we *know for a fact* that the coefficient of association between population size and the proportion of adults with a college education is 0. There is, in reality, no relationship between the two variables. But suppose further that we take a sample of only 30 of these countries and calculate the association between these two variables. It might come out as 0, but this is actually unlikely, because the strength of association is now based not on all the countries but on only 30 and will probably reflect their particular idiosyncrasies. In other words, the coefficient itself is determined by *which* 30 countries we pick. If, by chance, we pick 30 countries that are truly representative of all 200, we will in fact find no association. But chance might also lead us to pick 30 countries for which the association

---

[1] A full explanation of statistical significance is beyond the scope of this text; to pursue a deeper understanding of significance testing, you are encouraged to consult one of the statistics texts listed at the end of Chapter 18.

between population size and education level is unusually high, say, .60. In that case, our coefficient of association measures a characteristic of the particular sample in question, but if we generalize to the larger population, our conclusions will be incorrect. Knowing this, of course, we reject our measure of association based on this particular sample.

The problem is that in the real world we seldom know the underlying population parameter, which is the true degree of association in the whole population (as defined in Chapter 7). Indeed, the reason to draw samples in the first place is exactly because we often simply *cannot* study whole populations. It follows, then, that more often than not the *only* tests of association we will have will be those based on our sampling. Moreover, these calculations will usually be based on only *one* sample. Thus, the question becomes one of how confident we can be that a test of association based on a single subgroup of a population accurately reflects an underlying population characteristic. The job of the test of statistical significance is to pin a number on that confidence—that is, to measure the probability or likelihood that we are making an appropriate, or, conversely, an inappropriate, generalization.

To see how this works, let us continue our example. Suppose that we draw not one sample of 30 nations from our population of 200, but 1,000 separate and independent samples of the same size and that for each we calculate the coefficient of association. Because the true coefficient for the entire population is in fact 0, most of the coefficients for our 1,000 samples will also be at or relatively near 0. Some particular combinations of 30 countries may yield relatively higher values (that is, we might by chance happen to pick only countries scoring either high-high or low-low on the two variables), but the majority will be nearer to the population parameter. Indeed, the closer one gets to the true value, the more samples one finds represented. These distributions, in fact, often resemble the normal curve mentioned earlier. This is illustrated in Figure 17.2, where the height of the curve at any given point represents the number of samples for which the coefficient of association noted along the baseline has been calculated. As you can see, most of the sample coefficients cluster around the true population parameter.

What, then, is the likelihood that any particular coefficient is simply a chance variation around a true parameter of 0? Or, in other words, if we take a sample from some population and find in that sample a strong association, what are the chances that we will be wrong in generalizing so strong a relationship from the sample to the population? The normal curve has certain properties which enable us to answer this question with considerable precision.

Suppose, for example, we draw from our 200 nations a sample of 30 for which the coefficient of association is −.75. How likely is it that the corresponding coefficient for the population as a whole is 0? From Figure 17.2, the answer must be a resounding *Not very!*

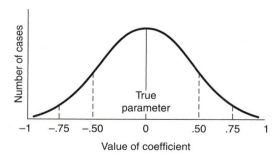

FIGURE 17.2 Normal distribution of coefficients of association for samples of 30 cases.

The area under the curve represents all 1,000 (actually any number of) sample coefficients when the true parameter is 0. The much smaller shaded area at and to the left of –.75 represents the proportion of such coefficients that are negative in direction and .75 or stronger in magnitude. Such cases constitute a very small proportion of the many sample coefficients. For this reason, the odds of drawing such a sample in any given try are quite slim. If 5 percent of all samples lie in this area, for instance, then only one time in twenty will we be likely to encounter a sample from a population with a true coefficient of 0 for which we find a coefficient in our sample of –.75. Yet that is precisely what we have found in this instance.

In other words, we have just drawn a sample with a characteristic that has a 5 percent likelihood of being an erroneous representation of a population in which the two variables in question are not associated with each other. Thus, if we claim on the basis of our sample that the two variables are in fact associated in the larger population (that is, if generalizing our results from the sample), we can expect to be wrong 5 percent of the time. That means, of course, that we will be right 95 percent of the time, and those are not bad odds. Indeed, levels of statistical significance of .05 (a 5 percent chance of erroneous generalization), .01 (a 1 percent chance of such error), and .001 (a 1/10 of 1 percent chance of such error) are commonly accepted standards in social science research.

If we look again at Figure 17.2, it should be apparent that more extreme values such as –.75 are less likely to give rise to this kind of error in generalization than are those closer to the center (for example, a greater proportion of samples from such a population will, by chance, show coefficients of –.50 or stronger, and so forth). It seems, then, that we can never be very confident of the trustworthiness of weaker associations, since we can never eliminate the heavy odds that they are simply chance occurrences in a population with a true coefficient of 0.

We can increase our confidence in our sample simply by increasing our sample size. If instead of 30 cases per sample we draw 100 or 150, each will be more likely to cluster around 0. In effect, the normal curve will be progressively squeezed toward the middle, as illustrated in Figure 17.3, until ultimately there is only one possible outcome—the true parameter. In the process, with a set of sufficiently large samples, even a coefficient of association of .10 or .01 can be shown to have acceptable levels of statistical significance. We can conclude, then, that some combination of sufficiently extreme scores and sufficiently large samples allows us to reduce to tolerable levels the likelihood of incorrectly generalizing from our data.

In the balance of this chapter we present a brief discussion of the most common measures of association and significance for each of the three levels of measurement. Although the procedures employed in calculating each of these measures differ, the purpose in each

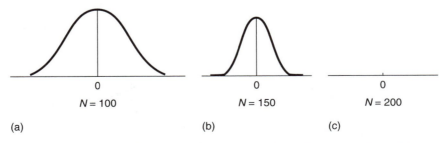

(a)	(b)	(c)
0	0	0
N = 100	N = 150	N = 200

FIGURE 17.3 Sampling distribution for differing numbers of cases in a population of 200.

case, as well as the interpretation of the result, will remain relatively consistent, for each co-efficient of association is designed to tell us to what extent our guessing of values on one variable is improved by knowledge of the corresponding values on another. Each test of significance tells us *the probability that any observed relationships in a sample result from bias in the sample rather than from an underlying relationship in the base population.*

The examples we use to illustrate these statistics involve comparisons of variables that are operationalized at the same level of measurement. However, researchers often want to look for relationships between variables that are at *different* levels of measurement (as in the case of an ordinal-level independent variable such as socioeconomic status and a nominal-level dependent variable such as party identification). To select the correct statistic in these situations, you need to be aware of a simple rule: You can use a statistic designed for a lower level of measurement with data at a higher level of measurement, but you may *not* do the reverse—doing so would produce statistically meaningless results. It would, for example, be legitimate to use a statistic designed for the nominal level with ordinal-level data, but illegitimate to use an ordinal-level statistic with nominal-level data. This means that when comparing variables that are measured at different levels of measurement, *you must choose a statistic suitable to the lower of the two levels.*

MEASURES OF ASSOCIATION AND SIGNIFICANCE FOR NOMINAL VARIABLES: LAMBDA

A widely used coefficient of association for two nominal variables where one is treated as independent and the other dependent is λ (lambda).[2] **Lambda** measures the *percentage of improvement* in guessing values on the dependent variable on the basis of knowledge of values on the independent variable when both variables consist of categories with neither rank, distance, nor direction.

An Example

Suppose we measure the party identification of 100 respondents and uncover the following frequency distribution:

Democrats	50
Republicans	30
Independents	20

Suppose further that we want to guess the party identification of each individual respondent, that we must make the same guess for all individuals, and that we want to make as few mistakes as possible. The obvious strategy is simply to guess the mode (the most populous category), or Democratic, every time. We will be correct 50 times (for the 50 Democrats) and incorrect 50 times (for the 30 Republicans and 20 Independents), not an especially noteworthy record but still the best we can do. For if we guess Republican each time, we will be wrong 70 times, and a guess of Independent will lead to 80 incorrect predictions. The mode, then, provides the best guess based on the available information.

---

[2] Actually, the statistic we shall describe here is λ_a, or lambda asymmetrical, a measure that tests association in only one direction (from the independent to the dependent variable). A test of mutual association, the true λ, is also available.

TABLE 17.1 Paternal Basis for Party Identification

Father's Party Identification	Respondent's Party Identification			
	Dem.	*Rep.*	*Ind.*	*Totals*
Democratic	45	5	10	60
Republican	2	23	5	30
Independent	3	2	5	10
Total	50	30	20	100

But suppose we have a second piece of information—the party identification of each respondent's father—with the following frequency distribution:

Democrats	60
Republicans	30
Independents	10

If these two variables are related to each other—that is, if one is likely to have the same party identification as one's father—then knowing the party preference of each respondent's father should help us to improve our guessing of that respondent's own preference. This will be the case if, by guessing for each respondent not the mode of the overall distribution, as we did before, but simply that person's father's party preference, we can reduce our incorrect predictions to fewer than the 50 cases we originally guessed wrongly.

To examine a possible association between these variables, we construct a crosstab summarizing the distribution of cases on these two variables. In Table 17.1, the independent, or predictor, variable (father's party identification) is the row variable, and its overall distribution is summarized to the right of the table. The dependent variable (respondent's party identification) is the column variable, and its overall distribution is summarized below the table. The numbers in the cells have been assigned arbitrarily, although in the real world they would, of course, be determined by the research itself.

With this table we can use parental preference to predict respondent's preference. To do this, we use the mode just as before, but apply it *within each category on the independent variable* rather than to the whole set of cases. Thus, for those respondents whose father is identified as a Democrat, we guess a preference for the same party. We are correct 45 times and incorrect 15 (for the 5 Republicans and 10 Independents). For those whose father is identified as a Republican, we guess Republican. We are correct 23 times and incorrect 7. And for those whose father is identified as an Independent, we guess a similar preference and are correct 5 out of 10 times. Combining these results, we find that we are now able to guess correctly 73 times and are still wrong 27 times. Thus, knowledge of the second variable has clearly improved our guessing. To ascertain the precise percentage of that improvement, we use *the general formula for a coefficient of association*:

$$\text{Association} = \frac{\text{Reduction in error in guessing}}{\text{Amount of original error}}$$

$$= \frac{\text{Amount of original error} - \text{Amount of remaining error}}{\text{Amount of original error}}$$

In the present instance, this is

$$\text{Association} = \frac{50 - (15 + 7 + 5)}{50}$$

$$= \frac{23}{50} = .46$$

By using father's party identification as a predictor of respondent's party identification, we are able to improve (reduce the error in) our guessing by some 46 percent.

The formula for calculating λ, which will bring us to the same result though by a slightly different route, is

$$\lambda = \frac{\Sigma f_i - F_d}{N - F_d}$$

where f_i = the maximum frequency *within each subclass or category* of the *independent* variable

F_d = the maximum frequency in the *totals* of the *dependent* variable

N = the number of cases.

Lambda ranges from 0 to 1, with higher values (those closer to 1) indicating a stronger association. Because nominal variables have no direction, λ will always be positive.

Our next step is to decide whether the relationship summarized by λ arises from a true population parameter or from mere chance. That is, we must decide whether the relationship is statistically significant.

Chi-Square

The test of statistical significance for nominal variables is χ^2 (**chi-square**). This coefficient tells us whether an apparent nominal-level association between two variables, such as the one we have just observed, is likely to result from chance. It does so by comparing the results actually observed with those that would be expected if no real relationship existed. Calculating χ^2 too, begins from a crosstab. Consider Table 17.2, which resembles Table 17.1 in that the marginals for each variable are the same as those of Table 17.1, but Table 17.2 does not include any distribution of cases within the cells.

To begin the determination of χ^2 we ask ourselves what value is *expected* in each cell, given these overall totals, if there is *no association* between the two variables. Of the 60 cases whose father was a Democrat, for instance, we might expect half (50/100) to be

TABLE 17.2 Paternal Basis for Party Identification: Marginal Values

Father's Party Identification	Respondent's Party Identification			
	Dem.	*Rep.*	*Ind.*	*Totals*
Democratic				60
Republican				30
Independent				10
Total	50	30	20	100

TABLE 17.3 Paternal Basis for Party Identification: Expected Values

Father's Party Identification	Respondent's Party Identification			
	Dem.	*Rep.*	*Ind.*	*Totals*
Democratic	30	18	12	60
Republican	15	9	6	30
Independent	5	3	2	10
Total	50	30	20	100

Democrats, almost a third (30/100) to be Republicans, and one in five (20/100) to be Independents, or, in other words, 30 Democrats, 18 Republicans, and 12 Independents. Similarly, we might arrive at expected values for those with a Republican or Independent father. These expected values are summarized in Table 17.3.

The question then becomes, are the values we have actually observed in Table 17.1 so different (so extreme) from those that Table 17.3 would lead us to expect if there were, in reality, no relationship between the two variables, that we can be reasonably confident of the validity of our result? Chi-square is a device for comparing the two tables to find an answer to this question. The equation for χ^2 is

$$\chi^2 = \Sigma \frac{(f_o - f_e)^2}{f_e}$$

where f_o = the frequency *observed* in each cell (Table 17.1)
f_e = the frequency *expected* in each cell (Table 17.3).

We calculate χ^2 by filling in the values in Table 17.4 for each cell in a given table. The ordering of the cells in the table is of no importance, but f_o from Table 17.1 and f_e from Table 17.3 for any particular line must refer to the same cell. The rationale for first squaring the differences between f_o and f_e and then dividing by f_e is essentially the same as that for the treatment of variations around the mean in determining the standard deviation. Chi-square is determined by adding together all the numbers in the last column. In the example, this yields a value of 56.07.

TABLE 17.4   Values Used in Deriving χ^2

f_o	f_e	$f_o - f_e$	$(f_o - f_e)^2$	$\dfrac{(f_o - f_e)^2}{f_e}$
45	30	15	225	7.50
5	18	−13	169	9.39
10	12	−2	4	.33
2	15	−13	169	11.27
23	9	14	196	21.78
5	6	−1	1	.17
3	5	−2	4	.80
2	3	−1	1	.33
5	2	3	9	4.50

Degrees of Freedom

Before interpreting this number, we must make one further calculation, that of the so-called degrees of freedom. The **degrees of freedom** (*df*) in a table simply consist of the number of cells of that table that can be filled with numbers before the entries in all remaining cells are fixed and unchangeable. The formula for determining the degrees of freedom in any particular table is

$$df = (r - 1)(c - 1)$$

where r = the number of categories of the row variable
  c = the number of categories of the column variable.

In the example, $df = (3 - 1)(3 - 1) = 4$.

We are now ready to evaluate the statistical significance of our data. Table A.4 in Appendix A summarizes the significant values of χ^2 for different degrees of freedom at the .001, .01, and .05 levels. If the value of χ^2 we have calculated (56.07) exceeds that listed in the table at any of these levels for a table with the specified degrees of freedom (4), the relationship we have observed is statistically significant at that level. In the present instance, for example, in order to be significant at the .001 level—that is, if when we accept the observed association as representative of the larger population we run a risk of being wrong one time in 1,000—our observed χ^2 must exceed 18.467. Since it does so, we are quite confident in our result.

MEASURES OF ASSOCIATION AND SIGNIFICANCE FOR ORDINAL VARIABLES: GAMMA

A widely used coefficient of association for ordinal variables is *G*, or **gamma**, which works according to the same principle of error reduction as λ, but focuses on predicting the ranking or relative position of cases rather than simply their membership in a particular class or category. The question treated by *G* is that of the degree to which the ranking of a case on one ordinal variable may be predicted if we know its ranking on a second ordinal variable.

When examining two such variables, there are two possible conditions of perfect predictability. The first, in which individual cases are ranked in exactly the same order on both variables (high scores with high scores, low scores with low), is termed *perfect agreement*. The second, in which cases are ranked in precisely the opposite order (highest scores on one variable with lowest on the other and the reverse), is termed *perfect inversion*. Therefore, predictability is a function of how close the rankings on these variables come to either perfect agreement (in which case *G* is positive and approaches 1) or perfect inversion (where *G* is negative and approaches –1). A value of *G* equal to 0 indicates the absence of association. The formula for calculating *G* is

$$G = \frac{f_a - f_i}{f_a + f_i}$$

where f_a = the frequency of agreements in the rankings of the two variables
  f_i = the frequency of inversions in the rankings of the two variables.

G is based on the relative positions of a set of cases on two variables. The cases are first arranged in ascending order on the independent variable. Their rankings on the dependent

TABLE 17.5   Centralized Crosstabulation

Independent Variable	Dependent Variable		
	Low	*Medium*	*High*
Low	a	b	c
Medium	d	e	f
High	g	h	i

variable are then compared. Those for which the original ordering is preserved are said to be in agreement, and those for which the original order is altered are said to be in inversion. Limitations of space do not permit us to consider this procedure in detail or to discuss the calculations of G when the number of cases is relatively small and/or no ties are present in the rankings. Rather, we shall focus on the procedures for calculating G under the more common circumstances, when ties (more than one case with the same rank) are present and the number of cases is large.[3] Here, as before, we work from a crosstab, as shown in Table 17.5.

To measure the association between these two variables, we determine the number of agreements and inversions relative to each cell in the table. An agreement occurs in any cell *below* (higher in its score on the independent variable) and to the *right* (higher in its score on the dependent variable) of the particular cell in question. Thus, agreements with those cases in cell a include all cases in cells e, f, h, and i, since these cases rank higher than those in cell a on *both* variables. An inversion occurs in any cell *below* (higher in its score on the independent variable) and to the *left* (lower in its score on the dependent variable) of the particular cell in question. Thus, inversions with those cases in cell c include all cases in cells d, e, g, and h, since these cases rank higher on one variable than those in cell c, but lower on the other. The frequency of agreements (f_a in the equation), then, is the sum for each cell of the number of cases in that cell multiplied by the number of cases in all cells below and to the right ($a[e + f + h + i] + b[f + i] + d[h + i] + e[i]$). The frequency of inversions (f_i in the equation) is the sum for each cell of the number of cases in that cell multiplied by the number of cases in all cells below and to the left ($b[d + g] + c[d + e + g + h] + e[g] + f[g + h]$). The resulting totals are simply substituted into the equation.

If, for example, the variables in Table 17.1 were ordinal, we could calculate G as follows:

$$f_a = 45(23 + 5 + 2 + 5) + 5(5 + 5) + 2(2 + 5) + 23(5)$$
$$= 1,575 + 50 + 14 + 115 = 1,754$$

$$f_i = 5(2 + 3) + 10(2 + 23 + 3 + 2) + 23(3) + 5(3 + 2)$$
$$= 25 + 300 + 69 + 25 = 419$$

$$G = \frac{f_a - f_i}{f_a + f_i} = \frac{1,754 - 419}{1,754 + 419} = \frac{1,335}{2,173} = .61$$

[3] In such applications, G may be unreliable, but it is included here to facilitate the discussion of association as a concept. A related statistic, Kendall's *tau*, may be more reliable, but its determination may be less intuitive to the beginning political scientist.

This tells us that there is 61 percent more agreement than disagreement in the rankings of the cases on the two variables. If f_i exceeded f_a, the sign of G would be negative, in order to indicate the existence of an inverse relationship.

The test of the statistical significance of G is based on the fact that the sampling distribution of G is approximately normal for a population with no true association, as was the sampling distribution of the hypothetical coefficient of association discussed earlier. Since this is so, we can determine the probability that any particular value of G has occurred by chance by calculating its standard score (z), locating its position under the normal curve, and assessing the probabilities. The actual calculation of z_G (**standard score of gamma**) will not be presented here, because the formula is complex and its understanding requires a more detailed knowledge of statistics than we have provided. Suffice it to say that when z_G exceeds ± 1.645 (when G lies at least 1.645 standard deviation units above or below the mean), G is sufficiently extreme to merit a significance level of .05, and that when z_G exceeds ± 2.326 (when G lies at least 2.326 standard deviation units above or below the mean), G achieves significance at the .01 level. The interpretation of these results is precisely the same as that in the earlier and more general example.

MEASURES OF ASSOCIATION AND SIGNIFICANCE FOR INTERVAL/RATIO VARIABLES: CORRELATION

The measure of association between two interval variables is the Pearson product-moment correlation (r), also known as the **correlation coefficient**. This coefficient summarizes the strength and direction of a relationship using the same notion we have already presented—about proportionate reduction in error in guessing values on one variable on the basis of known values of another—though the procedure, like the data for which it is designed, is more sophisticated than others we have discussed to this point. Here, rather than using the mean of the dependent variable (usually designated Y) to predict the values of individual cases, we use its geometric relationship with the independent variable (usually designated X) for this purpose. More particularly, we focus on the degree to which the equation of a particular straight line can help us to predict values of Y based on knowledge of corresponding values of X.

Graphing the Variables

The determination of r begins with the examination of a **scatter plot**, which is a graphic summary of the distribution of cases on two variables, in which the base line, or X-axis,

---

PRACTICAL RESEARCH ETHICS

What is the link between level of measurement and analytic techniques?

In doing initial bivariate analysis of your data, you need to always keep level of measurement in mind.

One of your most important duties as a researcher is to employ the proper analytic techniques (e.g., statistical measures), while maintaining close attention to each variable's level of measurement as you evaluate whether a hypothesized relationship achieves statistical significance.

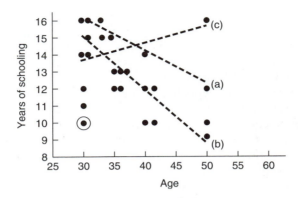

FIGURE 17.4 Scatter diagram showing relationship between age and years of schooling.

is denoted in units of the independent variable; the vertical line, or Y-axis, is denoted in units of the dependent variable; and each dot represents observations of one case on both variables. Such a plot is presented in Figure 17.4, in which the independent variable is age, the dependent variable is years of schooling completed, and the number of cases is twenty-five. The circled dot thus represents one case—a person thirty years old with ten years of schooling. The values in the figure have been arbitrarily assigned but would in reality be ascertained by the research itself.

The next step is to draw a straight line, called a **regression line**, through this field of dots so that no other line comes closer to touching all of the dots. This *line of best fit* for the relationship between two variables is analogous to the mean in univariate descriptive statistics. Just as the mean represents a most typical case in a frequency distribution, the regression line represents a most typical association between two variables. Just as we might use the mean to guess values of a variable in the absence of additional information, we can use the regression line to guess values of one variable on the basis of our knowledge of the values of another. If, for example, we know the value of *X* for a given case, we can project a vertical line from that point on the *X*-axis to the regression line, then a horizontal line from there to the *Y*-axis. The point of contact on the *Y*-axis gives us a predicted value of *Y*.

But just as a mean may be the single most typical value yet not be a good summary of a particular distribution, a regression line may be the best possible summary of a relationship between two variables yet not be a very useful summary. Accordingly, just as we use the standard deviation (*s*) as a measure of dispersion or goodness of fit around the mean, we use the correlation coefficient (*r*), or, more correctly, for purposes of interpretation, the square of that coefficient (r^2), as a measure of the *goodness of fit* of the various data points around the regression line. It is, in effect, a measure of how typical that line is of the *joint* distribution of values of the two variables.

Closeness of Association

Where all points actually fall directly on the line, as in Figure 17.5(a) and (e), the line provides a perfect description of the relationship between the two variables. Where the points are generally organized in the direction indicated by the line but do not all fall upon it, as in Figure 17.5(b) and (d), the line provides an approximation of the relationship

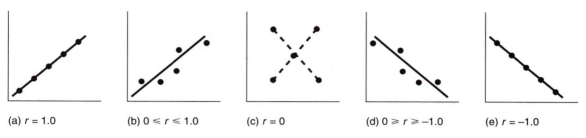

(a) $r = 1.0$ (b) $0 \leqslant r \leqslant 1.0$ (c) $r = 0$ (d) $0 \geqslant r \geqslant -1.0$ (e) $r = -1.0$

FIGURE 17.5   Summary of regression lines and values of r.

between the two variables. And where, as in Figure 17.5(c), there are multiple possible lines that equally fit the data, no association exists between the two variables. The problem, then, is twofold: First, what does this line of best fit look like? Second, how good a fit to the data does it in fact provide?

You may recall from your study of algebra that any straight line takes the form

$$Y_i = a + bX_i$$

where $a =$ the value of Y when $X = 0$
$b =$ the slope of the line
$X_i =$ the value of a given case on the independent variable.

The regression line is simply the one set of guessed values of this form that provides for the most accurate prediction of values of Y based on knowledge of values of X.

For reasons we shall not explore here, the slope b of that line will always take the form

$$b = \frac{\sum\limits_{i=1}^{N}(X_i - \overline{X})(Y_i - \overline{Y})}{\sum\limits_{i=1}^{N}(X_i - \overline{X})^2}$$

where X_i and Y_i are the corresponding values of the independent and dependent variables for case i, and $\overline{X}$ and $\overline{Y}$ are the respective means. Applying this formula and using a chart similar to the one we used in computing χ^2 we are able to ascertain the slope of any particular linear relationship between two interval variables. This process is illustrated in Table 17.6 for the data reported in Table 17.4. For these data, $\overline{X} = 37.08$ and $\overline{Y} = 12.88$. Substituting these values in the equation, we find

$$b = \frac{-136.79}{1,151.93} = -.12$$

In a **linear relationship**—one described or summarized by a straight line—a particular change in the value of the independent variable X is always accompanied by a particular change in the value of the dependent variable Y. Moreover, in such a relationship the rate of change is constant; that is, no matter what the particular values of X and Y, each change of one unit in X will be accompanied by a change in Y of some fixed size

TABLE 17.6 Values Used in Deriving the Equation of the Regression Line

X_1	$(X_1 - \overline{X})$	$(X_1 - \overline{X})^2$	Y_1	$(Y_1 - \overline{Y})$	$(X_1 - \overline{X})(Y_1 - \overline{Y})$
30	−7.08	50.13	10	−2.88	20.39
30	−7.08	50.13	11	−1.88	13.31
30	−7.08	50.13	12	−.88	6.23
30	−7.08	50.13	14	1.22	−7.93
30	−7.08	50.13	16	3.12	−22.09
31	−6.08	36.97	14	1.12	−6.81
31	−6.08	36.97	15	2.12	−12.89
31	−6.08	36.97	16	3.12	−18.99
33	−4.08	16.15	15	2.12	−8.65
33	−4.08	16.15	16	3.12	−12.73
35	−2.08	4.33	12	−.88	1.83
35	−2.08	4.33	13	.12	−.25
35	−2.08	4.33	15	2.12	−4.41
36	−1.08	1.17	12	−.88	.95
36	−1.08	1.17	13	.12	−.13
37	−.08	.01	13	.12	−.01
40	−2.92	8.53	10	−2.88	−8.41
40	−2.92	8.53	12	−.88	−2.57
40	−2.92	8.53	14	1.12	3.27
42	−4.92	24.21	10	−2.88	−14.17
42	−4.92	24.21	12	−.88	−4.33
50	−12.92	166.93	9	−3.88	−50.13
50	−12.92	166.93	10	−2.88	−37.12
50	−12.92	166.93	12	−.88	−11.37
50	−12.92	166.93	16	3.12	40.31
Totals	0	1,151.93		0	−136.79

determined by the slope of the regression line. Relationships in which slight changes in X are accompanied by relatively large changes in Y are summarized by lines that have a relatively steep slope ($|b| > 1$); this denotes the absolute value of b is greater than 1. Relationships in which large changes in X are accompanied by smaller changes in Y are summarized by lines that have a relatively flat slope ($|b| < 1$). Relationships in which one unit of change in X is accompanied by one unit of change in Y are summarized by lines for which b is equal to 1. Lines that slope upward from left to right, such as those in Figure 17.5(a) and (b), have a positive slope and represent relationships in which increases in X are accompanied by increases in Y. Those sloping downward from left to right, such as the lines in Figure 17.5(d) and (e), have a negative slope and represent relationships in which increases in X are accompanied by *decreases* in Y. Indeed, the slope of the line is simply the rate of change in Y for each unit of change in X. In our example, then, where b is equal to −.12, we know that the regression line will slope downward from left to right and will, if the two variables are drawn to the same scale, be relatively flat.

To arrive at the formula we used to compute the slope of the regression line, we had to assume that the line passes through the intersection of $\overline{X}$ and $\overline{Y}$ (the means of the respective variables). This is a reasonable assumption, because the means represent the central tendencies of these variables and because we are, in effect, seeking a joint or combined central tendency. Because we know both means and have now determined the value of b, we can easily find the value of a (the point at which the regression line intercepts the Y-axis) and solve the equation. The general equation of the regression line is

$$Y' = a + bX_i$$

and at the point where the line passes through the intersection of the two means

$$\overline{Y} = a + b\overline{X}$$

It must then follow that

$$a = \overline{Y} - b\overline{X}$$

Because all of these values are now known, we can determine that

$$a = 12.88 - (-.12)(37.08)$$
$$= 12.88 + 4.45 = 17.33$$

Thus, the equation of the regression line—the single best-fitting line—for the data reported in Figure 17.4 would be

$$Y' = 17.33 - .12X$$

Using this equation, we can predict the value of Y for any given value of X.

Once this equation has been determined, we may use the correlation coefficient (r) to assess the utility of the regression line. The formula for r_{XY} (the coefficient of correlation between X and Y) is

$$r_{XY} = \frac{N\Sigma XY - \Sigma X\Sigma Y}{\sqrt{\left[N\Sigma X^2 - (\Sigma X)^2\right]\left[N\Sigma Y^2 - (\Sigma Y)^2\right]}}$$

where

X = each value of the independent variable (the subscript i has been omitted here to simplify the presentation)
Y = each value of the dependent variable
N = the number of cases.

Although the assertion is certainly not obvious and although its algebraic proof lies beyond our present discussion, this working formula is derived from a comparison of the original error in guessing values of Y by using $\overline{Y}$ (the mean of the frequency distribution) with the error remaining when one guesses values of Y using Y' (the equation of the regression line). Thus, the procedure for computing r is analogous to that for computing both λ and G. It may best be accomplished by setting up a chart of the type with which we are now familiar in which the columns include X, Y, XY, X^2, and Y^2. The sums required by the equation are

TABLE 17.7 Values Used in Deriving the Correlation Coefficient (r)

	X	Y	XY	X^2	Y^2
	30	10	300	900	100
	30	11	330	900	121
	30	12	360	900	144
	30	14	420	900	196
	30	16	480	900	256
	31	14	434	961	196
	31	15	465	961	225
	31	16	496	961	256
	33	15	495	1,089	225
	33	16	528	1,089	256
	35	12	420	1,225	144
	35	13	455	1,225	169
	35	15	525	1,225	225
	36	12	432	1,296	144
	36	13	468	1,296	169
	37	13	481	1,369	169
	40	10	400	1,600	100
	40	12	480	1,600	144
	40	14	560	1,600	196
	42	10	420	1,764	100
	42	12	504	1,764	144
	50	9	450	2,500	81
	50	10	500	2,500	100
	50	12	600	2,500	144
	50	16	800	2,500	256
Totals	927	322	11,803	32,525	4,260

then provided by the column totals. Thus, for the data represented in Figure 17.4, whose regression line we have already determined, the chart is completed as in Table 17.7.

We substitute these totals in the equation

$$r = \frac{25(11,803) - (927)(322)}{\sqrt{\left[25(35,525) - (927)^2\right]\left[25(4,260) - (322)^2\right]}}$$

$$= \frac{295,075 - 298,494}{\sqrt{(888,125 - 589,329)(106,500 - 103,684)}}$$

$$= \frac{-3,419}{\sqrt{(28,796)(2,816)}}$$

$$= \frac{-3,419}{\sqrt{81,089,536}}$$

$$= \frac{-3,419}{9,005}$$

$$= -.38$$

This tells us that the slope of the regression line is negative and that the points cluster weakly to moderately around it (because r ranges from $+1$ to -1, with the weakest association at 0).

Explained Variance

Although r itself is not easily interpreted, r^2 may be interpreted as *the proportion of reduction in the variance of Y attributable to our knowledge of X*. In other words, r^2 is the proportion of variation in Y that is predictable (or explainable) on the basis of X. The quantity r^2 is often referred to as the percentage of *explained variance*, and the quantity $1 - r^2$ is often termed the percentage of *unexplained variance*. Thus, in our example, the r of $-.38$ means that differences on the independent variable *age* account for some 14 percent, or $(-.38)^2$, of the variance in the dependent variable *years of schooling* for the cases under analysis.

Computing Statistical Significance

For reasons that lie beyond the scope of the present discussion, we are able to specify the statistical significance of r only when *both* the independent *and* dependent variables are normally distributed. This is accomplished by using Table A.5 in Appendix A, for which purpose two pieces of information are needed. The first is r itself, which, of course, is known. The second, analogous to the χ^2 test, is the number of degrees of freedom of the regression line because two points determine a line (in this case, the intersection of) $\overline{X}$ and $\overline{Y}$ was the first and the intercept with the Y-axis the second), all other data points may fall freely, so df will always equal $(N - 2)$, where N is the number of cases. To use the table, then, we locate the appropriate degrees of freedom (in the example, $N - 2 = 25 - 2 = 23$) and the desired level of significance (for example, .05), just as we did for χ^2, and identify the threshold value of r necessary to achieve that level of significance; and evaluate our actual observation. In the present instance, this requires interpolating values in the table between $df = 20$ and $df = 25$. For $df = 23$, these values would be .3379, .3976, .5069, and .6194, respectively. Thus, our r of $-.38$ is statistically significant at the .10 level (it exceeds .3379), but not at the .05 level (it does not exceed .3976). The interpretation of this result is the same as those for other measures of statistical significance.

Conclusion

In this chapter we have introduced some of the more common statistics that are used to summarize the relationship between two variables. As in Chapter 16, we found that differing measures of association and statistical significance were appropriate, depending on the level of measurement that characterized the data being analyzed. Together with the techniques presented earlier, these various coefficients provide the researcher with some very useful basic tools with which to summarize research results. In the next chapter we outline some more sophisticated statistical techniques, which can further enrich our ability to analyze and understand what we have discovered.

Key Terms

association *290*
coefficient of association *291*
statistical significance *294*
lambda (λ) *297*
chi-square (χ^2) *299*

degrees of freedom (*df*) *301*
gamma (*G*) *301*
standard score of
   gamma (Z_G) *303*
correlation coefficient (*r*) *303*

scatter plot *303*
regression line *304*
linear relationship *305*

Research Examples

Given the complexity of political science research questions, it is unsurprising that few current articles employ simple two-way crosstabs or
bivariate correlations. Although excellent learning tools, these bivariate procedures have given
way to more sophisticated techniques that simultaneously control for multiple factors. Thus, we
are unable to provide current research examples
of this type.

Methodological Readings

A bibliography on statistics and related topics is
found at the end of Chapter 18.

CHAPTER 18

Statistics III: Examining Relationships among Several Variables

In this chapter you will learn:

- The primary analytic advantage of multiple regression techniques.
- The types of variables upon which regression analysis may be performed.

The univariate and bivariate statistics described in the preceding chapters often help us to understand the subjects we are researching. However, univariate and bivariate analyses rarely can provide convincing tests of hypotheses or the theories from which they were derived. To test a hypothesis convincingly, we must be able to rule out major alternative rival hypotheses. Although a sound research design can sometimes allow us to dismiss alternative rival hypotheses, social scientists commonly find that they must rely on data analysis rather than research design to examine the validity of rival hypotheses. This requires the use of **multivariate analysis**, which is analysis of the simultaneous relationship among three or more variables.

TABULAR ANALYSIS

Many of the statistical tools we have already discussed can be employed in multivariate analysis. To illustrate, we can use a highly simplified example to suggest the way in which crosstabs and bivariate statistics can be adapted in order to conduct a multivariate analysis.

An Example

Suppose we want to explore the relationship between political ideology and attending college. Reasoning that going to college gives people a stake in maintaining the status quo by preparing them to do relatively well within the existing socioeconomic system, we might begin with the hypothesis that those who have completed college will be more conservative than those who have not. To test this hypothesis, we might interview a sample of fifty people who have completed college and fifty people who have not completed college.

TABLE 18.1(a) Hypothetical Relationship between College Education and Political Ideology

Education	Ideology		Totals
	Liberal	Conservative	
College	40% (20)	60% (30)	(50)
No college	60% (30)	40% (20)	(50)
Totals	100% (50)	100% (50)	(100)

Imagine that we obtained the results shown in Table 18.1(a). The diagonal "loading" or trend in the cases in this table indicates that those who have attended college are more likely to be classified as conservative than those who have not attended college. By calculating a chi-square for this table, we find that the relationship between college and political ideology is statistically significant at the $p \leq .01$ level. All of these findings are consistent with our original hypothesis.

Before we rush to submit this finding to *American Political Science Review*, however, we need to test some alternative rival hypotheses to be sure that our result is valid. One approach is to extend our bivariate analysis into a multivariate analysis that will allow us to "control for" the effects of other variables on the relationship between college and ideology. For example, one alternative rival hypothesis that merits examination derives from the observation that men are more likely to be conservative than women. If, by chance, more of the people in our sample who went to college were male than female, the results shown in Table 18.1(a) may reflect gender differences rather than an actual effect of college attendance on political opinions.

Controlling for Other Factors

To explore this possibility, we could examine the relationship between college and ideology separately for men and for women by constructing two crosstabs such as Tables 18.1(b) and 18.1(c). If the alternative rival hypothesis is valid, the statistical relationship between college and ideology shown in Table 18.1(a) will *not* show up in these new tables because the effect of gender on that relationship will be eliminated. This process of holding constant the influence of a third variable on the relationship between two other variables is referred to as **controlling**, and is a major step in all forms of multivariate data analysis.

In this case, Tables 18.1(b) and 18.1(c) actually show that the relationship between college and ideology is essentially the same for men and women. Although the women in our sample are, as predicted, less likely than the men are to be classified as conservative, the "loadings" in these two tables are highly similar to each other, and calculation of the chi-square for each table shows that the relationships they represent are statistically significant. In such a situation, researchers say that the original relationship has "survived control" and that an alternative rival hypothesis can be "ruled out" as an explanation of the original findings. If a relationship survives enough such controls, it will be accepted as valid.

We have thus conducted a very simple multivariate analysis using techniques designed for bivariate analysis. We could extend this logic to evaluate more alternative rival hypotheses by controlling for two or more additional variables *at the same time*. To illustrate, one of

TABLE 18.1(b) Hypothetical Relationship between College Education and Political Ideology for Males

Education	Ideology		Totals
	Liberal	*Conservative*	*Totals*
College	33% (5)	57% (20)	(25)
No college	67% (10)	43% (15)	(25)
Totals	100% (15)	100% (35)	(50)

TABLE 18.1(c) Hypothetical Relationship between College Education and Political Ideology for Females

Education	Ideology		Totals
	Liberal	*Conservative*	*Totals*
College	43% (15)	67% (10)	(25)
No college	57% (20)	33% (5)	(25)
Totals	100% (35)	100% (15)	(50)

our alternative rival hypotheses might contend that racial differences between whites and nonwhites in terms of both political values and the likelihood of attending college created the apparent relationship between college and ideology shown in Table 18.1(a). To hold constant the effects of both race and gender on the relationship between college and ideology, we would have to set up four crosstabs tables showing the relationship between college and ideology: one for white males, one for white females, one for nonwhite males, and one for nonwhite females.

Limitations of Tabular Multivariate Analysis

Under many circumstances, generating separate tables can be a quite useful multivariate approach to evaluating hypotheses. However, it has important limitations. First, tables become very cumbersome to use and the results become difficult to interpret if the variables involved have many possible values. This makes it impractical for analysis of interval/ratio-level data and difficult to use with many nominal and ordinal variables. For instance, to compare an independent and dependent variable each having five values while controlling for a third variable with ten values would require an analysis of ten tables with twenty-five cells each. In that situation, unless we have an exceptionally large and diverse sample, many of the cells in the tables will have no cases in them, which can make it impossible to calculate some measures of association and significance. We might try to avoid this by collapsing certain categories of the variables in order to create fewer values and hold down the number of tables and cells needed (as when we reduce the measure "years of education" to a dichotomy of "less than 12 years" and "12 years or more"). However, it would mean giving up potentially important information contained in our original measures and may produce misleading results. Moreover, the same problem will appear, even after collapsing categories, if we tried to apply several control variables at once in order to examine the *combined effects* of different variables. Second, even if we can complete such an analysis, its results may be difficult to report because the patterns are likely to be complex and there are no overall statistics with which to summarize the results.

Fortunately, there is a variety of statistical procedures designed specifically for multivariate analyses that can be used in a wide range of situations, and that provide easily interpretable results. The procedures are important because of their value in hypothesis testing (allowing us to examine the relationship between two variables while holding the effects of other variables on each constant), but their greatest value may come from the ways in which they help us understand the complex and subtle networks of relationships within which social phenomena are usually embedded. In this chapter we introduce you to two of the most commonly used multivariate techniques so that you can know when and how to apply them in your research and can judge the skill with which others have applied them when you are reading research reports. We selected these techniques from among the many that are available because (1) they are very widely applicable, (2) they illustrate many basic principles of multivariate analysis, and (3) they are based on the same basic mathematical techniques and can therefore be explained more quickly than techniques that rest on different mathematical foundations.

MULTIPLE REGRESSION

The bivariate correlation and regression procedures described in Chapter 17 can be extended to cases in which you want to explore the relationship between one dependent variable (DV) and several independent variables (IVs). The purpose of **multiple regression** is to (1) yield an estimate of the *independent* effect of a change in the value of *each* IV on the value of the DV and (2) provide an empirical basis for predicting values of the DV from knowledge of the joint values of the IVs.

Analysis begins with your statement of an equation that you feel accurately describes the causal influences being investigated. Because this equation can be viewed as a **model** of the process in which you are interested, this step is referred to as **model specification**. It involves translating your verbal theory of the phenomenon into a mathematical equation. The general form for a **multiple regression equation** is

$$Y' = a_0 + b_1X_1 + b_2X_2 + b_3X_3 \ldots b_nX_n + e$$

which you should recognize as an extension of the bivariate regression equation explained in Chapter 17. Understanding this equation is simplified by the introduction of a concrete example.

An Example

Let us say that we are interested in assessing the validity of the theory that election to the U.S. Senate can be "bought" by heavy spending on a media campaign, because advertising messages reach voters not already predisposed by partisanship to vote for either candidate. We might begin by analyzing hypotheses that explain the percentage of the vote that candidates get as a function of (1) the amount they spend on media advertising and (2) the percentage of the electorate in their state that has the same party identification as the candidate. These hypotheses yield this simple model of the electoral process:

$$Y' = a_0 + b_1X_1 + b_2X_2 + e$$

where Y' = the predicted percent of the vote received by the candidate

$\qquad a_0$ = the average value of Y' when each Independent Variable equals 0

$\qquad b_1$ = the average change in Y' associated with a unit change in X_1 (the amount spent on advertising), *when the effects of other variables are held constant*

$\qquad X_1$ = the amount the candidate spends on advertising (in units of $1,000)

$\qquad b_2$ = the average change in Y' associated with a unit change in X_2 (the percentage of the electorate that shared the candidate's party identification), *when the effects of other variables are held constant*

$\qquad X_2$ = the percentage of the electorate that shares the candidate's party identification

$\qquad e$ = an "error term" representing any variance in Y' that is not accounted for by variance in the IVs in the model.

We might test the accuracy of this model by collecting appropriate data on 100 races for U.S. Senate seats. Before analyzing the data, though, we need to ensure that our model does not violate the assumptions inherent to regression analysis.

Regression Assumptions

Successful application of multiple regression techniques to any task requires that our model and the data with which we hope to test it conform to five assumptions that underlie the regression procedure:

1. The model is *accurately specified* (it accurately describes the actual relationships in question). This includes the assumptions that
   a. the relationship among variables is linear,
   b. no important IVs have been excluded, and
   c. no irrelevant IVs have been included.
2. There is *no error in measurement* of the variables.
3. Variables are measured at the *interval/ratio level.*
4. The following are true of the error term, e:
   a. Its mean (the expected value for any given observation) is 0.
   b. The error terms for each observation are *un*correlated.
   c. The IVs are *un*correlated with the error term.
   d. The variance for the error term is constant for all values of the IVs.
   e. The error term has a *normal distribution.*
5. None of the IVs is perfectly correlated with any of the other IVs or with any linear combination of other IVs. If this is true, there is *no perfect multicollinearity.*[1]

If our study comes *close enough* to meeting these assumptions,[2] we can substitute actual values from our research for Y', X_1, and X_2 and solve the regression equation representing our theory for the unknown terms a, b_1, and b_2 using the logic of least squares estimation. One hypothetical result of such a solution could be

$$Y' = 10 + .1X_1 + 1X_2$$

---

[1] For an explanation of these assumptions and an extended general discussion of multiple regression, see Pedhazur (1997).

[2] Studies seldom meet these requirements fully, and it is often impossible to know in advance of analysis whether or not they are met in a given data set. In this context, "close enough" means that the effect of any violation of assumptions can be corrected for or at least estimated and taken into account in drawing conclusions. For further clarification, see Pedhazur (1997).

INTERPRETING MULTIPLE REGRESSIONS RESULTS

The *least squares procedure* for multiple regression works in a manner similar to bivariate regression in that it passes a line through a plotting of the values of cases on several variables in such a way as to minimize the sum of the squared distance of each point from that line. The difference is that the "line" in the case of multiple regression is a set of mathematically estimated points on a plane that cannot be represented in a two-dimensional scatterplot. The *a* or intercept term is generally of little practical interest, because the values of the IVs are rarely 0. However, the substantive interpretation of an *a* of 10 in the equation is that even if the candidate spent no money on advertising and 0 percent of the voters in the state shared the candidate's party identification, the candidate would receive 10 percent of the vote just by being on the ballot.

Interpreting Coefficients

The key to interpreting multiple regression analyses is to understand the meaning of the b_i terms. They are referred to as **partial regression coefficients** and describe the unique contribution of each IV to the determination of the DV. In our electoral example, a b_1 of .1 would be substantively interpreted as meaning that every additional $1,000 spent on advertising increases the candidate's portion of the vote by one-tenth of a percentage point, and a b_2 of 1 would indicate that for every 1 percent increase in the percentage of voters that share the candidate's party identification there is a corresponding 1 percent increase in the share of the vote that goes to that candidate. In calculating these coefficients, regression statistically holds constant the effect of any variables that influence both the individual IV and the DV through use of the formula

$$b_i = \frac{\sum (X_n - X_n')(Y - Y')}{\sum (X_n - X_n')^2}$$

This statistical control simulates the control we might have obtained in an experimental setting and is thus valuable in two important respects. First, as we will explore shortly, it allows us to assess the *relative* importance of different IVs in determining the value of the DV. Second, it allows us to rule out the alternative hypothesis that the relationship between the DV and any given IV is spurious. If we are willing to assume that we have included all important causes of change in the DV in our model and find that the partial regression coefficient for any given IV is significantly different from 0, we can conclude that the relationship between that IV and the DV is *not* spurious. If, however, the *b* is near 0 or statistically insignificant, we must conclude that there is no independent relationship between that IV and the DV. In that case, we would drop the IV from our model in order to make it conform more closely to observed reality. Clearly, then, multiple regression can be a valuable tool in refining and improving our theories of political phenomena.

Interpreting R^2

We can assess the completeness of our theory by calculating a **coefficient of determination**, or R^2 (sometimes referred to as the *multiple R*), using the formula

$$R^2 = \frac{\sum (Y' - \overline{Y})^2}{\sum (Y' - \overline{Y})^2} = \frac{\text{Regression sum of squares}}{\text{Total sum of squares}}$$

This coefficient tells us how close all the data plots came to touching the "line" projected by our model and is commonly interpreted as the *proportion of the variation in the DV that is "explained"* (accounted for) *by variation in all of the IVs*. For example, an R^2 of .57 would be interpreted as showing that the IVs in the model from which it was calculated explain 57 percent of the variance in the DV. R^2 can range between 0 and 1; the closer it is to 1, the more complete the model is. The size of R^2 can almost always be increased by adding additional IVs to the model, but the researcher must ask if additional variables make the model too complex or add anything of value to our understanding of the phenomenon in question. In the case of our electoral example, for instance, we might marginally increase the R^2 by adding a variable to the equation that coded the number of letters in the candidate's last name. We will not do this for two reasons: (1) this variable violates the assumption that the regression contains no irrelevant variables, and (2) we only wish to include variables that our theory suggests—to do otherwise would rob our model of its potential predictive benefit.

SOLVING COMMON PROBLEMS IN MULTIPLE REGRESSION

Returning to the regression assumptions for a moment, we need to acknowledge that neither data nor reality always conforms to the conceptual model underlying multiple regression analysis. Relationships are not always linear, measurement error is almost always present, and so on. Fortunately, statisticians have devised ways for us to adapt multiple regression in order to compensate for some of these problems. In this section we discuss adaptations to three of the most commonly encountered problems so that you can (1) learn how to cope with these issues in your applications of multiple regression and (2) get a sense of the flexibility of multiple regression as an analytic technique.

Noninterval Data

In the social sciences, important variables often are not (and sometimes cannot be) measured at the interval/ratio level, thus violating the assumption of interval-level measurement. Noninterval data can, however, be used in multiple regression under two conditions.

First, if the measure is (or can be converted into) a *dichotomy*, it can be entered directly into the regression by simply coding the value of the dichotomy as 1 and the other as 0. For example, in a study of international trade, goods might be classified as "foreign" or "domestic," with a code of 1 being assigned to the value "foreign" and a code of 0 assigned to the value "domestic." Regression would treat this scheme as if it were interval because dichotomies have special mathematical properties. As a result, we can interpret the partial regression coefficient computed for any variable coded as a dichotomy just as if it were measured at the interval level.

Second, noninterval variables that have multiple categories can be incorporated into multiple regression by use of a system of *dummy variables*. For example, consider the case in which occupational status is measured only as "high," "medium," or "low" in a study that seeks to predict the number of political organizations to which a person belongs as a function of education (number of years of schooling) and occupational status. We can use the ordinal data on status in a multiple regression if we create two dichotomous dummy variables to represent the variable occupational status. The equation would be:

$$Y' = a + b_1X_1 + b_2X_2 + b_3X_3 + e$$

where Y' = the number of organizational memberships
X_1 = the number of years of schooling
X_2 = a dummy variable scored 1 if occupational status = "low" and 0 otherwise
X_3 = a dummy variable scored 1 if occupational status = "medium" and 0 otherwise.

Why use only two dummy variables to represent a noninterval variable with three categories? Because the value of the third dummy variable would be an exact linear function of the values of the other two, thus violating the assumption of no perfect multicollinearity and making it impossible to obtain a unique estimate of the various coefficients.

Whenever using dummy variables, we must follow the rule of creating *one fewer dummy variables than there are categories in the noninterval variable* being represented. In practice, it is usually advisable to leave out the category in which you expect the fewest cases. In our example, the "high" category was not represented by a dummy variable because there are relatively few high-status jobs.

Interaction Effects

Conventional least squares regression assumes that the effects of different IVs on the DV are independent of one another and can be added together to determine the total effect of a set of variables. In practice, the effects of many variables reinforce or amplify the effects of another variable. Whenever the impact of one IV depends on the value of another IV, an *interaction effect* exists. To return to the electoral example used earlier in this chapter, we might argue that the effect of advertising expenditures is different for incumbents (who tend to be well known) and challengers (who need to make voters aware of their qualifications).

Multiple regression can be adapted to this situation by including the interaction between advertising and incumbent status as a separate variable. Letting incumbent status be represented by a dummy variable (X_3) coded 1 for challengers and 0 for incumbents, the new regression model would be:

$$Y' = a + b_1X_1 + b_2X_2 + b_3(X_1X_3) + e$$

where X_1X_3 is an interaction variable created by multiplying X_1 by X_3. This procedure allows us to interpret b_1 as the unique contribution of advertising expenditures to vote percentage by breaking off the *joint* effects of advertising and incumbency into b_3, and it can yield more accurate predictions of Y.

Multicollinearity

Regression analysis requires that no IV be perfectly correlated with any other IV or any linear combination of other IVs. It is usually easy to meet this strict requirement because few social science variables can be perfectly predicted from knowledge of any other variable or set of variables. However, many important variables are highly correlated with each other. (Consider urbanization and industrialization, education and income, or party and ideology in Western Europe.) This condition is referred to as **multicollinearity**. If the correlations among IVs in a regression model are high enough, estimations of the coefficients become inaccurate and we cannot place any confidence in the results of the regression analysis. Significant multicollinearity can cause such large variances in the estimation of partial regression coefficients that it becomes impossible to compare the relative effects of different IVs on the DV. In addition, coefficients may fail to attain statistical significance even where there is a substantial relationship, leading us to falsely identify bivariate relationships as spurious.

It is therefore essential that researchers make a serious effort to determine if multicollinearity is present and to make the adjustments necessary to correct for it. Multicollinearity is usually indicated by one or more of the following symptoms:

1. A high R^2 for the equation but statistically insignificant regression coefficients (b's).
2. Dramatic changes in regression coefficients (b's) for given variables when other IVs are dropped from or added to the equation.
3. Regression coefficients that are *far* larger or smaller (either in absolute terms or in relation to the coefficients for other IVs) than theory and knowledge of other research results would lead us to expect.
4. Regression coefficients that have the wrong sign—that are negative when we have good reason to expect them to be positive or positive when we have good reason to expect them to be negative.

When any of these symptoms is noted in a regression analysis, it is important to test for multicollinearity. This is done by *regressing each IV on all other IVs*. We would, for example, test the equation

$$Y' = a + b_1X_1 + b_2X_2 + b_3(X_3) + e$$

by running the following equations:

$$X_1 = a + b_2X_2 + b_3X_3$$
$$X_2 = a + b_1X_1 + b_3X_3$$
$$X_3 = a + b_1X_1 + b_2X_2$$

If the R^2 for any of these equations were higher than, say, .8, we could conclude that substantial multicollinearity existed.

There are several possible approaches to correcting for multicollinearity. If we have the option of adding cases to our sample (as when we are collecting data from published records and can simply go back and resample), then increasing the sample size will sometimes eliminate multicollinearity. A second strategy would be to determine *which* of the IVs are highly related to each other and then combine them into a single indicator. If, for example, we had originally measured expenditures on radio, television, and newspaper advertising separately in our study of senatorial elections and found these three indicators to be highly correlated, we could combine the three into a single measure called *media expenditures* in order to eliminate the destabilizing effects of multicollinearity. Clearly, any such combining of variables works only when it is theoretically justified. We could not, for instance, solve a problem of multicollinearity by combining the incumbent status of the candidate with the regional location of the state because these are theoretically distinct concepts. Finally, we can attempt to cope with multicollinearity by discarding one or more of the highly intercorrelated variables. This can produce specification error, but by dropping first one and then the other correlated IV and comparing the results of different regressions, we can at least get a firm estimate of the damage done by both multicollinearity and misspecification.

Comparing IVs

It is often important to know which of several IVs exerts the most influence on a DV. If we wanted to encourage people to wear seat belts, for instance, we might want to know which of several factors that could lead to this behavior actually has the most impact on the decision to buckle up in order to invest our resources in the most efficient way. Multiple regression analysis is well suited for this purpose since it provides estimates of the unique contribution of each IV to variance in the DV in the form of its partial regression coefficients. Unfortunately, determining the relative effects of different IVs is not a simple matter of comparing the size of their regression coefficients.

When IVs are measured in different units (number of dollars versus percentage of voters, for instance), regression coefficients do not reflect the relative influence of IVs on the DV. One way to cope with this is to *standardize* the variables—so that they are measured in the same units—and obtain new estimates of the regression coefficients. Standardization of a case's score is achieved by converting the raw score into units of standard deviation from the mean value of the variable using the formula

$$X^* = \frac{X - \overline{X}}{s_X}$$

where the * indicates that the variable is standardized, X is the score for a given case, $\overline{X}$ is the mean score on that variable for all cases, and s is the standard deviation of the distribution of values on variable X (see Chapter 16).

When standardized scores are substituted for raw scores in the regression equation, the a term drops out because standardization forces it to 0, and the equation takes the general form

$$Y'^* = \beta_1 X_1^* + \beta_2 X_2^* \ldots \beta_n X_n + e$$

where β represents a *standardized partial regression coefficient*, referred to as a **beta weight or beta coefficient**. A beta weight corrects the unstandardized partial regression coefficient by the ratio of the standard deviation of the IV to the standard deviation of the DV and can be calculated by the formula

$$\beta_i = b_i \frac{s_{X_i}}{s_Y}$$

A beta weight can be interpreted as representing *the average standard deviation change in Y associated with a standard deviation change in X* when the effects of other IVs are held constant. Thus, a β of .5 would indicate that one standard deviation change in the value of an IV would be associated with a change of one-half standard deviation in the DV.

Standardizing thus allows us to compare the influence of different IVs *within a single sample*. However, when seeking to compare the influence of variables *across samples*, it can be misleading. If we wanted to compare the effects of campaign spending on the electoral success of candidates in the United States and Mexico, for example, we would find that there were substantial differences in the variance (and thus the standard deviation) of key variables because media campaigns cost more in the United States and election outcomes are usually significantly closer in one nation than in the other. Since the size of β is a function of variance (the larger the variance, the larger the β, other things being equal), we could be misled into thinking that spending had more of an effect in one nation than in the other simply because of mathematically determined differences in β. To avoid this error, it is important to use the *un*standardized partial regression slopes (b's) for a variable whenever we are seeking to compare the effects of an IV in different samples *if the variance for that variable differs considerably from sample to sample*.

Conclusion

We end this chapter with two notes of caution. First, it is important to recognize that we have discussed only a fraction of the many multivariate statistics that are available for the analysis of both interval and noninterval data. Each of these techniques is applicable to different analytical tasks. Among the most important, commonly used techniques that we have *not* discussed here are *logit regression*, which allows the use of a dichotomous dependent variable, a common condition

PRACTICAL RESEARCH ETHICS

The right tool for the job?

Now that you have read three chapters on data analysis, you may feel well prepared to load your data set into a statistics program (such as SPSS) and point-and-click your way through a multiple regression analysis.

Always temper your statistical enthusiasm by evaluating your data in light of the procedure's basic assumptions. Including hastily computed results in your term paper, thesis, conference presentation, dissertation, or published work tempts fate. If you rush into statistical analysis without fully assessing the qualities of your data, your future may well include an embarrassing public retraction of your research findings.

for voter turnout and other simple decision variables; *analysis of variance* (*ANOVA*), which is used to test hypotheses about differences of multiple means in various groups and can be especially valuable in identifying the effects of some "treatment" or intervention on the degree to which cases manifest a concept; and *factor analysis*, which is used to identify common factors that reflect the relatedness of apparently independent indicators. Explanations of when and how to use these and other techniques may be found in the readings suggested at the end of this chapter.

With such a wide variety of statistical techniques to choose from, the task of selecting the statistical procedure that is most appropriate to your data and research question can be quite challenging. Your academic librarian can help locate a number of volumes that offer flowcharts or other decision tools to aid in choosing which statistical techniques are most appropriate for your research, given your data. Ultimately, though, the best way to learn which technique is most useful for your data is through hands-on experimentation.

The second caution to bear in mind is that the overview of statistical techniques in this text has only introduced you to data analysis—it has not prepared you to actually execute more sophisticated data analysis techniques. Fortunately, you need not be a statistician to learn about and use the most common methods, since statistical analysis programs such as SPSS or SAS will carry out the calculations for you if the analysis is correctly set up. These programs have "help" functions that will enable you to learn both the statistics and the analytic requirements. Still, it is your responsibility to ensure that you are employing the correct procedure, and that you are correctly interpreting your analyses.

Key Terms

multivariate analysis *311*
controlling *312*
multiple regression *314*
model *314*

model specification *314*
multiple regression equation *314*
partial regression coefficients *316*

coefficient of determination (R^2) *317*
multicollinearity *319*
beta weight (β) or beta coefficient (β) *320*

Research Examples

Studying the election of women in dozens of countries using party list Proportional Representation, Schmidt (2009) comparatively evaluates various explanations for women's success using multivariate OLS regression. Additional examples of political science research using multivariate analysis are found in nearly every issue of the major journals listed in Chapter 3.

Methodological Readings

Among the many texts that provide a general introduction to statistics appropriate to the social sciences are *Statistics for Social Data Analysis* (Bohrnstedt and Knoke 1994), and *Statistics*, 9th ed. (McClave and Sincich 2003).

Applied Linear Regression (Weisberg 2005) provides a highly regarded, comprehensive examination of regression techniques. A detailed introduction to the types of statistics most often used in hypothesis testing is found in *Using Multivariate Statistics* (Tabachnick and Fidell 2001). Procedures for analyzing noninterval data are covered in detail in *Nonparametric Methods in Quantitative Analysis* (Gibbons 1997).

The Sage series: *Quantitative Applications in the Social Sciences* offers detailed and generally quite readable explanations of many specific analysis techniques. There are dozens of these monographs, each focusing on a specific social science quantitative procedure. Each analytic procedure is taught using concrete examples from the literature.

A useful introduction to SPSS, complete with step-by-step instructions for carrying out commands, is the *Quantitative Analysis Lab Manual* (Brians 2010) that accompanies this text. This lab manual, written with the beginning researcher in mind, includes weekly exercises for SPSS labs, as well as instruction in literature searching and citing your references.

References

Bohrnstedt, George W., and David Knoke. 1994. *Statistics for Social Data Analysis*, 3rd ed. Itasca, IL: F. E. Peacock.

Brians, Craig Leonard. 2010. *Quantitative Analysis Lab Manual*, 3rd ed. New York, NY: Pearson Longman.

Gibbons, Jean Dickinson. 1997. *Nonparametric Methods in Quantitative Analysis*, 3rd ed. Columbus, OH: American Sciences Press.

Kline, Rex B. 2005. *Principles and Practice of Structural Equation Modeling*, 2nd ed. New York: Guilford.

McClave, James T., and Terry Sincich. 2003. *Statistics*, 9th ed. Upper Saddle River, NJ: Prentice Hall.

Pedhazur, Elazar J. 1997. *Multiple Regression in Behavioral Research: Explanation and Prediction*, 3rd ed. Fort Worth, TX: Harcourt Brace.

Schmidt, Gregory D. 2009. "The Election of Women in List PR Systems: Testing the Conventional Wisdom." *Electoral Studies* 28(June): 190–203.

Tabachnick, Barbara G., and Linda S. Fidell. 2001. *Using Multivariate Statistics*, 4th ed. Needham Heights, MA: Allyn & Bacon.

Weisberg, Sanford. 2005. *Applied Linear Regression*, 3rd ed. New York, NY: John Wiley and Sons.

CHAPTER 19

Direct Observation: Systematically Watching Behavior

In this chapter you will learn:

- Why researchers sometimes need to observe political events directly as they occur.
- How to accomplish personal observations with scientific validity.
- The advantages and limitations of direct observation.
- The ethical issues posed by direct observation and how they might be addressed.

Remember looking at college information when you were in high school? You went to Web sites and heard stories from others who had visited various colleges. Recall how you had heard others talk about the college you were planning to attend, but you really wanted to tour the campus yourself to see if this was the place for you. My first foray into college occurred about four years after high school, when I decided to try to take some classes at the local community college. I had seen it hundreds of times: It was only about ten miles from my apartment, and it sat on a low hill about a mile from the major freeway in the area. I had even visited its pond and fed the ducks. But before signing up for any classes at Gavilan College, I wanted to walk around the buildings, meet some of the instructors, and learn more about what people actually do in college.

Personal, direct observations of people, locations, and events tell you things that no Web site, brochure, or interview can relay. You get the feel and smell of the setting. You hear and see things in ways that are impossible absent personal experience. In our society and businesses, we value those who have traveled to other countries and studied other cultures. Many feel that direct experience is a powerful teacher.

In political science, most research is conducted indirectly. Researchers must rely to some degree on others' experience with the political events they are seeking to understand. For example, with aggregate data, we usually rely on information collected by public or private agencies to represent the events we are studying; we do not actually observe coups, agricultural production, the distribution of income, or any of the other phenomena represented by the figures with which we work. Even when conducting surveys, we are relying on respondents' memories of their experiences or perceptions of their surroundings—we do not actually observe their actions or the setting in which those actions occurred.

Sometimes, though, researchers need to see and hear events for themselves in order to gain a full understanding of them. New phenomena may best be studied directly. For example, the alternative political parties that developed in the authoritarian states of Eastern Europe in the 1990s were a new phenomenon: political parties seeking to gain power through elections in previously nondemocratic Soviet bloc nations. To understand their functioning, we could try to apply theories of political party behavior that have been developed by observation of parties in democratic nations of the West. However, there are good reasons to suspect that these new parties will operate according to very different rules because they exist in a dramatically different context from, say, Canadian or French political parties. To formulate theories about their operation, we may need to observe them firsthand.

A second situation calling for direct contact with the subject of research is one in which we cannot be confident of the usefulness of others' reports of some ongoing behavior. In some cases, even though we could interview participants in the events that interest us, we may feel they would be unable to give us the understanding we need because they do not share our conceptual framework. We might, for instance, be looking for the effects of institutionalized ideology on the decisions of U.S. embassy personnel in handling requests for political asylum. If we ask the officials how they make decisions, they will quite sincerely cite the written rules they follow. If we see for ourselves the procedures followed, however, we might be able to identify unofficial ideological criteria at work.

Another situation in which we might not be willing to rely on others' accounts of events is one in which those who can supply the information might have an interest in misleading us. Real estate agents, for example, would have legal and professional reasons for giving the impression that they always comply with federal equal housing opportunity laws even if they knew that their practices often did not satisfy the requirements of that legislation.

In these and other circumstances, researchers may need to turn to **direct observation**. When we collect data by personal contact with the events we are studying *as they happen*, we are employing direct observation.

DIRECT OBSERVATION AND THE SCIENTIFIC METHOD

Despite its rich potential for providing insight, the use of direct observation is not common in political science. One reason for this is that many of the subjects that political scientists study are too large in scale to allow direct observation. Elections, for example, happen all over a nation simultaneously and therefore cannot be physically observed directly as complete events. Individual researchers must rely on indirect observation.

A second reason for the infrequent use of direct observation in political science is that we often do not have access to events that could be fruitfully studied by this method. Spontaneous popular uprisings, for example, such as those that unseated the Milosevic government in Serbia in 2000, occur too rapidly to allow us to plan a research project. Similarly, even ongoing phenomena may be inaccessible to us. We would be unlikely to get permission to observe the White House staff making national security decisions, for instance.

A third set of reasons why we do not see more use of direct observation relates to the nature of the method. First, it is usually a very time-consuming technique that may take months or years to produce results and can be quite expensive to carry out. Second, it often demands a great deal of the researcher, who may have to become immersed in the study to the exclusion of other activities, and it can seldom be carried out by assistants.

Political scientists, though, often choose not to use direct observation, even when it is appropriate and possible, because they question its scientific validity. This is usually a result of either or both of two concerns. First, there is often a perception that direct observation produces highly *subjective data* reflecting the unique insights and, perhaps, biases of the observer. Second, direct observation often produces *qualitative* data. Because some researchers think that only quantitative data can be scientific, they may view data collected through direct observation as "soft" (subjective and subject to challenge). Neither of these concerns is totally without foundation. Improperly done direct observation *can* produce highly subjective results that are influenced by the researcher's preconceptions. Even well-executed observations depend a great deal on the skill, energy, and insight of the observer and may be difficult to reproduce. In addition, much of the data that come from direct observation *are* qualitative in nature and do not lend themselves to standard data analysis techniques.

There are at least five reasons why these concerns should not deter social scientists from using direct observation under the right conditions:

1. Research has different purposes at different stages of the study of a topic and, as discussed in Chapters 1 and 4, the requirements for *scientific precision* differ with the *purpose* of research. Direct observation is especially well suited to the exploratory and descriptive stages of research, when we are seeking to *develop* theories rather than to test them. Descriptive research can be crucial to the scientific process in that it can provide an accurate picture of how a social or political process unfolds. A description of the process can serve as a foundation for using inductive logic to devise testable theories that provide a scientific understanding of the phenomenon in question. When used at the proper stage of the research process, direct observation is not only adequate to the task but often far superior to other methods of data collection.

2. Many of the concerns related to subjectivity in reporting results can be overcome by proper execution of direct observation. If researchers follow correct procedures in making and recording observations, it is possible for others to verify their conclusions or at least judge the degree of confidence that should be placed in them.

3. Even qualitative data can be analyzed in rigorous and objective ways if the analyst employs the right techniques. The fact that direct observation may produce primarily qualitative data, therefore, need not be taken as a major limitation on its applicability.

4. Under the right conditions and with the right approach, direct observation can even be used to *test* theories and should not be ruled out as a potential data gathering technique in explanatory research.

5. Against any of the limitations associated with the method, we must weigh the fact that direct observation has the distinct advantage of providing a very high level of *external validity* for our research. Because we observe *actual behavior* (not oral reports, written accounts, or simulations of it) and observe it *in the context in which it naturally occurs*, we can obtain a realistic view of events and can get highly valid measures of our concepts. Moreover, in some types of direct observation, *reactivity may be less of a problem than with more obvious data gathering techniques.*

In the rest of this chapter, we explore techniques of direct observation and suggest some methods for using it to its full potential.

DEGREE OF OBTRUSIVENESS

Direct observation can take several forms. First, we can distinguish between *obtrusive* and *unobtrusive* approaches. **Obtrusive research** occurs anytime the persons being studied are aware of being observed. It always carries some risk of provoking reactivity and, thus, producing at least partially invalid results. In **unobtrusive research**, subjects are unaware of being observed and, therefore, unlikely to alter their natural behaviors in response to the research itself. This has the advantage of increasing the chances of obtaining valid data.

Obtrusive Observation

In *obtrusive* observation, the researchers or trained assistants request permission to observe subjects and are identified as observers at the time of the data collection. An example of this approach is the case in which an investigator attends meetings of a committee of the state legislature and observes its decision-making processes. Committee members are aware of the observer and know the general purpose of the study.

Unobtrusive Observation

In *unobtrusive* observation, whether the researcher is concealed from those being studied or visible to them, the purpose of the observation is unknown to the subjects of the study. In the first type of study, the observer might be concealed from view or might use a hidden camera. An example would be a project in which the researcher is given permission to study the behavior of public personnel by observing the interaction of welfare clients and welfare agency caseworkers from behind a two-way mirror when neither the caseworkers nor the clients know they are being observed. In the second type, the observer may be in full view, but the purpose of the study is concealed. There are two versions of this type of unobtrusive observation.

The first is **passive observation**. It can be exemplified by a case in which a researcher attends all public meetings of a city council and openly sits with other citizens in the audience but carefully watches the debate to analyze patterns of influence on the council *without the knowledge of the council members*. A second form of unobtrusive observation is known as *participant observation*. When researchers actually become part of the events under study, they are engaging in **participant observation**. The researcher studying a given political organization who joined that group as any other citizen might, attended its meetings, served on its committees, took part in its fund-raising efforts, voted on its policies, and otherwise acted as a member *without the other members of the organization knowing that they were being observed as part of a study* would be using unobtrusive participant observation.

The obvious advantage of unobtrusive observation is that it virtually eliminates the possibility that subjects will alter their behavior in reaction to being studied so that it can yield highly valid information. However, unobtrusive observations can be very difficult to arrange and conduct and, as we discuss later in this chapter, often pose serious ethical questions for the scholar.

DEGREE OF STRUCTURE

A second division among approaches to direct observation is made between *structured* and *unstructured studies*. This distinction is made on the basis of the degree to which the researcher organizes or *structures* the process of observation by imposing a preconceived set of concepts and categories.

Structured Observation

In a **structured observation**, we use our understanding of the events under scrutiny to construct an **observation protocol** to guide the observer. The protocol tells the observer what to look for, the order in which to make observations, and the way to record the results. This approach is especially suited for gaining accurate descriptions of events.

As an illustration, we might want to study the ways in which members of the U.S. Congress use debate on the floor of the House of Representatives to gain support from interest groups and constituents. If we have a strong enough theory of how this is done, a checksheet could be developed listing the techniques that we expect to be used. We could then observe floor debates and use the checksheet to record whether or not each representative used the given techniques to send messages to potential supporters. The protocol would restrict our attention to a limited range of what was happening when representatives made public statements but would provide more objective data than a survey and would facilitate comparisons of the behavior of different House members.

Unstructured Observation

By contrast, if we were in an earlier stage of our study of this subject, we might be unwilling to restrict our observations to a list of items on a protocol. Such a situation would call for use of **unstructured observation**, in which we attempt to pay attention to all that goes on in a debate, take careful notes, and analyze the notes in an effort to discover patterns that can provide a basis for theorizing about how representatives use floor debate to influence potential supporters.

Structured and unstructured observation can be combined in a single research project. In fact, it is quite common for researchers using direct observation to mix the two approaches. A study may start with unstructured observation to gain a broad understanding of an event and formulate concepts with which to analyze it. The researcher may then use these insights to structure subsequent observations of the same phenomenon in order to test the utility of the conceptualizations. Alternatively, the two approaches may be combined by structuring portions of the observational task while leaving other parts unstructured.

It is important to recognize that the distinction between structured and unstructured observations is *not* a true dichotomy, with "pure" types of observation on either side. It is a continuum ranging from the least structured to the most structured methods of observation. Even the least formally structured observation involves an element of structure in that the researcher approaches the task with a set of questions about the event under study and with perceptions of how the event might work. Similarly, even in a highly structured observation, an alert researcher often notices unexpected qualities of the phenomena under study and may learn more than what is anticipated by the observation protocol. In this sense, the two approaches to observation are almost always blended to some degree.

TABLE 19.1	A Matrix of Observational Types	
	Unobtrusive	**Obtrusive**
Unstructured	A researcher walks her dog past a political demonstration on the corner of a busy intersection, and listens to the chants, reads the signs, and receives a flyer as she moves down the public street.	Looking to all of the world like the college professor he is, the observer introduces himself to those setting up a political booth near a busy walkway, and then moves across the way to learn by watching the interactions that occur.
Structured	Positioning himself within earshot of the open door to the kitchen, a researcher opens his laptop on a table in a fast food restaurant, looking at screen which contains a list of topics he will listen for.	A young college sophomore attends an AARP meeting in a college town to observe local political activity in comparison to a list of national AARP objectives. Her presence at the meeting is noted on the agenda, and she is introduced to the group.

Examples of observational types displaying varying degrees of obtrusiveness and structure are presented in Table 19.1.

TECHNIQUES OF UNSTRUCTURED OBSERVATION

Unstructured observation is used to develop a full understanding of the behaviors and relationships under study. It requires that investigators be open to discovering new dimensions to the behavior and willing to devise new ways of thinking about the topic. Observers are seeking to be taught by the world and want to get as close to the reality of the events as possible without being so constrained by preconceived notions of how things work that they overlook some important patterns.

The procedure for unstructured observation begins with identifying the set of behaviors that have to be observed in order to acquire a full understanding of the events in question. Refining the research question so that it provides a better guide to observation may require doing some background reading, talking with others who have had contact with the subject, and engaging in some very preliminary theorizing about what processes might be at work.

Next, the researcher needs to gain access to the subjects for purposes of observation. How this is done depends on whether he or she is using obtrusive or unobtrusive methods, and varies with the details of the project. It can be one of the most challenging portions of the work. Clearly, some subjects will be less willing to be observed than others, and most subjects will find some objectives in the study to be more acceptable than others. For example, revolutionaries conducting a guerrilla war will not be open to outsiders under almost any circumstances. By contrast, bureaucrats who may be willing to cooperate with research described as "a study of chains of command in public agencies" may be quite unwilling to participate in "a study of corruption in the management of public agencies."

This early step in the research process may very well present an ethical dilemma: Do you tell people they are being observed and, if so, do you tell them the real purpose of the study even if doing so risks losing their cooperation or at least creating a serious problem of reactivity? We address this and other ethical issues of direct observation later in this chapter. For now, assume that the ethical questions are resolved in favor of taking an obtrusive approach and that we can move to the third stage in the process.

The primary activity here is to observe and take careful notes on all that is seen and heard. The *written record of observations* is referred to as **field notes**. Though field notes are not as structured as interview notes, there are definite general rules for the proper taking of field notes.

1. You should *clearly define the objectives of the research* so that you know what you want to learn about the events under observation. From that you can develop a list of the types of things you are looking for, so as to focus your attention on those features of the events that are most important to observe. Having such a list is not inconsistent with keeping an open mind and being willing to change your focus as you gain a better understanding of the behaviors in question. It merely simplifies the task of reducing all that you will observe to a manageable number of entries for your notes.

   This list will be nothing more than a set of broad categories of information you hope to obtain about the events observed. For example, in observing meetings of opposing teams of negotiators who represented two sides of a civil war, you might want to note such things as (1) how often each side initiates proposals, (2) how eager each side seems to be to continue the talks as opposed to breaking them off, (3) how willing each side is to make concessions, and (4) whether each negotiating team is united or seems divided into factions. As you learn more about the process, you will want to refine these broad, overlapping categories into a more focused list of things to note, with each observation building on what you learned in the prior one.

2. *Avoid taking detailed notes in the presence of those who are being observed.* The primary reason for this is that open note taking can make your subjects even more aware of your presence and cause them to alter their normal behavior. Your objective is to put the subjects so at ease that they act exactly as they would if you were not present. This requires developing the skill of making *mental notes* of all that you see that is relevant to the study so that you can write up detailed notes later. This is a difficult task, so in advance of going to the field, it is wise to practice mental note taking by observing activities similar to those you are to study and then trying to re-create the events on paper later. If the practice subjects agree and you have the necessary equipment and setting, you can check on your accuracy by recording or filming the events observed and comparing the recordings of the events with the impressions conveyed by your field notes.

   Though you should not take detailed notes in the presence of subjects, it is sometimes possible to keep a small note pad concealed so you can inconspicuously jot down key words or phrases that will later serve to jog your memory of events when writing up field notes.

3. *Always write up field notes as soon as possible after actual observation* so that your memory of the events is clear. This is often difficult, because you may be tired at the end of several hours of observations and there may not be a convenient place to sit to write your notes. However, it is *essential* that you find a way to get the observations on paper as soon as possible so that you have a detailed and accurate record. Some investigators expedite this process by using a tape recorder to record their field notes verbally and then transcribe them later. If you choose this approach, it is

crucial to check the tape immediately to ensure that it worked properly; in that way, you will avoid discovering several days later, when you may find it difficult to re-create them from memory, that notes from an observation session have been lost.

It may take up to half as much time to make notes on observations as it took to actually make the observations, but this is time well spent because *field notes are the foundation of a direct observation project.*

4. *Make field notes as complete and detailed as possible.* Especially in the early stages of a project, it is important to put in almost everything that was observed. Facts that at first seemed unimportant may turn out to be crucial as you acquire a fuller under-standing of the topic.

5. *Always distinguish clearly in your notes between descriptions of actual behavior and your speculation about the meaning or importance of that behavior.* It should be clear to you, even after your memory of the events has faded, what was actually said and done by the subjects and what you *inferred* about their behavior at the time.

Because the content of field notes is dictated by the objectives of an individual proj-ect, it is difficult to state rules for what to include. In general, however, it is better to in-clude too much than to risk leaving out useful information. Excessive detail in field notes may complicate the task of analyzing them, but this problem can be handled. There is no way to remedy the problem of not having information if you failed to put it in at the time of the observation. Remember that one of the major objectives of direct observation is the creation of a complete and accurate description of a political phenomenon. More detail, therefore, is usually preferable to less.

Figure 19.1 provides an example of the kind of information that is recorded in field notes. It presents observations from a hypothetical study of several community organiza-tions in which the investigator is seeking to understand how leaders of these organiza-tions persuade residents of a neighborhood to join and remain in the group. Note the detail in which events are recorded. Notice also how notes on actual events are set off from interpretations or analysis of those events.

June 24, 2007. Observation of a demonstration by members of the Waterside Neighborhood Improvement Association to protest the announcement by the city government of plans to open a landfill on some abandoned property in the Waterside neighborhood.

Background: The Waterside community is composed of large old homes that were left behind as members of the upper class abandoned the city for the suburbs in the 1950s and 1960s. Today it is a fairly poor area with few remaining local businesses and inhabit-ed almost exclusively by Hispanics. The neighborhood organization was formed in 1985 to combat problems of crime, unemployment, and poor public services in the area.

Observations: The demonstration was held on the steps of city hall during the noon hour, when a large number of people were entering and leaving the building. The organization had obtained a permit from the police department, and all members remained on a grassy area beside the main entrance so that they did not block

(Continued)

FIGURE 19.1 Example of transcribed field notes from a hypothetical study of community organizations.

pedestrian traffic. Thirty-three members of the Waterside Association took part in the demonstration. In addition, there were two officials of the Catholic Church, the president of a statewide Hispanic political organization, and a member of the city council, who represents the neighborhood. The event was covered by two reporters from the local paper, a camera crew and reporter from each of the two local TV stations, and a reporter from National Public Radio.

The demonstration began promptly at noon and consisted of the following activities: (1) Throughout the demonstration, twelve of the participants waved handmade signs with slogans condemning the landfill. They were careful to face the TV cameras at all times. (2) The association president, the city councilman, and the state political leader (in that order) each stood on an old oil drum the demonstrators had brought to the site to make speeches lasting about ten minutes each. (3) Between each speech, a very energetic member of the group used a megaphone to lead chants about the injustice of the landfill decision. The chants were defiant in tone (e.g., "We won't take your trash!"), and one accused the mayor of "selling out." All members of the association who attended the demonstration were very active during the action, shouting, cheering, clapping, calling out to passersby, and shaking their fists in the cameras. The demonstration ended with a short speech and prayer by one of the priests. The signs and chants were in English, but the speeches were primarily in Spanish. Each speaker referred at least once to the fact that Waterside was a Hispanic community. Each asked at least once why the landfill was not put in Carlton (an affluent, predominantly white neighborhood at the edge of the city that had been recommended by a consultant's study as the most logical site).

When she was not speaking, the president of the Waterside Association was moving among the demonstrators, encouraging them to wave their signs, shout, and otherwise show their feelings. She pulled reporters into the middle of the group on three occasions and coached the camera crews on what to shoot. Comments made by the other speakers revealed she had personally invited them to attend and speak. While the group was returning to the neighborhood on a church bus borrowed for the occasion, the president made a statement about how she was sure that the event had made a difference and how important it was for Hispanics to stand up for their rights. She then went down the aisle and personally thanked everyone on the bus for taking part in the demonstration, using a lot of handshaking, backslapping, and hugs. Everyone else had carried out the tasks assigned to them, but no one seemed to share responsibility for making the demonstration work.

Comments: This group has a well-organized, highly disciplined core of active members and a good deal of support from other community institutions. The president, however, appears to be the main moving force. She seems to come up with most of the ideas and to mobilize others with her energy. The members seem to be motivated by a combination of ethnic pride and social solidarity. Much of what they do is predicated on their minority status, but they also seem to have developed a sense of comradeship in which each one carries on partly because they do not want to let the others down. The president apparently encourages both of these tendencies—perhaps because she knows that she cannot promise the members much in the way of material rewards. I cannot help but wonder how the organization would survive if she stepped down. She takes on so much responsibility that no one else seems to be getting any leadership training. Her strength may be the organization's weakness.

FIGURE 19.1   (Continued)

The next stage in the direct observation project is to analyze the field notes. With other methods there is a clear distinction between data collection and data analysis. This is not true of direct observation because the process of making field notes blends both data collection (writing down descriptions of what happened) and analysis (noting your impressions about the reasons for or importance of what happened). *Data analysis begins with the making of field notes.* Moreover, in direct observation, the researcher must *not* wait until all the data are in to begin analysis. It is vital that investigators review field notes from time to time during the period in which they are making observations. The purpose of this is to begin to look for patterns in what has been observed so as to be alert to the most important aspects of events in the next observation session.

Once all observation has been completed, you will formally shift to data analysis. With direct observation data, this means *using inductive reasoning to discover patterns among the many discrete facts recorded in the field notes.* The first step is usually to review the notes in order to find some meaningful categories to use in distinguishing among the events observed.

An Example

Consider a hypothetical study of legislative committees designed to investigate the degree to which they are subject to influence by organized interest groups. You might observe the meetings of several committees and then ask: Are there any systematic differences in the way these groups function? After examining your notes, you may decide that the groups differ along two important dimensions: the degree to which power is centralized in the formal leaders versus being widely shared among the members, and the degree to which the groups are businesslike and rule-driven in transacting their business versus being more collegial and relying on personal interaction. If we break these two dimensions in the middle and juxtapose them, we get the typology of committee operating styles presented in Figure 19.2, and we have a way of classifying committees for analysis.

The next step in analysis is to examine the field notes for evidence of differences *between* and *within* categories or types. For example, we might ask if committees of different types responded differently to interest groups and if the same type of committee treated different types of interest groups differently. We might ask if it seems to be easier for interest groups to gain access to some types of committees than to others or if the ease of access depends more on the characteristics of the interest group (such as how well financed it is, how professional its lobbying staff is, or how politically active it is in the representatives' home districts).

Style of Operation	Power Configuration	
	Decentralized	Centralized
Collegial	Populist	Machine
Rule-driven	Democratic	Authoritarian

FIGURE 19.2   Hypothetical typology of congressional committees.

The major challenge in both taking and analyzing field notes is to avoid the natural tendency to see only what you expect to see. If you are to gain a truly accurate understanding of these events, it is crucial to be open to the possibility that things do not work as expected and *to avoid imposing patterns* that are not there. One technique for keeping an open mind about your subject and ensuring that you are not overlooking important relationships is to occasionally ask trusted colleagues who are *not* involved with your research project to read over portions of your field notes and share with you their impressions of what is happening. They may be able to see patterns that your preconceived theory of the events has hidden from you.

TECHNIQUES OF STRUCTURED OBSERVATION

If unstructured observation is used to gain a more refined and accurate understanding of political behavior so that we can develop theories of it, structured observation is used to verify the utility of our understandings and to test hypotheses derived from our theories. Conducting a structured observation requires a clear idea of what we expect to see when we observe and what specific behaviors we are looking for. We are interested primarily in *recording specific behaviors*, not in finding the meaning our subjects attach to their behaviors or patterns in those behaviors. It is similar to carrying out a survey or a content analysis in that we are guided by an instrument that makes our observation very systematic and facilitates recording what we see in ways that make comparing cases easier. In direct observation, this instrument is known as an *observation schedule*.

Designing an Observation Schedule

An **observation schedule** is a detailed list of specific things to be observed and a system for recording them. The content and design of observation schedules depend on the nature of the research project and can vary widely, so that it is difficult to provide firm guidelines for their construction. Our objective here is merely to suggest some very general rules to follow and techniques to use in designing useful observation schedules.

Before we turn to a discussion of those rules, it is important to mention three features of structured observation that set the context for development of an observation schedule. First, recall that structured observations may be either obtrusive or unobtrusive. Because the observer must pay attention to a great many details and is most concerned with precision in recording events, *it is essential that observations be recorded as they are made.* As a result, structured observations run a greater risk of creating reactivity than unstructured ones do when they are done obtrusively. Subjects who see an observer busily taking notes on their actions are very likely to be keenly aware that they are being studied and may alter their behavior as a result. Structured techniques, then, are probably most effective when used unobtrusively.

An additional implication of the need in structured observation to record events as they happen is that *it is almost never possible to use structured techniques in a participant observation.* It would be virtually impossible to keep detailed records of behaviors while acting as a participant and would almost certainly give away your purpose in being there.

PRACTICAL RESEARCH ETHICS
Balance during immersion?

Direct observation provides a powerful research tool to political scientists. At best, this method may unlock political and social attitudes that are otherwise inaccessible, but it may also involve a potentially challenging ethical balancing act. Researchers' deep immersion in research subjects' lives and in issues that subjects personally value inherently increases the value of qualitative research, but may also raise substantial ethical challenges.

For example, in conducting an unobtrusive observation, you will attempt to build a close relationship based upon a false identity. How certain can you be that when you reveal yourself to your subject (as required by research standards), he or she will not experience a long-lasting emotional pain that exceeds the possible benefit of your research findings? Although this is a particularly dramatic example, this caveat to balance potential for harm versus benefit strongly applies to all qualitative research, and requires substantial forethought by researchers.

The second contextual feature of structured methods to consider before discussing the construction of observation schedules is that structured observations are often made by someone *other than the principal investigator.* Because the observations are more routine and often more numerous than those involved in unstructured methods, researchers commonly hire assistants to carry out the observations. This means that the observation schedule must be detailed and informative enough that it (1) can be used by an assistant *as the researcher intends it to be used* and (2) leaves very little discretion to the observer, so that the observations recorded by different assistants can legitimately be compared.

Finally, it is important to recognize the basic design of a structured observation in order to understand what is needed in an observation schedule. This design involves first identifying a *unit of analysis* for the study. In direct observation, units of analysis usually consist of recurring events. Examples include reaching a compromise at a negotiating session, debating a motion before the UN Security Council, and arguing between members of opposing groups at a demonstration in front of a clinic that provides abortions.

After identification of a unit of analysis, the next step is to *designate the aspects of that event to be observed.* Here is where the observation schedule comes in. An observation schedule is far more than a simple checklist in several ways: (1) It often provides more than simple *yes* or *no* options for recording behaviors. Observers are usually asked to record events in degrees or frequencies. (2) It usually contains instructions on *how* to conduct the observations by telling the observer what procedures to follow. (3) It generally includes some fairly detailed definitions of the behaviors to be observed so that observers know what to look for.

This last feature is vitally important. An observation schedule *is always based on operational definitions of the behaviors in question.* If it is to be useful, it must reduce a set of potentially complex events to basic elements, so that the observer can be sure when the event has been observed and can distinguish it from other, similar behaviors or events. To do this, an observation schedule breaks events into discrete variables, gives the observer an operational definition of each, and provides a scheme for recording observations of each variable.

An Example

Returning to the example of the study of the operating styles of congressional committees, one unit of analysis for such a study might be a public disagreement among members of the committee. The researcher would need to define what constitutes a disagreement and then identify the features of the event (the variables) to be observed—that is, the dimensions along which to classify each disagreement. These dimensions can be highly specific or quite broad. In the committee study, we might want to know something as specific as how often the parties to the disagreement interrupted each other, whether or not certain words were used by either side, and who spoke last. Alternatively, the dimensions may be as broad as whether the tone of the argument was hostile or cordial, whether or not it seemed to be conducted within mutually accepted norms, or what role the committee chair played in mediating the argument.

Which approach is better depends on the specific research project. However, *the broader the dimensions to be observed, the greater the discretion the observer has in classifying events*. Narrower dimensions may seem to trivialize the subject, but they have the advantage of limiting observers' discretion and, thereby, producing data that are more standardized and more comparable from observation to observation. Researchers are usually well advised to be *as specific as possible* in constructing an observation schedule.

A major reason for this is that one of the most important rules for designing an observation schedule is that *the categories used to classify events must be exhaustive and mutually exclusive*. It must be possible to place all observed events in some category. However, it must not be logically possible to place any single observation in more than one category. The best way to achieve this mutual exclusivity of categories is to be very specific—to break larger variables down into smaller ones. For example, rather than asking the general question about whether or not a disagreement seemed to be governed by mutually accepted norms, we might ask if the parties to the argument interrupted one another, raised their voices, or yielded the floor promptly when asked to do so by the chair.

Figure 19.3 is a segment of a hypothetical study of community organizations in which the meeting is the unit of analysis. Note that some items require only that the observer record objectively verifiable information about the meeting (when it started, how many people were in attendance, etc.), whereas other items require a judgment on the part of the observer (whether the members paid attention to the chair when he or she spoke, if the members were cordial and friendly to each other before the opening of the meeting, etc.). This mix is almost inevitable, but the investigator should provide observers with clear instructions on how to make a judgment about those matters that require judgment. It is wise to check their understanding of these instructions by having the assistant record observations of an event that the researcher also observes and then comparing the assistant's classification of events with those of the investigator.

Assessing Reliability and Validity

Those who use structured observation to gather data have to be just as concerned with the validity and reliability of their measurements as those who use other data collection techniques. It is therefore important to build into the data collection effort ways to check on this. When data from an observation schedule are quantitative, they can be analyzed with standard statistical techniques and are subject to the same tests of validity and reliability discussed in Chapter 5.

COMMUNITY ORGANIZATION OBSERVATION SCHEDULE

1. a. Name of organization _____
   b. Date and time of meeting _____
   c. Location of meeting _____
   d. Nature of meeting: *(1) regular business*
                            (2) annual meeting
                            (3) special or emergency
                            (8) other _____
   e. Purpose of meeting: *(1) routine business*
                            (2) to elect officers
                            (3) to discuss a problem
                            (4) social gathering
                            (5) to recognize members/accomplishments
                            (8) other _____

2. Pre-meeting socializing: *(1) less than half participated*
                              (2) about half participated
                              (3) most members participated

3. a. Was there a written agenda for the meeting?   YES   NO
   b. If yes, was it distributed to the members?   YES   NO
   c. If yes, when was it distributed?   *(1) before the day of the meeting*
                                          (2) just prior to the meeting
                                          (3) after the meeting

4. How many people attended the meeting? _____

5. a. Was the meeting open to the public?   YES   NO
   b. How many persons who were apparently not members attended? _____
   c. Were any nonmembers on the formal program?   YES   NO
   d. If yes, who (city council member, police officer, etc.)? _____

6. Who presided at the meeting (by office)? _____

7. What other persons had a formal role in the meeting (made a presentation, gave a report, etc.)? _____
   _____
   _____

8. Did the presiding officer say that members were encouraged to speak during the meeting?   YES   NO

9. How many members made comments or asked questions during the meeting? [Use tic marks to keep track.]
   _____

(Continued)

FIGURE 19.3 Partial observation schedule for a hypothetical study of community organizations.

10. How closely were parliamentary procedures followed in managing the meeting?

_____   *(1) not at all*

_____   *(2) loosely*

_____   *(3) fairly closely*

_____   *(4) strictly*

11. What were the main topics discussed during the program?

a. _____

b. _____

c. _____

d. _____

e. _____

12. a. How many formal votes were taken? [Use tic marks to keep track.]

b. How was voting done? *(1) show of hands*

(2) voice vote

(3) paper ballot

(8) other _____

c. What was the issue and outcome on each vote taken?

	ISSUE	OUTCOME
Vote 1:		
Vote 2:		
Vote 3:		
Vote 4:		
Vote 5:		

(CONTINUE ON BACK IF NEEDED)

FIGURE 19.3   (Continued)

However, the observation schedule almost always gives observers some degree of discretion about how to record events. Therefore, if more than one observer is used, it is also especially important to pay attention to **interobserver reliability**—the degree to which different observers classify similar events in the same way on the observation schedule. This is essentially the same as the problem of intercoder reliability in content analysis and can be verified by procedures similar to those discussed in Chapter 10. It is crucial, however, that investigators build into the instrument and data collection procedure the means of collecting the information they will need to verify the validity and reliability of their measures.

It is also a good idea to *pretest the observation schedule and procedure* before beginning actual fieldwork. A pretest involves the researcher and/or assistants using the schedule to record an event like the one you are studying to be sure that the categories are exhaustive and mutually exclusive, that the instructions on the form are easy to follow, and that the explanations of how to classify are clear enough that different observers can agree on the coding for the same or highly similar behaviors and events.

SAMPLING PROCEDURES IN DIRECT OBSERVATION

After identifying a set of behaviors to treat as a unit of analysis, we must decide which of these units to study. Because we cannot observe all instances of the behaviors that serve as our units of analysis, we are forced to select a sample of them.

Representative Sampling

The objective of this sampling—as in survey research or other methods of data collection—is *to examine a representative group of cases*. We want to understand how the events in question *usually* happen and do not want to be misled by observing atypical episodes. However, what we are sampling is not people or nations or publications, but events and behaviors. The important point about this is that we can seldom predict in advance when (and sometimes where) these events will take place. As a result, it is often impossible to apply standard random sampling procedures to the type of events that are most often studied through direct observation.

The sampling procedure that *is* used depends on the nature of the study. If the events reoccur on a regular basis and occur frequently enough, it may be possible to take a random sample of these events to study. For instance, if we were studying the way a large administrative agency processes citizens' complaints, and we knew that formal complaints were accepted in a specific office every workday between the hours of 2 P.M. and 5 P.M., and that the agency heard an average of fifteen complaints a day, we could set up rules for drawing a random sample of the anticipated complaints. In the room where complaints were received, we could station observers on random days with instructions to record the details of the handling of the eighth complaint brought each day until some statistically determined minimum number had been observed. We could have a good deal of confidence in the representativeness of this sample because of the number and regularity of the events.

However, if there are far fewer instances of our units of analysis or if we cannot predict when or where they will occur, then standard sampling procedures cannot be relied on to yield a good sample. To illustrate this, let us change the preceding example to say that the agency scheduled the hearing of complaints *only once a month* at a regular time and heard an average of only four complaints at each session. We could sample by way of the procedure just described, but would have to observe the organization over *many* months before our random procedure had produced a representative sample (because random procedures are not dependable with small numbers of cases). We may not be able to stretch our research out over such a long period.

To modify the example again, assume that the agency accepted complaints at a window in its offices *at any time of any workday*. Because we cannot predict when citizens will show up with complaints, it is impossible to apply standard sampling procedures to select complaints. However, if we had reason to believe that complaints were fairly evenly spaced throughout the day and the week, we could divide the workweek into hours and sample certain *time periods*. Observers could watch the window at preselected hours of specified days of the week and record any complaints filed at those times. With a sufficiently large number of complaints, this could provide a representative sample. However, if the number of complaints is small (only one or two each day, for instance), most observation periods would not include a complaint, and it would again take a *very* long time to observe enough complaints to have confidence in our sample. This would be both time consuming and extremely expensive.

When we turn from events that occur with some regularity to more sporadic events, sampling problems become even greater. To stay with our administrative example, say that we are concerned with complaints made only by certain types of citizens (elderly persons, minority-group members, etc.) or only with a certain type of complaint (like those that involve allegations of nonenforcement of a specific rule, or gender discrimination in service delivery). We have no way of knowing when and if such complaints will arise and cannot effectively sample them using some variant of random sampling.

Judgmental Sampling

When we are studying a behavior that occurs infrequently or without warning, we almost always have to rely on a *judgmental sample* as described in Chapter 7. We use what we know about the nature of the event to select a set of occurrences that will be *typical* of the behavior of interest if not representative in a strictly statistical sense. The task in judgmental sampling is to select for observation events that informed readers of the research can be persuaded are likely to be representative.

To illustrate, say that our study of complaint-handling was focused entirely on complaints about nonenforcement of agency rules and that we knew from agency records or prior research that complaints of this type came almost exclusively from low-income communities. We might choose to observe only complaints filed at those agency offices serving low-income neighborhoods in the hope of locating enough complaints of the desired type. If background research makes it possible to build a statistical profile of the events we want to study (when and where they happen most often, what types of people participate, how long they last, etc.), this information can assist in the judgmental selection of typical cases.

COPING WITH METHOD EFFECTS IN DIRECT OBSERVATION

In Chapter 1, using the example of the Hawthorne effect, we pointed out that researchers must always be alert to the possibility that their data collection efforts have, in some way, influenced the data that are obtained and have produced an inaccurate picture of the reality they hope to understand. For example, because people tend to give what they feel are socially acceptable answers to survey questions regardless of their true feelings, one effect of using the personal interview to gather data is a tendency to *understate* the occurrence of behaviors and attitudes that are contrary to dominant social norms. This impact is referred to as a **method effect**.

Minimizing Reactivity

The possibility of a method effect is especially high in direct observation for at least two reasons. First, in most direct observations, researchers are in closer and more extended contact with the subjects than with other methods, so there are more opportunities for the observer's actions or presence to influence subjects' behavior. We call this effect *reactivity*. Second, because observers exercise so much discretion in determining what to record and how to record it, direct-observation data are heavily influenced by observers' values and expectations. We call this effect *bias*. If we fail to minimize these method effects, we lose the main advantage of direct observation—the high degree of external validity it provides our research.

Which strategies are appropriate for minimizing method effects depends on the character of the specific project. We can, however, offer some general guidelines. The most effective means of coping with reactivity is to employ *unobtrusive observation*, because subjects who are not aware they are being observed do not react to being studied. Investigators should always consider the possibility of arranging an unobtrusive observation. However, as explained earlier, it is often impossible to use unobtrusive methods and, as will soon be discussed, it may sometimes be judged unethical to do so.

Moreover, one particular technique of unobtrusive study—participant observation—may not get around reactivity problems even when it is possible. Even if the observer's identity and purpose are concealed from members of the group, the observer's actions *as a member of the group* can cause other members to act differently from ways they otherwise would. If a researcher posing as a member of a political organization takes part in the group's debate about what action to take in response to some new threat to its interest, for example, that participation may sway the decision. Similarly, the researcher's work on one of the organization's projects may lead to its success when it otherwise would have failed or to its failure when it otherwise would have succeeded.

This sort of effect is difficult to avoid if the investigator is to retain credibility as a devoted member of the organization, but observers have to be very sensitive to it and attempt to strike the delicate balance between losing credibility and actually shaping the events they are trying to study. It is also important to attempt to judge the degree to which researcher participation influenced outcomes, so that this effect can be discounted in attempting to form an accurate picture of the processes under investigation.

When obtrusive methods are the only possibility, researchers can still take steps to minimize reactivity. The key to success in this lies in investigators' ability to *control their relationship to the subjects and the subjects' perception of the researcher*. Researchers must consciously manipulate subjects' perception of their character, values, and purpose in order to put the subjects so at ease that they behave as they normally would. Subjects must come either to ignore the observer as harmless, or to trust the observer enough to reveal their true feelings and behavior patterns. Researchers accomplish the first objective by **blending in**; they achieve the latter goal by **fitting in**.

Blending In

Observers can use several tactics to blend in. (1) They can physically stay in the background or at the margins of any action they are observing so that subjects easily forget their presence when focusing on the activity. (This practice often has the added advantage of placing observers in a location that provides a good vantage point from which to view the entire scene at once.) (2) Observers can adopt a passive manner, which makes it easy for others to overlook them or to consider them unthreatening. In this mode, they will certainly want to avoid commenting on what they see or confronting subjects in any way. (3) Observers can exercise patience and perseverance by showing up again and again so that they become commonplace and subjects begin to relax in their presence. The objective is to make the process of observation seem normal to the subjects—part of everyday life. This can take a great deal of time to accomplish. (4) Observers can blend into the group physically by grooming themselves and dressing in a manner that is inconspicuous under the circumstances. Wear what the subjects wear, but be careful to avoid violating any dress codes that may exist in the group by, for instance, wearing something recognized as a symbol of rank in the group or something reserved for persons with special status in the group. (5) Researchers can blend in socially by learning to converse comfortably with the subjects. This involves talking about things that are common topics of conversation among the subjects, using a personal style that is appropriate to the norms of the group (loud and outgoing or reserved and introspective, openly sharing feelings or putting up a front, frequently touching the subject or keeping your hands to yourself, etc.), and respecting any clear role definitions within the group such as a norm that says that women do not talk about politics or that younger members do not volunteer information about themselves unless asked by an elder. It is important not to carry this too far by trying to imitate subjects' speech patterns, mannerisms, or dress if it seems unnatural for the observer to act that way. An observer with a strong New England accent probably should *not* dress like a cowboy in an effort to study the political culture of western bars. Unnatural behavior will only attract attention and may be seen as an insult to the group.

Fitting In

Observers can fit in by using some of these same tactics. However, fitting in demands much more interaction between observer and subjects than blending in. It is a much greater concern in participant observation than in nonparticipant observation. Fitting in requires that the researcher consciously project an image as one of the group. This is done primarily by expressing values consistent with those of the subjects (perhaps a disregard for authority, prejudice toward some other group, or acceptance of a given political ideology). Behaving like one of the subject group may be necessary to build trust, but it has its dangers.

There is sometimes a risk that adopting the identity of a group member will make observers lose their objectivity about the study. Coming to see the world as subjects see it is known as **going native**. Investigators must be alert to this prospect because going native can prevent researchers from gaining scientifically useful insight into the behaviors under study. This is not a simple matter, because there is a fine line between going native and "getting inside" subjects to understand their motivations, values, and the like. Successful researchers are able to get close to subjects without losing sight of their objectives and interpretive framework.

Observers who seek to fit in also face ethical problems if they find that they must deceive subjects. They are very likely to have to lie about how they feel, what they have done, how they live, their background, and so on. We address this problem in the last section of this chapter.

Avoiding Personal Bias

Another method effect associated with direct observation is the bias that can result when observers' values or expectations influence their perception and interpretation of what they see. Direct observation is especially subject to this danger because, with this method, *the observer is the primary instrument of measurement*. Bias can result from a researcher's rigid adherence to preconceptions about the phenomena under study or from a researcher's uncritically accepting the perspective and interpretations of the subjects (going native). Avoiding bias requires being both open-minded about and detached from the subject of our studies. Several strategies can help achieve this end.

First, in obtrusive research, when observers and subjects can interact, observers can avoid letting their preconceptions lead them to wrong conclusions by periodically *checking their interpretations of what they see with the subjects*. For example, rather than simply assuming we know what motivates subjects to take a particular action, we can ask subjects why they did what they did. Their understandings of the situation or their values may be so different from ours that their motivations are just the opposite of what we had thought. Someone from an industrialized nation might think the harsh punishment of a Third World child by its parents is motivated by spite and the desire to inflict pain. In fact, the parents may act as they do because they love the child and want to make it strong enough to survive the hardships of life in a harsh environment. Similarly, researchers may assign meaning to events that subjects do not. An example would be the case in which an observer interprets as a danger signal a group of teenagers "hanging out" on a block, but a local resident knows the youths and views them as protecting the block from intruders by their presence.

It is wise to ask subjects how they interpret events before making assumptions. However, it is important to be subtle in asking these questions, phrasing them in terms familiar to the subjects, and presenting them as concerned inquiries, not demands for explanations. After observing a heated verbal exchange, for example, an observer should not ask, "Why were you so hostile toward her?" but may ask, "Do you think she will be mad about this?" to find out if the actor saw the exchange in the same terms as the observer. This does *not* mean that observers should let subjects determine their analysis of events, but only that they should check to see if subjects are thinking what the observers believe they are thinking.

RESEARCH EXERCISE

Directly Observing Your Campus

This exercise calls for you to look at your campus groups through the eyes of a social scientist.

1. Start with a research question or theoretical relationship that can be explored through direct observation of one of the politically oriented student groups on your campus—such as the Progressive Student Alliance or College Republicans. For example, you might ask questions such as:
   a. Is the role of female members different in liberal and conservative groups?
   b. What common values do members of the group share, beyond their political ideals?
2. Write out a list of the things you would have to observe in the group to answer your question.
3. Attend a meeting of the student group and observe what occurs, using the questions on the list you developed.
4. Keep mental notes and write up formal field notes immediately after leaving the meeting.
5. Write up a brief reaction to your observations that answers questions such as these:
   a. How did what you saw and heard differ from the way you thought things would work?
   b. How would you modify your list of things to look for in light of what you actually observed?
6. In class, compare students' experiences with their direct observations. What likely led to different experiences for different students?

Second, observers can avoid the mistake of seeing events too much as subjects see them by (1) periodically discussing with someone outside the study what they have seen and how they interpret it; and (2) soliciting the views of persons who are marginal to the group, such as the lone environmentalist on a city planning commission generally unconcerned about environmental issues or people who have recently moved back into a community after living elsewhere. Such people can be a valuable resource for researchers, because they have the insight born of close association with the events in question but can still take a critical perspective on those events.

Third, it is often useful to blend direct observation with some other form of data collection so the other data can be used to verify impressions formed from direct observation. A direct observation study of the effect of crime on citizens' behaviors might be augmented by a survey in which the same people who had been observed are asked direct questions about how fearful they are and how their behavior has changed as a result of their fear. The survey would not provide as much detailed data as the direct observation and may have less external validity. It could, however, be used to verify impressions gained from direct observation by asking such questions as, "Do respondents see the actions that observers attributed to fear (e.g., staying off the streets at night) as being motivated by fear of crime or do they have other explanations for this?" A wide variety of data sources (content analysis, public records, etc.) can serve this verification function.

FIGURE 19.4   An Example of Direct Observation:
- Why are the chairs facing the windows?
- Why are the chairs empty?
- What is the officer doing there?
- What is this room?

These and other means of *cross-validating* the conclusions drawn from observation can reduce the degree of subjectivity involved in the method and add significantly to the degree to which results are accepted as valid.

Conclusion

Direct observation techniques of information gathering are an important tool for social science inquiry. They can offer unique access to aspects of interesting phenomena that cannot effectively be studied using other methods. Both quantitative and qualitative researchers should actively consider these methods as a possible way of seeking answers to the questions they are investigating. However, direct observation must not be undertaken without a full understanding of its processes, serious consideration of its potential drawbacks, and careful planning and preparation. The challenges posed by this technique will become apparent as you try to answer the seemingly simple questions in Figure 19.4.

Direct observation techniques place field researchers in situations that can be both professionally and personally risky. They rely to a greater degree than most other methods on the judgment and skills of individual researchers, and can, in some circumstances, cause researchers to confront directly the most difficult questions of personal and professional ethics. Against these risks, researchers must balance the exceptional potential for gaining valid insights that direct observation can offer and the personal and professional growth that can result from meeting its unique challenges.

As you read research reports based on direct observation, you should keep all dimensions of this method in mind. In order to look carefully for evidence that biases have been introduced into the findings of the research by the peculiar features of direct observation, you will need to know as much about the research design and its implementation as possible. Always ask what steps the researchers(s) took to get around the potential pitfalls described in this chapter, and be cautious about accepting its conclusions until you are satisfied.

Key Terms

direct observation *325*	structured observation *328*	interobserver reliability *338*
obtrusive research *327*	observation protocol *328*	method effect *340*
unobtrusive research *327*	unstructured observation *328*	blending in *341*
passive observation *327*	field notes *330*	fitting in *341*
participant observation *327*	observation schedule *334*	going native *342*

Research Examples

Drawing on months of field work interacting with different groups in Japanese society, Ehrhardt (2009) argues that while political party affiliation in the past stemmed from personal identity, now it is more closely linked to policy preferences. Mitchell (2006) directly observed indigenous groups as a participant while examining the decision-making processes in the forests of Latin America. He identified key themes that emerged from these observations and his semistructured interviews in two Mexican communities.

Software

Arguably, two of the most popular programs among academics (and others) for the analysis of qualitative data are *Atlas.ti* developed by Scientific Software Development (www.atlasti.com) and *NVivo* developed by Qualitative Solutions and Research (www.qsrinternational.com). Each of these programs offers a platform for the transcription, viewing, grouping, and analysis of textual or visual data gathered in the course of qualitative research. As an added bonus for prospective users of these programs, many colleges and universities teach short training courses on using the programs and offer discounted pricing for the software. The manufacturers typically also offer trial versions and tutorials for those considering a purchase.

Methodological Readings

Many of the texts guiding direct observation are written by anthropologists and sociologists, home fields for this qualitative method. General introductions to direct observation methods include *Qualitative Researching* (Mason 2002) and *Learning in the Field: An Introduction to Qualitative Research* (Rossman and Rallis 2003). Close-contact participant-observation techniques are explained in considerable detail in *Participant Observation* (Dewalt and Dewalt 2002).

References

Dewalt, Kathleen Musante, and Billie R. Dewalt. 2002. *Participant Observation*. Lanham, MD: Rowman & Littlefield.

Ehrhardt, George. 2009. "Rethinking the Komeito Voter." *Japanese Journal of Political Science* 10(April): 1–20.

Mason, Jennifer. 2002. *Qualitative Researching*, 2nd ed. Thousand Oaks, CA: Sage.

Mitchell, Ross E. 2006. "Environmental Governance in Mexico: Two Case Studies of Oaxaca's Community Forest Sector." *Journal of Latin American Studies* 38(August): 519–548.

Rossman, Gretchen, and Sharon Rallis. 2003. *Learning in the Field: An Introduction to Qualitative Research*. Thousand Oaks, CA: Sage.

CHAPTER 20

Focus Group Research: Guided Conversations

In this chapter you will learn:

▪ What is focus group methodology and when it should be used.

▪ The advantages and limitations of focus groups.

▪ How focus groups are conducted and how their findings should be analyzed.

▪ How focus groups can be used in combination with other research methods.

Researchers sometimes want to study questions that others have not investigated, or they may want to gain a fresh perspective in an area where past research has failed to resolve major questions. In such cases, they will be unable to rely on prior theories or empirical studies to guide their efforts. If the phenomenon in question is new (or at least new to social science researchers), there may not even be firsthand knowledge of the events in question. In these situations, scholars may need to gather information through the use of focus groups.

At the most basic level, **focus group** methods involve bringing together small groups of carefully selected individuals for an in-depth discussion of some topic, guided by a **moderator**, in order to learn how people think about that topic. Most of us should be familiar with this basic idea of focus group research. We all have participated in group discussions that involved family members, friends, classmates or colleagues. Some of these discussions were more civilized and structured than others, for sure, but all of them focused on an issue or event that meant something to all participants. Instinctively, we try to reach some kind of agreement in these group discussions. If that is not the case, we have at least learned how others are thinking about the event or issue in question. That is, more or less, what focus groups try to do in a more formal research setting.

Focus groups can be used for different purposes at different stages of the research process. They can help formulate hypotheses for future studies, develop indicators to be used in data collection, improve the interpretation of data collected by other means, or produce data that are directly useful in answering a research question. During political elections, for example, most candidates try to pretest their campaign strategies with small groups of "regular" voters to see which issues might resonate among the electorate and which should be avoided. Focus groups also allow politicians to shape their public messages ("War on Terrorism") to ensure that policies will be perceived in the best light possible.

It is therefore not surprising that focus groups have become an enormously popular research methodology among those who like to predict public perceptions. This chapter explains why and when researchers might use focus group methods either as their primary methodology or in support of other data collection methods. It then describes some of the basic rules for conducting focus groups and using the information they produce.

WHY USE FOCUS GROUPS?

Focus group methods were developed in the 1940s by researchers who wanted to get as realistic a view of people's thinking as possible. Government agencies, political advisors, and social scientists have been making more use of focus groups in recent years, but the approach has been used most extensively in *market research* to help businesses explore aspects of consumer behavior as part of their effort to develop and sell products. Businesses often use focus groups to gain insights into such questions as how consumers will react to a new product, how effective a proposed advertising campaign might be, and why consumers prefer one product over another.

Limitations of Surveys

Survey research or individual interviews can often be used for these purposes, but early researchers recognized at least five limitations to survey-based methods:

1. Respondents can give us only the information we know to ask for, and many problems may have aspects that researchers will not think to ask about. For example, in a survey, we might ask a random sample of voters to rate two opposing candidates on each of five dimensions that we feel will determine how voters decide among candidates. We might then be surprised to find that the candidate who earned the higher rating did not win the election because voters used a different set of criteria in making their actual choice. Even if voters answered our questions honestly, we had asked the wrong questions.

2. Even if one uses open-ended questions, respondents may be influenced by the style in which questions are asked or by subtle aspects of their interaction with the interviewer and may not give valid answers.

3. Surveys are very expensive and time consuming. If we do not have a clear understanding of what we want to know and how to ask questions in order to get that information from respondents, we run the risk of making a large investment to obtain useless data.

4. Survey results are not always "self-explanatory" because it is always possible that respondents interpreted questions differently from the interpretations the researchers intended and that respondents' answers meant something different to them than they meant to the researchers.

5. People do not make decisions in isolation but are influenced by others' opinions and reactions. A survey interview, however, asks people to act in isolation from their social context in expressing opinions or making judgments. As a result, the data produced by a survey or interview may not accurately reflect social reality.

Limitations of Direct Observations

To avoid these limitations of interview-based data collection, researchers could turn to direct observation. Whereas that approach may be very valuable for certain research questions, it may be inappropriate for others. Scholars who are interested in a fairly narrow subject may face several problems with direct observation.

An Example

To illustrate the challenges of direct observations, let us use the subject of how heterosexuals perceive the goals of the gay rights movement. First, it may be difficult to find a site at which to observe interaction on this topic. Where can researchers go to be sure they will hear a discussion of the gay rights movement by nongays? Second, in a natural setting, it may be necessary to observe *many* hours of discussion of other topics in order to hear a few minutes of conversation about gay rights. Third, even if the subject comes up, the discussion may not address the aspects of the issue that are of interest to researchers since, in direct observation, researchers have no way to guide the discussion. Finally, even in natural settings, discussion may be artificially constrained. For example, people who work together may avoid expressing political disagreement for fear that they will damage relationships in the workplace. Properly designed and executed focus groups can help overcome all of these problems.

Advantages of Focus Groups

The central feature of focus group methods is that they *rely on interaction among the participants to generate insights into the subject under study*. As you will see when we describe the technique, focus groups enable their members to interact in a "safe" environment with very little direction from the researcher. As a result, participants have a chance to express their true feelings on the topic under study and can bring up any aspect of that topic that they feel is important. The group process may also allow them to come to understandings about the topic that none of them could have achieved alone.

This means that focus groups have three substantive advantages: (1) They *may* provide more accurate insights into what people actually think than do other techniques that involve more influence from the researcher; (2) they can produce results that reflect social realities more accurately than methods that ask people to act in isolation; and (3) they give us the ability to study *group dynamics* in ways that other techniques do not. In addition, focus groups offer some practical advantages. First, though they are *not* inexpensive, focus groups typically cost far less than a large survey and take far less time than direct observation. Second, because focus groups do not require elaborate measuring instruments and procedures, they can usually be conducted with far less preparation than interview-based research or even direct observation. This saves time and money.

Limitations of Focus Groups

Like other methods, focus group research has its potential drawbacks. We will describe four common limitations and suggest ways to cope with them. Each of the limitations may affect any given focus group session, but they do not all affect every focus group project equally. This is because there are many different ways to structure focus groups and because focus groups are held for many different purposes. If recognized and properly addressed, the limitations of focus groups need not damage the usefulness of the method.

First, focus group research may yield *subjective interpretations*. The primary product of a focus group is a transcript of what was said. To contribute to our understanding, this transcript must be interpreted by someone. Since the transcript does not consist of numerical data that can be subjected to statistical tests, its interpretation inevitably involves more subjectivity than do the analyses associated with other methods. As a result of differences in their own background or values, different observers may reach different conclusions about what "lessons" are to be learned from the focus group.

Remember that the interpretation of quantitative data can also be subject to debate. We are saying only that focus groups are more prone to the interpretation problem than some other methods are, and *not* that focus groups have this problem when other approaches do not.

Since subjectivity is inherent in the interpretation of focus group sessions, the only protection against being misled by it is some combination of the following steps. Researchers must be honest with themselves about their biases and try to be as objective as possible. They can bring in disinterested but qualified persons to do independent interpretations of the focus group results. Researchers can also share their work with other scholars who can judge the validity of their interpretation and suggest alternatives before considering their conclusions final. In addition, when writing up the study, researchers can faithfully describe enough of what was said to allow others to draw their own conclusions.

A second limitation is that the small number of people that can be involved in any focus group offers *limited representativeness* of any larger population. As a result, we cannot generalize to the larger population with the same precision or confidence that we can when larger samples are used. Additionally, there is always the chance that even carefully selected groups may be atypical of the population and thereby lead us to incorrect conclusions. Moreover, even if the focus groups are quite typical of the larger population, we have no objective measures to tell us this is the case in advance (as we do with probability sampling). We must wait until we can verify focus group results through some other method.

The appropriate responses to this problem consist of the researcher's awareness of the potentially unrepresentative nature of the results of focus groups and the researcher's avoidance of making unwarranted generalizations. Clearly it would be unwise to attempt very precise predictions of popular behavior on the basis of focus group results. For example, one could not, on the basis of focus group results, justifiably claim that "68.6 percent of citizens will vote against higher taxes to be used to retrain defense industry workers for civilian jobs." However, by observing focus groups, scholars might be able to reach conclusions like, "the participants tend to see the retraining of defense industry workers as a personal rather than a public responsibility."

A third limitation is that the *artificial setting* of a focus group may unpredictably affect subjects' behavior. The major purpose of focus groups is to get people to express themselves freely and reveal their true thinking without the restrictions imposed by a survey or interview. They often do this very well. However, we must recognize that the focus group is *not* a natural setting. Even if the moderator succeeds in creating a "permissive environment" that encourages self-expression, responses may be sincere but still unlike what they would have been in a different setting. As a result, we may not be able to generalize from the results of the focus group to the way people will behave in other social settings.

For example, the composition of the group may be unlike that of any group with which the participants are likely to interact on a regular basis. If we have intentionally selected participants of mixed socioeconomic backgrounds but who seldom cross socioeconomic lines in their daily life, the group dynamic that develops may not be typical of any that would occur in the real world. Similarly, the permissive environment of the focus group may allow people to express ideas they would never verbalize in naturally occurring groups that have more restrictive norms. As a result, a consensus may emerge that is unlike any that would be produced by a real-world interaction.

In addition, each focus group develops its own dynamic as a result of some chance factors such as who happens to express an opinion first or the direction or tone of the first set of comments. The same members might behave differently on another evening or if placed in another group. As a consequence, the results of any given focus group may be unrepresentative both of real-world outcomes and of the thinking of the group participants as individuals.

In short, even a carefully designed and well-run focus group may create false impressions because it is not itself a natural setting. There are two main avenues to coping with these issues. First, researchers can run a number of groups and form conclusions based on *patterns* rather than isolated results. Second, they must be sensitive to both the ways in which focus groups may differ from natural settings and the effects these differences may have on the outcome of the sessions, and they must incorporate that awareness into their analysis of the focus group observations.

A fourth limitation is that this technique may produce *method effects.* Most observational research methods carry the risk of influencing subjects' responses in some way. (Recall, for example, our discussion in Chapter 8 of biased question wording and resulting survey responses.) Focus groups are no exception. *Method effects* can arise from biases introduced by the behavior of the moderator, who could have preconceived notions about what the focus group will or "should" reveal and who may unconsciously steer the discussion in that direction. Moderators who conduct several focus groups on the same subject may have had early experiences that cause them to lead discussions in subsequent groups in the direction of being consistent with the early groups. Similarly, unintentional cues given to participants before the group session (through a description of the purpose of the group or simply the naming of its sponsor, for example) may shape the outcome.

WHEN ARE FOCUS GROUPS USEFUL?

Researchers must weigh the strengths and weaknesses of focus groups in the context of specific research situations and tasks. Focus groups can be of great value under some conditions and of little use under others. Here is a nonexhaustive list of some general situations in which focus groups' research is an advantageous method.

Conducting Exploratory Research

When researchers venture into an area that is so completely unexplored that they do not even know how to go about studying it or when they want a fresh perspective on an old but unresolved research question, focus groups can help them formulate ideas about both what questions to ask and what methods to use. An example of this can be found in study of the transformation of Eastern European nations from authoritarian to democratic political systems following the fall of communism after 1989. Researchers might want to know how citizens who have been denied any opportunity for meaningful participation in politics approach the tasks of democratic citizenship when they are given the chance. Because the transition from communism to democracy has never happened before, we have no prior theories or studies to guide us. Moreover, Western scholars have generally been unable to conduct surveys in those nations for decades and have little knowledge of how their citizens thought about politics before the transition. In this case, focus groups consisting of citizens of the changing nations could help researchers discover what is to be explained and develop hypotheses to guide research.

Refining Data Collection Instruments

Even when researchers know enough about an area to formulate hypotheses, they may be unsure about the best way to operationalize concepts. For example, standard question wording on a survey may not communicate effectively with unusual respondents. In the case of the Eastern European nations, we cannot even be sure that their citizens think about politics in the same terms as citizens of Western nations do. A series of focus groups could provide information that would assist in the development of appropriate wording for survey questions to be used with this population. Alternatively, researchers who plan to use direct observation to study political participation in Eastern European nations could use focus groups to learn the meaning of different expressions or actions so that they would know what significance the people being observed attached to their own words and deeds.

Interpreting Quantitative Findings

When researchers have used other methods to collect data that show clear patterns, they may still be unsure about how those patterns developed or what the patterns mean to the people who exhibit them. Again, focus groups can often provide answers. For example, many studies of environmental politics have found that women are far more likely than men to express concern about environmental hazards and to regard technologies as risky. Focus groups in which men and women discuss environmental issues may help researchers understand differences in the way the sexes tend to judge environmental hazards: what standards they use, how they process information, whom they trust as an authority, and so on. Scholars could then make more sense of the statistical relationships observed in their data.

Studying Group Processes

Whether they are legislative committees, juries, military units, law enforcement task forces, workplace teams, street gangs, or any of dozens of other collections of people, small groups make many of the decisions in our society. Understanding the processes by which groups influence their members' perceptions and reach decisions can, therefore, help us understand social phenomena or formulate public policies. Social scientists have long recognized that one behaves differently when in a group than when alone, and that the only way to understand *group* behavior is to study *group dynamics*. If our interest is in some aspect of group dynamics, then focus group methods offer an excellent way to observe efficiently and to avoid raising some of the ethical issues involved in direct observation.

Designing and Evaluating Public Policy

Focus groups can often help public officials and policy analysts gain an understanding of how citizens see problems, evaluate services, and are likely to react to new programs. Such insight can then be used to create new policies that address problems or to evaluate how well existing policies are working. To illustrate, public housing officials could conduct focus groups to help them anticipate how residents of a public housing development would react to a system of tenant management that gave the residents a voice in running the housing project. Based on what they learn, they could try to build into the tenant management program a realistic set of incentives for participation, rather than guess at what might motivate residents to take part.

An even more practice-oriented use of focus groups is to design and evaluate specific communication materials and strategies. To illustrate, imagine that public health officials want to convey to an immigrant community that has its own distinctive subculture certain information on a serious health hazard. The officials might use focus groups composed of members of the immigrant population to determine such things as what channels of communication would be most effective in reaching those residents and whether or not a given message would successfully capture residents' attention and be properly interpreted.

This use of social science methods to achieve very practical ends is commonly referred to as **applied research**, and focus groups constitute one of the most commonly used methods in "applied" settings. Such groups have, for example, proven especially valuable in designing election campaigns because they help campaign managers identify voters' most powerful concerns, thus enabling managers to get a feel for the ways that different appeals will be interpreted by voters.

PLANNING AND CONDUCTING FOCUS GROUPS

Once researchers have decided that focus groups are an appropriate method to use in a given study, they will confront several basic choices in planning and conducting the focus group sessions. We can explore these choices as responses to a series of questions.

The Role of Goals

The first step is to determine exactly what is to be learned from the focus groups. Objectives can range from the very general to the very specific. A relatively general goal might be "to gain insight into the impact of a localized environmental hazard on the lives of residents in order to formulate hypotheses about what determines how residents respond to the hazard." A more specific goal might be "to find out which of five possible sources of information about the hazard citizens are most likely to trust in order to devise a plan for conveying believable information to the public."

It is only when you are clear about what you hope to learn that you will know what to listen for in the focus group discussions. From a practical standpoint there are at least three reasons to identify goals as clearly as possible:

1. The goals will affect *the selection of participants and composition of groups*. If, for instance, you wanted to find out how the controversies surrounding a local environmental hazard had affected social relations within the community, you would want to be sure to include in the groups people on both sides of any issues. The statement

of goals should help researchers identify important characteristics to be considered in recruiting participants and assigning them to groups.

2. The goals will influence *the degree of moderator involvement*. Some goals will require that members of the focus group perform a task while others do not. You may, for example, want the group to reach a formal consensus, solve a hypothetical problem, or make a recommendation about how to address some issue. If so, you will need to have the moderator be more active in guiding the discussion to be sure that the task is completed. If the goals are very general, moderator involvement can be minimized. Selecting goals is therefore the first step in the planning of focus group sessions and the instructing of the moderator.

3. The goals will direct *the development of a "guide" for the moderator*. Even in largely unstructured focus groups, researchers will want the moderator to have a **guide** which sets forth some rules for the discussion and provides a very general outline of how the session should proceed in order to be sure that all of the important points are raised and addressed. A focus group guide is not as detailed as an interview schedule in survey research or even an observational schedule in direct observation. Each guide will be different and will reflect the objectives of the study. Most will cue the moderator to step in at appropriate times to move the discussion along or bring it back to the main issue if it strays too far. Most guides list the main points to be addressed in some appropriate order, suggest phrases to use in making the transition from one subtopic to another, and may even set time limits for the discussion of subtopics or lay out procedures to be used in performing tasks (for example, "Have the group break into three subgroups of equal size . . .").

Choosing How Many Sessions

It is almost always necessary to conduct more than one focus group session to rule out the possibility that there was something atypical about the participants or the group dynamic that developed in any one group. If similar patterns appear in more than one group, we can have more confidence that those patterns accurately reflect reality. Since two groups may give exactly opposite impressions or reach opposing conclusions, many practitioners consider *three* to be the minimum number of group sessions that should be held. Two other considerations, however, will weigh heavily in the choice of the number of sessions.

First, on the substantive side, your research objectives may dictate that you hold separate sessions for different subgroups within a general population or in different geographic locations. In the environmental contamination example, you may want to have separate sessions for citizens who choose to move away and for those who will stay in the contaminated community, or you may want to hold groups in various towns facing different types of environmental hazards so you can compare the groups' reactions. You would need to hold several sessions *for each subgroup* to have confidence in the results. These design considerations may dictate a larger minimum number of sessions.

Second, from a practical standpoint, focus groups are expensive and time consuming to plan, arrange, conduct, and analyze. The amount of time and money and the number of personnel available for the project may impose a limit on the number of sessions that can be held. The costs of *each* focus group session generally vary from $1,500 to $5,000 depending on such variables as whether a professional firm is hired to conduct the sessions, how much money participants must be paid, how transcription is done, and transportation costs.

Choosing an Appropriate Number of Participants

Experience has shown that focus groups rarely work well with fewer than six or more than ten participants. With smaller numbers of participants, especially strong personalities tend to exert too much influence on the outcomes, and individuals may feel too much pressure to carry a share of the conversation. With larger numbers, it is both difficult to give all members enough time to express their thoughts and hard to keep the discussion focused.

Again, the time and money available for the project will play some role in determining how many participants to include, given the decision to hold a certain number of sessions. One reason this is true is that it is frequently necessary to pay participants. The appropriate fee varies with the prevailing wage scale in a given area and with the characteristics of the participants. A group of, say, physicians or business executives may require far higher compensation than those who earn less. Occasionally, people can be persuaded to volunteer their time if the purpose of the research is one they value or if the sponsor of the research is one that commands respect and support. Local public health officials, for example, may be willing to take part in a study sponsored by their professional association and conducted for the purpose of improving public health services in the community.

Selecting Participants

Once the number of participants has been determined, the task of recruiting them begins. The first issue here is what kind of people you want to attract. The key is that you want people who are typical of the population group under study. Depending on the focus of the study, you may be able to work from a telephone book if any of the residents of a given community will do, or you may need more specialized lists of people such as welfare recipients, public school teachers, or members of local civic organizations. Once you have a list to work from, it is common to conduct a **screening interview** to determine whether specific individuals are suited for the study and are willing to take part. This is usually done by phone and followed with a written invitation and a follow-up call to confirm prospective participants' acceptance.

In the recruiting process, researchers must be alert to several additional issues. First, there is a tendency for people with unusually strong feelings about a subject to be more willing to participate than those with less emotional involvement in the issue. To keep this from distorting results, researchers should make a conscious effort to recruit some people with little initial interest in the subject. Second, unless friendship ties, work relationships, or family roles are a specific part of the research focus, it is usually better to recruit people who do not know one another. Strangers are usually less inhibited in their responses. Finally, researchers need to consider the effects of placing people who have different *social roles* in the same focus group. If the topic to be discussed relates to the expectations and interests associated with different social roles, participants in "mixed" groups may change their behavior as a result. Generally, it is unwise to put into the same focus group people with significantly different but interacting roles (like managers and workers or regulatory agency officials and members of the regulated industry) if those roles are relevant to the topic of the discussion. Unless interaction between people in different social roles is specifically part of the research objectives, it is better to select *relatively homogeneous groups* in order to have a sufficient basis for communication among the participants.

Selecting a Physical Setting

Since the main product of a focus group session is a transcript of what was said, it is important to arrange a high-quality audio recording of the event for later transcription. Audio equipment should be tested in advance to be sure it picks up comments from all positions in the room, and the moderator should have a backup system on hand in case the primary recording equipment fails. In some cases, it may also be desirable to videotape the sessions in order to capture the nonverbal communication that may occur. This advantage has to be weighed against the possibility that video cameras may make respondents self-conscious and that hidden cameras can seldom be positioned properly so as to pick up all the action.

In any case, it is important both to tell participants they are being recorded and to get their permission. Professional ethics require that such recordings and any transcripts made from them be kept strictly confidential by the project staff and not be used for any purpose beyond the research.

Focus groups are best conducted in a room large enough to allow participants to sit around a single table (or at least in a circle) but small enough to feel intimate. The room should be furnished and decorated in a manner that puts people at ease. Sometimes researchers want to observe the sessions in person and need a place to sit to the side. Other times they may not want to be seen and thus need a room with a one-way glass so they can observe without affecting the dynamics of the group. Actual discussions usually last about one and a half hours, but it is wise to allow two hours per session in case participants are late arriving, technical problems arise, or the discussion simply runs longer than anticipated.

Working with the Moderator

No single factor is more important to the success of a focus group than the competence of the moderator. The moderator is responsible for putting participants at ease, ensuring that all relevant topics are covered in the discussion, keeping more aggressive speakers from dominating the conversation, and helping to characterize the results of the session in a set of notes for the researchers. Accordingly, it is important to hire an experienced and skilled moderator if the budget allows or to invest substantial time in training someone to serve as moderator if an experienced one cannot be hired. It is generally unwise for a researcher to serve as the moderator because a researcher may unintentionally bias the results.

Moderators should share enough characteristics with focus group participants to help participants feel free to talk and to understand well enough what they *mean* by their remarks so as to respond properly. This is especially true with distinctive groups (for example, farmers, unemployed industrial workers, or female state legislators) and when the topic is one that touches on tensions between social groups.

An *assistant moderator* is almost always necessary. The assistant sits to the side and takes more detailed notes on the session than the moderator can take while interacting with the participants. The assistant may handle mechanical tasks such as greeting participants when they first arrive or distributing any written materials to be used in the session. Assistants can also serve as a backup since they often are familiar enough with the focus group process to step in if for some reason the moderator cannot attend a session. The assistant's most important function, however, may be to serve as a check on the moderator's perception of the sessions. The assistant works with the moderator in writing up an accurate set of notes after the session. If the two disagree on an event, both opinions should be included in the notes for the researcher to consider.

Once moderators are hired or trained, they must be instructed. As explained earlier, much of the moderator's role is dictated by the objectives of the project and outlined in the focus group guide. Even in those cases when moderators are expected to take a fairly active role in moving the discussion along, it is vital that they not influence the outcome. Doing this requires that they strike the proper balance between empathy and detachment, being accepting of all opinions expressed but not rewarding any particular type of statement. The emphasis must be on *having the participants express their opinions*.

At the end of the session, the moderator should write up a set of **field notes** summarizing themes or conclusions that emerged from the discussion, and pointing out any facts about the session that might influence the researcher's interpretation of the transcript. The moderator might note such issues as a high level of tension in the group, the exceptional influence of one or more participants over the group, or an apparent reluctance of some participants to express opinions. Moderators might also compare the results of different sessions they have conducted.

This raises the issue of whether to use *one or more than one main moderator*. Using the same moderator for all sessions offers more consistency in the way the sessions are run and provides a better basis for comparing sessions. It also allows a moderator to develop some insight into the topic and may help a moderator to anticipate problems and do a better job of running sessions subsequent to the first one or two.

However, researchers may want to use more than one moderator in several circumstances. One is the situation in which very different social groups are represented in different sessions and it is necessary to use different moderators to match participants' characteristics. For instance, if race relations is the topic and groups are racially homogeneous, it would be wise to select a moderator of the same race as the participants in each session. A second situation that calls for more than one moderator is one in which researchers want the results of each session or group of sessions to be totally independent of each other and there is some fear that a moderator might influence the outcomes on the basis of expectations developed in early sessions. Finally, logistical considerations such as geographically separated research sites or the need to conduct several sessions at once in order to meet a deadline or avoid "contamination" of the groups by news reports appearing between sessions might dictate the need for multiple moderators.

Conducting Sessions

Focus group meetings usually open with the moderator explaining the general purpose of the focus group and the ground rules for the discussion. One of the most important rules the moderator should stress at the beginning of each session is the idea that group members can agree or disagree with others' responses. In fact, the moderator should encourage divergent opinions because clients are often interested in why people disagree about a product or service. The moderator should also note that the session will be recorded and that all information will be kept confidential (participants usually have been asked to sign a consent form before the start of the session). This is commonly followed by an opening statement by each participant. Such statements usually tell a few basic facts about the individual. Having each person speak helps participants feel as if they have been introduced and makes the discussion more relaxed. It also encourages less outgoing individuals to speak up later in the session. The key objective of the opening moments of a session is to make it clear that the moderator wants to hear each member's story in his or her own words and that the purpose of the exercise is for the moderator and the session's sponsors to learn from the participants.

After the introduction, warm-up questions should be asked to draw the participants into the conversation. Moderators usually start with general, easy to answer questions that only indirectly relate to the actual topic of the session. A focus group designed to find out more about peoples' perceptions of Apple laptop computers, for example, might start with **warm-up questions** such as "Who has used laptop computers when traveling?" or "What do you think of the latest trend toward netbooks?" These questions can be answered by most people who have used computers and, as a consequence, are likely to jump-start the conversation.

Following the warm-up period, the moderator should start focusing on the key questions that need to be answered during the focus group session. Moderators should ask general, open-ended questions like, "How do you feel about X?" "What experience have you had with Y?" and "Does anyone want to respond to that?" This keeps things focused and moving. Questions that can be answered with a simple "yes" or "no," on the other hand, should be avoided for obvious reasons. Once the participants have become more comfortable discussing the topic in general terms, the moderator can ask more specific questions that probe opinions and perceptions more deeply. Truly skilled moderators will avoid questions that reinforce any particular viewpoint and will keep the conversation focused, even though some participants might interrupt the discussion, tell unrelated stories, or start arguing with each other. Another important point to remember is that the moderator should ask participants to talk to each other, not to the moderator. This strategy will ensure that participants will react to whatever has been said by others in the group, often generating new ideas and insights.

Towards the end of the session, the moderator should begin to wrap up the discussion by summarizing what has been said by the participants and how it might be understood by others. This summary gives all participants another chance to add further comments or to correct the moderator's perception of what has been mentioned. The goal of such a summary is to cross-check with all participants whether the moderator's interpretation of the group discussion actually is shared by the participants. Finally, the session should close with a brief statement by the moderator thanking all participants for their time and effort.

One variation on this procedure is to ask participants to fill out a questionnaire before and/or after the session. Such questionnaires can be used to gather background information on the participants that might not be evident from the discussion but that influences interpretation of participants' comments. They also show how participants' views changed as a result of the focus group discussion if the same questions are asked both before and after the session. Finally, they elicit from participants their assessments of the focus group process in order to improve the running of subsequent sessions. Pre-session questionnaires must be very carefully constructed so as not to influence the direction of the session by asking questions that suggest positions on issues or set up expectations about how the session will go. As a result, pre-session questionnaires should be used only if the benefits outweigh any threat of distorting the results of the sessions.

RESEARCH EXERCISE

Free or Constrained Speech?

Some commentators worry that a norm of political correctness threatens to stifle meaningful discussion of ideas, especially on college campuses. Others argue that there is no such danger and that advocates of "politically correct" language are simply calling attention to the biases inherent in everyday speech. Who is right?

1. Form teams within your class, with four to six students on each team. Each team will conduct a focus group to learn how college students perceive and are affected by the issue of "political correctness."
   a. The team will write a brief statement of objectives for a focus group, stating what it hopes to learn about political correctness from the group.
   b. Develop a "guide" to the focused discussion, in which you identify some questions about political correctness that you want explored in a focus group composed of college students. For example, you may want to know whether students are even aware of the issues raised by the idea of political correctness, whether they are receptive or hostile to the idea of politically correct language, whether they feel pressured to be politically correct, or how political correctness might be enforced (if at all) in their social circles.
   c. Devise a set of standards by which you would select participants for such a focus group.
2. Recruit six to ten students to take part in the group. The participants cannot be students in your research methods course, nor should you have previously discussed this exercise with them.
3. Conduct the focus group using one member of your team as the moderator, with the other members observing and taking notes. Video-record the session, if possible.
4. After the group leaves, go over the notes as a team:
   a. Come to an agreement about what was observed.
   b. Write a summary of the session.
5. Analyze the discussion and ask yourself if it offered answers to the questions around which you designed the focus group.

Note: Before conducting this exercise, check with your professor to ensure that your college or university's institutional review board will authorize a waiver for this educational illustration of human subject research.

Analyzing Focus Group Results

As a qualitative method, focus groups do not produce numerical data that can be analyzed using statistics to identify patterns and relationships. Focus groups produce a very large volume of verbal data in the form of transcripts, recordings of sessions, and moderators' field notes. The tasks of reducing all of this information to a readable summary and of drawing some justifiable conclusions from it can be daunting. We can provide no step-by-step guide for focus group analysis both because there is so much variation in project objectives and focus group procedures and because qualitative analysis relies heavily on insight and creativity. We can, however, suggest some general guidelines that will help you recognize a good analysis.

The first principle of focus group analysis is that researchers should always begin with a clear picture of what they hope to learn from the data. This step should have been taken in the identification of the purpose for the study as the first step in designing the project. Returning to that objective helps identify relevant information from the sessions and eliminate marginal information. It gives a benchmark as to how detailed the analysis must be. For example, if the purpose was largely descriptive (such as finding out what terms ordinary people use to discuss some political issue), only a summary may be needed. If the purpose was more analytical (such as determining why people were opposed to nuclear power), the analysis would have to be much more complex, and certain subtle features of the discussions might take on importance.

Once the objective has been established, researchers face the task of organizing the data for analysis. One approach is to read through the transcripts and literally cut out sections addressing specific topics. Researchers can then physically reassemble the sections so that all the comments relevant to a given subtopic are together. This approach can help reveal themes more clearly and can reduce the volume of data to be considered at any one time. It must be done skillfully to avoid taking comments out of their context and, thereby, concealing their *actual meaning*.

In analytical studies, it is especially important to listen to the recordings of the sessions in order to be sure that the context of members' comments is taken into account and their *meaning* understood. Transcripts can be produced so as to reflect some of the subtle texture of oral communication by means of certain conventions such as typing in all capitals those words that speakers stressed or putting interpretive comments in parentheses. For example: "Oh, I *never* believe what *my* mayor says" (*laughing*). However, even these practices may conceal subtle differences in meaning that only listening to the tape can reveal. Taken in context, for instance, the comment about the mayor may have been sarcastic, indicating that the speaker *does* believe the mayor. Researchers therefore rely on moderators to report significant *nonverbal communication* (body language) that went on in the group and that may influence the interpretation of verbal comments.

One potentially productive approach to interpreting focus group data is to use *content analysis* to help identify themes in the discussions. For example, if focus group participants were asked their reasons for opposing a hazardous waste incinerator, they would probably offer many different answers. A sophisticated content analysis of the transcripts might help by grouping those answers into a smaller set of related arguments that identified themes in the responses and indicated which occurred most often.

In all this, the researcher's job is to form an impression of how the participants felt about the topic and to produce a summary statement of their expressions. The object is not to explain why participants feel as they do in the scientific sense of explanation discussed in Chapters 2 and 6. Analysts might, however, draw on existing theories or their knowledge of the subject in order to offer interpretations of what participants meant by various comments, why participants said what they did in the manner in which they said it, or even how they developed these attitudes. Often the most useful insights derived from analyses of focus group results come from linking what was observed to larger theories or processes in order to highlight the *larger significance* of what was said in the focus groups. For instance, if focus groups reveal that residents of racially divided communities

PRACTICAL RESEARCH ETHICS

Communicating your commitment to ethical research?

Ethical considerations for focus groups are basically the same as for the other methods of social research mentioned in this book. For example, researchers must ensure that all participants are fully informed about the purpose of the focus group session and that the research procedures do not harm participants physically or psychologically.

Participants should also be aware that they cannot be pressured to speak during the group sessions and that they may decline to answer any questions with which they are not comfortable. Most importantly, all participants must know that their identity and responses will be kept strictly confidential and that the final transcripts and reports will not identify participants or anyone mentioned during the group sessions.

Of course, assuring confidentiality in focus groups is somewhat problematic because once something is said during a group session, it is instantly known to everyone else in the group. For that reason, at the beginning of each session your moderator needs to encourage participants to keep confidential what they hear or learn during the group session. In order to ensure complete understanding of and agreement with these ethical principles, you should require a signed consent form from all focus group participants.

At the conclusion of your focus group session, you will have a short "debriefing" component, which should provide a short explanation of the purpose of the session and a quick summary of what has been discussed. This will allow participants to talk about their reactions to the research topic and the conversations in which they have participated, and allow you, the researcher, to reiterate the confidential nature of the focus group conversation.

are denying the problem, a researcher may turn to theories of social psychology to interpret those residents' remarks as examples of coping mechanisms.

Reporting Focus Group Results

Reporting focus group results can be as challenging as analyzing them. Whereas quantitative data can be reduced to measures of association and presented in tables, it is difficult to reproduce the richness of qualitative data for simple presentation. It is worth putting a good deal of time into meeting this challenge because the report is very important to the success of a project.

Krueger and Casey (2005) suggest that reports perform three primary functions. First, and most obvious, a report communicates to a given audience information about the results of a study. Only if it is easy for the intended audience to understand, and clear in its message, will it actually have an impact on how that audience sees the topic of the study and thereby influence scholarship or public policy. Second, the act of writing a report assists researchers in developing their own personal understanding of a project and the subject it was designed to address. Third, a report provides a usable historical record of the results of a project. Because focus group data are so complex, it is especially important to have a compact summary if the results are ever to be used as background for future studies.

Researchers usually choose among three basic approaches for reporting focus group results: (1) They can *present enough carefully selected quotations* from the participants to convey an accurate picture of the discussions. This amounts to providing a representative sampling of what was said so readers can draw their own conclusions. (2) They can *summarize statements* by participants to point out major themes, using quotes only for illustrative purposes. This is a descriptive approach in which researchers assume responsibility for deciding what is important enough to report but also in which they offer little analysis. (3) They can *interpret what was said* so as to provide understanding, using description and quotes only to support their conclusions or illustrate points. Which strategy is appropriate depends on the purpose of the focus group project and the nature of the intended audience for the report.

To know what kind of report is called for, researchers must ask who will receive it and what use will be made of it. To understand the significance of this, recall the list of conditions under which focus groups are useful that was presented earlier in this chapter. If the focus groups were used to supplement another data collection technique, then the primary users of the report will be the researchers themselves. They will use understandings gained from the focus groups to formulate hypotheses, develop indicators, or assess their interpretation of data gathered by other means. Others may never see any more about the focus groups than a brief statement in a subsequent report to the effect that focus groups were used to frame the research question, design the project, or verify interpretations. In those cases, the report on the focus group results may be closer to the representative sampling of quotes just described, because the intended audience has the capability to draw informed conclusions from raw data.

If the focus groups were used to evaluate some aspect of public policy, assist in policy development, or design a campaign strategy, the audience for the report is likely to be persons who are less interested in the details of the sessions and more interested in the lessons to be learned from them. Such persons are, however, still also likely to want a strong sense of the thrust of the sessions. In this case, the report will probably rely heavily on summarized statements and a description of the key themes. Finally, if focus groups were used as a primary source of data collection (as in a study of small-group dynamics) and the results will appear in an academic publication, the report will have to be briefer and will have to stress interpretation of the sessions.

Online Focus Groups

Due to the growing cost of in-person focus groups, more and more research companies conduct focus groups over the Internet (see, for example, www.e-focusgroups.com). Participants in these **online focus groups** usually interact with one another and the moderator in real time through a Web-based chat or conferencing environment to discuss a particular topic. The main advantage of these "virtual discussion rooms" is that they allow respondents (and clients) from all over the world to gather electronicallly without leaving their homes or offices. This approach also eliminates all travel expenses and the need to rent focus group facilities for face-to-face gatherings. Moreover, because participants in online groups do not have to face each other directly and thus can remain anonymous, this methodology might be especially suited for discussing topics that are sensitive or potentially embarrassing. However, online focus groups also have some severe limitations that undermine the usability of this method for many research topics. For example, while people might be more willing to express themselves in an online chat by writing about their thoughts and feelings, it is much easier to talk about them in a face-to-face group session. In addition, it is likely that most people will not react the same way to text-based statements coming from some anonymous participant as they would to "real" people sitting just a few feet away in the same room. Finally, because most online focus groups do not have video feeds yet, all cues that might be gained from observing a respondent's body language will be lost in online groups. Thus, anybody considering the use of online groups in their research should carefully evaluate the advantages and disadvantages of this methodology in relation to the research topic at hand.

Conclusion

We want to highlight the point we made at the outset of this chapter. Focus groups can make a contribution at several stages of the research process. Not only can they serve as the primary data collection method for more qualitative studies, but they can also be integrated with quantitative methods. In the early stages of research, they can help clarify research questions or suggest new approaches to old problems. Once under way, they can help design measuring instruments to be used in interviews or direct observation. Additionally, this method may provide insights that more structured methods cannot, as well as allow researchers to explore people's thinking in detail. In the analysis stage, focus groups can improve our interpretation of quantitative data by shedding light on the meanings people attach to responses or actions. It is important to remember, though, that focus groups rely on brief but intense observation of carefully selected small groups of people to gain insights into social phenomena. Thus, focus groups are not statistically representative of larger populations, and produce data that must be analyzed subjectively.

Key Terms

focus group *347*

moderator *347*

applied research *353*

guide *354*

screening interview *355*

field notes *357*

warm-up questions *358*

online focus groups *362*

Research Examples

Manheim's (2005) *Strategic Public Diplomacy & American Foreign Policy* illustrates the use of focus groups in politics by providing an account of their use to design the presentation to the American public of the George H. W. Bush administration's rationale for U.S. involvement in the first Gulf War. More recently, Wanda (2009) used two focus groups of African American women to explore their responses to Obama's successful presidential election. Beeman et al. (2009), on the other hand, used focus groups and personal interviews to explore the meaning of democracy and democratic structures for women in Quebec.

The idea that online focus groups might one day replace or at least supplement traditional face-to-face focus groups is pursued in a study by Price, Nir, and Cappella (2006), who investigate the impact of such online group discussions on people's willingness to express their opinions during the 2000 presidential election campaign.

Methodological Readings

Two general introductions to focus group methods are Edmunds' (2000) *Focus Group Research Handbook* and Bader and Rossi's (2002) *Focus Groups: A Step-by-Step Guide*. Three books that explain the use of focus groups in social science research are *Focus Groups in Social Research* (Bloor et al. 2001), *Using Focus Groups in Research*

(Litosseliti 2003), and *Focus Groups: A Practical Guide for Applied Research* (Krueger and Casey 2005).

References

Bader, Gloria E., and Catherine A. Rossi. 2002. *Focus Groups: A Step-by-Step Guide*, 3rd ed. San Diego, CA: The Bader Group.

Beeman, Jennifer, Nancy Guberman, Jocelyne Lamoureux, Danielle Fournier, and Lise Gervais. 2009. "Beyond Structures to Democracy as Culture." *American Behavioral Scientist* 52(February): 867–884.

Bloor, Michael, Jane Frankland, Michelle Thomas, and Kate Stewart. 2001. *Focus Groups in Social Research*. Thousand Oaks, CA: Sage.

Edmunds, Holly. 2000. *Focus Group Research Handbook*. New York, NY: McGraw-Hill.

Krueger, Richard, and Mary Anne Casey. 2005. *Focus Groups: A Practical Guide for Applied Research*, 3rd ed. Thousand Oaks, CA: Sage.

Litosseliti, Lia. 2003. *Using Focus Groups in Research*. London, England: Continuum International Publishing Group.

Manheim, Jarol B. 2005. *Strategic Public Diplomacy & American Foreign Policy*. New York: Oxford University Press.

Price, Vincent, Lilach Nir, and Joseph N. Cappella. 2006. "Normative and Informational Influences in Online Political Discussions." *Communication Theory* 16(1): 47–74.

Wanda, Parham-Payne. 2009. "Through the Lens of Black Women: The Significance of Obama's Campaign." *Journal of African American Studies* 13(June): 131–138.

CHAPTER 21

Elite and Specialized Interviewing: Discussing to Garner Knowledge

In this chapter you will learn:

- How to study events that only a few people know about or that involve people outside the mainstream.
- How to conduct specialized interviewing and what specific challenges to look out for.
- How to ensure the validity of information obtained in personal interviews.
- How qualitative interview methods differ from quantitative methods.

Personal interviews with political elites such as presidents, prime ministers, or members of parliament are difficult to obtain. Even journalists, who depend on such interviews to do their jobs, struggle to get access to political leaders who often avoid the press or anybody asking critical questions. Nevertheless, in-depth interviews often reveal important pieces of information that cannot be gathered through any other research methodology. Katie Couric's now famous interviews for CBS News with the 2008 U.S. vice presidential nominee Sarah Palin, for example, revealed substantial gaps in Palin's knowledge of foreign affairs and subsequently undermined her political support among the American public.

Most of us, of course, are not famous journalists and therefore do not interview people on a regular basis. However, the basic idea of an interview—an in-depth conversation with another person—is something we are all familiar with. Long talks with friends or relatives, a brief chat with a colleague over lunch, conversations with people you met at a party, and even job interviews, are all examples of how we use "interviews" to gain information. Similarly, **intensive interviewing** techniques involving in-depth, one-on-one conversations with respondents are a primary instrument of qualitative research. They are used, not to obtain precise measures of concepts for testing theories, but as a means of gaining *in-depth understanding* of a phenomenon and discovering aspects of that phenomenon that researchers did not anticipate.

As you read this chapter about elite and specialized interviewing, be alert to the ways in which effective use of this technique requires attention to a different set of concerns than survey interviewing or any other quantitative data collection method. Pay special attention to the distinct "mind-set" required for qualitative inquiry. You will find that you will be less concerned with carrying out a precisely planned research design and measuring process than you are when conducting quantitative research, and more concerned with being open to learning what your subjects can uniquely teach you about the subject.

ELITE INTERVIEWING

Many important research questions in political science can be answered only if we can learn how certain individuals or types of individuals think and act. For example, whereas we can always speculate about reasons for the passage of a specific piece of legislation, we can learn the actual reasons only by finding out what the legislators thought. Answering these types of questions requires **elite interviewing** rather than surveys of the general population.

Defining Elites

In this context, people are referred to as *elite* if they have knowledge that, for the purposes of a given research project, requires that they be given individualized treatment in an interview. Their elite status depends not on their role in society but on their access to information that can help answer a given research question. Although people who get elite treatment in research *are* often persons of political, social, or economic importance, this is not a requirement. In a study of "extremist" groups like the Ku Klux Klan, for example, "elite" respondents (those with special knowledge of the organization) may not be persons of wealth or public notoriety.

Elite Interviewing versus Surveying

A central difference between sample survey interviewing and elite interviewing is the degree to which the interview is *standardized*. In sample surveys, each respondent is treated as much like every other respondent as possible. This is because the purpose of the interview is to obtain specific information that can be used to make quantitative comparisons between respondents in an effort to generalize to some larger population. In elite interviewing, each respondent is treated differently to the extent that obtaining the information possessed by that individual alone requires unique treatment. The purpose of elite interviewing is generally not the collection of prespecified data but the gathering of information to assist in reconstructing some event or discerning a pattern in specific behaviors.

A second major difference between elite interviewing and survey interviewing is that, whereas survey interviews are generally highly **scheduled interviews**, elite interviews are largely **unscheduled interviews**. An interview is highly *scheduled* if the questions to be asked and the order of their appearance are predetermined and inflexible. Highly scheduled interviews produce standardized data because they require that all respondents answer the same questions and select from the same options in answering. This has the advantage of allowing comparisons between respondents and facilitates data processing. Strict scheduling, however, has the disadvantage of restricting the information gained from interviews to that which the researcher has already decided is necessary for understanding the phenomena under study. Scheduling limits the researcher's opportunities to learn what respondents consider relevant or important and to gain new theoretical insights.

In a totally *unscheduled* interview, the interviewer is guided only by a general objective (for example, to find out how a given decision was made in a particular state agency) and has no predetermined set of questions to ask. Unscheduled interviews produce data that are difficult to condense and summarize and that may not allow precise comparisons among respondents. The asset accompanying this liability is a greater opportunity to learn from respondents and to acquire unexpected information that can lead to truly new ways of understanding the events being studied.

Unscheduled interviews are especially suited to elite interviewing, because in elite interviewing the researcher is interested in learning what the respondent perceives as important and relevant to the research and lets the respondent's observations suggest what questions should be asked in order to gain useful information. The interviewer is concerned with discovering facts and patterns rather than with measuring pre-selected phenomena.

Elite interviews can provide crucial information about political events that is otherwise unavailable. Elite interviewing involves some very real scientific risks, however. It generally means asking people who are deeply involved in a political process to shape the researcher's definition of the process. This may threaten the scientific validity of the information obtained if respondents (1) have so narrow a view of the events in question that they do not understand which aspects are important in explaining them; (2) have inaccurate information (either because they misperceived events in the first place or because they have forgotten important elements); (3) have convinced themselves, in order to rationalize their own actions, that things are one way when they are actually another; or (4) intentionally lie in order to protect themselves or others. For example, interviews with ranking members of George W. Bush's administration about the timing of their knowledge of the prisoner abuse at Abu Ghraib prison in Iraq might produce instances of invalid information for each of these reasons.

SEEKING VALIDITY

Though researchers cannot control what respondents say, they can guard against drawing invalid conclusions from elite interviews by following some general guidelines. First, never treat what interviewees say as factual data, but rather *treat the fact that they said it as data*. For an understanding of political behavior, it is often as important to know what people believe or claim to be true as it is to know what is true. For example, if you want to know why residents of a given community have organized to demand the closing of a nearby chemical plant, finding out how much of a safety hazard the plant actually poses may be less useful than finding out how much of a safety hazard residents *believe* the plant poses.

Second, never rely on a single respondent for information about any event, but obtain information about each event from as many respondents as possible before drawing conclusions.

Third, always seek ways of verifying information from elite interviews by comparing it with information from outside sources. If we interview party leaders to learn why a given candidate has been selected as the party's nominee in an election and respondents refer to "the obvious public support for the candidate" as their reason for supporting him or her, we will want to look for public opinion polls that supply evidence of the degree to which the public actually did support the candidate.

Fourth, learn enough about the subject to be able to recognize incorrect statements or to analyze responses perceptively for possible sources of invalidity. We should be able to answer questions such as the following before engaging in elite interviewing: Is there any reason why respondents might want to believe something other than the truth or want to have others believe something other than the truth? Do they stand to gain economically or politically from given statements? What answers are plausible given the facts we know about the subject from other, reliable sources?

Despite these possible complications, elite interviewing has tremendous potential for shedding light on important political phenomena and can often be a valuable supplement to studies relying principally on other data collection techniques, as well as provide the sole basis for important conclusions. It is crucial to remember, however, that information from people with inside knowledge is no substitute for a sound theoretical understanding of the subject. In order to reach scientifically valuable conclusions, political scientists must always impose their own analytic categories and conceptual schemes on the information gathered from elites.

TECHNIQUES OF ELITE INTERVIEWING

One of the first questions faced in elite interviewing is whom to interview. In survey interviewing, all of the respondents are treated as equally able to contribute information that can be used in answering the research question, and sampling methods determine whom to interview. Elite interviewers have to assume that potential respondents differ in how much they can contribute to the study and that each respondent has something unique to offer. Often, background research will identify the entire population of those likely to have relevant information. If we are studying the decisions of the presidential commission created to investigate the terrorist attacks of September 11, 2001, for instance, background research would identify the members of the commission, their staff personnel, and the people called to testify. By contrast, if we are doing a "community power study" to determine who controls public policy in a certain city, we will not find any official list of people who exercise political influence in the city. Finding out whom to interview in this case is one of the objectives of the interviews themselves.

Once a group of potential interviewees has been identified, the question of the order in which to see them arises. It is tempting to see first those people who should be most willing to talk and most sympathetic, or to want to see first the person believed to have the most information. Two things should be kept in mind, however. First, elite interviewing is a process of discovery. We seldom come to the interviews knowing everything important to ask. Early interviews may teach us things that help us get the most useful information from subsequent interviews. Often it is best to interview the most central figures late in the study.

Second, in elite interviewing, we are generally not dealing with isolated and uninvolved individuals. Each respondent is likely to have a unique (perhaps self-interested) view of the situation under study and may intentionally or unintentionally give inaccurate advice about whom should be interviewed. Under no circumstances should the researcher let early interviewees' suggestions *determine* the choice or order of subsequent interviews, although those suggestions can provide partial data on which to base such decisions. Sometimes the fact that early interviewees have suggested certain other persons is evidence in itself, as it may reveal alliances, communication patterns, or shared perceptions.

In addition, because elite respondents are likely to know one another and be involved with the subject matter, the researcher must be cautious that early interviews do not jeopardize the study by identifying it with a particular group among the potential respondents. If possible, it is best to avoid interviewing the most unusual persons first—the mavericks, opposition leaders, persons thought to have extreme views, or leaders of any dominant coalition. If word is passed to other interviewees that you have already spoken with those perceived to be outside of the norms or in positions of power, it may bias your other interviews.

Considering all this, researchers may find that the best initial interviews may be with people who are somewhat marginal to the situation but who are viewed as neutral or "mainstream" by most participants. In a study of politics in a state legislature, for example, it may be best to interview members of the legislative council (a general service agency used by all members of the legislature) first, rather than starting with key legislators. It is also wise to explain to the first respondents that the interview is preliminary and exploratory and that you may want to see them again. This is because you may learn what other questions to ask or how to interpret answers only after subsequent conversations.

Arranging Interviews

It may be difficult to schedule interviews with elites because such individuals are often busy people and this type of interview generally demands a large amount of their time (an hour or more is common). The following tips will generally help in securing interviews, *though it will sometimes be impossible or inadvisable to follow them in particular situations.*

1. Always call or write in advance to arrange for the interview rather than simply showing up, as is done in survey interviewing.
2. Be sure to request the interview by speaking with *the person to be interviewed* rather than a secretary or aide. You want to be certain the respondent understands the purpose of the meeting so he or she will not feel you are being deceitful.
3. Avoid highly detailed explanations of the purpose of the interview because these can bias responses or cause potential respondents to refer you to a staff person who has "expert" knowledge of the subject.
4. Always try to determine the reasons for refusals and try to see whether you can remove the cause. For example, if scheduling is a problem, you may offer to interview after work hours; if confidence is a problem, you may be able to secure references from people the potential respondent trusts, or agree to have a third party sit in on the interview as insurance against subsequent false claims.
5. Always have on hand materials that identify you and the sponsor of the research, in case questions arise. If possible, give contact information for someone who can verify the purpose and legitimacy of your study.

CONDUCTING ELITE INTERVIEWS

Once an interview has been arranged, it should *not* proceed by the rules given for survey interviewing. Elite interviewers have to be more flexible and have a wider range of interviewing styles than survey interviewers, but there are some general guidelines that will fit most situations:

1. Always introduce yourself and restate the broad purpose of the study at the beginning of each interview rather than assuming that the respondent remembers

these facts from a letter of introduction, phone call, or even a prior interview session.

2. The setting of an interview can be crucial. It is generally best to arrange a private interview away from potential distractions. Interviews over meals in restaurants or in the presence of the respondent's family usually do not go well. Occasionally, however, it is useful to have an interview in an unorthodox place (a city park, a bus, a logged forest) if it serves to put respondents at ease or jog their memory of past events.

3. Though group interviews can sometimes help produce a consensus on facts or reveal personal relationships, it is normally best to interview only one person at a time.

4. The tone of the interview should be reflective and conversational. Avoid firing questions in rapid succession. Do not be afraid of pauses as you or the respondent process information and collect thoughts.

5. Plan initial questions carefully. Though the bulk of the interview will be unscheduled, the first few questions are important in focusing respondents' attention, stimulating their memory, and clarifying their perception of what you want. Initial questions should be (a) clearly related to the stated purpose of the study, (b) likely to be answered with ease so that there is no threat to the interviewee's ego, (c) phrased to show the respondent that the interviewer has knowledge about the subject of the study, and (d) conducive to the kind of free-flowing answers that the researcher hopes to receive in the interview rather than to flat, factual answers. (If you need background information on the respondent, it can be obtained later in the interview.) Questions that stress the respondent's feelings about or definition of a situation can be especially useful opening questions.

6. Once you have successfully started the interview with some initial questions, it is time to keep the conversation going. The best way to do this is to use what Spradley (1979) called **grand tour questions**. These questions provide respondents with the opportunity to talk about something they know well. According to Leech (2002), there are three basic types of grand tour questions: (a) the "typical" grand tour question, which asks respondents to describe a typical day in their office (or job); (b) the "specific" grand tour question, which asks for a description based on some specific parameter decided by the interviewer (such as a specific day or event); and (c) the "task-related" grand tour question, which asks respondents to carry out a common task while describing it to the interviewer. According to Leech, the main benefit of these questions is that they get respondents talking about their daily life, but in a fairly focused way. However, while such questions might provide us with a good idea of what the respondent's average day might look like, the challenge of a successful interview will be to guess how accurately the respondent can describe a normal day. Leech (2002, p. 667) notes that "[r]espondents may have a tendency to focus on the interesting (which may not be usual), or on what they think should happen day to day (although it actually may not)."

7. Another way to get people to talk is to use **example questions**. According to Leech (2002), these questions focus on a single issue or event mentioned by the respondent and then ask for an example ("Can you give me an example of a time during which you did X?"). Related to this type of question are the so-called **native language questions**, which ask for an example in the respondents' own words ("How would you describe event X in your own words?"). The main benefit of these questions is to allow respondents to specify an event or an issue with an example from their own experience, which might provide additional insights.

8. Another important interview technique is the use of **prompts**. During interviews, prompts keep people talking even when they believe that they do not have to say much in response to a specific question. Many survey questions, for example, include planned prompts that the interviewer is supposed to mention if the respondents do not bring them up themselves. For example, during an interview about political media use, respondents might mention television news but might not say anything about online news. An appropriate prompt for such a question would be: "And how about online news . . . do you ever go online to read the news?" In cases where answers are not clear or precise enough, interviewers also might ask for clarification by using prompts such as "Could you explain this in more detail, please?" or "How is that?" While prompts are a common interview technique and can yield valuable information, it is important to remember that interviewers must use them without biasing or leading the respondents' answers. In particular, prompts that imply agreement or disagreement with the respondents' answers must be avoided at all cost.

9. In contrast to survey research, questions should often be subject to multiple interpretations. Remember that the objective is to learn how *respondents* see the situation and what they feel is relevant.

10. Comments, as well as questions, can be used to evoke a response. A remark like, "that is not the way it is usually done," for example, can lead to revelations about how respondents believe things do work.

11. Always maintain eye contact when possible (unless interviewees seem uncomfortable with this), and make it clear that you are listening intently and sympathetically. Phrases like *I see* or *of course* or simply a thoughtful *yes* can encourage respondents and keep them talking.

12. Remember that one of the chief rewards respondents get from granting in-depth interviews is the chance to "teach" someone who is knowledgeable about and genuinely interested in a subject of great importance to them. It can be important to let them realize that they are, in fact, helping and informing you.

13. It is generally best to appear to accept whatever comments respondents make. Do not appear to reject their opinions or challenge their statements of fact.

14. An exception to guideline 13 occurs when respondents are reluctant to reveal information you feel sure they have. In that situation, it may be necessary to employ what is often referred to as the **Nadel technique** (Nadel 1939). Here you play the role of critic or antagonist, questioning and challenging respondents' remarks in hopes of forcing them to reveal information in order to defend their views or prove a point.

15. Respondents who are reluctant to divulge information because they fear the way it may be used can sometimes be reassured by a reminder that the information will be kept confidential or that the researcher is really not in any position to affect the situation in any way.

16. Note-taking can be used as a tool to improve interviews. In elite interviewing, respondents can often be encouraged to give more information or stay on a given subject by the way an interviewer takes notes. Intense recording can serve as a cue that you find comments useful, and putting the pencil down altogether can signal that the respondent has ventured off the central topic. Because you have to take such extensive notes that it is probably impossible to be inconspicuous, you may as well use note-taking for all it is worth.

17. Always be sensitive to the interviewee's personality and personal style, and adapt your tactics to it. Some people are highly formal and others are very casual. Some deal in ideas almost exclusively, and others tend to personalize everything. Some people are accustomed to interacting mainly with superiors, and others mainly with subordinates. You may be able to get more information by adopting one of these roles. Never enter an interview with a fixed idea of the style you will use, but decide what is necessary when talking with the respondent.

18. Always review your interview notes as soon as possible after the interview to elaborate at points where you could get only an outline and to make comments about your interpretation of the interview. This may mean sitting in a cold parking lot or buying an unwanted cup of coffee in order to have a place to write, but it is important to trust to memory as little as possible.

19. Type up handwritten notes as soon as possible. Make several hard or electronic copies and store them in separate places to insure against loss.

Voice recorders are controversial tools in interviewing. Obviously they can help avoid mistakes about what is actually said, and they can capture subtle facts about the *way* in which things are said. Recorders can also help interviewers learn how they sound to respondents. This is useful because the way in which a question is asked can be an important consideration in interpreting a response. A drawback to recording interviews is that respondents are often inhibited by a recorder, because it denies them the chance of claiming that they have not made some remark if it later proves embarrassing. Sometimes they fear that the recording can be edited to make it appear as if they had said things they have not. Moreover, the mechanics of working the recorder can distract from the interview.

Researchers must decide about the use of recorders on the basis of the type of question they are investigating, the nature of the interviews they expect, and the character of the respondents. If the subject matter is highly sensitive or respondents are likely to be inhibited by recorders, the drawbacks of using them probably outweigh the advantages. If lengthy, detailed, and technical interviews are necessary and specific facts are crucial to the study, recorders may be necessary.

If a recorder is used, the researcher should ask permission to use it and should place the device in full view of the respondent. Pretest the recorder to ensure that it is suitable for the kind of interview anticipated (sufficiently sensitive, simple to operate, able to record long enough). *Never depend exclusively on a recorder.* It can malfunction and cause the loss of an irreplaceable interview. Always take written notes as well.

A final issue in elite interviewing is confidentiality. This can be more important with elite interviews than with surveys, because elites are often asked for information that, if revealed or misused, may have considerable public impact or personal consequences. If confidentiality is promised, and it generally must be, *researchers should make every reasonable effort to safeguard information.* This is often easier than in survey research, because large numbers of personnel are not generally required in elite studies, but interviewers can buy a little insurance by storing records in secure places and keeping the purpose of the study from becoming general knowledge, if possible. One threat to confidentiality occurs when a typist is used to type handwritten notes or transcribe recorded interviews. If researchers absolutely cannot do this work themselves, they should only employ dependable people to do it and conceal from the typist the identity of respondents when possible. Remember never to make interview records available to people not involved in the project.

RESEARCH EXERCISE

Preparing to Ask Interview Questions

This is a written exercise to practice preparing for conducting specialized interviews.

1. State three research questions that can be answered through elite interviewing. Try to think of diverse issues that relate to politics, culture, and the environment.
2. List the types of information needed in order to answer the questions, and identify either by name or by official position (for example, all members of Congress who support legislation to curb greenhouse gas emissions) the people you would expect to interview in gathering that information.
3. For each of the three topics, write at least one "grand tour question" and one "example question" (see guidelines 6 and 7 above) that could be used in the interview.
4. Discuss what steps you would take to ensure the validity of your conclusions. How would you check the accuracy of what respondents tell you?

SPECIALIZED INTERVIEWING

In some studies, political scientists do not want to obtain information from specific individuals, as in the case of elite interviewing, or from respondents who are representative of the general population, as in surveys, but need information from persons who are *representative or typical of some particular group.* This often calls for **specialized interviewing**.

A specialized interview is any interview in which the characteristics of respondents demand procedures different from those employed in standardized survey interviewing. Interviews with children, illiterate adults, prison inmates, homeless persons, non-English-speaking migrant workers, mental patients, and members of a religious cult are all examples.

Specialized versus Survey Interviewing

Specialized interviewing is called for when researchers cannot assume that they and their respondents share a *common vocabulary.* Words that researchers use frequently may not be understood by respondents. Similarly, respondents may use terms or slang with which the researcher is not familiar or may use conventional words in special ways the researcher does not understand. A second distinctive feature of specialized interviews is that interviewers often cannot assume that respondents can read or have the ability to follow a line of argument that would be expected of an average person in the culture. In addition, specialized interview situations often involve distinctive relationships between respondents and interviewers. Whereas ordinary respondents regard interviewers largely as equals who can be trusted to a degree and treated cordially, specialized subjects may view interviewers as authority figures or "outsiders" and may be hostile and suspicious. In these circumstances, communication can be difficult and the validity of responses can suffer.

All of these features of specialized interviews combine to create settings in which researchers cannot take communication for granted. Rather, interviewers have to carefully establish a basis for communication and then check to be sure that communication is occurring.

An Example

If we want to know the degree to which children consider the U.S. political system legitimate, we first need to define the concept of legitimacy and be sure that our young respondents know what we mean when we speak of the political system. Once we have verified their grasp of these concepts and have asked our central questions, we need to ask additional questions to determine whether the children's answers mean to them what we would expect the same answers to mean if they came from typical adults. One way to do this is first to give our child respondents examples of children acting in ways that suggest they accord either a high or a low level of legitimacy to some institution, then to ask our respondents to interpret the actions described as showing either high or low levels of respect for the political system, and then to tell us whether or not they would be likely to take these same actions. If children frequently misinterpret the fictitious actions or say they would take actions that are inconsistent with the level of legitimacy they have told us they accord the political system, we will not feel safe in assuming that they understand our questions or their answers in the same way we do.

PRACTICAL RESEARCH ETHICS

Can you obtain informed consent when you cannot guarantee anonymity?

As in other types of research, in elite interviews you are obligated to explain to the participants the nature, the risks (if any), and the purpose of the research project. In addition, you should be absolutely sure that the interview will not cause physical or emotional harm to your subjects. Ask yourself whether the information you collected might have any negative consequences for the interviewee—for example, getting fired for divulging "privileged" information or getting arrested for speaking out in a nation that does not support the idea of free speech.

The interviewees also should be aware that their participation is voluntary and that they can refuse to answer your questions. They should also know how the information gathered during the interviews will be used (for example, will it be used in an internal report only, or will it be published in an academic journal?).

Although research studies usually are conducted under the assumption that the findings are anonymous, elite interviews often cannot guarantee anonymity. In interviews with high-level officials, for example, it might be difficult to hide their true identity simply because they are the only (or most likely) person responsible for a particular aspect of your research. However, if it is possible to ensure anonymity, you should explain to the participants how you will keep what is being said during the interviews confidential and anonymous—such a pledge will make it easier for your participants to be frank and open with you.

When reporting your findings, it is important to represent accurately what you observed or were told in the interview. Be sure to avoid personal biases and opinions that might influence the way your research findings are explained.

Finally, if your interviews are conducted in order to be used in institutional research (particularly if you are a student or a faculty member), your research has to be approved by the ethics review board of your university to ensure that you are not violating any of the above-mentioned ethical considerations. In most of these cases, you also need to ask the subjects to agree to participate in your study by signing a consent form, which must explain the purpose of the study and the way the gathered information will be handled (guarantee of anonymity, use of data, etc.).

Conclusion

Intensive interviewing techniques, like direct observation, offer access to information about the world that cannot be obtained through other methods. When properly conducted, these interviews can yield valuable insights leading to further research, help us more fully develop our theories of some phenomenon, and let us discover *why* things happened as they did to a greater degree than more "detached" methods can.

Like direct observation, however, they also place special demands on the abilities and discipline of the researcher(s). They should never be the only approach used in answering a research question because you cannot be assured of access to the right people or of being able to validate the information you collect in this way in advance of actually doing the study. It is also important to be especially diligent in planning and training for your interviews, and careful to enlist the help of others in verifying your interpretations of the discussions. In addition, the information produced

by intensive interviewing methods is almost never quantitative and must be analyzed with techniques other than standard statistical analyses.

To ensure the validity of the conclusions drawn from elite and specialized interviewing you need to cross-check the researcher's reasoning and reporting of observations. This will be necessary in judging accurately the degree to which bias might have been introduced into the findings by the unique challenges of intensive interviewing.

Intensive interviews can be an enormously rich source of data for social scientists, but they require the development of almost artistic skills to be used effectively. Intensive interviewing of "special" respondents, who are unlikely to respond to questions the same way as "average" citizens, requires great sensitivity and in-depth knowledge of the circumstances of the respondents. In developing this skill, no amount of reading about in-depth interviews can substitute for experience with them.

Key Terms

intensive interviewing *365*
elite interviewing *366*
scheduled interviews *366*
unscheduled interviews *366*

grand tour questions *370*
example questions *370*
native language questions *370*
prompts *371*

Nadel technique *371*
specialized interviewing *373*

Research Examples

Although studies based on elite interviews are not common in political science journals, they can provide fascinating insights—especially when comparing the attitudes of elites with those of ordinary citizens. Albright (2008), for example, uses elite interviews to explore electoral strategies adopted by party leaders in Spain. Tallberg and Johansson (2008) employ elite interviews to examine the extent to which party politics influences European Council decision outcomes. Elite interviews can also be used together with other methodologies to generate more varied data. Lago

(2008), for example, conducts elite interviews and analyzes secondary survey data in Spain to explore the formation of electoral expectations in proportional representation political systems.

Methodological Readings

Two texts that explain intensive interviewing in detail are *Interviews: An Introduction to Qualitative Research Interviewing* (Kvale 2007) and *Qualitative Research Interviewing: Biographic Narrative and Semi-Structured Methods* (Wengraf

2001). For an examination of the role of interviewing in the larger context of qualitative methodologies, see *Analyzing Social Settings: A Guide to Qualitative Observation and Analysis* (Lofland et al. 2005).

References

Albright, Jeremy J. 2008. "Partisans or Independents? Evidence for Campaign Targets from Elite Interviews in Spain." *Electoral Studies* 27(December): 711–722.

Kvale, Steinar. 2007. *Interviews: An Introduction to Qualitative Research Interviewing*, 2nd ed. Thousand Oaks, CA: Sage.

Lago, Ignacio. 2008. "Rational Expectations or Heuristics?" *Party Politics* 14(1): 31–49.

Leech, Beth L. 2002. "Asking Questions: Techniques for Semistructured Interviews." *PS: Political Science & Politics* 35(December): 665–668.

Lofland, John, David A. Snow, Leon Anderson, and Lyn H. Lofland. 2005. *Analyzing Social Settings: A Guide to Qualitative Observation and Analysis*, 4th ed. Belmont, CA: Wadsworth.

Nadel, S. F. 1939. "The Interview Technique in Social Anthropology," in F. C. Bartlett, M. Ginsberg, E. J. Lindgren, and R. H. Thouless, eds. *The Study of Society* (pp. 317–327). London: Kegan Paul, Trench, Trubner & Co.

Spradley, James P. 1979. *The Ethnographic Interview*. New York: Holt, Rinehart and Winston.

Tallberg, Jonas, and Karl Magnus Johansson. 2008. "Party Politics in the European Council." *Journal of European Public Policy* 15(December): 1222–1242.

Wengraf, Tom. 2001. *Qualitative Research Interviewing: Biographic Narrative and Semi-Structured Methods*. Thousand Oaks, CA: Sage.

CHAPTER 22

The Research Report: Diagramming a Sample Article

In this chapter you will learn:

- How to plan your research report.
- The main components of a research report.

If the purpose of science is to discover or understand the world we live in, then the purpose of scientific writing must be to communicate our discoveries or understandings to others in as effective a manner as possible. Just as science, or social science, itself must be explicit, systematic, and controlled, the descriptions and assessments of scientific findings must be clear, complete, and—most especially—well organized. Because it often constitutes the first statement of discovery, and because it provides a primary means for developing a shared understanding, the research report is one of the most important, and potentially most effective, instruments of scientific communication.

Good research reports do not simply emerge, unassisted, from good research. Rather, the writing of a solid report requires every bit as much craftsmanship, and every bit as much practice, as any other stage of the research process. It requires the same planning, careful organization, clarity of thought and expression, and attention to detail that have been exercised all along the way. Although it is true that good research eases the writing of a good research report, it is equally true that a poorly written report can obscure the value of even the best research effort. After all, the research report is the *only* means we have to tell others of our work, and, conversely, it is the *only* means by which others can learn what we have accomplished. If we fail to communicate fully and effectively, the value of our research itself is greatly lessened.

In general, considerations of style, organization, proper grammar and usage, and other elements of effective writing lie well beyond the scope of this book. There are, however, a number of practical concerns that have a particular bearing on the writing of the research report and that do deserve some comment. In this chapter we examine several of these very briefly and present an annotated example of research reporting to help illustrate applications. Although the chapter itself is oriented toward writing a research report, the points presented also provide a basis for the *critical reading* of research reports prepared by others.

THE PLAN

Planning a research report should begin at the earliest stages of the research process. Recall that the six steps of the research process are: (1) the selection of a topic, (2) the systematic examination of related literature, (3) the formulation of a theory and hypotheses, (4) the determination of what type of evidence is required and (5) how it is to be obtained, and (6) the decision about how the resulting data are to be analyzed. Each of these actions contributes in an important way to the writing of the research report, and each should be undertaken with that fact in mind. Indeed, one of the greatest dangers the beginning researcher can confront is the tendency to compartmentalize the work, to treat each stage in the research process as if it were virtually independent of every other stage. In point of fact, the reverse is true. No stage of research, from problem formulation to the reporting of results, stands alone. Not only is each stage dependent on every other stage, but each must also be carried out with the others in mind. We may speak of six stages of the research process, but we speak of only one unified *process*.

Nowhere is this interdependence of parts clearer than in the writing of a research report, for it is in that report that we must join the pieces of our work together. We must precisely state our concepts and definitions; demonstrate the linkage between concept and research; describe, summarize, and evaluate our procedures and results; and assess our findings as they relate back to our concepts. In reality, then, the planning of a research report is inseparable from the planning of the research itself, and the writing of a report is inseparable from the conduct of our inquiry.

THE STRUCTURE

Because different subjects and different approaches to research can give rise to many different forms of research report, it is neither possible nor desirable to set forth hard-and-fast rules for the structure of these communications. We can, however, suggest the basic elements that should be present in any such report and point out the most commonly accepted way of organizing them. Those elements are (1) the introduction, (2) the literature review, (3) the statement of research methods, (4) the statement of findings, and (5) the conclusion.

The Introduction

The introduction to a research report should state clearly the theme or purpose of the research, the principal hypotheses (work that is primarily descriptive may not include hypotheses), and the rationale underlying both conducting the research and writing the report. In general, the purpose of the introduction is to set forth the *goals* of the work, to defend them, and to put them into what the author regards as the proper perspective.

It is at this point, too, that we alert readers to what we see as the major significance (the main contribution) of the research being reported. Only if the purpose of the work is stated clearly at the outset can readers judge the relevance to the central point of each argument or piece of data analysis presented. Surprise endings may be appropriate for short stories, but in a research report they only create extra work and confusion for readers.

PRACTICAL RESEARCH ETHICS

Writing the research report: Too late for ethics?

The research project culminates in writing your research report. Likewise, the ethical challenges discussed throughout this book come together as you write and submit your research to your professor or for publication.

Asking yourself a series of questions may help you maintain a high ethical standard. Have you carefully paraphrased and fully documented others' work in your citations? Have you clearly explained your research design, data gathering, and coding procedures so others may replicate your work, based solely upon your research report? Have you utilized the proper analytic tools, given the characteristics of your qualitative or quantitative data? Have you impartially explicated your research findings and limitations, as well as the broader implications of your work?

The Literature Review

The literature review in a research report is closely linked to, and builds upon, the introduction. A review of the relevant literature should cite and describe the research and the theories of those who have worked on related problems in the past. Our new theory may challenge or discount the existing literature, but we need to specifically identify (1) what we are improving upon in the current research, and (2) why our work constitutes an improvement.

In sum, the literature review places our research into a broader context within the discipline, substantiates the importance of your original research, and establishes the plausibility of your theory. How much attention others will pay to your research findings may be determined by the quality of the review of the literature: A literature review that precisely identifies the body of literature within political science to which you are contributing allows others to more easily incorporate your findings into later research. The literature review establishes the distinct contribution that your research will make to the existing body of research. Since no research stands completely on its own authority, reviewing the literature related to your research initially establishes the plausibility of your theory.

The Methods

The methods section should answer several questions. What was the source of data for the research? How were data gathered? Was there a sample? How was it selected? How many cases were included? How were the principal variables operationalized? Did the study encounter any special problems or develop any special instruments (for example, a new scale for measuring a particular attitude or behavior) worthy of note? The object here is to make a complete and precise statement of the steps taken in performing the research. As we pointed out in the introductory chapters, one important benefit of science as a way of knowing is that the findings of science are replicable—that the scientific method provides a way for sharing and evaluating both knowledge and the way to knowledge. Only by stating explicitly what we have done during the undertaking of our research can the results of our work be judged fully and critically by others. *The statement of the method of our study is the component of the research report that contributes most directly to such sharing.* For that reason, it must be written with honesty, thoroughness, care, and precision.

The Findings

The presentation of findings may include tables, graphs, or charts that help to summarize the results of our work, together with statistical or other analyses that prove germane. Researchers may be tempted at this point in their writing to include every shred of evidence and every table or chart that they examined when analyzing the data. The result is often a presentation that overwhelms the reader with unedited facts, some of which may be only marginally useful. It amounts to something of a *laissez-faire* approach to writing: Here are the facts—decipher them however you wish. Remember that no one is better positioned than you to identify and assess the meaning of your research results. Indeed, it is an obligation of the researcher to present in as clear a manner as possible only those results that speak most pointedly to the issues at hand.

Two suggestions, one general and one more specific, may offer some guidance here. First, the presentation of findings should be organized so as to illustrate the principal variables, hypotheses, or arguments set forth in the introduction to the report. Results not relating directly and importantly to these foci should not be included. By keeping this in mind, the researcher not only can eliminate a great deal of trivia from the report but also can present those findings that are included in a logical and meaningful manner. Second, it is a general rule of thumb that any table, chart, or graph included in a research report should be accompanied by at least two paragraphs of text in which the points are illustrated and their significance discussed. If the researcher cannot generate enough points of discussion to fill two paragraphs, it is quite likely that the particular table, chart, or graph in question is not sufficiently important to warrant inclusion in the report.

We also should emphasize that the researcher should not be reluctant to report either unexpected results or "nonfindings." The fact that a hypothesis is not supported by one's data may be just as important and scientifically interesting as the fact that it is. Thus, the criterion for including or excluding a piece of evidence in writing a research report is not whether or not it shows what was predicted, but, rather, whether what it shows is of any importance or interest.

The Conclusion

Finally, a research report generally concludes with a summary of findings, a discussion of the relationships between those findings and the theory in which the research was grounded, and, in some cases, an evaluation of the method of the study. Have we found anything of significance? If so, why is it significant, and what does it tell us? If not, why not? Were our hypotheses simply incorrect, or did we make some error or encounter some problem in designing or carrying out our research that prevented us from finding supporting evidence? Where do we go from here? This section of the report is, in effect, retrospective toward both the research paper and the research process. It presents the researcher with an opportunity to place the work in proper perspective between past and future scientific effort.

The placement of these several elements can vary somewhat depending on the development of a particular research report, but all or most will usually be present. In fact, these components can serve as an outline or organizing basis for most research reports, and the beginning researcher should take some care to see that each component is represented where appropriate and also that the relationship among them in the body of the report is both straightforward and logical.

Reading Research Reports

When reading research papers, it is useful to have a technique to summarize and critique the work.

1. Locate a scholarly political science article published in the last three months.
2. After reading the article, briefly summarize:
    a. The research question or theory
    b. The data or literature evidence used to evaluate part "a"
    c. The findings
3. Briefly critique the article:
    a. What are the two or three weaknesses?
    b. How would you address each weakness?

THE STYLE

Research reports are not written like novels or blogs. Unlike those writing for others' recreation, scientists often must communicate very complex technical information to a specialized audience in a relatively small space. Still, scientific writing should not be stodgy or overburdened with jargon. Our goal is to produce a report that balances readability with precision, and clarity with thoroughness. The following guidelines should help you to achieve these goals:

1. Work from an *outline*. Be sure the logic of your writing is clear to the reader.
2. Use words and phrases with which you are comfortable. Do not use big words just because they sound impressive. Use the word that most precisely defines your term.
3. Reread, revise, and rewrite. Reading your work aloud to see if it sounds right can help to identify and smooth out obvious rough spots. First drafts are *never* final drafts.
4. Seek others' opinions when possible. Have "new eyes" view your work; ask a roommate, friend, or colleague to read a draft of the report. She or he can alert you to errors that countless readings on your own will not reveal. Others' unfamiliarity with your field or methods is no hindrance to their proofreading; it may, in fact, be an asset. The best research is easily interpretable by an intelligent layperson.
5. Be sure to differentiate between observations and opinion; research reports rarely rest on one's own opinion (see the next point).
6. Fully document all of the research or popular work you reference in conducting your research and writing your report.

Continuing with the final point, clear citation of others' work is essential to the academic enterprise. Documentation is ethically required as it keeps us intellectually honest by preventing the fabrication of convenient evidence. It also provides a basis on which others can judge the validity of our arguments. By drawing evidence from dependable sources and/or relying on the opinions of informed authorities in reaching our own conclusions, the persuasiveness of our argument is increased.

Citations must be used *whenever* we borrow facts or ideas from another author. We must document references not only for direct quotations, but for *any* data or ideas we draw from the work of others. Information on the form and placement of citations and construction of a bibliography is best obtained from a style manual, several of which are listed at the end of this chapter. Alternatively, we might adopt the citation style of a major journal, such as the *American Political Science Review* or the *Journal of Politics*. Consistent form and complete information are the keys to documenting a research report correctly.

THE TITLE AND ABSTRACT

The title of a research report should be descriptive and complete, but it should not be overly detailed. It should give readers a good idea of what the report discusses, but not so good an idea that one need not read the paper. Compare, for example, the following alternative titles for the same research:

1. *Politics on the Day That Hell Freezes Over*
2. *Control over the Distribution of Scarce Resources at Such Time as the Temperature of Certain Regions Remains below 0° Celsius throughout the Month of July, as Measured on a Mercury Thermometer and through the Use of Pretested Survey Instruments, Including Guttman Scales, on a Small Population of Residents of Minot, North Dakota: An Experiment*
3. *The Effects of Climate on the Distribution of Political Resources*

Title 1 is short and to the point but not sufficiently descriptive to give the reader much idea of the article's content. Title 2 is so comprehensive as to be unwieldy. Only title 3 conveys the content of the report without undue attention to detail. The point is that the title should tell the reader the general topic of the report, but should not itself substitute for the sections of the report that deal with methods and findings.

Often, we find it useful to follow the title page of a report with an **abstract**, a brief statement, usually not more than 150 words and often no more than one or two sentences, in which we briefly summarize the contents of our report. The summary usually includes, in barest outline, a statement of what we have found, how we found it, and why it is important. Consider the following example:

ABSTRACT: THE EFFECTS OF CLIMATE ON THE DISTRIBUTION OF POLITICAL RESOURCES

Using both temperature and survey data from a study of Minot, North Dakota, the author concludes that resource allocations vary systematically with changes in the weather. More particularly, the data suggest that the poor are more adequately cared for and the downtrodden raised higher on the proverbial cold day in July than at other times. This finding offers considerable support for the hypotheses of Marx, Weber, and others.

By giving readers a concise summary of the accompanying report, the abstract tells one whether the material is likely to be of sufficient interest to warrant a close reading and thereby obviates the need for an extended title.

Conclusion

One final question about research reports that often arises is that of length. How long should a report be? There is no simple answer to this question. Most journals in political science prefer manuscripts of some twenty-five to thirty pages typed and double-spaced. A master's thesis may run to 100 or 150 pages, and a doctoral dissertation may take up to several hundred. Student research reports may run anywhere from ten to fifty pages, though fifteen to twenty is probably more common.

It is important to remember that the scope of your research project determines the report's length. Thus, if your outline threatens to exceed the paper's page limit, then you need to constrain your research more. Similarly, if from the outset you struggle to fill the outline, you may need to expand your research focus. Therefore, the material itself determines the length of the report. The argument should be adequately developed and the appropriate literature adequately reviewed. The method of the study should be fully expounded, and the results fully but judiciously reported. The conclusions should be both well developed and properly supported. Yet the length of each portion will vary from one report to the next. How long, then, should a research report be? As long as it needs to be to cover the subject, but succinct enough to maintain interest.

A CASE IN POINT

The remainder of this chapter is devoted to an annotated example of a research report. The example illustrates most of the elements we have described, and it should suggest to you the ways in which these components can be combined to produce an informative research report. The source of this report is Craig Leonard Brians and Steven Greene, "Elections: Voter Support and Partisans' (Mis)Perceptions of Presidential Candidates' Abortion Views in 2000," *Presidential Studies Quarterly*, 34(2004), pp. 412–419; reprinted by permission of the publisher.

Elections: Voter Support and Partisans' (Mis)Perceptions of Presidential Candidates' Abortion Views in 2000*

Title

CRAIG LEONARD BRIANS
STEVEN GREENE

Although the 2000 Republican and Democratic national party platforms show the parties at opposite poles on abortion policy, Governor George W. Bush publicly supported a vaguely defined "culture of life," rather than the constitutional amendment barring abortion that was advocated by his party. In light of Bush's campaign strategy, this article uses national

Abstract

---

* Authors' Note: The data used in this article were made available by the Inter-University Consortium for Political and Social Research. Neither the collector of the original data nor the consortium bears any responsibility for the analyses or interpretations presented here.

survey data to examine the accuracy of citizens' knowledge of the candidates' abortion pol-icy positions. Interestingly, pro-choice Republican voters were much less likely to defect from their party in 2000 than in 1996, suggesting that the Bush campaign's efforts to avoid public opposition to his abortion position were successful.

Introduction

Statement of research assertion

In August of 2000, a self-avowed fundamentalist Christian who had publicly pledged to "do everything in my power to restrict abortion" earned the Republican presidential nomination in Philadelphia.[1] In an apparent attempt to diffuse this controversial issue, throughout the nomination and presidential campaign Governor George W. Bush ob-scured his abortion views and avoided discussing the topic. His official position is that abortion should be outlawed except in cases of rape, incest, or to save the life of the mother.

Source citation

In a debate with Senator John McCain on *Larry King Live*, Governor Bush simulta-neously maintained that he completely endorsed and agreed with the Republican Party platform (which calls for a constitutional amendment barring all abortions) and he sup-ported the above-noted exceptions. Senator McCain apparently found it so frustrating to attempt to force Governor Bush to clarify these mutually exclusive positions that he even-tually quit discussing abortion (*Larry King Live* 2000).

The Bush campaign's efforts to obscure the candidate's abortion position reached their height during the first presidential debate when Bush refused to verify his previously stated plan to try to overturn the FDA's approval of the RU-486 abortion drug, saying he was only interested in doing whatever would protect women's health. He then linked his position on abortion to promoting a "culture of life," saying that while "abortions ought to be more rare in America," this culture would also lead to fighting laws that "allow doctors to take the lives of our seniors" and change the culture to discourage "youngsters who feel like they can take a neighbor's life with a gun" (Commission on Presidential Debates 2000). It would be difficult to find anyone who actively favors more abortions and more killing of older people and neighbors by teenagers. In the same debate, Vice President Al Gore clearly stated his support for a woman's right to choose abortion and RU-486, al-though he said he did not favor late-term or partial birth abortions (Commission on Presidential Debates 2000).

Importance of topic

Citation to relevant outside data

Explanatory footnote

During the campaign, disguising the Republican Party's long-standing strong oppo-sition to legal abortions could have advantaged Bush in several ways. First, only a small minority of Americans shares the Republican Party's official position—only 17 percent in the most recent Gallup poll (Gallup Organization and *USA Today* 2003). Publicly support-ing an unpopular policy is not likely to increase one's broad-based general election sup-port.[2] Second, even within the Republican Party, the abortion issue has generated tremendous conflict. The last several conventions have been characterized by a certain amount of rancor over abortion, although these disagreements are most visible when the platform is written before the convention. Third, Bush's campaign may have been trying to avoid having an abortion controversy attach itself to the candidate and increase the at-tention paid to this issue by voters.

---

[1] Quoted in the October 22, 1994, *Dallas Morning News.*
[2] Although Al Gore's issue positions were closer to more voters, the vice president often seemed unable to com-municate his shared ideas with voters during this campaign, leading to a widespread lack of accurate issue knowledge about the candidates in 2000 (Waldman and Jamieson 2003).

It seems reasonably clear that Bush attempted to obscure his abortion position to broaden his appeal to pro-choice voters, but on an issue as salient as abortion, how effective was this strategy? Was it, in fact, any more effective at preventing defection of pro-choice Republicans than Gore's clear statement of his abortion position was effective at preventing defection of pro-life Democrats? Because there are a roughly equal number of pro-life Democrats and pro-choice Republicans (Greene and Brians 2001), the most effective test may be to determine how many of each party's adherents defected in presidential voting. This comparison is facilitated by the fact that there are only small differences in the issue importance between those in the minority in either party—that is, pro-life Democrats or pro-choice Republicans (Greene and Brians 2001).

Those holding minority abortion policy views in a given political party may not defect and vote for the candidate closer to their view because the voters may not see the issue as that important, they may choose to ignore their party's and candidate's views on the issue, or they may not realize they do not hold the dominant view in the party. While candidates' actions and statements may facilitate each of these possibilities by making their issue position less obvious, voters who attribute their own position to their favored candidate—or at least "move" their favored candidate's attitudes closer to their own position—find it easier to vote for that candidate (Wilson and Gronke 2000; Krosnick 1990; Martinez 1988). The tendency of some voters to project policy positions onto candidates to rationalize their vote choice was empirically identified in the 1948 presidential election (Berelson, Lazarsfeld, and McPhee 1954, 219–223), the 1968 election (Brody and Page 1972; Page and Brody 1972), and the 1980 election (Wattenberg 1991, 111–116).[3]

Quantitatively testing an apparent campaign strategy, such as the obfuscation of an abortion policy position, poses serious challenges, because one cannot know what other outcomes might have occurred in the absence of the strategy. On the one hand, Governor Bush would seem to be successful if he did not do worse than Vice President Gore at preventing defections by abortion opinion minorities in his party through projection. On the other hand, an identical outcome could suggest that Gore was more successful, because he achieved no worse defections without obfuscating his abortion position. Alternatively, if abortion has been a more contentious issue for Republicans, Bush simply holding his defections equal to Gore's may connote success. Ultimately, it is not possible to know for certain what voters would have done if Bush had more clearly stated his abortion stance. Still, it would be instructive to compare the 2000 election data to 1996, when the Democratic nominee held Gore's position, but the Republican presidential nominee had been identified as open to a pro-choice position. This was particularly highlighted when Senator Bob Dole chose pro-choice New York Representative Susan Molinari to be the 1996 Republican National Convention keynote speaker, and proposed including language that tolerated alternative points of view on abortion in the party platform. Thus, to gain perspective, at several points in the analysis, 2000 data will be compared and contrasted with the 1996 results.

Margin notes:
- Statement of research question
- Rationale underlying approach to research
- Review of literature
- Assessment of strengths and weakness of the design
- Use of a control

---

[3] While Reagan benefited from rationalizations that citizens used to vote against Carter in 1980, voters seemed more comfortable acknowledging their policy differences with Reagan in 1984 while still supporting him at the polls (Wattenberg 1991, 116).

Method of
study

Secondary
analysis of
data

Identification
of the (inde-
pendent and
dependent)
variables

Discussion of
question
wording

Coding
procedure

Footnote
specifying the
coding
rationale

Restatement
of research
purpose and
cases and
time periods

Presentation
of the results

Discussion of
the graphic
presentation

Data

We primarily use data from the 2000 National Election Studies (NES), as well as the 1996 NES, in order to assess the role that abortion played in the 2000 campaign. Our analyses rely principally on several key variables: respondent's position on abortion, respondent's placement of the presidential candidates on abortion, respondent's partisanship, and re- spondent's two-party vote choice. The analyses are conducted by placing respondents into four groups based upon their partisanship and abortion position: pro-choice Democrats, pro-life Democrats, pro-choice Republicans, and pro-life Republicans.

The standard NES abortion question ranges from 1 to 4, with 1 being "abortion should never be permitted," 2 stating that "abortion should be permitted in case of rape, incest, and threat to mother's life," 3 indicating that "only after the need for the abortion has clearly been established," and 4 holding that "by law, a woman should always be able to obtain an abortion as a matter of personal choice." Respondents place themselves, as well as each candidate, on this scale. In order to categorize our respondents, we place those who indicated that their own position was 1 or 2 as pro-life and those indicating 4 as pro-choice. Unfortunately, the "clear need" category proves so problematic that we choose not to group respondents based upon this belief.[4] As for the partisanship basis of our group categorizations, because we are interested in how the supporters of each party stand on abortion, leaners may reasonably be grouped with self-identified party support- ers (Greene 2000). We use these four categories to analyze respondent vote choice and re- spondent placement of candidates' abortion position in both 1996 and 2000.

Data Analysis

Our analyses examine general voting patterns depending upon abortion attitudes and partisanship and evaluate more specific tests of the possibility that voters projected their own attitudes onto candidates. Although our main focus is the 2000 election, we include 1996 data as well, to provide a relative baseline for the 2000 candidates' performance. The primary goal of these analyses is to determine which candidate benefited most from his campaign's approach to abortion policy: whether it was Gore's more plainly stated position, or Bush's less clear abortion position. The secondary and related goal is to as- sess the relative impact of projection for the candidacies of Bush and Gore.

The initial examination of projection on the abortion issue indicates similar levels of misperception about both candidates by both Republicans and Democrats, regardless of abortion attitude. In Figure 1, we see that as Democrats become more liberal on abortion, the distance they see between Bush and Gore on the issue increases dramatically. Likewise, as Republicans become more conservative on abortion, the distance between Gore and Bush increases in a similarly pronounced fashion. In general, as respondents move in the direction of their party's core position, they are not only more in line with their party's candidate on the abortion issue but are more distant from the opposition party candidate as well. These figures thus further demonstrate the potentially important role for projection of abortion positions to play in voter decision making.

---

[4] When exploring how people with this attitude characterize "supporters of abortion" and "opponents of abor- tion" on the 1990 NES feeling thermometer measures, the mean values are close—45 and 55, respectively (on a 0 to 100 scale)—and the distribution of scores has large numbers at the extreme ends of both measures. This group seems to contain persons holding a range of moderate and situational abortion views, making it impossi- ble to accurately place them into either a pro-life or pro-choice category.

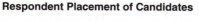

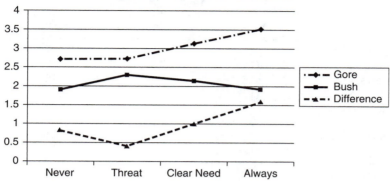

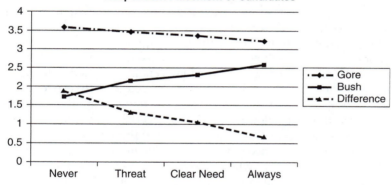

FIGURE 1 Presidential Candidates' Abortion Position as Rated by Voters Depending upon Citizen Abortion Position

Graphic presentation

Source: 2000 National Election Study.

Note: The *X*-axis represents respondents' positions on when abortion should be legal, and the *Y*-axis tracks respondents' perceptions of each candidate's abortion view. On the *X*-axis, *never* means "by law, abortion should never be permitted," *threat* indicates that "the law should permit abortion only in case of rape, incest, or when the woman's life is in danger," *clear need* means that "abortion should be permitted only after the need for the abortion has clearly been established," and *always* indicates that "by law, a woman should always be able to obtain an abortion as a matter of personal choice."

Comparing the two-party vote with partisans' abortion stances, it is apparent that Bush held the Republican Party together much better in 2000 than did Dole in 1996. Table 1 presents the percentage of voters in each of our four categories (pro-life Democrat, pro-choice Democrat, pro-life Republican, pro-choice Republican) who voted for each of the major party candidates in 1996 and 2000. This cross-tabulation of the two-party vote by a four-level combined measure of abortion stance and partisanship demonstrates that the GOP lost substantially more pro-choice Republican votes (29 versus 18 percent) in 1996 as opposed to 2000, and even saw 8 percent of the pro-life Republicans defect in 1996. On the other hand,

Discussion of the table

TABLE 1 Vote Percent by Partisanship and Abortion Attitude in 1996 and 2000

	1996		2000	
	Dole	Clinton	Bush	Gore
Pro-choice Democrats	5	95	7	93
	(15)	(266)	(22)	(273)
Pro-life Democrats	8	92	15	85
	(13)	(156)	(26)	(148)
Pro-choice Republicans	71	29	82	18
	(93)	(38)	(118)	(26)
Pro-life Republicans	92	8	96	4
	(217)	(18)	(226)	(10)

Source: 1996 and 2000 National Election Studies.

Note: The numbers in parentheses are cell frequencies.

Table even though Gore held onto pro-choice Democratic votes at a rate almost equal to Clinton (93 versus 95 percent), he lost 15 percent of pro-life Democrats, in contrast to only 8 percent for Clinton. Thus, even though the Democratic Party appeared to have an absolute advantage on the abortion issue in 2000, its position was weakened relative to 1996.

Discussion of the table Given the political salience and personal importance attached to the abortion issue, one might ask why there are not more defections in vote choice, especially among pro-life Democrats. Tables 2a and 2b present analyses demonstrating the high levels of projection taking place on the abortion issue. The projection on abortion is most evident in the pro-life Democrats' ratings of Gore and Clinton and pro-choice Republicans' ratings of Bush and Dole. One can clearly see that these groups are, in fact, dramatic outliers. Pro-life Democrats place Gore at 2.76, when objectively, his true position would have to be close to 4. Likewise, pro-choice Republicans place Bush at 2.70, when his actual position could objectively not be considered more than 2—which is almost exactly where the other groups placed him. The results follow a very similar pattern in 1996. The notable difference is that Bush is seen as more pro-choice, 2.70, by pro-choice Republicans, than is Dole, 2.46, who was actually the more liberal of the two on abortion. At least relative to Dole, Bush's strategy on abortion was clearly more effective.

Assessment of the correspondence between predictions based on theory and actual observations Additionally, Tables 2a and 2b provide strong evidence as to why the Democratic candidates are more effective at holding their party's minority abortion position voters. In both 1996 and 2000, pro-life Democrats saw themselves as 1.12 away from the Democratic candidate. In contrast, Bush was seen as 1.43 away from pro-choice Republicans. In sum, the results in Tables 2a and 2b suggest that Democratic candidates benefit from projection on the abortion issue more than Republicans. Crucially, in 2000's razor-thin outcome, Bush was much more successful in keeping pro-choice Republicans loyal, clearly in part from a campaign that allowed very substantial projection of their own abortion issue position onto him.[5]

---

[5] In an analysis not reported here, we found that abortion is not the only issue where Governor Bush benefited from voter projection in 2000. More voters projected their government spending views onto Bush in 2000 than had done the same with Dole in 1996.

TABLE 2A   Projection of Abortion Attitudes on 2000 Presidential Candidates

	Pro-choice Democrat	Pro-life Democrat	Pro-choice Republican	Pro-life Republican
Abortion rating for Gore	3.56	2.76	3.34	3.54
Abortion rating for Bush	2.02	2.30	2.70	2.07
Respondent-Gore abortion distance	0.48	1.12	0.78	1.84
Respondent-Bush abortion distance	2.07	0.76	1.43	1.22

Source: 2000 National Election Study.

Note: Gore's and Bush's abortion positions were rated by respondents on a scale ranging from 1 to 4, with 1 barring all legal abortions and 4 leaving the choice entirely to the woman. Respondent-Gore and Respondent-Bush distance shows the relative distance between the respondent's own abortion placement and where he placed Bush and where he placed Gore. The lower this number, the closer the respondent's own abortion position is to the candidate's perceived position.

TABLE 2B   Projection of Abortion Attitudes on 1996 Presidential Candidates

	Pro-choice Democrat	Pro-life Democrat	Pro-choice Republican	Pro-life Republican
Abortion rating for Clinton	3.56	2.76	3.26	3.59
Abortion rating for Dole	1.99	2.26	2.45	2.12
Respondent-Clinton abortion distance	0.44	1.12	0.74	1.86
Respondent-Dole abortion distance	2.00	0.94	1.55	0.47

Source: 1996 National Election Study.

Note: Clinton's and Dole's abortion positions were rated by respondents on a 1 to 4 abortion scale, where 1 bars all legal abortions and 4 leaves the choice entirely to the woman.

Conclusion

Conclusion

This study indicates that campaigns may be able to influence voters' level of misinformation about candidates' issue positions. These preliminary results suggest that Governor Bush was more successful in obscuring his, and his party's, abortion policy position among voters in 2000, than was Senator Dole in 1996. Vice President Gore's more straightforward approach may have cost him some support, when compared to President Bill Clinton in 1996.

Implication of the research

The salience of abortion will most likely only increase in upcoming elections. With recent controversies over "partial-birth" abortion and anticipation already building over what are likely to be among the most contentious Supreme Court appointments ever made—largely due to concerns over the continued legality of abortion—the ability of presidential candidates to strategically campaign on the abortion issue and take advantage of voters'? predilections toward projection will become even more important. The Democrats seem to have an advantage on the issue, for the time being, but Bush's 2000 performance suggests that this advantage can be dramatically diminished.

Addressing possible ethical concerns with others' use of the findings

Some may be concerned by this article's findings and the potential for future manipulation of public opinion by campaigns. Clearly, the degree to which candidates will be able to increase voters' misperceptions of their issue stances in the 2004 presidential election largely depends upon the news media's attention to the campaign. The substantially greater care most campaigns have used in preparing and documenting their advertising following the intense press attention to ads in the 1988 campaign demonstrates that candidates can regulate their own behavior when they know that the watchdogs are on duty. Thus, it is reasonable to conclude that if the press closely watches the candidates in 2004, the projection seen among voters in 2000 is less likely to be repeated.

References

Bibliography

Berelson, Bernard, Paul F. Lazarsfeld, and William N. McPhee. 1954. *Voting: A Study of Opinion Formation in a Presidential Campaign*. Chicago: University of Chicago Press.

Brody, Richard A., and Benjamin I. Page. 1972. "Comment: The Assessment of Policy Voting." *American Political Science Review* 66(June): 450–458.

Commission on Presidential Debates. 2000. *General Election Presidential Debates, October 3*. University of Massachusetts, Boston. Available from www.debates.org/pages/trans2000a .html.

Gallup Organization and *USA Today*. 2003. October 24–26, 2003. *National Survey of 1006 Adults*. Storrs, CT: Roper Center at the University of Connecticut.

Greene, Steven. 2000. "The Psychological Sources of Partisan-leaning Independence." *American Politics Quarterly* 28(October): 511–537.

Greene, Steven, and Craig Leonard Brians. 2001. "Elite Versus Popular Views on Abortion within American Political Parties." Paper prepared for presentation at the Annual Meeting of the Midwest Political Science Association, April 19–22, Chicago.

Krosnick, Jon A. 1990. "Americans' Perceptions of Presidential Candidates: A Test of the Projection Hypothesis." *Journal of Social Issues* 46(Summer): 159–182.

Larry King Live. 2000. GOP Debate with Senator John McCain and Governor George W. Bush. *CNN*, February 15.

Martinez, Michael D. 1988. "Political Involvement and the Projection Process." *Political Behavior* 10(Spring): 151–167.

Page, Benjamin I., and Richard A. Brody. 1972. "Policy Voting and the Electoral Process: The Vietnam War Issue." *American Political Science Review* 66(September): 979–995.

Waldman, Paul, and Kathleen Hall Jamieson. 2003. "Rhetorical Convergence and Issue Knowledge in the 2000 Presidential Election." *Presidential Studies Quarterly* 33(March): 145–163.

Wattenberg, Martin P. 1991. *The Rise of Candidate-Centered Politics*. Cambridge, MA: Harvard University Press.

Wilson, J. Matthew, and Paul Gronke. 2000. "Concordance and Projection in Citizen Perceptions of Congressional Roll-Call Voting." *Legislative Studies Quarterly* 25(August): 445–467.

Key Term

abstract *382*

Research Examples

The best place to find sample research reports is in the journals of political science and related disciplines that are listed at the end of Chapter 3. Excerpts from articles that illustrate many of the principles of research discussed in this text are found in *The Political Research Experience: Readings and Analysis* (Ethridge 2002).

Methodological Readings

A book that addresses all facets of writing political analyses is *Writing in Political Science: A Practical Guide* (Schmidt 2005). For excellent suggestions on ways to improve your writing style, see Strunk and White's classic *The Elements of Style* (2000). *Bartlett's Roget's Thesaurus* (1996) can contribute much to the clarity and variety of your presentation and can, on occasion, offer direction for reducing your reliance on jargon. For guidance on the proper form and placement of footnotes and bibliography, consult *The Style Manual for Political Science* (American Political Science Association 2001). A revised version of the classic by Kate Turabian, *A Manual for Writers of Term Papers, Theses, and Dissertations* (2007), is now available.

Examples of the APSA reference and citation format are available at the author's Web site (www.psci.vt.edu/brians).

References

American Political Science Association. 2001. *The Style Manual for Political Science*, rev. ed. Washington, DC.: American Political Science Association.

Bartlett's. 1996. *Bartlett's Roget's Thesaurus*. Boston: Little Brown.

Ethridge, Marcus E. 2002. *The Political Research Experience: Readings and Analysis*, 3rd ed. Armonk, NY: M.E Sharpe.

Schmidt, Diane E. 2005. *Writing in Political Science: A Practical Guide*, 3rd ed. New York: Pearson Longman.

Strunk Jr., William, with E. B. White. 2000. *The Elements of Style*, 4th ed. Boston: Allyn & Bacon.

Turabian, Kate L. 2007. *A Manual for Writers of Research Papers, Theses, and Dissertations*, 7th ed. Revised by Wayne C. Booth, Gregory G. Colomb, Joseph M. Williams, and University of Chicago Press Staff. Chicago: University of Chicago Press.

CHAPTER 23

Summary: Overview of a Research Project

You now have the basic information you need to plan and execute a complete research project. In Figure 5.6 in Chapter 5 we provided an overview of the research process. We have explored the components of that process at length in the remainder of the text. In this closing chapter, we review the research process as an integrated whole. We stress the ways in which the steps you have seen separated by chapter boundaries are, in practice, interwoven and interdependent. Our purpose is to facilitate your attacking research questions with a full understanding of the research process rather than a disjointed focus on each stage as it is reached. The value of an integrated understanding, of course, is that *many research problems can be avoided if the researcher is aware of the implications of decisions made at one stage of a project for subsequent stages.*

DEVELOPING THEORIES, HYPOTHESES, AND A RESEARCH DESIGN

Research begins with a research question that asks why things are as we observe them to be. We are generally seeking an explanation for observed events. The place to start looking for this explanation is in the social science literature pertaining to our general subject. If we are fortunate, a literature search will turn up a ready-made explanation in the form of a theory that others have developed to explain events like the one that interests us. More often, however, we have to use the literature more creatively to *devise* the best theory possible, given existing information about the subject. The remainder of the research process is then devoted to testing this explanation to see how much it adds to our understanding of the events in question.

Stating Hypotheses

The first step in this testing is to state some hypotheses that logic tells us must be accurate if our proposed answer to the research question is valid. These hypotheses serve several key functions. In the first place, they identify the units of analysis that must be observed in order to assess our explanation. Second, they isolate the variables for which we must develop indicators. Finally, hypotheses suggest ways in which our observations must be organized in order to provide useful evidence of the validity of our explanation. In stating hypotheses we also need to consider two questions: Can we observe the stated relationship? Can we locate the necessary data, or do we have the resources required to

PRACTICAL RESEARCH ETHICS
How do private efforts produce a public result?

In every chapter, this book has promoted ethical research in each facet of research. For political scientists, ethical responsibilities cannot be overemphasized, because we conduct our research on people's behavior, for people. This charge carries with it a substantial responsibility to care for the subjects of our research throughout the process.

For example, whereas most of the standards in Figure 23.1 focus on technical considerations, the final standard explicitly focuses on ethics. Yet, all thirty-three research standards implicitly call for ethical behavior by researchers. The questions in Figure 23.1 and the professional guidelines in Appendix B should offer concrete means to answer the myriad of ethical issues that are raised in research, ranging from the necessity of protecting research subjects from harm, to presenting analyses that fairly represent the underlying data.

Never forget, it is immaterial whether anyone else ever realizes the lengths to which you have gone to conduct your research and your life ethically. As the aphorism states, your personal ethics are most accurately measured when you do not think anyone is watching you. As fellow political scientists, we hope that you ethically measure up.

collect them for ourselves? It is essential that we select hypotheses that can be adequately tested with the time, skills, and resources available to us. To do otherwise is to ensure failure.

Researching the Literature

As we build our theories and hypotheses, we need to consult the literature to learn what is already known about our topic(s), and how others have previously researched these relationships. However, the examination of the literature does not end when research starts. In Chapter 3 we offered a comprehensive system that can be used throughout the research project. Knowing the differences between scholarly and popular publications allows you to draw from the broadest possible range of literature, using different sources for different purposes.

Selecting a Research Design

The next step is the development of a research design to guide the application of our measuring procedures. The central purpose of a research design is to ensure that we can feel confident that any relationships observed are the result of the processes described in our explanation and not of some other set of processes. Research designs provide this confidence by allowing us to rule out alternative rival hypotheses. A good research design, then, begins with a review of the literature. That review (along with logical analysis of situations) can suggest the major alternative rival hypotheses that must be ruled out before we can place confidence in our central explanation of observed events.

Research designs are developed by (1) identifying the comparisons that must be made in order to test a hypothesis, (2) deciding what observations must be made (of whom or what, in what order, by what means, under what conditions) before those comparisons can be made, (3) anticipating all results that might be obtained from making the comparisons (no relationship, a positive relationship, a negative relationship, and so forth), (4) identifying the major alternative rival hypotheses that can explain each possible result, and (5) organizing a set of observations that will allow the additional comparisons necessary to test the validity of the most important of these alternative rival hypotheses as explanations of whatever results are observed.

Operationalizing Hypotheses

Next, the variables identified in the hypotheses must be operationalized so that we can obtain measures to compare in reaching a conclusion about the accuracy of our predictions. In selecting operationalizations or measurement procedures, we must be acutely sensitive to the resources required to apply them. If we do not have the necessary time, money, or cooperation of subjects, we cannot use the measuring procedure. In addition, it is necessary to ask whether we are altering the meaning of any of the concepts included in our explanation when we let the results of any given measuring procedure represent them in our research. Though validity can often be assessed in data analysis, the question of validity must be faced well in advance of data collection, for no amount of clever data analysis can make invalid measures useful.

Selecting Data Analysis

It is essential that we know what analyses to perform when developing a research design, for it is the design that determines what data will be available for analysis. For example, if we anticipate controlling for many variables in the data analysis stage, we must be certain that our research design will yield enough cases to allow for such a complex breakdown of the sample. If we want to hold party affiliation constant by examining measures of association between two key variables for members of each party separately, we must include enough members of each party for computation of valid measures of association and we must plan to obtain information on subjects' party affiliation. If we plan to use time-series analysis in a study employing aggregate data, we must be sure that data on values of our independent variable come from a period prior to the time at which data on the dependent variable are collected if we have theoretical reasons to believe that there is a lag in the impact of the IV on the DV.

In the design of research, as in the selection of hypotheses and the devising of measures, it is essential to ask whether we are setting ourselves too ambitious a task. The best research design in the world is useless if the researcher lacks the resources to execute it. We must give careful consideration to the costs and logistics of data collection in designing research projects.

DATA COLLECTION AND ANALYSIS

As we have presented the research process, data collection and analysis are carried out in order to test hypotheses. We have discussed the primary rules to be observed in using various methods of data collection and analysis and, in Chapter 2, described the process of reasoning from empirical results to theory, thereby completing the research circle. There is no need to repeat those discussions here. We would, however, like to make two final points about the research process.

Using Multiple Methods

The first point is that, although we have presented the various data collection techniques separately, they need not be kept separate in the research process. In fact, there are good reasons for *mixing* methods of data collection in a study. In the first place, different methods can serve different purposes. Researchers may, for example, use focus groups to determine the breadth and nature of people's concerns about a set of political issues, then use survey research to estimate the *distribution* of those same views among the general population. In addition, it is often useful to employ a variety of methods in the data collection stage of a study because of the added confidence *multiple methods of measurement* can give us in the validity of results, as discussed in Chapters 4, 5, and 11. For example, in studying variations in the quality of public services among a city's neighborhoods, one will find it useful to confirm assessments of service quality obtained from survey research by means of aggregate data, official records, interviews with public officials, and the judgments of trained observers. If all these methods of measurement produce a similar ranking of neighborhoods, researchers can feel quite confident that they have accurately measured service quality.

Exploring Your Topic

A second point is that empirical research can be exploratory in nature. Rather than using it to test hypotheses derived from explanations, we can use it to provide data for use in devising explanations in the first place. Each research project generally raises new questions, suggests new explanations, and leads to new research. Looking back at Figure 5.6, you will see a shortcut from *generalization of observed relationships to hypotheses* and back to *data analysis*. This shortcut is the result of applying inductive logic in data analysis. A feedback loop serves an important function in empirical inquiry, for it suggests new data analyses that allow researchers to refine and elaborate explanations in ways they did not anticipate when designing a project, or to test explanations they did not anticipate.

A CHECKLIST FOR JUDGING RESEARCH

In an evaluation of others' research or in the design of your own, it is often helpful to step back from the details of each stage and try to get an overview of the research, asking whether it meets certain general but clearly stated requirements of sound empirical inquiry. To facilitate doing this, we have provided, in Figure 23.1, a list of things to look for. The questions are listed in approximately the sequence in which you might expect to encounter different problems in a report of research or in the execution of a project. The rules suggested by these questions are broad, and a project that "checks out" on all these items may still contain subtle or highly technical errors. Nonetheless, if you can answer "yes" to each of the questions in the figure, the research being assessed is probably free of any error that this book has prepared you to identify and exhibits the basics of sound research.

Use the Checklist Carefully

In using the checklist, be aware of three cautions. First, not all questions will apply to any one research project. Exploratory research, for example, will not be designed to test hypotheses, and research based on elite interviews will probably not require a random

A CHECKLIST FOR EVALUATING EMPIRICAL RESEARCH

☐ 1. Is the research question clearly stated? Do we know what the objectives of the research are so that we can assess the overall project? Is the research clearly related to some larger political issue or problem? Is this an important subject to study?

☐ 2. Are the units of analysis clearly identified, correctly chosen, and consistently used throughout the project?

☐ 3. Are the concepts employed in the research clearly specified and adequately developed? Do the concepts have identifiable referents?

☐ 4. Is it clear what explanations are being tested? If a theory is used, is it logically correct? Do the concepts have identifiable empirical referents?

☐ 5. Is the theory or explanation consistent with existing literature on the subject? Is there evidence of a thorough literature review? Is the relationship of this research to prior research and larger political issues made clear?

☐ 6. Are hypotheses to be tested identified clearly and stated correctly? Do they logically follow from the explanation or theory being examined? Are they empirically testable?

☐ 7. If more than one hypothesis is being tested, are the relationships between them specified? Are all hypotheses clearly related to the theory, and their role in testing it made explicit?

☐ 8. Are the variables under investigation clearly identified and their status (independent, dependent, intervening, antecedent) specified in the hypotheses?

☐ 9. Are variables that might be expected to modify predicted relationships included in the study? (For example, can we expect relationships to hold for both men and women, or, in both industrialized and nonindustrialized nations?)

☐ 10. Are operationalizations of concepts stated clearly and measurement procedures specified in sufficient detail that others can replicate them? Have others used these operationalizations?

☐ 11. Are the measures likely to be valid and reliable? Are tests of validity and reliability anticipated? Are threats to validity and reliability recognized and provisions made to control them?

☐ 12. Is the research design clearly stated and appropriate for testing the hypotheses being examined? Are major alternative rival hypotheses recognized and provision made in the research design for examining these hypotheses as alternative explanations? Will the design provide a logically sound basis for causal inferences?

☐ 13. Is the population of interest to the researcher identified clearly? Is the sample used representative of that population? If not, does the researcher recognize the limitations this places on how results can be generalized? Are sampling procedures adequately described?

☐ 14. Is the data collection technique employed (survey research, content analysis, and so forth) appropriate to the study given its units of analysis and the type of information being sought? Are all procedural rules observed that pertain to the particular method of data collection?

☐ 15. Is the data collection fully described? Are outside primary data sources fully identified so others can locate them?

☐ 16. Are coding systems that might affect measurement (such as collapsing various income groups into broad categories or treating certain types of responses as supportive or nonsupportive) fully described and justified? (continued)

FIGURE 23.1 Checklist.

☐ 17. Is the construction of any indices or scales fully described? Do these summary measures preserve the meaning of the concepts? Do they seem to be unidimensional (to reflect a single underlying concept or pattern)?

☐ 18. Have instruments been pretested?

☐ 19. Have efforts been made to verify results? (For example, have follow-up calls been made to survey respondents, or have alternative sources of aggregate data been sought?)

☐ 20. In presenting the data, are the tables and figures appropriate for illustrating the point they are intended to make? Are they fully discussed in the text and their central significance pointed out? Do they represent the results accurately?

☐ 21. Are the tables and figures clearly and completely labeled so that they can be easily interpreted?

☐ 22. Are the interpretations of the tables and figures offered correct, or do they suggest a misreading of the data?

☐ 23. Are appropriate descriptive statistics (such as mean and standard deviation) used to summarize the data and supplement tables and figures?

☐ 24. In examining relationships between variables, do the researchers provide evidence of the strength, direction, form, and significance of relationships?

☐ 25. Do the researchers explore the possible effects of antecedent, intervening, and suppressor variables? Do they attempt to control these effects in the data analysis?

☐ 26. Are all statistics used appropriate for the level at which variables are measured, and are they suited to the purpose for which they are used?

☐ 27. Do the data conform to the assumptions (random sampling, normal distribution, and so forth) involved in legitimate application of the statistics used? Have the researchers investigated the degree to which their data fit these assumptions?

☐ 28. Are measures of statistical significance applied only where appropriate and correctly interpreted? Have the researchers avoided confusing statistical significance with substantive significance?

☐ 29. Are major alternative rival hypotheses statistically explored and the results both reported and correctly interpreted?

☐ 30. Is each piece of data analysis clearly related to the major conclusions drawn from the study? Are the interpretations consistent with the data and with the theory or explanation being tested?

☐ 31. Does the research report:
  a. contain a precise statement of the purpose of the study?
  b. review enough of the relevant literature to demonstrate the contribution of this study?
  c. adequately describe the research design, data, and methods used?
  d. follow a clear and appropriate organization in presenting findings?
  e. state conclusions clearly?

☐ 32. Are the conclusions reached actually warranted by the data presented and the research design used? Does the study make the kind of contribution to the literature the authors claim it does, or have the authors generalized too far beyond the limits of their research?

☐ 33. Have the authors been sensitive to ethical issues raised by the research? Have they satisfactorily resolved these issues?

FIGURE 23.1 (Continued)

sample. Second, the questions refer to technical rather than substantive aspects of research. A researcher may do everything correctly and still be investigating a trivial subject. *Valuable research is both technically correct and substantively important.* In judging research, ask whether its proper execution will add useful knowledge to our attempts to understand significant political events. Sometimes, lower levels of technical sophistication are justified by the complexity and magnitude of an important subject. On the whole, the project that adds a little to our knowledge of an important subject is more valuable than a project that adds a lot to our knowledge of a trivial matter. Third, few projects can be free of limitations. For instance, it may be impossible to obtain a representative sample of an entire large population within the resource limits of a given study. It may be necessary to sample only one subgroup (as when a study of American political behavior is conducted with a sample from one city only). Such limitations become errors only when the researcher fails to recognize them and modify accordingly the conclusions drawn from the study.

The checklist can be used to assess others' research as well as to evaluate your own. As a research exercise, you may want to locate an article reporting the results of a research project and evaluate it using the checklist in Figure 23.1, identifying any errors you may find and explaining why they are errors. We have presented the table in a way that makes it easy to photocopy for repeated use.

Conclusion

Armed only with the information contained in this book, you could successfully carry out a wide range of empirical investigations. You should recognize, however, that this text has just scratched the surface of the huge subject of empirical political research. The dozens of other books and articles listed in our suggestions for further reading in every chapter should convince you that there is much more to be said and much you cannot learn from this book.

In the process of research, you may discover the importance of the things you do *not* know. Even if you carefully and properly follow every guideline and rule presented in this text, you may find yourself either (1) unable to complete some research projects or (2) producing a set of research results that more experienced social scientists recognize as seriously flawed because you have made errors we did not warn you against. If you follow the suggestions presented in the first five chapters, you should make very few errors in

stating hypotheses, operationalizing concepts, searching the literature, or devising a research design. Our chapters on sampling and data management probably provide less complete guides, however, because those processes are both more technical and more closely tied to the situations encountered in individual research projects. Similarly, we have only been able to provide you a partial guide to the various data collection and data analysis techniques because of the scope and technical nature of these subjects; you are well advised to study them further before claiming expertise in empirical analysis. The research examples and methodological readings at the ends of chapters provide good *starting places* for acquiring genuine expertise.

We have provided a sound foundation on which you can build your competence as a political scientist. We hope you find that task as exciting and rewarding as we have and that in the future you will agree that getting there was half the fun.

APPENDIX A

Statistical Tables

TABLE A.1	Random Digits								
10097	32533	76520	13586	34673	54876	80959	09117	39292	74945
37542	04805	64894	74296	24805	24037	20636	10402	00822	91665
08422	68953	19645	09303	23209	02560	15953	34764	35080	33606
99019	02529	09376	70715	38311	31165	88676	74397	04436	27659
12807	99970	80157	36147	64032	36653	98951	16877	12171	76833
66065	74717	34072	76850	36697	36170	65813	39885	11199	29170
31060	10805	45571	82406	35303	42614	86799	07439	23403	09732
85269	77602	02051	65692	68665	74818	73053	85247	18623	88579
63573	32135	05325	47048	90553	57548	28468	28709	83491	25624
73796	45753	03529	64778	35808	34282	60935	20344	35273	88435
98520	17767	14905	68607	22109	40558	60970	93433	50500	73998
11805	05431	39808	27732	50725	68248	29405	24201	52775	67851
83452	99634	06288	98083	13746	70078	18475	40610	68711	77817
88685	40200	86507	58401	36766	67951	90364	76493	29609	11062
99594	67348	87517	64969	91826	08928	93785	61368	23478	34113
65481	17674	17468	50950	58047	76974	73039	57186	40218	16544
80124	35635	17727	08015	45318	22374	21115	78253	14385	53763
74350	99817	77402	77214	43236	00201	45521	64237	96286	02655
69916	26803	66252	29148	36936	87203	76621	13990	94400	56418
09893	20505	14225	68514	46427	56788	96297	78822	54382	14598
91499	14523	68479	27686	46162	83554	94750	89923	37089	20048
80336	94598	26490	36858	70297	34135	53140	33340	42050	82341
44104	81949	85157	47954	32979	26575	57600	40881	22222	06413
12550	73742	11100	02040	12860	74697	96644	89439	28707	25815
63606	49329	16505	34484	40219	52563	43651	77082	07207	31790
61196	90446	26457	47774	51924	33729	65394	59593	42582	60527
5474	45266	95270	79953	59367	83848	82396	10118	33211	59466
94557	28573	67897	54387	54622	44431	91190	42592	92927	45973
42481	16213	97344	08721	16868	48767	03071	12059	25701	46670
23523	78317	73208	89837	68935	91416	26252	29663	05522	82562
04493	52494	75246	33824	45826	51025	61962	79335	65337	12472
00549	97654	64501	88159	96119	63896	54692	82391	23287	29529
35963	15307	26898	09354	33351	35462	77974	50024	90103	39333
59808	08391	45427	26842	83609	49700	13021	24892	78565	20106
46058	85236	01390	92286	77281	44077	93910	83647	70617	42941

(continued)

TABLE A.1 Random Digits (Continued)

32179	00597	87379	25241	05567	07007	86743	17157	85394	11838
69234	61406	20117	45204	15956	60000	18743	92423	97118	96338
19565	41430	01758	75379	40419	21585	66674	36806	84962	85207
45155	14938	19476	07246	43667	94543	59047	90033	20826	69541
94864	31994	36168	10851	81553	34888	01540	35456	05014	51176
98086	24826	45240	28404	44999	08896	39094	73407	35441	31880
33185	16232	41941	50949	89435	48581	88695	41994	37548	73043
80951	00406	96382	70774	20151	23387	25016	25298	94624	61171
79752	49140	71961	28296	69861	02591	74852	20539	00387	59579
18633	32537	98145	06571	31010	24674	05455	61427	77938	91936
74029	43902	77557	32270	97790	17119	52527	58021	80814	51748
54178	45611	80993	37143	05335	12969	56127	19255	36040	90324
11664	49883	52079	84827	59381	71539	09973	33440	88461	23356
48324	77928	31249	64710	02295	36870	32307	57546	15020	09994
69074	94138	87637	91976	35584	04401	10518	21615	01848	76938

Source: The RAND Corporation. *A Million Random Digits with 100,000 Normal Deviates* (New York: Free Press, 1966), p. 1.
Reprinted with permission.

TABLE A.2 Sample Size for Sampling Attributes at Specified Levels of Precision (in percent with a 95% confidence interval, p = .05)*

Population Size	Sample Size for Precision of					
	± 1%	± 2%	± 3%	± 4%	± 5%	± 10%
500	†	†	†	†	222	83
1,000	†	†	†	385	286	91
1,500	†	†	638	441	316	94
2,000	†	†	714	476	333	95
2,500	†	1,250	769	500	345	96
3,000	†	1,364	811	517	353	97
3,500	†	1,458	843	530	359	97
4,000	†	1,538	870	541	364	98
4,500	†	1,607	891	549	367	98
5,000	†	1,667	909	556	370	98
6,000	†	1,765	938	566	375	98
7,000	†	1,842	959	574	378	99
8,000	†	1,905	976	580	381	99
9,000	†	1,957	989	584	383	99
10,000	5,000	2,000	1,000	588	385	99
15,000	6,000	2,143	1,034	600	390	99
20,000	6,667	2,222	1,053	606	392	100
25,000	7,143	2,273	1,064	610	394	100
50,000	8,333	2,381	1,087	617	397	100
100,000	9,091	2,439	1,099	621	398	100
→ ∞	10,000	2,500	1,111	625	400	100

Source: Taro Yamane, *Elementary Sampling Theory* (Englewood Cliffs, NJ: Prentice Hall, 1967), p. 398. Adapted and reprinted with permission of the publisher.

*Proportion of units in the sample possessing the characteristic being measured; for other values of p, the required sample size will be smaller.

†In these cases, 50% of the universe in the sample will give more than the required accuracy. Since the formal distribution is a poor approximation of the hypergeometrical distribution when n is more than 50% of N, the formula used in this calculation does not apply.

TABLE A.3 Sample Size for Sampling Attributes at Specified Levels of Precision (in percent with a 99% confidence interval, p = .01)*

Population Size	Sample Size for Precision of				
	±1%	±2%	±3%	±4%	±5%
500	†	†	†	†	†
1,000	†	†	†	†	474
1,500	†	†	†	726	563
2,000	†	†	†	826	621
2,500	†	†	†	900	662
3,000	†	†	1,364	958	692
3,500	†	†	1,458	1,003	716
4,000	†	†	1,539	1,041	735
4,500	†	†	1,607	1,071	750
5,000	†	†	1,667	1,098	763
6,000	†	2,903	1,765	1,139	783
7,000	†	3,119	1,842	1,171	798
8,000	†	3,303	1,905	1,196	809
9,000	†	3,462	1,957	1,216	818
10,000	†	3,600	2,000	1,233	826
15,000	†	4,091	2,143	1,286	849
20,000	†	4,390	2,222	1,314	861
25,000	11,842	4,592	2,273	1,331	869
50,000	15,517	5,056	2,381	1,368	884
100,000	18,367	5,325	2,439	1,387	892
→ ∞	22,500	5,625	2,500	1,406	900

Source: Taro Yamane, *Elementary Sampling Theory* (Englewood Cliffs, NJ: Prentice Hall, 1967), p. 399. Adapted and reprinted with permission of the publisher.

*Proportion of units in the sample possessing the characteristic being measured; for other values of p, the required sample size will be smaller.

†In these cases 50% of the universe in the sample will give more than the required accuracy. Since the formal distribution is a poor approximation of the hypergeometrical distribution when n is more than 50% of N, the formula used in this calculation does not apply.

TABLE A.4 Distribution of χ^2

df	.05	.01	.001	df	.05	.01	.001
1	3.841	6.635	10.827	26	38.885	45.642	54.052
2	5.991	9.210	13.815	27	40.113	46.963	55.476
3	7.815	11.345	16.266	28	41.337	48.278	56.893
4	9.488	13.277	18.467	29	42.557	49.588	58.302
5	11.070	15.086	20.515	30	43.773	50.892	59.703
6	12.592	16.812	22.457	32	46.194	53.486	62.487
7	14.067	18.475	24.322	34	48.602	56.061	65.247
8	15.507	20.090	26.125	36	50.999	58.619	67.985
9	16.919	21.666	27.877	38	53.384	61.162	70.703
10	18.307	23.209	29.588	40	55.759	63.691	73.402
11	19.675	24.725	31.264	42	58.124	66.206	76.084
12	21.026	26.217	32.909	44	60.481	68.710	78.750
13	22.362	27.688	34.528	46	62.830	71.201	81.400
14	23.685	29.141	36.123	48	65.171	73.683	84.037
15	24.996	30.578	37.697	50	67.505	76.154	86.661
16	26.296	32.000	39.252	52	69.832	78.616	89.272
17	27.587	33.409	40.790	54	72.153	81.069	91.872
18	28.869	34.805	42.312	56	74.468	83.513	94.461
19	30.144	36.191	43.820	58	76.778	85.950	97.039
20	31.410	37.566	45.315	60	79.082	88.379	99.607
21	32.671	38.932	46.797	62	81.381	90.802	102.166
22	33.924	40.289	48.268	64	83.675	93.217	104.716
23	35.172	41.638	49.728	66	85.965	95.626	107.258
24	36.415	42.980	51.179	68	88.250	98.028	109.791
25	37.652	44.314	52.620	70	90.531	100.425	112.317

Source: From Table IV of Ronald A. Fisher and Frank Yates, *Statistical Tables for Biological, Agricultural and Medical Research*, 6th ed., published by Longman Group, Ltd., London (previously published by Oliver & Boyd, Edinburgh). Reprinted with permission of the authors and the publisher.

Note: For odd values of n between 30 and 70, the mean of the tabular values for $df - 1$ and $df + 1$ may be taken. For larger values of n, the expression $\sqrt{2x^2} - \sqrt{2df - 1}$ may be used as a normal deviate with unit variance, remembering that the probability for χ^2 corresponds with that of a single tail of the normal curve.

TABLE A.5 Values of the Correlation Coefficient for Different Levels of Significance

df	.1	.05	.01	.001	df	.1	.05	.01	.001
1	.98769	.99692	.999877	.9999988	16	.4000	.4683	.5897	.7084
2	.90000	.95000	.990000	.99900	17	.3887	.4555	.5751	.6932
3	.8054	.878	.9587	.99116	18	.3783	.4438	.5614	.6787
4	.7293	.8114	.91720	.97406	19	.3687	.4329	.5487	.6652
5	.6694	.7545	.8745	.95274	20	.3598	.4227	.5368	.6524
6	.6215	.7067	.8343	.92493	25	.3233	.3809	.4869	.5974
7	.5822	.6664	.7977	.8982	30	.2960	.3494	.4487	.5541
8	.5494	.6319	.7646	.8721	35	.2746	.3246	.4182	.5189
9	.5214	.6021	.7348	.8471	40	.2573	.3044	.3932	.4896
10	.4973	.5760	.7079	.8233	45	.2428	.2875	.3721	.4648
11	.4762	.5529	.6835	.8010	50	.2306	.2732	.3541	.4433
12	.4575	.5324	.6614	.7800	60	.2108	.2500	.3248	.4078
13	.4409	.5139	.6411	.7603	70	.1954	.2319	.3017	.3799
14	.4259	.497	.6226	.7420	80	.1829	.2172	.2830	.3568
15	.4124	.482	.6055	.7246	90	.1726	.2050	.2673	.3375
					100	.1638	.1946	.2540	.3211

Source: From Table VII of Ronald A. Fisher and Frank Yates, *Statistical Tables for Biological, Agricultural and Medical Research,* 6th ed., published by Longman Group, Ltd., London (previously published by Oliver & Boyd, Edinburgh). Reprinted with permission of the authors and the publishers.

TABLE A.6 Portions of Area Under the Normal Curve

(A) z	(B) Area between mean and z	(C) Area beyond z	(A) z	(B) Area between mean and z	(C) Area beyond z	(A) z	(B) Area between mean and z	(C) Area beyond z
0.00	.0000	.5000	0.43	.1664	.3336	0.86	.3051	.1949
0.01	.0040	.4960	0.44	.1700	.3300	0.87	.3078	.1922
0.02	.0080	.4920	0.45	.1736	.3264	0.88	.3106	.1894
0.03	.0120	.4880	0.46	.1772	.3228	0.89	.3133	.1867
0.04	.0160	.4840	0.47	.1808	.3192	0.90	.3159	.1841
0.05	.0199	.4801	0.48	.1844	.3156	0.91	.3186	.1814
0.06	.0239	.4761	0.49	.1879	.3121	0.92	.3212	.1788
0.07	.0279	.4721	0.50	.1915	.3085	0.93	.3238	.1788
0.08	.0319	.4681	0.51	.1950	.3050	0.94	.3264	.1736
0.09	.0359	.4641	0.52	.1985	.3015	0.95	.3289	.1711
0.10	.0398	.4602	0.53	.2019	.2981	0.96	.3315	.1685
0.11	.0438	.4562	0.54	.2054	.2946	0.97	.3340	.1660
0.12	.0478	.4522	0.55	.2088	.2912	0.98	.3365	.1635
0.13	.0517	.4483	0.56	.2123	.2877	0.99	.3389	.1611
0.14	.0557	.4443	0.57	.2157	.2843	1.00	.3413	.1587
0.15	.0596	.4404	0.58	.2190	.2810	1.01	.3438	.1562
0.16	.0636	.4364	0.59	.2224	.2776	1.02	.3461	.1539
0.17	.0675	.4325	0.60	.2257	.2743	1.03	.3485	.1515
0.18	.0714	.4286	0.61	.2291	.2709	1.04	.3508	.1492
0.19	.0753	.4247	0.62	.2324	.2676	1.05	.3531	.1469
0.20	.0793	.4207	0.63	.2357	.2643	1.06	.3554	.1446
0.21	.0832	.4168	0.64	.2389	.2611	1.07	.3577	.1423
0.22	.0871	.4129	0.65	.2422	.2578	1.08	.3599	.1401
0.23	.0910	.4090	0.66	.2454	.2546	1.09	.3621	.1379
0.24	.0948	.4052	0.67	.2486	.2514	1.10	.3643	.1357
0.25	.0987	.4013	0.68	.2517	.2483	1.11	.3665	.1335
0.26	.1026	.3974	0.69	.2549	.2451	1.12	.3686	.1314
0.27	.1064	.3936	0.70	.2580	.2420	1.13	.3708	.1292
0.28	.1103	.3897	0.71	.2611	.2389	1.14	.3729	.1271
0.29	.1141	.3859	0.72	.2642	.2358	1.15	.3748	.1251
0.30	.1179	.3821	0.73	.2673	.2327	1.16	.3770	.1230
0.31	.1217	.3783	0.74	.2704	.2296	1.17	.3790	.1210
0.32	.1255	.3745	0.75	.2734	.2266	1.18	.3810	.1190
0.33	.1293	.3707	0.76	.2764	.2236	1.19	.3830	.1170
0.34	.1331	.3669	0.77	.2794	.2206	1.20	.3849	.1151
0.35	.1368	.3632	0.78	.2823	.2177	1.21	.3869	.1131
0.36	.1406	.3594	0.79	.2852	.2148	1.22	.3888	.1112
0.37	.1443	.3557	0.80	.2881	.2119	1.23	.3907	.1093
0.38	.1480	.3520	0.81	.2910	.2090	1.24	.3925	.1075
0.39	.1517	.3483	0.82	.2936	.2061	1.25	.3944	.1056
0.40	.1554	.3446	0.83	.2967	.2033	1.26	.3962	.1038
0.41	.1591	.3409	0.84	.2995	.2005	1.27	.3980	.1020

(continued)

TABLE A.6 Portions of Area Under the Normal Curve (Continued)

(A) z	(B) Area between mean and z	(C) Area beyond z	(A) z	(B) Area between mean and z	(C) Area beyond z	(A) z	(B) Area between mean and z	(C) Area beyond z
0.42	.1628	.3372	0.85	.3023	.1977	1.28	.3997	.1003
1.29	.4015	.0985	1.71	.4564	.0436	2.13	.4834	.0166
1.30	.4032	.0968	1.72	.4573	.0427	2.14	.4838	.0162
1.31	.4049	.0951	1.73	.4582	.0418	2.15	.4842	.0158
1.32	.4066	.0934	1.74	.4591	.0409	2.16	.4846	.0154
1.33	.4082	.0918	1.75	.4599	.0401	2.17	.4850	.0150
1.34	.4099	.0901	1.76	.4608	.0392	2.18	.4854	.0146
1.35	.4115	.0885	1.77	.4616	.0384	2.19	.4857	.0143
1.36	.4131	.0869	1.78	.4625	.0375	2.20	.4861	.0139
1.37	.4147	.0853	1.79	.4633	.0367	2.21	.4864	.0136
1.38	.4162	.0838	1.80	.4641	.0359	2.22	.4868	.0132
1.39	.4177	.0823	1.81	.4649	.0351	2.23	.4871	.0129
1.40	.4192	.0808	1.82	.4656	.0344	2.24	.4875	.0125
1.41	.4207	.0793	1.83	.4664	.0336	2.25	.4878	.0122
1.42	.4222	.0778	1.84	.4671	.0329	2.26	.4881	.0119
1.43	.4236	.0764	1.85	.4678	.0322	2.27	.4884	.0116
1.44	.4251	.0749	1.86	.4686	.0314	2.28	.4887	.0113
1.45	.4265	.0735	1.87	.4693	.0307	2.29	.4890	.0110
1.46	.4279	.0721	1.88	.4699	.0301	2.30	.4893	.0107
1.47	.4292	.0708	1.89	.4706	.0294	2.31	.4896	.0104
1.48	.4306	.0694	1.90	.4713	.0287	2.32	.4898	.0102
1.49	.4319	.0681	1.91	.4719	.0281	2.33	.4901	.0099
1.50	.4332	.0668	1.92	.4726	.0274	2.34	.4904	.0096
1.51	.4345	.0655	1.93	.4732	.0268	2.35	.4906	.0094
1.52	.4357	.0643	1.94	.4738	.0262	2.36	.4909	.0091
1.53	.4370	.0630	1.95	.4744	.0256	2.37	.4911	.0089
1.54	.4382	.0618	1.96	.4750	.0250	2.38	.4913	.0087
1.55	.4394	.0606	1.97	.4556	.0244	2.39	.4916	.0084
1.56	.4406	.0594	1.98	.4761	.0239	2.40	.4918	.0082
1.57	.4418	.0582	1.99	.4767	.0233	2.41	.4920	.0080
1.58	.4429	.0571	2.00	.4772	.0228	2.42	.4922	.0078
1.59	.4441	.0559	2.01	.4778	.0222	2.43	.4925	.0075
1.60	.4452	.0548	2.02	.4783	.0217	2.44	.4927	.0073
1.61	.4463	.0537	2.03	.4788	.0212	2.45	.4929	.0071
1.62	.4474	.0526	2.04	.4793	.0207	2.46	.4931	.0069
1.63	.4484	.0516	2.05	.4798	.0202	2.47	.4932	.0068
1.64	.4495	.0505	2.06	.4803	.0197	2.48	.4934	.0064
1.65	.4505	.0495	2.07	.4808	.0192	2.49	.4936	.0064
1.66	.4515	.0485	2.08	.4812	.0188	2.50	.4938	.0064
1.67	.4525	.0475	2.09	.4817	.0183	2.51	.4940	.0064
1.68	.4535	.0465	2.10	.4821	.0179	2.52	.4941	.0054
1.69	.4545	.0455	2.11	.4826	.0174	2.53	.4943	.0057
1.70	.4554	.0446	2.12	.4830	.0170	2.54	.4945	.0055

TABLE A.6 Portions of Area Under the Normal Curve (Continued)

(A) z	(B) Area between mean and z	(C) Area beyond z	(A) z	(B) Area between mean and z	(C) Area beyond z	(A) z	(B) Area between mean and z	(C) Area beyond z
2.55	.4946	.0054	2.82	.4976	.0024	3.09	.4990	.0010
2.56	.4948	.0052	2.83	.4977	.0023	3.10	.4990	.0010
2.57	.4949	.0051	2.84	.4977	.0023	3.11	.4991	.0009
2.58	.4951	.0049	2.85	.4978	.0022	3.12	.4991	.0009
2.59	.4952	.0048	2.86	.4979	.0021	3.13	.4991	.0009
2.60	.4953	.0047	2.87	.4979	.0021	3.14	.4992	.0008
2.61	.4955	.0045	2.88	.4980	.0020	3.15	.4992	.0008
2.62	.4956	.0044	2.89	.4981	.0019	3.16	.4992	.0008
2.63	.4957	.0043	2.90	.4981	.0019	3.17	.4992	.0008
2.64	.4959	.0041	2.91	.4982	.0018	3.18	.4993	.0007
2.65	.4960	.0040	2.92	.4982	.0018	3.19	.4993	.0007
2.66	.4961	.0039	2.93	.4983	.0017	3.20	.4993	.0007
2.67	.4962	.0038	2.94	.7984	.0016	3.21	.4993	.0007
2.68	.4963	.0037	2.95	.4984	.0016	3.22	.4994	.0006
2.69	.4964	.0036	2.96	.4985	.0015	3.23	.4994	.0006
2.70	.4965	.0035	2.97	.4985	.0015	3.24	.4994	.0006
2.71	.4966	.0034	2.98	.4986	.0014	3.25	.4994	.0006
2.72	.4967	.0033	2.99	.4986	.0014	3.30	.4995	.0005
2.73	.4968	.0032	3.00	.4987	.0013	3.35	.4996	.0004
2.74	.4969	.0031	3.01	.4987	.0013	3.40	.4997	.0003
2.75	.4970	.0030	3.02	.4987	.0013	3.45	.4997	.0003
2.76	.4971	.0029	3.03	.4988	.0012	3.50	.4998	.0002
2.77	.4972	.0028	3.04	.4988	.0012	3.60	.4998	.0002
2.78	.4973	.0027	3.05	.4989	.0011	3.70	.4999	.0001
2.79	.4974	.0026	3.06	.4989	.0011	3.80	.4999	.0001
2.80	.4974	.0026	3.07	.4989	.0011	3.90	.49995	.00005
2.81	.4975	.0025	3.08	.4990	.0010	4.00	.49997	.00003

Source: Richard P. Runyon and Audrey Haber, *Fundamentals of Behavioral Statistics*, 3d ed. (Reading, MA: Addison-Wesley, 1976), pp. 378–79.

APPENDIX B

Ethical Standards in Empirical Research

AMERICAN POLITICAL SCIENCE ASSOCIATION

The American Political Science Association has adopted a set of "Principles of Professional Conduct." The following rules are excerpted from the section on ethical research practices.[1]

---

1. Openness concerning material support of research is a basic principle of scholarship. . . .
3. In applying for research funds, the individual researcher should:
    3.1 clearly state the reasons for applying for support and not resort to stratagems of ambiguity to make the research more acceptable to a funding agency;
    3.2 indicate clearly the actual amount of time the researcher personally plans to spend on the research;
    3.3 indicate other sources of support of the research, if any; and
    3.4 refuse to accept terms and conditions that the researcher believes will undermine his or her freedom and integrity as a scholar.
4. In conducting research so supported, the individual bears sole responsibility for the procedures, methods, and content of research. The researcher:
    4.1 must avoid any deception or misrepresentation concerning his or her personal involvement or the involvement of respondents or subjects, and must avoid use of research as a cover for intelligence work or for partisan political purposes;
    4.2 must refrain from using his or her professional status to obtain data and research materials for purposes other than scholarship;
    4.3 with respect to research abroad, should not concurrently accept any additional support from agencies of the government for purposes that cannot be disclosed;
    4.4 should carefully comply with the time, reporting, accounting, and other requirements set forth in the project instrument, and cooperate with institutional grant administrators in meeting these requirements; and
    4.5 should avoid commingling project funds with personal funds, or funds of one project with those of another.
5. With respect to any public scholarly activity including publication of the results of research, the individual researcher:
    5.1 bears sole responsibility for publication;
    5.2 should disclose all relevant sources of financial support;
    5.3 should indicate any condition imposed by financial sponsors or others on research publication, or other scholarly activities; and
    5.4 should conscientiously acknowledge any assistance received in conducting research.

---

[1]Reproduced with the permission of the American Political Science Association. The full text of A Guide to Professional Ethics in Political Science, 2nd edition (2008) is available from www.apsanet.org/imgtest/ethicsguideweb.pdf

5.5 Authors are obliged to reveal the bases of any of their statements that are challenged specifically, except where confidentiality is involved.

6. Scholars have an ethical obligation to make a full and complete disclosure of all nonconfidential sources involved in their research so that their work can be tested or replicated.

6.1 As citizens they have an obligation to cooperate with grand juries, other law enforcement agencies, and institutional officials.

6.2 Conversely, scholars also have a professional duty not to divulge the identity of confidential sources of information or data developed in the course of research, whether to governmental or nongovernmental officials or bodies, even though in the present state of American law they run the risk of suffering an applicable penalty.

6.3 Scholars must, however, exercise appropriate restraint in making claims as to the confidential nature of their sources, and resolve all reasonable doubts in favor of full disclosure.

7. Political scientists, like all scholars, are expected to practice intellectual honesty and to uphold the scholarly standards of their discipline.

7.1 Plagiarism, the deliberate appropriation of the work of others represented as one's own, not only may constitute a violation of the civil law but represents a serious breach of professional ethics.

AMERICAN ASSOCIATION FOR PUBLIC OPINION RESEARCH

The American Association for Public Opinion Research has adopted the following Code of Professional Ethics and Practices.[2]

I. Principles of professional practice in the conduct of our work

A. We shall exercise due care in developing research designs and survey instruments, and in collecting, processing, and analyzing data, taking all reasonable steps to assure the reliability and validity of results.

1. We shall recommend and employ only those tools of analysis which . . . are well suited to the research problem at hand.

2. We shall not select research tools and methods of analysis because of their capacity to yield misleading conclusions.

3. We shall not knowingly make interpretations of research results, nor shall we tacitly permit interpretations that are inconsistent with the data available.

4. We shall not knowingly imply that interpretations should be accorded greater confidence than the data actually warrant.

B. We shall describe our methods and findings accurately and in appropriate detail in all research reports, adhering to the standards for minimal disclosure specified in Section III below. . . .

---

[2]*Code of Professional Ethics and Practices* (2005), courtesy of the American Association for Public Opinion Research. The full text is available from www.aapor.org/AAPOR_Code.htm

II. Principles of professional responsibility in our dealings with people

   A. The public

      1. If we become aware of the appearance in public of serious distortions of our research, we shall publicly disclose what is required to correct these distortions. . . .

   D. The respondent

      1. We shall strive to avoid the use of practices or methods that may harm, humiliate, or seriously mislead survey respondents.

      2. Unless the respondent waives confidentiality for specified uses, we shall hold as privileged and confidential all information that might identify a respondent with his or her responses. We shall also not disclose or use the names of respondents for nonresearch purposes unless the respondents grant us permission to do so.

III. Standard for minimal disclosure

   1. Who sponsored the survey, and who conducted it.

   2. The exact wording of questions asked, including the text of any preceding instruction or explanation to the interviewer or respondent that might reasonably be expected to affect the response.

   3. A definition of the population under study, and a description of the sampling frame used to identify this population.

   4. A description of the sample selection procedure, giving a clear indication of the method by which the respondents were selected by the researcher, or whether the respondents were entirely self-selected.

   5. Size of sample and, if applicable, completion rates and information on eligibility criteria and screening procedures.

   6. A discussion of the precision of the findings, including, if appropriate, estimates of sampling error, and a description of any weighting or estimating procedures used.

   7. Which results are based on parts of the sample, rather than on the total sample.

   8. Method, location, and dates of data collection.

GLOSSARY

Abstract A brief statement summarizing the contents of a report.

Additive index A measure created by combining indicators of different aspects of the same concept.

Aggregate data Data pertaining to groups of cases or to collectivities.

Alternative rival hypothesis An alternative explanation for obtained results that logically cannot be accurate if the initial hypothesis is accurate.

Annotated bibliography A list of information sources that includes both complete citation information and brief summaries, often with evaluations.

Antecedent variable A variable that precedes another variable and, for a given hypothesis, is regarded as the independent variable.

Applied research Research that has the primary purpose of examining or resolving particular policy problems.

Areal group A group defined by residence within a particular geographic area.

Association A relationship in which two (or more) variables co-vary.

Assumption (also *axiom* or *postulate*) An abstract assertion about relationships that serves as a foundation for theoretical reasoning but is not subject to empirical test.

Authenticating A process for confirming that one belongs to a group of people authorized to access restricted information over a digital network.

Bar chart A graphic device in which bars are used to represent observations.

Basic research Research the primary purpose of which is to develop or test a scientific theory.

Beta weight or **beta coefficient** A standardized partial regression coefficient used to compare the relative effects of independent variables on a dependent variable.

Bibliographic record Similar to citation, but also provides additional information to find related works in a library catalog or database.

Bibliographic sources Systematic listings of publications organized to assist in literature reviews.

Bibliography A compilation of the publication information of books, articles, and other materials on a given topic.

Bilateral bar chart A two-directional graphic device in which bars are used to represent variation above or below some norm.

Bivariate statistics Statistics summarizing the relationship between two variables.

Blending in A technique used by qualitative observers to stimulate subjects to ignore the researcher.

Boolean operators Words such as *and, or,* or *not* that provide linkages among concepts during a computerized literature search, and in programming languages used for statistical analysis.

Causal model A model that graphically specifies a set of relationships between concepts or variables such that change in one or more precedes and gives rise to change in another.

Causal relationship A relationship in which change in one or more concepts or variables leads to or "forces" changes in one or more other concepts or variables.

Central tendency (measure of) Device for determining the value or score that best represents a set of cases on a given variable.

Chi-square (χ^2) A test of the statistical significance of the association between two nominal variables.

Citation Acknowledgment of one's use of another's work; provides a basic description of an information source.

Cited reference searching Technique for tracing how an author's work has been cited by later authors, showing the evolution of knowledge.

Closed-ended questions Questions that force respondents to choose an answer from a limited number of options.

Cluster sampling *See* multistage random area sample.

Codebook A listing of variables and values indicating how they are coded in a study.

Coder A person who assigns scores to cases or responses, usually with reference to content analysis coded in a study.

Codes Numbers assigned to represent different values on variables for purposes of data analysis.

Coding The process of assigning numerical values to represent values on variables.

Coding sheet A structured form for recording data.

Coefficient of association A measure of the degree and direction of association between two variables.

Coefficient of determination (R^2) The multiple regression coefficient tells how much of the variance in the values on a dependent variable is "explained" by variance in a *set* of independent variables.

Cohort study A study based on repeated surveys of a specific group (for example, persons born in a given year) at different points in time.

Collectively exhaustive A characteristic of measures by which all cases can be assigned to at least one category.

Computer-assisted telephone interviewing (CATI) Interviewing using computer display of instrument, usually includes continual calculation of summary statistics.

Concept A word or phrase that represents some idea or phenomenon.

Concept search grid An organizational framework that lists related search terms.

Concurrent validation The characteristic of a measure that allows accurate sorting of cases on the basis of related concurrent traits.

Confidence interval An indicator of the accuracy with which a population parameter can be predicted from a sample statistic stated in terms of the range of values above or below the sample statistic the population parameter is likely to fall.

Confidence level An indicator of the likelihood that a sample is representative stated in terms of the probability that a sample statistic is within a given confidence interval of a population parameter.

Construct validity The characteristic of a measure by which it behaves as we would expect on the basis of theory.

Content analysis A technique used in the study of communication-related materials and behaviors.

Contingency question A filtering device used in survey research to ascertain the appropriateness of asking a subsequent question.

Control In experimental design, to limit the factors influencing a variable under observation; in data analysis, to hold the values of one variable constant while examining the relationship(s) between two or more other variables.

Control group Subjects in an experiment not exposed to the independent variable (experimental event).

Controlled time-series design A research design that uses control groups to assess the impact of an event.

Controlling Holding constant the effect of one variable on the relationship between two other variables in order to obtain an accurate measure of that relationship.

Convergent validity A characteristic whereby several measures of a common concept provide essentially the same result.

Correlation coefficient (r) The coefficient of association between two interval variables measuring the closeness of fit of data points around the regression line.

Covariational relationship A relationship in which two or more concepts or variables tend to change together for unspecified reasons.

Cross-sectional survey A survey that compares data from different cases at a single point in time.

Cross tabulation A tabular presentation summarizing the relationship(s) between two or more variables.

Data Observations of or information about reality arising from the research process.

Data archives Collections of the results of previous research.

Data specifications Detailed descriptions of the data that are to be recorded for each case and variable.

Data transformation Modification of data to meet the requirements of a particular analysis technique.

Deduction Reasoning that moves from abstract statements about general relationships to concrete statements about specific behaviors.

Degrees of freedom (df) The number of cells in a table or points along a regression line that may be entered without being determined by prior entries.

Demographic group A group defined by some personal characteristic(s) of its members.

Dependent variable A variable whose value changes in response to changes in the value of some other variable.

Descriptive research Research concerned primarily with measuring some aspect of reality for its own sake rather than with developing or testing some theory.

Direct observation A technique used primarily in the study of group norms and behaviors.

Discriminant validation A characteristic whereby a measure is valid for one concept alone as opposed to several concepts.

Dispersion (measure of) An indicator of variation around the measure of central tendency, that is, an indicator of its representativeness.

Ecological fallacy The improper use of aggregate data to draw conclusions about the characteristics of individual cases or groups.

Elite interviewing Gathering data through interviews designed to tap the unique knowledge of the respondents.

Empirical Pertaining to or characterized by observations or descriptions of reality.

Empirically grounded A type of theory that is based on induction from actual observation.

Empirical referent An observable object or event that corresponds to a concept.

Enumerative table A simple tabular listing of research data.

Equivalent measures Indicators that measure the same phenomena in more than one system.

Experimental design A research strategy in which the relationship between a given stimulus, event, or other variable and some observable behavior is isolated.

Experimental group Subjects exposed to the independent variable (experimental stimulus).

Explanatory research Research that uses observations of reality to test hypotheses and to help identify or develop an understanding of patterns of behavior in the context of a theory.

Exploratory research Research designed to discover factors that should be included in theorizing and research on a subject.

Ex post facto experiment A research design in which experimental controls are simulated in data analysis.

External validity See also generalizability, pertains to the degree to which a given study relates to other populations.

Face validity A characteristic of a measure that gives it intuitive appeal.

Field experiment A partial application of experimental design in a real-world setting, as distinct from a laboratory.

Field notes Written records made during direct observation.

Fitting in A technique used by qualitative observers to pursuade subjects to trust the observer enough to reveal their true feelings and behavior patterns.

Focus group A small group used for in-depth study of a subject through directed discussion.

Free Web That part of the Internet that is identified by common Web search engines, specifically the portion that does not charge access fees.

Frequency distribution An ordered count of the number of cases that take on each value of a variable.

Frequency distribution control A procedure by which experimental and control groups can be made equivalent by selection of combinations of subjects with comparable aggregate characteristics.

Galton's problem The task of testing for the effects of diffusion in comparative research.

Gamma (G) A coefficient of association between two ordinal variables.

Generalizability The characteristic that permits the results of research on a limited set of cases to be extended to the population from which those cases are drawn.

Going native When a researcher involved in participant observation adopts the values and mind-set of those being observed and loses objectivity.

Guide A set of instructions to aid a moderator in conducting a focus group.

Guttman scaling A method of scale creation that provides internal criteria for determining the degree to which a set of items exhibit unidimensionality (measure a single concept).

Histogram A bar chart showing the distribution of values on a variable.

Homogeneity The degree to which members of a given population are like one another.

Hypothesis A statement predicting the relationship(s) between variables.

Independent variable A variable whose own value changes influence the value of some other variable.

In-depth interviewing A technique for gathering information by interviewing subjects at length while being highly flexible in the structure and content of the questions asked in order to discover unexpected facts.

Index 1. A list identifying the location of a word in a book or encyclopedia or of an article in a set of periodicals; plural: **Indexes**. 2. A statistical indicator calculated from several variables; plural: **Indices**.

Index construction Combining two or more related indicators into a single, more comprehensive indicator.

Indicator A specific measure of a variable.

Indirect causation The phenomenon by which one variable exerts causal influence on another only by changing the value of other variables that directly affect it.

Induction Reasoning that generalizes from what has been observed to what has not—that is, in which an abstract theory is developed from concrete evidence.

Information Environmental Scan A technique of casting the widest net to immerse oneself in information that may be related to one's theory (or story), from any number of sources both scholarly and popular—the first step of our word mining sequence

Inference Reasoning from either observation or a logical system to reach conclusions not already apparent.

In-person interview A survey interview in which the interviewer questions the respondent face-to-face.

Instrument A device or procedure used for taking a measurement.

Instrumentation The specification of steps to take in making observations; the creation of measurement devices.

Intercoder reliability Agreement in the values assigned to the same or similar cases by independent observers.

Interlibrary loan A national system for libraries to lend and borrow materials from their own collections for the use of patrons of other libraries.

Internal validity A form of construct validity that evaluates if the measures are accurately evaluating the theoretical concepts.

Interobserver reliability The degree to which two or more individuals agree on the details of an event they have observed as part of a research project.

Interval measurement Measurement that classifies and rank orders cases so that the distance between cases is known by using a standard unit of measurement.

Intervening variable A variable that influences the effect of an independent variable on a dependent variable.

Interview schedule The questionnaire used with in-person interviews.

Judgmental sample A sample in which specific cases are purposely selected.

Key The explanation of symbols used in a graphic presentation.

Key word or key phrase A word or phrase that is meaningfully related to a given concept, used for bibliographic search.

Lambda (λ) A coefficient of association between two nominal variables.

Level of measurement The amount of information provided by a set of instruments.

Likert scaling A method of scale creation based on asking respondents to report the degree to which they agree or disagree with a series of statements selected to represent a trait.

Line graph A graphic device using lines to connect points representing observations so as to suggest trends or other relationships.

Linear relationship A relationship between two variables that can be graphically represented as a straight line.

Longitudinal survey A survey that compares the attributes or behaviors of a given set of cases at different points in time.

Mail surveys Surveys conducted by mailing questionnaires to respondents and asking that they complete and return them.

Marginals The frequency distribution as it appears in the row and column totals of a contingency table.

Mean A measure of central tendency for interval variables.

Measurement The application of an instrument to count or in some other way quantify observations of reality.

Measurement error Inaccuracies in the observation of reality; differences between reality and recorded observations of it.

Measurement theory A statement of why one expects values on an indicator to change when the value of the variable it represents changes.

Median A measure of central tendency for ordinal variables.

Method effect Any misleading impact of the particular method used to study a subject on the results of that study.

Mode A measure of central tendency for nominal variables.

Model A simplified representation of reality.

Model specification The process of selecting the variables to be included in a regression model and specifying their relationship to one another.

Moderator The person who directs discussion in a focus group and reports on its results.

Most different systems design A strategy for comparative research in which characteristics that differ between units of analysis can be ruled out as explanations for others that are shared.

Most similar systems design A strategy for comparative research that focuses on units of analysis that are very similar, on the theory that shared characteristics can be held constant when differences between the units are examined.

Multicollinearity The condition in which one or more of the independent variables in a regression equation are perfect linear functions of one or more other independent variables in the equation.

Multidimensional Having several facets or elements.

Multiple causation The common situation in the social sciences in which an effect is the result of more than one cause.

Multiple indicators More than one measure of the same variable, especially useful for enhancing the validity of indicators.

Multiple regression A statistical procedure for examining the relationship among a dependent variable and several independent variables.

Multiple regression equation The mathematical equation that represents the conceptual process described by a regression model and is used as a basis for multiple regression analysis.

Multiplicative index A single measure constructed from a combination of measures of different but related concepts.

Multistage random area sample A sample in which geographic units or their analogs rather than individuals are selected for analysis.

Multivariate analysis Any statistical analysis examining the relationship between *more than two* variables simultaneously.

Multivariate statistics Statistics relating to the relationships among more than two variables.

Mutually exclusive Characteristic of measures by which a given case can be assigned to only one category.

Negative relationship The relationship said to exist when corresponding values on two variables change in *opposite* directions.

Nominal measurement Measurement that merely classifies cases without regard to rank or distances between cases.

Nonexperimental studies Studies in which there is no research design to provide a logical basis for causal inference.

Nonrecursive The term describing a causal model in which at least one variable influences another variable that occurs earlier in the model.

Normal distribution A distribution that is unimodal and symmetrical, with the peak at the center, and in which the mode, median, and mean take on the same value.

Normative Pertaining to or characterized by preferences or value judgments.

Observation In science, the application of an instrument to assign values to cases on indicators.

Observation point The time of observation or measurement.

Observation schedule A form facilitating systematic recording of data observations.

Obtrusive measure A measurement that is evident to the research subjects.

Obtrusive research Research employing obtrusive measures.

Open-ended questions Questions that allow respondents to answer in their own words.

Operational definition Set of observations that represent abstract concepts.

Operationalization The process of designating sets of observations to represent abstract concepts.

Ordinal measurement Measurement that classifies and ranks cases without regard to the distance between them.

Pair-comparison scaling A technique employed in content analysis to measure the intensity of evaluative statements.

Panel study A study that employs the same group of subjects for a series of observations at different points in time.

Parameter Any characteristic of a population, as distinct from a characteristic of a sample.

Parsimony The presentation of material as efficiently as possible; simplicity in a theory.

Partial regression coefficient A statistic that indicates the effect of an independent variable on a dependent variable when the effects of all other variables in a model are controlled.

Participant observation A form of direct observation in which the researcher becomes more or less actively involved in the behaviors of the group that is being studied.

Path analysis A statistical technique for assessing the relative influence of variables in a causal model.

Pie chart A graphic device in which sectored circles are used to represent observations.

Pilot study A small-scale trial of measures and procedures used to identify in advance any weaknesses in the research plan or instrumentation.

Population A set of cases about which one wishes to draw some conclusions.

Portals Web pages that provide a common front end to diverse sources.

Positive relationship The relationship said to exist when corresponding values on two variables change in the same direction.

Posttest In an experiment, a measurement taken after the introduction of the experimental event.

Pragmatic validation The process of determining the pragmatic (practical) validity of an indicator.

Pragmatic validity The validity of an indicator as a measure of a concept that is demonstrated by the ability to use it to predict the values of indicators of other concepts.

Precision matching A procedure by which experimental and control groups may be made equivalent through the selection of comparable individuals.

Predictive validity A characteristic of a measure that allows the accurate prediction of future events.

Pretest In an experiment, a measurement taken before the introduction of the experimental event.

Proposition A statement of the relationship between concepts that is logically derived from the assumptions of a theory; a component of a theory.

Q-sort A technique employed in content analysis to measure the intensity of evaluative statements.

Qualitative Research based on the researcher's informed understanding of the events under study, often based upon his or her personal involvement in the research narrative, and avoiding numerical comparisons of cases.

Qualitative methods Research strategies designed to gather qualitative information, usually in narrative form, in order to describe or understand people and events in their natural setting.

Quantile A measure of position within a distribution.

Quantile range A measure of dispersion for ordinal variables.

Quantitative Research based on statistical comparisons of the characteristics of the numerical measurement representing cases being studied.

Quantitative methods Techniques emphasizing detached observation, documenting phenomena numerically, and statistical comparisons of the characteristics of the cases being studied.

Quasi-experimental design Research in which data analysis techniques or data-gathering strategies are used to approximate the degree of control associated with experimental research.

Question branching Ordering survey questions based on responses to earlier questions.

Question format The technique by which survey questions are presented and answered.

Questionnaire A survey instrument intended for use in mailed or self-administered surveys.

Quota sample A sample in which cases are selected to fill a predesignated distribution of attributes.

Random errors Nonsystematic measurement errors that render indicators invalid and unreliable as measures of a concept.

Randomization A procedure for selecting cases for study (or for obtaining equivalence in experiments) in which each case in a population, and each combination of cases of a given size, has an equal chance of selection.

Random sample A sample in which cases are selected from a population in accordance with the principle of randomization.

Raw data The product of unstandardized or otherwise unprocessed observations.

Reactivity The circumstance in which persons under study modify their behavior in reaction to the research itself.

Recording form The form used to transfer aggregate data from a source document to machine-readable form.

Recursive The term describing a causal model in which no variable influences any variable that occurs before it in the model and thus contains no "feedback."

Regression line The line that best summarizes the distribution of data points on a scatter diagram and the slope of which characterizes the relationship in units of change between two internal variables.

Regression toward the mean The natural tendency for extreme values to move toward more typical values over time.

Reliability The consistency with which a measuring instrument allows assignment of values to cases.

Representativeness The degree to which a relatively small number of cases resemble the larger number of cases from which they are drawn.

Representative sample A sample in which all major traits of the population being sampled are present in the same proportion as in the population itself.

Research design The plan of a study that organizes observations in such a way as to establish a sound logical basis for causal inference.

Research question A question identifying the basic information we are seeking in a research project.

Respondents Persons who respond to an interview or questionnaire.

Sample A small group of cases drawn from and used to represent some larger group.

Sampling error Differences between the attributes of a sample and those of the population from which the sample is drawn.

Scale A series of indicators that can be ordered so as to rank cases according to the degree to which they manifest a concept.

Scale score A single measure of how much a subject has of a given attribute measured by a scale.

Scaling The process of combining several indicators of a given concept into a single complex indicator of that concept.

Scatter plot A graphic summary of the distribution of cases on two variables, using dots to represent observations.

Scheduled interviews Elite or specialized interviews that are guided by an interview schedule specifying the questions to be asked.

Scholarly journal Periodicals that have been peer-reviewed, with articles written by scholars for an academic audience; antonym; popular periodical.

Scientific research A method of testing theories and hypotheses by applying certain rules of analysis to the observation and interpretation of reality under strictly delineated circumstances.

Screening interview An interview conducted to select participants for a focus group.

Searching Using digital tools to identify potentially relevant information sources.

Secondary analysis Analysis of data that have been gathered previously, usually by another researcher.

Segmented bar chart A graphic display of data with bars divided into segments to show the distribution of a second characteristic in the population represented by the bar.

Solomon three-control-group research design A variation on the classic experimental design intended to allow researchers to identify any influence of *maturation* on the results of an experiment.

Solomon two-control-group research design A variation on the classic experimental design intended to allow researchers to identify any *test effect* present in the experiment.

Specialized interviewing Interviews with respondents who require nonstandard procedures to ensure communication.

Spurious relationship A relationship in which two variables co-vary but only because of chance or because of the action of some other variable.

Standard deviation (s) The measure of dispersion for interval variables.

Standardized measures Indicators adjusted so as to allow valid comparisons among units of different sizes in the analysis of aggregate data.

Standard score (z) The measure of location in an interval distribution based on standard deviation units about the mean.

Standard score of gamma (Z_G) A test of the statistical significance of an association between two ordinal variables.

Statistical significance The likelihood that an association noted between two variables, based on analysis of a sample, might have occurred by chance and might not exist in the larger population.

Statistics Numbers that summarize either the distributions of values on or the relationships between or among variables; in sampling, the characteristics of a sample that correspond to the parameters of a population.

Stimulus The independent variable in an experiment.

Stratified sampling A procedure in which subgroups are selected on the basis of one or more shared characteristics and then sampled separately.

Structural content analysis Analysis focusing on the format of a communication.

Structured observation Direct observation using a prepared schedule or protocol to record data.

Subjects Persons who are being studied in a research project.

Subject encyclopedia An authoritative compendium of articles summarizing knowledge on a particular subject.

Substantive content analysis Analysis focusing on the meaning of a communication.

Summative indicator A measure of group characteristics created by combining the individual characteristics of group members.

Survey research A technique used in the study of individual attitudes, attributes, or behaviors.

Syntality indicator A measure of some quality or characteristic of a group as a whole.

Systematic errors Measurement errors that affect all applications of an instrument and render indicators invalid as measures of a concept.

Systematic random sample A sample in which cases are drawn from a master list by random selection of the first case and application of a selection interval for choosing subsequent cases.

Telephone surveys Surveys in which interviews are conducted over the telephone.

Test effect Any difference in the pretest and posttest scores of a subject due exclusively to a response to the pretest.

Theoretical import The degree to which a concept plays an important part in a conceptual explanation of an event.

Theorizing The process of stating conceptual explanations for real-world events by asserting systems of relationships among concepts.

Theory A possible explanation for events, often a set of logically related assumptions and propositions.

Theory elaboration The result of theory testing that refines a theory rather than confirming or refuting the theory.

Theory testing An effort to demonstrate the utility of a theory through research.

Thurston scaling A technique of scale construction in which some members of the group being studied are asked to act as "judges" to assign values to items to be used in a scale in order to increase its validity as a measure of some underlying concept.

Time-series analysis A data analysis technique based on regression that seeks to establish causal relationships through temporal ordering.

Time-series design A research design that seeks to establish causal relationships through analysis across time.

Trend study Analysis based on a comparison of the same general population (such as persons of voting age in a certain state) at different times.

Unit of analysis The smallest component or element about which generalizations are to be made.

Univariate statistics Statistics relating to or describing one variable.

Unobtrusive research or measure A measurement that intentionally avoids influencing the behavior of research subjects.

Unscheduled Free-form, without a specific format or instrument; said of interviews, observations, etc.

Unscheduled interviews Elite or specialized interviews that are *not* guided by an interview schedule listing questions to be asked.

Unstructured observation Direct observation using notes but not a prepared schedule or protocol, to record data.

Validation The process of assessing the degree to which an indicator accurately reflects the concept it is intended to measure.

Validity The extent to which measures correspond to the concepts they are intended to reflect.

Value The characteristic or score of a particular case on a given variable.

Variable A characteristic that takes on different values from one case to another or, for a given case, from one time to another.

Variation ratio The measure of dispersion for nominal variables.

Weight To alter the relative importance of items in an index or cases in a sample; the differential value assigned to a particular item or case to accomplish this.

Weighted index An index in which scores on one variable have been standardized by reference to scores on some other variable in order to facilitate valid comparison of index scores for different cases.

Wildcard characters Keyboard characters used to stand in for letters or numbers, especially suffixes, in online searching, expanding the search.

Word Mining Our name for a technique to develop search terms for the literature review drawing words from each reference—literally, extracting search terms for subsequent searches from each source you locate.

Working hypothesis A statement predicting a relationship between indicators.

INDEX

A

Abstract concepts, 21–22, 30
  quantification of, 88–90
  variables and, 89–92, 94
Abstract of research report, 382, 383–384
Accuracy, aggregate data and, 214
  of multivariate model specification, 315
  sample size and, 146–148
Activities of survey research, 152–153
Additive index, 216
Adequacy of research design, 75, 81
Administration of measuring instrument, 104, 105
Aggregate data, 209–225
  for cross-national studies, 234–235
All-channel network, 245–246
Alternative form method, 108–109
Alternative rival hypotheses, 34
  explanatory surveys and, 154
  field experiments and, 123
  and other hypotheses, 81
  randomization and, 121
  research design and, 77–80
  survey questions and, 156
Ambiguous questions, 158
American Association for Public Opinion Research (AAPOR),
    code of ethics, 176, 409–410
American Political Science Association (APSA), ethical
    guidelines, 408–409
American Political Science Association (APSA), style, 39
American Political Science Review, 37, 43, 66, 73, 312
American Statistical Index, 220
Analysis of data, 4, 11–12
  in direct observation, 333–334
  from focus groups, 359–361
  and measurement errors, 104
  multivariate, 311–323
  preparation for, 252–254
  presentation of, 386–389
  of survey research, 155, 156, 173
  units of. *See* Unit of
Analysis of variance, 322
Antecedent variables, 32
Applied research, 5, 353
Appropriate codes, 256–257
  measures, 94, 97
  operational definitions, 176
  qualities for secondary analysis, 174–175
  research techniques, 8
Areal groups, 210
Argumentativeness in interview questions, 159
Assistant moderator, for focus groups, 356–357
Assistants, structured direct observations by, 326, 335, 336
Association between variables, 290–310, 311–323
  measures of, 290–294
  interval/ratio variables, 303–309
  nominal variables, 297–301
  ordinal variables, 301–303

Association, coefficient of, 294–295
Assumptions, 21–22, 23, 25
  hypotheses and, 33
  for regression procedure, 315
Asymmetrical matrix, 242, 243, 244
Attitudes, defined, 152
Attrition from sample, panel studies, 155
Audience for reports of focus groups, 361–362
Author search, defined, 44
Average, 279–280, 284–286
Axes of graphs, 268, 269
  of scatterplots, 303–304
Axioms. *See* Assumptions

B

Babbie, Earl, 161
Background characteristics of survey respondents,
    152, 156
Balance point, mean as, 284–285
Bar chart, 271–273
Basic research, 5
Behavior, and direct observation, 327, 340–342, 350
  of interviewers, 168–169
  observation of, 9–10
  operational definition of, 335–336
Best fit, line of, 304–309
Beta weight (or coefficient), 330–331
Bias, comparative analysis and, 228–229, 232
  in cross-national studies, 232–233, 236
  in direct observation, 350, 356, 359
  in interview questions, 155, 158–159
  mail surveys and, 163–164
  online bibliographic references, 43, 48, 53
  from personal interviews, 163
  response set, 159
  in samples, 134–135, 138–139, 143, 163–164
  in surveys, 155, 156, 158–159, 161, 164
Bibliographic entries, 382
  in research report, 390
Bibliographic records, 39–43
Bibliographic search techniques, 36–74
Bibliography, defined, 39
Bilateral bar charts, 272–273
Bimodal distributions, 282
Bivariate analysis, 288, 290–310
  with several variables, 311–312
Blogs, 47, 61, 67
Boolean operators, and Boolean logic, 59, 63, 71–72
Brians, Craig Leonard, 383, 385, 390
Briefing for survey research, 153, 168–169

C

Catalog of United States Census Publications, 220
Catalogs, library, 37, 38, 40, 43–44
Categories of study, and sample size, 146
Causal chains, 32
Causal inference, 117–118, 123

Causal relationships, 25–26
  model of, 26
  standardized coefficients and, 321
Causation, 25–26
Cells, in crosstabulations, 274
Census data, 211
Central tendency, 279–281
Chain network, 245–246, 248
Chain of reasoning, 68–70
Characteristics, causing measurement error, 102–104
  desirable, of interviewers, 168–169
Charts, in reports, 387
Checklist for evaluation of research, 395–397
Chi-square, 299–300
Circle network, 245, 246
Classic experiment, 118–122
Closed-ended questions, 156–157
Cluster sampling, 135, 139–142
Coalition of Environmentally Responsible Economies
    (CERES), 247–249
Codebook, 176, 257–260, 261
Coders, for content analysis, 197, 199, 200
Coding, of aggregate data, 222–223
  of data, 251–252
  procedure, 379, 386
Coding sheets, 260–261
Coefficient of association, 291–299, 301–303
  beta, 320–321
  of multiple determination, 317
  partial regression, 316
Cohort studies, 154
Collapsing categories, 99, 256–257, 313–314
Collection of data. See Data collection
Collectively exhaustive categories, 95, 156
Column variables, crosstabulation, 298
Communicable theories, 23
Comparative research, 226–239
Comparison in research design, 78, 80
Complete measures, 105
Components of theory, 23–25
Composite scores, 114
Compound meaning in questions, 158
Computers, data entry into software, 262
  random number generator program, 136
  and telephone interviewing, 165
Concepts, 23–25
  operationalization of, 89–92
  for survey research, 152
  variables, and, 89–90
Conceptualization, 19
Conclusions, 3–4
  of research report, 378, 380
Concrete observations, 7, 88
Conditioned responses to interview questions, 158, 159
Confidence interval and sampling, 146–148
Confidence level and sampling, 132–133
Confidentiality in elite interviewing, 371, 372, 374
Congressional District Data Book, 220
Congressional districts, cluster sampling, 139, 140
Congressional Record, 194
Construct validation, 110, 111–113
Contamination of groups, in focus groups, 357
Contamination of population, 174

Content analysis, 194–208
  aggregate data from, 213–214
Contextual judgment, content analysis, 194, 201
Control groups, 119–120, 123
Control in research design, 78–80
  in multivariate analysis, 312–313, 316
Controlled time-series design, 124
Convergent validation, 110, 112
Co-op America, 247, 248, 249
Correlation coefficient, 206–207, 303–309
  statistical significance of, 404
Costs, of 2010 US Census, 131
  of data collection, 394
  of focus groups, 349, 354
  of Internet surveys, 165, 166
  of mail surveys, 163
  of panel studies, 155
  of personal interviews, 148, 163
  and sampling error, 148
  of survey research, 163
Country-specific indicators, cross-national
    studies, 231
County and City Data Book, 220
County Yearbook, 221
Covariational relationships, 25
Cronbach's alpha, 184
Cross-cultural research, 228–229
Cross-national research, 226–239
Cross-sectional surveys, 154,
Crosstabulation (or Crosstabs), 273–275
  in multivariate analysis, 311–314
Culture-bound results, 227–228

D

Data, 9
  archives, 175
  coding of, 252–264
  for cross-national studies, 234–237
  demographic, 210, 211, 220–221
  individual level, 174–175, 222
  judgmental, 214
  processing of, 252–264
  qualitative, 76, 84–85, 325–326, 359–360
  raw, 216
  for secondary analysis, 174–175
  specifications, 222–223
  survey, sources of, 175
  tabular presentation of, 265–268
  transformations, 217
Data analysis, controlling in, 312–313
  of direct observation, 326
  and focus groups, 359–361
  and qualitative versus quantitative methods, 84–85
Data collection, 222–223, 394–395
Deduction, 21, 22, 32–33
Degrees of freedom, 301, 309
Demographic data, 210, 211, 220–221
  items in survey instrument, 156, 160, 161
Demographic Yearbook, 211, 221
Dependent variables (DV), 26, 30–31
  experimental research design, 118–121
  research report, 386

Description of data, 265–277
Descriptive research, 76, 81
    direct observation and, 326
    surveys, 153–154
Descriptors. *See also* Subject headings
Design of research, 75–81, 83, 229, 232–233,
        393–394
    of research report, 379–380
    assessment of strengths and weaknesses, 385
    of surveys, 152–168
Dewey Decimal system, 43
Dichotomy, noninterval data as, 317–318
Diffusion in cross-national studies, 234
Direct measures, 89, 102, 105
Direct observation, 324–346
Direction of relationship, 11–12, 26–27, 290, 291, 294
Disclosure, ethical standards, 409, 410
Discriminant validation, 110, 114
Discussion of tables in research report, 268, 388
Dispersion, measure of, 280–281, 282, 283, 284, 286
Distributions, coefficients of association, 295–296, 303
    mean and, 284–285
    normal, 287–288
    on one variable, 278–288
    sampling, 295–297
Documentation of sources, 48, 382
Double-barreled questions. *See* Compound questions
Dummy variables, 318
Dynamics, group, 349, 351, 352, 354, 356, 362

E

EbscoHost, 54
Ecological fallacy, 215, 224
Elaboration of theories, 27–29
Elections, U.S., data on, 221, 222
Elements of research design, 76
Elite interviewing, 365–376
Empirical evidence, 6
Empirical political science, 45
Empirical referents, 24–25, 30
Empirical research, 2–3, 17–18, 24
    concepts, 24–25
    evaluation of, 395–397
    measures for, 113
    and quantification, 88–89
    theories and, 17–18
Environmental scan, information, 47–54, 65, 71, 72
Equivalent measures, 228
    in cross-national surveys, 229–231
Error, 187
    in measurement, 102–105
    in regression assumptions, 315
    in sampling, 146
Error terms, multiple regression, 314–315
Ethics, research, 3, 393, 397
    and aggregate data, 222
    when coding data, 263
    in comparative research, 236
    when constructing scales, 188
    and content analysis, 199
    and data presentation, 270
    and designing research, 78
    when directly observing subjects, 327, 329–330, 335

    and elite interviewing, 374
    and focus groups, 352, 356, 361
    use of Internet resources, 48
    Obedience to Authority, 78, 122, 130
    in operationalization, 98
    in qualitative research, 335, 361, 374
    in quantitative research, 280, 303, 321
    in researching the literature, 48
    and sampling, 149
    in social network analysis, 241
    Stanford Prison Experiment, 78, 122
    in survey research, 173, 176
    and theory building, 24
    and writing research reports, 379, 381, 390
European Union (EU), 175
Eurostat Yearbook, 221
Evaluating public policy, 14, 353, 361
Event data, 213–214, 221, 223
Exhaustive categories, in direct observation schedule,
        336, 338
    in nominal measurement, 95
    in survey questions, 156
Experimental groups, 121–122, 124
Experimental research design, 118–123
Explanation in surveys, 154
Explanatory research, 76–80, 81, 392–395
    direct observation and, 326
    research design and, 76
    surveys and, 153–155
Exploratory research, 19, 33
    focus groups and, 351–352
    surveys and, 153, 154
Ex post facto experiments, 124
External validation, 110, 111–112
External validity of direct observation, 326, 340, 344
    of measures, 105, 107
    versus internal validity, 105–107
Extreme cases and the mean (i.e., outliers),
        284–286
    and regression toward the mean, 127

F

Face-to-face interviews, 152, 163
    monitoring of, 163, 172
Face validity, 110, 114
Factors, external, 120
Facts about survey respondents, 152
    theory and, 18
Facts-on-File, 221
Feeling thermometer, 157
Field experiments, 123
Field notes of direct observations, 330–333
Financial support of research disclosure of
        sources, 408
Findings, presentation of, 380
Focus group methods, 347–364
Follow-up mailings, survey research, 164, 172
Footnotes, in research report, 384, 386
Format, of bar charts, 271–273
    of crosstabulations, 273–275
    of line graphs, 268–269
    of pie charts, 269–271
    of tables, 265–268

Format, of bar charts (*continued*)
    of survey instrument, 153, 155, 160, 161–162, 165, 170
    of survey questions, 157, 158–160
Freedom House, 235
Frequency distribution control, 122
Frequency distributions, 275, 281, 283–284, 286–287, 297–298, 304, 307
    in crosstabulations, 275
Funding for research, 174
    ethical considerations, 408

G
Galton's problem, 234
Gamma, and ordinal variables, 301–303
General Social Survey (GSS), 175
General theories, 23
Generalizability, of research, 132
    coefficients of association and, 296
    comparative research, 228, 229
    content analysis, 205–206
    deduction, 21, 22
    ecological fallacies, 215
    external validity and, 105–106
    from focus groups, 350
    induction, 20, 21
    from observation, 9–10, 28
    sampling and, 132–133, 135, 140, 143, 144
Generalization, in data analysis, 395
    from sample to population, 132–133
Goals of focus groups, 353–354
Goodness of fit, 304
Google, 36, 38, 40, 53, 64, 71
Google Scholar, 55, 60, 66
Government agencies, data compiled by, 211–212, 220–221
Governmental cooperation in cross-national surveys, 235
Governmental support of research, ethical considerations, 408, 409
Graphs, bar charts, 271–273
    line graphs, 268–269
    pie charts, 269–271
Greene, Steven, 383, 385, 386, 390
Group dynamics, 349, 351, 352, 354, 356, 362
Groups, characteristics, aggregate data, 209–210
    in experimental research, 121–122
Guide, for focus groups, 354
Guide to US Elections, 221
Guttman coefficient of reproducibility (C_R), 187–188
Guttman scaling, 184–188

H
Hawthorne effect, 10, 84
Heterogeneity, and sample size, 145–146
Histograms, 281
Homogeneity, and sample size, 145–146
Hypotheses, 29–30, 89–90. *See also* Alternative rival hypotheses; Working hypotheses
    formulation of, 32–34
    functions of, 29, 392–393
    multivariate analysis, 313–314
    operationalization of, 89–90
    regression analysis, 314
    testing of, 31–32

I
Identical indicators, cross-national studies, 230
Inappropriate measures, 105
Incomplete measures, 105
Incremental nature of research, 34
Independent observations, for cross-national studies, 233–234
Independent variables (IV), 26, 30–31, 106, 290
    comparison of, 313
    in crosstabulations, 274–275
    experimental research design, 118–121
    multiple regression, 314, 318
    research report, 386
Indexes, research literature, 38, 41
Indicators, 90–92
    Valid, for aggregate data, 209–210
Indices, construction, 216–217
Indirect causation, 26
Individuals, data on, 209–210, 215
    and populations, 132
    rights of, in research, 409, 410
    survey research and, 152
Induction, 20–22
    in data analysis, 115
    in direct observation, 326
Inductive generalization, 20, 32, 395
Inductive logic, 20
    in data analysis, 395
Inference, causal, 75, 76, 118
    in construct validation, 110, 111
Information environmental scan, 47–54, 65, 71, 72
Infotrac Expanded Academic ASAP, 257–258
Instability, in quasi-experiments, 126–127
Instrument, measuring, 90, 93
    refining through focus groups, 352
Instrumentation, 89
    in direct observation, 334, 338, 342
    in experiments, 118
    of survey research, 155–162
Interaction effects and multiple regression, 318–319
Intercoder reliability, 206–207
Interfaith Center for Corporate Responsibility (ICCR), 248–249
Internal validation, 112, 113
Internal validity in research design, 105–106
International Social Survey Programme (ISSP), 175
Internet research, 64–67
    search strategies, 64–66
    subject directories, 65
Internet surveys, 165–168
Interobserver reliability, structured observations, 338
Interpretation of results, 12–13
    of focus groups, 359–361
    in multiple regression, 316–317
Inter-university Consortium for Political and Social Research (ICPSR), xi, 175, 213, 383
Interval/ratio measurement, 95–96, 97
Interval/ratio variables, 97
    coding of, 253, 256–257
    descriptive statistics for, 284–288
    multiple regression, 313, 315
    relationships between two, 303–309

Intervening variables, 31
Interviewers, training for survey research, 153, 168
Interviewing, 170–172
  elite, 366–367
  specialized, 373–374
  pretesting, 169–170
  and test-retest method, 108
  unscheduled, 366–367
Interview schedules, 155–156
Introduction, in interviews, 171
  of research report, 378
  of research report, example, 384
Invalid indicators, 105, 107, 108
Invalid information from elite interviews, 367
Items, content analysis, 198

J

Journals, scholarly, 37–38, 43, 47, 53, 60, 62, 64, 73–74
JSTOR, 60, 61, 62
Judges for substantive content analysis, 197
Judgmental data, 214
Judgmental samples, 143

K

Keesing's Contemporary Archives, 221–222
Kendall's tau, 302–303
Key to line graph, 269
Key Word In Context (KWIC), 63, 200
Keywords or phrases, bibliographic search, 40, 42, 43, 44, 45, 46, 49, 57, 58–59, 61, 62, 64, 65, 70
Knowledge, scientific research and, 3–4
  theories and, 19
Knowledge Networks, 167
Krueger, Richard, 361
Kuder-Richardson 20 (KR20), 184

L

Lambda, and nominal variables, 297–299
Language of inquiry, 3
Least squares regression, 314–317
Legal decisions, research and, 3, 13, 14
Length, of interviews, 155–156
  of research report, 383
  of survey questions, 158
  of table or figure description, 380
Level of analysis, ecological fallacy and, 215, 219
Levels of measurement, 94–96, 97
  and coding, 253–254
  Interval/ratio, 95–96, 97
  Nominal, 95, 97
  Ordinal, 95, 97
  statistical analysis and, 279
LexisNexis Academic, 38, 55, 61, 63, 198
Libraries, bibliographic search, 37–52, 54–64, 70–72
  EbscoHost, 54
  Infotrac Expanded Academic ASAP, 257–258
  WorldCat, 52
  Worldwide Political Science Abstracts, 38, 41, 42
Library of Congress Classification system, 43–44
Library of Congress Subject Headings (LCSH), 43–44
Likert scaling, 183–184

Limits of research, 397, 398
Linear network, 245. *See also* Chain network
Linear relationships, 305
Line of best fit, 304, 305
Line graphs, 268–269
Linguistically equivalent surveys, 235
Links, 241, 242
Lists, for mail surveys, 163
Literary Digest, 134
Literature, of political science research report, 379
  search of, 36–74
Loaded questions, 158–159
Logarithmic transformation, 217
Logic, deductive, 21, 22, 32, 33
  inductive, 20, 21, 22, 32, 33
  of theory building, 17–20, 22
Logical structure of theory, 23
Longitudinal surveys, 154–155
Louis Harris Data Center at the *Odum Institute*, 173

M

Mail surveys, 163–164
  questionnaires, 164
  response rates, 164
Manipulation, in experimental research design, 118, 119
  of variables in field experiments, 123
Marginals, in crosstabulations, 275
Market research, 248
Matching, in experimental groups, 121–122
Maturation, in experiments, 79
Maturation, internal validity and, 106
Mean, 284–286
Meaning, in focus group results, 359–361
Meaningless statistical results, 280
Measurement, 89–90, 92, 94
  error, 102–105
  instruments of, 103–105
  levels of, 94–99
  theory, 101
Median, 282–284
Mental note taking, 330, 343
Meta-search engines, 66
Method effects, in direct observation, 340–345
  in focus groups, 351
Misleading evidence, from pie charts, 271
Misuse of research role, 408
Modal category, 282
Mode, 282
Models, causal, 26–27
Moderator, for focus groups, 347, 350, 351, 354, 356–358
Monitoring in survey research, 153, 163, 166, 171, 172
Monthly Catalog of U.S. Government Publications, 221
Monthly Checklists of State Publications, 221
Most different systems design, 232–233
Most similar systems design, 232, 233
Multidimensional concepts, 91–92
Multilingual interviews, 172
Multimethod designs, 80, 207
Multiple causation, 26, 81
Multiple indicators, 91–92, 110, 113, 217, 219, 223
Multiple methods of measurement, 76, 89

Multiple regression, 314–321
  equation for, 314
  and multicollinearity, 315, 318, 319–320
Multiplicative index, 216
Multistage random area sampling, 139–142
Multivariate analysis, 311–323
Municipal Yearbook, 221
Mutually exclusive categories, in coding, 254, 255, 256
  in direct observation schedule, 336, 338
  in nominal measurement, 95
  in survey questions, 156

N

Nadel technique, 371
National Election Studies (NES), or *ANES*, 175, 386
Negative relationships, 12, 27, 294, 296, 303, 305
News Dictionary, 221
New York Times index, 221
Nodes, 241, 242, 244
NOIR table, 97
Nominal measurement, 95
Nominal variables, 95
  coding, 254–255
  descriptive statistics for, 281–282
  multiple regression and, 318
  relationship between two, 297–301
Nonfindings, report of, 380
Noninterval data, multiple regression, 318
Nonverbal communication, 356, 360
Normal curve, 295–296, 303, 403, 405–407
Normal distribution, 287–288
  of error terms in multiple regression, 315
  logarithmic transformations and, 217
  and statistical significance, 295–296
Normative analysis, 2–3
Note-taking, literature research, 61
Numerical codes, 254–257

O

Objectives, of direct observation, 331
  of elite interviewing, 368
  of focus groups, 353
Observable phenomena, 24
Observation, 76, 88–89
  and alternative rival hypotheses, 77–80
  of behavior, 9–10
  in cross-national studies, independent, 228, 233–234
  direct, 324–346
  generalization from, 395
  in survey research, 152
Observation point, 80
Observation schedule, 334–338
Obtrusive research, 327
Open-ended questions, 156, 157, 161, 170, 171
Open mind, in direct observation, 330, 334, 342
Operational definitions, 92–93, 228–229
Operationalization, 7–8, 89–92
  and alternative rival hypotheses, 79–80
  appropriate, for secondary analysis, 174
  coding and, 257
  in content analysis, 197, 198, 206
  in cross-national studies, 228

level of measurement, 96–97
  and measurement theory, 99, 100
  in survey research, 152–155, 174
  validation and, 110, 113
Opinions, 152
Order of questions in survey instrument, 160–161
Ordinal measurement, 95
Ordinal variables, 95, 97
  coding, 253, 255–256
  descriptive statistics for, 282–284
  in multiple regression, 318
  relationships between two, 301–303
Organizational statistics, 212–213, 223
Outliers. *See* Extreme cases
Outline, of research report, 70, 380, 381

P

Pair-comparison scaling, 202
Panel studies, 155
Paper-and-pencil method, 171
Parameter, population, 134, 146, 295–296, 299
Parsimony, in coding, 254, 255
  in theories, 23
Partial regression coefficients, 316, 318
Participant observation, 327, 334
Participant selection, in focus groups, 355
Passive observation, 327
Patterns in direct observation, 329, 333–334, 341
Paying, focus group participants, 355
Pearson product-moment correlation, 206–207, 303–304
  statistical significance of, 404
Perceptions, 152
  direct observation and, 324, 328, 341
Perfect agreement, 301
Perfect inversion, 301
Perfect scale type, Guttman scale, 186
Periodical indexes, 41, 54–55, 59–60
  EbscoHost, 54
  Infotrac Expanded Academic ASAP, 257–258
  JSTOR, 60, 61, 62
  LexisNexis Academic, 38, 55, 61, 63, 198
  Social Science Citation Index, 59
  Worldwide Political Science Abstracts, 38, 41, 42
"Person-in-the-street" interviews, 152
Personal information about respondents, 156, 161
Personal interviews. *See* Face-to-face interviews
Personnel for survey research, 168–169
Perspectives on Politics, 73
Pew Research Center for the People and the Press, 175
Phenomena, relationships between, 29–30, 291
Pie chart, 270–271
Pilot study, 169–170
Pluralism, 30
Political behavior, 5
  and survey research, 152
Political inquiry, 3
Political science, 4, 43, 46, 228
  journals, 73–74
  literature of, 36–74
  research, 4
  and sampling error, 148

Political scientists, 2, 65, 77, 123, 124, 209, 325, 326
  Will I ever be a political scientist? 13
Political systems, 23–24, 227–228
Polity IV, 235
Popular press, research use, 53, 198. *See also LexisNexis*
    Academic
Population, 131–133, 290–291
  aggregate data, 209–210
  appropriate for secondary analysis, 174
  contamination of, 174
  parameter, 134, 146, 295–296, 299
  and sample precision, 145–148
  and sample size, 146–147
Positive relationships, 26–27, 294, 301
Posttest, in experimental design, 118
Postulates. *See* Assumptions
Pragmatic validation, 110
Precision, of concepts, 25
  of judgmental data, 214
  in measurement, 94, 96–99
  of sample; population size and, 146–147
Precision matching, 121
Predictability, 301
Predictive validity, 110
Presentation of findings, ethical considerations, 408–410
  research report, 380
Pretest, in experimental design, 118
Pretesting, of measures, 103, 104
  of observation schedules, 338
  of survey instruments, 153, 169–170
  for validity and reliability, 103, 106, 107, 108, 109
Problems, of aggregate data, 214–219
  of content analysis, 204–207
  of multiple regression, 317–321
Processing of data, 261–263
  measurement errors in, 104
Professional standards of research, 78, 408–410
Propositions, 25, 99, 101, 115
Publications' content, aggregate data from, 213, 220
Public opinion polls, 151
  aggregate data from, 212
  sample size, 146–148
Public policy, and empirical research, 14, 353, 361–362

Q

Qualitative analysis, 2
  and direct observation, 325–326
  and elite interviews, 365
  and focus groups, 347
  versus quantitative analysis, 81–85
Qualitative methods, 81
Quantile ranges, 283–284
Quantitative analysis, 2, 81, 379
Quasi-experimental designs, 123–129
Question branching, 171
Questionnaires, 155
  format of, 161–162
  mail surveys, 163–164
  organization of, 160–161
Questions, cross-cultural, 228–229
  differing interpretations, error from, 103
  discussion of wording, 386

  for elite interviews, wording of, 370–371
  in surveys, wording of, 158–160
Quota samples, 145

R

Random-digit dialing (RDD), 165
Random errors, 105
  reliability and, 105, 108, 113
  validity and, 105, 108, 113
Random number table, 136, 399–400
Random samples, 135–137
  for content analysis, 196
  direct observations, 339–340
Randomization, in experimental research designs, 121
Ranking of cases, 95
Rates, computation of, 209
Raw data, 216
Reactivity, 10, 84
  in direct observation, 326, 327, 330, 334, 340–341
  in experiments, 119
  in panel studies, 155
  in personal interviews, 168
Recording form for aggregate data, 223
Records of communication, for content analysis, 195
Regression artifact, in experiments, 127
Regression, multiple, 314
  assumptions, 315
  line of, 304
Regression toward the mean, 127
  internal validity and, 127
Relationships, 11–12
  between concepts, 25–27, 89–92
  between indicators and concepts, 99–102
  between variables, 29–31, 99–102
  statistical, 12
Relevant research literature, identification of, 36–74
Reliability, 107–109
  of census data, 211
  of content analysis data, 206–207
  of event data, 213
  intercoder, 206
  interobserver, 338
  of judgmental data, 214
  of measures, 107–109
  of scales, 182
  of structured direct observation, 336
  of survey data, 212
Reports of research, 361–362, 377–391
Representative samples, 132–133
  for direct observation, 339–340
  in focus groups, 350
  in panel studies, 154
Research, 4
  bibliographic search, 36–74
  comparative, 226–239
  cross-cultural, 228–229
  deductive reasoning, 22, 32–33
  design, 75–81
  evaluation of, 396–397
  exploratory, 19, 33
  model of, 115
  overview and summary, 392–398

Research (*continued*)
  process of, 1–15
  report, 377–391
  selection of techniques, 8–9
  testing of theories, 27–29
Research ethics, 3, 393, 397
  and aggregate data, 222
  when coding data, 263
  in comparative research, 236
  when constructing scales, 188
  and content analysis, 199
  and data presentation, 270
  and designing research, 78
  when directly observing subjects, 327, 329–330, 335
  and elite interviewing, 374
  and focus groups, 352, 356, 361
  use of Internet resources, 48
  Obedience to Authority, 78, 122, 130
  in operationalization, 98
  in qualitative research, 335, 361, 374
  in quantitative research, 280, 303, 321
  in researching the literature, 48
  and sampling, 149
  in social network analysis, 241
  Stanford Prison Experiment, 78, 122
  in survey research, 173, 176
  and theory building, 24
  and writing research reports, 379, 381, 390
Research questions, 5, 12
  appropriate operationalization, 174
  definition in research report, 385
Research reports, 377–391
  from focus groups, 361–362
Respondents, 152
  in elite interviews, 366–372
Response rates, 163, 164, 165, 168
Response set bias, 159
Review of literature, research report, 379
Roper Opinion Research Center, 175
Row variables in crosstabulations, 274–275

S

Salient references, content analysis, 197–198, 201
Samples, 131–135
  in comparative research, 228
  and conceptualization of survey, 153
  for content analysis, 200, 205–206
  for cross-national studies, 228
  for direct observation, 339–340
  research report, 379
  size, 145–148
  for surveys, 139–143
Sampling error, 146
  content analysis, 196
Scale, 181
Scale score, 181
Scaling techniques, 180–193
Scatter plots, 275, 303–304
Scheduled interviews, 366
Scholarly journals, 37–38, 43, 47, 53, 60, 62, 64, 73–74
  indexes, 38, 41
  list of, 41, 54–55, 59–60

Scientific method, 4
  direct observation and, 325–327
Scientific research, 3–4
  public policy and, 14, 353
  theory building and, 19–25
Screening interview, for focus groups, 355
Searching, research literature, 36–74
  Concept search grid, 48–49
  Internet – Free Web, 64–66
  Periodical indexes and databases, 41, 54–55, 59–60
  Systematic literature search, 36–74
Secondary analysis of survey data, 174–176, 386
Segmented bar charts, 271
Selection, in experiments, 120–121
Selection-maturation, in experiments, 79
Self-administered questionnaires, 152, 154, 161, 165
  demographic items, 161
Self-mailing questionnaires, 164
Semantic differential, 190–192
Settings, of elite interviews, 370, 373
Shively, W. Philips, 100
Significance of research, statement of, 378, 384
Significance, statistical, 309
Simple random samples, 135–137
Simple tables, 265–267
Size of samples, 145–148
Social desirability bias. *See* Socially approved answers
Social Investment Forum (SIF), 247, 248, 249
Social network, 240
Social network analysis, 240–251
  applications, 247–249
Social network matrices, 242–244
  asymmetrical matrix, 243–244
  symmetrical matrix, 243–244
Social science, research design and, 75–76
  hypothesis, 29–30
  theory, 23–25
Socially approved answers, 159
Socioeconomic status (SES), 5
Solomon, R. L., 119
Solomon three-control-group research design, 120
Solomon two-control-group research design, 119
Sources of data, aggregate, 220–221
  for cross-national studies, 234–237
Specialized interviewing, 373–374
Specification error, multicollinearity and, 319–320
Specification of multivariate model, 314–315
Spreadsheet, 275
Spurious relationships, 26, 34
Stable characteristics, causing measurement error, 102–103
Standard deviation, 286–287
Standardization, 316
  in multiple regression, 320
  of variables, for comparison, 218–219
Standardized regression coefficients, 320–321
Standards, professional, 408–410
Standard score, 287
  of gamma, 303
Standard unit in measurement, 95
Star network, 245, 246
The State and Metropolitan Area Data Book, 220
Statesman's Yearbook, 221

Statistical Abstract of the United States, 220
Statistical analyses, 278–323
Statistical control, 312–313, 316
SPSS (Statistical Package for the Social Sciences), 275
Statistical relationships, 11
Statistical significance, 290–297
   correlation coefficient tables, 404
   for interval/ratio variables, 309
   measures, 290–295, 299, 303, 309
   and multicollinearity, 319
   for nominal variables, 298
   for ordinal variables, 301
   standards for, 294
Statistical tables, 399–407
Statistical Yearbook (UNESCO), 221
Statistics, 278–323
Stimulus. *See* Independent variables
Stratified sampling, 142–143
Straw poll, 134, 135
Street corner interviews, 135
Structural content analysis, 202–203
Structured observation, 328, 329
Structure of research reports, 378–380
Style guides, 39
Style of research reports, 381–382
Subgroups, in sample, 132
Subject and U.S. Area Reports, 220
Subject directory, 65–66
Subject headings, 43, 52, 56–57, 63, 65, 70
Subject index, defined, 41
Subjective data from direct observation, perception of, 326
Subjects, in experiments, 118
   in direct observation, 327, 328
Subsample method, 109
Substantive content analysis, 200–201
Substantive questions in survey instrument, 160
Substantive value of research, 398
Successive cross-sectional surveys, 154–155
Summative indicators, 209
Survey data, 174–176, 212, 222
Survey design, 153–155
Survey research, 151–179
   aggregate data from, 222
   for cross-national studies, 235
   samples for, 139–143
Surveys, descriptive, 153–154
   explanatory, 154
   exploratory, 153
Symmetrical matrix, 242, 243
Systematic bias, 138–139
Systematic bibliographic search, 36–74
Systematic errors, 104–105
Systematic random sample, 137–138
System level traits, 210, 227–228
System level variables, 210

T

Tables, crosstabulations (crosstabs), 273–275, 298, 299, 302, 311–313
   discussion of, in research report, 387–388
   simple, 265–267
Tabular analysis as multivariate analysis, 311–314

Tabular presentation, of data, 311–314
Techniques, appropriate, 8–9
Telephone surveys, 164–165, 171–172
   monitoring of, 172
Temporary characteristics, causing measurement error, 103
Test effect, 119
   internal validity and, 106
   in panel studies, 155
Testing, in experiments, 118
Testing, of hypotheses, 34
   of measures, 102
   of reliability, 108–109
   of theories, 27–34
Test-retest method, 108, 109
Theoretical import of concepts, 25
Theorizing, 16–18
Theory, 18
   building of, 16–35
   elaboration, 27–29
   logical structure of, 22
   measurement, 101
   operationalization of, 7–8
   testing, 27–29
Threats to validity, 106–107
Three-control-group experimental design, 119–120
Thurstone scaling, 188–190
Time-series designs, 124–129
Times of London index, 221
Title search, 44
Title, of research report, 382
Topics for research. *See also* Research questions
Training for survey research, 168–169
Transcript, of direct observation notes, 330–331
   of elite interviews, 372
   of focus group sessions, 350, 354, 356–357
Transformation of data, 217
Translation, of concepts into variables, 30, 89, 94
   of hypotheses into working hypotheses, 99
Trend line, in time-series designs, 124, 127
Trend studies, 154
True population parameter, 295
Two-control-group experimental design, 119
Types of networks, 245–246
   all-channel, 245–246
   chain, 245–246
   circle, 245–246
   linear, 245–246
   star, 245–246

U

UNESCO, *Statistical Yearbook*, 221
Unit of analysis, 196
   for content analysis, 245–246
   for structural content analysis, 245–246
   structured direct observation, 335
United States, demographic data, 221
   governmental data, 220
U.S. Government Printing Office, 44
Univariate statistics, 280, 288
Universe. *See* Population
Unobtrusive research, 327

Unreliable measures, 105, 107, 108, 109
Unscheduled interviews, 366–367
Unstandardized regression coefficients, 320
Unstructured observation, 328–331
Usable studies for secondary analysis, 174–175
Useful concepts, 23–24
Useful theories, 22–23

V

Validation, 110–114
Validity, 105–107
    aggregate data and, 211–214
    of census data, 211
    of event data, 213
    external, of direct observation, 34
    internal, 105
    of measures, 105
    multiple methods of measurement and, 113
    pretesting, 106
    reliability and, 107
    in research design, 83
    research design and, 83
    of scales, 181
    in structured direct observation, 340
    of survey data, 212
Valuable research, 395
Values, and ethical dilemmas, 342–343
    and normative analysis, 2
    and research design, 81
    on variables, 90, 91, 92, 94n1
Variables, 30–32
    association between, 290–294
    coding of, 254–257
    in cross-national studies, 228
    dummy, 318
    indicators and, 90
    operational definitions, 92–93

relationships between, 25–27, 30, 89–91
    several, 317–318
    simple tables, 265–267
    spurious, 26
    in survey research, 154
    two, 290–310
    values and, 88, 90, 94n1
Variation ratio, 282
Verification of surveys, 173–174
Visual aides in survey research, 157, 163, 165
Voting data, 221

W

Warm-up questions in survey instrument, 160
Web, free, 37, 38, 40, 53, 56, 62, 64–66
Web pages, evaluating, 66–67
Web sites, academic, 55
Weblogs. *See* Blogs
Weighted index, 216
Weighting, 216–217
Word count for content analysis, 197, 199
Word mining, 46–66
    Step 1: information environment, 46–54
    Step 2: bibliographic records, 54–61
    Step 3: full text, 61–64
    Step 4: the free Web, 64–66
Working hypotheses, 79–80, 99, 101
World Almanac, 221
WorldCat, 52
World Factbook (CIA), 234
Worldmark Encyclopedia of Nations, 221
Worldwide Political Science Abstracts, 38, 41, 42

X–Z

Yearbook of International Trade Statistics, 221
Yearbook of National Accounts Statistics, 221
Zero point, in interval/ratio measures, 96